ENCYCLOPEDIA OF HUMAN RESOURCE MANAGEMENT

Encyclopedia of Human Resource Management

Edited by

Adrian Wilkinson

Professor of Employment Relations, Griffith University, Australia

and

Stewart Johnstone

Senior Lecturer in Human Resource Management, Newcastle University Business School, UK

 Edward Elgar
PUBLISHING

Cheltenham, UK • Northampton, MA, USA

Published by
Edward Elgar Publishing Limited
The Lypiatts
15 Lansdown Road
Cheltenham
Glos GL50 2JA
UK

Edward Elgar Publishing, Inc.
William Pratt House
9 Dewey Court
Northampton
Massachusetts 01060
USA

Paperback edition 2017

A catalogue record for this book
is available from the British Library

Library of Congress Control Number: 2015950509

This book is available electronically in the **Elgar**online
Business subject collection
DOI 10.4337/9781783475469

ISBN 978 1 78347 545 2 (cased)
ISBN 978 1 78347 546 9 (eBook)
ISBN 978 1 78811 326 7 (paperback)

Typeset by Servis Filmsetting Ltd, Stockport, Cheshire

Contents

Contributors

Stephen Ackroyd, Professor Emeritus, Lancaster University School of Management; Honorary Professor, Cardiff Business School

Maha Alfarhan, Doctoral Researcher, Nottingham Business School, Nottingham Trent University

Cameron Allan, Senior Analyst, Workplace Health and Safety Queensland

Bethania Antunes, Senior Lecturer in Reward Management, Business School, University of Greenwich

Katsuki Aoki, Associate Professor, Meiji University School of Business Administration

James Arrowsmith, Professor, School of Management, Massey University

Maurizio Atzeni, Researcher, Centre for Labour Relations, National Research Council of Argentina (CEIL/CONICET)

Silvia Bagdadli, Associate Professor, Department of Management and Technology, Bocconi University

Catherine Bailey (née Truss), Professor of Management, Sussex University

Janis Bailey, Associate Professor, Griffith Business School, Griffith University

Marian Baird, Professor of Employment Relations and Director of the Women and Work Research Group, University of Sydney Business School

Arnold B. Bakker, Professor of Work and Organizational Psychology, Erasmus University Rotterdam

Angela Baron, PhD Candidate, Bournemouth University

Edward Barratt, Senior Lecturer in Human Resource Management, Essex University

Nick Barter, Academic Director, Griffith Online, Griffith University

Yehuda Baruch, Professor of Management, Southampton Business School, University of Southampton

John Benson, Professor, Head, School of Business, Monash University Malaysia

Ioulia Bessa, University Academic Fellow in the area of the 'new worlds of work' at the Centre for Employment Relations Innovation and Change, University of Leeds

Peter F. Beszter, Senior Lecturer, Staffordshire University

Tanya Bondarouk, Professor of Human Resource Management, Human Resource Management Department, University of Twente

Corine Boon, Assistant Professor of HRM, University of Amsterdam

Paul Boselie, Professor, Utrecht School of Governance, Utrecht University

George Boyce, Acas

Nikos Bozionelos, Professor of Organizational Behaviour and Human Resource Management, Audencia Nantes School of Management

Jelena Brcic, Postdoctoral Fellow, Rotman School of Management, Toronto

Chris Brewster, Professor of Human Resource Management, Henley Business School, University of Reading

John W. Budd, Professor of Work and Organizations, Carlson School of Management, University of Minnesota

Pawan S. Budhwar, Professor of International Human Resource Management, Aston Business School, Aston University

John Burgess, Professor of Human Resource Management, School of Management, Curtin University

Bernard Burnes, Professor of Organizational Change, Stirling University

Alan Burton-Jones, Senior Lecturer, Griffith Business School, Griffith University

Clare Butler, Lecturer in Work and Employment, University of Newcastle upon Tyne

David Cabrelli, Senior Lecturer in Commercial Law, Edinburgh University and Solicitor (non-practising)

Tim Campbell, Visiting Fellow Nottingham Business School, Nottingham Trent University

Joseph A. Carpini, PhD Candidate, Business School, University of Western Australia

Brianna Barker Caza, Associate Professor of Organizational Behaviour, Asper School of Business, University of Manitoba

Alistair Cheyne, Professor of Organizational Psychology, Loughborough University

Stephen Clibborn, Associate Lecturer, University of Sydney Business School

David G. Collings, Professor of Human Resource Management, Dublin City University

Neil Conway, Professor of Organizational Behaviour, Royal Holloway University of London

Fang Lee Cooke, Professor of HRM and Asia Studies, Monash University

Nelarine Cornelious, Professor of HRM and Organization Studies, University of Bradford

Rick Csiernik, Professor, King's University College at Western University, Ontario

Niall Cullinane, Lecturer, Queens Belfast University

Daniel J. Cummings, School of Applied Psychology, Griffith University

Jean Cushen, Lecturer, School of Business, National University of Ireland, Maynooth

Marie T. Dasborough, Assistant Professor, School of Business and Administration, University of Miami

Gill Dix, Head of Strategy, ACAS

Jimmy Donaghey, Professor of Industrial Relations, Warwick Business School, Warwick University

Tony Dundon, Professor of Human Resource Management and Employment Relations, University of Manchester

Mike Emmott, CIPD

Elaine Farndale, Associate Professor of Human Resource Management, Center for International Human Resource Studies, School of Labor and Employment Relations, Pennsylvania State University

David Farnham, Professor of Employment Relations Emeritus, Portsmouth University

Charles H. Fay, Professor of Human Resource Management, School of Management and Labor Relations, Rutgers University of New Jersey

Erich C. Fein, Senior Lecturer, School of Psychology and Counselling, University of Southern Queensland

Alan Felstead, Research Professor, Cardiff School of Social Sciences, Cardiff University

Patricia Findlay, Professor of Work and Employment Relations, University of Strathclyde

Matt Flynn, Associate Professor, Xi'an Jiaotong Liverpool University

Chris Forde, Professor of Employment Studies at the Centre for Employment Relations Innovation and Change, University of Leeds

Helen Francis, Emeritus Professor of Human Resource Management, Edinburgh Napier University Business School

Erica French, Associate Professor of Management, Queensland University of Technology

Gregor Gall, Professor of Industrial Relations, School of Management, University of Bradford

Thomas Garavan, Professor, Edinburg Napier Business School, University of Napier

Mark Gilman, Professor of SME Growth & Development, Birmingham City University

Paul J. Gollan, Professor of Management and Director of the Australian Institute for Business and Economics, Faculty of Business, Economics and Law, University of Queensland

María C. González Menéndez, Professor of Sociology, University of Oviedo (Spain)

Michelle Greenwood, Senior Lecturer, Monash University

Michael Gregson, Head of Commercial, Acivico Ltd, Birmingham

Damian Grimshaw, Professor of Employment Studies, University of Manchester

Monika Hamori, Professor of Human Resource Management, IE Business School

Bill Harley, Professor, Department of Management and Marketing, Melbourne University

Brian Harney, Senior Lecturer in Strategy and HRM, Dublin City University

Christopher M. Harris, Assistant Professor in Human Resources, Texas Women's University

Geraldine Healy, Professor of Employment Relations, Centre for Research in Equality and Diversity, Queen Mary University of London

Rebecca Hewett, Senior Lecturer in Human Resource Management, Business School, University of Greenwich

Jason Heyes, Professor of Employment Relations at the Work, Organisation and Employment Relations Research Centre, University of Sheffield

Donald Hislop, Reader in Sociology of Contemporary Work, Loughborough University

Andy Hodder, Lecturer in Employment Relations, University of Birmingham

Anni Hollings, Principal Lecturer in HRM, Staffordshire University

Steve Hughes, Professor of International Organizations, University of Newcastle upon Tyne

Scott A. Hurrell, Senior Lecturer, Adam Smith Business School, University of Glasgow

Sue Hutchinson, Associate Professor in HRM, Bristol Business School, University of West of England

Pia Ingold, Assistant Professor, Department of Psychology, University of Zurich

Michael Isichei, PhD Candidate, Dublin City University

Stewart Johnstone, Senior Lecturer in HRM, University of Newcastle upon Tyne

Clare Kelliher, Professor of Work and Organization, Cranfield University

John Kimberley, Associate Professor of HRM, Birmingham City University

Daniel King, Senior Lecturer, Nottingham Business School, Nottingham Trent University

Martin Kleinmann, Full Professor, Department of Psychology, University of Zurich

Eva Knies, Assistant Professor, Utrecht University

Gary Latham, Secretary of State Professor of Organizational Effectiveness, Rotman School of Management, University of Toronto

Paul Latreille, Professor of Management at the Work, Organisation and Employment Relations Research Centre, University of Sheffield

Joan Lewis, HR and Employment Law Consultant

Dirk Lindebaum, Reader in Management, University of Liverpool, and Professor in Management, Hanken School of Economics, Helsinki

Stephanie Luce, Associate Professor of Labor Studies, CUNY

Marco Maatman, Business Consultant and Competence Leader, Atos

Oliver Mallett, Lecturer in Management, Durham University

Ashish Malik, Lecturer, Newcastle Business School, University of Newcastle

Teresa Marchant, Senior Lecturer, Griffith Business School, Griffith University

Mick Marchington, Emeritus Professor of Human Resource Management, Manchester Business School

Miguel Martínez Lucio, Professor at the Manchester Business School, University of Manchester

Maggie May, Griffith Business School, Griffith University

Ian McAndrew, Associate Professor, University of Otago

Jo McBride, Senior Lecturer in Industrial Relations, Work and Employment, University of Newcastle upon Tyne

Anthony McDonnell, Reader in Management, Queen's University, Belfast

Jeroen Meijerink, Assistant Professor of Human Resource Management, University of Twente

John P. Meyer, Professor in Industrial/Organizational Psychology, University of Western University, Canada

Marcia P. Miceli, Professor of Management, McDonough School of Business, Georgetown University

Jill Miller, Research Adviser, CIPD

Michael Moran, PhD Candidate, Department of Management, National University of Ireland, Galway

Michael J. Morley, Professor of Management, Kemmy Business School, University of Limerick

Rachel Morrison, Senior Lecturer, Faculty of Business and Law, AUT University

Kathryn Moura, PhD Candidate, Griffith Business School, Griffith University

Paula K. Mowbray, PhD Candidate, Griffith Business School, Griffith University

Daniel Muzio, Professor of Professions and Organizations, University of Newcastle upon Tyne

Christine Naschberger, Associate Professor in Human Resource Management,

Management, Organization and Law Department, Audencia Nantes School of Management

Janet P. Near, Coleman Chair and Professor of Management, Kelley School of Business, Indiana University

Margarita Nyfoudi, Senior Lecturer, Human Resource Management, Birmingham City University

Wayne O'Donohue, Senior Lecturer, Griffith Business School, Griffith University

John G. O'Gorman, Emeritus Professor, Griffith Health Institute, Griffith University

Joe O'Mahoney, Reader, Cardiff Business School, Cardiff University

Liz Oliver, Lecturer in Employment Law, University of Leeds

Antonios Panagiotakopoulos, Senior Lecturer of HRM at New York College, Greece and Visiting Research Fellow in HRM at CERIC, University of Leeds

Sharon K. Parker, Winthrop Professor, Business School, University of Western Australia

Marcello Pedaci, Researcher, University of Teramo

David Peetz, Professor of Employment Relations, Griffith Business School, Griffith University

Silvia Pirrioni, Doctoral Researcher, Nottingham Business School, Nottingham Trent University

Arthur Poropat, Senior Lecturer, School of Applied Psychology, Griffith University

Erik Poutsma, Associate Professor Comparative Research of Employment Relations, Radboud University

Vincenza Priola, Senior Lecturer in Organization Studies, Open University (UK)

Stephen Procter, Alcan Chair of Management, University of Newcastle upon Tyne

Alexandros Psychogios, Senior Lecturer in OB and HRM, Hull University

Amanda Pyman, Professor, Deakin University

Nagiah Ramasamy, Associate Professor, Sunway University

Sheryl Ramsay, Griffith Business School, Griffith University

Raymond Randall, Senior Lecturer in Organizational Behaviour and Human Resource Management, School of Business and Economics, Loughborough University

Tom Redman, Professor of Human Resource Management, Durham University

Douglas W.S. Renwick, Lecturer in HRM, Sheffield University

Susan Ressia, Lecturer, Griffith Business School, Griffith University

Fiona Robson, Deputy Director, Roehampton Business School, University of Roehampton

Maree Roche, Senior Lecturer in Organizational Psychology, University of Waikato

Jenny K. Rodriguez, Lecturer in Employment Studies, University of Manchester

Philip Rose, Chair, Department of Global Business, Hannam University

Peter Ross, Senior Lecturer, Griffith Business School, Griffith University

Kevin Rowan, Head of Organization and Services, TUC

Chris Rowley, Professor, Cass Business School, City University, London; IHCR, Korea University, Korea; Institute of Asia and Pacific Studies, Nottingham University

Bob Russell, Associate Professor, Griffith Business School, Griffith University

Karin Sanders, Professor of Human Resource Management and Organizational Behaviour, School of Management, University of New South Wales Business School

Judy Scully, Senior Lecturer in Work and Organizational Psychology, Aston University

Kate Shacklock, HRM and ER Discipline Leader, Griffith Business School, Griffith University

Dhara Shah, Lecturer, Griffith Business School, Griffith University

Maura Sheehan, Professor of International Management, Edinburgh Napier University

Peter Sheldon, Associate Professor, School of Management, University of New South Wales

Helen Shipton, Professor of International Human Resource Management, Nottingham Business School, Nottingham Trent University

David H.K. Shum, Professor, Griffith Health Institute, Griffith University

Melanie Simms, Professor of Work and Employment, Leicester University

Natalie Skinner, Senior Research Fellow, School of Management, University of South Australia

Gary Slater, Senior Teaching Fellow in Economics and Member of the Centre for Employment Relations Innovation and Change, University of Leeds

Alison Smith, Head of Executive Education and Corporate Relations Nottingham Business School, Nottingham Trent University

Mark Smith, Professor, Grenoble Ecole de Management, France

Ebrahim Soltani, Professor, Quality and Operation Management Department Chair, Hamdan Bin Mohammed Smart University

Christine Soo, Assistant Professor of Management and Organizations, UWA Business School, University of Western Australia

Amie Southcombe, Lecturer, Griffith Business School, Griffith University

Jim Stewart, Professor of Human Resource Development, Coventry University

John Stirling, Senior Teacher, University of Newcastle upon Tyne

Mark Stuart, Montague Burton Professor of HRM and Employment Relations, and Director of the Centre for Employment Relations Innovation and Change, University of Leeds

John Storey, Professor in Human Resource Management, Open University

Dimitrinka Stoyanova Russell, Lecturer in Human Resource Management, Cardiff Business School

Glenda Strachan, Professor of Management, Griffith Business School, Griffith University

Linda Tallberg, Lecturer, Griffith Business School, Griffith University

Stephen Taylor, Senior Lecturer, Human Resource Management, Exeter

Stephen T.T. Teo, Professor of HRM, RMIT University, Australia

Paul Thompson, Professor, Department of HRM, Strathclyde University

Amy Wei Tian, Lecturer in Management and Organizations, UWA Business School, University of Western Australia

Andrew R. Timming, Reader in Management, University of St Andrews

Olga Tregaskis, Professor of International HRM, Norwich Business School, University of East Anglia

John Trehy, PhD Student, Dublin City University

Herman H.M. Tse, Associate Professor, Monash Business School, Monash University, Australia

Paul Turner, Professor of Management Practice, Leeds Beckett University Business School

Paul S. Turner, Director of Portfolio, Georgia Group Consulting Limited, UK and Australia

Karina Van De Voorde, Assistant Professor, Tilburg University

Marc Van Veldhoven, Professor of Work, Health and Wellbeing, Tilburg University

Monique Veld, Assistant Professor, Faculty of Management, Science and Technology, Open University of the Netherlands

Robert Wapshott, Senior Lecturer in Entrepreneurship, University of Sheffield

Qi Wei, Lecturer in Human Resource Management, Business School, Kingston University

Geoff White, Professor of HRM, Greenwich University

Annika Wilhelmy, Assistant Professor, Department of Psychology, University of Zurich

Adrian Wilkinson, Professor, Griffith Business School, Griffith University

Morgen Witzel, University of Exeter Business School, Exeter University

Carol Wolkowitz, Reader, Warwick University

Geoff Wood, Professor, Essex Business School

Stephen Wood, Professor of Management, University of Leicester

Angela Wright, Senior Lecturer in HRM, Westminster University

Chris F. Wright, Research Fellow, University of Sydney

Ning Wu, Senior Lecturer in Human Resource Management, Nottingham Business School, Nottingham Trent University

Matthew Xerri, Lecturer, Griffith Business School, Griffith University

Ying Xu, Lecturer, Faculty of Business and Economics, Macquarie University

Kevin You, PhD Candidate, Griffith Business School, Griffith University

Vimolwan Yukongdi, Assistant Professor, Asian Institute of Technology, Thailand

Introduction

This book arises out of a continued and widening interest in the theory and practice of HRM in recent years. Organizational interest in HRM has also seen a steep growth in the number of students enrolling in HRM degree and individual courses. All managers have learnt that they do HRM for better or worse and with varied consequences but they cannot escape being involved in it.

In order to meet the needs of students studying HRM, there has been a large increase in the production of HRM texts and journals (see the lists below) and, as such, *The Encyclopaedia of Human Resource Management* has been designed to be a companion to, rather than a replacement for, a standard text on HRM.

The target audience of this book are researchers, academics, practitioners and students. The book is designed as a valuable reference resource for HRM professionals, and in addition, the encyclopaedia provides students new to the field with information about unfamiliar HRM terminology, technical 'jargon' and acronyms in a user-friendly way. The encyclopaedia provides easily accessible information that enables readers to understand key theoretical concepts such as the employment relationship, employee engagement and psychological contracts. In addition, HR practices such as broadbanding, zero-hour contracts and competencies are explained. We believe that this book, with its concise entries, will provide students with a compact companion that will complement their studies of HRM, as well as being a useful examination revision aid.

Our overall aim has been to produce an authoritative and comprehensive reference book covering a broad range of key HRM topics, with over 400 entries, each reflecting the views of an expert and authoritative author. The encyclopaedia is arranged in an alphabetical sequence to enable the reader to quickly locate the entry of interest. Each entry then provides a short introductory overview of the topic area, theory, technique or practice. Each term is defined and then there is an evaluative commentary. In addition, each entry provides a list of references and further readings that will guide the user to resources enabling them to gain a deeper awareness and understanding of each topic. The selected readings provide a wide range of appropriate material from classic texts, theoretical and empirical journal articles, and seminal and up-to-date papers for the reader to follow up.

The completing of such a work is not without complexity as there are no clearly defined limits to the subject of HRM and the boundaries between, for example, HRM and 'organizational behaviour' and 'management' are somewhat elusive. Thus entries can be found on 'core' HR areas as performance appraisal, industrial conflict, and key organizational behaviour terms including organizational culture and organizational commitment, and on broader management terms such as strategy, diversity, and employment law. The rationale is that these terms are likely to be used in a HRM course that seeks to link HR issues into broader management practice. Entries are also cross-referenced to other relevant entries where appropriate.

We would like to thank the authors and the in-house publishing team for their invaluable contribution to this project. We are also grateful to Susan Ressia for her work in putting the book together.

ADRIAN WILKINSON AND STEWART JOHNSTONE

General texts on HRM

Armstrong, A. and S. Taylor (2014), *Armstrong's Handbook of Human Resource Management Practice*, 13th edn, Philadelphia: Kogan Page Ltd.

Bach, S. and M. Edwards (eds) (2013), *Managing Human Resources: Human Resource Management in Transition*, 5th edn, Chichester: John Wiley & Sons Inc.

Banfield, P. and R. Kay (2012), *Introduction to Human Resource Management*, 2nd edn, Oxford: Oxford University Press.

Beardwell, I. and A. Thompson (2014), *Human Resource Management: A Contemporary Approach*, 7th edn, Boston: Pearson.

Bratton, J. and J. Gold (2012), *Human Resource Management: Theory and Practice*, 5th edn, Basingstoke: Palgrave Macmillan.

Carbery, R. and C. Cross (2013), *Human Resource Management: A Concise Introduction*, New York: Palgrave Macmillan.

Holland, P., C. Sheehan, R. Donohoe, A. Pyman and B. Allen (2014), *Contemporary Issues and Challenges in HRM*, 3rd revised edn, Prahan: Tilde Publishing.

Kramer, R., T. Bartram, H. De Cieri, R.A. Noe, J.R. Hollenbeck, B. Gerhart and P.M. Wright (2014), *Human Resource Management in Australia: Strategy, People, Performance*, 5th edn, North Ryde: McGraw Hill.

Leatherbarrow, C. and J.A. Fletcher (2014), *Introduction to Human Resource Management: A Guide to HR in Practice*, 3rd edn, London: Chartered Institute of Personnel and Development.

Legge, K. (2005), *Human Resource Management: Rhetorics and Realities*, Anniversary edn, New York: Palgrave Macmillan.

Mabey, C., G. Salaman and J. Storey (eds) (1998), *Strategic Human Resource Management: A Reader*, Thousand Oaks, CA: Sage.

Marchington, M. and A. Wilkinson (2012), *Human Resource Management at Work: People Management and Development*, 5th edn, London: Chartered Institute of Personnel and Development.

Noe, R.A., J.R. Hollenbeck, B. Gerhart and P.M. Wright (2014), *Fundamentals of Human Resource Management*, 5th edn, New York: McGraw-Hill.

Redman, T. and A. Wilkinson (eds) (2013), *Contemporary Human Resource Management: Text and Cases*, 4th edn, Harlow: Pearson.

Schuler, R. and S.E. Jackson (eds) (2007), *Strategic Human Resource Management*, Malden, MA: Blackwell.

Sparrow, P., M. Hird and C. Cooper (2015), *Do We Need HR?* Basingstoke: Palgrave Macmillan.

Stone, R. (2014), *Managing Human Resources*, 8th edn, Milton: John Wiley & Sons.

Storey, J. (ed.) (2007), *Human Resource Management: A Critical Text*, 3rd edn, London: Thomson Learning.

Thomson, R., E. Arney and A. Thomson (2015), *Managing People: A Practical Guide For Front-Line Managers*, 4th revised edn, London: Routledge.

Torrington, D., L. Hall, S. Taylor and C. Atkinson (2014), *Human Resource Management*, 9th edn, Pearson: Harlow.

Tyson, S. (2015), *Essentials of Human Resource Management*, 6th edn, London: Routledge.

Wilkinson, A., T. Redman, S. Snell and N. Bacon (eds) (2009), *The Sage Handbook of Human Resource Management*, London: Sage.

HRM journals

Asia Pacific Journal of Human Resources http://onlinelibrary.wiley.com/journal/10.1111/%28ISSN%291744-7941

British Journal of Industrial Relations http://onlinelibrary.wiley.com/journal/10.1111/%28ISSN%291467-8543

Employee Relations www.emeraldinsight.com/loi/er

Employment Relations Record http://search.informit.com.au/browseJournalTitle;res=IELBUS;issn=1444-7053

Human Resource Management Journal (UK) http://onlinelibrary.wiley.com/journal/10.1111/%28ISSN%291748-8583

Human Resource Management (US) http://onlinelibrary.wiley.com/journal/10.1002/%28ISSN%291099-050X

Industrial Relations Journal (UK) http://onlinelibrary.wiley.com/journal/10.1111/%28ISSN%291468-2338

Industrial Relations: A Journal of Economy and Society http://onlinelibrary.wiley.com/doi/10.1111/irel.2015.54.issue-2/issuetoc

International Journal of Employment Studies http://search.informit.com.au/browseJournalTitle;res=IELBUS;issn=1039-6993

International Journal of Human Resource Management www.tandfonline.com/toc/rijh20/current#
Journal of Industrial Relations http://jir.sagepub.com
Journal of Labour and Industry: A Journal of the Social and Economic Relations of Work www.tandfonline.com/
   toc/rlab20/current
Journal of Organizational Effectiveness: People and Performance www.emeraldinsight.com/journals.
   htm?issn=2051-6614&volume=1&issue=1
Personnel Review www.emeraldinsight.com/loi/PR
Work, Employment and Society http://wes.sagepub.com/content/by/year

Useful websites

Acas (Advisory Conciliation and Arbitration Service) www.acas.org.uk
Academy of Human Resource Development, global organization sharing resources and networking www.
   ahrd.org
American Society for Human Resource Management www.shrm.org
Australian Human Resources Institute, useful resources and networking www.ahri.com.au
CBI www.cbi.org.uk
Chartered Institute of Personnel and Development www.cipd.co.uk
Company information including financial statements and company profiles www.dnb.co.uk/solutions/
   sales-and-marketing/hoovers
Department for Business, Innovation and Skills (UK) www.gov.uk/government/organisations/department-
   for-business-innovation-skills
Department of Employment (Australia) https://employment.gov.au
Department of Labor (US) https://www.dol.gov
Employing people www.gov.uk/browse/employing-people
EUR-Lex   http://eur-lex.europa.eu/summary/chapter/employment_and_social_policy.html?root_default=
   SUM_1_CODED=17, provides access to European Union law. This site links to employment and social
   policy.
European Foundation for the Improvement of Living and Working Conditions www.eurofound.europa.eu
Fairwork Commission Australia www.fwc.gov.au
Health and Safety Executive www.hse.gov.uk
Hong Kong Institute of Human Resource Management www.hkihrm.org
Human Resources Processionals Association, Canada www.hrpa.ca/Pages/Default.aspx
Incomes Data Services Limited (includes useful articles on HRM topics) www.incomesdata.co.uk
Investors in People www.investorsinpeople.co.uk
Law Rights – UK Employment Law www.compactlaw.co.uk/free-legal-information/employment-law.html
National Institute of Economic and Social Research http://niesr.ac.uk
National Institute of Personnel Management http://nipm.in
Occupational Health and Safety (US), Department of Labor www.osha.gov
People Management (magazine produced by the CIPD with topical articles) www.peoplemanagement.co.uk
Recruitment and salary information www.hays.com.au/index.htm
Safe Work Australia www.safeworkaustralia.gov.au/sites/SWA
TUC (main confederation of British trade unions) www.tuc.org.uk
UKCES www.gov.uk/government/organisations/uk-commission-for-employment-and-skills
Workplace Occupational Health and Safety Australia www.australia.gov.au/topics/health-and-safety/
   occupational-health-and-safety
Work Foundation www.theworkfoundation.com
Worksmart https://worksmart.org.uk
World at Work, US compensation/remuneration and total rewards information www.worldatwork.org/home/
   html/home.jsp

Absence

Absence from work generally falls into two categories: planned and unplanned. Planned absence is time off work that can be scheduled in advance, such as annual leave and training. On the whole, the employer has some time to prepare and organize cover, or there's time available for project handovers to another member of staff. These planned absences are usually for a set duration, as set out in an organization's policies and with consideration of legal requirements. In contrast, unplanned absence is when an employee is absent from work at very short notice. This could be due to sickness absence, to care for dependents or for bereavement. The timing and duration of these absences is not as predictable as for planned absences. When we talk about absence management, it is usually unplanned absence that we are referring to.

Effectively managing absence from work is important, as it is a significant cost to business. An independent review of the sickness absence system in Great Britain in 2011 estimated that 140 million working days are lost to sickness absence each year. Employers pay sick pay and associated costs of £9 billion a year, and the state spends £13 billion annually on health-related benefits. The 2014 CIPD/*Simplyhealth* Absence Management survey estimates that sickness absence in the UK costs an organization around £600 per employee per year.

Sickness absence tends to be categorized as either short-term (up to seven days), medium-term (up to four weeks) or long-term (four weeks or more). The survey found most UK absence is classified as short-term (common causes are minor illness, including colds/flu, headaches; back pain; musculoskeletal injuries; stress and home/family responsibilities). The most common causes of long-term absence are acute medical conditions (stroke, heart attack and cancer), musculoskeletal injuries, stress, mental ill-health and back pain. Some absences are unavoidable; however, employers can try to minimize absence costs through promoting employee health and wellbeing, and taking firm action against illegitimate absence (persistent lateness and unauthorized absence). Not taking such action can have a negative effect on employee morale and colleagues' workloads. However, people also need to be discouraged from coming to work when they're genuinely ill.

If organizations are to most effectively manage absence, it is important to first accurately measure and monitor it, identifying trends and then exploring underlying causes and examine why absence may be higher in some parts of the organization than others. The two most common measures of absence are the number of days absent per employee per year, and the percentage of working time lost. Some organizations have introduced 'trigger mechanisms' to review attendance and alert line managers to any patterns of absence such as if an employee exceeds a certain number of days absent within a set time period, or regular patterns, such as taking every Friday off. Organizations need to have a formal policy in place that clearly states the expectations of employees when they need to take time off work, for example, who they should notify that they won't be in work, and how long they can take off work before any requirements of a note from a healthcare professional. The policy should also make it clear what employees can expect from their employer, such as for how long and at what rate they are entitled to sick pay.

Responsibility for managing absence usually falls to the HR department and line managers. However, research has revealed that line managers are seldom receiving the training and support they need to do so effectively. Line managers are ideally placed to spot the early warning signs of issues and provide support where necessary. They need to have good communication skills and create a trusting culture so employees feel able to flag a potential issue before it becomes a real problem. In short, line managers need to be trained in:

- the organization's absence management policies and procedures;
- the legal issues around absence management that exist in each of the countries the organization operates in;
- the management of complex cases and how to address sensitive issues, in particular 'myth-busting' about what they can and cannot do;
- having effective conversations with staff when an issue becomes apparent, including discussing possible adjustments to work or the work environment that could help someone stay in work;
- how to hold effective return-to-work interviews;
- the role of occupational health services and proactive measures to support staff health and wellbeing.

One of the most effective ways to manage absence is for managers to hold return-to-work interviews with staff. These discussions provide managers with an opportunity to have a dialogue with staff about underlying issues that might be causing the absence and to discuss possible adjustments to the work itself or the work environment. If investigation into absence from work deems that absence is unacceptable or illegitimate, disciplinary procedures may be deemed appropriate. Over recent years, flexible working has increasingly been recognized as an effective method of managing absence, especially given the wider benefits for employee satisfaction and engagement. Offering flexible working options, such as flexible working hours or leave for family circumstances, enables people to better manage their work and home responsibilities, and supports employee well-being.

Overall, having a well-thought-out absence management approach, that is appropriate for your business, is essential to maximize productivity and minimize absence costs. It is generally accepted that the most effective absence management approaches and strategies don't just focus on reactively managing absence, but should also take a preventative stance. Investing in the areas of employee wellbeing that are most relevant for the workforce will help create a great place to work where employees feel valued and engaged.

JILL MILLER

See also:
Flexible working; Presenteeism; Wellbeing.

References and selected further readings

Acas (2014), *Managing Attendance and Employee Turnover*, London: Acas.
Black, C. and D. Frost (2011), *Health at Work: An Independent Review of Sickness Absence*, Cm 8205, London: Department for Work and Pensions, www.dwp.gov.uk/docs/health-at-work.pdf.
CIPD (2006), *Absence – Online Tool*, London: Chartered Institute of Personnel and Development, www.cipd.co.uk/hr-resources/practical-tools/absence-management.aspx.
CIPD (2014), *Absence Management Survey*, London: Chartered Institute of Personnel and Development.

Embleton, S. and L. Brown (2014), Long-term sickness absence: five tricky issues for employers, *Employers' Law*, September, pp. 14–15.
Gov.uk (2014), *Fit for Work*, www.gov.uk/government/uploads/system/uploads/attachment_data/file/362480/fit-for-work.pdf.

Acas

The Advisory, Conciliation and Arbitration Service (Acas) was established in the UK as a statutory body under the Employment Protection Act (1975). The then-Department of Employment's role in industrial disputes was facing criticism in part as its conciliation role was felt to be compromised at a time when the department was responsible for running an incomes' policy. An organization was therefore needed that was independent of government and Acas was established to meet this need (see Hawes, 2000; Sisson and Taylor, 2006).

A largely publicly funded body, Acas' independence is assured by its governance arrangement with a council made up of members drawn from employers, trade unions and independent backgrounds. The Act creating Acas also provided that the service should not be subject to directions from any minister of the Crown.

Acas has a duty to promote the improvement of industrial relations in Great Britain. The discharge of this role has changed over the past 40 years in the light of an ever-evolving industrial relations landscape.

In its early days and up to the mid-1980s, Acas' work was dominated by collective employment relations and Acas regularly handled some 2,000–3,000 requests for collective dispute resolution each year. Collective bargaining was regarded as the ideal mechanism for regulating voluntary employment relations and Acas had a statutory duty to promote its use and extension.

The late 1980s saw changes in the law surrounding trade unions and industrial disputes. The volume of requests for Acas conciliation in collective disputes declined, while individual employment disputes, particularly as expressed in employment tribunal claims grew (Saundry and Dix, 2014). In 1988 there were 29,000 applications to industrial (now employment) tribunals, but by 1999 that number had increased to more than 100,000 (Dix et al., 2008). This rise in tribunal cases saw the balance of Acas' work shift towards individual dispute resolution, which remains the case today. In 1993 Acas' statutory duty to encourage the extension of collective bargaining was removed. This is not to say that Acas has no current role in collective issues and the service still conciliates in around 800–900 collective disputes per year.

The increase in tribunal cases during the 1990s aroused governmental concern and led to a growing interest in alternative dispute resolution approaches to resolving workplace disputes such as mediation. In April 2014, Acas launched a new Early Conciliation service, which requires all potential employment tribunal applicants to approach Acas first to see if their dispute can be settled through conciliation before it is lodged with the employment tribunal.

Acas is best known, certainly domestically, for its dispute resolution work but preventing disputes is also an important part of its duty to promote the improvement of employment relations. From its earliest days Acas has carried out advisory projects inside organizations.

Acas has also played a prominent role over the years as a commentator on workplace issues and a commissioner of employment relations research. Acas also publishes policy discussion papers and is one of the co-sponsors of the Workplace Employment Relations Study, the nationally and internationally renowned survey of British workplaces. The series dates back to 1980 with the sixth survey conducted in 2011 (van Wanrooy et al., 2013).

GILL DIX AND GEORGE BOYCE

See also:

Alternative dispute resolution; Arbitration; Conciliation; Employment tribunal; Mediation.

References and selected further readings

Acas (2014), *Measuring the Value and Impacts of Acas*, research paper, www.acas.org.uk/media/pdf/j/e/TRI14-Measuring-the-Value-and-Impacts-of-Acas-2014.pdf.

Dix, G., J. Forth and K. Sisson (2008), Conflict at work: the pattern of disputes in Britain since 1980, in W. Brown, A. Bryson, J. Forth and K. Whitfield (eds), *The Evolution of the Modern Workplace*, Cambridge: Cambridge University Press.

Hawes, W. (2000), Setting the pace or running alongside: Acas and the changing employment relationship, in B. Towers and W. Brown (eds), *Employment Relations in Britain: 25 Years of the Advisory, Conciliation and Arbitration Service*, Oxford: Blackwell.

Saundry, R. and G. Dix (2014), Conflict resolution in the UK, in W.K. Roche, P. Teague and A.J.S. Colvin (eds), *Oxford Handbook of Conflict Management in Organisations*, Oxford: Oxford University Press.

Sisson, K. and J. Taylor (2006), The changing face of British employment relations, in L. Dickens and A. Neal (eds), *The Changing Institutional Face of British Employment Relations*, New York: Kluwer Law International.

van Wanrooy, B., H. Bewley, A. Bryson, J. Forth, S. Freeth, L. Stokes and S. Wood (2013), *Employment Relations in the Shadow of Recession*, Basingstoke: Palgrave McMillan.

Aesthetic labour

Aesthetic labour refers to the embodied attributes and characteristics of employees, especially in interactive service work. It focuses on how an employee's appearance contributes (either positively or negatively) to the consumer experience as it unfolds in the workplace.

Aesthetic labour has its roots in the field of impression management. Scholars of aesthetic labour are thus mostly interested in understanding how employees' physical appearance can positively convey the 'brand' of the organization. One example is a retail clothing store that only hires attractive saleswomen in order to target a young and female demographic of customer. Another example is a security company that only hires visibly tattooed job candidates because security guards are supposed to appear tough and intimidating. In both cases, the 'look' of the employee is as important as his or her skills or experiences.

The literature on aesthetic labour can be broadly divided into two strands. The first strand examines how having the right 'look' can often result in positive employment and consumer experience outcomes. The right 'look' depends on the context of the organization and its target demographic, but often it corresponds to beauty and attractiveness.

The second strand of literature examines how having the wrong 'look' can result in negative employment and consumer experience outcomes. Thus, employees and job candidates with a physical stigma often encounter prejudice and outright discrimination in the labour market because they do not conform to the aesthetic standards of the organization and the broader society.

Aesthetic labour is an important area of research because it recognizes the reality that employment success is, contrary to popular opinion, not simply a matter of bringing the right skills and experiences to the labour market. Success also depends in large part on the physical attributes of employees and job candidates. This is especially true in the service sector where employees represent the 'image' of the company to the customer.

ANDREW R. TIMMING

See also:

Direct discrimination; Diversity management; Impression management; Recruitment; Selection.

References and selected further readings

Gatta, M. (2011), In the 'blink' of an eye — American high end small retail businesses and the public workforce system, in I. Grugulis and O. Bozkurt (eds), *Retail Work*, Basingstoke: Palgrave Macmillan.

Nickson, D., C. Warhurst, A. Witz and A.M. Cullen (2001), The importance of being aesthetic: work, employment and service organization, in A. Sturdy, I. Grugulis and H. Willmott (eds), *Customer Service*, Basingstoke: Palgrave.

Pettinger, L. (2004), Brand culture and branded workers: service work and aesthetic labour in fashion retail, *Consumption, Markets & Culture*, **7**(2), pp. 165–184.

Timming, A.R. (2015), Visible tattoos in the service sector: a new challenge to recruitment and selection, *Work, Employment & Society*, **29**(1), pp. 60–78.

Warhurst, C. and D. Nickson (2007), Employee experience of aesthetic labour in retail and hospitality, *Work, Employment & Society*, **21**(1), pp. 103–120.

Williams, C.L. and C. Connell (2010), 'Looking good and sounding right': aesthetic labor and social inequality in the retail industry, *Work and Occupations*, **37**(3), pp. 349–377.

Age discrimination

Age discrimination (or ageism) within a workplace context is defined as the treatment of an employee in a way that is influenced by his or her age. This can be in the form of stereotyping based on age; restricting opportunities for employment, career development or workplace accommodation; or bullying and harassment. Like other forms of discrimination, ageism can be both direct – such as setting pay based on age – or indirect, such as paying employees more for long service, a condition that older workers would be more likely to meet than younger ones (Acas, 2011).

Age discrimination can affect both older and younger employees. The 2001 Employment Equality (Age) Directive was transposed into law of EU member states to protect workers of all ages (although the US ADEA only prohibits age discrimination against people 40 years old and older). Generally however, research on age discrimination has focused on that experienced by older workers, especially with respect to recruitment and retention. While employers generally have some positive perceptions of older workers (such as having valuable experience or being customer-friendly), employers also see older workers as lacking up-to-date skills, being resistant to change and vulnerable to health problems (Carnegie Trust, 1996). The term 'master narrative of decline' has been coined to identify the deterministic relationship between age and physical and mental capacity (Tretheway, 2001). However, there is little, if any, evidence of declining mental capacity that would negatively impact on work capacity, at least before the age of 70 (Meadows, 2004). Older people may process information slower than their younger colleagues, but are better able to set new information in a wider context, relying on experience, and can therefore process larger batches of information. While physical capacity does decline with age, advances in technology have meant that a healthy 60-year-old is physically capable of doing most jobs (Harper, 2011).

MATT FLYNN

See also:

Direct discrimination; Diversity management; Older worker; Young workers.

References and selected further readings

Acas (2011), *Age and the Workplace*, London: Acas.
Carnegie Trust (1996), *The Third Age: The Continuing Challenge*, Dunfermline: Carnegie United Kingdom Trust.
Harper, S. (2011), Health and wellbeing in older workers: capacity change with age, in E. Parry and S. Tyson (eds), *Managing an Age Diverse Workforce*, London: Palgrave Macmillan, pp. 206–222.
Meadows, P. (2004), *Retirement Ages in the UK: A Review of the Literature*, London: DTI, www.dti.gov.uk/er/emar/errs18.pdf.
Tretheway, A. (2001), Reproducing and resisting the master narrative of decline: midlife professional women's experiences of aging, *Management Communication Quarterly*, **15**(2), pp. 183–226.

Ageing workforce

As populations age, both governments and employers are looking for ways to encourage (and to a certain extent compel) people to delay retirement. Although the main drivers for public and HRM policies to extend working life are to remove strain from, and ensure the viability of, state and occupational pension systems, Western European countries are also facing chronic skills shortages due to low fertility rates (Van Berkel et al., 2007). Employers have been encouraged by both EU and national governments to facilitate longer working lives through a combination of 'Active Ageing' HRM policies and practices (Eurofound, 2013). These have generally included:

- Flexible working hours arrangements in order to support a gradual exit from the labor market. Many EU countries also have statutes to require employers to provide flexible working hours arrangements for employees with eldercare responsibilities.
- Lifelong learning to support later-life career changes and to encourage older workers to keep their skills up to date. There is evidence that older workers are less likely to both be offered and take up training opportunities, in part because employer-sponsored training focuses primarily on new employees through induction training.
- Healthy workplaces in order to mitigate the onset of and support older workers in managing long-term health conditions. The Workability Index (Ilmarinen, 1999), as designed by the Finnish Institute of Occupational Health, is a system that has generated a great deal of both academic and practitioner interest as it has played a major role in raising Finland's real retirement age from 59 to 63.4 since 2005.

- Career management in order to facilitate the transition of older workers from physically demanding work toward employment in which they can use their skills and experience. A recent initiative led by employers and unions in the UK National Health Service is reviewing career routes for all healthcare professionals.
- Financial literacy in order to raise awareness of workers of their income from pension and savings once they leave the labor market. Employer provided pre-retirement planning is less prevalent now, but some governments, including the UK, are providing universal access to financial advisory services.

More recent good practice age management guidance has emphasized not only HRM policies, but labor processes as well. In particular, managers have been encouraged to conduct appraisals with older workers in order to facilitate dialogue on work and retirement plans (McNair and Flynn, 2012).

MATT FLYNN

See also:

Default retirement age; Older worker; Retirement.

References and selected further readings

Eurofound (2013), *Role of Governments and Social Partners in Keeping Older Workers in the Labour Market*, Dublin: Eurofound.
Ilmarinen, J. (1999), *Ageing Workers in the European Union: Status and Promotion of Working Ability, Employability and Employment*, Helsinki: Finnish Institute of Occupational Health.
McNair, S. and M. Flynn (2012), *Managing a Healthy Ageing Workforce: A Business Imperative*, Glasgow: HWL.
Van Berkel, R., V. Borghi, E. Carmel, K. Hamblin and T. Papadopoulos (2007), Governing the activation of older workers in the European Union, *International Journal of Sociology and Social Policy*, **27**(9/10), pp. 387–400.

Alienation

Alienation is an all-encompassing concept central to our understanding of work and life within capitalism. In general terms and following Marx, we can say that alienation expresses the dissociation existing between work, intended as fundamental, creative and enriching human life activity, and the particular form it takes under capitalism. Within this system, based on the exchange of commodities privately owned, work is performed as labour – the only commodity workers own – and sold to employers in exchange for a wage, which is, in turn, used to satisfy immediate needs. This particular economic structure – that compels workers to sell their work to survive – alienate workers in so far as it deprives them of control over their labour process, now managed and organized by the employer in search of profitability, and over the product of their work, now the legitimate property of the employers. Instead of finding in their work a creative and fulfilling activity in which mind and hands contribute to create a product that can satisfy an immediate human need, workers see their work as a pure necessity performed under the pressure to earn a wage. The alienation of workers due to the lack of control of their labour process it is further exacerbated by workers' powerlessness in the face of processes of work intensification, automation, costs reduction that the logic of competition among individual capitals, which drives the system, imposes on societies.

Marx saw these dimensions of alienation originated within the capitalist work process not just affecting individual workers in their attitude toward work (seen often just as an unpleasant reality and 'shunned as a plague' as Marx would have put it) but also as directly connected to the way in which social relationships are shaped. Since school age, capitalism imbues individuals in economic categories that respond to the logic of commodities exchanged in the market. Thus it seems normal to have bosses enforce orders, rely on an employer for a wage, compete with other workers, or ignore the work done by other workers when buying in a supermarket. This logic, individualizing, separating and alienating human beings from each other, disguises the social relations that substantiate the nature of commodities into 'the fantastic form of a relation between things' (Marx, 1976, p. 165). Looking at the way in which capitalism reproduces itself, concealing its truly unhuman and dehumanizing nature in the common sense of things, Marx argued that a general social alienation affect all classes within societies, including capitalists, whose actions and relations are dictated by dynamics that they cannot independently control.

MAURIZIO ATZENI

See also:

Deskilling; Division of labour; Self-management.

References and selected further readings

Hyman, R. (2006), Marxist thought and the analysis of work, in M. Korczynski, R. Hodson and P. Edwards (eds), *Social Theory at Work*, Oxford: Oxford University Press.
Marx, K. (1976), *Capital, Vol. 1*, section on the labour process and the fetishism of commodities, London: Penguin.
Spencer, D. (2014), Marx and Marxist views on work, in M. Atzeni (ed.), *Workers and Labour in a Globalised Capitalism*, Basingstoke: Palgrave.
Swain, D. (2012), *An Introduction to Marx's Theory of Alienation*, London: Bookmarks.

Alternative dispute resolution

Alternative dispute resolution (ADR) refers to a range of third-party intervention techniques and strategies intended to assist parties in conflict achieve a mutually acceptable outcome. A key definitional issue concerns what such processes are an alternative to: in the workplace context this might be external arbitral via (labour) courts/tribunals, but also more formal internal adjudicatory arrangements such as grievance procedures. To the extent that ADR processes have become increasingly structured/institutionalized, various commentators/practitioners instead prefer the term 'appropriate' dispute resolution.

The range of ADR processes embraces negotiation, mediation, conciliation, arbitration and various hybrids, the last including specific techniques such as 'med-arb,' 'arb-med,' early neutral evaluation, fact-finding, private judging, mini-trial, ombuds, etc. The significance of such approaches is revealed by their growing prevalence in both Europe (Purcell, 2010) and the US (Stipanowich and Lamare, 2013), with mediation, for example, almost ubiquitous in large corporations in the latter.

As Menkel-Meadow (2010) explains, the empirical literature generally falls into two categories: descriptive studies of ADR and its effects, and comparative studies that seek to assess various forms of ADR against more conventional processes on dimensions such as efficacy, fairness, etc. A critical concern for some commentators is the extent to which such processes offer appropriate protections for vulnerable participants or instead privatize justice. Processes may be further delineated empirically (Menkel-Meadow, 2010) according to the number of participants, whether participation is voluntary or (court) mandated (or indeed annexed), the extent to which parties control outcomes, and whether processes are public or private. These dimensions render the comparative field especially challenging, although a small number of studies that seek to evaluate ADR processes using methods that account for selection and control groups with random allocation is emerging. Relatedly, in the face of the variety of possible processes, some authorities have also sought to establish heuristics for 'fitting the forum to the fuss' (Sander and Goldberg, 2007). The availability of a range of dispute resolution options is also integral to the notion of 'conflict management systems' gaining in popularity, most notably in large US corporations.

PAUL LATREILLE

See also:
Arbitration; Conciliation; Employment tribunal; Mediation.

References and selected further readings

Green, M.Z. (2005), Tackling employment discrimination with ADR: does mediation offer a shield for the haves nor real opportunity for the have-nots, *Berkeley Journal of Employment and Labor Law*, **26**(2), pp. 321–361.

Menkel-Meadow, C.J. (2010), Dispute resolution, in P. Cane and H.M. Kritzer (eds), *The Oxford Handbook of Empirical Legal Research*, Oxford: Oxford University Press.

Purcell, J. (2010), Individual Disputes at the Workplace: Alternative Disputes Resolution, Dublin: Eurofound.

Roche, W.K., P. Teague and A.J.S. Colvin (2014), *The Oxford Handbook of Conflict Management in Organizations*, Oxford: Oxford University Press.

Sander, F.E.A. and S.B. Goldberg (2007), Fitting the forum to the fuss: a user-friendly guide to selecting an ADR procedure, *Negotiation Journal*, **10**(1), pp. 49–68.

Stipanowich, T. and J.R. Lamare (2013), Living with ADR: evolving perceptions and use of mediation, arbitration and conflict management in Fortune 1,000 corporations, *Harvard Negotiation Law Review*, **19**, pp. 1–68.

AMO model

The AMO model is one of the most often used theories in HRM research. The aim of the model is to explain the mechanisms linking HRM and performance. The AMO model is a comprehensive model that combines insights from several underlying theories, such as social exchange theory and the job characteristics model. Appelbaum and colleagues (200) were among the first to introduce the AMO model in the HRM literature in their well-cited book *Manufacturing Advantage: Why High-Performance Work Systems Pay Off*.

The rationale of the AMO model is that individuals perform well when they have the ability (A), motivation (M) and opportunities to perform (O). Employees are able to do their job if they possess the necessary knowledge and skills. They are willing to do their job if they feel adequately interested and incentivized. Employees have the opportunities to perform if their work structure and environment provides them with the necessary support and avenues for expression. Boxall and Purcell (2008, p. 173) summarize the reasoning behind the AMO framework by stating that 'individual attributes have a huge impact but even the most able and motivated people cannot perform well if they lack "the tools to finish the job" or work in an unsupportive social environment.' The AMO model is often expressed in the following mathematical equation: $P = f\,(A,M,O)$.

The AMO model is not just a conceptual tool, it is based on research by industrial psychologists in the 1980s and 1990s. However, most of these studies include only one or two AMO variables. There are very few studies that have included all three AMO variables in a comprehensive study. A notable exception is a recent study by Knies and Leisink (2014), which supports the theoretical assumption that employees' abilities, motivation and opportunities to perform mediate the relationship between HRM and performance. Moreover, this study helped to clarify how the AMO variables are interrelated. The results show that individual characteristics (that is, ability and motivation) are directly related to individual performance, whereas job characteristics (that is, opportunity) have an indirect effect through motivation.

EVA KNIES

See also:

High-performance work systems; Strategic HRM.

References and selected further readings

Appelbaum, E., T. Bailey, P. Berg and A.L. Kalleberg (2001), *Manufacturing Advantage: Why High-Performance Work Systems Pay Off*, Ithaca, NY: Cornell University Press.
Boxall, P. and J. Purcell (2008), *Strategy and Human Resource Management*, Basingstoke: Palgrave.
Jiang, K., D.P. Lepak, J. Hu and J.C. Baer (2012), How does human resource management influence organizational outcomes? A meta-analytic investigation of mediating mechanisms, *Academy of Management Journal*, **55**(6), pp. 1264–1294.
Knies, E. and P.L.M. Leisink (2014), Linking people management and extra-role behaviour: results of a longitudinal study, *Human Resource Management Journal*, **24**(1), pp. 57–76.
Liu, Y., J.G. Combs, D.J. Ketchen and R.D. Ireland (2007), The value of human resource management for organizational performance, *Business Horizons*, **50**(6), pp. 503–511.

Annualized hours

An annualized hours arrangement involves the scheduling of working time over a year rather than a basic working week. A hypothetical system might start from a year of 52.2 weeks of 39 working hours (2035.8 hours), deducting 25 days leave (195 hours) and eight days public holidays (62.4 hours) to leave 1,778.4 hours available for rostering, which may be scheduled as shifts. Typically, a certain number of hours (e.g., 200) are allocated as 'reserve' or 'floating' hours. These are used as a form of compulsory overtime, subject to certain agreements around notice periods. Similar arrangements that operate over shorter periods, such as a quarter or a month, are commonly known as 'working time accounts'.

The annualized hours system provides employers with long-term flexibility (as required in seasonal industries) and short-term flexibility since it allows for managers to draw down reserve hours as required. Annualized hours are attractive as a substitute for overtime or temporary work as they permit accurate labour scheduling while avoiding the costs associated with conventional overtime or adding to headcount. The increased variation of working time for employees is often compensated for by greater overall time off work, whether by reducing the nominal basic week, increasing leave entitlement or waiving non-utilized reserve hours. This is usually cost-effective, given the higher productivity and financial savings associated with annualized hours. Workers also often receive higher pay and the consolidation of earnings into salaries by way of compensation.

However, annualized hours systems can be complex to introduce and administer. Individual working time must be continually monitored and employees must be willing to deliver their contracted flexible hours. Managers need to ensure that 'banked hours' are not unduly over- or under-accumulated, and must normally be willing to write off those that are not used. There is also scope for conflict in transitions to the system as annualized hours arrangements lead to long-hour workers losing overtime pay, while others are effectively conscripted into periodic extra work. As a result, annualized hours are most commonly in evidence in countries with robust collective bargaining arrangements, such as Germany, or legal support, such as France.

JAMES ARROWSMITH

See also:

Long hours culture; Overtime; Shift work; Unsocial hours; Work–life balance; Working time.

References and selected further readings

Arrowsmith, J. (2007), Why is there not more 'annualised hours' working in Britain? *Industrial Relations Journal*, **38**(5), pp. 423–438.

Corominas, A. and R. Pastor (2010), Replanning working time under annualised working hours, *International Journal of Production Research*, *11*(1), pp. 1493–1515.

Heyes, J. (1997), Annualised hours and the 'knock': the organisation of working time in a chemicals plant, *Work Employment & Society*, **11**(1), pp. 65–81.

Apprenticeship

The term 'apprenticeship' has varied meanings depending on time and place. It is mostly associated with a European tradition which originated and developed in the later Middle Ages as a system of training young people for entry to craft and technical level occupations. The system was at that time generally managed by what were known as 'guilds', sometimes seen as forerunners of both trade unions and professional associations. Members of these guilds were expert practitioners of a trade or craft, known as 'masters'. A master would take on a young person as an apprentice for a defined period of time, often around seven years, providing the master with access to labour and often some payment, and the apprenticeship provided the young person with access to learning and development. The relationship between master and apprentice was often governed by an 'indenture', which was a form of legal contract specifying terms and conditions of the apprenticeship.

The original forms of apprenticeship have developed over time and have encompassed increased numbers and types of occupation. These developments have varied in different parts of the world and in different countries. As originally practised, apprenticeships were based on arrangements organized outside of state control. However, more recent and current forms of apprenticeship have been subject to state intervention. For example, in the USA, the National Apprenticeship Act was passed into law in 1937 and, while amended, still operates. In Germany, the national Vocational Training Act of 2005 is the latest in legislation governing, among other things, apprenticeships. In the UK, the Industrial Training Act of 1964 had impact on the design and operation of apprenticeships. However, government interventions have had varying motivations and purposes. In Germany, for example, legislation enshrines and requires cooperation between what are termed the social partners; representative bodies of employers, employees and education providers; in the design and operation of apprenticeships to ensure high quality and standards. The German approach to vocational training and apprenticeships is known as the dual system involving defined periods of study of at least three years, which includes work-based learning with an employer and class-based learning with an education provider, leading to a recognized qualification at craft or technical levels. In contrast, the UK state intervention has recently become more concerned with number of apprentices rather than the quality of learning. This has led to employers being the dominant player in apprenticeships where shorter periods of study and lower level qualifications are achieved by apprentices. These recent developments have been termed as 'apprenticeship lite' (Sloman, 2014) and 'restricted' apprenticeships in contrast to traditional apprenticeships, which they term 'expansive' (Fuller and Unwin, 2008). Fuller and Unwin (2008) make an argument for the greater quality and benefits to all stakeholders of an 'expansive' apprenticeship.

JIM STEWART

See also:

Employability; Human resource development; Off-the-job learning; On-the-job learning; Skill; Training; Vocational and education training.

References and selected further readings

Allen, M. and P. Ainley (2014), A great train robbery or a real alternative for young people? Apprenticeships at the start of the 21st century, https://radicaledbks.files.wordpress.com/2013/09/apprenticeships.pdf.
Fuller, A. and L. Unwin (2008), Towards Expansive Apprenticeships: A Commentary, Teaching and Learning Research Programme, ESRC, www.tlrp.org/pub/documents/apprenticeshipcommentaryFINAL.pdf.
Sloman, M. (2014), A long journey to a cul-de-sac: a reflection on UK skills policy, Human Resource Development International, 17(2), pp. 222–230.

Aptitude test

Many jobs are complex and multifaceted, meaning that successful employees require a diverse range of skills and a job-specific knowledge to perform the task well. In many situations, employees are selected for their potential to succeed in these roles after a period of training and development. Aptitude refers to the underlying ability or potential to develop the knowledge, skills and any other qualities that will be required for successful performance in a work role.

An aptitude is a useful cluster of psychological and physical qualities. An aptitude test is designed to assess a group of specific abilities that have long-term implications for performance in specific, well-defined work roles. These tests are often used early on in a person's career to help identify the roles in which they are more likely to succeed and can be especially useful for selecting individuals for specialized long-term training and development programs.

Aptitude tests often consist of a number of different job-related psychometric tests of specific abilities (called a test battery) with the combined results indicating the test-taker's potential. For example, someone with the potential to be a successful accountant may need to demonstrate above-average levels of numerical ability and strong verbal reasoning ability. The questions within the test may also be constructed to reflect the content or the context of the work role. For example, a measure of numerical ability used to select trainees into the construction industry may include questions involving calculations of weights, areas and distances. Rigorous job analysis needs to be conducted in order to identify the abilities required for the job and the specific tests for inclusion in the test battery.

It is important to note that those being tested do not need specialized knowledge of the work or well-developed skills. However, tests of existing knowledge may be included if it is needed to engage in, and benefit from, job-related training (e.g., a good knowledge of mathematical and scientific principles is needed at the start of many apprenticeships). Depending on the demands of the work role, these test batteries may also include tests of physical ability such as manual dexterity or hand–eye coordination.

Aptitude tests have been shown to be useful in a variety of work contexts, often because they include reliable tests of ability that have been shown to predict work performance. When appropriately tailored to the work content and context, taking an aptitude test can also provide a prospective employee with a useful insight into the type demands they may face in the work role.

RAYMOND RANDALL

See also:
Job analysis; Psychometric testing.

References and selected further readings

Ghiselli, E. (1973), The validity of aptitude tests in personnel selection, *Personnel Psychology*, **26**, pp. 461–477.
Kirkup, C., R. Wheater, J. Morrison, B. Durbin and M. Pomati (2010), *Use of an Aptitude Test in University Entrance: A Validity Study*, London: Department for Business, Innovation and Skills.
Muchinsky, P.M. (1993), Validation of intelligence and mechanical aptitude tests in selecting employees for manufacturing jobs, *Journal of Business and Psychology*, **7**, pp. 373–382.
Muchinsky, P.M. (2002), Mechanical aptitude and spatial ability testing, in J. Thomas (ed.), *Comprehensive Handbook of Psychological Assessment*, Vol. 4, New York: Wiley, pp. 21–34.

Arbitration

Arbitration is a type of alternative dispute resolution process in which a neutral third party, with the agreement of and often chosen by the parties, reviews the evidence in a dispute and reaches a decision on the merits of the case. That decision is generally binding, although arbitration can be of a non-binding, advisory form, representing the arbitrator's assessment of the relative strengths and weaknesses of the case. In the US, in particular, there has been longstanding use of arbitration to resolve collective disputes, although there has been growing use of mandatory arbitration stipulations in the event of individual employment disputes, preventing the employee pursuing a legal case, class action or appeal.

In conventional arbitration, the arbitrator makes a decision on the merits of the case as presented by the disputants. In contrast, final offer (or 'pendulum') arbitration involves the arbitrator selecting one of the parties' positions. The uncertainty induced under this arrangement might be expected to lead risk-averse parties to adopt more moderate bargaining positions rather than risk losing altogether, and thus lead to more negotiated settlements, but has received mixed support empirically and is contradicted by laboratory studies that have been argued to provide a cleaner test (Dickinson, 2014).

Ongoing controversy also continues to surround the concept of compulsory employment arbitration, despite its relative speed and cost advantages over litigation. Early studies of grievance/discharge arbitration provided substantial evidence of gender effects. Concerns also include the potential for and evidence of repeat player advantages, with lower employee success rates and awards compared with court outcomes when faced by experienced (typically large) organizations. Given that employers typically pay the arbitrator's fee, there is a further concern – also evidenced empirically – of significant effects arising from repeat employer use of particular arbitrators (Colvin, 2011). Despite such advantages, however, US evidence suggests the popularity of binding arbitration in large organizations may be waning, with such organizations turning to more consensual, problem-solving alternatives such as mediation, accompanied in some cases by the adoption of sophisticated internal conflict management systems (Stipanowich and Lamare, 2013). Nonetheless, as Dickinson (2014) argues, a non-binding arbitration stage in negotiations may be helpful as a means of overcoming negotiator overconfidence.

PAUL LATREILLE

See also:
Alternative dispute resolution; Conciliation; Employment tribunal; Mediation.

References and selected further readings

Bales, R.A. (1997), *Compulsory Arbitration: The Grand Experiment in Employment*, Ithaca, NY: Cornell University Press.
Bemmels, B. (1988), Gender effects in discharge arbitration, *Industrial and Labor Relations Review*, **42**(1), pp. 63–76.
Bingham, L.B. (1997), Employment arbitration: the repeat player effect, *Employee Rights and Employment Policy Journal*, **1**, pp. 189–220.
Colvin, A.J.S. (2011), An empirical study of employment arbitration: case outcomes and processes, *Journal of Empirical Legal Studies*, **8**, pp. 1–23.
Dickinson, D.L. (2014), Alternative dispute resolution: how different procedures might succeed in settling disputes, *IZA World of Labor*, **71**.
Stipanowich, T. and J.R. Lamare (2013), Living with ADR: evolving perceptions and use of mediation, arbitration and conflict management in Fortune 1,000 corporations, *Harvard Negotiation Law Review*, **19**, pp. 1–68.

Assessment centres

The assessment centre is not a place, it is a process. As such it may comprise anything from a few hours spent administering a range of selection techniques, to a two-day residential where candidates can be put through a variety of tests and assessments procedures, but may also be required to interact both with each other and a range of employees from the recruiting business.

As such no single definition is available to describe the assessment centre but it is most typically described as an integrated system of tests and other measures, including simulation exercises, designed to generate behaviour similar to that required for success in a target job or job level. As well as simulation exercises, psychometric testing, group exercises and various interviews may also take place to determine an individual's values, potential for development, and preferred team roles.

It is popular in organizations because it has been demonstrated to have the highest validity of all selection tools. Robertson and Smith (2001) found a combination of selection methods has a higher predictive value for job success as opposed to only structured interviews.

Assessment centres are primarily used for recruitment but they may also be used for development purposes. In this instance, they are usually designed to assess potential and enable individuals to identify their own development needs alongside their career aspirations.

Assessments centres work by assessing candidates' knowledge, skills, abilities and attitudes in a fair and objective way rather than relying on secondary evidence such as success in a previous job, qualifications or third-party opinion. They also give assessors the opportunity to test candidates' claims about their ability to cope under pressure or to respond positively in certain circumstances.

The advantages of using assessment centres are that they predict future potential as well as current performance with greater accuracy than any other form of assessment. They also give fairer opportunities to candidates because they rely on objective criteria rather than a superficial judgement about capabilities from limited and sometimes irrelevant information. They give a realistic preview of the job enabling candidates to self-select and they enable lots of different people to be involved in the selection process.

However, the disadvantages of using assessment centres are that they are costly and time-consuming. Often they are reserved for large-scale recruitment, such as graduate recruitment or recruitment for senior positions.

ANGELA BARON

See also:

Management development; Recruitment; Selection; Selection method; Selection test.

References and selected further readings

Lievens, F. (2009), Assessment centres: a tale about dimensions, exercises, and dancing bears, *European Journal of Work and Organizational Psychology*, **18**(1), pp.102–121.
Povah, N. and L. Povah (2009), *Succeeding at Assessment Centres for Dummies*, Chichester: Wiley.
Povah, N. and G. Thornton (eds) (2012), *Assessment Centres and Global Talent Management*, London: Gower Publishing Ltd.

Robertson, I. and M. Smith (2001), Personnel selection, *Journal of Occupational and Organizational Psychology*, **74**(4), pp. 441–472.

Taylor, S. (2014), *Resourcing and Talent Management*, 6th edn, London: CIPD.

Woodruffe, C. (2007), *Development and assessment Centres: Identifying and Developing Competence*, 4th edn, London: Human Assets.

Attitude survey

The attitude survey, also known as an employee engagement or climate survey, is a tool used by management to monitor employee attitudes, satisfaction and commitment towards management and its policies. The survey can also be used to identify areas of employee concern and to enable employees to express their opinions or suggestions for improvement to management. Typically, an attitude survey will take the form of an anonymous questionnaire to ensure honest feedback. The survey may include questions on various organizational and employee aspects, and employees will rate these various factors on a satisfaction scale. The questionnaire may also include a qualitative component, with open-ended questions posed where employees may provide comments.

Attitude testing has a long history, beginning in the 1920s in the United States when J. David Hauser of Hauser Associates developed a quantitative approach to measuring employees' attitudes and demonstrated its utility to employers. In the postwar boom, there was an increase in the number of organizations using attitude surveys, as more industrial psychologists were employed by organizations. However, there were issues with poor survey design and lack of external norms. These issues were resolved by the involvement of the academic community in the study of attitude testing. In 1950, the Industrial Relations Centre at the University of Chicago developed the Employee Inventory (EI) for Sears, which was a sophisticated self-administering instrument that companies could use. The EI was later published and commercialized for use by other firms, and became the industry's most popular employee attitude questionnaire. The Institute for Social Research at the University of Michigan also contributed to the field of attitude testing following their landmark employee morale studies and the development of a technique called 'survey feedback', which identified the importance of consultation between management and employees and the communication of results following the administration of the questionnaire (see Jacoby, 1988, for an historical perspective).

The two most extensively validated employee attitude survey measures are the Job Descriptive Index (JDI; Smith et al., 1969) and the Minnesota Satisfaction Questionnaire (MSQ; Weiss et al., 1967). Attitude surveys can be faceted or provide global measures. For example, the JDI is faceted and measures various dimensions of the job, while others may be global and measure a single overall feeling toward the job. Important considerations when designing and using attitude surveys include the use of norms, comparison of data and numerical accuracy, country/cultural differences, and linking employee attitudes to business measures (Saari and Judge 2004). Consultancy firms have also driven the development and commercialization of attitude surveys, with Gallup and Towers Watson two of the key organizations providing engagement surveys.

PAULA K. MOWBRAY

See also:

Communication; Consultation; Employee involvement; Employee voice; Suggestion scheme.

Reference list and selected further readings

www.gallup.com
www.towerswatson.com
Jacoby, S.M. (1988), Employee attitude surveys in historical perspective, *Industrial Relations: A Journal of Economy and Society*, **27**(1), pp. 74–93.
Saari, L.M. and T.A. Judge (2004), Employee attitudes and job satisfaction, *Human Resource Management*, **43**(4), pp. 395–407.
Smith, P.C., L.M. Kendall and C.L. Hulin (1969), *The Measurement of Satisfaction in Work and Retirement*, Chicago: Rand McNally.
Weiss, D.J., R.V. Dawis, G.W. England and L.H. Lofquist (1967), *Manual for the Minnesota Satisfaction Questionnaire*, Minneapolis: Industrial Relations Center, University of Minnesota.

Bargaining levels

Bargaining levels refers to that point within an employing organization or groupings of such organizations where collective agreements are concluded. Bargaining levels may 'overlap' and different elements of a collective agreement may be negotiated at different levels. Bargaining levels may also change over time as different levels might gain greater or lesser significance or even be abandoned altogether. Different countries may also have preferences for different bargaining levels with their employment relations systems being characterized by centralized or decentralized structures.

Theoretically, there is a potential range of bargaining levels: a work group; a workplace; an organization; an economic sector; a national region; a nation-state; an international 'region' such as the European Union and globally. The bargaining at different levels may range from relatively informal agreements over specific issues within a workgroup to formalized agreements across companies and establishing more general principles.

The level at which bargaining takes place is dependent on a range of factors, including the particular preferences of the actors. However, a key factor is the existence of competent representative groupings of employers and employees with the authority to implement agreements. For workers, this normally means trade union organization, while employers may be more broadly organized in sectoral and national groupings.

Both worker and employer organizations are commonly less authorative beyond national boundaries. A second important factor in determining level is the policies of national and supra-national states. For example, social democratic governments in Scandinavian countries have traditionally encouraged centralized and national collective bargaining levels in contrast to conservative or liberal governments in Europe with a preference for decentralized bargaining.

Bargaining levels have often been areas of contention both within and beyond national boundaries as the following examples serve to illustrate.

A major issue in UK employment relations in the post-war period was that of 'wage drift' – effectively the shift from what the Donovan Commission (1968) described as being from the formal to the informal. That is, from increasingly ineffective national collective agreements towards workplace bargaining often led by shop stewards. A further UK example was the protracted dispute around the withdrawal by employers from the National Engineering Agreement against the opposition of the unions. Private sector bargaining at this level in the UK has virtually disappeared alongside a more widespread decline in collective bargaining. Public sector bargaining has continued at this level in the UK, but has also been under pressure from governments committed to decentralization.

Beyond national boundaries, trade unions have sought to bargain at the European Union level for supportive directives and also to use European Works Councils as a new mechanism to extend bargaining. There have also been a small number of cases of International Framework Agreements establishing general bargaining principles.

JOHN STIRLING

See also:
Collective bargaining; Employers; associations; Trade unions.

References and selected further readings

Beszter, P., P. Ackers and D. Hislop (2015), Understanding continuity in public sector HRM through neo-institutional theory: why national collective bargaining has survived in English local government, *Human Resource Management Journal*, **25**(3), pp. 364–381.

Brown, W. (1993), The contraction of collective bargaining in Britain, *British Journal of Industrial Relations*, **31**(2), pp. 189–200.

Bryson, A., J. Forth and N. Millward (2002), *All Change at Work? British Employment Relations 1980–98, Portrayed by the Workplace Industrial Relations Survey Series*, London and New York: Routledge.

Donovan Commission (1968), The Royal Commission on Trade Unions & Employers' Associations 1965–1968, *British Journal of Industrial Relations*, **6**(3), pp. 275–286.

Druker, J. and R. Croucher (2000), National collective bargaining and employment flexibility in the European building and civil engineering industries, *Construction Management and Economics*, **18**(6), pp. 699–709.

Gospel, H. and J. Druker (1998), The survival of national bargaining in the electrical contracting industry: a deviant case? *British Journal of Industrial Relations*, **36**(2), pp. 249–267.

Van Wanrooy, B., H. Bewley, A. Bryson, J. Forth, S. Freeth, L. Stokes and S. Wood (2013), *Employment Relations in the Shadow of Recession: Findings from the 2011 Workplace Employment Relations Study*, Basingstoke: Palgrave Macmillan, pp. 190–191.

Bargaining scope

Bargaining scope may most briefly be defined as those issues covered by a collective agreement. However, precisely what those issues are reflects a shifting balance in the power relations between employers and workers, the role of governments and an indefinable 'zeitgeist'. There are also differences as to what is within and outside the scope of an agreement in relation to the level at which bargaining takes place. Finally, there are shifts in the balance of what might be considered matters for bargaining and those that are considered matters for consultation. The boundaries between these concepts themselves may also be a fuzzy one, with unions and managements seeking to shift issues from one category to the other.

There is generally a core of issues that fall within the scope of collective bargaining and these may be regarded as pay and related matters – the matters most directly affecting employers costs and workers standards of living. Thus we might expect to see basic rates of pay and bonuses along with overtime and shift premiums in the majority of collective agreements. Alongside this, we could expect to see wage related matters such as hours of work, holiday and sick pay. Beyond this, we begin to see the fluidity in scope that reflects the power of employers and unions respectively and the role of government.

In the most general sense we can expect employers to seek to reduce the scope of bargaining; that is, to retain decisions as managerial prerogatives. The opposite is true for trade unions seeking the joint regulation of the employment relationship or even their own unilateral control. In the UK in the 1970s, for example, the TUC advised workplace representatives to seek agreements on a range of issues including workplace rights (time off work for union meetings); training; maternity pay and workplace nurseries; new technology; local government policies and pensions (BBC, 1977). This was in a 'zeitgeist' context of broader political demands for workers' control expressed through workers plans such as that at Lucas Aerospace.

Employers response from the 1980s onwards have been the focus on human resource management strategies that individualize the employment contract and, inevitably, remove issues from the scope of collective bargaining and diminish its long-term relevance.

Inevitably, government policy and legal enactment impacts on bargaining scope either encouraging or restricting change. At the most basic level of pay bargaining, government policies of pay restraint as in the anti-inflation policies of UK governments in the 1970s or restrictions on public sector bargaining as in the 'austerity policies' of the Conservative–Liberal coalition restrict the scope to raise pay. Legislation on minimum wage can also take pay out of bargaining by establishing a norm rather than a base to bargain from. Equally significantly, issues which were formerly collective bargaining matters simply become transferred to legislation.

JOHN STIRLING

See also:

Collective bargaining; Consultation; Trade unions.

References and selected further readings

BBC (1977), *Trade Union Studies: Democracy at Work*, London: British Broadcasting Corporation.
Brown, W. (1993), The contraction of collective bargaining in Britain, *British Journal of Industrial Relations*, **31**(2), pp. 189–200.
Bryson, A., J. Forth and N. Millward (2002), *All Change at Work? British Employment Relations 1980–98, Portrayed by the Workplace Industrial Relations Survey Series*, London and New York: Routledge.
Glassner, V., M. Keune and P. Marginson (2011), Collective bargaining in a time of crisis: developments in the private sector in Europe, *Transfer: European Review of Labour and Research*, **17**(3), 303–322.
Van Wanrooy, B., H. Bewley, A. Bryson, J. Forth, S. Freeth, L. Stokes and S. Wood (2013), *Employment Relations in the Shadow of Recession: Findings from the 2011 Workplace Employment Relations Study*, Basingstoke: Palgrave Macmillan, pp. 190–191.
Wainwright, H. and D. Elliott (1981), *The Lucas Plan: A New Trade Unionism in the Making*, London: Allison & Busby.

Benefits

Benefits are a major component in any reward management system. In general benefits (or 'fringe benefits' as they are sometimes termed) are those additional parts of the remuneration package that are not delivered in cash form, although clearly some benefits (e.g., holidays, sick pay and maternity leave) provide payment while absent. Although such benefits are not normally included in the monthly pay statement for employees, they have a clear cost to the employer and a value to employees. Smith (2000) estimated that the cost of benefits can form up to half the cost of the total remuneration package. Benefits can have different functions – some are to provide employee welfare and income security (e.g., annual leave, sick pay, maternity pay) while others may confer status (e.g., company cars) or serve as an aid to recruitment and retention (e.g., gym membership, discounts on company products). Yet others provide reimbursement of expenses incurred by the employee (e.g., travel and subsistence allowances). Pensions are also a major component of the benefits package for many employees in many countries, and these have seen major changes in recent years because of the effects of demographic change.

Despite the importance of benefits in terms of costs and value to employees, there is little evidence or theory underpinning their provision. There has been scant research on the impact of benefits on employee motivation and engagement (Milkovich and

Newman, 2008) and employer provision in the past has been largely driven by particular labour market pressures or legislative requirements. There are significant differences in the range of benefits offered by organizations and also considerable disparities between countries, depending on the degree to which the state requires employers to provide particular benefits or the degree of state provision of welfare to citizens. In the USA, a major part of the employers' benefits cost is derived from the provision of private health insurance and this element has been particularly important in driving up costs. In Europe legislation requiring minimum leave and maternity/paternity leave has been a major influence on organizational provision (IDS, 2010). Forth and Millward (2000) argue that, from an economic perspective, some employers choose to provide generous benefits as a means to compensate for lower salaries. Milkovich and Newman (2008) refer to two US studies that indicate that benefits do reduce staff turnover but further studies found that this was due to just two benefits – pensions and healthcare.

In recent times, the US practice of providing flexible or 'cafeteria' benefits, whereby employees are each given an individual budget to choose from a list of benefits, has spread beyond North America but take-up in the UK has been patchy, largely because the tax regime is not conducive to swapping benefits for cash (Wright, 2009). Benefits have also become an important element in Total Reward strategies, forming a significant part of the reward proposition, but the scale of benefits provision in the UK has probably diminished in recent recessionary times, especially final salary pension schemes (Government Actuary's Department 2014).

GEOFF WHITE

See also:
Reward management; Total reward.

References and selected further readings

Forth, J. and N. Millward (2000), *The Determinants of Pay Levels and Fringe Benefit Provision in Britain*, discussion paper 171, London: NIESR.
GAD (2014), *Annual Report 2013–2014*, London: Government Actuary's Department.
IDS (2010), *Hours and Holidays*, IDS HR Study 907, London: Incomes Data Services.
Milkovich, G.T. and J.M. Newman (2008), *Compensation*, 9th edn, Boston, MA: McGraw-Hill.
Smith, I. (2000), Benefits, in G. White and J. Druker (eds), *Reward Management: A Critical Text*, London: Routledge.
Wright, A. (2009), Benefits, in G. White and J. Drucker (eds), *Reward Management: A Critical Text*, 2nd edn, London: Routledge.

Best fit

In the strategic HRM field, two normative models of how firms should make strategic choices in HRM are distinguished (Boxall and Purcell, 2000): the best practice and best fit approaches. While the best practice approach assumes that certain HR practices universally outperform others, the best fit approach argues that the effectiveness of HR practices depends on contextual factors – for example, sector, country, strategy, systems or employee groups. Achieving a 'fit' between the HR system and its context is supposed to be associated with high performance.

The best fit approach started with the basic premise that organizations adopting a particular strategy require HR practices that are different from those required by organizations adopting alternative strategies (Delery and Doty, 1996). This alignment between HR practices and the competitive strategy has been labelled vertical or strategic fit. For example, Schuler and Jackson (1987) linked three generic competitive strategies to a set of HR practices, through identifying role behaviours employees need to show to effectively implement these strategies. Besides achieving an alignment with strategy, it is also important to align HR practices with each other into a coherent and consistent system or bundle in order to achieve the desired results. This fit is called horizontal or internal fit, because it focuses at the relationship between the separate HR practices within an HR system. Delery (1998), for example, distinguishes between different types of relationships between HR practices, such as synergistic, additive and substitutive relationships.

Many researchers have emphasized the importance of strategic and internal fit for achieving high performance (Arthur, 1994; Huselid, 1995). However, there may also be other contextual factors that affect the effectiveness of HRM, such as the institutional environment, the workforce, the organization's culture, technology and the organization of work. Therefore, more types of fit have been distinguished, such as environmental or institutional fit, which covers the match between the institutional environment and HR practices.

Although the idea of fit seems to be theoretically convincing, empirical evidence is mixed, particularly in studies that compare the best practice and best fit approach (Boxall and Purcell, 2000; Delery and Doty, 1996). The best fit approach has received some criticism because the operationalizations of the types of fit seem rather simplistic and do not reflect the complexity of the construct. However, recent studies which include more types of fit and use more sophisticated models do seem to find evidence for the importance of fit.

CORINE BOON

See also:

Best practice; Configurational model; Strategic HRM; Strategy.

References and selected further readings

Arthur, J.B. (1994), Effects of human resource systems on manufacturing performance and turnover, *Academy of Management Journal*, 37(3), pp. 670–687.
Boxall, P. and J. Purcell (2000), Strategic human resource management: where have we come from and where should we be going? *International Journal of Human Resource Management*, 2(2), pp. 183–203.
Delery, J.E. (1998), Issues of fit in strategic human resource management: implications for research, *Human Resource Management Review*, 8(3), pp. 289–309.
Delery, J.E. and D.H. Doty (1996), Modes of theorizing in strategic human resource management: tests of universalistic, contingency, and configurational performance predictions, *Academy of Management Journal*, 39(4), pp. 802–835.
Huselid, M.A. (1995), The impact of human resource management practices on turnover, productivity, and corporate financial performance, *Academy of Management Journal*, 38(3), pp. 635–672.
Schuler, R.S. and S.E. Jackson (1987), Linking competitive strategies with human resource management practices, *Academy of Management Executive*, 1(3), pp. 207–219.

Best practice

In the strategic HRM field, two normative models of how firms should make strategic choices in HRM are distinguished (Boxall and Purcell, 2000): the best practice and best fit approaches. While the best practice approach assumes that certain HR practices universally outperform others, the best fit approach argues that the effectiveness of HR practices depends on contextual factors, for example sector, country, strategy, systems, or employee groups.

Interest in the notion of best practice is, at least in part, inspired by the work of Pfeffer (1994, 1998). Pfeffer argues that a particular set of human resource (HR) practices can increase company profits, irrespective of the context. He also argues that the impact is more pronounced when HR practices are used together in a bundle or system. Pfeffer (1994) proposed a set of 16 best practices, which he later summarized down to seven: employment security; selective hiring; self-managed teams or teamworking; high pay contingent on company performance; extensive training; reduction of status differences; and sharing information (Pfeffer, 1998). This list is based on research on the effectiveness of separate HR practices such as selection, training, performance appraisal and compensation.

There are some criticisms of best practices. First of all, best practice lists vary significantly. Second, it remains relatively unclear what goals and whose goals are being served (Boxall and Purcell, 2000). Will implementing a set of best practices in your firm enhance profits or rather long-term viability? And do best practices benefit only shareholder interests or also employee interests? The best practice view does not provide clear answers to these questions.

However, despite the criticisms, the best practice approach does receive a lot of empirical support. Many studies find that a set of best practices is associated with higher organizational performance. Also, when compared with the best fit approach, best practice receives more support (e.g., Delery and Doty, 1996). More recently, Boxall and Purcell (2008) have proposed a model that combines best practice and best fit. In this model, best practices serve as an underpinning layer, reflecting generic best practices that are effective in any organization, whereas on the surface level, these best practices need to be matched with the unique character and context of the organization in order to achieve a competitive advantage, which reflects the best fit approach.

CORINE BOON

See also:
Best fit; Strategic HRM.

References and selected further readings

Boxall, P. and J. Purcell (2000), Strategic human resource management: where have we come from and where should we be going? *International Journal of Human Resource Management*, **2**(2), pp. 183–203.
Boxall, P. and J. Purcell (2008), *Strategy and Human Resource Management*, 2nd edn, New York: Palgrave Macmillan.
Delery, J.E. and D.H. Doty (1996), Modes of theorizing in strategic human resource management: tests of universalistic, contingency, and configurational performance predictions, *Academy of Management Journal*, **39**(4), pp. 802–835.
Pfeffer, J. (1994), *Competitive Advantage Through People*, Boston: Harvard Business School Press.
Pfeffer, J. (1998), *The Human Equation: Building Profits by Putting People First*, Boston: Harvard Business School Press.

Big Five

The 'Big Five' refers to a model of human personality that has come to dominate research and practice on personality assessment since the early 1990s. Otherwise referred to as the Five-Factor Model, the Big Five is comprised of the following dimensions: agreeableness (reflecting affability and friendliness), conscientiousness (dependability and effort), emotional stability (emotional adjustment versus worry and anxiety), extraversion (outgoing and socially-dominant), and openness (curiosity, intellectual interests, and broad-mindedness).

Although long used in HRM, prior to 1990 there was limited evidence supporting the application of personality assessments within work organizations (Guion and Gottier, 1965). This position was largely accepted by researchers until the advent of the Big Five enabled comprehensive reviews of personality in the workplace (especially Barrick and Mount, 1991). Unlike intelligence, the structure of which has been commonly (if not universally) accepted for nearly a century, generally accepted models of personality assessment are relatively recent.

Many personality instruments, for both selection and development, are based upon the Big Five factor structure. This is because a large body of research has validated the Big Five as reliable and consistent predictors of important behavioural and life outcomes, including important behaviours and outcomes in the workplace. While the Big Five is the most used personality structure in both research and applied settings, it is not without its criticisms. These criticisms largely come in three forms: the fact that the Big Five is descriptive, not explanatory; the possibility of a different factor structure, particularly across cultures; and disagreements about the lower order facets on the factors.

The Big Five is a comprehensive taxonomy of personality, is based upon an impressive body of research, and each of the traits are reliable and relatively consistent predictors of a number of important organizational outcomes. Much of the value of the Big Five comes from the fact that this relatively simple set of personality dimensions encompasses much of the variance in personality (Funder, 2001), and provides a ready method for assessing the persistent, motivational aspects of individuals that contribute to their work performance. As argued by Blumberg and Pringle (1982), performance depends on ability, opportunity and motivation. Although organizational circumstances have a large effect on motivation, the Big Five has proven to be a valuable framework within which to assess the motivational propensities that individuals bring to the organization. Although it does not represent a 'final' model of personality, its practical utility is likely to make the Big Five the dominant approach for personality assessment in both research and organizational practice for many years to come.

DANIEL J. CUMMINGS AND ARTHUR POROPAT

See also:

Person specification; Personality test; Personality traits.

References and selected further readings

Barrick, M.R. and M.K. Mount (1991), The Big Five personality dimensions and job performance: a meta-analysis, *Personnel Psychology*, **44**(1), pp. 1–26.

Blumberg, M. and C.D. Pringle (1982), The missing opportunity in organizational research: some implications for a theory of work performance, *The Academy of Management Review*, 7(4), pp. 560–569.

Funder, D.C. (2001), Personality, *Annual Review of Psychology*, **52**, pp. 197–221.

Guion, R.M. and R.F. Gottier (1965), Validity of personality measures in personnel selection, *Personnel Psychology*, **18**, pp. 135–164.

Biodata

Biodata are items of information from an individual's personal history (their biography) found empirically (i.e., through observation) to predict aspects of work performance. For example, the number of jobs previously held might be found for a sufficiently large sample of applicants for a job to predict the length of time individual's stay with the organization. The item might then be used as part of a package of techniques for job selection.

Good items of biodata have a number of characteristics. One is objectivity. That is, the answer to the item does not depend on the subjective experience of the person responding as much as on the situation referred to. Asking a person to list the jobs they have held and the periods during which they held them provides a basis for a count of the number of jobs and a check on the fullness of disclosure (assuming of course that the person is being honest and has a reasonable memory). A second characteristic is that the item is not overly invasive. That is, the details asked are not too personal (e.g., a person's sexual orientation).

Biodata were initially identified in terms of empirical relationships alone. Associations were sought between a wide range of items from people's life histories as well as measures of their job performance. Where associations were found to reach some acceptable level of magnitude or statistical significance, the item was retained, irrespective of its content.

Use of biodata can be unstable and regular monitoring of its relevance is usually required. Work requirements may alter, rendering previously useful items of information no longer relevant. The applicant pool might change in character as a result of fluctuations in the labour market, again making some items previously useful very rare or very common and hence reducing their value in distinguishing among applicants.

The use of rationally chosen items that meet appropriate standards, such as objectivity and non-invasiveness, is readily understood by applicants and is usually readily accepted by them, more so than some of the more esoteric techniques used in job selection. They are seldom, however, used alone but more frequently as part of a package or battery of techniques, such as interview and intelligence test.

JOHN G. O'GORMAN AND DAVID H.K. SHUM

References and selected further readings

Landy, F.J. and J.M. Conte (2007), *Work in the 21st Century*, Malden, MA: Blackwell.

Mitchell, T.W. (1994), The utility of biodata, in G.S. Stokes and M.D. Mumford (eds), *Biodata Handbook: Theory, Research, and the Use of Biographical Information in Selection and Performance Prediction*, Palo Alto, CA: Consulting Psychologists Press.

Schmidt, F.L. and J.E. Hunter (1998), The validity and utility of selection methods in personnel psychology: practical and theoretical implications of 85 years of research findings, *Psychological Bulletin*, **124**(2), pp. 262–274.

Wood, R. and T. Payne (1998), *Competency-Based Recruitment and Selection*, West Sussex: Wiley.

Blacklisting

Blacklisting is the practice of employers and employment agencies using lists of workers whom are regarded to be 'undesirable' to prevent these workers from gaining employment. Thus, blacklisting is a pre-employment stage process whereby managers check names of prospective workers against the blacklist. Those whose names are on the blacklist are not interviewed and/or offered work even if they are suitable by virtue of being well-qualified and experienced. Occasionally, there is no formal list when individuals become relatively well-known and occasionally workers are sacked after gaining employment because the list was not checked prior to employment. The term is not racist in derivation.

Those deemed 'undesirable' are regarded as 'troublemakers' (such as left-wing union activists) by virtue of their willingness to challenge managerial prerogative, especially over health and safety and through collective actions such as strikes. The lists are necessarily secret and secretive in order that the practice – which is widely regarded in liberal societies as immoral and abhorrent – is kept not only from public view but from those subject to it, lest it is exposed and challenged. The consequences of allowing the opportunity to challenge the blacklist to arise – through removing its veil of secrecy – is not just to threaten its continued operation but also to expose employers and employment agencies to industrial disputes and legal action.

Blacklisting is most commonly found in economic sectors characterized by discontinuous employment, required skills or experience being limited to the few, labour costs being a high proportion of production costs, delays to production having financial consequences (through penalty clauses, overrun costs, etc.) and extensive subcontracting of labour. Consequently, sectors such as construction, food processing and media production (films, television) are known to have practised blacklisting. However, it is the use of short-term employment contracts under which workers continually move from one job and/or employer to another that provides the structural opportunity to operate blacklisting.

Blacklisting presents a problem for HRM because, at one level, the practice is clearly illiberal, unenlightened and does not ideologically attempt to persuade workers of virtues of management. However, at another level, it physically prevents those who would disrupt management attaining its goals from being in the workplace. Companies in construction who subscribe to HRM have widely practised blacklisting.

Historically, the most famous case of blacklisting took place in the US film and entertainment industry, especially in Hollywood. From 1947 to the 1960s, hundreds of actors, directors, producers, screenwriters and entertainers such as musicians were denied work because of their suspected political beliefs or associations, specifically their alleged membership of or sympathy with the Communist Party, involvement in progressive political causes associated with communism and refusal to assist investigations into Communist Party activities.

More recently, and facilitated by the introduction of freedom of information and data protection measures, widespread blacklisting has been in exposed in the construction industry in Britain. Those blacklisted were barred from work, leading to poverty, mental illnesses such as depression, and relationship breakups. Blacklisting has long been suspected through the activities of the Economic League but in 2009 its successor organization, the Consulting Association (established in 1993), was revealed to have been used by more than 40 major construction companies in order to blacklist more than 3,200 workers.

GREGOR GALL

See also:
Non-unionism; Strikes; Trade unions.

References and selected further readings

Smith, D. and P. Chamberlain (2015), *Blacklisted: The Secret War between Big Business and Union Activists*, London: New Internationalist Books.
Vaughn, R. (2004), *Only Victims: A Study of Show Business Blacklisting*, Milwaukee, IL: Limelight Editions.

Blended learning

At its simplest level blended learning (BL) is about 'blending' different modes of learning. A more commonly understood definition of BL is mixing and matching aspects of traditional face-to-face approaches of instruction with new technologies for the purposes of imparting learning. However, the second part of the definition is more problematic, as it can imply a major role for new technologies in delivering BL. Critics of this approach would argue that BL has been in existence for a very long time, as face-to-face instruction has often integrated and mixed with other forms of instruction, such as practicums, supervised distance education and learning, and self-paced and directed learning, which have nothing to do with online or e-learning. Colloquially speaking, BL often implies using some degree of blend between online and face-to-face learning environments, although the degree to which one does the 'blending' is debatable. The nature and extent of blending is better answered by considering the nature of the learning initiative at hand. For example, looking at the hierarchy of learning outcomes approach (Delahaye, 2005), the extent of use of online and other independent and self-directed modes of learning typically increase as one attempts to deliver higher order learning outcomes.

The need to embrace BL is embedded in both pedagogical rationales and socio-demographic profiles of the learners. For instance, one estimate suggests that nearly a third of all students enrolled in the American education system in the last decade, nearly 6.7 million, enrolled in one online course (Allen and Seaman, 2013). The approaches to BL do vary from the context in which it is applied. Broadly, the major learning contexts that exist are from school (kindergarten to Year 12), higher education and business or corporate industry contexts. The objectives and motivations for each context differs and, thus, affects the choices available. For example, in the latter context, the relevance and cost of learning to a business has a significant impact on its design and use. As a relatively young approach, the challenge for educators and practitioners is deal with the diversity of learners, dynamic environment, changing technology as well as the content that needs to be learned and decide what to blend, how to blend, to what extent, under what conditions and how to evaluate the effectiveness of each as well as the synergistic effects of each learning mode.

CHRIS ROWLEY AND ASHISH MALIK

See also:

E-Learning; Online learning.

References and selected further readings

Allen, I.E. and J. Seaman (2013), *Changing Course: Ten Years of Tracking Online Education in the United States*, Newburyport, MA: Sloan Consortium.
Bonk, C. and C. Graham (eds) (2012), *The Handbook of Blended Learning*, San Francisco: Pfeiffer.
Delahaye, B.L. (2005), *Human Resource Development: Adult Learning and Knowledge Management*, 2nd edn, Brisbane: John Wiley & Sons.
Graham, C., S. Allen and D. Ure (2005), Benefits and challenges of blending learning environments, in M. Khosrow-Pour (ed.), *Encyclopaedia of Information Science and Technology*, Hershey, PA: Idea Group, pp. 253–259.
Picciano, A.G., C.D. Dziuban and C.R. Graham (eds) (2014), *Research Perspectives in Blended Learning: Research Perspectives*, Vol. 2, New York: Routledge.

Body work

'Body work' may be defined as paid work focusing 'directly on the bodies of others: assessing, diagnosing, handling, and manipulating bodies that thus become the object of the worker's labour' (Twigg et al., 2011; Wolkowitz et al., 2013; Kang, 2010). It extends interest in (unpaid) work on one's own body (Gimlin, 2007) to other ways in which bodies are involved in the production of value. 'Body work', as defined above, overlaps with McDowell (2009), who includes as body work all service sector interactions requiring co-presence, and 'intimate labour' (Parreñas and Boris, 2010), who highlight the purchase of forms of intimacy previously located outside market relations. However, the more restrictive definition of body work discussed here encourages researchers to consider how the materiality of inter-corporeal interactions affects work relations, including the incorporation of gendered relations to others' bodies (e.g., nurturing, distant, controlling) into the division of labour. The concept of 'body work' also overlaps with 'reproductive labour' (Duffy, 2005), which includes work that does not involve touch. It too challenges terms like 'affective labour' that obscure the hard physical labour and stigma associated with body work (Bolton and Wibberley, 2014).

Empirical research adopting the concept of body work shows the relevance of inter-corporeality for the organization and meaning of work. More than 10 per cent of jobs in the UK involve body work, including body work in health and social care (e.g., nursing, personal care); aesthetic services (hairdressing); and protective services (prison warders, bouncers), but excluding sex work. Cohen (in Twigg et al., 2011) argues that the temporal and spatial requirements of body work make it difficult to organize according to capitalist rationality. Hence, except for elite professional work such as medicine, profits can be made only if wages are kept low and working hours flexible. Further implications of the meaning of bodies for body work employment include, for instance, the power relations between workers and customers, clients and customers; the disproportionate recruitment of migrant and racialized labour; and the organization of sex work and sex worker identities.

CAROL WOLKOWITZ

See also:
Aesthetic labour; Emotional labour; Labour; Work.

References and selected further readings
Bolton, S.C. and G. Wibberley (2014), Domiciliary care: the formal and informal labour process, *Sociology*, **48**(41), pp. 682–697.
Duffy, M. (2005), Reproducing labor inequalities: challenges for feminists conceptualizing care at the intersections of gender, race, and class, *Gender & Society*, **19**(1), pp. 66–82.
Gimlin, D. (2007), What is 'body work'? *Sociology Compass*, **1**(1), pp. 353–370.
Kang, M. (2010), *The Managed Hand: Race, Gender, and the Body in Beauty Service Work*, Berkeley, CA: University of California Press.
McDowell, L. (2009), *Working Bodies: Interactive Service Employment and Workplace Identities*, Chichester: Wiley-Blackwell.
Parreñas, R.S. and E. Boris (eds) (2010), *Intimate Labors: Cultures, Technologies, and the Politics of Care*, Stanford, CA: Stanford University Press.
Twigg, J., C. Wolkowitz, R. Cohen and S. Nettleton (eds) (2011), *Body Work in Health and Social Care*, Chichester: Wiley-Blackwell.
Wolkowitz, C., R. Cohen, T. Sanders and K. Hardy (eds) (2013), *Body/Sex/Work: Intimate, Embodied and Sexualised Labour*, Basingstoke: Palgrave Macmillan.

Bonuses/incentives

A bonus is a cash payment (or in some cases shares) to employees that is usually related to performance of the individual, the group, the organization or some combination of any of these. The objective of such schemes is to incite greater effort through motivating or encouraging employees to do something, as a reward offered for increased productivity. Therefore a bonus aims to stimulate greater output, or even desired actions and behaviours.

There are two types of bonus scheme, discretionary and contractual. Discretionary schemes allow an employer to withhold payment of a bonus as long as it is not acting irrationally in so doing. By contrast, if a bonus agreed under a contractual basis is not paid, especially where employees have met the criteria for payment, an employee can apply to an employment tribunal for unlawful deductions of wages. Bonuses can even be consolidated into an employee's wages or unconsolidated and paid as a one-off lump sum.

Definitions of incentive pay are problematic not least because more recently the term has become part of the rhetoric of 'new pay', a complete reward system prescribed for the modern strategically minded organization (see Lawler, 1990, 1995). In the UK sense, however, it is fair to say that the term is more often referred to under the umbrella of variable pay. Incentive pay is described as a system of payment in which a proportion of earnings is related to either the level of worker effort (input) or the level of output (Gilman, 2001).

Incentive pay can therefore include systems that have a direct relationship with output, such as payment by results. It is, however, also used to cover schemes in which workers may be encouraged to perform with only an indirect relationship with output (e.g., merit pay and performance-related pay). More recently, it is used to describe reward systems in which there is no necessary relationship at all with individual performance, but where workers are entitled to a share in the company's performance and profitability, such as profit-related pay and employee share ownership plans.

MARK GILMAN

See also:

Employee share ownership plans; Payment by results; Performance-related pay; Profit-related pay; Variable pay.

References and selected further readings

Armstrong, M. (2012), *Armstrong's Handbook of Reward Management*, London: Kogan Page.
Gilman, M. (2001), *Variable Pay: The Case of the UK*, Dublin: European Industrial Relations Observatory.
Gilman, M. (2013), Reward management, in T. Redman and A. Wilkinson (eds), *Contemporary Human Resource Management: Text and Cases*, New York: Pearson.
Lawler, E.E. (1990), Strategic Pay: Aligning Organizational Strategies and Pay Systems, San Francisco and Oxford: Jossey-Bass.
Lawler, E.E. (1995), The new pay: a strategic approach, *Compensation & Benefits Review*, **27**, pp. 14–22.
Perkins, S.J. and G. White (2008), *Employee Reward: Alternatives, Consequences and Contexts*, London: CIPD.

Broadbanding

Broad bands are a form of pay structure (which groups similar roles or jobs together and applies a range of pay or band of pay from a minimum to a maximusm) in which the span of the pay range is wide. They have been variously defined in practice with the Institute of Personnel and Development (IPD, 2000) saying that salary bands that have widths from 70 per cent to 100 per cent – that is the maximum of the pay range can be twice the minimum salary level for each role – are defined as broad bands.

More broadly, Milkovich and Newman (2005) refer to broad bands as a form of delayering of pay structures as the extended width of each pay band typically allows the employer to have fewer bands than if the bands or grades (similar terms) are narrower. The aim of broad bands is for employers to have more flexibility over the progression of individuals' pay. This enables people to progress their pay based on assessments of their performance, their acquisition of additional competencies or skills, taking on of additional responsibilities or because the market gives a higher value to particular roles (and the employer wishes to retain people in these roles). This mix of potential rationales can lead to some downsides – there may be less transparency or it may be too difficult for managers to communicate to employees why their pay is at a particular level and it may therefore be harder for managers to make fair judgements. In a European law jurisdiction, the lack of transparency could make it harder for employer to defend equal pay claims.

The proponents of broad bands argue there are substantial benefits for organizations and individuals from a career progression perspective since people can take on extra responsibilities or make lateral moves in the organization to further their careers and be rewarded in a more flexible way that would be the case if they needed formally to seek and be granted a promotion to take on new role. However, Arnold and Scott (2002) find mixed evidence that this improves career management processes in organizations. In practice, as Milkovich and Newman (2014) argue broad bands are often 'zoned' so that they are – in effect – each divided into narrower sub-ranges of pay, either because employers wish to apply different marker-based salary reference points within the same band or to apply 'bars' to progression within bands if performance or development criteria have not been met. As Milkovich and Newman (2014) further comment, this zoning starts to look a lot like narrower grades or ranges – although reference points and bars may be used more for manager guidance in broad bands and less as a more formal control mechanism, as they would be in narrow pay bands or grades.

ANGELA WRIGHT

See also:
Reward management.

References and selected further readings

Arnold, E. and C. Scott (2002), Does broad banding improve pay system effectiveness? *Southern Business Review*, **27**(2).
IPD (2000), *Study of broad-banded and job family pay structures*, London: Institute of Personnel and Development.
Milkovich, G. and J. Newman (2005), *Compensation*, 8th edn, New York: McGraw Hill.
Milkovich, G. and J. Newman (2014), *Compensation*, 11th edn, New York: McGraw Hill International.

Bullying

Workplace bullying refers to repeated, negative and serious actions directed to one or more persons, where unequal power makes self-defence by the target/s very difficult (Einarsen et al., 2011).

Both formal and informal power processes operate as perpetrators are often hierarchically superior, but can be co-workers and subordinates. The actions, often psychological in nature, can involve activities, interactions or processes that evolve in a cumulative fashion over time and are perceived as threatening, intimidating or demeaning, and noted to cause humiliation, offence and distress to target/s (Neilsen and Einarsen, 2012). The actions are not prescribed, especially as they relate to subjective perceptions on the target/s part, but can include patterns of overt (e.g., non-verbal, verbal and physical intimidation) and covert behaviours (e.g., spreading rumours; sabotaging work), and non-behaviours (e.g., lack of relevant communication; exclusion) (Branch et al., 2013) by perpetrator/s.

Research in workplace bullying, which originated in Scandinavia in the 1980s, influenced by school bullying research and workplace problems identified in psychotherapy (Einarsen et al., 2011), has grown rapidly into a multidimensional, worldwide endeavour. Some debate over the term continues, with 'mobbing' sometimes used instead, reflecting its group-based nature in many cases. It can also be termed 'harassment' (distinct from sexual harassment).

Workplace bullying has serious, costly implications for individual, group, and organizational functioning and effectiveness through its negative disruptions across areas including teamwork, mental and physical health, job satisfaction, and organizational commitment (Neilsen and Einarsen, 2012). Accordingly, researchers and practitioners are tackling many challenges, including gaining a deep understanding of its processes with the aim of ultimately preventing its occurrence. It is associated with deficient leadership, team and management skills, organizational cultures and complex communication processes, policies and procedures within organizations, and national legal frameworks (Branch et al., 2013). A national response in Australia is reflected in changes to the Fair Work Act (2013), the success of which will be evaluated over time (French et al., 2014).

SHERYL RAMSAY

See also:
Wellbeing.

References and selected further readings

Branch, S., S. Ramsay and M. Barker (2013), Workplace bullying, mobbing and general harassment: a review, *International Journal of Management Reviews*, 15, 280–299.
Einarsen, S., H. Hoel, D. Zapf and C.L. Cooper (2011), The concept of bullying and harassment at work: the European tradition, in S. Einarsen, H. Hoel, D. Zapf and C.L. Cooper (eds), *Bullying and Harassment in the Workplace: Developments in Theory, Research and Practice*, 2nd edn, Boca Raton, FL: CRC Press, pp. 3–40.
French, B., M.V. Boyle and O. Muurlink (2014), Workplace bullying in Australia: the Fair Work Act and its impact, *New Zealand Journal of Human Resource Management*, 14(2), pp. 69–81.
Laschinger, H.K.S. and R. Fida (2014), A time-lagged analysis of the effect of authentic leadership on workplace bullying, burnout, and occupational turnover intentions, *European Journal of Work and Organizational Psychology*, 23(5), 739–753.
Neilsen, M.B. and S. Einarsen (2012), Outcomes of exposure to workplace bullying: a meta-analytic review, *Work & Stress*, 26(4), 309–332.
Ramsay, S., A. Troth and S. Branch (2011), Work-place bullying: a group processes framework, *Journal of Occupational and Organizational Psychology*, 84, 799–816.

Bureaucracy

The term 'bureaucracy' is French in origin, joining the word *bureau*, meaning office or desk, to the Greek word *kratos*, meaning rule or political power. From its first uses in the eighteenth century, bureaucracy took on a pejorative connotation, suggesting an excessive attention to rules and procedures and slow and inefficient task performance. For Max Weber by contrast, its pre-eminent theorist, bureaucracy was a rational method of organizing that broke the hold of traditional practices. Weber's ideal typical bureaucracy entailed control and coordination of work tasks through a hierarchy of suitably qualified office-holders, with rules and procedures providing the most appropriate means of achieving specified ends. Salaried and pensionable appointment, security of tenure and a career deprived the individual post office-holder of the need to seek personal material advantage from office, encouraging dutiful, impersonal service. Breaking with arbitrary rule, assignment by patronage or particularistic criteria, bureaucracy was a necessary accompaniment to democratic government. It was also emerging in diverse fields as the dominant organizational form by virtue of its technical superiority.

Weber interpreted the scientific schemes of management in industry in the United States as exemplifying this rationalizing tendency. But it would not be until later, after the Second World War, with the widespread development of career ladders and more extensive employment rules by larger enterprises, that bureaucratization would flourish in a business context. Familiar intellectual criticisms of such regimes have been that they are unresponsive and ineffective in the face of change, that bureaucratic procedures stifle desirable 'human qualities'. In recent years, critics have argued that bureaucracy has been rendered effectively obsolete in a new epoch. In response, it has been claimed, organizations are becoming more reliant on informal networks with employees enjoying greater autonomy.

Yet it is difficult to reconcile such claims of change with the available evidence. Bureaucracy, though commonly subject to modification in large private sector enterprises, remains very much alive today. Familiar modern management aims involve both innovation in the application of techniques of management and employee self-discipline and the adaptation of familiar bureaucratic methods to new ends. Certain employment rules, concerning, for example, the demarcation of jobs, have undoubtedly been relaxed. But in other respects – for example, in the display of emotions in many service sector roles – workplace rules often appear more all-encompassing today.

The modifications to bureaucracy in business have encouraged debate on ethics, with critics drawing attention to dangers associated with increasing line manager autonomy in decision-making, the intensification of effort and control of employees as well as the growing casualization of work. But it is in the public sector that the risks of the diminishing influence of bureaucracy have been most clearly highlighted. Here, significant changes to administrative style – the enhanced role of personal responsibility, entrepreneurial ideals and techniques adapted from the commercial enterprise – have been contrasted with an alternative 'tradition' of bureaucratic impartiality, fairness and consistency in a way that Weber would have appreciated. Critics argue that trust in the operation of government is threatened by reform. And without trust, democratic citizenship will atrophy.

EDWARD BARRATT

See also:

Empowerment; Hierarchy; Public sector.

References and selected further readings

Allbrow, M. (1970), *Bureaucracy*, Basingstoke: Macmillan.
Alvesson, M. and P. Thompson (2005), Bureaucracy at work, in P. du Gay (ed.), *The Values of Bureaucracy*, Oxford: Oxford University Press.
Du Gay, P. (2000), *In Praise of Bureaucracy*, London: Sage.
Perrow, C. (1979), *Complex Organizations: A Critical Essay*, Brattleboro, VT: Echo Point.
Weber, M. (1978), *Economy and Society*, 2 volumes, Los Angeles: University of California Press.

Burnout

The term 'burnout' was first coined in the 1970s by Freudenberger to describe the gradual emotional depletion and loss of motivation he observed among people who had volunteered to work for aid organizations in New York. Freudenberger (1974) defined burnout as 'a state of mental and physical exhaustion caused by one's professional life', and he referred to 'the extinction of motivation or incentive, especially where one's devotion to a cause or relationship fails to produce the desired results'. Employees who burn out from their work deplete their energetic resources and lose their dedication to work. On the basis of interviews with human service workers in California, Maslach and her colleagues defined burnout as a chronic form of work-related stress that is characterized by three main symptoms, namely emotional exhaustion, depersonalization and reduced personal accomplishment (Maslach et al., 2001).

Burned-out individuals feel chronically fatigued, and endorse a negative callous attitude towards their work and the people with whom they work. They often believe that they no longer make a meaningful contribution to the organization. Research has shown that people burn out in their work as a consequence of prolonged exposure to high job demands and low job resources. Having to deal with a high workload and emotionally demanding clients seems to particularly increase the risk of burnout when there are not sufficient job resources available, including autonomy, social support, skill variety and performance feedback.

Employees with higher levels of burnout are more likely to report a range of psychological and physical health problems, including depression, sleep disturbance, memory impairment and neck pain. The burnout syndrome has also been found to be an independent risk factor for infections, Type 2 diabetes and cardiovascular diseases (see Leiter et al., 2014). Consequently, burned-out employees are likely to withdraw from their work in the form of lateness, absence or turnover (Maslach et al., 2001). Moreover, individual performance is compromised because burned-out workers need to invest extra time and effort in performing their job.

Most research on burnout focuses on possible causes and consequences of the syndrome. Scholars have also started to investigate work engagement as the positive antipode of burnout to find out what should be done to prevent burnout. These studies typically show that engaged workers differ from burned-out workers in that the former group has more job and personal resources available to cope with their high job demands. In addition, engaged workers use personal initiative to change their job demands and resources if needed – this latter behaviour is called 'job crafting'.

ARNOLD B. BAKKER

See also:

Employee engagement; Stress; Wellbeing.

References and selected further readings

Bakker, A.B. and P. Costa (2014), Chronic job burnout and daily functioning: a theoretical analysis, *Burnout Research*, **1**, 112–119.
Bakker, A.B., E. Demerouti and A.I. Sanz-Vergel (2014), Burnout and work engagement: the JD-R approach, *Annual Review of Organizational Psychology and Organizational Behavior*, **1**, 389–411.
Demerouti, E., A.B. Bakker, F. Nachreiner and W.B. Schaufeli (2001), The job demands – resources model of burnout, *Journal of Applied Psychology*, **86**, 499–512.
Freudenberger, H.J. (1974), Staff burnout, *Journal of Social Issues*, **30**, 159–165.
Leiter, M.P., A.B. Bakker and C. Maslach (2014), *Burnout at Work: A Psychological Perspective*, Hove: Psychology Press.
Maslach, C., W.B. Schaufeli and M.P. Leiter (2001), Job burnout, *Annual Review of Psychology*, **52**, 397–422.

Call centres

Call centres are actual workplaces. In other words they are, in the first instance, an empirical phenomena. Although a 'call centre industry' is commonly referred to, this term is misleading and certainly requires qualification. This is on account of the fact that most industries today make use of call centres in their operation. Consequently, it is more accurate to define a call centre as a way of organizing communication or the production and exchange of immense volumes of information. The call centre represents a labour process for accomplishing work in an information- and service-oriented economy.

At a basic level, call centres may provide in-bound functionality, whereby callers place calls to an organization for a service, which may include the ordering of a physical product. Thus, potential patients may call a public health hotline for medical attention, or an airline for an international travel booking. Other call centres provide outbound call capacity and they are usually associated with product/service marketing, fundraising, or data collection of one sort or another (e.g., polling). In actual fact, most call centres are hybrid operations that both receive and make calls to/from a public. This organization of work, or labour process, is made possible through the employment of a suite of digital technologies that include automated call distribution systems for the queuing of inquiries to waiting service representatives, predictive dialling for the continuous placement of outbound telemarketing type calls and computer systems that host the input of data that is provided to and collected from callers. Other information based technologies have also quickly been appropriated by call centres, including real time chat, email communication and social media. Consequently, it is more common today to refer to 'contact' rather than to 'call' centres.

Call centres, as described above began to appear in the early 1990s, initially in the finance sector, where they came to replace local branch facilities. They quickly spread to many other activities that included not only commodity exchange but also public goods provision. By the end of that decade, the vast majority of service encounters in developed economies were conducted through call centres.

Call centres involved two sorts of problems for HR professionals. First, there were the practical problems associated with organizing work in this fashion. Early researchers characterized call centres as informational assembly lines staffed by an emergent cybertariat. Job dissatisfaction, alienation, high rates of voluntary turnover, job stress, burnout and the associated issue of maintaining employee motivation gave rise to a host of HR challenges. Related to these issues, call centres were also the research sites for some novel HR theorizing and theory-testing, in particular around high-performance work alternatives to the highly routinized work that some saw as the hallmark of the call centre. HR theorists suggested that higher-end, relational work, perhaps involving genuine work teams, could break the cycle of 'burn and churn' that was identified with call centre work. Others turned their attention to more traditional human relations approaches to employment issues in call centres, including investment in workplace cultural initiatives that invariably involved work teams, although not necessarily teamwork. Critical researchers retained a healthy scepticism towards all such possibilities. In the meantime, the outsourcing of large swathes of this type of work to offshore destinations in the developing world, including India and the Philippines, attendant on the rise of a networked global economy has given fresh impetus to these debates.

BOB RUSSELL

See also:

Alienation; High-performance work systems; Job satisfaction; Labour process/theory; Outsourcing.

References and selected further readings

Batt, R. (2000), Strategic segmentation in front-line services: matching customers, employees and human resource systems, *International Journal of Human Resource Management*, **11**(3), pp. 540–561.

Callaghan, G. and P. Thompson (2001), Edwards revisited: technical control and call centres, *Economic and Industrial Democracy*, **22**(1), pp. 13–37.

Russell, B. (2008), Call centres: a decade of research, *International Journal of Management Reviews*, **10**(3), pp. 195–219.

Russell, B. (2009), *Smiling Down the Line: Info-Service Work in the Global Economy*, Toronto: University of Toronto Press.

Taylor, P. and P. Bain (1999), 'An assembly line in the head': work and employee relations in the call centre, *Industrial Relations Journal*, **30**(2), pp. 101–117.

Taylor, P. and P. Bain (2005), India calling to the far away towns: the call centre labour process and globalisation, *Work, Employment and Society*, **19**(2), pp. 261–282.

Capability procedure

Work performance has been defined by Banfield and Kay (2008, pp. 275–276) as 'what people are capable of achieving and what is actually achieved'. Formal capability procedures can be used when an individual's work performance falls well below organizational requirements due to skills, knowledge or attitudinal limitations. Prior to any formal process, it is vital that a fair, accurate and auditable account of underperformance is developed through standard practices, as part of performance appraisal or other formalized evaluations. Underperformance is not necessarily indicative of a *capability* problem, as there are a range of possible work-related and extramural causes: for example, a new position, illness, bullying, harassment, work over/underload or career duties. Most of these can be overcome with targeted organizational guidance and support, or proficient, formal investigation in the case of bullying or harassment. However, if it is established that there is a skills, knowledge or motivational gap effecting performance, then proactive interventions to improve performance are required.

Although addressing capabilities issues needs to be approached with sensitivity, for individuals early in their career it may be easier to accept the organization's findings, given their relative inexperience. Closing the capability gap is often best done through additional guidance support and training, alongside systematic, constructive and encouraging monitoring and feedback. Effective mentoring, coupled with clear direction and targets, and a clarification of expectations is also important.

For experienced staff, promotion or allocation to one-off projects could result in a capability gap. Pre-emptive, effective identification of training and development needs and induction may reduce or avoid underperformance. Motivational-based capability issues may be more difficult to explore, with lack of progression, work overload or underload, unhappiness with policy or procedural changes among some of the causal factors. Most difficult are skills and knowledge gaps that may not have been identified or addressed. Once again, informal discussions can go some way to ameliorating underlying issues, paving the way for effectively managed resolution/s.

Formal capability procedures should only follow exhaustive and demonstrable informal action when there has been a failure by individuals to meet set targets in the informal phase. For newcomers and established staff alike, formalization of capability issues can yield mixed results, from relief to despondency, demotivation, feeling bullied by management or career progress undermined. Outcomes can be improved through sensitive handing and well-drafted HRM policies with clear written guidelines, procedures, time-scales and flowcharts. In combination with effective line management training on managing informal and formal practice, capability procedures are likely to provide the best outcomes for all. Cross-cultural issues need to be considered also, especially given the importance of status and standing in many cultures, further emphasizing the importance of effective guidance and training for informal methods and that best practice should be embedded within national, organizational and managerial cultural norms.

NELARINE CORNELIOUS

See also:

Hard and soft HRM; Human resource development; International human resource management.

Reference list and selected further readings

Banfield, P. and R. Kay (2008), *Introduction to Human Resource Management*, Oxford: Oxford University Press.
Ituma, A., R. Simpson, F. Ovadje, N. Cornelius and C. Mordi (2011), Four domains of career success: how managers in Nigeria evaluate career success, *International Journal of Human Resource Management*, **22**(17), pp. 3638–3660.

Career breaks

Careers are sequential work experiences over the life course. Taking from the definition of career, a career break is a period of time during which the individual discontinues one's regular work activities. The length of that period is typically specified in advance, although deviations from the initial plan are likely.

Reasons behind career breaks include: travelling or engaging in activities that enrich and update one's professional knowledge and experience (often termed as 'sabbatical'); developing new professional skills and knowledge that may enable change in career direction and career reinvigoration (e.g., gaining an MBA degree); engaging in activities that enhance personal growth, such as attending classes in art, music or literature; engaging in self-reflection and in career strategizing; but also giving birth, raising one's children and fulfilling a national obligation, such as serving compulsory military service. The typical length of a career break is in the range of three months to three years.

Career breaks differ from pauses due to unemployment because career breaks are planned and are taken under the volition and initiation of the individual him/herself. They are also different from 'gap years' or 'overseas experience', which refer to the year many individuals take in-between secondary and tertiary education in order to further mature and explore the world.

In most cases, the individual comes into agreement with the employer about the timing, duration and other conditions of the career break. Legislation in certain countries facilitates this. For example, Belgian law entitles everyone to a break of one year over their work life. In other cases, however, individuals develop and execute a plan of timely resignation from their current employment in order to have the career break.

The effects of breaks on careers are contingent upon the type of the break, the industry and the way the break is utilized. From the perspective of objective success (e.g., hierarchical, status or financial attainment), career breaks due to maternity or fulfilment of obligations (e.g., military service) tend to be detrimental. Individuals can find themselves behind their cohort because of skills depreciation during the break. Nevertheless, it may be possible to harness the negative consequences with engagement in skills updating before career re-entry. Career breaks taken simply for recreation purposes also tend to harm career attainment. On the other hand, for carefully thought-out professional reasons, career breaks may have positive effects on objective success. This, however, is contingent upon factors including the timing of the break and economic conditions.

NIKOS BOZIONELOS

See also:

Careers; Human capital; Skill.

References and selected further readings

Lovejoy, M. and P. Stone (2012), Opting back in: the influence of time at home on professional women's career redirection after opting out, *Gender, Work and Organization*, **19**(6), pp. 631–653.
Shaw, S., M. Taylor and I. Harris (1999), Jobs for the girls: a study of the careers of professional women returners following participation in a European funded updating programme, *International Journal of Manpower*, **20**(3–4), pp. 179–188.
Skans, O.N. and L. Liljeberg (2014), The wage effects of subsidized career breaks, *Empirical Economics*, **47**(2), pp. 593–617.

Careers

The term 'career' comes from the French for racetrack. Until the late 1970s, a career consisted of long-term employment in an organization, with upward progression. This was an ideal type. It did not represent all workers, but received substantial research attention. Following significant organizational restructuring in the 1980s and 1990s, a new movement proposed more flexible and diverse careers such as boundaryless (Arthur, 1994), protean (Hall, 1996) and kaleidoscope (Mainiero and Sullivan, 2005). The commonly accepted definition of careers is individuals' sequences of work experiences over time, involving a lifelong series of identity changes, continuous learning and self-evaluation (Arthur et al., 1989; Hall, 1996).

Careers play an essential role in individuals' lives, at the very minimum work provides basic subsistence. Careers also have more complex roles defining individuals' identity and giving meaning to life (Briscoe et al., 2012b). Organizations use career management to retain key employees and develop elite talent. Individuals expect achievement and growth opportunities from their careers and will move elsewhere if necessary.

A significant issue currently debated today is whether individuals or organizations should take responsibility for careers. The shifts in previous decades towards more flexible careers also moved responsibility of career management to the individual. Some criticized this as neoliberal discourse in putting too much onus on individuals and allowing organizations to abrogate their responsibilities (Roper et al., 2010). The outworking of this new discourse can be seen when organizations make workers redundant, contrasting organizations that intend to be strategic in their human resource management, and emphasize the importance of long-term career management for their employees. Other factors determining careers include individuals' circumstances, networks and skills, where careers cannot be viewed as 'boundaryless' or under the control of the individual (Unite et al., 2012). On the other hand, some individuals are active agents exploiting organizational resources to advance their personal career goals (Inkson, 2008).

Two key components of careers are career success and career transition. Career success is defined in similar ways around the world, although there are subtle variations between countries. External or objective success can be seen in achievements such as salary. Internal or subjective success can be seen in satisfaction, which is also a widespread career need except in China, Japan and Malaysia. Gen Y defines career success by more idiosyncratic criteria (Unite et al. 2012). Consequently, multinational corporations need different career management practices in different countries and for different generations (Demel et al., 2012). Career transitions are any shift within or between jobs, into and out of self-employment and between occupations. Many career changes are initiated by individuals, displaying a protean approach (Unite et al. 2012). Self-initiated career change is more likely to occur in countries with an egalitarian culture, such as Australia.

Significant institutional and social change means that younger individuals have different experiences from their elders (Unite et al. 2012). For example, careers in China were traditionally influenced by the Confucian values of hierarchy, discipline and face. Before the recent opening up to a market economy, individuals were assigned to jobs through centralized state planning and careers previously consisted of lifetime employment in state-owned enterprises, but this option no longer has the same cachet. With the new economy there is a trend towards competitive and individualistic values (Shen, 2012). In South Africa until apartheid ended, certain careers were closed to certain races (Briscoe et al., 2012b). The US has the most individualistic culture in the world. Individuals made redundant will often blame themselves and seek answers about how they were responsible for their demise. They may not desire constant change but accept it as inevitable, while Gen Y is demanding work–life balance in ways that have never been seen before (Briscoe et al., 2012a).

Teresa Marchant

See also:

Downsizing; Generations; Multinational companies; National culture; Retention; Talent management; Training and development.

References and selected further readings

Arthur, M.B. (1994), The boundaryless career: a new perspective for organizational inquiry, *Journal of Organizational Behaviour*, **15**, pp. 295–306.
Arthur M.B., D.T. Hall and B.S. Lawrence (1989), Generating new directions in career theory: the case for a transdisciplinary approach, in M.B. Arthur, D.T. Hall and B.S. Lawrence (eds), *Handbook of Career Theory*, Cambridge: Cambridge University Press, pp. 7–25.

Briscoe, J.P., D.T. Hall, M. Las Heras and J. Unite (2012a), Careers in the United States, in J.P. Briscoe, D.T. Hall and W. Mayrhofer (eds), *Careers Around the World: Individual and Contextual Perspectives*, New York: Routledge, pp. 355–370.

Briscoe J.P., D.T. Hall and W. Mayrhofer (2012b), Careers around the world, in J.P. Briscoe, D.T. Hall and W. Mayrhofer (eds), *Careers Around the World: Individual and Contextual Perspectives*, New York: Routledge, pp. 3–14.

Demel, B., Y. Shen, M. Las Heras, D.T. Hall and J. Unite (2012), Career success around the world: its meaning and perceived influences in 11 countries, in J.P. Briscoe, D.T. Hall and W. Mayrhofer (eds), *Careers Around the World: Individual and Contextual Perspectives*, New York: Routledge, pp. 59–87.

Hall, D.T. (1996), Protean careers in the 21st century, *Academy of Management Executive*, **10**(4), pp. 8–16.

Inkson, K. (2008), Are humans resources? *Career Development International*, **13**(3), pp. 270–279.

Mainiero, L.A. and S.E. Sullivan (2005), Kaleidoscope careers: an alternative explanation for the 'opt-out generation', *Academy of Management Executive*, **19**(1), pp. 106–123.

Roper, J., S. Ganesh and K. Inkson (2010), Neoliberalism and knowledge interests in boundaryless careers discourse, *Work, Employment and Society*, **24**, pp. 661–679.

Shen, Y. (2012), Careers in China, in J.P. Briscoe, D.T. Hall and W. Mayrhofer (eds), *Careers Around the World: Individual and Contextual Perspectives*, New York: Routledge, pp. 224–237.

Unite, J., E. Parry, J.P. Briscoe and K. Chudzikowski (2012), Careers and age: career success for older and younger workers, in J.P. Briscoe, D.T. Hall and W. Mayrhofer (eds), *Careers Around the World: Individual and Contextual Perspectives*, New York: Routledge, pp. 118–144.

Change management

Change management refers to conscious attempts to bring about changes in organizations. Although the term can be defined in a number of ways, it basically refers to any technical, structural, economic, psychological or social event that affects the way an organization or its stakeholders behave. Such changes can range from small-scale fine-tuning, such as team-building and continuous improvement projects, to large-scale transformations, such as organizational restructuring, culture change and mergers and acquisitions.

Organizational change has existed as long as there have been organizations, i.e., thousands of years. For much of this time, those who controlled organizations, whether they were sovereigns, religious leaders or guild masters, preferred stability over change, as change was seen as potentially undermining their authority and standing. However, with the advent of the Industrial Revolution, those who controlled the emerging factory system began to see change as preferable to stability because change offered greater opportunities to increase their profits.

As a consequence, in the late eighteenth and nineteenth century, owners, managers and engineers began to take an interest in how organizations could be developed and improved. Perhaps the best-known example at this time was Adam Smith's pin factory. Smith argued that through the division of labour, whereby each worker was made to specialize in one narrowly defined task, production could be greatly increased and costs greatly decreased. While good for factory owners, this process was less good for employees, which is why employer-led change tended to be accompanied by employee-led resistance.

It was partly to address resistance and partly to identify the 'one best way' to organize work that Frederick Taylor developed scientific management at the beginning of the twentieth century, which could be considered as the first real attempt to offer a systematic approach to managing change. Although scientific management still has its adherents in terms of its approach to work organization, it never really took off as an approach to change management. However, in the 1940s, an approach to change management emerged that is still highly influential today – organization development (OD). This is an approach that has evolved over the past 80 years into an integrated framework of theories and practices that, it is claimed, is capable of addressing most of the important problems confronting the human side of organizations.

Kurt Lewin is credited with laying the groundwork for OD, his main contributions being:

- Planned change – this comprises four interrelated elements: field theory, group dynamics, action research and the three-step model of change.
- Showing how psychological theories and techniques developed and used in laboratory experiments to study group behaviour could be applied to studying and changing group behaviour in the real world.
- Providing a set of ethical values and 'utopian aspirations' that emphasized the need to promote democratic and participative management in order to bring about beneficial change in organizations.

Although originally focussing on small-group change, OD began in the 1970s and 1980s to pay more attention to organization-wide issues through four main developments:

- Influenced by socio-technical and contingency theories, OD practitioners came to adopt an open-systems perspective that viewed organizations in their totality and within their environment.
- A change of focus from group norms and values to organizational culture.
- A shift of emphasis from individual and group learning to organizational learning.
- Devoting increasing attention to organizational transformation rather than just group change.

By the end of 1980s, OD had assembled a widely-used range of tried-and-tested approaches, including practices developed outside the OD field such as Six Sigma, Total Quality Management (TQM) and Business Process Reengineering. However, despite its efforts to develop a more organization-wide focus, its most popular approaches still tended to be slow, participative and group-level based. Perhaps not surprisingly, therefore, in an era when swift and decisive top-down, imposed change was becoming the norm, OD was beginning to be challenged by newer approaches to understanding organizations and organizational change.

These newer approaches tended to take a holistic-contextual view of organizations and their environments; they challenged the notion of change as an ordered, rational and linear process; and there was an emphasis on change as a continuous process that is heavily influenced by culture, power and politics. By the end of the 1980s, these different strands had loosely coalesced under the umbrella of 'emergent change'. Despite the great interest in emergent change over the past 30 years or so, and despite the theoretical insights it offers into how organizations operate and change, it has not provided a practical alternative to OD. This is because it has failed to provide clear directions for implementing emergent change or develop a range of tools and techniques for managing change.

OD, on the other hand, has continued to develop in terms of theory and practice, and has extended its user base. For example, OD practices have been incorporated into HRM and HRD, creating strong overlaps between the three areas. It has also expanded globally, with OD networks appearing in Asia and Africa. In addition, it has incorporated newer perspectives on the nature of organizational life, such as social constructionism, postmodernism and complexity theories. Lastly, in an era when ethical behaviour, social awareness and environmental behaviour have grown in importance, OD's ethical values and participative approach are seen as being in tune with the way society wishes organizations to operate.

BERNARD BURNES

See also:

Employee involvement; Ethics; Scientific management.

References and selected further readings

Burnes, B. (2014), *Managing Change*, 6th edn, Pearson: Harlow.
Burnes, B. and B. Cooke (2012), The past, present and future of organization development: taking the long view, *Human Relations*, **65**(11), pp. 1395–1429.
Pettigrew, A.M. (1997), What is a processual analysis? *Scandinavian Journal of Management*, **13**(4), pp. 337–348.
Weick, K.E. and R.E. Quinn (1999), Organizational change and development, *Annual Review of Psychology*, **50**, 361–386.
Wooten, K.C. and L.P. White (1999), Linking OD's philosophy with justice theory: postmodern implications, *Journal of Organizational Change Management*, **12**(1), pp. 7–20.

CIPD

The Chartered Institute of Personnel and Development (CIPD) is the professional body for HR and people development. It represents the voice of a worldwide community of 140,000 members working in HR, learning and development, people management and consulting across the private, public and voluntary sectors. As an independent and not-for-profit organization, it is committed to championing better work and working lives for the benefit of individuals, business and wider society.

The Institute provides thought leadership, practical advice and guidance, as well as professional development, rigorous professional standards and career support for its members. It seeks to improve understanding of how organizations operate and perform, and how they manage and develop their people.

The CIPD has links with more than 100 similar institutions and associations across the world, including the European Association for People Management (EAPM) and the Australian Human Resources Institute (AHRI). In recent years, it has expanded its activities in international markets, particularly in Southeast Asia, building from its Singapore office, and the Middle East.

The CIPD started life in 1913 as the Welfare Workers' Association (WWA) with a membership of just 34 people. In 1994, the Institute of Personnel and Development was formed when the Institute of Personnel Management merged with the Institute of

Training and Development. The Institute was granted chartered status as the CIPD in 2000, which means that it can confer individual chartered status on members who meet the required standards of knowledge, practice and behaviours.

In 2009, the CIPD's Profession Map was launched. The Map is a dynamic set of standards, setting the benchmark for what effective HR and learning and development (L&D) people do across every aspect of the profession. CIPD supports continuing professional development and recognition for members at all stages of their career. CIPD qualifications provide students with the underpinning knowledge they need to pursue successful careers in HR and L&D, while *Experience Assessment* provides a more direct route to professional membership. The CIPD encourages senior HR professionals to share their experiences and contribute to research and public policy debates.

The Institute's research programme informs its engagement with policymakers and other opinion formers on behalf of the profession. It has published important studies of many core HR issues, including the psychological contract, links between people and performance, and employee engagement.

In addition, the Institute's public policy work helps inform and shape debate, government policy and legislation. For example, its *Learning to Work* programme, launched in 2012, is focused on bridging the gap between education and work to both tackle youth unemployment and encourage employers to take responsibility for building their own talent pipelines. The campaign draws on the resources of members through its extensive local branch network and has parallels to the purpose and priorities that drove the formation of the Workers Welfare Association in 1913.

MIKE EMMOTT

See also:

Human resource management; Human resource manager.

References and selected further readings

CIPD Annual Review 2012–13, www.cipd.co.uk/binaries/Annual-review-2012-2013.pdf.

Coaching

The word 'coach' emerged in the sixteenth century and originates from the Hungarian word *kocsi*, which means wagon. It was introduced in management literature in 1950 (Mace, 1950), but it only started gaining momentum with the work of Fournies (1978). Within the past decade, it has evolved as one of the most important workplace interventions and is widely used in organizations today.

Coaching as a workplace practice may be defined as the developmental interaction whereby a coach provides an employee with motivation, help, guidance and feedback with the aim to empower the latter to set and achieve specific personal, professional and performance objectives. In the beginning of the coaching relationship, the coach–coachee interaction is essential for the coachee to establish goals and act upon them. During the process, the coach uses a set of techniques that include active listening and questioning in order to involve the coachee in critical reflection and appreciation of the current and aspired situation. Thereafter, the coachee is encouraged to inform their practice by what they have learnt through reflection. Coaching is usually a short-term intervention, at the end of which the employee is able to set and achieve similar to the above objectives without the presence of the coach.

Both the coach and the coachee are equivalent and important members of the process. The coach needs to possess a wide range of abilities, from being a good listener and communicator to being able to adjust style and approach depending on the context and situation. Respectively, it is essential that the coachee is willing to involve in coaching and, therefore, personal, professional or performance development. Indeed, unless the employee is eager and motivated to learn and change, even the work of the most experienced and skilful coach may render fruitless.

Segers et al. (2011) classified the numerous types of workplace coaching depending on the agenda (skills, performance, life), type of coach (external, internal, line manager, self) and espoused school of thought (emotionality, rationality, activity, awareness, context). Although the most common form is the one received from line managers, substantial consideration should be given to selecting the most suitable type. For instance, power imbalance and the long-term relationship between a manager and an employee may hinder the latter from discussing openly career choices or personal issues.

Contemporary coaching research has shown that it is related to various positive employee outcomes, including improved employees' satisfaction and individual performance. Nevertheless, it is still in its infancy. Additional and more robust research is necessary to highlight the importance of each coaching type per se.

MARGARITA NYFOUDI

See also:

Continuing professional development; Organizational learning; Performance appraisal; Performance appraisal interview.

References and selected further readings

Fournies, F.F. (1978), *Coaching for Improved Work Performance*, Bridgewater, NJ: Van Nostrand Reinhold Co.

Mace, M. (1950), *The Growth and Development of Executives*, Cambridge, MA: Harvard University Press.

Segers, J., D. Vloeberghs, E. Henderickx and I. Inceoglu (2011), Structuring and understanding the coaching industry: the coaching cube, *Academy of Management Learning & Education*, **10**(2), pp. 204–221.

Co-determination

The question of worker democracy and control of enterprises is one that has been discussed for some time. It can take many forms from providing suggestions to management as to how the firm and workplace practices can improve to actually jointly managing and indeed determining the way organizations develop and evolve (see Marchington and Wilkinson, 2000). There is a scale of power that varies according to the influence a worker can have. Within the European context there has been an interest in co-determination for a long time and specific countries such as Germany have been known for their development of such forms. The German model is seen as a good example of co-determination where workers through various representatives have an input into the affairs of company management. The role of co-determination in current post-Second World War Germany is more than just linked to the role of works councils and worker representatives on these bodies (these works councils where trade union representatives and other worker representatives discuss matters of work and employment with management and in some cases even sign collective agreements). In Germany co-determination involves a supervisory board, in this case where there will be worker directors who attempt to influence decisions at the highest level. Such bodies continue to be dominated by the employers in the final instance, however they do allow workers and their representatives some say on key strategic issues as such or at least advance notice of changes to come. There are many instances in Europe and in other contexts where companies have worker representatives on the board of directors, although these are usually a small minority of individuals that are easily outnumbered by management. In addition, the ability of worker representatives to influence proceedings may be impaired by the lack of training and support they receive, as well as their isolation from the customs and networks of management. However, in some contexts there is a growing interest in such a presence. With the increasing influence of company pension funds who in turn own a range of other company shares we are seeing a growing interest in worker representatives becoming more active as trustees and representatives in such bodies that will influence the conduct of HRM to some extent in organizations in the near future.

MIGUEL MARTÍNEZ LUCIO

See also:

Consultation; Representative participation; Workplace democracy.

References and selected further readings

FitzRoy, F. and K. Kraft (2005), Co-determination, efficiency and productivity, *British Journal of Industrial Relations*, **43**(2), pp. 233–247.
Marchington M. and A. Wilkinson (2005), Direct participation and involvement, in S. Bach (ed.), *Managing Human Resources: Personnel Management in Transition*, Oxford: Blackwell, pp. 398–423.
Wächter, H. and M. Muller-Camen (2002), Co-determination and strategic integration in German firms, *Human Resource Management Journal*, **12**(3), pp. 76–87.

Collective agreements

A collective agreement is an agreement negotiated collectively between a management, representing an employer's interest, and a trade union, representing the interest of workers. A collective agreement enshrines the rules relating to regulating the employment relationship between employer and workers. The rules are differentiated into two types – substantive rules that establish the norms in the form of specific conditions of employment and cover: pay, hours of work, overtime payments, holiday payments, discipline, grievances, sickness and accident payments, redundancy and termination of employment. Procedural rules set the standards of conduct between the employer and workers in resolving differences that arise from creating and maintaining a collective agreement.

The scope and content of collective agreements may be determined by the procedural agreement between an employer and trade union(s). The procedural arrangements may limit the range of subjective matter that lies within a substantive agreement and they may specify particular types of workers that are within or outside the scope of the agreement. The scope of a collective agreement is often dependent on the bargaining rights that have been conferred by an employer in recognizing a particular trade union and how this recognition might be limited to specific bargaining units.

In the majority of democratic societies, collective agreements between employers and trade unions are legally binding and enforceable through the courts. In the European Union, countries such as Germany have promoted collective agreements through Works Councils. The exception to this is the United Kingdom, where collective agreements are not legally binding on the parties who have signed them. If either the union or management do not comply there is no recourse to the law and therefore an agreement is only binding in honour. This is reflective of the voluntarist tradition in UK employment relations, which historically has seen government and the law have a minimum of involvement in the regulation of employment relations, instead leaving it to employers and trade unions to regulate their own affairs. However, with the decline in trade union membership and a consequent decline in joint regulation and collective bargaining and the increasing influence of European Community laws on UK domestic laws, there has been a move towards greater legal regulation of UK employment relations.

PETER F. BESZTER

See also:

Bargaining scope; Collective bargaining; Joint consultation.

References and selected further readings

Bain, G.S. (ed.) (1983), *Industrial Relations in Britain*, Oxford: Basil Blackwell.
Blyton, P. and P. Turnbull (2004), *The Dynamics of Employee Relations*, 3rd edn, Basingstoke: Palgrave Macmillan.
Colling, T. and M. Terry (eds) (2010), *Industrial Relations Theory & Practice*, 3rd edn, Oxford: Blackwell.

Collective bargaining

Collective bargaining is the process whereby representatives of employers and workers jointly determine, regulate and agree terms on decisions relating to substantive and procedural matters that shape the employment relationship.

The term collective bargaining was invented by Sidney and Beatrice Webb to describe the process of agreeing terms and conditions of employment through representatives of employers – possibly their associations and representatives of the workers – probably their trade unions. The Webbs saw collective bargaining as a substitute for employer bargaining individually with each worker and establishing such terms and conditions for each through the contract of employment. A major factor behind worker organization has been the recognition of the uneven balance in bargaining power between employer and the individual worker. Collective bargaining is essentially a representative process – in which representatives of capital reach agreements or compromise with representatives of labour.

Collective bargaining is a dynamic, continuous process, which depends on maintaining, regulating and supplementing agreements on a day-by-day basis. Where collective bargaining takes place, it is an important determinant of the rules that govern the relationship between workers and employers in the workplace.

The literature on collective bargaining focuses on the functions of collective bargaining rather than societal context in which bargaining takes place. Some of the key contributors are:

- Sidney and Beatrice Webb, argue in their work *Industrial Democracy* (1902) that collective bargaining is an economic institution.
- Alan Flanders argues in his paper 'Collective bargaining: theoretical analysis' in the *British Journal of Industrial Relations*, November 1968, that collective bargaining should be seen as a political institution.
- Neil Chamberlain and James Kuhn argue in *Collective Bargaining* (1965) the distinction between collective bargaining as an economic process, as argued by the Webbs, and collective bargaining as a political process, as argued by Flanders, does not mean that there are two self-contained types of collective bargaining. They argue that collective bargaining can be considered from three perspectives that represent different stages of its development and are not necessarily in conflict but rather reflect the historical development of collective bargaining. The three perspectives are: the marketing theory; the government theory and the managerial theory. The market perspective sees trade unions acting as a labour alliance in collective bargaining. The governmental perspective presents an autonomous and agreed rule of law into industrial relations. The managerial perspective emphasizes the contribution of the trade unions towards making management more democratic and promoting industrial democracy.

Collective bargaining from the pluralist perspective is seen as an effective and efficient way of dealing with inherent conflict within the workplace, recognizing differences between trade unions and employers. Collective bargaining simplifies the rule making process by avoiding dealing with individual workers and making settlements that cover groups of workers. Philosophically, it has been argued that in every civilized society workers should have a right of representation in any decisions affecting their working lives and that collective bargaining brings about the means of doing this. However, from the unitarist perspective, collective bargaining by standardizing terms and conditions of employment limits the free flow of labour in response to market forces. It does not fit in with the human resource management approach, which focuses on incentives and motivation of the individual worker rather than the collective workforce.

In the United Kingdom and elsewhere, collective bargaining is in decline. In the case of the UK, this decline has been tracked by the Workplace Industrial/Employment Relations Surveys over the past 35 years. The latest survey in 2011 showed that workplaces with any collective bargaining, the overall collective bargaining coverage was 13 per cent (public sector 57 per cent; private sector 7 per cent). Workers covered by collective bargaining was overall 23 per cent (public sector 44 per cent; private sector 16 per cent).

Despite its decline, collective bargaining is still an integral part of the employment relations landscape in the European Community, the UK, the US and Commonwealth countries such as Australia, New Zealand and Canada. It remains a valuable conduit for promoting and facilitating joint regulation in the workplace.

PETER F. BESZTER

See also:
Collective agreements; Joint consultation; Pluralism; Unitarism.

References and selected further reading

Bain, G.S. (ed.) (1983), *Industrial Relations in Britain*, Oxford: Basil Blackwell.
Blyton, P. and P. Turnbull (2004), *The Dynamics of Employee Relations*, 3rd edn, Basingstoke: Palgrave Macmillan.
Burchill, F. (1992), *Labour Relations*, Basingstoke: Palgrave Macmillan.
Colling, T. and M. Terry (eds) (2010), *Industrial Relations Theory & Practice*, 3rd edn, Oxford: Blackwell.
Rose, E. (2008), *Employment Relations*, 3rd edn, London: Prentice Hall.
van Wanrooy, B., H. Bewley, A. Bryson, J. Forth, S. Freeth, L. Stokes and S. Wood (2013), *The Workplace Employment Relations Study – First Findings*, London: Department of Business, Innovation, and Skills.

Collectivism

In general, this term can have a variety of applications, although in HRM and the field of industrial relations it refers more to the collective orientation of the employment relationship. This is whereby workers collectively organize themselves, generally through joining trade unions, to exert some power in determining and regulating the employment contract through collective bargaining. Collectively, workers have greater power than as an individual and thereby collectively will gain more influence and have more involvement in the decision-making process of their employment.

However, it is argued that we cannot speak of collectivism as a simple term or narrative (McBride and Martinez Lucio, 2011). Collectivism is a flexible and rich concept and should not be defined in a one-dimensional manner but consideration should be taken of the different approaches in varying debates. First, it should be noted that the 'individual' and 'collective' are usually interlinked: individual tensions can be a source of collective organization. (Martinez Lucio and Stewart, 1997). From a different approach, collectivism can be linked to the occupational identity and extended to a sense of class identity and solidarity (McBride, 2006; MacKenzie et al., 2006). Stephenson and Stewart (2001) identify three different categories of collectivism: 'trade union collectivism', 'workplace collectivism' and the 'collectivism of everyday life'. There are a series of other interventions on gender and ethnic relations (Healy et al., 2004a, 2004b) and the experience of work that nourish our understanding of collectivism as a more complex and broader concept. The community unionism literature (see McBride and Greenwood, 2009) focuses on how trade unions are extending their role out of the workplace and into the community, thereby broadening collectivism. Other studies focus on regional community initiatives (Holgate and Wills, 2007) in the combination of a variety of community groups with varying identities, such as ethnicity, gender, faith, age and past experience, who developed strategies to give support to groups of workers in the local community. Then there are debates as to the 'collective memory', 'historical' changes in the understanding of collectivism and also the role of the 'political', which requires a more concerted role in current understandings of collectivism (McBride and Martinez Lucio, 2011).

JO MCBRIDE

See also:

Community unionism; Employment relationship; Trade unions.

References and selected further readings

Healy, G., H. Bradley and N. Mukherjee (2004a), Inspiring activists: the experience of minority ethnic women in trade unions, in G. Healy, E. Heery, P. Taylor and W. Brown (eds), *The Future of Worker Representation*, Basingstoke: Palgrave Macmillan.

Healy, G., H. Bradley and N. Mukherjee (2004b), Individualism and collectivism revisited: a study of black and minority ethnic women, *Industrial Relations Journal*, **35**(5), pp. 451–466.

Holgate, J. and J. Wills (2007), Placing labour in London: trade union strategy and practice, in L. Turner and D. Cornfield (eds), *Seeking Solidarity: Labor and the Politics of Urban Coalition Building*, Ithaca, NY: Cornell University Press.

MacKenzie, R., M. Stuart, C. Forde, I. Greenwood, J. Gardiner and R. Perrett (2006), All that is solid? Class, identity and the maintenance of a collective orientation amongst redundant steel workers, *Sociology*, **40**(5), pp. 833–855.

Martinez Lucio, M. and P. Stewart (1997), The paradox of contemporary labour process theory: the rediscovery of the 'employee' and the disappearance of collectivism, *Capital and Class*, **62**, pp. 49–78.

McBride, J. (2006), Research note: mapping worker collectivism: some evidence from industries on the River Tyne, *Work, Employment and Society*, **20**(3), pp. 583–591.

McBride, J. and I. Greenwood (eds) (2009), Community Unionism: A Comparative Analysis of Concepts and Contexts, Basingstoke: Palgrave Macmillan.

McBride, J. and M. Martinez Lucio (2011), Dimensions of collectivism: occupation, community and the increasing role of memory and personal dynamics in the debate, *Work, Employment and Society*, **25**(4), pp. 794–805.

Stephenson, C. and P. Stewart (2001), The whispering shadow: collectivism and individualism at Ikeda-Hoover and Nissan UK, *Sociological Research Online*, **6**(3), pp. 1–15.

Commitment

There is general agreement that commitment has important implications for behaviour – people are more likely to continue a course of action (e.g., remaining with an organization) when they make a commitment. There is less agreement about what commitment is and how it should be measured. In their three-component model of organizational commitment, Meyer and Allen (1997) attempted to consolidate differing perspectives by proposing that commitments can take different forms, or be characterized by different mindsets, including emotional attachment (affective commitment), sense of obligation (normative commitment) or perceived cost of discontinuing a relationship or course of action (continuance commitment). Each of these mindsets serves as a motivational force that binds an individual to an entity and/or course of action. Indeed, affective, normative, and continuance commitment to the organization all correlate negatively with turnover intention and actual voluntary turnover. However, the mindsets have different implications for discretionary behaviours not included within the terms of the commitment. For example, employees with strong affective commitment perform more effectively and are more likely to engage in organizational citizenship behaviours than are those with strong normative or continuance commitment (Meyer et al., 2002). More recently, it has been demonstrated that the individual mindsets can combine in different ways to form 'commitment profiles', and that some profiles are associated with more positive outcomes than others. Most notably, the combination of strong affective and normative commitment, experienced as a moral duty (i.e., desire to do the right thing), has been found to be associated with higher levels of retention, job performance, and citizenship behaviours than other profiles.

Some scholars continue to seek a unitary definition of commitment, viewing it as a bond with (Klein et al., 2012) or positive attitude toward (Solinger et al., 2008) an entity or action – concepts quite similar to affective commitment. Although these scholars do not deny the existence and potential impact of obligations and perceived costs, they do not include them within the realm of commitment. One benefit of this approach is simplicity in measurement. Another is ease with which parallel measures of commitment to different entities can be developed.

Early theory and research focused primarily on commitment to the organization, but employees can commit to multiple constituencies, or targets, within (supervisor, team) and outside (union, profession, customers) the organization, and that these can combine to influence behaviour. Meyer and Herscovitch (2001) proposed that the affective, normative and continuance commitment mindsets apply to all commitments. Again, they all bind an individual to an entity and/or course of action, but differ with regard to their implications for discretionary behaviour. For example, employees with affective commitment to an organizational change initiative want to see the change succeed and will exert more discretionary effort in support of the change, even if it involves some sacrifice, than those with strong continuance commitment – the latter tend to do only what is required of them. Recognizing that employees can form multiple commitments is important for several reasons. First, commitment to a particular target (e.g., project) will generally have a stronger effect on target-relevant behaviour than will more global commitments (e.g., commitment to the organization). Second, commitments to different targets can complement, conflict with or serve as substitutes for one another. For example, when the goals of an organization are aligned with those of an individual's profession, commitment to the profession will complement commitment to the organization, and might serve as a substitute for organizational commitment under certain conditions (e.g., economic conditions preclude the establishment of a long-term relationship). However, when goals and values are not aligned, commitments to different targets can lead to role conflict.

Although individuals can differ in their propensity to form commitments, situational factors have been found to play the strongest role in the development of commitment. Among the strongest correlates of affective and normative organizational commitment are perceived organizational support, organizational justice, person–organization fit, and transformational leadership (Meyer et al., 2002). All of these can be controlled to some degree by organizations and used as levers to foster positive commitment within their workforces. Creating conditions such as these helps to satisfy basic psychological needs and serves as the basis for mutually beneficial social exchange relationships. Consequently, it is not surprising that positive commitments are also associated with employee wellbeing, both physical and psychological. For a more detailed review of commitment theory and research, and how it can be applied effectively for the mutual benefit of organizations and their employees, see Klein et al. (2009).

JOHN P. MEYER

See also:

Labour turnover; Organizational citizenship behaviour; Person–environment fit; Retention; Transformational leadership; Wellbeing.

References and selected further readings

Klein, H.J., T.E. Becker and J.P. Meyer (eds) (2009), *Commitment in Organizations: Accumulated Wisdom and New Directions*, London and New York: Routledge.

Klein, H.J., J.C. Molloy and C.T. Brinsfield (2012), Reconceptualizing workplace commitment to redress a stretched construct: revisiting assumptions and removing confounds, *Academy of Management Review*, **37**, pp. 130–151.

Meyer, J.P. and N.J. Allen (1997), *Commitment in the workplace: Theory, research, and application*, Thousand Oaks, CA: Sage Publications.

Meyer, J.P. and L. Herscovitch (2001), Commitment in the workplace: toward a general model, *Human Resource Management Review*, **11**, pp. 299–326.

Meyer, J.P., D.J. Stanley, L. Herscovitch and L. Topolnytsky (2002), Affective, continuance, and normative commitment to the organization: a meta-analysis of antecedents, correlates, and consequences, *Journal of Vocational Behavior*, **61**, pp. 20–52.

Solinger, O.N., W. van Olffen and R.A. Roe (2008), Beyond the three-component model of organizational commitment, *Journal of Applied Psychology*, **93**, pp. 70–83.

Communication

The first model of communication was developed in 1949 by Shannon and Weaver, and considered the role of the sender in encoding the message, the channel and the role of the receiver in decoding the message. Accordingly, our understanding of communication requires an information source, at least two people and a mechanism or channel to transmit the message. Therefore, organizational communication refers to the processes, systems and patterns of formal and informal interpersonal and group interaction in the workplace. These communication systems may provide for two-way communication, enabling management to inform employees on matters that concern them, and enabling employees to raise issues with management. Communication does not, however, infer that employees will be consulted and have a voice or a genuine say over decision-making. Rather, communication refers to the exchange of information, which may in turn provide employees with a voice.

The types of information communicated by management to employees can include broad organizational issues, such as the values, goals, strategic plan and the performance of the organization. Management may also communicate to employees on issues related to their employment and working conditions, such as organizational changes, HR policies, health and safety, and learning and development programmes. The line manager is usually responsible for the daily interaction with employees, and therefore plays a key role in transmitting information from management to employees as well as communicating job expectations and work tasks. Effective communication in the workplace can encourage trust between employees and management and commitment to the organization (Thomas et al., 2009; Zeffane et al., 2011). Therefore, managers need to provide open communication in order to transmit information clearly, and to enhance their relationship with their employees.

Employees can communicate both to their peers and management on work-related issues. When an organization is undergoing change, employees should be given the opportunity to express their concerns and opinions. Employees should also be able to discuss terms and conditions of their employment, health and safety, learning and development requirements and to discuss work tasks.

There are a variety of mechanisms that can be used to enable communication within the workplace. Management will often utilize formal means such as management briefings, magazines, noticeboards, intranet, newsletters and bulletins to convey organizational information. These forms of communication are typically one-way from management to employees. Staff surveys, such as engagement surveys or attitude surveys, often provide employees with the opportunity for one way communication to management. Two-way communication can be enhanced by team briefings, consultative committees, speak-up programmes, staff appraisals and face-to-face interaction.

PAULA K. MOWBRAY

See also:

Attitude survey; Consultation; Employee involvement; Employee voice; Suggestion scheme; Upward problem-solving.

References and selected further readings

Barrett, D. (2011), *Leadership Communication*, New York: McGraw-Hill Irwin.
Rosengren, K.E. (2013), *Communication*, London: Sage.
Shannon, C. and W. Weaver (1963), *The Mathematical Theory of Communication*, Illinois: University of Illinois Press.
Thomas, G.F., R. Zolin and J.L. Hartman (2009), The central role of communication in developing trust and its effects on employee involvement, *Journal of Business Communication*, 46(3), pp. 287–310.
Zeffane, R., S.A. Tipu and J.C. Ryan (2011), Communication, commitment & trust: exploring the triad, *International Journal of Business and Management*, 6(6), pp. 77–87.

Community unionism

Trade unions are traditionally considered to be the primary vehicle for employees to voice their concerns and seek representation through industrial (workplace) relations. However, trade unionism has often been regarded as an inherently workplace-based concept. Trade unions are, by definition, membership-based organizations that seek to collectivize workers in a particular sphere of interest to bargain on issues of terms and conditions of employment. In the UK, the provisions of the Employment Act 1999 enable trade unions to pursue statutory recognition for workers in a defined 'bargaining unit', confirming the workplace orientation of trade unions. As direct trade union influence has waned with the decline of collective bargaining coverage, trade unions and workers have increasingly sought alternative routes to seek influence over the actions of employers. Wills (2002) argues that this is a deliberate strategy informed by declining union coverage and reach, stimulating a groundswell of activism from underserved, underpaid and underrepresented workers.

Holgate (2009) and Fitzgerald (2009) demonstrate the 'bottom-up' dynamic in different sources of community. Holgate exposes the apparent tension between community-based Living Wage campaigns and the direct concerns that conflict between the traditional role of trade unions in bargaining and negotiating over pay. Fitzgerald articulates the cultural and organizational gap between traditional union organizing and new groups of workers through social and economic change resulting from migration patterns.

The effectiveness of community organizing dynamics is far from certain but Williams et al. (2011) argue that there is an environmental effect. While there is little evidence to support theories of direct negotiating and bargaining outcomes, there is evidence to suggest that community campaigning has an influence on employer actions. Reports of the Living Wage Campaign (www.livingwage.org.uk) demonstrate the concern that some employers have to be seen to be 'decent' living wage employers, while migrant worker campaigns have led to changes in the legislative framework, including the introduction of the Gangmasters Licensing Authority following the 2004 Act.

Trade unions themselves are responding to this new environment. Unite the Union has a specific 'Community' section within the organization, reaching out to workers in non-traditional ways, offering advice on a range of issues and 'linking' communities of interest (http://unitetheunion.org), rather than advice on collective bargaining and representation. Anti-austerity campaigns have also led unions to seek coalition building with community-based groups and organizations, from the disability alliance Hardest Hit group to foodbank providers the Trussell Trust.

Trade unions are increasingly recognizing and responding to the lack of a direct workplace route to influence employers. The trade union 'community' has traditionally been the workplace, once a 'closed shop', where union membership was required in organized workplaces. Trade unions are now redefining that 'community' and placing increased emphasis upon common interests rather than by common employers.

KEVIN ROWAN

See also:

Collective bargaining; Collectivism; Living wage; Trade unions.

References and selected further readings

Fitzgerald, I. (2009), Polish migrant workers in the north – new communities, new opportunities? in J. McBride and I. Greenwood (eds), *Community Unionism: A Comparative Analysis of Concepts and Contexts*, Basingstoke: Palgrave Macmillan, pp. 93–118.
Holgate, J. (2009), Contested terrain: London's living wage campaign and the tensions between community and union organising, in J McBride and I Greenwood (eds), *Community Unionism: A Comparative Analysis of Concepts and Contexts*, Basingstoke: Palgrave Macmillan, pp. 49–74.
Williams, S., B. Abbot and E. Heery (2011), Non-union worker representation through civil society organisations: evidence from the United Kingdom, *Industrial Relations Journal*, **42**, pp. 69–85.
Wills, J. (2002), Community unionism and trade union renewal in the UK; moving beyond the fragments at last, *Transactions of the Institute of British Geographers*, **26**(4), pp. 465–483.

Comparative HRM

Comparative human resource management (CHRM) assumes that HRM varies by country and/or groups of countries and attempts to understand (and sometimes explain) those differences. It can also refer to geographical differences within countries (Dutch-speaking north of Belgium versus the French-speaking south, for example), but this is rare.

CHRM is almost by definition a critical approach to HRM. HRM research originated in and is dominated by work from the USA. Comparative HRM argues that in other countries people are managed differently from the 'good practice' models presented by many business schools, consultants and gurus but that these variations in what HRM is and does are evidence of rational adaptation to different situations rather than evidence of backwardness. Fundamental to CHRM is the notion of contextual fit; what works in one context may not work well in another. CHRM has the further advantage that understanding our own context is always made much clearer by comparing it with another context.

HRM policies and practices differ in every part of the world: HRM is conducted very differently in Japan, Turkey, Finland, Vietnam and the USA. Practices are not only conducted differently, but defined, thought about and judged differently by various stakeholders and over different timescales. In many subjects, the importance of context would be unremarkable, but in HRM the hegemony of best practice approaches means that alternatives have to be argued for. In HRM there is now considerable evidence that different policies and practices fit better in some contexts than in others.

National or regional differences would not matter all that much if the notion of globalization applied to HRM. If countries were converging over time to a best practice model in their HRM policies and practices, then it would make sense to concentrate on that model and just wait for the other locations to 'catch up'. It has been argued that the influence of multinational companies (MNCs) bringing their own innovative globalized practices into host countries is gradually reducing the differences. There is an extensive standardization/differentiation debate in international HRM, examining the drive MNCs have to enforce worldwide policies and the need or desire they have to adapt to local circumstances (such as labour markets, legislation, trade unions). The limited evidence that we have, however, argues that if there is a pressure towards convergence, it is taking a long time to have an effect and that, in practice, countries and regions remain very different in how they manage their people.

How are we to explain these differences? Two main theories have been advanced; the cultural and the institutional. Cultural theories assume that there are (measurable) differences between the fundamental value held in different countries in areas such as the importance of hierarchy, acceptance of individualism and the allowable variation in behaviours that create the differences in the way people are managed. The institutional theories argue that it is the (measurable) differences between national institutions – such as education, social security, legal and political systems. Cultural theories argue that the way people are managed is a reflection of deep-seated differences in societal values. There is clearly truth in this, as anyone who travels a lot will know. It seems likely that, for example, in societies where hierarchy is very important, there will be less opportunity to question the boss. In societies where uncertainty is seen as something to be avoided, there will be more rules, and in societies where individualism is seen as of less value than being part of the group, pay systems that depend on employees competing with each other will not be popular. However, there are two problems with applying this to HRM. First, the measures used by various cultural experts differ and are indeed incompatible and, second, that, even if the measures are accepted, organizations have scope to manage their cultural mix. All cultures are some form of normal distribution curve with many people being culturally typical and others being cultural outliers. It is relatively straightforward for an organization to select people who are not typical of the society; maybe, depending on the organization, less individualistic or prepared to take risks. Organizational cultures will also impact these national cultures.

Organizations are generally less able to manage their institutional context. If they operate in a society, they have to cope with the country's education system, welfare system, regulations and laws, trade unions and a host of other external factors. It is not sensible to expect similar recruitment policies in a country with high unemployment and one with labour shortages, or to expect similar staff development policies in a country with an excellent education system and one where only a small elite is well-educated. As another example, diversity laws in the USA may require attention to quotas – this would be unlawful under diversity laws in Europe. Laws in Saudi Arabia are different again.

So, while both cultural theories and institutional theories are needed to help us understand fully the differences in HRM between countries, the former is more manageable for organizations. There is now clear evidence that the institutional differences are directly related to differences in HRM policies and practices. However, there is much that remains under-researched in CHRM. There are many countries and large regions of the world where we know very little about their HRM or how it compares to HRM in other places. There are significant aspects of HRM that have not been studied much in comparative work. Our understanding of how the cultural and institutional differences between countries impacts human resource management falls well short of any notion of a comprehensive theory.

CHRIS BREWSTER

See also:

Convergence theory; International human resource management; Multinational companies; National culture.

References and selected further readings

Barry, M. and A. Wilkinson (eds) (2011), *Research Handbook of Comparative Employment Relations*, Cheltenham: Edward Elgar.

Boxall, P. (1995), Building the theory of comparative HRM, *Human Resource Management Journal*, 5(5), pp. 5–17.

Brewster, C. and M. Mayrhofer (2012), *A Handbook of Research on Comparative Human Resource Management*, Cheltenham: Edward Elgar.

Sparrow, P., R. Schuler and S. Jackson (1994), Convergence or divergence: human resource practices and policies for competitive advantage worldwide, *International Journal of Human Resource Management*, 5(2), pp. 267–299.

Vaiman, V. and C. Brewster (2015), Comparative explanations of comparative HRM: assessing cultural and institutional theories, *International Journal of Human Resource Management*, 26(2), pp. 151–164.

Competence

'Competence' is generally understood as an ability to do something successfully or efficiently and is attributed to both human agents and organizations. The application of competence is referred to as competency. Competence was understood by the ancient Greeks as a broadly based quality that individuals used throughout their lives and in many contexts whereas interpretations of human competence in the contemporary business and management literatures have tended to associate it more narrowly with specific roles, jobs and tasks in organizations. The time and motion studies used by F.W. Taylor in the early 1900s are sometimes cited as early examples of this narrower application of competence.

In the 1970s, psychologist David McClelland (1973) advocated testing employees' levels of job or task competence rather than their general intelligence. This notion became popular and has subsequently influenced approaches to employee selection, training, succession planning and performance management. Subcategories of job-related competence include cognitive, social and motor skills. The idea of measuring and valuing human competence in organizations has led to the development of a wide variety of tools and techniques, including competence models, competence audits, competency frameworks and competency management.

Despite the widespread use of human competence-related tools and techniques, the nature of human competence remains elusive and no commonly accepted standard exists for measuring or valuing it. A degree of semantic and conceptual confusion is also apparent in the practitioner literature with some writers conflating competence with competency and others using the plural form of competency (competencies) to refer to multiple competences. Some researchers have noted that while job or task performance is directly observable competence cannot be observed and thus the attribution of performance to a particular underlying competence can only be conjectural. Others have questioned the 'objectivistic' linking of competence to jobs and tasks, citing research showing that different individuals and groups of employees may interpret the same job or task differently (Sandberg, 2000) and consequently the competence they use may be different to that identified in standard job-competence models. A further problem surrounds the connections between human competence and organizational competence; while cross-level linkages are widely assumed they remain comparatively under-researched and poorly understood.

ALAN BURTON-JONES

See also:

Human capital.

References and selected further readings

Campion, M.A., A.A. Fink, B.J. Ruggeberg, L. Carr, G.M. Phillips and R.B. Odman (2011), Doing competencies well: best practices in competency modeling, *Personnel Psychology*, **64**, pp. 225–262.
Dubois, D. and W. Rothwell (2004), *Competency-Based Human Resource Management*, Palo Alto: Davies-Black Publishing.
McClelland, D.C. (1973), Testing for competence rather than for intelligence, *American Psychologist*, **28**, pp. 1–14.
Moliterno, T. and R.E. Ployhart (2011), Emergence of the human capital resource: a multilevel model, *Academy of Management Review*, **36**(1), pp. 127–150.
Pinnington, A.H. (2011), Competence development and career advancement in professional service firms, *Personnel Review*, **40**(4), pp. 443–465.
Sandberg, J. (2000), Understanding human competence at work: an interpretive approach, *Academy of Management Journal*, **43**, pp. 9–25.

Competency-based pay

Competency-based pay progression grew in popularity during the 1990s, spurred on by the arguments of Lawler (1994) that to promote innovation and a more outward focus organizations should move from what he termed 'job-based' to 'competency-based' approaches to organization structures and processes – moving away from bureaucratic systems, in effect. Hence, he suggested people should be rewarded more for their competency and skill as distinct from their position in a hierarchy. The term competency harks back to the work of Boyatzis (1982) on manager competencies. He defined 'competencies' as the underlying characteristics of individuals that cause them to perform well – hence, partly skill, partly behaviour. Competencies or competences are rather confusingly defined and spelt differently in different contexts.

Neathey and Reilly (2003) identify three uses of competency and/or competence within reward systems:

1. Input or the capacity people have to do job well, which encompasses their knowledge, skills and personal attributes.
2. Process – the behaviour required to convert inputs into outputs.
3. Outputs – actual performance in the job.

A number of organizations began to use competency-based pay progression within their pay structures, in particular as a response to the inadequacies of performance pay progression. There were particular concerns about linking employee development with pay progression for knowledge workers. This led to the use of pay progression systems that linked managerial assessment of individuals' competencies in terms of their inputs and behaviour with their output in terms of assessed performance. Neathey and Reilly (2003) found a diverse range of practice in competency-related pay systems with almost as many individual approaches as there are organizations practicing them. They identified three broad categories:

1. A matrix approach where pay increases are determined by competence assessment and position in pay range.
2. Pay progression systems in which competence assessment determines incremental progression within pay ranges.
3. Systems in which there are much looser links between competency and pay in which competency assessment is just one of a number of factors determining pay, with others including market, internal relativities and performance.

The use of competencies within HRM and reward practices was critiqued by Sparrow (1996) on both theoretical and practical grounds. He argued they were not a sufficiently robust concept on which to base pay or other important employment decisions. More practically, systematically measuring competencies is not an objective process as managers find it difficult to make complex assessment across a range of competencies within a competency framework (which sets out the competencies relevant to different roles).

Angela Wright

See also:
Competence; Skills-based pay.

References and selected further readings
Boyatzis, R. (1982), *The Competent Manager: A Model for Effective Performance*, New York: John Wiley & Sons.
Lawler, E. (1994), From job-based to competency-based organizations, *Journal of Organizational Behavior*, **15**, pp. 3–15.
Neathey, F. and P. Reilly (2003), *Competency-Based Pay*, Sussex: Institute for Employment Studies.
Sparrow, P. (1996), Too good to be true? *People Management*, December 5, pp. 22–29.

Competitive advantage

Competitive advantage refers to the nature of an organization's performance relative to competitors. An organization is said to have obtained a competitive advantage when it holds a unique advantage that is sustained even despite competitors' constant attempts at replication. The concept of competitive advantage emerged in the 1980s as a means to better assess the value proposition and sustainability of organizational activities beyond mere financial performance. The term is largely attributable to the work of Michael Porter who drew attention to the attributes enabling firms, and later nations, to outperform the competition. A competitive advantage is said to exist when an organization meets the threefold criteria of (a) offering a proven value-based proposition that benefits end users, (b) this value proposition is delivered through organizational activities in a manner that competitors find hard to imitate and (c) the advantage is sustainable in the face of environmental change and competitor actions (Cunningham and Harney, 2012). There are a number of means by which competitive advantage can be achieved, including through the use of HRM, organizational culture or via technological innovation.

The logic of competitive advantage has been useful in a number of respects. First, it has a temporal dimension moving beyond narrow and short-term financial criteria to examine the ability of a firm to achieve differential performance over time. Second, understanding how competitive advantage may be achieved has directed attention inwards towards firm-level activities, thereby emphasizing the value of HRM. Third, the desire to achieve competitive advantage has become the ultimate overarching purpose for organizations. It follows that much research over the past three decades has been consumed with demonstrating how HRM can help in building and sustaining competitive advantage.

The popularity of competitive advantage means that it is frequently advanced as an ideology or article of faith without due attention to critical scrutiny. Yet at the most basic level, some question whether the concept has empirical validity; many of the organizations once highlighted as having achieved the status of competitive advantage have since fallen from grace. A recent argument finds the term self-defeating as it implies an endpoint that has been achieved as opposed to a process or constant quest. One consequence is a stress on the 'sustainable' component of competitive advantage with 'temporary' or 'transient' advantage suggested as more appropriate labels. Philosophical critique finds a term founded upon tautological reasoning; competitive advantage serves as both the foundation for, and outcome of, firm success (Powell, 2001). Nonetheless the missionary zeal of competitive advantage has served as an important catalyst for research efforts. The term has also been expanded to capture the significance of broader network and relationship management manifest as 'collaborative advantage'.

BRIAN HARNEY

See also:
Resource-based view; Strategic human resource management; Strategy.

References and selected further readings

D'Aveni, R.A., G. Dagnino and K.G. Smith (2010), The age of temporary advantage, *Strategic Management Journal*, **31**(3), pp. 1371–1385.
Cunningham, J. and B. Harney (2012), *Strategy and Strategists*, Oxford: Oxford University Press.
McGrath, R.G. (2013), Transient advantage, *Harvard Business Review*, **91**(6), pp. 62–70.
Porter, M. (1980), *Competitive Advantage: Creating and Sustaining Competitive Performance*, New York: Free Press.
Powell, T. (2001), Competitive advantage: logical and philosophical considerations, *Strategic Management Journal*, **22**(9), pp. 875–888.

Compressed working time

Compressed working time (CWT) refers to rescheduling working hours into fewer days during the week than is standard for the workplace by increasing the number of hours an employee is required to work per day. It does not normally require a reduction in total hours and is not the same as shift-working. One of the most common forms is to compress a 40-hour week into four ten-hour days (often expressed as 4/40) rather than work five eight-hour days, thus giving the fifth day off. An alternative is the 'nine-day fortnight' requiring an employee to work nine 8.9-hour days every two weeks, leaving the tenth day off.

The benefits to employees are that they are able to have additional leisure time while still preserving their income, reduced travel to work time and reduced stress. This would suggest more positive employee attitudes and several studies have shown that CWT schedules positively affects job satisfaction and satisfaction with work schedule (e.g., Baltes et al., 1999). Potential organizational gains include extended daily coverage, reduced overtime payments and decreased absenteeism (because CWT enables more time off for personal business). Such arrangements may also help retain valuable staff, particularly those with family responsibilities, and are easy to implement. The impact on productivity, however, is less clear, with research showing productivity either improving or staying the same. For example, Vega and Gilbert's (1997) study of police officers reported productivity improvements with CWT arrangements, whereas Baltes et al.'s (1999) review concluded no impact on productivity. On the downside, longer working days can be physically and mentally draining and fatigue can increase, providing sufficient cover on the off day may be problematic, and where employees are highly interdependent, time off needs to be rotated.

In Great Britain both availability and take-up of this form of rescheduling work has increased over the past decade. According to the Work Life Balance (WLB) Employer Survey (BIS, 2014) of workplaces in Britain around two fifths (41 per cent) of employers reported that CWT was available in their establishment in 2013 compared to just 19 per cent in 2003, and 13 per cent of employees worked on this basis compared with just 3 per cent of employees in 2000. The WLB Employee Survey (BIS, 2012) shows that this form of working was most commonly reported in banking, insurance professional and support services industry, but least likely to be found in construction and manufacturing.

SUE HUTCHINSON

See also:

Absence; Family-friendly policies; Flexible working; Flexitime; Job satisfaction; Work–life balance.

References and selected further readings

Baltes, B.B., T.E. Briggs, J.W. Huff, J.A. Wright and G.A. Neuman (1999), Flexible and compressed work-week schedules: a meta-analysis of their effects on work-related criteria, *Journal of Applied Psychology*, **84**(4), pp. 496–513.
BIS (2012), *The Fourth Work–Life Balance Employee Survey*, Employment Relations Research Series 122, www.gov.uk/government/uploads/system/uploads/attachment_data/file/32153/12-p151-fourth-work-life-balance-employee-survey.pdf.
BIS (2014), *The Fourth Work–Life Balance Employer Survey (2013)*, Research Paper No. 184, www.gov.uk/government/uploads/system/uploads/attachment_data/file/398557/bis-14-1027-fourth-work-life-balance-employer-survey-2013.pdf.
Ronen, S. and S.B. Primps (1981), The compressed work week as organizational change: behavioral and atti-tudinal outcomes, *Academy of Management Review*, **6**(1), pp. 61–74.
Vega, A. and M.J. Gilbert (1997), Longer days, shorter weeks: compressed work weeks in policing, *Public Personnel Management*, **26**(3), pp. 391–402.

Conciliation

Conciliation is a form of dispute resolution process falling under the broad heading of alternative dispute resolution. It is similar to mediation in that it involves a neutral third party seeking to assist disputants work towards resolving their differences by improving communication, and indeed the two terms are often used interchangeably. This reflects the difficulty, both theoretically and in practice, of distinguishing the two approaches, attempts to do so focusing on 'the degree of initiative taken by the third party' (Corby, 1999, p. 3). However, there appears little (international) consistency as to which permits the more directive approach, the distinction depending also on the model of mediation considered. In general, conciliation is a rather less structured and time-bound process and may involve greater technical assistance, and is more commonly deployed in the context of collective disputes where it is often state-sponsored. In Britain, as well as this last function, conciliation is also used to describe the statutory duty of its Advisory, Conciliation and Arbitration Service (Acas) to promote resolution in employment tribunal cases, as well as its role in collective disputes.

Taking conciliation to describe the process of improving communication flows with a view to encouraging conflict resolution *without making suggestions*, and drawing on earlier work by Kressel and Pruitt (1985, 1989), Dix (2000) provides a useful account of conciliator roles and styles. Key elements the former include being reflexive (estab-lishing trust and rapport), information provision (clarifying issues and conveying technical/legal/procedural information) and substantive involvement (promoting resolu-tion through exploring parties' interests, exploring strengths and weaknesses of cases, etc.). Conciliation styles are conceptualized in relation to three dimensions: reactive/ proactive, message-bearer/influencing and passive/forceful. Evidence from representatives in employment tribunal cases in Britain suggests these various roles/styles have empirical validity in the context of Acas' individual conciliation work (Latreille et al., 2007).

The decline of collective forms of industrial conflict in most developed countries has reduced the demand for collective conciliation. In the context of (individual) employment disputes, conciliation is increasingly being used to resolve prior to (labour) court hearings, for example, including France, Germany and South Africa. In some cases attendance at conciliation is mandatory. More recently in Britain, 'early conciliation' is being offered to parties before claims are lodged.

PAUL LATREILLE

See also:

Acas; Alternative dispute resolution; Arbitration; Employment tribunal; Mediation.

References and selected further readings

Acas (2015), *Conciliation Explained*, www.acas.org.uk/media/pdf/c/1/Conciliation-Explained-Acas.pdf.
Corby, S. (1999), Resolving employment rights disputes through mediation: the New Zealand experience, *Comparative Notes*, no. 2, Institute of Employment Rights.
Dix, G. (2000), Operating with style: the work of the ACAS conciliator in individual employment disputes, in B. Towers and W. Brown (eds), *Employment Relations in Britain: 25 years of the Advisory, Conciliation and Arbitration Service*, Oxford: Blackwell.
Kressel, K. and D.G. Pruitt (1985), Themes in the mediation of social conflict, *Journal of Social Issues*, **41**, pp. 179–198.
Kressel, K. and D.G. Pruitt (1989), A research perspective on the mediation of social conflict, in Kressel, K. and D.G. Pruitt (eds), *Mediation Research: The Process and Effectiveness of Third-Party Intervention*, San Francisco: Jossey-Bass.
Latreille, P.L., J.A. Latreille and K.G. Knight (2007), Employment tribunals and Acas: evidence from a survey of representatives, *Industrial Relations Journal*, **38**(2), pp. 136–154.

Configurational model

Configurational models are perhaps one of the most comprehensive but also complex ways of examining HRM. A configurational model provides a holistic overview of the HRM system, examining how a pattern of multiple independent variables are related to a given dependent variable. In technical terms a configuration model refers to 'any multidimensional constellation of conceptually distinct characteristic that commonly occur together' (Meyer et al., 1993, p. 1175). This holistic basis of inquiry makes configuration models distinct from universal approaches that examine simple and direct relationships. Likewise, in contrast to contingency theory, configurational models adopt the logic of equifinality, i.e., that there are multiple, equally effective ways of meeting the same desired outcome. Configurational models therefore propose a systems-based analysis that captures both the intended objective and the various means of achieving that objective. As a result, configurational approaches typically propose typologies or ideal types.

One of the most influential configurational models in HRM comes from the work of Miles and Snow (1984), who suggested a number of organizational strategies (analyser, defender, prospector, reactor) and the various HR configurations likely to be aligned with each. For example a prospector strategy founded on innovation is likely to require sophisticated, skill-based recruitment, results-orientated performance and external competitiveness in terms of compensation. In contrast an organization pursuing a defender strategy in a stable market might develop talent internally and have a more process-orientated performance appraisal and hierarchical-based compensation.

Configurational models stress both vertical and horizontal alignment, with an ideal configuration being one that maximizes the degree of internal fit and consistency in the HRM system. The systems-based approach is useful as it captures all dimensions of the business and HRM system, arguing that the whole may be more than the sum of its parts. However, this holistic focus and non-linear logic also makes configurational models more difficult to apply so that they are frequently conceptually evoked, but less often empirically examined. Likewise, with a stress on patterns of unique factors, some configurational theorists emphasize that configurations emerge and form over time. The recurrent dilemma faced by configurational approaches is that 'while they come closest to modelling the complexity of organizations, they must stop short for analytical manageability' (Colbert, 2004, p. 346). Advocates of configurational theory argue that the purpose is to present ideal states as opposed to empirical realities and that these in turn have proved useful tools to encourage conversation and self-reflection among HR practitioners.

BRIAN HARNEY

See also:

Context; Contingency theory; Strategic HRM; Universalistic theory.

References and selected further readings

Colbert, B. (2004), The complex resource-based view: implications for theory and practice in strategic human resource management, *Academy of Management Review*, **29**(3), pp. 341–358.
Delery, J. and D. Doty (1996), Models of theorising in strategic human resource management: tests of universalistic, contingency and configurational performance predictions, *Academy of Management Journal*, **39**(4), pp. 802–835.
Meyer, A., A. Tsui and C.R. Hinings (1993), Configurational approaches to organisational analysis, *Academy of Management Journal*, **36**(6), pp. 1175–1195.
Miles, R. and C. Snow (1984), Designing strategic human resource systems, *Organizational Dynamics*, Summer, pp. 36–52.

Conflict

Conflict at work is normally associated with strikes and industrial action but it covers a much larger repertoire of actions based upon a wide arrange of attitudes and behaviours of the actors in employment relations. Indeed, strikes are but a symptom or expression of conflict, not synonymous with conflict itself. Moreover, conflict at work can seep out into conflict in wider society and vice versa in a process of osmosis, because conflict within employment is part and parcel of the processes that inform how politics and economics work in wider society.

Conflict arises as a result of the interconnected clashing of differing material interests, ideologies and power resources between different groups in the employment relationship and over the organization of work and employment. This means that although the major axis is that between the employee or worker and the manager or employer (sometimes known as between capital and labour), there is also a myriad of other axes of relationship of conflict – for example, among workers, within management and between professions.

While there are different views and expectations concerning the level and nature of conflict at work (see below), it is important to recognize that conflict can be hidden or open. Whether conflict over material interests, ideologies and power resources becomes open depends upon the ability of one or more of the parties involved to move from constructing conflictual attitudes to expressing these attitudes in different forms of behaviour. In other words, the existence of open conflict depends upon a process by which grievances come into being, a process involving attribution and mobilization (Kelly, 1998).

Conflict can be individual, semi-collective or collective based and be in pursuit of moderate or militant aims (Kelly, 1996), or to support or undermine the status quo. The form it takes in regard of these three social category foundations are many and varied – sabotage, pilfering, humour, fiddling, soldiering, suicide (sometimes through self-immolation), absenteeism and whistleblowing are just some examples. Others are encompassed within the category 'organizational misbehaviour' (see Richards, 2008). Hamper (1992) told how some workers cooperated with each other in a car factory in order that they only worked every second day because two workers' jobs could be done by one worker. This example of the car factory indicates that such manifestations of conflict and subversion may only be coping mechanisms which do not fundamentally challenge the managerial order. Indeed, Ackroyd and Thompson (1999) emphasize that not all forms of organizational misbehaviour are necessarily opposed by managers, as they can oil the wheels of regimes of work.

Conflict does not exist in a vacuum over space and time. It can co-exist with cooperation between groups (but especially between workers and management), whether of a conscious organized kind or by default. Cooperation can be willing or grudging. Periods can be dominated by conflict, then giving rise to eras of cooperation. The expression of cooperation tends to be the direct or indirect instigation of capital as it benefits most from this while the expression of open conflict tends to be at the instigation of workers because not only are management actions held to be legitimate but management has the greater ability to dominate workers.

Conflict at work can not only be studied by using a range of perspectives but these perspectives are also approximations of ideological positions of parties within the employment relationship itself. The most important ones are unitarism, pluralism and radicalism/Marxism. Unitarism views conflict between employees and employers as not only dysfunctional but also deviant and illegitimate. Where conflict exists, it is deemed to be the result of the actions of so-called 'troublemakers' such as union activists. Unitarism unconditionally supports the managerial prerogative, denouncing any challenges to it and for this reason it is the hegemonic perspective among managers and employers themselves (especially under the era of HRM). By contrast, pluralism essentially regards that differing interests and the representation of these is legitimate so long as the conflict that these may generate does not become debilitating. In order to resolve such conflicts, managers negotiate with unions through processes of collective bargaining and establish mechanisms for limiting and managing conflict. It is almost unheard of for employers or managers to be of a radical or Marxist perspective for herein conflict at work is viewed as not only inevitable but also progressive and legitimate. For Marxists, the conflict provides the opportunity to generate the means to supersede the existing order at work and in society. Under capitalism, conflicts of interests, ideology and resources are endemic even if they are not always expressed openly and these transcend the boundaries of the workplace.

With the development of new forms of labour such as emotional and aesthetic labour as well as how advanced technologies are now central to the production, distribution and exchange of goods, services and information, the terrain on which conflict can be expressed and manifest has changed. Thus, the 'smile strike' is a form of resistance in customer facing jobs – either by refusing to physically smile as a cabin crew member or shop assistant or to smile in tone of voice and demeanour on the phone in a call centre. However, cases of sabotage are not widely known of regardless of the prevalence of information technologies and 'just-in-time' production systems. Although necessarily secretive in nature, the secrecy involved with sabotage cannot be fully maintained if it is to be used as a bargaining tool by employees (rather than just 'kicking back' against the employer), suggesting relatively few cases do, indeed, take place. Equally significant for the terrain on which conflict at work can be expressed is the expansion of capitalist employment relations to newly industrializing economies such as China and Indonesia. Riots and suicides have become relatively common in such countries because strikes are unlawful or independent unions are prevented from operating effectively.

Notwithstanding the prevalence of general strikes in some Southern European countries, strikes are in decline in many advanced economies. In this context of the decline in the traditional means, there is relatively little evidence of method replacement whereby new methods provide alternative ways of expression. 'Bossnapping' is one example but has been confined to France. That is not to suggest that the absence of openly expressed conflict is an indication of happiness among employees and harmony with employers. It may be that within the significant recent increase in sickness/absence levels is to be found evidence of employee expressing conflict.

GREGOR GALL

See also:

Collective bargaining; Frames of reference; Industrial action; Organizational misbehaviour; Sabotage; Strikes.

References and selected further readings

Ackroyd, S. and P. Thompson (1999), *Organisational Misbehaviour*, London: Sage.
Gall, G. (2013), Labour quiescence continued? Recent strike activity in Western Europe, *Economic and Industrial Democracy*, **34**(3), pp. 667–669.
Hamper, B. (1992), *Rivethead: Tales from the Assembly Line*, New York: Warner.
Kelly, J. (1996), Union militancy and social partnership, in P. Ackers, C. Smith and P. Smith (eds), *The New Workplace and Trade Unionism: Critical Perspectives on Work and Organisation*, London: Routledge, pp. 77–109.
Kelly, J. (1998), *Rethinking Industrial Relations: Collectivism, Mobilisation and Long Waves*, London: Routledge.
Richards, J. (2008), The many approaches to organisational misbehaviour: a review, map and research agenda, *Employee Relations*, **30**(6), pp. 653–678.

Constructive dismissal

The term 'constructive dismissal' describes a situation where an employee is entitled to end their contract of employment because of something that the employer has done. An employee will be entitled to end their contract of employment where the employer has breached a fundamental term in that contract (*Western Excavating (ECC) Ltd v Sharp*). It should be noted that not all contract terms will be considered fundamental terms such that a breach would repudiate the contract, only those terms that are central or 'go to the root of the contract' are fundamental. A breach of a fundamental term might arise where an employer fails to fulfil an important contractual obligation – for example, a failure to pay for work done (pay being central to the work wage bargain) – or where the employer seeks to unilaterally change a central term in the contract. A fundamental breach of contract gives the innocent party (here the worker or employee) a choice as to whether to accept the other party's (employer's) repudiation and rescind the contract or to affirm and continue the contract. If the employee or worker chooses to rescind the contract, the contract would come to an end and the parties would no longer be bound by it. The Employment Rights Act 1996 recognises this as a dismissal for the purposes of the statutory right not to be unfairly dismissed (section 95(1)(c)).

LIZ OLIVER

See also:

Contract of employment; Dismissal; Unfair dismissal.

References and selected further readings

Cabrelli, D. (2009), Re-establishing orthodoxy in the law of constructive dismissal: *Claridge v Daler Rowney Ltd* [2008] IRLR 672 and *Bournemouth University Higher Education Corporation v Buckland* [2009] IRLR 606, *Industrial Law Journal*, **38**(4), pp. 403–411.
Willey, B. (2012), *Employment Law in Context: An Introduction for HR Professionals*, 4th edn, Harlow: Pearson.

Consultation

Consultation is an integral element of strategic human resource management designed to generate employee engagement, commitment and organizational effectiveness in globally competitive markets. The intellectual origins of consultation lie in the human relations approach that placed a premium on management–employee communications. Consultation can be defined as the exchange of employers and employees (and/or their representatives) views on workplace issues. Consultation takes different forms: direct communication, upward problem-solving, representative participation and financial participation. These forms are distinguished by the degree to which they empower employees with decision-making rights vis-à-vis information-sharing. Requirements for successful consultation include: organizational stakeholders' support and trust and embeddedness (alignment with the organizational climate and external environment).

There are clear differences in the form and extent of consultation across countries. National variations exist due to differences in institutions and regulations. For example, a difference between Australia and the United Kingdom (UK) is the presence of

Information and Consultation Regulations for firms with 50 or more employees in the UK. These regulations stem from employees' statutory rights to information and consultation in the European Union. The degree of legal support for consultation is therefore a factor that influences the nature, processes, outcomes and power of consultation in practice, and remains a controversial issue.

Managerial attitudes to consultation also shape its form(s), process and outcomes. For example, management values in liberal market economies focus on the short term; cost minimization and the primacy of shareholder value, inhibiting power-sharing and long-term investment in consultation. In contrast, in coordinated market economies, joint governance is a valued and institutionalized process: management and labour engage in joint decision-making on matters of mutual concern. Another important theme is trade union attitudes. Unions in many countries are ambivalent to direct consultation: it is seen as a threat, potentially encroaching upon bargaining; thus reducing unions' power and influence. The extent to which consultation is mutually supportive of or antagonistic toward unions is linked to managerial attitudes.

AMANDA PYMAN

See also:
Collective bargaining; Employee voice; Varieties of capitalism.

References and selected further readings

Charlwood, A. and M. Terry (2007), 21st century models of employee representation: structures, processes and outcomes, *Industrial Relations Journal*, **38**(4), pp. 320–337.
Cox, A., S. Zagelmeyer and M. Marchington (2006), Embedding employee involvement and participation at work, *Human Resource Management Journal*, **16**(3), pp. 250–267.
Dundon, T., A. Wilkinson, M. Marchington and P. Ackers (2004), The meanings and purpose of employee voice, *International Journal of Human Resource Management*, **15**, pp. 1149–1170.
Kochan, T.A. and P. Osterman (1994), *The Mutual Gains Enterprise: Forging a Winning Partnership Among Labour, Management and Government*, Boston: Harvard University Press.
Teicher, J., P. Holland, A. Pyman and B. Cooper (2007), Employee voice in Australia, in R. Freeman, P. Boxall and P. Haynes (eds), *What Workers Say: Employee Voice in the Anglo-American World*, Ithaca: ILR Press, pp. 125–144.
Wilkinson, A., P.J. Gollan, M. Marchington and D. Lewin (2010), *The Oxford Handbook of Participation in Organizations*, New York: Oxford University Press.

Context

In any organization, management do not develop HRM procedures, processes, systems, and strategies autonomously, independently or *in vacuo*; these HR activities are contextualized. This means, in practice, that HRM in an organization at any one time is the product of its current internal and external contexts – sometimes called 'environments', less usually 'settings' or 'milieus'. Internally, for example, managerial politics determine the status, legitimacy and scope of the HR function. External to an organization, the law or legal context is a major determinant of how employees are managed. The law, for example, provides opportunities and limitations on how an organization recruits, selects, determines pay and rewards, disciplines and dismisses employees. Similarly, an organization's microeconomic or market context affects the supply, demand and wages for labour, the price of corporate borrowing, and demand for the organization's products or services. All these contextual factors (and others) influence the numbers of workers that the enterprise employs, the jobs they do, how they do them, what they are paid, and people management practices.

Older textbooks in 'personnel management' in the English-speaking world and 'personnel administration' in some other countries rarely considered explicitly how 'contexts', whether internal or external, affected personnel management and personnel practices. They typically described the ambiguous nature of the personnel function and the techniques employed in personnel management practice. These included 'manpower planning', employment resourcing, pay and payment systems, training and development, industrial relations and the welfare function. Some texts also examined, again largely through descriptive narratives, limited aspects of social psychology, the roles of individuals and groups in organizations, and managerial communications with employees. Often unitary in their perspective, these universalistic texts, with only a few exceptions, were essentially static, descriptive studies. They took the internal and external contexts of personnel management as givens and viewed them as relatively stable, unchanging and common frameworks affecting all organizations in similar ways.

With the expansion of economic globalization, powerful multinational corporations (MNCs), intensive international product market competition, and contemporary HRM, the increasing importance of the changing contexts of the human resources function became generally recognized by both managers and academic writers in the field. Starting in the United States and then spreading to other parts of the English-speaking world, a new business consensus emerged in leading-edge private-sector organizations and to a lesser degree in public and third-sector enterprises. If firms were to compete effectively in tight product markets and market-driven economies, then senior managers had to develop integrated business and HR strategies. In doing this, top managers needed to analyse and respond to the dynamic internal and external contexts within which their organizations operated.

The internal factors included organizational culture, styles of management, the finance and other management functions and HRM issues. The external factors typically covered: the sector in which the organization was located; macro-environmental issues such as the national economy; national institutions affecting HRM; global factors, such as the international economy; social issues (such as demography and changing social structures); and national and international politics. As a result, business leaders began taking account of a series of inward-facing and outward-facing contextual factors when developing business strategy, HR strategy and HRM activities in their firms.

Jackson and Schuler (1995, p. 1) were among the first scholars to provide an integrative framework for understanding HRM in context. For them, HRM encompasses three elements: HR practices, HR policies and 'overarching human resource philosophies'. To understand HRM in context, they argue, it is necessary to consider how these three components of HRM are affected by what they call the internal and external 'environments' of organizations. They specify the internal contextual factors as: technology, structure, size, organizational lifecycle stage and business strategy. Their external contexts are: legal, social, and political environments; unionization; labour market conditions; industry characteristics; and national cultures. However, Jackson and Schuler treat organizational culture as inextricably connected with HRM and not separate from it. Whatever the details of their model, the importance of their analysis is that if HRM is to be an effective part of managerial planning, it has to shift its focus from an overwhelming variety of specific HR practices and policies to the more abstract and fundamental dimensions of contexts, HRM systems and expected employee behaviours.

Various other contextual classifications have been proposed. Typical internal contexts of an organization include: culture; size; technology; structure and social components (such as rules, systems and coordinating mechanisms); issues of power and control; and business and managerial contexts (such as managerial functions; managerial power, authority and influence; and managerial politics). The external contexts are typically conceptualized in terms of the socio-cultural, technological, economic, environmental, political and ethical (STEEPLE) contexts of an organization.

The contextual factors outlined above are neither exclusive nor exhaustive. Indeed, there are variations in what are considered to be the critical contexts of organizations; there is no consensus on what they are. The examples provided here are simply indicative of the typologies used. But their importance is twofold.

First, there is explicit recognition that corporate HRM strategies, processes and procedures are affected by the varied, dynamic contexts within which organizations and the HR function operate. These contexts need to be acknowledged and drawn upon in organizational decision-making and in the determination of HR policy and practices. Second, these dynamic contexts – internal (such as when a new chief executive or head of HR is appointed) and external (such as developments in macroeconomic policy) – affect organizations differentially. Thus changes in senior management staffing affect that organization specifically; macroeconomic policy, in turn, affects all organizations subject to it, but its impact on each one varies. HRM contexts are important, therefore, but they do not generate universalistic HRM solutions.

A wide choice of tools, techniques and data-collection methods is available to managements when they do contextual analyses. Internal tools of contextual analysis in relation to HR and non-HR issues are organizationally specific, highly political and need careful handling. One example is SWOT analyses. These focus on the internal strengths and weaknesses of an organization and its external opportunities and threats. Other examples include reviewing an organization's 'core competencies' or drawing on McKinsey's '7-S' framework (structure, systems, style, staff, skills, strategy, shared values). STEEPLE, in turn, is one of the most common tools for analysing the external contexts of organizations, identifying their key drivers and developing appropriate actions.

The practical techniques used in external contextual analyses commonly involve four analytical stages: *scanning* the environment or its contexts; *monitoring* specific environmental-contextual trends; *forecasting* the direction of contextual changes; and *assessing* current and future contextual changes for their organizational implications. Two approaches are normally used. One is a 'macro' outside-in approach; the other is a 'micro' inside-out approach. The first reviews any future external forces likely to affect an organization, where the aim is to make sure its top managers understand the dynamics of change before determining explicit organizational responses to them. The second takes the organization as the starting point, such as its workforce, products or services, and technologies, and then reviews those elements of its contexts needing to be scanned, monitored, forecasted and assessed.

Various data-collection and forecasting methods are used in context analysis. Data-collection methods specify data sources and gather them, whereas forecasting methods transform data to answer questions posed by contextual analysts. Sources of data are either primary (internal) or secondary (external) and involve individuals, sampled populations and expert panels. Forecasting methods, such as Delphi forecasting or scenarios, serve three purposes: they verify 'hunches', answer 'what if' questions, and facilitate the forecasting of trends, events and patterns of activity.

The HR world has moved on significantly since the static model of personnel management to the dynamic inward-facing and outward-facing HRM models of managing people at work today. Reviewing the internal and external contexts of HRM in the development of strategy and HR rules and processes is now a central feature of the HR function. This demands strategic vision by HR leaders, ability to work with other senior managers, and a dynamic approach when dealing with contextual changes. Thus the contexts of HRM matter. Analysing these contexts is not an exact science, but doing so provides indicative contextual categories, a variety of diagnostic techniques, and different methods of data-collection and forecasting. By identifying, measuring and responding to the contexts of HRM, senior managers help shape customized HRM strategies and practices in organizations, in conditions of change.

DAVID FARNHAM

See also:

Comparative HRM; International human resource management; Multinational companies; Strategic HRM.

References and selected further readings

Fahey, L. and V. Narayanam (1986), *Macroenvironmental Analysis for Strategic Management*, St. Paul, MN: West Publishing Company.
Farnham, D. (2014), *The Changing Faces of Employment Relations: Global, Comparative and Theoretical Perspectives*, London: Palgrave Macmillan.
Farnham, D. (2015), *Human Resource Management in Context: Insights, Strategy and solutions*, 4th edn, London: Chartered Institute of Personnel and Development.
Jackson, S.E. and R.S. Schuler (1995), Understanding human resource management in the context of organizations and their environments, *Annual Review of Psychology*, **46**, pp. 237–264.
Newell, S. and H. Scarbrough (2001), *Human Resource Management in Context: A Case Study Approach*, Basingstoke: Palgrave Macmillan.
Yoder, D. (1956), *Personnel Management and Industrial Relations*, 4th edn, Michigan: Prentice-Hall.

Contingency theory

Contingency theory suggests that in order to be effective, HRM must be consistent with other aspects of the organization and/or external environment. Whereas universalistic theory suggests that HRM will have a direct impact on organizational performance, contingency theory implies interactions rather than simple linear relationships. According to contingency theory, a one-size-fits-all approach is inappropriate, as the effectiveness of HR practices is dependent on the context in which they are applied. Contingency decisions within HRM have largely been understood on the basis of external and internal fit. External fit, also termed vertical alignment, requires that the HRM practices of the organization must match the organizational strategy or environmental conditions faced by the organization. A failure to achieve this fit between context and HR practice will ultimately lead to suboptimal performance. The main emphasis in HRM has been on 'best fit' or 'matching models' whereby HRM practices are required to be consistent with a firm's organizational strategy (e.g., cost, quality, innovation). However, external fit has also been understood as matching HRM to the stage of growth in the organizational lifecycle (e.g. start-up, growth, maturity). In addition, and also reflecting the logic of contingency theory, it is important that HRM practices exhibit internal fit (also termed horizontal alignment) so that they work together to communicate the same message and deliver the same desired outcome.

The logic of contingency theory underpins much research on HRM. The functional imperative of aligning HRM with strategy served as one of the key factors differentiating HRM from personnel management, while a current stream of research examines industry, firm size and environmental intensity as the moderating or boundary conditions informing the HRM–performance relationship. Attention has also turned to differentiating HRM within firms so that, contingent on the value and uniqueness of employee groups in realizing strategy, certain types of HR practices are said to be more optimal than others (Lepak and Snell, 1999). The limits of contingency theory, however, is that it risks proposing a limited range of options which takes things as a given and thereby narrows the role of choice and the agency of HR managers to do things differently. Frequently absent are the dynamics of change or considerations that HR managers may proactively influence, avoid, or navigate key contingencies themselves. Contingency theory also seems to relegate implementation to something as unproblematic once a decision is made. Politics, power, resistance and, for the most part, employees are assumed out of existence. In advancing contingency research, HRM researchers have called for consideration of broader contingencies including institutional fit and also more micro-level research, including implementation as a locus of fit. This is symbolic of the long-standing dilemma that contingency theorists face, namely which contingencies should be privileged and how many contingencies can logically be examined before analysis collapses under the weight of a chimera.

BRIAN HARNEY

See also:

Best fit; Context; Strategic choice; Strategy; Universalistic theory.

References and selected further readings

Baird, L. and I. Meshoulam (1988), Managing two fits of strategic human resource management, *Academy of Management Review*, **13**(1), pp. 116–128.
Delery, J. and D. Doty (1996), Models of theorising in strategic human resource management: tests of universalistic, contingency and configurational performance prediction, *Academy of Management Journal*, **39**(4), pp. 802–835.
Lepak, D.P. and S.A. Snell (1999), The human resource architecture: toward a theory of human capital allocation and development, *Academy of Management Review*, **24**(1), pp. 31–48.
Purcell, J. (1999), Best practice and best fit: chimera or cul-de-sac? *Human Resource Management Journal*, **9**(3), pp. 26–41.

Continuing professional development

Continuing professional development (CPD) is a self-directed process that is used as a practical tool to facilitate lifelong learning. It is not a one-off intervention but a regular and systematic practice that needs to be owned by the learner in order to be successful. As Megginson and Whitaker (2007, p. 3) argue, CPD is 'a process by which individuals take control of their own learning and development' highlighting that it is 'an on-going process of reflection and action'. Indeed, reflection sits at the heart of CPD not only because it facilitates individual learning, but also for the reason that it empowers the learner to understand how they learn best and to critically plan their future development based on their career aspirations.

CPD may be experienced in various forms within the premises of an employer organization or externally. Employees typically learn on-the-job, both formally (e.g., during job shadowing) and informally (e.g., while interacting with colleagues). Organizations may also offer employees in-house or externally provided classroom-based workshops, while some employees may be given the opportunity to study for an accredited course or qualification. In line with a shift of focus from training to learning, employees may also engage in self-study, including individual reading and online courses. Given the numerous CPD options available, critical reflection is necessary for the learners to successfully navigate through the opportunities and take the right action for their professional development.

CPD has received much recognition over the past couple of decades as a best practice towards career development and accreditation. Indeed, the rapid changes in today's turbulent environment may render the skills, knowledge and competencies of professionals obsolete in an instant. Therefore, individuals embrace CPD as a medium for maintaining their competitiveness and also facilitating their career progression. Likewise, employers promote employees' CPD, given that a workforce with up-to-date skills and competencies contribute to organizational success. In addition, cultivating an environment that supports CPD attracts like-minded candidates and thus, creates an upward spiral of talent and growth within the organization. Finally, most professional bodies regard CPD as an essential condition for a chartered membership and expect their members to practise it regularly. The underlying rationale is to highlight the importance of CPD for maintaining respect and continuity for the profession.

Despite the widespread promotion of CPD, past literature is mostly prescriptive while theoretical or empirical substantiation of the concept is scarce and mainly focused on learners' attitudes. Further research needs to examine the links of CPD with important employee and organizational outcomes.

MARGARITA NYFOUDI

See also:
Coaching; Mentoring; Performance appraisal; Personal development plan.

References and selected further readings
Megginson, D. and V. Whitaker (2007), *Continuing Professional Development*, 2nd edn, London: CIPD.
Rothwell, A. and J. Arnold (2005), How HR professionals rate 'continuing professional development', *Human Resource Management Journal*, **15**(3), pp. 18–32.
Sadler-Smith, E., C.W. Allinson and J. Hayes (2000), Learning preferences and cognitive style: some implications for continuing professional development, *Management Learning*, **31**(2), pp. 239–256.

Contract of employment

The law of contract recognises different forms of contract and one of these is known as a contract 'of service'. Within the context of a contract of service, the common law (judge made law) implies certain generic terms into the contract. These terms represent the implicit expectations of employers and employees generally when entering into a contract of service and include such obligations as the obligation to follow reasonable instructions (on the part of the employee) and an obligation to maintain mutual trust and confidence (on the part of the employer). The courts have faced considerable challenges in distinguishing contracts of service from other forms of economic relationship whereby one person performs work for another. The classic distinction is between a contract of service (a contract of employment) and a contract for services (self-employment). However, as forms of work contract have become more diverse and complex, this distinction becomes more diffuse. This is to the detriment of groups of workers who cannot be classified as working under a contract of service and yet are dependent on the other contractor and clearly not entrepreneurs in business on their own. A series of tests to identify a contract of service emerged through the common law (judge made law). It is now settled law that the appropriate test is a multiple test (*Ready Mixed Concrete Ltd (South East) v Minister of Pensions and National Insurance*), which takes into account personal service, mutuality of obligations, control and other factors consistent with a contract of service.

The designation of a contract as a contract of service has significance beyond the construction of the terms of the contract; this is because key employment statutes borrow from the common law definition to determine the personal scope of their provisions. For example, the definition of 'employee' within the Employment Rights Act 1996 means an individual who has entered into or works under a 'contract of employment' (section 230(1)) and in turn a contract of employment means 'a contract of service or apprenticeship' (section 230(2)). Certain key employment rights such as the right not to be unfairly dismissed (section 94) are available only to employees to the exclusion of other forms of worker.

A situation has arisen whereby certain vulnerable workers are excluded from important employment rights and the courts have called on parliament to resolve this using statute.

Some 'in between' statuses have been developed such as the broader category of 'worker' to which some employment rights are available. Yet the situation remains largely unresolved.

LIZ OLIVER

See also:

Employee; Employment relationship; Self-employment; Worker.

References and selected further readings

Freedland, M.R. (2011), *The Legal Construction of Personal Work Relations*, Oxford: Oxford University Press.
Leighton, P. and M. Wynn (2011), Classifying employment relationships — more sliding doors or a better regulatory framework? *Industrial Law Journal*, **40**(1), pp. 5–44.
Willey, B. (2012), *Employment Law in Context: An Introduction for HR Professionals*, 4th edn, Harlow: Pearson.

Convergence theory

Convergence approach suggests that management aspects become more alike globally. Globalization, with its main economic and technological drivers, enhances convergence among models of organization and management practices as countries demonstrate similar frameworks of economic growth and political stability. In particular, convergence theory supports the view that values are developed within a particular society and they have been impacted by technological and economic advancements. As societies become more similar because of globalization, in terms of industrialization and use of technology, values will eventually converge to the dominant political and economic paradigm. This is the Western capitalism, given that this is where most industrialization has traditionally occurred (Ralston, 2008). This practically means that organizations are globally converged with Western (mainly US-oriented) types of organizing, managing operations and leading people.

Convergence theory is the opposite of divergent, which argues that each country has a unique approach to organization and management, suggesting that local social and cultural aspects dominate and lead individuals and organizations to adopt specific values independently of globalization forces and pressures.

There are various forms of convergence approach, confirming the differentiation around its meaning. For example, Mayrhofer et al. (2004) in examining evolution of human resource management (HRM) demonstrated that convergence is a complex issue within HRM agenda. They also identified different forms of HRM evolution, namely *directional convergence, final convergence, stasis* and *divergence*. The first is related to the extent HRM change follows the same direction in two or more countries. Final convergence refers to the extent that HRM practices reach a similar point in two or more countries. Stasis is related to the lack of change in HRM development within different countries. Finally, divergence refers to the extent HRM changes follow different directions in two or more countries.

A critical role towards a convergence approach of HRM is played by super-national political entities like the European Union (EU) as well as international economic institutions such as the International Monetary Fund (IMF). These institutions produce policies and legislation that countries need to follow in order to achieve specific levels of social stability and economic development. For instance, although there are different legal systems that determine employee relations within European countries, EU directives related to labour market and trade unions can facilitate convergence of social and employment legislation among EU member states. Similarly, the IMF enhances the implementations of similar policies among weaker economies, targeting at labour relations' deregulation in order to become more attractive to foreign direct investments (FDIs).

The latest development in convergence theory is the concept of bounded convergence. This concept argues that sometimes people management practices follow hybrid models of HRM. This concept is also known as crossvergence theory arguing that it is in fact a combination of social, cultural forces as well as business/management paradigms that are the main drivers of value system formation.

ALEXANDROS PSYCHOGIOS

See also:

Globalization; Institutional theories; International human resource management; multinational companies; National cultures.

References and selected further readings

Barry, M. and A. Wilkinson (eds) (2011), *Research Handbook of Comparative Employment Relations*, Cheltenham: Edward Elgar.

Brewster, C. and M. Mayrhofer (2012), *A Handbook of Research on Comparative Human Resource Management*, Cheltenham: Edward Elgar.

Mayrhofer, W., M. Morley and C. Brewster (2004), Convergence, stasis or divergence? in C. Brewster, W. Mayrhofer and M. Morley (eds), *European Human Resource Management: Evidence of Convergence?* Oxford: Butterworth-Heinemann, pp. 415–437.

Mayrhofer, W., C. Brewster, M. Morley and J. Ledolter (2011), Hearing a different drummer? Convergence of human resource management in Europe — a longitudinal analysis, *Human Resource Management Review*, **21**(1), pp. 50–67.

Ralston, D.A. (2008), The crossvergence perspective: reflections and projections, *Journal of International Business Studies*, **39**(1), pp. 27–40.

Sparrow, P., R. Schuler and S. Jackson (1994), Convergence or divergence: human resource practices and policies for competitive advantage worldwide, *International Journal of Human Resource Management*, **5**(2), pp. 267–299.

Coordinated market economy

Coordinated market economy (CME) is a term that has come into widespread usage since Hall and Soskice (2001) denoted the developed economies of Continental north-western and Alpine Europe, Scandinavia and Japan. Other terms include 'stakeholder capitalism' (Dore), Rhineland capitalism, collaborative business systems (Whitley, 1999) and 'Continental European and social democratic capitalism' (Amable). Such economies are characterized by dense ties between key actors, allowing for a sharing of ideas, and the promotion of practices founded on compromise (Hall and Soskice, 2001). In practical terms, this is associated with the dominance of patient long-term investors, a relatively strong emphasis on stakeholder and environmental wellbeing, regulated labour markets and a high degree of social protection. Within the workplace, CMEs are associated with relatively strong worker rights and voice, and co-determination in the organization. The literature on comparative capitalism makes the assumption that CMEs are superior in terms of generating sustainable growth and societal wellbeing than liberal market economies (LMEs).

There are three major debates surrounding the concept. First, it is argued that much of the literature does not take account of the diversity encountered in CMEs, and indeed other capitalist archetypes, notably smaller firms and those in peripheral regions where practices can be quite far removed from the CME ideal (Lane and Wood, 2012). This does not necessarily make the concept less valuable, however, a degree of caution in its deployment is in order. Second, much of the present literature is imbued with a certain pessimism, and suggests that the CME model is gradually eroding in favour of lighter regulation and the debasement of labour standards. However, more optimistic accounts point to the revival of the patient investor paradigm in Germany (which was previously undermined through a process of corporate unbundling in the late 1990s and 2000s). It has also been argued that the decline in worker and stakeholder rights in LMEs is even more rapid, making the differences between the two greater, rather than less. Finally, the argument that CMEs are associated with the greater usage of alternative energy sources will insulate them to some extent from future volatility in energy prices, thus reducing opportunities for speculation. This requires longer-term investment horizons, again rewarding patient investors over speculators, and in turn will give workers greater security, and more incentives to develop their organization specific human capital.

GEOFF WOOD

See also:
Comparative HRM; Liberal market economy; Varieties of capitalism.

References and selected further readings

Hall, P. and D. Soskice (2001), An introduction to the varieties of capitalism, in P. Hall and D. Soskice (eds), *Varieties of Capitalism: The Institutional Basis of Competitive Advantage*, Oxford: Oxford University Press.
Hancke, B., M. Rhodes and M. Thatcher (2007), Introduction, in B. Hancke, M. Rhodes and M. Thatcher (eds), *Beyond Varieties of Capitalism: Conflict, Contradiction, and Complementarities in the European Economy*, Oxford: Oxford University Press.
Lane, C. and G. Wood (eds) (2012), *Capitalist Diversity and Diversity within Capitalism*, London: Routledge.
Whitley, R. (1999), *Divergent Capitalisms: The Social Structuring and Change of Business Systems*, Oxford: Oxford University Press.
Wood, G., P. Dibben and S. Ogden (2014), Comparative capitalism without capitalism, and production without workers: the limits and possibilities of contemporary institutional analysis, *International Journal of Management Reviews*, **16**(4), pp. 384–396.

Core worker

Core workers refer to those employees who typically work full-time, are highly skilled and relatively well-paid, and enjoy employment security, workplace-based fringe benefits, and extensive social security. They may also enjoy opportunities such as training and development, promotion, with well-defined internal career paths. They may be unionized, particularly in the manufacturing and public sectors, and are covered by collective bargaining which may further enhance, or at least protect, their employment terms and conditions. They tend to be carefully selected by the employing organization, enjoy more autonomy at work and may have more opportunities in participating in decision-making of the organization than peripheral workers. Core workers are considered to be those carrying out important activities for the organization that required unique skills and firm-specific knowledge critical to organizational competitiveness.

The term 'core worker' is part of the concept of 'core-peripheral model' advanced by Atkinson (1985). It is a staffing strategy increasingly adopted by employers since the mid-1980s, initially in the Anglo-Saxon context and now much more widespread. The core-peripheral model sparked considerable academic debate and entered the human resource management literature in the mid-1980s. In this model, the workforce is divided into classes, with the core workforce enjoying privileged employment terms and conditions that are arguably at the expense of the peripheral workforce. Core employees tend to be treated as an investment and therefore high-performance management systems tend to be deployed to manage this group of the workforce in order to elicit a higher level of employee commitment and engagement essential to improving organisational performance.

Since the mid-1980s, the size of the core workforce (i.e., 'good jobs') has been in contraction across a range of economies, even in countries that have traditionally operated in a strong internal labour market system, such as Japan, Korea and China. The shrinking of good employment has been particularly pronounced in the 1990s as employers in the public and private sector alike are struggling to remain competitive following a number of regional and global economic crisis, including the 1992 Japanese bubble burst, the 1997 Asian financial crisis and the 2008 global financial crisis. As a result, core business activities once performed by core workers are now increasingly carried out by peripheral workers.

Some human resource management scholars have proposed specific human resource architecture to tailor for these two groups of workforce in the organization to enhance their competitiveness (e.g., Lepak and Snell, 1999). Others (e.g., Kalleberg, 2009) have questioned the ethnical dimension of deploying such a two-tier workforce and contemplate the broader social and economic implications of this deliberate employer strategy.

FANG LEE COOKE

See also:

High-performance work systems; Peripheral worker.

References and selected further readings

Atkinson, J. (1985), *Flexibility, Uncertainty and Manpower Management*, Brighton: Institute of Manpower Studies.

Atkinson, J. and N. Meager (1986), *Changing Working Patterns: How Companies Achieve Flexibility to Meet New Needs*, London: Institute of Manpower Studies, National Economic Development Office.

Felstead, A. and N. Jewson (eds) (1999), *Global Trends in Flexible Labour: Critical Perspectives on Work and Organisations*, Basingstoke: Palgrave Macmillan.

Kalleberg, A. (2009), Precarious work, insecure workers: Employment relations in transition, *American Sociological Review*, **74**(1), pp. 1–22.

Lepak, D. P. and S.A. Snell (1999), The human resource architecture: toward a theory of human capital allocation and development, *Academy of Management Review*, **24**(1), pp. 31–48.

Payne, J. and C. Payne (1993), Unemployment and peripheral work, *Work, Employment and Society*, **7**(4), pp. 513–534.

Corporate social responsibility

Corporate social responsibility (CSR) is defined as 'context-specific organizational actions and policies that take into account stakeholders' expectations and the triple bottom line of economic, social, and environmental performance' (Aguinis, 2011, p. 855).

In many organizations, CSR has evolved from being viewed as an extra cost or burden to being central for the competitive advantage of businesses, especially employer branding. CSR initiatives can be actions within the firm such as changing methods of production or service delivery with regard to the environment. On the other hand, CSR may involve initiatives outside the firm such as supply-chain practices or employee volunteering. The human resource management (HRM) function has been recognized as having potentially a pivotal role in the design and implementation of CSR because of its ethical scope, contribution to sustained competitive advantage, and especially through its inherent links to employees. It has been found that CSR has the potential to increase employees' trust, commitment and motivation, creates meaning and identity and thereby strengthens the psychological contract and the associated performance outcomes (Mirvis, 2012).

Such initiatives are relatively new and have emerged from the shadow cast by Milton Friedman's influential article in the 1970s 'The social responsibility of business is to increase its profits', which argued for shareholder dominance over all other potential stakeholders, contributed to the marginalization of many organizations' policies in relation to social responsibility and significantly influenced corporate mindsets, especially in liberal market economies. In subsequent decades, there has been a gradual shift to a greater focus on the stakeholders of organizations, including employees.

CSR is now often viewed as a strategic source of competitive advantage (McWilliams and Siegel, 2011; Porter and Kramer, 2006). Apart from CSR improving access to finance, firm reputation and attractiveness as employers, it has also been linked to enhanced financial performance (Orlitzky, 2011). Evidence suggests that transforming CSR into financial performance involves vertically and horizontally integrating CSR and high-performance work practices (HPWPs) (Chang et al., 2013). With close parallels to the HR-performance literature, a strong CSR-performance association may only be viewed as a priority by organizations if it is seen to generate profit. This, of course, spurs a debate on whether organizations are motivated primarily by a genuine ethical commitment or simply by profit in relation to their CSR initiatives.

MICHAEL MORAN AND MAURA SHEEHAN

See also:

HR function and business partnering; Performance appraisal; Training and development.

Reference list and selected further readings

Aguinis, H. (2011), Organizational responsibility: doing good and doing well, in *APA Handbook of Industrial and Organizational Psychology, Vol 3: Maintaining, Expanding, and Contracting the Organization*, Washington, DC: APA, pp. 855–879.

Chang, Y.K., W.-Y. Oh and J.G. Messersmith (2013), Translating corporate social performance into financial performance: exploring the moderating role of high-performance work practices, *International Journal of Human Resource Management*, **24**(19), pp. 3738–3756.

McWilliams, A. and D.S. Siegel (2011), Creating and capturing value: strategic corporate social responsibility, resource-based theory, and sustainable competitive advantage, *Journal of Management*, **37**(5), pp. 1480–1495.

Mirvis, P. (2012), Employee engagement and CSR: transactional, relational and developmental approaches, *California Management Review*, **54**(4), pp. 93–117.

Orlitzky, M. (2011), Institutional logics in the study of organizations, *Business Ethics Quarterly*, **21**(3), pp. 409–444.

Porter, M.E. and M.R. Kramer (2006), Strategy & society: the link between competitive advantage and corporate social responsibility, *Harvard Business Review*, **84**(12), pp. 78–92.

Cross-cultural training

For multinational companies (MNCs) to implement their expatriation strategies success-fully, organizations need to ensure their expatriates adjust to the new environment and are competent in a global context. Indeed, a successful assignment depends largely upon how expatriates react or adjust to the culture and norms of their host country, and the new work environment. Cross-cultural training (CCT) commonly used by MNCs to dis-seminate cultural knowledge is a programme tailored to prepare expatriates for an inter-national assignment. CCT is an educative process used to improve intercultural learning when interacting with diverse cultures, thereby it can help expatriates to understand and accept the host culture prior to embarking on the assignment. Brislin (1979) identified three main techniques for effective CCT namely: cognitive; affective and behavioural. Tung (1981) further suggests that the training methods should be chosen according to the type of assignment, similarity between cultures and degree of interpersonal interaction between managers and host nationals. The main objective of a CCT should be to educate members of one culture to effectively communicate with members of another to ensure effective adjustment in the new country (Waxin and Panaccio, 2005).

One of the main themes in the CCT literature is expatriate cross-cultural adjustment. For an expatriate to successfully adjust while on an international assignment, research suggests that acculturation and adaptation together with the need to gain an under-standing of the host country's culture is of critical importance. Individuals tend to make anticipatory adjustments before they encounter a new environment; thus, it is important that expatriates have realistic expectations that can be achieved when they are provided with appropriate CCT. The need to develop cross-cultural skills is even greater where the gap between cultures is wide. One of the most widely used conceptual frameworks in cross-cultural research is Hofstede's Cultural Values Framework (Hofstede, 1983). It has provided scholars with much needed insight and understanding into the structure of national cultures.

DHARA SHAH

See also:
Expatriate; National culture.

References and selected further readings

Bennett, R., A. Aston and T. Colquhoun (2000), Cross-cultural training: a critical step in ensuring the success of international assignments, *Human Resource Management*, **39**, pp. 239–250.

Black, J.S. and M. Mendenhall (1990), Cross-cultural training effectiveness: a review and a theoretical frame-work for future research, *Academy of Management Review*, **15**, pp. 113–136.

Brislin, R.W. (1979), Orientation programs for cross-cultural preparation, in A.J. Marsella, G. Tharp and T.J. Ciborowski (eds), *Perspectives on Cross-Cultural Psychology*, Orlando: Academic Press, pp. 87–304.

Hofstede, G. (1983), Dimensions of national culture in fifty countries and three regions, in J.B. Deregowski, S. Dziurawiec and R.C. Annis (eds), *Expiscations in Cross-Cultural Psychology*, Lisse: Swets and Zeitlinger, pp. 335–355.

Tung, R.L. (1981), Selection and training of personnel for overseas assignments, *Columbia Journal of World Business*, **16**(1), pp. 68–78.

Waxin, M.F. and A. Panaccio (2005), Cross-cultural training to facilitate expatriate adjustment: it works! *Personnel Review*, **34**(1), pp. 51–68.

Custom and practice

Custom and practice played a very important part in the establishment of the terms by which employers and employees were intended to conduct their relationship before written contracts of employment were widely used. It reflected the ways in which work had always been done and took on the status of a term of contract, albeit implied, that was passed on to new recruits as being 'the way that we do things here'. While today, written contracts of employment are widely issued, custom and practice may not be as important as a source of law. However, it may still find its way into contracts of employment where a gap in the employment relationship has necessitated a form of collective response to establish precedent and continued action. As such, the practice starts as an informal response to something that is seen as being poorly managed or ambiguous – perhaps in terms of inadequate job design or required employee action – that is then adopted by employees in a customized response to that problem. This in turn becomes the normal practice for all employees affected by that problem, and is essentially formalized as an implied term within the employment contract. Of course, if a custom and practice was interpreted as being useful to management, it may well have found itself converted into an expressed term within the employment contract. Custom and practice helps define the employment contract provided it meets three criteria: it is definite and precisely defined; it is reasonable and generally applied and fits within the accepted practices of the organization; and it is well-known by all those in the area to whom it relates. It is also important to consider how long the practice has been in place before it could be described as being the customary way in which employees behave.

Not all custom and practice has been of benefit to management. When union power and collective bargaining were far more significant in establishing substantive employee experiences, custom and practice was often the result of union challenges to the expressed terms of the contract. An example is 'clocking off' times when workers established customs associated with putting tools away or going to the washroom to clean up ten minutes or so before the shift was completed. While reasonable behaviour, it was found to cost thousands of pounds of lost productivity. Management found themselves having to 'buy-out' custom and practice – often at considerable expense – despite the custom and practice being in breach of the expressed term of the employment contract.

While custom and practice may be more associated with the employment relations before the dominance of unitarism, there is some linkage with the contemporary emphasis given to the psychological contract and expectations of employee engagement, as both have an implied term of going beyond contract in a demonstration of loyalty and support for the employer.

ANNI HOLLINGS

See also:
Collective bargaining; Contract of employment; Labour law; Terms and conditions.

References and selected further readings

Aylott, E. (2014), *Employment Law*, London: Kogan Page.
Cushway, B. (2015), *The Employer's Handbook 2014–15: An Essential Guide to Employment Law, Personnel Policies and Procedure*, Bristol: Punter Southall.

Dibben, P., G. Klerk and G. Wood (2011), *Employment Relations: A Critical and International Approach*, London: Chartered Institute of Personnel and Development.

Marchington, M. and A. Wilkinson (2012), *Human Resource Management at Work*, 5th edn, London: Chartered Institute of Personnel and Development.

Customer appraisal

Quality and customer care programmes are very widespread in the service sector. One impact of these initiatives is that organizations are now increasingly setting employee performance standards based upon customer care indicators and appraising staff against these (Gamble, 2007). The use of service guarantees, which involve the payment of compensatory moneys to customers if the organizations do not reach service standards, has also led to a greater use of customer data in performance appraisal ratings.

Customer service data for use in appraising employees is gathered in a variety of methods. First, there is the use of a range of customer surveys, such as via the completion of customer care cards, telephone surveys, interviews with customers and online surveys. Organizations are now using such surveys more frequently and are increasingly sophisticated in how they gather customer views. Second, there is a range of surveillance techniques used by managers to sample the service encounter, for example the recording of service encounters in call centres. Third, there is a large increase in the use of so-called 'mystery shopping'. For some commentators, customer service can only be really effectively evaluated at the boundary been between customer and organization and this view has fuelled the growth of mystery shopping as a data-capturing process. Here staff are employed by a specialist agency, purport to be real shoppers and observe and record their experience of the service encounter. It is now commonly used in banks, insurance companies, supermarkets, restaurants and pubs and parts of the public sector.

Mystery shopping is argued to give a company a rich source of data that cannot be uncovered by other means, such as customer surveys. Such surveys, although useful for some purposes, are often conducted sometime after the service encounter and thus exact service problems are difficult to recollect. Mystery shopping is also seen as being particularly useful in revealing staff performance that causes customers to leave without purchasing. In many service sector organizations, a natural consequence of the use of mystery shoppers has been to utilize the data in the performance evaluations of staff (Fuller and Smith, 1991).

However, these data-gathering methods are, as one could well expect, not very popular with staff. Employees often question the ethics of introducing shoppers and feel that it represents a distinct lack of managerial trust in them. Thus employees describe shoppers in terms of 'spies' and 'snoopers' and react with hostility and 'shopper spotting' to their introduction. The introduction of mystery shopping for largely negative reasons of catching staff performing poorly only fuels such reactions. Some researchers advise that using mystery shopping as a source of data to help to coach staff produces improved performance (Latham et al., 2012) rather than punishing them for poor performance.

TOM REDMAN

References and selected further readings

Fuller, L. and V. Smith (1991), Consumers' reports: management by customers in a changing economy, *Work, Employment & Society*, **5**(1), pp. 1–16.

Gamble, J. (2007), The rhetoric of the consumer and customer control in China, *Work, Employment & Society*, **21**(1), pp. 7–25.

Latham, G.P., R.C. Ford and D. Tzabbar (2012), Enhancing employee and organisational performance through coaching based on mystery shopper feedback: a quasi-experimental study, *Human Resource Management*, **51**(2), pp. 213–229.

CV/Résumé

A curriculum vitae (CV) or résumé are tools used by students or job seekers in job applications with the objective to be invited for a job interview in order to obtain an internship or a job. The CV and résumé are important career management tools for individuals and organizations. Both tools are used for job promotions and more recently for personal branding and e-branding through social media sites like LinkedIn.

Some practitioners consider that there is no differentiation between a CV and a résumé – they use both terms interchangeably. Other practitioners see differences between a CV and a résumé concerning length, content and purpose. Therefore a résumé is shorter and more concise (one or two pages) while a CV is longer and more detailed (more than two pages). Usually the content of a résumé includes the skills, experience and education of the job seeker.

Recruiters often receive a considerable number of CVs/résumés for a given vacant position and on average will spend around 30 seconds reading a CV/résumé. This fact shows the importance of knowing how to present a CV/résumé. The content of a CV/résumé also depends on the job seeker's age, job experience, etc. There are also vast differences between applying for an internship or a job in different countries (see Canada Career Guide, 2011) and therefore country-specific requirements and rules should be respected. In addition, there are often sector specific requirements such as in the banking sector where an applicant's CV/résumé would have a rather conservative and traditional form and content, compared to a job seeker applying for a job in an advertising agency, and so would be more likely to show their creativity and innovative skills.

One of the recognized issues in recruitment is the role of unconscious bias in the corporate world (Naschberger et al., 2012). A recent study conducted by scientists (Moos-Racusin et al., 2012) shows the influence of gender bias in selection where male candidates were rated as significantly more competent and hireable than his identical female counterparts. Therefore recruiters must be trained and build awareness in order to reduce subjectivity and bias in the hiring process.

CHRISTINE NASCHBERGER

See also:

Careers; Promotion; Recruitment.

References and selected further readings

Canada Career Guide (2011), *Going Global: Career & Employment Resource Guide for Canada, Résumé/CV Guidelines and Samples*, Canada: Going Global, pp. 157–166.

Marlowe, C.M., S.L. Schneider and C.E. Nelson (1996), Gender and attractiveness biases in hiring decisions: are more experienced managers less biased? *Journal of Applied Psychology*, **81**(1), pp. 11–21.

Moos-Racusin, C.A., J.F. Dovidio, V.L. Brescoll, M.J. Graham and J. Handelsman (2012), Science faculty's subtle gender biases favor male students, *Proceedings of the National Academy of Sciences of the United States of America (PNAS)*, **109**(41), pp. 16474–16479.

Naschberger, C., C. Quental and C. Legrand (2012), Le parcours de carrière des femmes cadres: pourquoi est-il si compliqué et comment le faciliter? *Gestion: Revue Internationale de Gestion*, **37**(3), pp. 43–50.

Osoian, D., M. Zaharie and A. Miron (2011), Career management tools: curriculum vitae design, *Managerial Challenges of the Contemporary Society*, **2**, pp. 220–213.

Default retirement age

The default retirement age (DRA) is a term used to discuss the UK government regulation of mandatory retirement as set out in the Employment Equality (Age) Regulations 2006 (now part of the Single Equality Act 2010). The regulations prohibited workplace age discrimination, but permitted some flexibility for employers in setting age-based HRM policies in terms of service-related pay systems, pensions and redundancy. While drafting the Age Regulations, one of the most difficult issues that the Department of Trade and Industry (DTI, now the Department for Business Innovation and Skills) faced was whether or not to allow employers to set mandatory retirement ages. In the end, the government accepted the employers' case and opted to set a default retirement age of 65, after which an employer could lawfully dismiss an employee based on age (DTI, 2005). Under the regulations, an employer could set a retirement age below the DRA, but would face what the government called a 'tough test' (Age Positive Campaign, 2006). Although employers are allowed to compulsorily retire employees at 65 (or in some cases even younger), the Age Regulations do impose a duty to consider requests to delay retirement (DTI, 2005). So long as the employer follows the procedure set out in the Age Regulations for informing and consulting the employee on the decision to retire, it can compulsorily retire the employee without needing to justify its decision. Although employers were allowed to compulsorily retire employees at 65 (or in some cases even younger), the Age Regulations do impose a 'duty to consider' requests to delay retirement. Although most requests to delay retirement resulted in negotiated outcomes, employers tended to grant extended work arrangements on a fixed-term basis (Flynn, 2010b).

In 2010, the UK government abolished the DRA. However, employers are permitted to retain a mandatory retirement age where they can objectively justify doing so. Such objective justification can be based on the requirements of an occupation that older workers would be significantly less likely to fulfil than younger ones, for example, the Home Office has retained a mandatory retirement age for constables (Flynn, 2010a). However a 2012 Supreme Court ruling has expanded objective justification reasoning to include workforce planning, such as creating promotion opportunities for younger workers. Oxford and Cambridge universities have introduced mandatory retirement ages for professors at 67, justifying the HR policy as necessary to enable younger academics to develop their careers (Flynn, 2014).

MATT FLYNN

See also:
Ageing workforce; Older worker; Retirement.

References and selected further readings

Age Positive Campaign (2006), *Age Legislation Factsheet*, London: DWP.
DTI (2005), *Equality and Diversity, Coming of Age: Consultation on the Employment Equality Regulations 2006*, London: DTI.
Flynn, M. (2010a), Mandatory retirement in the police service: the case of the London MPS, *Policing: An International Journal of Police Strategies & Management*, **33**(2), pp. 376–391.
Flynn, M. (2010b), The United Kingdom government's 'business case' approach to the regulation of retirement, *Ageing and Society*, **30**(3), pp. 421–443.

Flynn, M. (2014), *Representing an Ageing Workforce: Challenges and Opportunities for Britain's Unions*, London: TUC.

Deskilling

The idea that capitalist dynamics of accumulation produce a generalized reduction in the content of the skills required for a specific production and thus a constant degradation of work and of the work experience, has been first put forward by the social theorist Harry Braverman in his 1974 seminal book *Labor and Monopoly Capital*. What Braverman tried to demonstrate in his book was that work processes and workplace transformations had to be understood in connection with the processes of valorization and accumulation taking place in a historically specific form of capitalism. He showed how management in the twentieth century in the USA, through the introduction of scientific management, moved progressively to appropriate workers' knowledge of the production process, controlling the planning and conceptual aspect of production, simplifying jobs and segmenting task. By this deskilling process, Braverman argued, employers were able to substitute machine to labour force, to reduce salary levels and to curb workers' resistance, traditionally focused on the defence of work knowledge and skills. Braverman's original thesis on deskilling was later to be discussed and criticized within the so-called labour process debate that developed in the UK from the end of the 1970s. He was accused of being too determinist and of misinterpreting the diversity of empirical reality with law-like general assumptions. A closer look to Braverman's writings, however, put in evidence how, within the general tendency of capitalism to deskill workers, management always encounters tensions and contradictions in the practical application of deskilling. This either from straightforward workers' opposition or from the difficulties and inadequacies of certain production processes to sustained forms of deskilling. Braverman thus identified rather than fixed laws, context-specific, cyclical and continuous processes of deskilling and reskilling unevenly distributed across different production/technological processes and geographical areas.

Forty years after the publication of his influential book and after a new leap in technology, Braverman's deskilling thesis remains a powerful tool to understand long-term work patterns and processes within the evolution of capitalism. Once we consider how skills requirements have evolved in the development of the computers and software industries in the light of Braverman's thesis, for instance, we cannot but find confirmation of many of Braverman's assumptions. Whereas the first computers required a team of highly qualified scientists to project and produce these machines, today's knowledge has been patented and codified to allow Chinese factories to assemble computers under the most rigorous principle of scientific management, employing a virtually unskilled workforce. Similarly, the simplification of software language, the relative accessibility and widespread use of computer-related technologies and communication processes have deskilled jobs across all sectors of economic activities while simultaneously upgrading the skills of societies at large. Braverman's insights on the cyclical and continuous processes of deskilling and reskilling remain important today.

Maurizio Atzeni

See also:
Alienation; Division of labour; Labour process/theory; Self-management.

References and selected further readings
Braverman, H. (1974), *Labor and Monopoly Capital: The Degradation of Work in the Twentieth Century*, New York: Monthly Review Press.
Thompson, P. (1989), *The Nature of Work*, 2nd edn, Basingstoke: Palgrave.
Spencer, D. (2000), Braverman and the contribution of labour process analysis to the critique of capitalist production – twenty five years on, *Work, Employment and Society*, **14**(2), 223–243.

Direct discrimination

Direct discrimination broadly addresses individual disadvantage linked to a protected characteristic. Measures that seek to prevent direct discrimination are underpinned by liberal notions of procedural or formal equality and require equal treatment between those who share particular characteristics and those who do not. Within the framework of anti-discrimination law in Great Britain employers must not discriminate against job applicants or employees (Equality Act 2010 section 39). Discrimination is defined with reference to certain characteristics that are designated as protected under the Equality Act 2010. All of the characteristics protected under the Equality Act 2010 are relevant to direct discrimination (age, disability, gender reassignment, marriage and civil partnership, pregnancy and maternity, race, religion or belief, sex and sexual orientation). Direct discrimination arises where, because of a protected characteristic, an employer treats an employee or applicant less favourably than the employer treats or would treat others (section 13(1)). The wording 'because of a protected characteristic' is broad enough to encompass associative discrimination and this means that the less favourable treatment does not have to be because of the protected characteristic of the employee or applicant themselves, but can be because of the protected characteristic of another (for example, an employee is treated less favourably because he or she has a disabled child). This wording also encompasses perceptive discrimination; here the less favourable treatment would be because the employer perceives the employee or applicant to have a particular characteristic when in fact they do not (for example, an applicant is treated less favourably because the employers thinks that he or she is gay when in fact they are not). The words 'or would treat' allow for deterred discrimination that arises when a suitably qualified applicant is 'put off' from applying for a job because the employer signals that applicants with a particular characteristic would not be considered.

In order to establish that he or she has been treated 'less favourably', an employee or applicant must identify a comparator who does not share the protected characteristic but is in the same circumstances (section 23). This can be a real or a hypothetical person.

Where the protected characteristic is age, employers can defend a claim of direct discrimination if they can show that their treatment of the employee or applicant was a proportionate means of meeting a legitimate aim (section 13(2)). There is no such defence for any of the other protected characteristics.

Liz Oliver

See also:

Equal opportunity; Indirect discrimination.

References and selected further readings

Bamforth, N., M. Malik and C. O'Cinneide (2008), *Discrimination Law: Theory and Context: Text and Materials*, London: Sweet & Maxwell.

Kirton, G. and A. Greene (2010), *The Dynamics of Managing Diversity a Critical Approach*, 3rd edn, Oxford: Elsevier Butterworth-Heinemann.

Willey, B. (2012), *Employment Law in Context: An Introduction for HR Professionals*, 4th edn, Harlow: Pearson.

Dirty work

The scholarly term 'dirty work' is attributed to Everett C. Hughes who in 1958 wrote *Men and Their Work*. It has predominantly been used in sociology, but in recent years the term has been used in different fields of management. Dirty work is largely a social construct that can change over time as societal attitudes differ towards certain professions and work tasks. Dirty work is also highly dependent on the culture within which the work is done. It is also worth noting that today there is a colloquial usage of the term.

The key aspect of dirty work is that the occupation has some form of physical, social or moral taint. It is the proximity of this taint within the work that leads to a stigmatization of dirty workers in a wider societal context. For example, work that can be seen as having a physical taint includes working with 'dirty subjects' such as waste sanitation workers. A social taint can come from working with other stigmatized populations, such as work involving prisoners for prison guards. A moral taint can come from 'performing work of a morally dubious nature' such as exotic dancers (Baran et al., 2012, p. 598).

The research literature has taken an occupational perspective on dirty work focusing on how such workers are stigmatized. The main questions here have been why dirty workers do the work they do and how they normalize it. Different ways of normalizing the work have been suggested such as creating occupational ideologies, social buffers, confronting clients and the public about the stigma and taint, using different defensive tactics, and gaining a habituation/desensitization of the work over time (Ashforth and Kreiner, 2002). As such, the dirty work literature recognizes that negative experiences of dirty work can be 'reframed' in a more positive light. This 'reframing' is done by ascribing to ulterior motives (e.g., limited education, pressing need for money, financial downturns, providing for the family), thus limiting stickiness (a key construct within dirty work). There has also been investigation into how the stigmatization of former dirty workers presents challenges in applying for non-dirty work roles (Bergman and Chalkey, 2007). In this way, there are some issues that seem to 'stick' with dirty workers even after they leave dirty work, implying that the 'dirtiness' is somehow inherent not only for the work-role but also to the actual individual.

LINDA TALLBERG

References and selected further readings

Ashforth, B. and G. Kreiner (2002), Normalizing emotion in organizations: making the extraordinary seem ordinary, *Human Resource Management Review*, **12**, pp. 215–235.

Ashforth, B., G. Kreiner, M. Clark and M. Fugate (2007), Normalizing dirty work: managerial tactics for countering occupational taint, *Academy of Management Journal*, **50**(1), pp. 149–174.
Baran, B., S. Rogelberg, E. Lopina, J. Allen, C. Spitzmüller and M. Bergman (2012), Shouldering a silent burden: the toll of dirty tasks, *Human Relations*, **65**(5), pp. 597–626.
Bergman, M. and K. Chalkley (2007), 'Ex' marks a spot: the stickiness of dirty work and other removed stigmas, *Journal of Occupational Health Psychology*, **12**(3), pp. 251–265.

Disability discrimination

Legislation addressing disability discrimination has been in force in Britain since 1995 when the Disability Discrimination Act came into being. Like in many other national contexts, this followed the growth and development of a disability rights movement that exerted political pressure and called for the removal of barriers to participation in social activity including employment. At the EU level, the introduction, in 1998 of a treaty article allowing for action to prevent discrimination based on disability (now found in Article 19 of the Treaty on the Functioning of the European Union) was later followed by Directive 2000/78/EC, establishing a general framework for equal treatment in employment and occupation. This Directive deals with discrimination on a number of grounds including disability and its provisions were implemented nationally in 2004. The Equality Act 2010 now addresses disability discrimination.

Under the Equality Act 2010, employers must not discriminate against job applicants or employees (section 39). Discrimination is defined with reference to certain characteristics that are designated as protected. Disability is a protected characteristic (section 4). For the purposes of the 2010 Act, a person has a disability if they have a physical or mental impairment and the impairment has a substantial and long-term effect on their ability to carry out normal day-to-day activities (section 6). Certain medical conditions are pre-designated as a disability, these include cancer, HIV infection and multiple sclerosis (section 1(6)). Controversially this definition draws from a medical model of disability rather than the social model, which views disability as created by the environment rather than individual impairment. The Equality Act prohibits certain forms of conduct. Prohibited conduct includes several forms of discrimination as well as harassment and victimization. Disability is a relevant protected characteristic for direct (see 'Direct discrimination' in this volume) and indirect discrimination (see 'Indirect discrimination' in this volume) as well as harassment and disability discrimination allegations or claims are relevant to victimization. In addition some specific forms of disability discrimination are classed as prohibited conduct, these are discussed next.

'Discrimination arising from disability' (section 15), this form of discrimination will only occur where the employer knows or could reasonably be expected to know that the person (an employee or applicant) has a disability (section 15(2)). An employer will discriminate against the person if the employer treats them unfavourably because of something arising in consequence of their disability. The disabled person does not have to identify a non-disabled comparator in order to establish that discrimination has occurred. Employers can defend a claim of discrimination arising from disability by showing that the treatment was a proportionate means of achieving a legitimate aim (section 15(1)(b)).

The Equality Act imposes a duty on employers to make reasonable adjustments in relation to disabled employees and applicants (section 39(5)). This measure is rooted in the social model of disability which requires the removal of barriers to the participation of disabled people. A failure to comply with the duty constitutes discrimination (section 21). The duty is a form of proactive measure (see 'Positive discrimination' in this volume) that arises in relation to employment and recruitment and it entails a requirement to take such steps as is reasonable to have to take to avoid a disadvantage (section 20(3)). This requirement arises in three circumstances. The first is where a provision, criterion or practice of the employer puts a disabled person at a substantial disadvantage in comparison to persons who are not disabled; the second is where a physical feature puts a disabled person at a substantial disadvantage in comparison to persons who are not disabled. In these circumstances the employer is required to take such steps as is reasonable to have to take to avoid the disadvantage (section 20(3)). The third requirement arises where a disabled person would, but for the provision of an auxiliary aid, be put at a substantial disadvantage in comparison to persons who are not disabled. Here the requirement is to take such steps as is reasonable to have to take to provide the auxiliary aid.

LIZ OLIVER

See also:

Direct discrimination; Equal opportunity; Indirect discrimination; Positive discrimination.

References and selected further readings

Barnes, C. and G. Mercer (2005), Disability, work, and welfare challenging the social exclusion of disabled people, *Work Employment & Society*, **19**(3), pp. 527–545.

Jones, M. and V. Wass (2013), Understanding changing disability-related employment gaps in Britain 1998–2011, *Work, Employment & Society*, **27**(6), pp. 982–1003.

Lawson, A. (2008), *Disability and Equality Law in Britain: The Role of Reasonable Adjustment*, Oxford: Hart.

Willey, B. (2012), *Employment Law in Context: An Introduction for HR Professionals*, 4th edn, Harlow: Pearson.

Disciplinary procedure

No precise legal definition of the expression 'disciplinary procedure' is provided by UK law. However, the Foreword to the *Code of Practice 1 on Disciplinary and Grievance Procedures* produced by the Advisory, Conciliation and Arbitration Service (Acas, 2015) provides a helpful narrative. It provides that a disciplinary procedure is one designed to furnish 'practical guidance to employers, employees and their representatives and sets out principles for handling disciplinary and grievance situations in the workplace'. Prior to the coming into force of the Employment Act 2008, it was a legal requirement for an employer to adhere to a statutorily prescribed disciplinary procedure in the UK. If the employer failed to follow the statutory disciplinary procedure, then this would render an employee's dismissal as an automatically unfair dismissal under Part X of the Employment Rights Act, which would entitle him/her to receive compensation. The law in the UK was modified in 2009 and such statutory disciplinary procedures were abolished, owing to the extent of the litigation that they had generated. Instead, the law now provides that an employer who fails to adhere to the requirements of Acas' *Code of Practice 1 on Disciplinary and Grievance Procedures* will be subject to an order from a tribunal or court that a dismissed employee will be treated as automatically unfairly dismissed, enabling that employee to claim compensation.

The application of a disciplinary procedure will be appropriate where it is alleged that an employee has committed an act of misconduct or is no longer capable to do his/her job; for example, owing to incompetence or long-term illness. As for the basic ingredients of a disciplinary procedure, these consist of the following in sequential order:

1. A letter informing the employee of the allegations against the employee or the problem.
2. Suspension with pay, if necessary.
3. Reasonable investigation.
4. Discussion and consultation with the employee.
5. A disciplinary hearing.
6. A managerial decision to impose a disciplinary sanction.
7. An appeal hearing.

Over the past 20 years, the prevailing theory behind the incentivization of employers to adopt pre-dismissal disciplinary procedures has been to afford an employee a measure of procedural justice prior to any decision to dismiss him/her from his post. The thinking is that if employers prescribe and follow impartial and fair disciplinary procedures, a far greater number of employees will accept that the process behind their dismissal was fair. This will have the likely consequence that the tribunal and court system will have fewer disputes to resolve, since the parties will settle their disputes about dismissals outside the tribunal system.

DAVID CABRELLI

See also:
Grievance procedure; Gross misconduct; Misconduct; Notice period.

References and selected further readings
Acas (2015), *Code of Practice 1 on Disciplinary and Grievance Procedures*, www.acas.org.uk/media/pdf/f/m/ Acas-Code-of-Practice-1-on-disciplinary-and-grievance-procedures.pdf.
Collins, H. (1992), *Justice in Dismissal*, London: Clarendon Press.
Fredman, S. (1986), Natural justice for employees: the unacceptable faith of proceduralism, *Industrial Law Journal*, **15**, pp. 15–31.
Sanders, A. (2009), Part One of the Employment Act 2008: 'Better Dispute Resolution?' *Industrial Law Journal*, **38**, pp. 30–49.
Sanders, A. (2010), A right to legal representation (in the workplace) during disciplinary proceedings? *Industrial Law Journal*, **39**, pp. 166–182.
Sanders, A. (2013), Does Article 6 of the European Convention on Human Rights apply to disciplinary procedures in the workplace? *Oxford Journal of Legal Studies*, **33**, pp. 791–819.
Sanders, A. (2014), The law of unfair dismissal and behaviour outside work, *Legal Studies*, **34**, pp. 328–352.

Discipline and grievance

Employment relationships are defined by their terms, which spell out the rights, entitlements and obligations of employers and employees.

Particularly where employment relationships are well-defined and enforceable, discipline and grievance processes are the mechanisms for policing the relationship and enforcing its terms. Discipline is the employer's response to a perceived breach of the terms of the relationship by the employee. Grievance, in strict definition, is the employee's mechanism for addressing an alleged breach of the terms of the relationship by an employer.

Employees' obligations may be written in an employment contract or in an employer's rules. Or they may be implied, as, for example, implied obligations of competence, obedience and fidelity. While employees can come to the disciplinary attention of employers for many reasons, in reality most discipline arises from poor performance or some type of misconduct.

An effective disciplinary process begins with positive intent and ends with closure of the problem. It should be aimed at correcting the employee's unsatisfactory performance or behaviour, with termination of the relationship only a last resort.

There are some essential elements to any effective and fair disciplinary process. The first is getting the facts. Confronted with a suspicion of misconduct, for example, the employer should undertake a sufficient investigation to form as accurate a belief as reasonably possible about what happened. The next step depends on the findings.

In instances of minor performance or behaviour issues, it will often be best to talk to the employee informally to point out the deficiency and the expected standards.

Where an investigation turns up a more serious problem that may lead to disciplinary action, principles of natural justice require that the specific concern or allegation, and the evidence supporting it, be put to the employee for a response before any decision on disciplinary action is taken. Advance notice of the meeting, the possible disciplinary consequences and the right to representation are also in the spirit of natural justice, and may be required by law or contract in some jurisdictions.

In terms of discipline itself, it is widely accepted that there are 'first time dismissible offences', usually reserved for incidents of serious misconduct. Dishonesty offences, assault, intimidation, alcohol and drug offences and conflicts of interest would all typically qualify as 'serious misconduct' and often result in instant dismissal for a single occurrence.

For less serious misconduct, and for most performance problems, a remedial approach – starting with verbal warnings, followed by a written warning for a second offence or escalation of the problem, but allowing for ultimate dismissal if warnings were not heeded – would be usual and preferred. A remedial focus also requires that warnings should often be accompanied by counselling and training to assist the struggling employee.

A grievance, as noted, is the employee's vehicle for protesting an alleged breach of employment terms by the employer, although in some jurisdictions, employees may be able to raise any employment relationship problem or dissatisfaction through a grievance procedure. Sometimes employees file a grievance because they are unhappy with the terms of employment and want something changed. That is an extension of the grievance procedure beyond its usual role of interpreting and enforcing the existing terms of employment.

Employees' rights and entitlements may be set out in the express or implied terms of an employment contract (for example, wage rates and the right to fair treatment), in the employer's policies (free childcare perhaps, or transportation, or wash-up time), or in legislation or regulation (such as protection against discrimination and harassment).

A generally accepted principle is that grievances are best resolved as close as possible to where they originated. Accordingly, the supervisor or manager closest to the matter being grieved should have the first opportunity to resolve the grievance informally, although this will sometimes be limited by authority or the need for consistency across the organization.

Grievances should ordinarily be put in writing, identifying the problem, the evidence and the proposed resolution. Again, prior to providing a response, the employer should investigate to establish the facts, understand the employee's view of the problem, consider whether the grievance has validity and if so, consider possible solutions.

Grievance meetings should ideally be held quickly after the grievance is filed. Notice of the meeting, attendances, the grievant's right to representation, sensitivity to vulnerable employees, the right to be heard and the need for accurate documentation are all matters equally important to grievance hearings as to discipline hearings. On the other hand, depending on the subject matter, grievance hearings often hold more opportunities and options than disciplinary hearings. An employer will be reluctant to negotiate where a grievant seeks 'reinterpretation' of a contractual term, but may be more flexible where the grievance addresses a gap in employment terms or a non-contractual matter. Eventually, failing agreement, in most jurisdictions the employer will issue a decision on the grievance.

With both discipline and grievances, the right to some sort of meaningful appeal is seen as an essential characteristic of an effective and fair process. Internally, first appeal steps will usually involve reconsideration by a higher level of management, with union or works council involvement in some jurisdictions and circumstances. Externally, appeals of denied grievances and imposed discipline through industrial or employment tribunals, specialist courts or the general civil courts is provided for in many jurisdictions, with mediation assistance also often available in the first instance. In the USA, employer-sponsored 'employment arbitration' has seen some growth, although not without contention, and union grievance procedures remain available under union contracts in the USA and elsewhere.

IAN MCANDREW

See also:

Disciplinary procedure; Grievance procedure; Mediation; Misconduct; Negotiation.

References and selected further readings

Colvin, A. (2014), Grievance procedures in non-union firms, in W. Roche, P. Teague and A. Colvin (eds), *Conflict Management in Organizations*, Oxford: Oxford University Press.

Lamare, J.R. and D. Lipsky (2014), Employment arbitration in the securities industry: lessons drawn from recent empirical research, *Berkeley Journal of Employment & Labor Law*, 35(1/2), pp. 113–133.

Saundry, R., C. Jones and V. Antcliff (2011), Discipline, representation and dispute resolution — exploring the role of trade unions and employee companions in workplace discipline, *Industrial Relations Journal*, 42(2), pp. 195–211.

Walker, B. and R. Hamilton (2011), Employee–employer grievances: a review, *International Journal of Management Reviews*, 13, pp. 40–58.

Disconnected capitalism

The concept of disconnected capitalism derives from an explanatory framework developed by Thompson (2003) to link the growth of financialization in the economy to largely negative outcomes in the employment relationship. 'Financialization' refers to the increased significance of capital markets as drivers of firm behaviour. Firms must engage in a variety of short-term measures and perpetual restructuring to meet shareholder value valuations, metrics and targets. Corporate executives are incentivized to support such measures through rewards tied to stock options.

Corporations become more 'disposable' and that undermines the stable conditions necessary for the sustainability of the kinds of high-performance work systems promoted in HRM discourses are severely weakened. Although managers at local level may enter into such productivity bargains in good faith and they may be capable of generating mutual gains, such bargains are increasingly fragile or broken by decisions taken at corporate level. The core disconnect is between the objectives of managers in the work sphere (engagement, commitment, discretionary effort) and the inability of employers to provide the supportive conditions in the employment relationship (job security, career development, investment in training and skill enhancement). This puts into question the human capital model that has traditionally underpinned commitment-led HR discourses and practices.

The DCT has diffused rapidly in debates and research on contemporary work and employment practices (see Thompson, 2013). Researchers have applied the concept to different circumstances, such as McCann's (2013) study of falling attachment levels among finance employees. One of the limitations of the original argument was that it didn't provide enough clarity on how financialization worked through particular mechanisms and agents. Clark's (2009) work on the significance of private equity firms helped fill that gap. In later work with American colleagues (Appelbaum et al., 2013), further confirmation was provided of the negative impact of capital markets and financial engineering of a variety of breaches of trust with employees, supplier and other stakeholders. They also argue that financialization produces a disconnect to the study of the employment relationship itself given that firms seek to extract value through a greater variety of means than just the labour process. This offers a challenge to industrial relations, HRM and labour process theory.

PAUL THOMPSON

See also:

Financialization; High-performance work systems; Labour process/theory.

References and selected further reading

Appelbaum, E., R. Batt and I. Clark (2013), Implications of financial capitalism for employment relations research: evidence from breach of trust and implicit contracts in private equity buyouts, *British Journal of Industrial Relations*, **51**(3), pp. 498–518.

Clark, I. (2009), Owners and managers: disconnecting managerial capitalism? Understanding the private-equity business model, *Work, Employment and Society*, **23**(4), pp. 775–786.

McCann, L. (2013), Disconnected amid the networks and chains: employee detachment from company and union after offshoring, *British Journal of Industrial Relations*, **52**(2), pp. 237–260.

Thompson, P. (2003), Disconnected capitalism: or why employers can't keep their side of the bargain, *Work, Employment and Society*, **17**(2), pp. 359–378.

Thompson, P. (2011), The trouble with HRM, *Human Resource Management Journal*, **21**(4), pp. 355–367.
Thompson, P. (2013), Financialization and the workplace: extending and applying the disconnected capitalism thesis, *Work, Employment and Society*, **27**(3), pp. 472–488.

Dismissal

The term 'dismissal' ordinarily implies that an employment contract has been or is being brought to an end at the instigation of the employer. Within the law of contract there are various ways in which contracts can be brought to an end (all of the obligations between the parties are discharged and the parties are no longer bound). Some of the ways in which contractual obligations can be discharged will be in line with the contract (such as discharge by performance of the contract), and some will be contrary to the contract (such as termination for breach of contract). Not all of the ways in which a contract can be discharged will be classed as a dismissal for the purposes of the statutory rights of employees (those with a contract of service) in the context of contract termination.

For the purposes of the statutory right not to be unfairly dismissed (granted to qualifying employees by section 94 of the Employment Rights Act 1996; see 'Unfair dismissal' in this volume) a dismissal occurs in the following circumstances: the employee's contract of employment is terminated by the employer (whether with or without notice); the employee is employed under a limited-term contract and the contract terminates by virtue of the limiting event without being renewed under the same contract; the employee terminates the contract in circumstances in which she or he is entitled to terminate it by reason of the employer's conduct (Employment Rights Act 1996 section 95(1)). The latter refers to a 'constructive dismissal' (see 'Constructive dismissal' in this volume). Under these provisions, an employee will also be dismissed if she or he resigns when they are already under notice of dismissal (section 95(2)). For the purposes of the statutory redundancy provisions, the definition of dismissal is virtually the same as that set out above, but with some important differences. For example, for redundancy purposes (such as access to a redundancy payment) an employee will not be deemed to have been dismissed where their contact is renewed or they are re-engaged (section 138). The offer of further employment must have been made before the end of the contract and the renewal or re-engagement must take effect immediately or within four weeks following the end of the employment (section 138). The rationale for provision is to encourage employers to offer suitable alternative employment to employees who are at risk of redundancy. There are other circumstances where statute either requires or prevents a termination from being classed as a dismissal for the purposes of redundancy (for an example of the former see section 136(5) and for the latter see section 136(2)).

LIZ OLIVER

See also:
Constructive dismissal; Contract of employment; Unfair dismissal; Wrongful dismissal.

Reference list and selected further readings

Willey, B. (2012), *Employment Law in Context: An Introduction for HR Professionals*, 4th edn, Harlow: Pearson.
See also reading for 'Unfair dismissal' and 'Wrongful dismissal'.

Distance learning

Distance learning is almost self-defining. It is simply learning that occurs at a distance through organizations that design the distance learning and plan and organize its delivery. Such organizations include universities and colleges. A famous example is the UK's Open University (OU), which was established in 1969. Since then, the concept and mode of operation of the OU has been exported around the world. The focus is primarily educational qualifications, from first degrees to doctorate-level credentials. Commercial providers of distance learning existed long before the OU and are generally and collectively known as 'correspondence colleges'. The products of these colleges also include qualifications but usually at the sub-degree level and with a vocational focus associated with specific occupations and trades.

Those responsible for the delivery of the learning may or may not have also been responsible for its design. The title of this person will vary according to the organization responsible for the distance learning; for example, lecturer or tutor if a university, or trainer or facilitator if a correspondence college. Those who uptake distance learning are termed 'colleague learners'. These are the individuals who are engaged in distance learning generally and do so at a distance from other learners engaged in the same learning and so in isolation.

However, from its earliest days, the OU designed and implemented as part of its courses various interventions to overcome the isolation of lone individual learners. These included telephone tutorials with a tutor; geographically based self-study groups of learners that also benefit from being tutor-facilitated, and annual week-long residential summer schools held, usually, at the campus of a traditional university. Similar interventions were and remain part of the provision of commercial providers of distance learning. It is rare for an individual distance learner to experience no interaction with tutors/ trainers or other learners. The need for direct face-to-face interaction is primarily associated with the media originally used in distance learning. This was primarily print based with study packs of specially written learning materials, supplemented by textbooks and other pre-existing materials, such as journal articles. Print-based materials were, and still are, supplemented by audio and video materials and, in the case of the OU, radio and TV broadcasts. However, in recent years and currently, use of information and communication technology (ICT) is common. Thus, online learning is now a very common feature of distance learning. This technology enables contact and interaction between individual learners and tutors/trainers, and between learners as a group. So, there is less need to have expensive face-to-face interaction in a fixed time and place. Even so, there remain current examples of distance learning that rely almost exclusively on print-based materials with interventions such as workshops of two or three days duration in fixed places and times (see www.icslearn.co.uk for examples). Attendance at such workshops may, however, be optional.

In summary, distance learning is an approach to education, training and development that is designed and intended to overcome the barriers and restrictions of time and place to access to learning opportunities.

JIM STEWART

See also:
Blended learning; E-learning; Off-the-job learning; Online learning; Qualifications; Training.

Reference list and selected further readings

Simonson, M., S. Smaldino and S.M. Zvacek (2014), *Teaching and Learning at a Distance: Foundations of Distance Education*, 6th edn, Charlotte, NC: Information Age Publishing.
Simpson, O. (2012), *Supporting Students for Success in Online and Distance Education*, 3rd edn, London and New York: Routledge.
Stewart, J. (2010), E-learning for managers and leaders, in J. Gold and R. Thorpe (eds), *Gower Handbook of Leadership and Management Development*, 5th edn, Farnham: Gower Publishing.

Diversity management

'Diversity management' has a number of different meanings depending on its use and the philosophical position of the user. In the name of diversity management, businesses have instituted specific diversity policies and programmes to value difference and enhance the inclusion of all employees. This is in contrast to national regulations, which often focus on particular disadvantaged identity groups (e.g. based on sex, race/ethnicity, age, disability, sexuality, religion) rather than individuals. Diversity management – with its American origins – is often seen as an alternative or even a paradigm shift to 'equal opportunities' and considered a backlash to the use of affirmative action in the USA. Diversity management was positioned as adopting a business case approach aimed at improving organizational competitiveness and efficiency. The business case is contrasted with the equal opportunities approach, which is seen as driven by a social justice case to diversity. However, these hard and fast distinctions are flawed; for example, equal opportunities by focusing on the underrepresentation of particular identity groups have also recognized the business case with respect to the labour market shortages and the benefits of a diverse workforce. Further binary differences are highlighted with diversity characterized by individualism rather than collectivism, voluntarism rather than regulation, business interests rather than social justice, yet the binary of equal opportunities *or* diversity management has been the target of well-evidenced criticism. Despite the shift to voluntarism characterized by diversity management, key HRM policies are influenced by national (and in Europe, EU) equality legislation, such as discrimination, recruitment, selection, appraisal and promotion policies; however, operationally there is often a gap between policy and practice.

Thus the debates around diversity are contested and are complicated by the different perspectives and approaches of authors. Kirton (2008) seeks to unpick this complexity by distilling the main ways in which diversity is understood:

1. Diversity can be used as a *descriptor* of differences (workforce diversity).
2. Diversity is an organizational policy approach explicitly focused on utilizing and valuing employee differences – usually referred to as 'diversity management' or 'managing diversity'.
3. Diversity can be seen as a *conceptual construct*. While diversity management in practice is related to the earlier policy approaches of 'equal opportunities', diversity as a concept has philosophical origins that are different to concepts of equality (Young, 1990).

4. Diversity can be seen as a discourse or discursive practice when, for example, organizations position the business case as a 'normalized mega discourse' that enshrines the achievement of organizational economic goals as the ultimate guiding principle, which shifts the focus away from redressing inequalities to the achievement of economic goals.

The literature on diversity management often encompasses one or more of the above approaches, which will often be interrelated and sometimes contradictory. For the student of diversity management, this can present a challenge, but recognizing these differences can lead to a stronger and more critical analysis of diversity research and practice.

Studies on diversity management are often set in one national context, whereas comparative research demonstrates further complexities across national boundaries often influenced by cultural and institutional differences. Healy and Oikelome's (2011) comparative study of diversity in the health sector in the UK and US demonstrated sharp similarities in the use of the international labour market through which healthcare is provided. In contrast it demonstrated clear differences in approach to diversity management in the same sector with the American healthcare organizations focusing in particular on individualistic approaches in contrast to the more collectivist approaches in the UK. The study also widened the strands covered by diversity management to include 'place of qualification' when qualifications gained outside the UK and US proved a potential source of discrimination and differential management strategy. Healy and Oikelome (2011) also explained the role of national diversity policies in an African country using the example of Nigeria and pointed to the importance of history, in particular colonial history, in enabling a more complete understanding of national diversity contexts and how diversity and migration may intersect. The case for an intersectional sensibility, first made by black feminists, also reveals the different career experiences of those with multiple identities. Further, empirical work drawing on inequality regimes concepts derived from Joan Acker's work, reveals how the processes and practices (including diversity management) operate within organizations.

Critical writers, guided by emancipatory principles, point to the value-loaded nature of diversity policies and practices. Iris Marion Young's work, for example, argues for the affirmation of group-based differences and makes a strong case for affirmative action and takes the view that basic equality in life is a moral value and that injustices demand institutional changes (Young, 1990, p. 14). Healy et al. (2010) draw on Max Weber's complex understandings of rationalities to expose the value oriented nature of a diversity management approach with respect to an espoused 'objective' method of selection (assessment centres) and Tatli and Özbilgin (2012) use Bourdieu's approach to capitals to expose new categories of difference in intersectional studies of diversity at work. These approaches bring into sharp relief the complexity that characterizes diversity management and exposes the career hurdles faced by identity groups.

In conclusion, diversity management is far more than a tool of management and its study demands a critical, theoretical and empirically informed approach.

GERALDINE HEALY

See also:

Assessment centres; Careers; Comparative HRM; Equal opportunity; National culture.

References and suggested further readings

Bendl, R., I. Bleijenbergh, E. Henttonen and A.J. Mills (eds) (2015), *The Oxford Handbook of Diversity in Organizations*, Oxford: Oxford University Press.

Healy, G. and F. Oikelome (2011), *Diversity, Ethnicity, Migration and Work: An International Perspective*, Basingstoke: Palgrave Macmillan.

Healy, G., G. Kirton, M.F. Özbilgin and F. Oikelome (2010), Competing rationalities in the diversity project of the UK judiciary: the politics of assessment centres, *Human Relations*, **63**(6), pp. 807–834.

Kirton, G. (2008), Managing multi-culturally in organizations in a diverse society, in S. Clegg and C. Cooper (eds), *Handbook of Macro Organizational Behaviour*, London: Sage, pp. 309–322.

Kirton, G. and A. Greene (2015), *The Dynamics of Managing Diversity*, 4th edn, London: Routledge.

Tatli, A. and M.F. Özbilgin (2012), An emic approach to intersectional study of diversity at work: a Bourdieuan framing, *International Journal of Management Reviews*, **14**(2), pp. 180–200.

Young, I.M. (1990), *Justice and the Politics of Difference*, Princeton: Princeton University Press.

Division of Labour

Changes in the organization of work and increasingly globalized production processes force us to rethink the concept of the division of labour beyond its narrow technical definition. Today the division of labour, the segmentation of complex operations into simple task distributed to individual workers, has gone beyond the simple organizational sphere. Organizational processes of companies continue to be based on a division and specialization of labour. This remains necessary to cheapen the production process by unskilling jobs and to allow a better control of the labour force. But internal organizational divisions of labour are interlinked with broader processes of social division of labour driven by capitalist development. Communication technology has allowed global companies to outsource services to developing countries, dividing work within the organization's international structure through the exploitation of capitalism's uneven geography. Similarly, global commodities chains use this geographical division of labour to assemble different production phases in 'cheap labour' parts of the world. By contrast, high levels of consumption in the rich part of the world have made the work of migrants in cleaning, food, care, health, retail and distribution essential to these economies. The work of social reproduction, which is necessary to the reproduction of human beings and of workers but that is unproductive from an economic point of view, continues to be invisible and so the work of the women who continue to bear the responsibilities of this.

All these divisions of labour – whether based on gender, social status and class or uneven geographical development – have been historically used by capital in order to reproduce itself. As Marx pointed out, one thing is to highlight the economic importance of the division of labour in terms of speeding up processes and overall social productivity. But quite a different thing is to use the technical advantage coming from the division and cooperation of labour as an excuse to create or reproduce social patterns and power relationships based on exclusion and inequality.

MAURIZIO ATZENI

See also:

Alienation; Deskilling; Labour.

References and selected further readings

Atzeni, M. (ed.) (2014), *Workers and Labour in a Globalised Capitalism: Contemporary Themes and Theoretical Issues*, Basingstoke: Palgrave Macmillan.

Huws, U. (2014), *Labour in the Global Digital Economy: The Cybertariat Comes of Age*, New York: Monthly Review Press.

Mies, M. (2014), *Patriarchy and Accumulation on a World Scale: Women in the International Division of Labour*, London: Zed Books.

Mezzadra, S. and B. Neilson (2013), *Border as Method or, the Multiplication of Labour*, Durham and London: Duke University Press.

Thompson, P. (1989), *The Nature of Work: An Introduction to Debates on the Labour Process*, Basingstoke: Palgrave Macmillan.

Downsizing

Organizational downsizing can be defined as 'a planned set of organisational policies and practices aimed at workforce reduction with the goal of improving firm performance' (Datta et al., 2010, p. 282). Dealing with organizational downsizing and redundancy has been a growing demand on the HR departments' time and expertise following the great financial crisis of the past decade. One estimate of the job loss impact of the crisis was that more than seven million jobs were lost in the developed world (PwC, 2013). Other estimates suggest much higher level levels of redundancy, with one estimate of the US economy alone reporting that nearly nine million jobs were lost between 2007 and 2008 (Goodwin et al., 2014).

Effectively managing workforce reduction is thus of increasing importance in HRM practice, not least because of its greater scale and frequency but also because of the potentially serious negative effects of when it is badly handled. The mismanagement of workforce reduction can cause major damage to both the organization's employment and general business reputations. Damage to the former can seriously effect an organization's selection attractiveness and employment brand with potential future employees by producing an uncaring, 'hire and fire' image. Similarly, bad publicity over downsizing can cause customers to worry that the firm may go out of business or give rise to problems in the continuity or quality of supplies and services.

More recently, there have been increasing concerns about the broader impacts of downsizing on overall organizational effectiveness of the post-downsized 'anorexic organization'. The benefits that organizations claim to be seeking from downsizing typically centre on savings in labour costs, speedier decision-making, better communication, reduced product development time, enhanced involvement of employees and greater responsiveness, which all add up to improved organizational performance. However, research often suggests that such outcomes of downsizing are difficult to realize and that robust evidence for improved organizational performance as a result of downsizing is hard to find.

Critics of downsizing argue it can have a damaging effect on corporate performance. Paradoxically, restructuring has often been seen as a sign of 'corporate virility' and stock market prices have been suggested to rise in periods of high downsizing activity.

However, there is a suggestion from the downsizing literature that while there is some evidence in a few studies that downsizing improves market performance, the overall picture is that the large majority of studies find that downsizing announcements result in negative impacts on market returns (Datta et al., 2010). The research on downsizing and profitability is more mixed in the studies reported so far with limited evidence in some studies of improved profitability two to three years later but also evidence of reduced future profit. Other studies have examined the relationship between downsizing and organizational outcomes, such as sales growth, productivity, R&D investment, innovation, technological investment, etc., have also found mixed results. The overall picture from empirical research on organizations using lay-offs as a strategy for financial, market and organizational improvement is that in general most fail to achieve the positive benefits they seek and in many, performance continues to deteriorate, sometimes at an even faster rate than pre-downsizing.

The potential negative impact of downsizing is not restricted to organizational outcomes but has major consequences for employees. Downsizing and redundancy affects those who leave the organization in a range of ways. First, it is generally well-established that redundant employees have higher risk of long-term unemployment and lower-paid jobs on their return to the labour market if they can find work. It seems being made redundant marks you out as a 'labour market lemon' (Turnbull and Wass, 1997), sending a strong signal to other potential employers that the redundant employee is of inferior quality. Second, protracted unemployment has also well-known consequences of poor general health and particularly poor mental health as a result of the psychological distress of redundancy.

Downsizing has also has considerable consequences for the employees who remain in the organization. Such employees are by their very nature much more important to the employer, and often have to do more work, but are mainly overlooked in downsizing situations with many downsizing employers considering them lucky to have a job. The impact of downsizing on the remaining employees is such that commentators talk of 'survivor syndrome'. This is the term given to the collection of behaviours such as decreased motivation, morale and loyalty to the organization, and increased stress levels and scepticism that are exhibited by those who are still in employment following restructuring. Other symptoms of survivor syndrome are argued to include increased absenteeism, quit rates, job insecurity and decreased work quality, productivity and trust in management (Gandolfi, 2008). Downsizing survivor syndrome has often been referred to as a long-lasting 'aftershock' or 'aftermath' of the redundancy process. The work behaviours and attitudes of downsizing survivors are likely to be strongly dysfunctional for their personal work performance in a post downsizing period. It is perhaps no surprise then, as we discuss above, that the collective performance of organizations also often declines post-downsizing.

Tom Redman

References and selected further readings

Datta, D.K., J.P. Guthrie, D. Basuil and A. Pandey (2010), Causes and effects of employee downsizing: a review and synthesis, *Journal of Management*, **36**, pp. 281–348.

Gandolfi, F. (2008), Reflecting on downsizing: what have managers learned? *SAM Advanced Management Journal*, **73**(2), pp. 46–55.

Goodwin, N., J. Harris, J. Nelson, B. Roach and M. Torras (2014), *Macroeconomics in Context*, London: Routledge.

PwC (2013), *Being Better Informed Report*, London: PricewaterhouseCoopers.

Turnbull, P. and V. Wass (1997), Job insecurity and labour market lemons: the (mis)management of redundancy in steel making, coal mining, and port transport, *Journal of Management Studies*, **34**(1), pp. 27–51.

Early retirement

Early retirement is defined as retirement (i.e., leaving the labour market completely) before the age at which one would normally be eligible to draw the majority of one's pension. The marker for normal retirement age is the state pension age (SPA), it should be noted that many second-tier pension schemes in the UK and USA have pension ages below SPA, at least for the current cohort of older workers (OECD, 2003). Retiring at an occupational pension age below SPA is not normally considered 'early retirement'.

There are two sets of reasons why people retire early. First, they may be 'pulled' out of the labour market by financial or other incentives to leave work. An example of an early retirement incentive might be a 'top-up' by the employer of the employee's pension fund such that s/he can retire before reaching pension age without suffering a financial penalty. Older workers may also be 'pushed' into early retirement by the physical and mental strain associated with work. Often, early retirement is a result of a mix of both (Tillsley et al., 2000). For example, many occupational pension schemes have routes out of work for incapacity reasons, especially for workers in stressful or physically demanding work such as teaching or health services (Muller-Camen et al., 2011).

Throughout most of the second half of the twentieth century, most Western European countries had used state- and employer-sponsored early retirement routes as a way to manage unemployment. For example, the German government has sponsored since the 1990s a scheme known as Altersteilzeitgesetz (ATZ), part-time employment prior to retirement law, which allows employees in certain declining industries to be eligible for retiring two years before the state pension age (or working part-time for the four years before full retirement) so long as the older employee is replaced by a younger one (BMAS, 2010). Ebbinghaus (2001) coined the phrase 'collusion toward early retirement' to describe the attraction of such schemes for industrial social partners. For unions and government, early retirement was seen as a way to reduce youth unemployment while protecting the 'right to retire' of older workers (Flynn, 2014). For business, early retirement is a way to shed higher-paid employees with out-of-date skills. Generally, state-sponsored early retirement has been more prevalent in coordinated market economies in which employers are more constrained in being able to shed staff for performance reasons or through redundancy.

The idea that older workers who retire early 'make way' for younger ones to take their places has been challenged by academics who raise the 'lump of labour fallacy' argument. This argument raises two broad points: first, removing able employees from the labour market leads to lower national productivity, thus negatively affecting job growth. This is particularly the case in countries such as the UK, which face chronic skills shortages. Second, job attrition does not occur uniformly across the workforce, so employers who 'pension off' older workers in certain targeted occupations (for example middle management positions) rarely replace them with younger workers (Engelhardt, 2003).

MATT FLYNN

See also:
Downsizing; Older worker; Retirement.

References and selected further readings

BMAS (2010), *Altersteilzeitgesetz*, www.bmas.de/portal/9346/alttzg.html.
Ebbinghaus, B. (2001), When labour and capital collude: the political economy of early retirement in Europe, Japan and the USA, in *Comparing Welfare Capitalism: Social Policy and Political Economy in Europe, Japan and the USA*, London and New York: Routledge, pp. 76–104.
Engelhardt, G.V. (2003), Reasons for job change and the disposition of pre-retirement lump-sum pension distributions, *Economics Letters*, **81**(3), pp. 333–339.
Flynn, M. (2014), *Representing an Ageing Workforce: Challenges and Opportunities for Britain's Unions*, London: TUC.
Muller-Camen, M., R. Croucher, M. Flynn and H. Schroeder (2011), National institutions and employers' age management practices in Britain and Germany: 'path dependence' and option creation, *Human Relations*, **64**(4), pp. 507–530.
OECD (2003), *Ageing and Employment Policies/Vieillissement et politiques de l'emploi United Kingdom*, Paris: Organisation for Economic Co-operation and Development.
Tillsley, C., P. Taylor and J. Beausoleil (2000), *Factors Affecting Retirement*, London: DfEE.

E-learning

E-learning is a relatively new term introduced into the learning and development lexicon to reflect the growing use of information and communication technology (ICT) primarily, but not exclusively, in the delivery of learning and development. Such use is characterized by some researchers and writers as constituting a revolution in learning. A perhaps more considered view argues that it is more an evolution, since technology has always formed part of and supported learning delivery; a chalkboard or whiteboard and associated writing instruments, for example, were the advanced technologies of their time (Stewart, 2010). E-learning is also arguably only the latest approach to and method of delivering what is termed open and distance learning (ODL). Technologies utilized in ODL have always been those available at different points in time; for example, print media, radio, television, videos and CDs. More direct forerunners of e-learning include machine-based learning (MBL), computer-enhanced learning (CEL) and computer-based training (CBT). The latter two of these relied on ICT, as does e-learning. The most significant changes have been in the development and spread of the internet, especially Web 2.0, which enables direct creation of content by participants; software developments such as virtual learning platforms, streaming of visual and audio content and face-to-face interactions enabled by Skype; and hardware developments such as smartphones and pocket-sized tablets.

The major application of e-learning has been in supporting ODL. This has occurred in three contexts (Holden and Stewart, 2013). The first of these is formal education. ICT-based solutions delivering learning to individuals independent of time and space is associated with the global rise of higher education and the development of global education markets. What is generally referred to as 'online learning' now represents significant proportions of higher education delivery. The second context is work organization. This context is explained in part by the combination of ICT developments and globalization (Stewart, 2010). The latter phenomenon and the associated growth of multinational companies (MNCs) with geographically dispersed operations and staff mean that e-learning provides previously unavailable opportunities to reach large numbers of employees in many different locations with standardized learning. Employers with only domestic operations are also embracing e-learning. The third context of use is within societies and communities through state-sponsored and funded initiatives.

E-learning does have some limitations. An obvious one is access to hardware and another is the need for basic knowledge and skills to navigate advanced hardware and software (Sambrook, 2003). A third is the specialist skills needed to design and facilitate e-learning (Salmon, 2013).

JIM STEWART

See also:

Blended learning; Distance learning; Off-the-job learning; Online learning; Qualifications; Training.

References and selected further readings

Holden, R. and J. Stewart (2013), E-learning, in J. Gold, R. Holden, J. Stewart, P. Iles and J. Beardwell (eds), *Human Resource Development: Theory and Practice*, Basingstoke: Palgrave Macmillan.
Salmon, G. (2013), *E-Tivities: The Key to Active Online Learning*, 2nd edn, London: Routledge.
Sambrook, S. (2003), E-learning in small organizations, *Education and Training*, **45**(8/9), pp. 506–516.
Stewart, J. (2010), E-learning for managers and leaders, in J. Gold and R. Thorpe (eds), *Gower Handbook of Leadership and Management Development*, 5th edn, Farnham: Gower Publishing.

Electronic HRM

Electronic HRM (e-HRM) covers all possible integration mechanisms and contents between HRM and information technologies (IT) aiming at creating value within and across organizations for targeted employees and management. By definition, the e-HRM territory as a field of inquiry is of an interdisciplinary nature. It focuses on all integration mechanisms and all HRM content shared via IT that aim to make HRM processes distinctive and consistent, more efficient, high in quality, which creates long-term opportunities within and across organizations for targeted users.

Unlike many (IT) applications, e-HRM has a greater target scope in organizations involving up to 90 per cent of all employees within a firm. The second aspect relates to differences in technological cognitive frames of user-groups associated with the different intended goals of e-HRM, which service specific target groups or tasks and processes to be performed with e-HRM. Third is the balance between the mandatory and voluntarily use of e-HRM. For HR professionals, operating with e-HRM may be a part of their everyday work routine. Employees however, may only update their address, bank information or family status (through an e-HR portal) once or twice a year. The fourth important aspect is the potential misinterpretation of e-HRM which is grounded in a firm's business case based on the dominance of the voluntary use of e-HRM. For example, an employee is encouraged (not obliged) to fill in online documents that are later taken into HR transactions as a mandated process. This brings significant cost savings to the business due to the voluntary use of e-HRM processes. The final difference derives from all of the above. If the use of e-HRM is not necessarily binding for all groups of users, and different target groups develop their own ways of dealing with e-HRM, then organizations often face the situation where an individual's technological enthusiasm and decision to first use e-HRM is different from the decision to enact and continuously work with e-HRM. While e-HRM usage is directly related to the job tasks of HR professionals, line managers and employees are expected to use e-HRM for reasons other than direct job-related outcomes. Therefore employees will not be expected to use e-HRM that often, which may result in them having to repetitively rediscover the ways to perform seemingly simple HR tasks within the complicated technology.

TANYA BONDAROUK

See also:

Human resource information systems; Human resource management.

References and selected further readings

Bondarouk, T. and E. Furtmueller (2012), Electronic human resource management: four decades of empirical evidence, *Best Paper Proceedings of the Academy of Management Meeting 2012*, Boston, August 3–7.
Bondarouk, T. and R. Harms (2009), *Does E-HRM Appropriation Lead to Improvements in HRM Services? Quantitative Results from a Public Sector Organization*, paper presented at the 2009 Annual Academy of Management Meeting, Chicago.
Marler, J.H. and J.H. Dulebohn (2005), A model of employee self-service technology acceptance, *Research in Personnel and Human Resources Management*, **24**, pp. 137–180.
Marler, J. and S. Fisher (2013), An evidence-based review of e-HRM and strategic human resource management, *Human Resource Management Review*, **22**, pp. 18–36.
Ruël, H.J.M., T.V. Bondarouk and J.C. Looise (2004), *E-HRM: Innovation or Irritation? An Exploration of Web-Based Human Resource Management in Large Companies*, Utrecht: Lemma.
Strohmeier, S. (2007), Research in e-HRM: review and implications, *HRM Review*, **17**(1), pp. 19–37.

Electronic recruitment

Electronic recruitment (e-recruitment) includes all recruitment related practices carried out by the use of various electronic means. Online, internet or web-based recruiting are used to identify and attract potential employees. An e-recruitment system can be also seen as a back-office system for administrating the recruitment process, and is normally designed to allow applicants to submit their data electronically.

The traditional, face-to-face recruitment process varies in complexity and degree of difficulty depending on the recruitment objectives and the recruitment sources chosen. Through the years, external recruitment instruments included newspaper advertisements, private and public employment agencies, internet job boards, corporate websites, employee referrals, colleges and universities, employment agencies, job fairs, etc. The core of e-recruitment includes automation of the entire recruitment process, sophisticated online screening systems, automated pre-screening, communicating with applicants and automated long-term candidate-relationship management.

Traditional recruitment and e-recruitment cover similar tasks and steps that are performed sequentially to fulfil organizational and HRM goals include identification, attraction, processing incoming applicants and communicating with them. The e-recruitment process also serves a marketing purpose of selling jobs through building a company's reputation, internet communications and relationship marketing. E-recruitment has changed face-to-face recruitment from a batch to a continuous 'just-in-time' mode, with some activities being performed concurrently.

With some caution, empirical studies have reported changes in the performance based on automated recruitment practices, such as the shorter time-to-hire, larger pools of candidates, convenience for recruiters and applicants, and even improvements in the quality of job candidates. The question remains, how scholars and practitioners should measure the success of e-recruitment. Probably, e-recruitment research and practice might be useful to consider from a services point of view, assessing its performance based on connections between employee satisfaction, the size of an organization, the number of e-recruitment practices, the extent of use and the integration of e-recruiting and the overall perceived quality of personally tailored feedback to applicants, can affect their reactions in the application process. Examination of how tailored feedback influences applicant attraction, self-selection and associated financial outcomes for an organization can also be measured. E-recruitment may support diversity management in organizations by enabling the examination of demographic characteristics of individuals recruited online, determining yield ratios, retention and developing turnover measures. Consequently, in the future, outcome measures such as job performance, job satisfaction and organizational commitment could then be compared between individuals who were recruited online with those recruited via traditional newspaper advertisements, career fairs or personal recommendations.

TANYA BONDAROUK

See also:

Electronic HRM; Human resource information systems.

References and selected further readings

Braddy, P.W., A.W. Meade, J.J. Michael, and J.W. Fleenor (2009), Internet recruiting: effects of website content features on viewers' perceptions of organizational culture, *International Journal of Selection and Assessment*, **17**(1), pp. 19–34.

Cappelli, P. (2001), Making the most of on-line recruiting, *Harvard Business Review*, **79**(3), pp. 139–146.

Holm, A. (2012), E-recruitment: towards an ubiquitous recruitment process and candidate relationship management, *Zeitschrift für Personalforschung (ZfP)*, **26**(3), pp. 241–259.

Lee, I. (2007), An architecture for a next-generation holistic e-recruiting system, *Communications of the ACM*, **50**(7), pp. 81–85.

Wolfswinkel, J.F., E. Furtmueller and C.P.M. Wilderom (2013), Using grounded theory as a method for rigorously reviewing literature, *European Journal of Information Systems*, **22**, pp. 45–55.

Emotional intelligence

Emotional intelligence (EI) is defined as actual *or* self-perceived abilities in processing emotional information. The abilities in question typically pertain to perceiving, using, understanding and regulating emotions. The difference between actual and self-perceived abilities is crucial; it locates EI in independent scientific domains. Conceived as actual ability, EI marks a factor in human intelligence theory. Relevant performance-based tests employ scoring protocols allowing for an objective determination of correct or incorrect responses (e.g., the MSCEIT). Conceptualized as self-perceived abilities (or trait EI), it is embedded in personality theory. These traits reflect behavioral preferences rather than abilities. Trait EI measures often use Likert-type scales (e.g., the TEIQue). Distinguishing ability and trait EI is practically relevant for HRM researchers and practitioners, especially with regard to EI interventions: ability EI increases with age, but the evidence for trait EI is less persuasive. In this light, ability EI-based interventions would seem preferable, since scores are more likely to increase, although other issues remain, as suggested below.

In terms of research, one key issue of ability EI has been its predictive validity over and above personality and cognitive ability. Research suggests that ability EI can predict important outcomes, such as leadership emergence, job performance, life satisfaction and wellbeing, albeit some scholars remain unconvinced. However, recent debates have moved toward questioning the linear assumptions behind ability EI (i.e., that EI is *always* related in a linear fashion to 'positive' outcomes). For one thing, questions are asked whether there can be too much EI, implying a curvilinear relationship with outcome variables (e.g., mental health). For another, some scholars suggest that ability EI might be an example of a value-driven construct definition (as imposed by researchers), where the processes that underlie ability EI (i.e., as captured in the four abilities mentioned above) are conflated with its outcomes. Specifically, the definition of ability EI is often followed by the annex 'to promote emotional and intellectual growth'. Thus, research on the 'dark side' of ability EI (e.g., when individuals use their emotional abilities manipulatively) only emerged recently. Doubt also persists about the understanding of emotional-cognitive process underlying ability EI. For instance, little is known *why* exactly ability EI increases with age. This lack of understanding affects HRM researchers and practitioners wishing to develop EI. Interventions need to be sensitive to how these processes can be influenced to obtain a desired change in a given outcome variable (e.g., stress resilience).

The domain of trait EI features less controversy. There are several validated questionnaires available for research purposes and practical applications in the workplace. Trait EI has demonstrated incremental validity over and above existing personality measures to predict several work-related outcomes, such as life satisfaction, rumination, coping styles and job performance. It also negatively correlates with alcohol consumption. Less is known whether trait EI can be developed and whether this affects various outcomes. While some studies suggest that trait EI interventions can be successful (i.e., increased trait EI improved wellbeing, but not work performance), other studies found that trait EI does not correlate with age. Thus, it is not clear yet whether trait EI interventions have lasting effects on individuals. No matter how EI is measured, rigorously designed studies have repeatedly refuted popular claims about the magnitude of what EI can predict.

DIRK LINDEBAUM

See also:

Personality traits; Stress; Wellbeing.

References and selected further readings

Antonakis, J., N.M. Ashkanasy and M.T. Dasborough (2009), Does leadership need emotional intelligence? *The Leadership Quarterly*, **20**(2), pp. 247–261.

Lindebaum, D. (2009), Rhetoric or remedy? A critique on developing emotional intelligence, *Academy of Management Learning and Education*, **8**(2), pp. 225–237.

Lindebaum, D. (2015), A qualitative study of emotional intelligence and its underlying processes and outcomes in management studies, in C.E.J. Härtel, W.J. Zerbe and N.M. Ashkanasy (eds), *Research on Emotion in Organizations*, Bingley: Emerald.

Lindebaum, D. and J.P. Jordan (2014), When it can be good to feel bad and bad to feel good: exploring asymmetries in workplace emotional outcomes, *Human Relations*, **67**(9), pp. 1037–1050.

Mayer, J.D., R.D. Roberts and S.G. Barsade (2008), Human abilities: emotional intelligence, *Annual Review of Psychology*, **59**, pp. 507–536.

Petrides, K.V., R. Pita and F. Kokkinaki (2007), The location of trait emotional intelligence in personality factor space, *British Journal of Psychology*, **98**(2), pp. 273–289.

Salovey, P. and J.D. Mayer (1990), Emotional intelligence, *Imagination, Cognition and Personality*, **9**, pp. 185–211.

Emotional labour

The term 'emotional labour' was introduced by Arlie Hochschild in her seminal book, *The Managed Heart: Commercialization of Human Feeling*. Detailing the work of flight attendants and debt collectors, *The Managed Heart* highlighted that, along with physical labour, the workers were required to perform emotional labour. Emotional labour describes the effort made by workers to manage their feelings in order to create the desired emotional state in themselves, and in others, with the express aim of aligning with organizational display rules and fulfilling their work role requirements (Hochschild, 1983). Hochschild argues that emotional labour involves the transmutation and commercialization of workers' 'private sphere' feelings into a commodity that is consumed in the 'public sphere', and can make workers feel inauthentic and estranged from their own emotions.

Workers can enact emotional labour in two ways: deep acting and surface acting. Deep acting sees workers regulate their own feelings to match their emotional display. If successful, this process of regulation can result in a fusion of 'real' and acted emotions. Surface acting involves workers suppressing their personal feelings and faking an appropriate emotional display. Hochschild argues that this behavioural compliance results in ultimate alienation, and has been linked with emotional exhaustion and burnout. In either case, deep acting or surface acting, Hochschild's thesis emphasizes the shift of control of worker's emotions from the individual to the organization and the potential human cost of this process (Brook, 2009).

Yet, critics have accused Hochschild of generating a false distinction between the private self and the commodified public self, and in so doing producing a one-dimensional view of emotion at work. They have questioned if the commodification of emotions is intrinsically alienating, arguing that for some workers, customer interaction increases job satisfaction (Ashforth and Humphrey 1993). Korczynski (2002) proposes that it is the lack of discretion over the performance of emotional labour, rather than emotional labour itself, that is most detrimental. Bolton (2005) argues that emotional labour is appropriate for describing some but not all practices involving the management of emotion at work and suggests the term inadequately captures the complex and sometimes contradictory nature of workplace emotionality. Bolton recommends that the examination of emotion at work needs to consider the factors that motivate workers to enact feeling rules: remembering that workers' emotional displays are embedded in social situations and interpersonal relationships that, in turn, are set within wider institutional practices, hierarchical power relationships and societal roles.

CLARE BUTLER

See also:
Aesthetic labour; Burnout; Emotional intelligence; Impression management.

References and selected further readings
Ashforth, B.E. and R.H. Humphrey (1993), Emotional labor in service roles: the influence of identity, *Academy of Management Review*, **18**(1), pp. 88–115.
Bolton, S.C. (2005), *Emotion Management in the Workplace*, London: Palgrave Macmillan.
Brook, P. (2009), The alienated heart: Hochschild's 'emotional labour' thesis and the anticapitalist politics of alienation, *Capital and Class*, **33**(2), pp. 7–31.
Hochschild, A.R. (1983), *The Managed Heart: Commercialization of Human Feeling*, London: University of California Press.
Korczynski, M. (2002), *Human Resource Management in Service Work*, Basingstoke: Palgrave.

Employability

The concept of employability has become ubiquitous in policy debates relating to the labour market and education. Although the precise meaning of employability has been interpreted in a variety of ways (McQuaid and Lindsay, 2006), in broad terms it refers to the extent to which individuals are equipped to participate successfully in the labour market. It captures the idea that workers should take responsibility for equipping themselves with new skills, knowledge and attributes so as to maximize their chances of obtaining and retaining employment in organizational and labour market contexts that are assumed to be less stable than in the past.

The importance that policymakers have come to attach to employability as a determinant of a country's employment rate reflects the wider shift in labour market policy orthodoxy that took place in Western economies after the 1970s. The Keynesian emphasis on aggregate demand as the key determinant of employment, which dominated policy thinking from the 1940s onwards, gave way to a focus on supply-side phenomena and a belief that the root causes of unemployment should be understood in 'individualistic and behavioural terms' (Peck and Theodore, 2000, p. 729). Governments have thus exhorted workers to enhance their employability while simultaneously linking entitlements to unemployment benefits more closely to unemployed workers' willingness to actively search for work and accept available jobs.

Key international bodies, such as the World Bank and the Organisation for Economic Co-operation and Development (OECD), have encouraged governments to promote employability and it has been a prominent theme in the European Commission's social policy programmes since the 1990s. A key assumption underpinning the Commission's 'flexicurity' agenda, which encourages European Union (EU) member countries to pursue policies that deliver labour market flexibility while maintaining a basic level of security for workers, is that globalization and technological change have rendered job security unachievable. The objective for European policymakers should therefore be to promote employment security – enabling workers to remain in employment, but not necessarily with their current employer (European Commission, 2007).

The exact meaning of employability, its proper place in labour market and education policies and the means by which employability might be ensured continues to be debated. The recent economic crisis has demonstrated that 'employability' does not necessarily lead to employment security. Many academics have argued that greater attention should be paid to the factors that influence labour demand (e.g., McQuaid and Lindsay, 2006), while others, drawing on the work of Amartya Sen, have advocated that policymakers should promote workers' 'capabilities', providing collective supports aimed at empowering workers and increasing their freedom to select appropriate labour market pathways (see Zimmermann, 2014).

JASON HEYES

References and selected further readings

European Commission (2007), *Towards Common Principles of Flexicurity: More and Better Jobs Through Flexibility and Security*, Luxembourg: Office for Official Publications of the European Communities.

Heyes, J. and H. Rainbird (2009), Vocational education and training, in M. Gold (ed.), *Employment Policy in the European Union: Origins, Themes and Prospects*, Basingstoke: Palgrave Macmillan.

McQuaid, R.W. and C. Lindsay (2006), The concept of employability, in R.W. McQuaid, A. Green and M. Dawson (eds), *Employability and Local Labour Market Policy*, New York: Routledge.

Peck, J. and N. Theodore (2000), Beyond 'employability', *Cambridge Journal of Economics*, **24**, 729–749.

Zimmermann, B. (2014), From flexicurity to capabilities: in search of professional development, in M. Keune and A. Serrano (eds), *Deconstructing Flexicurity and Developing Alternative Approaches: Towards New Concepts and Approaches for Employment and Social Policy*, New York: Routledge.

Employee

Section 230(1) and (2) of the Employment Rights Act 1996 (ERA) and section 295(1) of the Trade Union and Labour Relations (Consolidation) Act 1992 both prescribe that an employee is 'an individual who has entered into or works under (or, where the employment has ceased, worked under) a contract of employment', which is then defined as a 'contract of service or of apprenticeship'. The common law goes on to explore the ingredients of the contract of service and prescribes three irreducible criteria. First, the purported employer must enjoy the right to control the work done by the individual. Second, the individual must agree that, in consideration of a wage or other remuneration, he will provide his own work and skill in the performance of some service for the purported employer on a personal basis. Finally, the arrangement struck between the purported employer and employee must be such that the former makes an ongoing commitment to provide a reasonable and minimum amount of work in the future and pay for it with a corresponding obligation imposed on the latter to perform that reasonable and minimum amount of work when offered in the future. As such, in order to qualify as an employee, as a bare minimum, the individual must be engaged on the basis of a contract, involving the provision of personal services to the purported employer, whereby the latter has the power to control the work of the former and both are subject to ongoing mutual obligations.

The significance of the concept of 'employee' lies in the fact that such an individual is entitled to the benefit of all statutory employment rights, such as the right to protection from unfair dismissal under Part X of the ERA, the right to receive a statutory redundancy payment in terms of Part XI of the ERA, the right to be paid the national minimum wage under the National Minimum Wage Act 1998, and the right to holiday leave and pay under the Working Time Regulations 1998. In recent years, there have been many debates concerning the proper criteria that ought to be applied for the establishment of employment status. In particular, it is argued that the concept is ill-equipped to cope with the myriad of ways in which enterprises contract for the individual supply of labour; for example, the growth in self-employment, casualization, and flexibilization of the labour market, with the exponential surge in atypical working relationships, such as zero-hours contract working, part-time working, fixed-term working, casual working, agency working, etc. In response to these changes in the labour market, much of the literature focussing on the 'employee' construct addresses whether the contractual model underpinning employment status ought to be abandoned (Hepple, 1986; Wedderburn, 1987), or retained, subject to important modifications (Freedland, 2003).

DAVID CABRELLI

See also:

Contract of employment; Temporary worker; Worker.

References and selected further readings

Freedland, M. (2003), *The Personal Employment Contract*, Oxford: Oxford University Press.
Hepple, B. (1986), Restructuring employment rights, *Industrial Law Journal*, **15**, pp. 68–83.
Wedderburn, B. (1987), From here to autonomy? *Industrial Law Journal*, **16**, pp. 1–29.

Employee assistance programmes

Employee assistance programmes (EAPs) are voluntary counselling and health promotion initiatives used by employees and their families to address issues such as addiction, separation and divorce, bereavement, mental health and concerns arising from the nature of work and the workplace. EAP emerged at the turn of the twentieth century in North America as a response to industrialization, beginning as welfare capitalism, a management-inspired movement whose goal was to improve workplace conditions in order to increase productivity and minimize unionization. As welfare capitalism was fading during the 1930s, Alcoholism Anonymous arose and as part of its mission assisted men in industry with alcohol problems initiating the Occupational Alcoholism Program (OAP) movement. OAPs functioned primarily through the efforts of volunteers with recovery histories referring fellow employees to AA meetings or internal occupational health professionals. The North American labour movement in conjunction with the United Way (UW) also trained volunteer union counsellors to act as liaisons between workers and UW agencies. Occupational assistance was dominated by volunteers until the 1970s, when helping began to become more professionalized and the broader range of behavioural issues began to be identified as being more problematic than alcohol abuse in the workplace. James Wrich is credited with coining the term EAP to reflect this broader approach. EAP development witnessed an influx of counselling professionals some who worked for organizations and some who worked as external for-profit EAP providers. EAPs expanded the OAP mandate to include entire families and what had been the purview of large organizations became a standard employee benefit. External service provision led to competition not only between internal and externally located counsellors but also directly between EAP vendors vying for customers. A major impact of the commodification of EAP was the capping of services such that no longer could an employee or family member receive the needed counselling but now they were limited to a set number of sessions, typically six or less as negotiated with the vendor. Which is better, internal or external service provision underscored the major debate of EAP: who is served? A core question underscoring EAP is whether it is an employee benefit or a means of social control, which was further intensified when some programmes added drug-testing as an outcome measure. EAP is an unregulated practice, with no mandatory accreditation body. While the majority of counsellors belong to professional associations and voluntary bodies exist, the provision of corporate services and contracts comes under no mandated guidelines of practice. Despite distinct limits in the nature of EAP it does provides access to on-demand counselling, often with 48 hours to a segment of the population that otherwise not be able to afford or readily access this resource.

RICK CSIERNIK

See also:
Occupational health; Welfare; Wellbeing.

References and selected further readings

Csiernik, R. (2014), *Workplace Wellness*, Toronto: Canadian Scholars Press.
Garza, G. (2014), *Occupational Social Work: An International Perspective*, Monterrey: Universidad Autonoma de Nuevo León.
Kurzman, P. and R. Maiden (2010), *Union Contributions to Labor Welfare Policy and Practice*, New York: Routledge.

Employee engagement

Employee engagement is an umbrella term that is used to encompass the constructs of work engagement, role engagement and personal engagement as well as employee engagement itself, or even simply 'engagement'. There is no consistent use of terminology or single agreed definition. Broadly, approaches to engagement can be classified either as a psychological state, 'being engaged', or as an approach to managing employees, 'doing engagement' (Truss et al., 2013).

- **Being engaged:** the social psychologist William Kahn (1990) is widely recognized as the founding father of the engagement field. He referred to personal engagement with work as the cognitive, emotional and physical expression of one's authentic self when performing work tasks. Kahn argued that individuals will express themselves fully and thus experience high levels of engagement when they find their work meaningful, they feel that it is safe to be themselves and they are emotionally and physically available to be engaged. However, among the academic community, it is the work of the Utrecht Group led by Wilmar Schaufeli that has come to dominate the field with their tripartite definition of engagement as 'a positive, fulfilling work related state of mind that is characterized by vigor, dedication and absorption' (Schaufeli et al., 2002, p. 74). Others have argued that employee engagement is a composite positive attitude comprising general satisfaction with such aspects of work as leadership, job design and management style (Harter et al., 2002).

- **Doing engagement:** recently, employee engagement has been referred to as a unitarist form of employment relations practice associated with high levels of involvement and participation, which may have alternative variants such as 'soft' employee-centred approaches and 'hard' performance focused approaches (Jenkins and Delbridge, 2013). This perspective on engagement is akin to the popular use of the term among the practitioner community (e.g., www.engagefor-success.org).

Employee engagement is a topic that has gained significant popularity among practitioners following evidence emanating largely from consultancy firms that highly engaged workers are likely to perform better, take less sick leave and enjoy higher levels of personal wellbeing (www.engageforsuccess.org). However, the evidence base surrounding engagement 'as practice' on which this is founded is highly controversial. Guest (2013), for example, has pointed out that some of the popular measures used by consultancy firms lack validity and reliability and may amount to no more than old wine in new bottles. Engagement in this sense therefore risks being dismissed as the latest management fad.

Engagement has also become an important topic amongst the academic community; one recent evidence synthesis found over 700,000 published items relating to the topic (Truss et al., 2015). Here, the field has been described as emergent and characterized by a proliferation of competing definitions and measures that makes it difficult to form a clear overview of the quality of the evidence base. Although the predominance of the Utrecht definition and measure of engagement and its use in a wide range of countries have been widely acknowledged, some have suggested that uncertainties remain over the robustness of the three-factor structure of the measure and its applicability across different cultural settings (Wefald et al., 2012).

Alongside the debate over how to define and measure engagement, some have also argued that although engagement is normally presented as a uniformly positive psychological state, there may be downsides as well, such as the risk of burnout, which have not yet been fully explored.

A further complication is the recent emergence of a body of literature from the HRM community that defines engagement as a variant of the employment relationship. This small collection of studies uses qualitative data to interrogate engagement from a critical HRM perspective and points out the potential power political dimensions of imposing engagement strategies on the workforce (Truss et al., 2013).

Catherine Bailey (née Truss)

See also:

Employee involvement; Industrial relations; Job satisfaction; Participation.

References and selected further readings

Guest, D. (2013), Employee engagement: fashionable fad or long-term fixture?, in C. Truss, K. Alfes, R. Delbridge, A. Shantz and E.C. Soane (eds), *Employee Engagement in Theory and Practice*, London: Routledge.

Harter, J.K., F.L. Schmidt and T.L. Hayes (2002), Business-unit-level relationship between employee satisfaction, employee engagement, and business outcomes: a meta-analysis, *Journal of Applied Psychology*, **87**, pp. 268–279.

Jenkins, S. and R. Delbridge (2013), Context matters: examining 'soft' and 'hard' approaches to employee engagement in two workplaces, *International Journal of Human Resource Management*, **24**(14), pp. 2670–2691.

Kahn, W.A. (1990), Psychological conditions of personal engagement and disengagement at work, *Academy of Management Journal*, **33**, pp. 692–724.

Schaufeli, W.B., M. Salanova, V. Gonzalez-Roma and A.B. Bakker (2002), The measurement of engagement and burnout: a two sample confirmatory factor analytic approach, *Journal of Happiness Studies*, **3**, pp. 71–92.

Truss, C., E. Soane, A. Shantz, K. Alfes and R. Delbridge (2013), Employee engagement, organisational performance and individual wellbeing: exploring the evidence, developing the theory, *International Journal of Human Resource Management*, **24**(14), pp. 2657–2669.

Truss, C., A. Madden, K. Alfes, D. Robinson, L. Fletcher, J. Holmes, J. Buzzeo and G. Currie (2015), *Evaluating the Evidence on Employee Engagement and its Potential Benefits to NHS Staff: A Narrative Synthesis of the Literature*, Southampton: NIHR.

Wefald, A.J., M.J. Mills, M.R. Smith and R.G. Downey (2012), A comparison of three job engagement measures: examining their factorial and criterion-related validity, *Applied Psychology: Health and Well-Being*, **4**(1), pp. 67–90.

Employee involvement

Direct employee involvement (EI) refers to formal and informal consultation and communication practices – such as workforce meetings – that involve individual employees and work-teams. It can be contrasted with industrial democracy, which assumes employees have a *right* to exercise voice through their representatives, while EI works on the principle that employers *choose* to involve employees because it is likely to improve organizational performance and employee wellbeing (Wilkinson et al., 2010). It has become increasingly widespread since the 1980s, coinciding with a decline in representative participation and union coverage in most developed economies. In the UK the 2011 WERS survey found that 95 per cent of workplaces with at least 20 employees held regular workforce meetings, up from 35 per cent in 1990.

Formal direct EI comprises downward communications and upward problem-solving (Wilkinson et al., 2013). The former includes practices such as team briefing, town hall meetings, newsletters and blogs, all of which are aim to ensure employees find out what is happening at their workplace and, ideally, across the wider organization. Team briefing, for example, typically involves line managers passing information to their teams about how the business is doing, compiling rosters and social events. In customer-facing organizations, such meetings could occur daily or weekly while in offices or factories they would typically take place every month or quarter. They often allow time for questions and discussion about the issues raised. Upward problem-solving includes practices such as quality improvement groups and engagement surveys, with the latter having grown significantly in usage during the last decade. The former provide opportunities for employees to contribute to discussions at workplace level, perhaps via multidisciplinary groups, to improve work processes by tapping into a range of ideas. The latter offer less chance to put forward ideas but they do provide a check on how employees feel about their line manager, various aspects of their work and the organization as a whole.

Informal EI refers to ad hoc interactions between line managers and their staff that encourage information-passing and consultation on an ad hoc basis. Despite receiving only limited attention, research suggests informal EIP is important not just in small firms where formal practices are less likely but also in larger organizations to lubricate trust and commitment (Townsend et al., 2012; Marchington and Suter, 2013). The distinction between informal and formal EIP is not totally clear but the former is more common in organizations where line managers are expected to be accessible and responsive to their teams such as in hotels, restaurants and retail outlets.

It is important to measure the extent to which EI is embedded within organizations because this can provide an evaluation of its effectiveness (Cox et al., 2006). *Breadth* refers to the number of discrete practices used and, while it is possible that different EIP practices contradict one another, the prevailing view is that impact is greater if multiple channels are deployed. Moreover, these give employees the chance to be involved in different ways because information received from line managers stimulates ideas for problem-solving groups and gives employees greater confidence to speak up at meetings. Assessing *depth* is more complex and requires careful analysis of how EI operates in practice. Drawing on several studies, Marchington (2015) argues this depends on four criteria: degree of proactive management support for EI; opportunities for employees to contribute to decisions; relevance and meaningfulness of subject matter; and regularity and sustainability of each EI practice. This shows depth can vary considerably between organizations, as well as over time.

Breadth and depth of EI is shaped by a number of forces at and beyond organization level, the precise mix depending on the type of economy and the role government plays in regulating employment relations. In liberal market economies (LMEs), regulatory space is filled by professional associations, management consultants and organizations with a specific interest in EI such as Engage for Success in the UK. In some LMEs, temporary support for partnership has helped to develop EI within the context of a commitment to mutuality. At organization level, breadth and depth is shaped by product and labour market forces, level of union organization, size of the organization and of individual establishments, strength of organization culture and role of line managers in promoting EI. While forces beyond the organization influence breadth, depth is shaped more by senior managerial commitment to sustaining EI (Marchington, 2015).

MICK MARCHINGTON

See also:
Joint consultation; Partnership.

References and selected further readings

Cox, A., S. Zagelmeyer and M. Marchington (2006), Embedding employee involvement and participation at work, *Human Resource Management Journal*, **16**(3), pp. 250–267.
Marchington, M. (2015), Analysing the forces shaping employee involvement and participation in liberal market economies, *Human Resource Management Journal*, **25**(1), pp. 1–18.
Marchington, M. and J. Suter (2013), Where informality really matters: patterns of employee involvement and participation in a non-union firm, *Industrial Relations*, **52**(S1), pp. 284–313.
Townsend, K., A. Wilkinson and J. Burgess (2012), Filling the gaps: patterns of formal and informal participation, *Economic and Industrial Democracy*, **34**(2), pp. 337–354.
Wilkinson, A., P. Gollan, M. Marchington and D. Lewin (eds) (2010), *The Oxford Handbook of Participation in Organisations*, Oxford: Oxford University Press.
Wilkinson, A., T. Dundon and M. Marchington (2013), Participation and involvement, in S. Bach and M. Edwards (eds), *Managing Human Resources*, London, Blackwell.

Employee share ownership plans

Employee share ownership provides for employee participation in enterprise results in an indirect way, either by receiving dividends or by the appreciation of employee-owned capital, or a combination of both.

There are several types of employee share ownership plan (ESOP). The first is the award of free shares to employees. Alternatively, share ownership plans may provide for employees to purchase shares in the company, possibly on advantageous terms. In some plans employers may match the purchases made by employees. There may be a link with pensions in that the share purchases may be part of larger and wider portfolios of investments made by the employee in conjunction with their employer (as in 401k plans in the USA).

In some cases, shares are held collectively for employees, and are not distributed to individual employees. In this instance, the dividends received by the trust are then distributed to employees as a profit-share. Alternatively, shares may initially be held collectively but then distributed to individual employees over time. This is typically what occurs in ESOPs. In this form of share ownership, shares are initially passed to an employee benefits trust, financed either by loans, profits, or a gift from the company owner. These types of ESOPs have acquired a specific meaning in the USA, where they have grown tremendously over the past 30 years, largely as a result of favourable tax considerations for companies that establish them.

Another form of share acquisition is the stock option plan. Employees may be granted the right to acquire shares at some point in the future. Although this does not necessarily lead to ownership, because the employee may simultaneously exercise the option and sell the shares, in most all-employee plans of this sort, some employees will exercise and hold. Further variants include producer cooperatives, in which all the firm's shares (if the provided legal form) are collectively owned by its workforce.

Government regulation mainly consists of regulation of the amount of contributions by employees and employers, eligibility criteria to prevent discrimination, and retention periods for tax exemption. For promotion of savings, in some countries governments provide for bonuses when there is defined contribution from employees.

Since the 1970s, a large number of studies investigated the effect of share plans on the favourable attitudes and behaviour of employees as well as the organizational performance. A majority of studies found favourable effects of share plans on identification, satisfaction, commitment, turnover and productivity. This relationship is stronger when there is a more widespread distribution, i.e., a majority of the employees have a stake in the company. Problem of causality remains because most studies are cross-sectional, i.e., done at a single point in time.

Erik Poutsma

See also:

Financial participation; Profit-related pay and gainsharing; Profit-sharing.

References and selected further readings

Kaarsemaker, E.C.A., A. Pendleton and F. Poutsma (2010), Employee share ownership, in A. Wilkinson, P.J. Gollan, M. Marchington and D. Lewin (eds), *The Oxford Handbook of Participation in Organizations*, Oxford: Oxford University Press, pp. 315–337.

Poutsma, E. and E. Kaarsemaker (2015), Added value of employee financial participation, in M. Andresen and C. Nowak (eds), *Human Resource Management Practices, Management for Professionals*, New York: Springer, pp. 181–196.

Employee voice

Employee voice concerns the ways and means through which employees attempt to have a say and potentially influence organizational affairs about issues that affect their work and the interests of the organization. This can involve a variety of voice mechanisms (e.g., formal and informal, direct and indirect, union and non-union). In general, employee voice is about how employees are able to have a say over work activities and decisions within the organization in which they work, regardless of the institutional channel through which it operates. Voice encompasses individual discretionary employee behaviours but also includes the ways in which employees challenge managerial behaviour, either individually or through collective behaviours and mechanisms, and also includes self-determining efforts by employees to identify themselves in ways that are set aside from the interests of the firm (Wilkinson et al., 2014). The term 'voice' is weaker than that of other related terms such as 'participation' because it does not denote influence or power-sharing and may thus be at times no more than trickle-up voice.

The way voice initiatives actually work may depend on whether participants perceive them as faddish or as being embedded within the organization. Clearly, forms of employee voice can differ in the extent they influence management. Some forms are purposely designed to give workers a voice but only a modest role in decision-making, while others are intended to give the workforce a more significant say in organizational governance.

Most studies focus on managers as policy actors operating within a framework of legislation or public policy prescriptions. Management plays a key part in adapting and interpreting legislation, corporate initiatives and management fashions to the workplace. In many European countries, the state plays a role in supporting employee voice. Other countries, including the USA and Australia, have much less emphasis on statutory provisions for employee voice with more emphasis on the preferences of managers and unions to establish their own arrangements.

We also see the growth and importance of informal voice – that is non-programmed interactions between managers and workers – which provides opportunities for information-passing and consultation. Most employees appear to want the opportunity to have a say and to contribute to the work issues that matter to them, and they also want a menu of voice choices rather than a single channel: in short varieties of voice. However, the existence of voice schemes may tell us little about the quality of the employee voice process.

ADRIAN WILKINSON

See also:

Communication; Consultation; Employee involvement; Empowerment.

References and selected further readings

Barry, M. and A. Wilkinson (2015), Pro-social or pro management: a critique of the conception of employee voice as a pro-social behaviour within organisational behaviour, *British Journal of Industrial Relations*.

Dundon, T., A. Wilkinson, M. Marchington and P. Ackers (2004), The meanings and purpose of employee voice, *International Journal of Human Resource Management*, **15**(6), pp. 1150–1171.

Freeman, R., P. Boxall and P. Haynes (eds) (2007), *What Workers Say: Employee Voice in the Anglo-American World*, Ithaca: Cornell University Press.

Marchington, M. (2008), Employee voice systems, in P. Boxall, J. Purcell and P. Wright (eds), *The Oxford Handbook of Human Resource Management*, Oxford: Oxford University Press.

Mowbray, P., A. Wilkinson and H. Tse (2015), An integrative review of employee voice: identifying the common conceptualisation and research agenda, *International Journal of Management Reviews*, **17**(3), pp. 382–400.

Wilkinson, A. and C. Fay (2011), New times for employee voice? *Human Resource Management*, **20**(1), pp. 65–74.

Wilkinson, A., J. Donaghey, T. Dundon and R. Freeman (eds) (2014), *The Handbook of Research on Employee Voice: Participation and Involvement in the Workplace*, Cheltenham: Edward Elgar.

Employer branding

The notion of an employer brand is a fairly recent phenomenon. The assumption is that employers with a positive brand image, as a good employer will find it easier to attract and retain good quality employees. The CIPD factsheet on the topic describes employer branding as follows:

> The term 'employer branding' describes how an organization markets what it has to offer to potential and existing employees. Marketers have developed techniques to help attract customers, communicate with them effectively and maintain their loyalty to a consumer brand. Employer branding involves applying a similar approach to people management.

As such, it positions itself very firmly as a marketing strategy. It is how the firm markets itself to attract the best talent.

Some of the reasons why employer branding has increased in importance in HR are in relation to increased competition in labour markets for talented labour or the so called 'war for talent'.

Employer branding also reflects a move away from recruiting for jobs to recruiting for talent. Recruiting for jobs meant a heavy reliance on a job description and attracting candidates who would provide the best fit for that description. Recruiting for talent is more about attracting the best talent possible and then fitting them into roles where their potential can best be exploited.

In addition, as the idea of the corporate image has become more important and consumer power more potent, companies are applying marketing techniques to corporate advertising to reflect their brand. They have consequently found it beneficial to reflect this in their advertising strategies for human resources to ensure a positive and consistent message to strengthen their brand. Another complication is the advent of social media, meaning that brand management is becoming even more complex and employers have recognized the need to ensure their employees also reflect a positive brand image to potential future employees and customers alike.

One of the dangers of employer branding is that the internal experience does not match the projected brand. This means that employers concerned with projecting a positive internal brand need also to ensure this is promoted among their existing employees, as well as reflected in their attraction strategies for new employees. This is reflected in the relative importance ascribed to employer awards such as 'Great Place to Work' or the *Times* Best Companies list. It also means that greater emphasis needs to be placed on management of the psychological contract or employee engagement to ensure current employees are positive about the organization as an employer.

ANGELA BARON

See also:
Recruitment.

References and selected further readings

Dodd, L. (2011), Bringing a more inclusive approach to internal branding, *Strategic Communication Management*, **15**(9), pp. 32–35.
Erikson, T. and L. Grattion (2007), What it means to work here, *Harvard Business Review*, **85**(3), pp. 104–112.
Incomes Data Services (2012), *Employer Branding*, London: IDS.
Rosethorn, H. (2009), *The Employer Brand: Keeping Faith with the Deal*, Aldershot: Gower.

Employers' associations

Employers' associations are voluntary, collective, representative organizations of employers specializing in labour market matters. Associations provide their members with collective strengths and resources unavailable to companies acting alone. They are a subset of business associations, many of which focus only on 'trade' (product market) matters or perhaps combine these with industrial relations functions. As 'pure' employers' associations specialize almost entirely on labour market issues, they are sometimes colloquially called 'bosses' unions'. Associations are highly influential in much of Europe, Southern and Eastern Asia, Latin America and Australia, and have formed international confederations.

As voluntary organizations, associations face challenges of 'associability' and 'governability' (Traxler, 1993, pp. 677–678). That is, they must attract and retain members, while effectively representing the often differing interests of member firms who also can choose to act alone and against association policy. How associations 'structure' themselves can assist associability and governability. Territorial associations recruit all firms within a geographical area, irrespective of industry. Sectoral associations recruit within one or a few related industries. National federations of associations can bring together sectoral and territorial bodies.

Institutional factors have also helped foster and consolidate associations. Employers traditionally formed associations when facing threats from unions and government regulation, but also from employers whose behaviours undermined broader employer interests. Associations' main respective responses – resistance to and then multi-employer collective bargaining with unions, lobbying and publicity campaigns aimed at governments, and measures to discipline errant competitors – are 'collective goods' (Olson, 1971, pp. 14–16), activities on behalf of all employers, members or not. They allow employers to express collective industrial relations and HRM preferences in the wider labour market; for example, on minimum wages, workplace health and safety regulation or training policy.

Yet, reliance on collective goods leaves associations vulnerable to 'free-riding'; non-members benefit without contributing financially. To encourage and reward membership, many associations therefore provide 'selective goods' (Olson, 1971, pp. 60–64). These are free services solely for members, like information on industry trends, published advice on regulations and call centre advisory services.

As multi-employer collective bargaining has long provided associations with central institutional roles, its recent decline in some countries brings associations severe associability challenges, like those that undercut US associations after the 1970s. Some associations are responding by marketing 'elective goods': customized, commercially priced products and services to members and non-members (Sheldon et al., 2014).

PETER SHELDON

See also:
Collective bargaining; Industrial relations; Labour market; Trade unions.

References and selected further reading

Olson, M. (1971), *The Logic of Collective Action: Public Goods and the Theory of Groups*, Cambridge, MA: Harvard University Press.
Schmitter, P. and W. Streeck (1999), *The Organization of Business Interests: Studying the Associative Action of Business in Advanced Industrial Societies*, MPIfG Discussion Paper 99/1, Cologne.
Sheldon, P., R. Nacamulli, F. Paoletti and D.E. Morgan (2014), Employer association responses to the effects of bargaining decentralization in Australia and Italy: seeking explanations from organizational theory, *British Journal of Industrial Relations*, http://onlinelibrary.wiley.com/doi/10.1111/bjir.12061/abstract.
Traxler, F. (1993), Business associations and labour unions in comparison: theoretical perspectives and empirical findings on social class, collective action and associational organizability, *British Journal of Sociology*, **44**, pp. 673–691.

Employment agency

The term 'employment agency' covers a wide range of labor market intermediaries, including private sector temporary employment agencies, 'permanent placement' firms, and government-run employment services. Employment agencies have existed since at least the late 19th century, and the private employment agency industry has grown rapidly globally since the 1970s. The intervention of an employment agency between employer and worker creates a distinct triangular relationship between the three parties. In the case of permanent placement, the agency 'steps out of the picture' once a worker has been placed. In the case of temporary employment agencies, an ongoing relationship between the three parties is created, in which the agency receives a mark-up fee for every hour that a worker ('temp') is placed within a client firm (Gonos, 1997). It is this distinctive arrangement that has been of most interest to scholars in the field of HRM and the sociology of work (Forde, 2001).

Employers seek recourse to employment agencies for a range of reasons, to provide numerical flexibility, for specialist one-off tasks, and to save on labor costs. Increasingly, employers are utilizing employment agencies to service core tasks in firms, with temporary agency temps in particular being used in large numbers by firms, on a long-term or permanent basis. The use of employment agencies raises important issues for human resources, as well as for the understanding of precarious and insecure forms of work. There has been debate over which party (agency or client firm) has legal obligations for workers provided via employment agencies, how temps can be managed and motivated, how effective partnerships can be established between employers and employment agencies, and the quality of jobs acquired through employment agencies (Fudge and Strauss, 2013; Hoque et al., 2008; Smith and Neuwirth, 2008).

The role of employment agencies varies markedly from country to country. National and supra-national regulation plays an increasingly important role in shaping the activities of employment agencies. In many countries, equal treatment provisions for agency workers have been implemented. In Europe, the Agency Working Directive, passed in 2011 has sought to ensure that temps are given equal treatment in terms of pay to comparable permanent workers. The triangular relationship creates significant challenges to ensuring equal treatment and it is widely accepted that on average, terms and conditions for agency temps are inferior to directly employed workers.

CHRIS FORDE AND GARY SLATER

See also:

Temporary work; Temporary worker.

References and selected further readings

Forde, C. (2001), Temporary arrangements: the activities of employment agencies in the UK, *Work, Employment and Society*, **15**(3), pp. 631–644.

Fudge, J. and K. Strauss (eds) (2013), *Temporary Work, Agencies and Unfree Labour: Insecurity in the New World of Work*, London: Routledge.

Gonos, G. (1997), The contest over 'employer' status in the postwar United States: the case of temporary help firms, *Law & Society Review*, **31**(1), pp. 81–110.

Hoque, K., I. Kirkpatrick, A. De Ruyter and C. Lonsdale (2008), New contractual relationships in the agency worker market: the case of the UK's National Health Service, *British Journal Of Industrial Relations*, **46**, pp. 389–412.

Smith, V. and E. Neuwirth (2008), *The Good Temp*, Ithaca: Cornell University Press.

Employment relationship

The employment relationship is the connection between employees and organizations through which individuals sell their labour to an employer. In practice, employment relationships can be short-term or long-term, can be governed by informal understandings or an explicit contract, and can involve workers and organizations of all types. From a legal perspective, the laws in each country define what is considered an employment relationship covered by employment and labour law as well as other public policies such as unemployment insurance or social security.

By definition, the employment relationship requires an employer and an employee. To think about their employment relationship, one should consider each of their interests. That is, what does each want to get out the employment relationship? This relationship is then mediated by states and markets. States regulate the employment relationship directly and indirectly, such as through the enforcement of property rights, as well as establish the broader socio-economic context. Markets mediate the employment relationship by determining alternative opportunities and thus power. Lastly, a contract captures the terms, conditions, and expectations under which an employee sells his or her labour to an employer. This might be an explicit written document, as is often the case for CEOs, professional athletes and unionized workers. In other cases, the contract might be verbal or implied. In almost every case, contracts are incomplete because all of the tasks and performance expectations cannot be specified in advance. Consequently, it is common to think of the employment relationship as also governed by implicit contracts of informal, legally unenforceable promises that are economic, psychological, or social in nature.

Different perspectives on the interests of employers and employees as well as the power dynamics established by states and markets yield contrasting frames of reference or schools of thought on the employment relationship: (a) a mutually advantageous trade among self-interested agents in a free market (a 'free market' frame of reference); (b) a long-term partnership between employees and employers with common interests ('unitarism'); (c) a bargain between unequal stakeholders with some competing economic interests ('pluralism'); and (d) a distinctly unequal power relation embedded in complex social hierarchies (critical, heterodox, or radical frame of reference). It is important for HRM to appreciate these alternative perspectives because they help explain contrasting views on the nature of HRM, the desirability of trade unions, the need for regulatory standards for the employment relationship and other important issues.

JOHN W. BUDD

See also:

Contract of employment; Frames of reference; Labour market; Trade unions; Work.

References and selected further readings

Ackers, P. and A. Wilkinson (eds) (2003), *Understanding Work and Employment: Industrial Relations in Transition*, Oxford: Oxford University Press.
Budd, J.W. and D. Bhave (2008), Values, ideologies, and frames of reference in industrial relations, in P. Blyton, E. Heery, N.A. Bacon and J. Fiorito (eds), *Sage Handbook of Industrial Relations*, London: Sage.
Budd, J.W. and D. Bhave (2010), The employment relationship, in A. Wilkinson, N. Bacon, T. Redman and S. Snell (eds), *Sage Handbook of Human Resource Management*, London: Sage.
Kaufman, B.E. (ed.) (2004), *Theoretical Perspectives on Work and the Employment Relationship*, Champaign, IL: Industrial Relations Research Association.
Thompson, P. and D. McHugh (2002), *Work Organisations: A Critical Introduction*, Basingstoke: Palgrave Macmillan.

Employment tribunal

Employment tribunals (ETs) are judicial bodies with responsibility for adjudicating disputes arising from alleged violations of statutory employment rights in Britain (similar 'labour courts' exist elsewhere). Originally established in 1964 as industrial tribunals to hear employer appeals against state-imposed training levies, they now consider a wide range of party-versus-party claim types (jurisdictions) including unfair dismissal, redundancy payments, breach of contract and discrimination. Mirroring the decline of collective disputes, the number of claims has risen from around 40,000 a year in the early

1980s to more than 230,000 in 2009/2010, revealing the (growing) importance of ETs as labour market institutions.

The composition of ETs has traditionally been tripartite, with a legally qualified chair/employment judge plus two lay members – one each from panel representative of employers and employees – determining liability and remedy. Appeals – on points of law only – are made to the Employment Appeal Tribunal (EAT). As with the civil courts – which some commentators have argued they have increasingly come to resemble (Corby and Latreille, 2012) – most claims are resolved prior to a full hearing, for example, being settled with the assistance of the Advisory, Conciliation and Arbitration Service (Acas). Of the 15–20 per cent that are heard, around half are successful.

Empirical studies have explored issues across the ET lifecycle, including the determinants of claim instigation, settlement/conciliation, judgments and post-tribunal experiences, while thematic work has explored the roles inter alia of firm size, representation, Acas and lay members. The growing number of claims has also made this an area of active policy intervention by successive governments, much of it focused around promoting earlier resolution of problems. Particular controversy exists in relation to recent reforms however, most notably the introduction of fees for bringing and hearing claims, introduced on the basis of reducing the risk of litigation to business, thereby promoting job creation, and of making the parties contribute to the cost of the system. Together with an increased qualifying period for unfair dismissal, this has resulted in a drop of around two-thirds in the number of claims since 2013.

Paul Latreille

See also:

Acas; Alternative dispute resolution; Arbitration; Conciliation; Mediation.

References and selected further readings

Corby, S. and P. Burgess (2014), *Adjudicating Employment Rights*, Basingstoke: Palgrave Macmillan.
Corby, S. and P. Latreille (2012), Employment tribunals and the civil courts: isomorphism exemplified, *Industrial Law Journal*, 41(4), pp. 387–406.
Gibbons, M. (2007), *Better Dispute Resolution: A Review of Employment Dispute Resolution in Great Britain*, London: DTI.
Harding, C., S. Ghezelayagh, A. Busby and N. Coleman (2014), *Findings from the Survey of Employment Tribunal Applications 2013*, Department for Business, Innovation and Skills Research Series, no. 177.
Hepple, B. (2013), Back to the future: employment law under the coalition government, *Industrial Law Journal*, 42(3), pp. 203–223.
Saridakis, G., S. Sen-Gupta, P. Edwards and D.J. Storey (2008), The impact of enterprise size on employment tribunal incidence and outcomes: evidence from Britain, *British Journal of Industrial Relations*, 46(3), pp. 469–499.

Empowerment

The term 'empowerment' is used in HRM (and management) to refer to the process of allowing employees to make decisions relating to work matters. However, unlike industrial democracy, it is not based on workers having a right to a say. The empowerment process in most organizations starts from the basis that it is for employers to decide whether to, and how to empower employees. Thus 'empowerment' in practice is based on individuals or small groups being authorized by management to carry out specific activities.

While 'empowerment' may be a new label, the underlying ideas have a long history. As part of a reaction to the dehumanizing effects of scientific management there were movements to fuse technical and social components to develop socio-technical systems. Equally the notion of citizenship was also important concerning the rights afforded to industrial citizens. However, there is also a business case for empowerment that has received more attention in the HRM literature, acknowledging that workers are closer to the work situation and have the knowledge of work processes, which enables them to suggest improvements and hence improve efficiency (Wilkinson, 2008).

Furthermore, empowerment contributes to effectiveness where it involves staff taking on additional responsibilities that others (such as senior managers) would otherwise have to perform. However, the most important potential benefit of empowerment results are due the potential to improve employee competence.

It is often assumed that employees will welcome empowerment and regard it as beneficial to them, but there is little detailed discussion of the issues likely to arise when implementing empowerment, or the conditions that are necessary for such an approach to be successful.

ADRIAN WILKINSON

See also:
Employee involvement; Employee voice.

References and selected further readings
Conger, J. and R. Kanungo (1988), The empowerment process: integrating theory and practice, *Academy of Management Review*, **13**(3), pp. 471–482.
Denham Lincoln, N., C. Travers, P. Ackers and A. Wilkinson (2002), The meaning of empowerment: the interdisciplinary etymology of a new management concept, *International Journal of Management Reviews*, **4**(3), pp. 271–290.
Foy, N. (1994), *Empowering People at Work*, London: Gower.
Wall, T., S. Wood and D. Leach (2004), Empowerment and performance, *International Review of Industrial and Organizational Psychology*, **19**, pp. 1–46.
Wilkinson, A. (1998), Empowerment: a review and a critique, *Personnel Review*, **27**(1), pp. 40–56.
Wilkinson, A. (2008), Empowerment, in S. Clegg and J. Bailey (eds), *Encyclopaedia of Organizational Studies*, New York: Sage, pp. 441–442.

Equal opportunity

Equal opportunity is an umbrella term that includes a range of corrective responses to discrimination, past and present and recognizes that certain groups of people have been (or remain) advantaged or disadvantaged in the labour market based on observable characteristics (for example sex and ethnicity). It is based on 'a concept of ensuring fair treatment for all employees (or prospective employees)' (Heery and Noon, 2001, p. 106) and can cover other social structures such as education. Most countries have legislation that addresses issues of equity in workplace practices and generally prohibits various types of employment discrimination and sets minimum standards for organizational behaviour. A plethora of terms are used in English (employment equity, affirmative action and recently terms including diversity) and there is a lack of agreed definitions, particularly outside of a legislative context.

The origins of equal opportunity concepts lie in the human rights or social justice framework that arose from international conventions signed in the wake of the Second World War and the Civil Rights Movements of the 1960s and 1970s (Strachan et al., 2011). The influence of international treaties, national culture, demography and make-up of the labour market have all played a part in the variety of ways in which countries approach issues of equal opportunity in employment. Equal opportunity policies and programmes have a variety of legislative bases (French et al., 2010). All incorporate a social justice framework, although they can also be 'marketed' as having a business case, most effectively when there is a tight labour market. In the majority of countries, the legislation and policies target women, ethnic minorities, religious groups and, to a lesser extent, people with a disability. However, there are countries where employment equity policies are designed to assist the majority population, for example, South Africa and Malaysia (Jain et al., 2003, pp. 1–55).

Equal opportunity legislation advocates a proactive means of addressing group disadvantage based on characteristics that are difficult or impossible to change and stereotypes that are often incorrect. This recognizes that market forces can be oppressive and unjust, and at times need to be tempered by institutions that promote more equitable relations at work (Kirton and Greene, 2005, pp. 115–117). Within this broad concept, there are a variety of approaches that can be taken, and a number of ways of describing and categorizing the approaches have been developed. Jewson and Mason (1986) divided these into the liberal and radical approaches. The liberal approach, in principle, argues that 'equality of opportunity exists when all individuals are enabled freely and equally to compete for social rewards'. Its focus is the 'rules of the game' and the policymaker has the role of umpire who ensures that 'the rules of competition are not discriminatory and that they are fairly enforced on all' (Jewson and Mason, 1986, pp. 315, 313). Selection on merit is a cornerstone of this approach (Thornton, 1990). In contrast to this focus on process, the radical approach focuses on outcomes. It 'seeks to intervene directly in workplace practices in order to achieve a fair distribution of rewards among employees' with the focus on 'the fairness of the distribution of rewards' (Jewson and Mason, 1986, p. 315). This approach can include practices such as the implementation of employment quotas from the group judged as disadvantaged, for example, in India for scheduled castes or Norway's requirement for minimum numbers of women on company boards (Jain et al. 2003, pp. 6–15; Seierstad and Opsahl 2011). Often referred to as 'positive discrimination', 'employment practices are deliberately manipulated in order to obtain a fair distribution' of disadvantaged groups (Kirton and Greene, 2005, p. 117).

In most countries, legislation and organizational practice implements the liberal approach. Implemented through what Konrad and Linnehan (1995) describe as 'identity-conscious structures', decision-makers must consider individual merit and demographic group identity in order to remedy current discrimination, redress past injustices and achieve fair and visible representation across all positions. This occurs by monitoring personnel decisions made about members of protected groups more stringently; comparing the numbers, experiences and outcomes of protected groups with those of others and making special efforts to employ and promote the career progress of protected groups. While the merit principle is maintained in this approach, programmes targeted at the disadvantaged group are included. Other policies developed under the broad umbrella of equal opportunity target all employees, but may be of particular relevance to one group, such as parental leave, which, in most countries, is particularly important for maintaining women's attachment to the labour force. However, elements of both approaches do mix to some degree; for example, in the UK the overall approach is voluntarist with the exception of some specific legislation in Northern Ireland (Dickens, 2007).

GLENDA STRACHAN, ERICA FRENCH AND JOHN BURGESS

See also:

Direct discrimination; Gender; Gender pay gap; Indirect discrimination.

References and selected further readings

Dickens, L. (2007), The road is long: thirty years of equality legislation in Britain, *British Journal of Industrial Relations*, **45**(3), pp. 463–494.

French, E., G. Strachan and J. Burgess (2010), Approaches to equity and diversity: conflicting beliefs and competing ideals, in G. Strachan, E. French and J. Burgess (eds), *Managing Diversity in Australia: Theory and Practice*, Sydney: McGraw Hill, pp. 41–56.

Heery, E. and M. Noon (2001), *A Dictionary of Human Resource Management*, Oxford: Oxford University Press.

Jain, H., P. Sloane and F. Horwitz (2003), *Employment Equity and Affirmative Action: An International Comparison*, Armonk, NY: M.E. Sharpe.

Jewson, N. and D. Mason (1986), The theory and practice of equal opportunities policies: liberal and radical approaches, *The Sociological Review*, **34**(2), pp. 307–334.

Kirton, G. and A.-M. Greene (2005), *The Dynamics of Managing Diversity: A Critical Approach*, 2nd edn, Oxford: Elsevier.

Konrad, A. and F. Linnehan (1995), Formalized HRM Structures: coordinating equal employment opportunity or concealing organisational practices? *Academy of Management Journal*, **18**(3), pp. 787–820.

Seierstad, C. and T. Opsahl (2011), For the few not the many? The effects of affirmative action on presence, prominence, and social capital of women directors in Norway, *Scandinavian Journal of Management*, **27**(1), pp. 44–54.

Strachan, G., J. Burgess and E. French (2011), Equity in the twenty-first century workplace, in K. Townsend and A. Wilkinson (eds), *Research Handbook on the Future of Work and Employment Relations*, Cheltenham: Edward Elgar, pp. 345–369.

Thornton, M. (1990), *The Liberal Promise: Anti-Discrimination Legislation in Australia*, Sydney: Oxford University Press.

Equal pay

Equal pay is the legal requirement for employees to be paid equally when they are doing equal work. There are two dimensions to equal pay. First, equal pay for equal work means that people doing the same type of work under the same conditions should not be paid differently because of who they are; for example, on account of their sex or race. Second, equal pay for work of equal value means that jobs requiring similar levels of skills, decision-making and effort are not paid differently. This second aspect of equal pay is important for closing pay gaps since occupational segregation – for example, the propensity of women and men to work in different occupations – often means that disadvantaged groups find themselves in activities that are lower valued and lower paid (England, 1992). In the US, the term 'comparable worth' is often used to mean equal pay for work of equal value.

Across much of the world there is legislation to support equal pay. In the EU, equal pay was part of the 1957 founding Treaty and the implementation of the equal pay laws is a requirement for membership of the Union (Heide, 1999). Similarly in the US, equal pay legislation was implemented in the early 1960s forbidding pay differences for jobs requiring equal effort, responsibility and skill, and performed under similar working conditions. Equal pay claims can only be made where employees work for the same organization so pay inequalities across firms for similar jobs are not affected.

A key element of equal pay relies on job evaluations for the assessment of skills, effort and responsibilities. This process of evaluation is complex since gendered social norms may reinforce inequalities that equal pay policies aim to close (Acker, 1989). Even where jobs are evaluated as equal, employees may still have uneven access to other benefits such as bonuses or other payments, often more prevalent in certain male-dominated occupations.

Claims for equal pay require an employee or group of employees to make a legal claim against their employer. Here a considerable body of case law has developed at national and supra-national levels around the interpretation of equal pay and equal treatment (see Heide, 1999). Trade unions have been active in leveraging equality legislation to address inequalities for low-paid workers, particularly women (Deakin et al., 2015).

MARK SMITH

See also:
Direct discrimination; Gender; Gender pay gap; Job evaluation; Low pay.

References and selected further readings
Acker, J. (1989), *Doing Comparable Worth: Gender, Class and Pay Equity*, Philadelphia: Temple University Press.
Deakin, S., S. Fraser Butlin, C. McLaughlin and A. Polanska (2015), Are litigation and collective bargaining complements or substitutes for achieving gender equality? A study of the British Equal Pay Act, *Cambridge Journal of Economics*, **39**, pp. 381–403.
England, P. (1992), *Comparable Worth Theory and Evidence*, New York: Aldine de Gruyter.
Heide, I. (1999), Supranational action against sex discrimination: equal pay and equal treatment in the European Union, *International Labour Review*, **138**(4), pp. 381–410.

Equity

Equity is a standard of fair employment standards covering both material outcomes and personal treatment. Equity is important for HRM because workers, public policymakers and societies have expectations about fair employment standards; organizations that fall short may experience consequences such as employee turnover, low morale and productivity, demands for additional employment regulation, and a negative public image. But equity standards can be challenging because there are diverse perspectives on equity that yield different criteria for what is seen as fair or unfair.

From perspectives rooted in psychological theorizing, equity is typically seen as individual fairness or justice. In an early approach, J. Stacy Adams' (1965) equity theory says that a person who perceives that the ratio of her outcomes to inputs is not equal to this ratio for some comparison person will feel that she is being treated unfairly. For example, a worker who perceives herself to have similar qualifications, responsibilities and performance to another worker, and yet is paid less, will feel inequitably treated. Today, this kind of focus on outcomes is the 'distributive justice' part of scholarship on employee justice in organizations. The other key dimension is procedural justice that considers the fairness of a process. For example, using consistent standards in performance reviews might be seen as procedurally fair by employees. HRM might also be concerned with interactional justice, which is the degree of fairness perceived by employees when they are informed about decisions.

From a different perspective that emphasizes economic markets, fairness can be seen as what autonomous parties voluntarily agree to in a market transaction. From an employment relations perspective, however, excessive labour market competition can lead to employment practices that are abusive and exploitive. From this perspective, then, equitable employment outcomes require the meeting of standards that allow workers to achieve human dignity. Such standards are usually seen as requiring institutional intervention, whether through the enhanced bargaining power of trade unions or through legislative mandates for minimum wages, safety standards, protections against arbitrary discharge and restrictions on child labour.

It is also important for HRM to consider whether equity supports or conflicts with other objectives. In market-based perspectives, productivity, profitability and related concerns ('efficiency') are more important than equity concerns. In the organizational justice approach, it is common to see equity as serving efficiency because employees who are fairly treated will be more productive. In employment relations theorizing, efficiency and equity can sometimes be in conflict with each other, but both are legitimate goals that need to be balanced.

JOHN W. BUDD

See also:

Employment relationship; Ethics; Regulation.

References and selected further readings

Adams, J.S. (1965), Inequity in social exchange, in L. Berkowitz (ed.), *Advances in Experimental Social Psychology, Vol. 2*, New York: Academic Press.
Budd, J.W. (2004), *Employment with a Human Face: Balancing Efficiency, Equity, and Voice*, Ithaca, NY: Cornell University Press.
Greenberg, J. (2011), Organizational justice: the dynamics of fairness in the workplace, in S. Zedeck (ed.), *APA Handbook of Industrial and Organizational Psychology, Vol. 3*, Washington, DC: American Psychological Association.
Greenberg, J. and J.A. Colquitt (eds) (2005), *Handbook of Organizational Justice*, Mahwah, NJ: Erlbaum.

Ethics

Human resource management – as a field of research, study and practice – is by its very nature a deeply ethical endeavour. The term 'ethical' in this context should be understood as *consideration of* the moral, rather than moral as such. Hence, to label a subject as ethical is not to say it is moral, but rather to question if it is so. In making this distinction I hope to discourage interpretations of the ethical as merely compliance or 'best practice', and mitigate any rush to action (Winstanley and Woodall, 2000), in the belief that such foreclosure potentially place 'ethics' at risk of causing more harm than good. The question to be asked is 'is HRM moral?' (Legge, 1996).

Traditionally, ethical examinations of HRM have tended to apply the modern rationalist trilogy of ethical theories – deontology, utilitarianism and rights/justice theories – to individual (micro) phenomena. Deontology is an ethical theory based on the concept of the inherent rightness or wrongness of actions, independent of their consequences. Utilitarianism is an ethical view that considers actions as good based on their consequences and aims, maximizing outcomes for the collective good. Justice ethics are based on the duty to treat all parties fairly and to distribute risks and benefits equitably. For example, justice-based principles, such as fairness and equity, have been applied to specific HRM practices (e.g., equal opportunity in recruitment, remuneration); and rights-based principles have been considered with respect to employment issues (e.g., privacy, whistleblowing). To some extent this focus reflects the fundamental concerns of employee advocates such as trade unions, national governments (e.g., UK, Australia and Germany), intergovernmental institutions (e.g., the International Labour Organization and the United Nations). However, traditional ethical theories are problematic as they can be used to argue that HRM is either ethical *or* unethical depending on how the theories are applied and in what context.

Furthermore, focus at the micro-level of HRM has significant limitations. Compliance with fairness and equity principles can promulgate minimalistic adherence. Mere lists of employees' rights can be ambiguous and open to a variety of interpretations and applications. There is a tendency with such approaches to concentrate on apparent problems at the expense of the broader ethical questions related to the management of employees. Additionally, such analyses are limited by the degree to which they suggest that ethical behaviour is related to individual behaviour (managers and employees) and individual HRM practices, and in doing so neglect the employment relationship as a site for construction of ethics, and ignore background broader political and social contexts.

As alternative to traditional ethical theories, and resultant problems of reductionism and pursuit of 'solutions', two developing streams of research hold promise: social-political (macro) analyses of HRM and post-foundational approaches at the relational (micro) level of HRM. Socio-political macro-level analyses have focused on 'soft' HRM and high engagement practices (Greenwood, 2002; Legge, 1996) and the domination of unitarism and strategy in HRM (Kamoche, 2001; Kochan, 2007), and have advanced a pragmatic pluralist approach using stakeholder theory (Greenwood and Freeman, 2011). In this vein, various debates have opened recently about links between corporate social responsibility and HRM: the rights and responsibilities of employees as stakeholders in the firm; the involvement of civil society organizations in governing employment; and responsibility of HRM at a societal level.

Post-foundational writings in philosophy (e.g., Levinas, Bauman) and psychoanalysis (e.g., Lacan, Klein) have been used to theorize ethical framings of the capitalist employment relationship and advance conceptual analyses of the outcomes of such framings for the ethical subjectivity of employees (Jack et al., 2012). Relational ethics (or ethics of alterity) suggest that it is through the face-to-face encounter, which is fundamental to human social relations, that the subject is called to morally respond to the Other. This stream of research questions positivist and humanist understandings of individuals and organizations as entities in their own right that that can be characterized as ethical or unethical and, as such, whether it is possible and desirable to 'inject' more ethics into HRM. In contrast, it is held that ethics, along with other constructed organizational phenomenon such as power and culture, only come into being in our experience of the world, in particular in our relationships with others. Research from this approach provokes debate in areas such as the ethical prerogative of HRM, the manner in which HRM reifies employees at the risk of their dignity, the way in which employees are positioned as both consuming subjects and consumed objects through HRM, and the self-disciplining power of HRM technologies (e.g., performance measurement and employability) (see Jack et al., 2012).

The ethical challenge for HRM goes far beyond equal employment opportunity or preventing employee theft; such a narrow depiction of ethics as compliance or risk prevention falls well short of HRM's influence and our expectations. HRM and HRM practitioners are socially and politically embedded and therefore hold roles and responsibilities, not only across organization, but also in society at large. The question of whether and how it may be possible for HRM to shift from risk aversion and codified behaviours to moral responsiveness is being examined though post-foundational lens with particular focus on ethics of power/knowledge and ethics of subjectivity. HRM ethics are central to any understanding of what it means to manage humans as resources.

MICHELLE GREENWOOD

See also:

Corporate social responsibility; Equity; Pluralism.

References and selected further readings

Greenwood, M. (2002), Ethics and HRM: a review and conceptual analysis, *Journal of Business Ethics*, **36**(3), pp. 261–279.
Greenwood, M. and R.E. Freeman (2011). Ethics and HRM: the contribution of stakeholder theory, *Business and Professional Ethics Journal*, **30**(3/4), pp. 269–292.
Jack, G., M. Greenwood and J. Schapper (2012), Frontiers, intersections and engagements of Ethics and HRM, *Journal of Business Ethics*, **111**(1), pp. 1–12.
Kamoche, K.N. (2001), *Understanding Human Resource Management*, Buckingham: Open University Press.
Kochan, T. (2007), Social legitimacy of the HRM profession: a US perspective, in P. Boxall and J. Purcell (eds), *The Oxford Handbook of HRM*, Oxford: Oxford University Press, pp. 599–619.
Legge, K. (1996), Morality bound, *People Management*, **25**(2), pp. 34–36.
Winstanley, D. and J. Woodall (2000), The ethical dimensions of human resource management, *Human Resource Management Journal*, **10**(2), pp. 5–20.

Ethnocentric management

Ethnocentric management refers to a staffing policy adopted by multinational companies (MNCs), where they primarily appoint parent country nationals (PCNs) to key executive positions in their overseas affiliates. MNCs with an ethnocentric approach also impose home-country cultural norms to define the organization of work and country-of-origin bias in their subsidiary operations (Reiche and Harzing, 2011). Harzing's (2001) study gave some insight into factors that influence MNCs' decisions for adopting an ethnocentric approach of using PCNs for top management positions in their subsidiaries; namely, transfer of know-how, position filling, exercising control of the subsidiary, compensating for lack of qualified local national managers and training of host country managers.

While control and intellectual capital, manifested by the transfer of PCNs to subsidiaries is critical for sustaining competitive advantage, there are many issues faced by MNCs and expatriates in the host country. PCNs and their families may endure difficulties in adapting to the foreign language, cultural and legal environment; moreover, for the MNC the cost of selecting, training and maintaining an expatriate and their families for an assignment in the subsidiary can be very high, and in some host countries there may be insistence on localizing operations, which can cause further difficulties. However while PCNs may represent costly and sometimes unsuccessful endeavours, they still remain a viable staffing strategy among MNCs as:

- they can facilitate the communication process between the parent location and its subsidiaries, as well as across subsidiaries;
- they can aid in establishing country linkages;
- they bring strong technical and management competence and are familiar with home office goals, policies and practices; and
- they can assist MNCs in exercising control of subsidiaries and increase the firm's understanding of international operations (Reiche and Harzing, 2011).

As such, the practice of employing PCNs may be a strategic move on the part of an MNC to increase their international experience and knowledge-base of present and future managers, and gather and maintain a resident base of knowledge about the complexities of international operations. There is growing research on emerging economies' MNCs and global HR practices due to the rapid rise of MNCs from these countries. Thite et al. (2012) developed a conceptual framework of global HR practices in MNCs from emerging economies across their subsidiaries. Their study identified that the universal or US model was not applicable to the emerging MNCs and there was a need to develop alternative models to aid understanding of the staffing approaches of these MNCs.

DHARA SHAH

See also:

Expatriate; Geocentric management; International human resource management; Polycentric management.

References and selected further readings

Harzing, A. (2001), Who's in charge? An empirical study of executive staffing practices in foreign subsidiaries, *Human Resource Management*, **40**(2), pp. 139–158.
Reiche, S.B. and A. Harzing (2011), International assignments, in A. Harzing and A. Pinnington (eds), *International Human Resource Management*, 3rd edn, Thousand Oaks, CA: Sage, pp. 185–227.
Thite, M., A. Wilkinson and D. Shah (2012), Internationalization and HRM strategies across subsidiaries in multinational corporations from emerging economies — a conceptual framework, *Journal of World Business*, **47**(2), pp. 251–258.

European works councils

European works councils are legally mandated, company-level information and consultation forums attached to large, multinational corporations operating in Europe. They are the result of the transposition of European Directive 94/45/EC into national labour law across the member states of the European Union. All large multinational companies with operations in Europe must convene at least yearly and fund a European works council so that workers' representatives elected by the workforce can be informed and consulted about strategic decision-making. Different companies convene different types of European works councils, with some chaired by employers' representatives and others chaired by workers' representatives. But in all cases, the European works council is a type of labour-management committee meant to provide the workforce with an avenue for representative employee voice.

The key debate surrounding European works councils centres around the question of 'value added': *cui bono*? The extent to which employees and organizations benefit from these forums is open to interpretation. In respect to potential employee benefits, some scholars have argued that European works councils serve as stepping stones toward greater cross-national solidarity and trust between workers, thus levelling the playing field between capital and labour. Others have argued that the forums do not lead to any increased labour internationalism. In respect to potential organizational benefits, the extent to which companies can improve performance and efficiency through European works councils is questionable. Some scholars have argued that increased transparency resulting from information and consultation leads to improved organizational problem-solving, while others have argued that European works councils are generally a waste of company money and time. In short, case study research on the extent to which European works councils 'add value' to employees and organizations is mixed.

Regardless of the benefits (or perceived lack thereof), European works councils are an important area of study because they represent the first real attempt at transnational employment regulation at the level of the European Union. They have also introduced the hitherto foreign concept of statutory information and consultation to traditionally liberal market countries that have no history of works councils, like the United Kingdom and Ireland. Thus, they have had a substantive impact on employment relations in Europe.

ANDREW R. TIMMING

See also:

Consultation; Employee voice; Labour law; Workplace democracy.

References and selected further readings

Fitzgerald, I. and J. Stirling (eds) (2004), *European Works Councils: Pessimism of the Intellect, Optimism of the Will?* London: Routledge.
Streeck, W. (1997), Neither European nor works councils: a reply to Paul Knutsen, *Economic and Industrial Democracy*, **18**(2), pp. 325–337.
Timming, A.R. (2009) Trust in cross-national labour relations: a case study of an Anglo–Dutch European works council, *European Sociological Review*, **25**(4), pp. 505–516.
Waddington, J. (2011), *European Works Councils: A Transnational Industrial Relations Institution in the Making*, New York: Routledge.

Whittall, M, H. Knudsen and F. Huijgen (eds) (2007), *Towards a European Labour Identity: The Case of the European Works Council*, London: Routledge.
Wills, J. (1998), Taking on the CosmoCorps? Experiments in transnational labor organization, *Economic Geography*, **74**(2), pp. 111–130.

Executive search firms

Executive search firms oversee the process of matching executives and hiring organizations: they supply information on the two parties, mediate between them, and in most cases guarantee the quality of the placement. Most often they work on a 'retained' basis: they have an exclusive contract with clients and are paid for their services even if they do not secure a placement.

The past 25 years have seen a growing demand for the services of executive search firms. Revenue growth in the employment services industry overall was three times as high as, for example, in the US economy, mainly due to the erosion of employee loyalty to organizations and the growth in new executive hires who came from outside the organization. The most significant source of these outside hires, apart from executives' own social networks, was executive search firms.

Among the handful of academic papers that focus on search firms, by far the greatest effort has concentrated on understanding why search firms exist and what roles they play in the corporate hiring process. Economists argue that search firms present efficiency-based advantages to hiring organizations: due to the large number of searches that they do, they are more skilled in executing searches. They are also more likely to establish a higher-quality match between the hiring organization and the candidate as a result of the expertise that they amassed. Sociologists propose that the primary task of search firms is to mediate between two parties with different interests: search firms gauge the intentions of both parties, buffer them from each other, ensure confidentiality and resolve conflictive issues such as the final compensation package.

The second important stream of research concerns the biases that search firms bring to the search process. They were shown to favour a highly visible, narrow group of executives working for large-sized, high-performing organizations. Several studies found that they were less likely to keep records on female executives and racial minorities than on white male executives. Search firms were shown to shape executive careers in other ways, too: executives whose moves they mediated were more likely to get a promotion or move to a larger and more reputable new employer. At the same time, they were just as likely to move to a new job function or industry as their counterparts who moved without such mediation. That is, search firms matched executives to open positions based on their existing knowledge and skills, while they were unlikely to lead them to areas where their skills had not been tested yet.

MONIKA HAMORI

See also:

Headhunting; Selection.

References and selected further readings

Bonet, R., P. Cappelli and M. Hamori (2013), Labor market intermediaries and the new paradigm for human resources, *Academy of Management Annals*, **7**(1), pp. 341–392.

Cappelli, P. and M. Hamori (2014), Understanding executive job search, *Organization Science*, **25**(5), pp. 1511–1529.

Dreher, G.F., J. Lee and T.A. Clerkin (2011), Mobility and cash compensation: the moderating effects of gender, race, and executive search firms, *Journal of Management*, **37**(3), pp. 651–681.

Hamori, M. (2010), Who gets headhunted and who gets ahead? The impact of search firms on executive careers, *Academy of Management Perspectives*, **24**(4), pp. 46–59.

Exit interview

An exit interview is a purposeful discussion about organizational separation or disengagement between an employer and a departing employee. Exit interviews seek to discover the employee's reasons for wanting to leave the organization and to maintain good public relations with exiting employees. Specifically the reasons include:

- Providing the employer with better insights into what is right or wrong about the company's policies and practices.
- Identifying the conditions under which the exiting employee would have stayed; for example, better supervisory practices.
- Discovering the factors that could improve the organization in the future; for example, improving human resource practices such as recruitment, selection and compensation practices; as well as redesigning vacated jobs.
- Identifying the compensation package in the new organization and generally collecting information on the terms and conditions of service offered by other organizations as doing so would enable the organization to identify best practices to replicate.
- Minimizing, if not eliminating, potential legal action if such exists, for example, in matters such as sexual harassment or bullying.
- Seeking feedback on improving initiatives, such as diversity and affirmative action.

Organizations need to differentiate between 'push' and 'pull' factors, if they wish to deal with employee turnover issues and improve employee retention. While exit interviews can point towards why an employee is leaving the organization, often they do not identify the cause. Are there pull factors encouraging the employee to leave? An employee might say that they are departing to join another organization that offers better pay or other working conditions, but this does not explain what led the person to start looking for another job in the first place. Or is the departing employee being 'pushed out' of the organization? Push factors include poor supervision, problems with certain colleagues, limited or no career opportunities, insecurity of employment and dissatisfaction with compensation schemes.

If the exit interviewer does not ask the pertinent questions to determine the genuine reasons for the employee leaving, the actual reasons may not be known. Some employees may also be unwilling to disclose the actual reason for leaving for fear that this may cause problems.

Exit interviews are often supported with the completion of a questionnaire, requesting departing employees to state the main reasons for leaving. This provides more accurate information than a formal exit interview. Some organizations also send questionnaires to people once they have left the organization, on the belief that they would be more willing to compete them at this point.

CHRIS ROWLEY AND NAGIAH RAMASAMY

See also:

Prejudice; Retention; Security of employment.

References and selected further readings

Carvin, B.N. (2011), New strategies for making exit interviews count, *Employment Relations Today*, **38**(2), pp 1–6.

Cushen, J. (2013), Financialization in the workplace: hegemonic narratives, performative interventions and the angry knowledge worker, *Accounting, Organizations and Society*, **38**(4), pp. 314–331.

Davenport, T.H. (2013), *Thinking for a Living: How to Get Better Performances and Results from Knowledge Workers*, Cambridge, MA: Harvard Business Press.

Gordon, M.E. (2011), The dialectics of the exit interview: a fresh look at conversations about organizational disengagement, *Management Communication Quarterly*, **25**(4), pp. 59–86.

Macafee, M. (2007), How to conduct exit interviews, *People Management*, **13**(14), pp. 42–43.

Taylor, S. (2010), *Resourcing and Talent Management*, 5th edn, London: Chartered Institute of Personnel and Development.

Expatriate

In today's competitive global market, organizations are seeking to increase their overseas presence through the assignment of expatriate managers. Expatriates are traditionally the employees who move across national boundaries into various roles within a firm's foreign operations, temporarily or for a short- or long-term assignment (Dowling et al., 2013). The literature on international human resource management (IHRM) has identified several reasons for international assignments and employment of expatriates; the most common reasons are to fill the skills gap; to launch a new business; to transfer technology; to develop and train staff; and to develop organizations in terms of knowledge, competence and procedure transfer. Other than the traditional company-sponsored expatriates, there are various other forms of international employees and work/employment, namely: immigrants, global careerists, self-initiated expatriates, commuter assignments, short-term assignments and virtual assignments (Collings et al., 2007).

Despite the strategic role that international transfers can play, many organizations do not appear to use them effectively. A major challenge for organizations involved in the internationalization of businesses is managing expatriates. As well as the strategic importance of international assignments for organizations and their overall HRM approaches, there are enormous costs involved. As such, researchers and practitioners are interested in determining ways to ensure expatriates' success on international assignments. In a global economy, expatriates encounter many challenges, which has compelled multinationals to review their IHRM practices. For decades, much of the literature has focused on investigating the methods used by organizations to respond to the challenges of international growth from an economic viewpoint and from managerial perspectives. While

IHRM has traditionally been researched using mainly Western theoretical perspectives, there is a recognized need to study IHRM from different cultural perspectives and from workers and professionals', rather than managerial perspectives.

Considering the complexities of the expatriation process, analysis of assignment success or failure becomes crucial for organizations with a high share of internationally mobile employees. Thereby, investigation into factors that influence success of the assignment has become a main focus of research (e.g., intention to stay on the assignment until it is successfully completed).

DHARA SHAH

See also:

International human resource management; Multinational companies; National culture.

References and selected further readings

Bonache, J., C. Brewster, C. Suutari and P. De Saa (2010), Expatriation: traditional criticisms and international careers introducing the special issue, *Thunderbird International Business Review*, **52**(4), pp. 263–274.

Collings, D., H. Scullion and M. Morley (2007), Changing patterns of global staffing in the multinational enterprise: challenges to the conventional expatriate assignment and emerging alternatives, *Journal of World Business*, **42**(2), pp. 198–213.

Dowling, P., M. Festing and A. Engle (2013), *International Human Resource Management*, 6th edn, London: Cengage Learning EMEA.

Harvey, M. and M. Moeller (2009), Expatriate managers: a historical review, *International Journal of Management Reviews*, **11**, pp. 275–296.

Reiche, B.S., M.L. Kraimer and A.W. Harzing (2011), Why do international assignees stay? An organizational embeddedness perspective, *Journal of International Business Studies*, **42**(4), pp. 521–544.

Expectancy theory

Expectancy theory is a process theory of motivation, which presents a more complex picture of motivation than the content theories of Maslow and Herzberg that preceded it. Expectancy theory was first developed by Vroom (1964) and the extended by Porter and Lawler (1968) who, it may be argued, developed Vroom's original theory to take into account contextual organizational influences and arguably also goal theory and equity theory.

The theory says that people will be motivated when they expect that they will be able to achieve what they want from the effort that they put in. Hence, there is a relationship between effort and reward if certain conditions are met. First, people need to sufficiently value the outcome or reward (valance – V): second, to feel that there is a causal relationship between their effort and the likely reward or outcome (instrumentality – I) and third, to feel they are capable of actually achieving or performing (expectancy – E). The theory was expressed by Vroom in a mathematical formula:

$$\text{Force of motivation} = E \times I \times V.$$

If people feel that, in spite of their efforts, they will not be able to achieve the reward or goal then there will be little motivation force.

Expectancy theory has fed into the work of reward practitioners with respect to the adoption of the 'line of sight' principle in performance pay or bonus scheme design (Gomez-Mejia and Balkin, 1992). Gerhart and Rynes (2003) support the general principles of expectancy theory as part of a theoretical framework to explain empirical findings on reward, but they take issue with the use of formulae within it, saying there is a lack of support for such a mathematical approach.

Expectancy theory as extended by Porter and Lawler (1968) implies a complex web of individual and organizational relationships. Wannus et al. (1983) argue that an individual's experience inside and outside the organization are important contextual factors on motivation, which might not be as rational in real life as the model suggests. This leads to important caveats on the effectiveness of pay as a motivator. Rynes et al. (2004) argued that while pay might be used as a general motivator, it is not equally important in all organizational situations or for all individuals (for example, high performers tend to expect to be well-paid).

ANGELA WRIGHT

See also:

Herzberg; Maslow; Work motivation.

References and selected further readings

Gerhart, B. and S. Rynes (2003), *Compensation: Theory, Evidence, and Strategic Implications*, Thousand Oaks, CA: Sage.
Gomez-Mejia, L. and D. Balkin (1992), *Compensation, Organizational Strategy and Firm Performance*, Cincinnati, OH: South-West Publishing Co.
Latham, G.P. (2007), *Work Motivation: History, Theory, Research, and Practice*, London: Sage.
Porter, L. and E. Lawler (1968), *Managerial Attitudes and Performance*, Homewood: R.D. Irwin.
Rynes, S., B. Gerhart and K. Minette (2004), The importance of pay in employee motivation: discrepancies between what people say and what they do, *Human Resource Management*, **43**(4), pp. 381–394.
Vroom, V. (1964), *Work and Motivation*, Chichester: John Wiley
Wannus, J., T. Keon and J. Latick (1983), Expectancy theory and occupational choices: review and test, *Organisational Behaviour and Human Performance*, **29**, pp. 66–86.

Experiential learning

The concept of experiential learning is developing in popularity and credibility. In basic terms it is described as 'learning by doing' or learning 'on the job'. On occasions this has been negatively translated as learning by making mistakes and also copying the mistakes of others. However, on-the-job learning has its place and this has been recognized, if not universally applauded, by the introduction of National Vocational Qualifications (NVQs) which assess competence in the workplace.

A more 'rounded' view of experiential learning is understood as learning through reflection on doing, and thus the Kolb learning cycle which developed into the Experiential Learning Model (ELM) (Kolb, 2015) is pertinent. The cycle begins with the concrete experience, moving through reflective and observation of that experience to abstract conceptualization (i.e., the analysis of the experience and implementation of problem-solving) and finally to active experimentation, which will develop the experience further.

This form of learning has become very popular, particularly in business schools, where the application of learning to real-life experience is seen as key to developing not only business knowledge but also professional skills, making students employable. It requires the learner to be active and fully participate in the learning process, which thereby devolves much of the responsibility of learning to the learner.

Business schools have led the way in experiential learning through the use of case-based education and exercises that focus upon live problem-solving. In recent years, executive education models (whereby groups of company executives take development opportunities that focus learning upon the exploration of specific company issues) have been used to develop undergraduate work-based degrees. The ultimate in experiential learning is where students are employed full-time in organizations, undertaking short, sharp, knowledge-based study blocks and in-house company consultancy projects. These degrees require students with high levels of confidence and autonomy and an ability to reflect and learn, and are increasing in popularity with employers who feel they have work-ready graduate employees rather than graduates at the end of their learning, who require further training.

ALISON SMITH

See also:

On-the-job learning.

References and selected further reading

Caza, A., H.A. Brower and J.H. Wayne (2015), Effects of a holistic, experiential curriculum on business students' satisfaction and career confidence, *The International Journal of Management Education*, **13**(1), pp. 75–83.

Finch, D., M. Peacock, D. Lazdowski and M. Hwang (2015), Managing emotions: a case study exploring the relationship between experiential learning, emotions, and student performance, *The International Journal of Management Education*, **13**(1), pp. 23–36.

Hodge, L., K.L. Proudford and H. Holt (2014), From periphery to core: the increasing relevance of experiential learning in undergraduate business education, *Research in Higher Education*, 26, www.www.aabri.com/manuscripts/142030.pdf.

Jackson, D. (2015), Employability skill development in work-integrated learning: barriers and best practice, *Studies in Higher Education*, **40**(2), pp. 350–367.

Karia, M., H. Bathula and M. Abbott (2014), An experiential learning approach to teaching business planning: connecting students to the real world, in M. Li and Y. Zhao (eds), *Exploring Learning & Teaching in Higher Education*, Heidelberg: Springer, pp. 123–144.

Kolb, D.A. (2015), *Experiential Learning: Experience as the Source of Learning and Development*, New Jersey: Pearson Education.

External labour markets

External labour markets comprise an organization's labour supply that is external to the organization. Other terms synonymous with external labour markets are 'external recruiting' and 'external labour forces'. External recruitment refers to the attraction of people from the external labour market to a job/position being offered by an organization. The source of the external labour can come from a multitude of different geographic locations including local, regional, national and international labour markets. The choice between internal or external labour sources should be dependent on the organization's strategy, policies (e.g., equal opportunity for women) and/or financial motives (e.g., requirement to reduce recruitment expenditure). Aside from geography, external labour markets can be segmented by knowledge, skills, abilities and other attributes (KSAOs); education; worker characteristics and occupational groups. It is important to be able to distinguish between types of external labour because they differ in terms of their perspectives on motivation, control and career advancement/development.

The external labour market usually includes a few different types of candidates. These are people actively seeking a job (active job-seekers); those who are interested in a position, but search for a job infrequently (semi-passive) and those who currently have a job but are not seeking other employment, but may be persuaded to take another position if an attractive offer arises (passive job-seekers). While it is often easier, quicker and cheaper to recruit and select active job-seekers, many of the highest-quality employees are not actively seeking new employment opportunities. To recruit such people, often a more proactive and strategic approach is required.

The external labour market is also inherently associated with a range of pros and cons. The pros include new employees that can be selected to bring in novel KSAOs and new ideas that enable the organization to achieve their strategic objectives. While it can be argued that internal employees could be trained and developed to meet strategic needs, often such an approach is not feasible and/or some KSAOs can take a long time to learn/develop. In addition, employees hired from the external market can be used to shake up organizational status quo to assist organizational change. The cons when compared to internal sourcing include an increased amount of time to maximize the productivity of new hires, disgruntled employees who feel the position should have been offered to internal candidates, and it is often more expensive and time-consuming to recruit and select externally.

MATTHEW XERRI

See also:
Recruitment.

References and selected further readings

Compton, R.L., W.J. Morrissey, A.R. Nankervis and B. Morrissey (2009), *Effective Recruitment and Selection Practices*, 5th edn, Sydney: CCH Australia Limited.
Connell, J. and S. Teo (eds) (2010), *Strategic HRM: Contemporary Issues in the Asia Pacific Region*, Prahran: Tilde University Press.
Kramar, R., T. Bartram, H. De Cieri, R.A. Noe, J.R. Hollenbeck, B. Gerhart and P.M. Wright (2013), *Human Resource Management in Australia*, 5th edn, Sydney: McGraw-Hill Australia.
Phillips, J. and S. Gully (2014), *Strategic Staffing*, Essex: Pearson Education.
Wilton, N. (2013), *An Introduction to Human Resource Management*, 2nd edn, London: Sage.

Family-friendly policies

Family-friendly policies provide options for work arrangements that assist employees to combine paid work with family and care responsibilities. Three main policy areas are: employee-centred flexibility (e.g., changing the location, scheduling or hours of work), paid and unpaid leave (e.g., parental leave) and childcare (e.g., onsite childcare). Family-friendly policies can exist as government legislation, within enterprise bargaining/collective agreements and/or as organizational policy.

Family-friendly policies were developed in response to profound changes in workforce demographics, including increased participation by women, parents (sole and partnered) and carers (e.g., workers caring for an elder or disabled relative). Family-friendly policies have a positive effect on gender equality and work–family balance by supporting mothers' capacity to combine paid employment with caregiving, and increasing fathers' participation in care (Hegewisch and Gornick, 2011).

Work–family policies also benefit organizations via increased job satisfaction and commitment and reduced turnover (Butts et al., 2013). However, significant gaps between the policy availability and uptake are common, due to concerns over negative consequences of policy uptake such as reductions in career opportunities or job security. For work–life policies to be truly effective they must be accepted and integrated into the mainstream for all workers (Kossek et al., 2014).

More recently, the *ethical* argument for family-friendly policies has received considerable attention, which is argued to enhance policy impact via voluntary efforts by organizations (Tziner et al., 2014). Stakeholder theory has been used to argue for better strategy initiatives when setting directions in organizations (Orlitzky and Benjamin, 2001) and for the inclusion of wellbeing metrics when evaluating the effectiveness of organizations (Tziner et al. 2014). While the use of voluntary implementation of work–family policies by human resource departments will not replace the need for government legislation to support such policies, it would be best to see both methods of implementation used more frequently in practice.

NATALIE SKINNER AND ERICH C. FEIN

See also:

Flexible working; Job quality; Wellbeing.

References and selected further readings

Butts, M.M., W.J. Casper and T.S. (2013), How important are work–family support policies? A meta-analytic investigation of their effects on employee outcomes, *Journal of Applied Psychology*, **98**(1), pp.1–25.
Hegewisch, A. and J.C. Gornick (2011), The impact of work-family policies on women's employment: a review of research from OECD countries, *Community, Work and Family*, **14**(2), pp.119–138.
Kossek, E.E., M. Valcour and P. Lirio (2014), The sustainable work force: organizational strategies for promoting work-life balance and wellbeing, in P.Y Chen and C.L Cooper (eds), *Wellbeing: A Complete Reference Guide, Volume III*, New York: Wiley & Sons, pp.295–319.
Orlitzky, M. and J.D. Benjamin (2001), Corporate social responsibility and firm risk: a meta-analytic review, *Business and Society*, **40**(4), pp.369–396.
Skinner, N. and J. Chapman (2013), Work–life balance and family friendly policies, *Evidence Base*, **4**, pp.1–25.
Tziner, A., E.C. Fein and A. Birati (2014), Tempering hard times: integrating well-being metrics into utility analysis, *Industrial and Organizational Psychology: Perspectives on Science and Practice*, **7**(4), pp.554–568.

Financial participation

Financial participation is the participation of employees in enterprise profits and outcomes. In the European Union (EU), financial participation is often referred to as PEPPER – promotion of employee participation in profits and enterprise results – and a number of studies have been referred to as PEPPER reports. In the USA, 'shared capitalism arrangements' is the preferred term. Financial participation can take many different forms. The literature distinguishes three major categories of schemes: profit-sharing, ownership of employee shares and stock options.

With profit-sharing, the employees receive in addition to their fixed salary a variable part of income, which depends directly on the profits or other measure of results. Contrary to individual bonuses, profit-sharing is a collective scheme applied to all or most employees. The scheme can provide immediate or deferred benefits to employees; paid in cash, shares or other securities; or it can be allocated to specific funds invested for the benefit of employees (such as in France and Finland). Related to the profit-sharing schemes are so-called 'gain-sharing' arrangements. Such schemes are not dependent on the financial performance of a company, but other criteria, such as productivity gains, cost savings or certain quality objectives.

With ownership of employee shares, workers share in the results through the payment of dividends and/or capital appreciation of the shares held. It can be allocated as free shares or available for purchase, usually on advantageous terms. Employee share ownership can be both individual and collective. When collectively held, a trust (or other body) receives the dividend and distribute the amount to employees as a profit share. Also, the collectively held shares may be distributed to individual employees over time, such as is the case in the USA type employee share ownership plans (ESOPs).

Stock options are closely related to employee share, where employees receive a right to buy company shares in a given period and for a certain price. They can ultimately lead to shareholding, but unlike share schemes, there may be tax exemption attached to this form in order to promote savings as in save-as-you-earn schemes in the UK.

Reasons for establishing employee financial participation are that it intends to lead to significant behavioural effects, such as increased effort, improved collaboration, reduced turnover and increased binding to the company. These behavioural effects will have a positive impact on the performance of the company as a whole. Research partly confirms these effects.

ERIK POUTSMA

See also:
Employee share ownership plans; Profit-related pay and gainsharing; Profit-sharing.

References and selected further readings
Kruse, D.L., R.B. Freeman and J.R. Blasi (eds) (2010), *Shared Capitalism at Work: Employee Ownership, Profit and Gain Sharing, and Broad-Based Stock Options*, Chicago: University of Chicago Press.
Pendleton, A. and E. Poutsma (2013), Financial participation, in C. Brewster and W. Mayrhofer (eds), *Handbook of Research in Comparative Human Resource Management*, dg: Cheltenham: Edward Elgar Publishing, pp. 345–368.
Poutsma, E. and E. Kaarsemaker (2015), Added value of employee financial participation, in M. Andresen

and C. Nowak (eds), *Human Resource Management Practices: Management for Professionals*, New York: Springer, pp. 181–196.

Poutsma, E., P.E.M. Ligthart, A. Pendleton and C. Brewster (2013), The development of employee financial participation in Europe, in E. Parry, E. Stravrou and M. Lazarove (eds), *Global Trends in Human Resource Management*, Basingstoke: Palgrave Macmillan.

Financialization

Since the 1980s, organizations have been operating within an era of 'financialized' capitalism (Van der Zwan, 2014). 'Financialization' prompts top organization management to prioritize shareholder value creation over – and often to the detriment of – other stakeholders. Contemporary shareholders are typically transient, institutional investors who care less about improving the performance of individual firms in their portfolio than they do about making the correct prediction on a firm's performance in order to outperform the index and/or peer group they are benchmarked against. The short-term nature of investment means top management must continuously stimulate a market for organizational shares, prompting them to direct firm activities around achievement of investor-favoured novel financialized performance metrics. Achieving financialized performance metrics goes hand-in-hand with depleting internal organizational investment as top management heighten returns to shareholders; a trend that is claimed to be fundamentally damaging the long-term productive and innovative capacity of organizations (Mukunda, 2014).

Financialization undermines top managements' ability to adopt a 'human capital' or 'resource based' approach to HRM (Thompson, 2013). These aforementioned approaches depict employees as a valuable resource organizations should commit to, engage and develop. However, dominant financialized performance metrics categorize employee-related expenditure, not as an investment yielding productive return, but a cost to be minimized. Consequently financialization prompts perpetual organizational restructuring involving headcount reduction, centralization, outsourcing and use of fixed-term and peripheral employment; even in times of strong organizational profit and growth. Financialization is associated with a reduction in relative employee remuneration and since the early 1980s, advanced capitalist economies have reduced labour's share of national income. Macroeconomic inequality is mirrored within organizations and there is a consistent pattern of increased wage inequality within firms due to the acceleration of top management pay amid falling real employee remuneration. Financialization has seen a transfer of benefit risk from employers to employees; particularly in the area of retirement benefits. The cumulative effect of financialized pressures is that employees are being asked to do more with and for less in work environments characterized by pervasive job and financial insecurity. For HRM professionals, the dominance of financialized pressures make achieving high levels of employee engagement and commitment a difficult, and arguably counterproductive, endeavour as employees increasingly view themselves as an insecure disposable commodity rather than a valuable organizational asset (Cushen, 2013).

Jean Cushen

See also:

Disconnected capitalism; Human capital; Resource-based view; Unitarism.

References and selected further readings

Christensen, C.M. and D. van Bever (2014), The capitalist's dilemma, *Harvard Business Review*, **92**(6), pp. 60–68.
Cushen, J. (2013), Financialization in the workplace: hegemonic narratives, performative interventions and the angry knowledge worker, *Accounting, Organizations and Society*, **38**(4), pp. 314–331.
Mintzberg, H., R. Simons and K. Basu (2002), Beyond selfishness, *MIT Sloan Management Review*, **44**(1), pp. 67–74.
Mukunda, G. (2014), The price of Wall Street's power, *Harvard Business Review*, **92**(6), pp. 70–78.
Thompson, P. (2013), Financialization and the workplace: extending and applying the disconnected capitalism thesis, *Work. Employment and Society*, **27**, pp. 472–488.
Van der Zwan, N. (2014), Making sense of Financialization, *Socio-Economic Review*, **12**(1), pp. 99–129.

Fixed-term contract

Fixed-term contracts are contracts related either to the undertaking of a specific task, or to a predetermined period of time, which may be a number of months or even years. While there is a long history of non-standard employment, the growth in fixed-term contracts in many countries has been (at least partially) attributed to the increased deregulation of labour markets as a widespread policy response to unemployment since the 1980s.

Traditionally used in seasonal work, the use of fixed-term contracts can be linked to the increasing use of numerical flexibility by organizations (Kalleberg, 2000) and therefore offers a number of benefits to employers and organizations.

Fixed-term contracts can negate the negative costs associated with sacking employees, as those employed on fixed-term contracts have considerably lower levels of employment protection than permanent workers (Goux et al., 2001, pp. 533–534). Those on fixed-term contracts are also generally paid less and provided with fewer opportunities for training and development than permanent workers. Employers are also able to stipulate non-renewal clauses into fixed-term contracts, further illustrating the precarious nature of such forms of employment.

There are also a number of potential negatives for organizations, which make use of this type of contract. The precarious nature of such work can lead to problems both of recruitment and retention, although it is noted that the aim of using fixed contracts may be purposefully to generate worker turnover (Portugal and Varejão, 2009). Nevertheless, with such an approach, there will be a cost to the organization in terms of continuity and stability and potential problems with commitment and motivation.

There is evidence of benefit to employees to suggest that fixed-term contracts can act as a stepping stone to more permanent work for the unemployed (Booth et al., 2002). However, fixed-term contracts are considered to be a form of casual, precarious employment due to the lack of permanency and limited degree of labour market power of workers on such contracts, often being associated with poor pay, fewer benefits and limited long-term career prospects. Despite this, it has been claimed that there are no negative health consequences associated with being employed on a fixed-term contract (Guest, 2004, pp. 13–15).

ANDY HODDER

See also:

Flexible firm; Flexible working; Precarious employment.

References and selected further readings

Booth, A., M. Francesconi and J. Frank (2002), Temporary jobs: stepping stones or dead ends? *The Economic Journal*, 112(480), pp. f189–f213.

Gash, V. and F. McGinnity (2007), Fixed-term contracts — the new European inequality? Comparing men and women in West Germany and France, *Socio-Economic Review*, 5(3), pp. 467–496.

Goux, D., E. Maurin and M. Pauchet (2001), Fixed-term contracts and the dynamics of labour demand, *European Economic Review*, 45, pp. 533–552.

Guest, D. (2004), Flexible employment contracts, the psychological contract and employee outcomes: an analysis and review of the evidence, *International Journal of Management Reviews*, 5/6(1), pp. 1–19.

Kalleberg, A. (2000), Nonstandard employment relations: part-time, temporary and contract work, *Annual Review of Sociology*, 26, pp. 341–365.

Portugal, P. and J. Varejão (2009), *Why Do Firms Use Fixed-Term Contracts?* IZA Discussion Paper Series, No. 4380.

Flexible firm

The idea of the 'flexible firm' emerged in the early 1980s, a time of economic restructuring in the UK. Put forward by John Atkinson and others (Atkinson, 1984; NEDO, 1986), the model claimed that firms were increasingly seeking and achieving greater flexibility from their workforce. This flexibility was of two main kinds: numerical, the ability of firms to adjust numbers employed and hours worked; and functional, the ability of firms to match the skill profiles of their workforce to changing patterns of demand. As part of these developments, it was argued, the workforce was being divided into two basic groups: core workers, who were expected to display functional flexibility in return for security of employment; and peripheral workers, such as those on temporary and part-time contracts, who were expected to provide the firm with the numerical flexibility it required.

The idea of the flexible firm model gave rise to an extensive and often heated debate (see, e.g., Pollert, 1991). There was enough evidence to offer the model *prima facie* support: the size of certain 'peripheral' groups of workers, for example, did seem to be on the increase (Hakim, 1990). It was less easy, however, to fit all the various elements into the pattern that the model suggested. Thus functional flexibility, rather than representing the development of a core group of polyvalent super-craftspersons, was more often both negative in nature – involving the breaking down of boundaries between what different groups of workers were expected to do – and limited in degree. There was little to suggest in any case that so-called 'core' workers were gaining security of employment in exchange for being functionally more flexible, either in the UK (Cully et al., 1999) or in the US (Cappelli, 1995).

An attempt to develop the model in the light of the available evidence was made by Ackroyd and Procter (1998) in their 'new flexible firm'. Segmentation of the labour force, they argued, was based not on a core/periphery distinction but on the product-focused way in which many firms were restructuring their operations. Beyond a small group of senior management, there was no protected 'core' workforce: in that sense, all were subject to a heightened degree of insecurity as firms attempted to achieve flexibility through the manipulation of product-focused and finance-driven segments of activity.

STEPHEN PROCTER

See also:

Core worker; Flexible working; Peripheral worker.

References and selected further readings

Ackroyd, S. and S. Procter (1998), British manufacturing organization and workplace industrial relations: some attributes of the new flexible firm, *British Journal of Industrial Relations*, **36**(2), pp. 163–183.

Atkinson, J. (1984), Manpower strategies for flexible organizations, *Personnel Management*, August, pp. 28–31.

Cappelli, P. (1995), Rethinking employment, *British Journal of Industrial Relations*, **33**(4), pp. 563–602.

Cully, M., S. Woodland, A. O'Reilly and G. Dix (1999), *Britain at Work: as Depicted by the 1998 Workplace Employee Relations Survey*, London and New York: Routledge.

Hakim, C. (1990), Core and periphery in employers' workforce strategies: evidence from the 1987 ELUS Survey, *Work, Employment and Society*, **4**(2), pp. 157–188.

NEDO (1986), *Changing Working Patterns: How Companies Achieve Flexibility to Meet New Needs*, London: National Economic Development Office.

Pollert, A. (ed.) (1991) *Farewell to Flexibility?* Oxford: Blackwell.

Flexible working

Flexibility or flexible working is a very broad and poorly defined concept and is used as an umbrella term to describe a wide range of practices associated with the utilization of labour. The definition is important, however, because different interpretations hold different implications for employers and employees. The CIPD (2014) uses the term 'flexible working' to describe 'a type of working arrangement which gives some degree of flexibility on how long, where, when and at what times employees work. The flexibility can be in terms of working time, working location or the pattern of working.' Examples of practices associated with this definition are part-time work, term-time working, job sharing, flexitime, compressed hours, annual hours, homeworking, mobile or telework-ing and career breaks. This interpretation is increasingly used in policy debates and the practitioner literature and is often associated with practices that promote a better work–life balance, suggesting that flexibility is good for employees. Other terms include 'atypical working', 'non-standard' and 'contingent employment'. This latter type of work includes part-time work, temporary jobs, fixed-term jobs, agency work, subcon-tract work, casual employment and sometimes self-employment. Critics argue that this type of work has negative implications for workers, with suggestions that it is less stable and secure than traditional work.

An alternative perspective, which focuses on the employers need for flexibility, but captures most of the aforementioned forms of flexibility, is to conceptualize it as having the following dimensions:

- **Functional or task flexibility**, which is the ability to redeploy employees across a range of tasks according to work demand. This can involve taking on tasks at a different or the same job level. Examples include multi-skilling, job rotation and teamwork.

- **Numerical flexibility**, which involves adjusting the labour supply by increasing or decreasing the number of employees and/or the number of hours worked. This type of arrangement is common in very cyclical businesses such as tourism, agriculture and retail. Examples include part-time working, temporary jobs and job share.
- **Temporal flexibility**, which allows employers to vary the number and pattern of working hours in response to work demands. This maximizes productive time and minimizes unproductive or idle time. Examples include annual hours, flexitime, overtime and zero-hours contracts.
- **Geographical or distance flexibility**, which is the ability to work remotely, for example at home or at different locations.

This conceptualization of flexibility, which builds on an early model of the flexible firm developed by Atkinson (1984), clearly illustrates the choices available to employers to meet the need for flexibility. It emphasizes how employers can adjust labour supply to product or service demand, thus enabling them to become more responsive to market conditions and make more efficient and economic use of labour. Additional forms of flexibility are outsourcing, or the transfer of products or services to another vendor or supplier, which is a longer term type of flexibility with implications for labour, and financial or wage flexibility, such as performance-related pay, which enables greater financial flexibility for the price of labour. However, in the main it is the short-term forms of flexibility – numerical, functional and temporal flexibility – that the literature refers to when discussing flexible working arrangements. Debates have focused on asking who benefits from these types of working – employers or employees? Some critics argue that in practice it means flexibility *of* the employee rather than flexibility *for* the employee. Others view flexibility as potentially beneficial for both sides.

Increasingly in the UK, policymakers and organizations are promoting flexible working arrangements as being of mutual benefit to employers and employees. The business benefits are seen to include increased productivity, reduced absence and improved ability to recruit and retain staff. For employees it provides greater control over how, when and where they work, a greater sense of empowerment, a better work–life balance and improved wellbeing. In the workplace this can translate into improved attitudes and behaviours. This win-win view is reinforced by growing legislation (in both the UK and Europe), most recently the right for employees to request flexible working. However, it is important to note that the practices being referred to here are narrowly focused on those that are predominantly employee-led – for example, part-time work, homework, flexitime, term-time working and compressed working hours. There are also costs to be acknowledged (for example, implementation and administrative costs), and difficulties in implementing such schemes. Also of significance is the fact that, although cases study evidence supports the benefits of these types of working, the empirical evidence is more mixed. For example, De Menezes and Kelliher's (2011) review of the literature found no consistent evidence of a business case for these types of arrangements. The evidence, however, is more supportive of a positive link between job satisfaction and these flexible work arrangements.

Many of the criticisms of flexible working concern temporary work, which includes fixed-term contracts, agency work and casual work. This form of flexibility is generally considered to be employer-led with the benefits covering improved ability to adjust staffing levels to demand, reduced employment costs, cover for short-term absences and screening for permanent jobs. Critics, however, argue that temporary workers are peripheral workers and as such are marginalized and disadvantaged. They are often employed in lower-quality jobs, lack the training and development opportunities open to permanent staff and face job insecurity. Nevertheless there is evidence that some people prefer temporary work, since it gives them more discretion over when and what kind of work they do, can be less stressful and provides a stepping stone to more permanent work. A review of the empirical research (de Cuyper et al., 2008) on the psychological impact of temporary employment reveals mixed results, with both positive and negative findings. Part of the explanations for this may lie in the fact that the make-up of temporary workers is extremely varied, including skilled professional workers who probably enjoy high salaries and job autonomy, but also low-paid casual workers who have little employment security and less meaningful work.

Some forms of functional flexibility, such as teamworking and multi-skilling are also criticized for leading to work intensification, increased pressure and stress. Again, the evidence is mixed. Employees who are functionally flexible can have more fulfilling and satisfying jobs and be more productive. While this form of flexibility allows employers to reorganize, reallocate and retrain their staff to respond to changing work demands, it is expensive to implement because training is required and can result in a dilution of skills.

In summary, flexible working has many different meanings and the outcomes for employers and employees depends on the form that it takes, its implementation and a range of individual factors.

SUE HUTCHINSON

See also:

Compressed working time; Family-friendly policies; Flexitime; Part-time work; Teamwork; Temporary work; Term-time working; Work–life balance.

References and selected further readings

Atkinson, J. (1984), Manpower strategies for flexible organisations, *Personnel Management*, August, pp. 28–31.
BIS (2014), *Costings and Benefits to Business of Adopting Work Life Balance Working Practices: A literature Review*, London: Policy Studies Institute, www.gov.uk/government/uploads/system/uploads/attachment_data/file/323290/bis-14-903-costs-and-benefits-to-business-of-adopting-work-life-balance-working-practices-a-literature-review.pdf.
CIPD (2014), *Flexible Working Factsheet*, www.cipd.co.uk/hr-resources/factsheets/flexible-working.aspx.
de Cuyper, N., J. Jong, H. De Witte, K. Isaksson, T. Rogotti and R. Schalk (2008), Literature review of the theory and research on the psychological impact of temporary employment: towards a conceptual model, *International Journal of Management Reviews*, **10**(1), pp. 25–51.
De Menezes, L.M. and C. Kelliher (2011), Flexible working and performance: a systematic review of the evidence for a business case, *International Journal of Management Reviews*, **13**, pp. 452–474.
Hutchinson, S. (2014), Flexibleworking, in G. Rees, and P.E Smith (eds), *Strategic Human Resource Management: An International Perspective*, London: Sage, pp. 183–225.

Flexicurity

As a concept, flexicurity emerged in the mid-1990s, in reference to Dutch and Danish labour market models, which in that period had remarkable performance.

It has come to occupy a central place in the political and academic debate after the European Commission has adopted it as key target within the European Employment Strategy, addressing it in a number of summits, strategy papers and guidelines.

While the concept has gained great currency, it is still employed in different ways. The dominant discourse, as it is put forward also by European institutions, defines flexicurity as a policy strategy aimed at simultaneously increasing labour flexibility and security. In other words, as a combination of measures promoting workers' adaptability and, at the same time, securing them from the potential detrimental effects (through employment services, training and retraining initiatives, and welfare provisions). In this light, an accurate systematization of the concept suggests the possibility of various types of combinations between different forms of flexibility (external-numerical, internal-numerical, functional, variable pay) and security (job, employment, income and 'combination' security) (Wilthagen and Tros, 2004).

Flexicurity is optimistically considered the most effective response to the challenges of a globalized economy. In the dominant discourse, it promises competitiveness, economic and employment growth, while safeguarding social cohesion. It should lead to win-win solutions, furthering the interests of both workers and employers.

Criticisms focus first of all on the ambiguity of the concept and openness to political capture; not least because it does not specify what level of flexibility and security are appropriate and which types of measures are compatible and able to balance their effects. In addition, core critiques are the lack of attention to conflicts of interests and heterogeneity in labour market and the reductionist view of the sources of flexibility and security (Burroni and Keune, 2011). Several scholars emphasize the role of collective bargaining. A broader critical discussion raises questions also on its theoretical assumptions. Flexicurity is considered an alternative way of naming problems and assigning responsibility for addressing them: it promotes a further individualization of social protection and could intensify inequalities, dualisms, vulnerability (Keune and Amparo, 2014).

Finally, recent contributions focus on whether flexicurity, having been developed in times of good economic and labour market performance, would also work in times of economic difficulties, job losses and high unemployment, and how it could be implemented.

MARCELLO PEDACI

See also:

Flexible firm; Job security; Regulation.

References and selected further readings

Burroni, L. and M. Keune (2011), Flexicurity: a conceptual critique, *European Journal of Industrial Relations*, **17**(1), pp. 75–91.
Eurofound (2012), *The Second Phase of Flexicurity: An Analysis of Practices and Policies in the Member States*, Luxembourg: Publications Office of the European Union.
European Commission (2007), *Towards Common Principles of Flexicurity: More and better Jobs Through Flexibility and Security*, Luxembourg: Publications Office of the European Union.
Ibsen, C.L. and M. Mailand (2010), Striking a balance? Flexibility and security in collective bargaining, *Economic and Industrial Democracy*, **32**(2), pp. 161–180.
Keune, M. and S. Amparo (eds) (2014), *Deconstructing Flexicurity and Developing Alternative Approaches:*

Towards New Concepts and Approaches for Employment and Social Policy, New York and London: Routledge.

Wilthagen, T. and F. Tros (2004), The concept of 'flexicurity': a new approach to regulating employment and labour markets, *Transfer: European Review of Labour and Research*, **10**(2), pp.166–186.

Flexitime

Flexitime allows employees to choose, within certain set limits, when to start and finish work, and is one of the most common forms of working time flexibility. Normally certain 'core' hours are required, for example 10am–3pm every day when all employees are expected to be present and some organizations allow employees to flex their lunchtime, provided a minimum period is taken (e.g., 30 minutes). Typically, hours of attendance are recorded and added up over a set accounting period – for example, four weeks or a calendar month – using timesheets or clock cards. At the end of this period, employees are expected to balance the hours they have worked with their contractual hours. Within limits, employees can carry over a credit or debit of hours to the next period and some schemes allow employees to build up a bank of hours to take as additional holiday or time off.

Employer surveys indicate that flexitime is available in around half of all workplaces in Britain, and take up by employees is increasing. For example, the Work–Life Balance Employer Survey (BIS 2014a) reports that in 2013 just over half (54 per cent) of employers in Britain reported that flexitime was available in their establishment, and 29 per cent of employees worked on this basis compared with 12 per cent of employees in 2000. This form of working was most commonly reported in banking, insurance professional and support services industries, and least common in manufacturing (BIS, 2012).

Flexitime is generally considered to be more desirable to employees and surveys indicate it shows the highest level of unmet demand, meaning that employees who do not have access to this type of arrangement would like to work in that way (BIS, 2014b). The obvious attraction to employees is the flexibility it gives around start and finish times, thus enabling individuals to fit their personal commitments with work. It also provides the opportunity to avoid travelling in rush hour, to undertake work during quieter times and accrue extra time off. These benefits are reflected in studies that show that flexitime has positive effects on job satisfaction and satisfaction with work schedule (Baltes et al., 1999). It follows therefore that, from an employer's perspective, flexitime can be an aid to recruitment and retention. It can also help in managing peaks and troughs in the workload and potentially provides an opportunity for scheduling work across a longer period of the day. Surveys also show that that flexible work schedules have a positive effect on employee productivity and employee absenteeism.

However flexitime is not suitable for all types of work, such as shift workers, continuous production lines or where direct contact with the customer is required. The organization may also be too small to accommodate such flexibility and it may be incompatible with team working (Smeaton and Young, 2007). There is also the potential risk of abuse, particularly where employees are trusted to record their own hours. The clocking in and out of work or recording hours on a time sheet does not fit with a culture based on trust and for this reason is considered undesirable by many organizations. It can also result in increased administration costs and there may be difficulties in providing adequate supervision outside the core hours.

SUE HUTCHINSON

See also:

Absence; Compressed working time; Family-friendly policies; Flexible working; Job satisfaction; Work–life balance.

References and selected further readings

Baltes, B.B., T.E. Briggs, J.W. Huff, J.A. Wright and G.A. Neuman (1999), Flexible and compressed work-week schedules: a meta-analysis of their effects on work-related criteria, *Journal of Applied Psychology*, **84**(4), pp. 496–513.

BIS (2012), *The Fourth Work–Life Balance Employee Survey*, Employment Relations Research Series 122, www.gov.uk/government/uploads/system/uploads/attachment_data/file/32153/12-p151-fourth-work-life-balance-employee-survey.pdf.

BIS (2014a), *The Fourth Work–Life Balance Employer Survey (2013)*, Research Paper No. 184, www.gov.uk/government/uploads/system/uploads/attachment_data/file/398557/bis-14-1027-fourth-work-life-balance-employer-survey-2013.pdf.

BIS (2014b), *Costings and Benefits to Business of Adopting Work–Life Balance Working Practices: A Literature Review*, London: Policy Studies Institute, BIS, www.gov.uk/government/uploads/system/uploads/attachment_data/file/323290/bis-14-903-costs-and-benefits-to-business-of-adopting-work-life-balance-working-practices-a-literature-review.pdf.

IDS (2012), *Flexitime in Practice*, https://ids.thomsonreuters.com/hr-in-practice/features-analysis/flexitime-in-practice?filters=10603&index=2&content=61373.

Smeaton, D. and V. Young (2007), *Work in the Future: Employers and Workplace Transformation*, Manchester: Equal Opportunities Commission.

Frames of reference

The frames of reference concept has a long pedigree in studies of managing employment and human resource management (HRM). Its influence can be traced to a seminal research paper written by the industrial sociologist Alan Fox (1966). Reflecting on the problem of 'workplace disorder', Fox elaborated on the contribution of employer attitudes. In considering such attitudes, Fox borrowed from industrial psychology the concept of a frame of reference. A frame of reference was noted to be a 'conceptual structure of generalizations', 'assumptions' and 'ideas' that aided the perception and interpretation of events. Such frames of reference influenced how individuals perceived social phenomena, swaying their judgement and impacting on their subsequent behaviour. Fox posited that among employers, two frames of references might be identified: 'unitarism' and 'pluralism'. In their different ways, unitarist and pluralist frames of reference coloured employer attitudes towards the exercise of authority, the existence of workplace conflict and the role of trade unions. The frames of reference concept would later be identified as relevant not only to understanding employer attitudes, but also those of workers and the 'wider public'. Allied to this, the consideration of reference frames would broaden to incorporate an appreciation of 'radicalism', while Budd and Bhave (2008) have recently referred to an 'egoist' frame that celebrates free-market individualism and an interpretation of labour markets aligned to neoclassical economics.

Since Fox's seminal work, the frames of reference concept has regularly featured in the literature, typically in introductory chapters to texts on employment relations and HRM. The idea that workplace actors adhere to a collection of assumptions that, in some way, serve to inform subsequent behaviour is a useful one. By way of simple example, an employer adhering to a unitarist frame of reference will look unfavourably on trade unions and act in ways that prevent or frustrate their presence in the workplace. In contrast, a trade unionist, inclined to a radical frame of reference, will remain deeply suspicious of HRM attempts to generate 'employee engagement': viewing it as managerial ploy to incorporate workers into a company agenda and loosen their ties to the union. Of course the putative frames of unitarism, pluralism and radicalism are merely ideal-type classifications, useful for offering some point of initial entry into establishing and understanding different attitudinal postures in HRM and employment relations. In reality, workplace actors may well adhere to a hotchpotch of assorted notions that belie neat categorization. Nonetheless, by being aware of an individual's frame of reference, we can begin to make some sense of their behaviour at work.

NIALL CULLINANE

See also:

Employment relationship; Pluralism; Radicalism; Unitarism.

References and selected further readings

Budd, J. and D. Bhave (2008), Values, ideologies and frames of reference in employment relations, in N. Bacon, P. Blyton, J. Fiorito and E. Heery (eds), *Sage Handbook of Industrial and Employment Relations*, London: Sage.
Fox, A. (1966), *Industrial Sociology and Industrial Relations*, Royal Commission on Trade Unions and Employer Associations, Research Paper No. 3, London: HMSO.

Freelance work

Freelance work is generally considered a form of self-employment that does not require the employment of others and involves relative autonomy in delivering work for a client. However, this is a fuzzy area and, for example, in the UK, freelance work does not hold an official or widely accepted definition (Kitching and Smallbone, 2012). Nevertheless, it is a common form of work and Kitching and Smallbone (2012) estimate there are as many as 1.56 million freelance workers in the UK.

The relatively recent prominence of freelance work reflects the changing nature of work and employment through periods of organizational downsizing and the externalization of labour (Storey et al., 2005); for example, allowing businesses to lower wage costs or avoid forms of employment regulation. In this way, employees were pushed out of organizations and into self-employment, often working for their former employers (Stanworth and Stanworth, 1997). This pattern created a new type of career path, emphasizing individualism, the development of high-quality networks and strategies (Born and Witteloostuijn, 2013). However, Stanworth and Stanworth (1997) highlight the dependency that can develop on particular clients, coupled with job insecurity owing to decisions over recruiting or retaining freelancers being informal and ad hoc. Further, the work itself carries the potential for a lack of social protection, employee rights and for forms of self-exploitation in order to compete on price in highly competitive markets.

Research on freelance work has paid particular attention to the media industry. For example, Storey et al. (2005, p. 1051) report on media freelance workers who aspired to independence and autonomy, but experienced vulnerability amid 'the constraints and power asymmetries of the market place'. Grugulis and Stoyanova (2011) highlight further problems where, after a fracturing of the labour market and lacking organization, junior freelancers lack easy access to experienced colleagues from whom they can learn or seek advice. Yet, there is no 'standard' freelance worker and greater research is needed to understand this form of work (Kitching and Smallbone, 2012).

OLIVER MALLETT AND ROBERT WAPSHOTT

See also:

Self-employment.

References and selected further readings

Born, A. and A. Witteloostuijn (2013), Drivers of freelance career success, *Journal of Organizational Behavior*, **34**(1), pp. 24–46.

Fraser, J. and M. Gold (2001), 'Portfolio workers': autonomy and control amongst freelance translators, *Work, Employment & Society*, **15**(4), pp. 679–697.

Grugulis, I. and D. Stoyanova (2011), The missing middle: communities of practice in a freelance labour market, *Work, Employment & Society*, **25**(2), pp. 342–351.

Kitching, J. and D. Smallbone (2012), Are freelancers a neglected form of small business? *Journal of Small Business and Enterprise Development*, **19**(1), pp. 74–91.

Stanworth, C. and J. Stanworth (1997), Reluctant entrepreneurs and their clients: the case of self-employed freelance workers in the British book publishing industry, *International Small Business Journal*, **16**(1), pp. 58–73.

Storey, J., G. Salaman and K. Platman (2005), Living with enterprise in an enterprise economy: freelance and contract workers in the media, *Human Relations*, **58**(8), pp. 1033–1054.

Gender

Gender refers to the roles, behaviours, values and meanings culturally associated to women and men. Gender differences do not necessarily correspond to differences in biological sex. Gender differs from biological sex in that it refers to socially constructed expectations, practices and behaviours of what it means to be a man or a woman within a specific society.

The distinction between sex and gender became widespread from the 1970s with the advancement of feminist theory. Within the social sciences the categories associated to gender are more commonly that of 'masculinity' and 'femininity' (rather than man and woman), which refer to identities, practices and symbols and provide a means for gender signification. The analysis of masculinity and femininity in the social sciences allows for a discussion of gender and gender identities that is not tied to the biological sexes. By avoiding a comparison between men and women as distinctive groups, the use of the constructs of masculinity and femininity permits the decoupling between femininity and women and masculinity and men and thus allows the possibility for considering heterogeneities among women and among men (Priola, 2009). However, one of the risks of distinguishing between categories is the reinforcement of stereotypes that bestow women and men according to a few essentialist, fixed attributes such as women are nurturing, emotional, supportive and intuitive, while men are rational, competitive and analytical (Brannan and Priola, 2012).

Research in the past 40 years has shown that social inequalities in terms of gender are often reproduced in the workplace and that work organizations are the site for the production and reproduction of gender differences. Analysis of gender and work have focused on a wide range of aspect including: gender vertical and horizontal segregation; gendered processes and practices in the workplace; gender identities and organizational culture; gender discrimination and equal opportunities policies; women and men in management. While scholars distinguish among several theoretical approaches to gender, a basic distinction is that between liberal and radical perspectives. The liberal perspective focuses on women's ability to maintain equality through their own choices and actions, and calls for political and legal reforms that guarantee equality of opportunities. The radical approach aims to challenge the patriarchal order within society, and calls for a reorganization of the social and economic systems in order to achieve equality of outcomes.

VINCENZA PRIOLA

See also:
Direct discrimination; Diversity management; Equal opportunity.

Reference list and selected further readings
Brannan, M.J. and V. Priola (2012), Girls who do boys like they're girls'? Exploring the role of gender in the junior management of contemporary service work, *Gender, Work and Organization*, **19**(2), pp. 119–141.
Broadbridge, A. and S.L. Fielden (eds) (2015), *Handbook of Gendered Careers in Management: Getting In, Getting On, Getting Out*, Cheltenham: Edward Elgar.
Jeanes, E., D. Knights and P. Yancey Martin (eds) (2011), *Handbook of Gender, Work and Organization*, Chichester: Wiley-Blackwell.

Parsons, E. and V. Priola (2013), Agents for change and changed agents: the micro-politics of change and feminism in the academy, *Gender, Work and Organization*, **20**(5), pp. 580–598.

Priola, V. (2009), Masculinity and femininity, in A. Mills, G. Durepos and E. Wiebe (eds), *Sage Encyclopedia of Case Study Research*, London: Sage.

Gender gap

The gender gap refers to the percentage difference between women and men in relation to a variable or a specific context/setting, and is calculated by separating the rate of women and men and identifying the gap between the rates. Given women's struggles of presence and legitimacy in occupations, workplaces and labour markets, the gender gap is used to understand, explain and tackle the underrepresentation of women: in organizations, in male-dominated fields, such as science, technology, engineering and math (STEM), and in management.

The gender gap is helpful to describe the situation and relative position of women in relation to men (e.g., women in corporate boards); make visible and measure magnitude and causes of gender inequality (e.g., household responsibilities and their impact on women's ability to enter labour markets) and highlight changes and trends in the situation of women in relation to men (e.g., mentoring programmes that challenge the male-dominated orientation of some fields and encourage girls to consider them as career paths).

Gender-sensitive indicators (e.g., education, salary and occupation) are used to identify, characterize or quantify inequalities that exist between women and men; to monitor socio-historical transformations that impact inequalities, and to assess outcomes and impact of gender mainstreaming: initiatives that utilize gender perspectives and prioritize the goal of gender equality in policymaking, regulation and resourcing. The indicators are used to create indexes of concentration, distribution and feminization, which highlight group distribution (for example, occupational segregation or the jobs that women and men primarily do within a specific sector); representational differences between groups (for example, the overall number of men and women in a specific sector), and over/underrepresentation of women in relation to men (for example, masculinization of the construction sector or feminization of the teaching profession).

The strength of the gap depends on the magnitude of the difference and the values themselves: a smaller difference suggests more equality and a larger difference suggests more inequality. Conversely, negative values suggest a difference in favour of men and positive values suggests a difference in favour of women. However, gender indicators alone do not improve gender equality, so the quantified representation of inequality should be combined with qualitative analyses of assumptions and stereotypes about individuals, and how these operate as part of wider institutional, structural and organizational dynamics to (re)create and perpetuate inequalities.

Embedding notions of gender as a fluid system of social relations, recent discussions recognize that positioning gender in a binary is insufficient. Discussions no longer focus primarily on women; for example, looking at men in female-dominated occupations (e.g., teaching and nursing) and transgender women and men. In addition, discussions have moved away from gender as a single-axis category, instead exploring dynamics of intersectional inequality.

JENNY RODRIGUEZ

See also:
Diversity management; Gender.

References and selected further readings

de Vries, J.A. (2015), Champions of gender equality: female and male executives as leaders of gender change, *Equality, Diversity and Inclusion: An International Journal*, **34**(1), pp. 21–36.
Kakabadse, N.K., C. Figueira, K. Nicolopoulou, J. Hong Yang, A.P. Kakabadse and M.F. Özbilgin (2015), Gender diversity and board performance: women's experiences and perspectives, *Human Resource Management*, **54**(2), pp. 265–281.
Schilt, K. (2010), *Just One of the Guys? Transgender Men and the Persistence of Gender Inequality*, London: University of Chicago Press.
Woodhams, C., B. Lupton and M. Cowling (2014), The presence of ethnic minority and disabled men in feminised work: intersectionality, vertical segregation and the glass escalator, *Sex Roles*, pp. 1–17.
World Economic Forum (2014), *Global Gender Gap Report 2014*, Geneva: World Economic Forum, www3.weforum.org/docs/GGGR14/GGGR_CompleteReport_2014.pdf.

Gender pay gap

The gender pay gap measures the difference between women and men's earnings. It is often measured on an hourly basis to avoid the impact of gendered differences between weekly or annual working times. Whatever way it is measured, the gap exists and persists in all countries, even in those societies characterized by strong equality values. In one sense, the pay gap simply captures the differences in pay of women and men but this in fact reflects many gendered inequalities in and out of the labour market (Whitehouse, 2003).

Scholars often talk about the unadjusted and the adjusted gender pay gap. The unadjusted measures the average gap for all workers regardless of their characteristics. The latter relates to the gap adjusted for the differences between women and men that may help explain pay levels for example age, education job tenure, occupation and sector (Blau and Kahn, 2007). The part of the gap that then remains unexplained is often put down to discrimination. While much research has focused on the adjusted gap, it is important to recognize that many of the elements used to explain the gap may also be subject to discriminatory processes such as access to certain jobs, adopting uninterrupted career patterns and segregation of education disciplines (Smith, 2012).

There are many explanations for the gender pay gap (Rubery and Grimshaw, 2015). Economic approaches have tended to focus on women's and men's investment in their careers and education in order to explain the gap. However, although there have been rapid rises in the women's educational levels, exceeding men's in many countries, this has not been accompanied by a concomitant closure of the pay gap. The approaches of other disciplines have tended to focus on the institutions and actors on the labour market in order to explain the continuation of the gap including the presence of minimum wage regulation, the behaviour of trade unions, employers and regulations promoting equality of pay. Similarly, the differential valuation of skills associated with female-dominated occupations has also been identified as a key factor.

More recent scholarship has focused on gender pay gaps within particular groups of workers for example by occupations, sectors or by ethnicity (O'Reilly et al., 2015). These studies demonstrate how pay gaps vary across groups of workers and can be larger than average among the highest-paying jobs. The inclusion of other demographic characteristics illustrates the problem of intersectionality – the fact that some women may experience multiple disadvantages because they are also from an ethnic minority or disabled.

MARK SMITH

See also:

Direct discrimination; Equal pay; Gender; Low pay.

References and selected further readings

Blau, F. and L. Kahn (2007), The gender pay gap: have women gone as far as they can? *Academy of Management Perspectives*, **21**, pp. 7–23.

O'Reilly, J., M. Smith, S. Deakin and B. Burchell (2015), Equal pay as a moving target: international perspectives on forty-years of addressing the gender pay gap, *Cambridge Journal of Economics*, **39**, pp. 299–317.

Rubery, J. and D. Grimshaw (2015), The 40-year pursuit of equal pay: a case of constantly moving goalposts, *Cambridge Journal of Economics*, **39**, pp. 319–344.

Smith, M. (2012), Social regulation of the gender pay gap, *European Journal of Industrial Relations*, **18**(4), pp. 365–380.

Whitehouse, G. (2003), Gender and pay equity: future research directions, *Asia Pacific Journal of Human Resources*, **41**(1), pp. 116–128.

Generations

There is no single agreed definition of a 'generation' and the birth years differ between countries and authors. A typical definition of a generational cohort is a group of people sharing similar birth years and consequently experiencing similar historic events framing their beliefs, values and preferences (Palese et al., 2006). According to Lowe et al. (2008), there are four generational cohorts in the current Australian workplace: Matures/Veterans (born before 1945), Baby Boomers (born 1946–1965), Generation X (1966–1980) and Generation Y (also called Millennials, 1980–2000).

The idea that there are generational differences in work values is popular among practitioners; however, there continues to be debate within academic circles as to the validity of this idea. Sociology provides a strong basis for the concept of generations, but empirical results are somewhat mixed. There is insufficient generational research to be sure that age, experience or career or life stage, for example, are not also impacting the results. Longitudinal research is needed to confirm (or not) the predictive ability of an employee's generation on work values.

KATE SHACKLOCK

See also:

Careers.

References and selected further readings

Hansen, J.-I. C. and M.E. Leuty (2012), Work values across generations, *Journal of Career Assessment*, **20**(1), pp. 34–52.
Jin, J. and J. Rounds (2012), Stability and change of work values: a meta-analysis of longitudinal studies, *Journal of Vocational Behavior*, **80**, pp. 326–339.
Lowe, D., K.J. Levitt and T. Wilson (2008), Solutions for retaining Generation Y employees in the workplace, *Business Renaissance Quarterly*, **3**(3), pp. 43–57.
Lyons, S. and L. Kuron (2014), Generational differences in the workplace: a review of the evidence and directions for future research, *Journal of Organizational Behavior*, **35**(S1), pp. 139–157.
Palese, A., G. Pantali and L. Saiani (2006), The management of a multigenerational nursing team with differing qualifications: a qualitative study, *The Health Care Manager*, **25**(2), pp. 173–193.
Parry, E. and P. Urwin (2011), Generational differences in work values: a review of theory and evidence, *International Journal of Management Reviews*, **13**(1), pp. 79–96.
Shacklock, K.H. and Y. Brunetto (2011), The intention to continue nursing: work variables affecting three nurse generations in Australia, *Journal of Advanced Nursing*, **68**(1), pp. 36–46.

Geocentric management

Geocentric management can be broadly defined as an approach to managing a multinational enterprise's (MNE) international units that is based on the adoption of a global orientation. Specifically, the approach advocates the adoption of best practice and the promotion of managers based on the value added or performance rather than nationality. From a staffing perspective, in filling international management positions geocentric organisations do not favour home or host country nationals, but rather select managers that are best for the job. Geocentric management therefore implies that 'the skill of the person is more important than their passport' (Evans Pucik and Barsoux 2002, p. 25).

The term 'geocentric management' originated from Howard Perlmutter's (1969) seminal article 'The tortuous evolution of the multinational corporation', in which Perlmutter established a taxonomy of MNEs based on their attitude towards foreign people, ideas and resources in both the home and host environment. The original taxonomy consisted of three approaches to the management of international business units namely, the ethnocentric, polycentric and geocentric approach. In contrast to the ethnocentric and polycentric approaches to management in which there is a strong orientation to the home or host country respectively, the geocentric approach represents a global orientation whereby corporate culture is more strongly emphasised than national culture (Edstrom and Galbraith, 1977). It resonates with Bartlett and Ghoshal's (1989) transnational orientation which is charcterised by flexible organisational strategy and responsiveness to emerging developments in the business environment.

Adopting a geocentric approach means that MNEs are better placed to develop and implement policies and practices that are appropriate from one country to another, thereby maintaining consistency in their global operations. A geocentric perspective may act as a buffer against nationality biases in the recruitment, selection and international deployment of senior managers, aiding MNEs in selecting the best candidates for jobs and international assignments, and in subsequently maintaining a quality network of global managers. Geocentric management encourages the interdependence of home and host country facilities and thus facilitates independent business units becoming part of an integrated global structure. Managers working in MNEs that adopt a geocentric management approach are likely to have a more global mindset than those working in MNEs that adopt an ethnocentric or polycentric management approach.

MICHAEL ISICHEI AND DAVID G. COLLINGS

See also:

Ethnocentric management; Expatriate; Globalization; International human resource management; Polycentric management.

References and selected further readings

Bartlett, C.A. and S. Ghoshal (1989), *Managing Across Borders: The Transnational Solution*, Boston, MA: Harvard Business School Press.
Collings, D.G. and H. Scullion (2006), Approaches to international staffing, in H. Scullion and D.G. Collings (eds), *Global Staffing*, New York: Routledge.
Collings, D.G., H. Scullion and M.J. Morley (2007), Changing patterns of global staffing in the multinational enterprise: challenges to the conventional expatriate assignment and emerging alternatives, *Journal of World Business*, **42**(2), pp. 198–213.
Edström, A. and J.R. Gaibraith (1977), Transfer of managers as a coordination and control strategy in multinational organizations, *Administrative Science Quarterly*, **22**(2), pp. 248–263.
Evans, P., V. Pucik and J.-L. Barsoux (2002), *The Global Challenge: International Human Resource Management*, New York: McGraw-Hill.
Perlmutter, H.V. (1969), The tortuous evolution of the multinational corporation, *Columbia Journal of World Business*, **4**, pp. 9–18.

Glass ceiling

The 'glass ceiling' is a metaphor used since the 1980s to describe the invisible (in that they are neither formal, nor explicit) obstacles that women face in advancing to senior management in organizational hierarchies. More widely, it refers to a set of social and organizational values and processes that hinder women's equal access to high-level decision-making positions in a society. It is also often used as a short-cut term to describe gender discrimination as a determinant of vertical gender segregation (i.e., women's underrepresentation at top jobs).

Explanations based on human capital theory and on social history are often used to explain the underrepresentation of women in top jobs. Women's late mass incorporation to education and to the labour market from the 1970s, their industry specialization (horizontal gender segregation) and their devoting more time to the family than men means that the pool of available women with the requisite experience is very narrow. Yet, this argument fails to explain the underrepresentation of women in top jobs in feminized sectors, the sluggish rate of overall incorporation of women to these positions, the mounting experiences of women that arrived to them by being 'twice as good as men', as well as the differences in the rate of incorporation of women to these jobs in countries that follow the same socio-demographic patterns.

Thus, other cultural and societal dynamics embedded in organizations must be considered to explain the 'glass ceiling'. One key explanation is that recruitment, selection and promotion processes for senior management, board members, top judiciary roles and other elite jobs are gendered. Recruitment for these posts relies heavily on personal recommendations and informal approaches for which men's networks are crucial. Gender stereotyping that views women as less ambitious, less confident, less skilled at leadership or with a distinct style of management is widespread and further positions women as outsiders, and as women rather than individuals. Also, the work profile typically required in order to be promoted (i.e., a full-time career working long hours) is easier for men to acquire as it ignores the role of the person in the reproductive sphere.

Such obstacles exist in all societies, although their extent, the institutional mechanisms behind them and the degree of attempts to tackle the problem vary widely. To address this bias, some countries have in recent years issued codes of corporate governance or even quota legislation (Norway, Spain, France and more recently Germany) to ensure a minimum of women are appointed to corporate boards. Some countries have also made it compulsory for firms of a certain size to develop gender equality plans encompassing all organizational levels and HRM practices.

MARÍA C. GONZÁLEZ MENÉNDEZ

See also:

Corporate social responsibility; Diversity management; Equal opportunity; Gender pay gap.

References and selected further readings

Fagan, C., M.C. González Menéndez and S. Gómez Ansón (2012), *Women on Corporate Boards and In Top Management: European Trends and Policy*, Basingstoke: Palgrave Macmillan.
Kanter, R. (1977), *Men and Women of the Corporation*, New York: Basic Books.
Oakley, J.G. (2000), Gender-based barriers to senior management positions: understanding the scarcity of female CEOs, *Journal of Business Ethics*, **7**(4), pp. 321–334.
Terjesen, S., R.V. Aguilera and R. Lorenz (2015), Legislating a woman's seat on the board: institutional factors driving gender quotas for boards of directors, *Journal of Business Ethics*, **128**, pp. 233–251.

Global supply chains

Global supply chains can be thought of as the interorganizational and intraorganizational linkages between the raw materials that go into production and the ultimate consumers of the goods. Global supply chains have become particularly important with the rise in techniques such as just-in-time, lean production and outsourcing to reduce the cost base of production or reduce inventories of raw materials and produce. Three competing terms are often used to describe global supply chains in the employment relations literature: global commodity chains (GCC), global value chains (GVC) and global production networks (GPN). The stress in GCC is on commodities passing through multiple stages of ownership before meeting the ultimate consumer in a linear fashion. In GVC, stress is placed upon the adding of value on transfer of goods between stages in a linear fashion. The GPN approach views both the GCC and GVC approaches as being too linear and instead stresses the embedding of supply within wider networks in society.

The key debate in the area lies around the governance of global supply chains, i.e., who controls the chain and what are the effects of this on workplace relations. Firms that have the most power are often referred to as 'lead firms'. One of the key issues in the governance debate is where the lead firm lies within the global supply chain, in particular, whether the supply chain is buyer-driven or supplier-driven. Buyer-driven supply chains are those where power lies close to the ultimate consumer. Supplier-driven supply chains are those where power is concentrated close to the raw material end

(Gereffi, 1994). A second conceptualization provided by Gereffi and colleagues (2005) categorizes global supply chains into five types: market, where parties have options to shift between buyers and suppliers with relative ease; modular, where bespoke goods are made for buyers with little other interactions; relational, where relations are built over a long period and there is mutual dependence between buyers and suppliers; captive, where small suppliers or buyers are wholly dependent on links to larger organizations; and hierarchy, where the lead organization wholly controls the others in the supply chain.

Global supply chains have been a key focus of corporate social responsibility policies of many multinational corporations, as global supply chains often present a paradox that the company moves there to take advantage of lower regulation but ends up regulating itself. Donaghey and colleagues (2014) outline that global supply chains often are susceptible to consumer-led pressure over labour rights on lead firm brands rather than the direct use of labour power as brands often source from where workers have very limited power resources.

JIMMY DONAGHEY

See also:

Corporate social responsibility; Multinational companies.

References and selected further readings

Donaghey, J., J. Reinecke, C. Niforou and B. Lawson (2014), From employment relations to consumption relations: balancing labor governance in global supply chains, *Human Resource Management*, 53(2), pp. 229–252.
Gereffi, G. (1994), The organization of buyer-driven global commodity chains: how US retailers shape overseas production networks, in G. Gereffi and M. Korzeniewicz (eds), *Commodity Chains and Global Capitalism*, Westport, CT: Praeger, pp. 95–122.
Gereffi, G., J. Humphrey and T. Sturgeon (2005), The governance of global value chains, *Review of International Political Economy*, 12(1), pp. 78–104.
Humphrey, J. (2001), Governance in global value chains, *IDS Bulletin*, 32(3), pp. 19–29.

Globalization

Globalization is a broad term that may be taken to refer to the integration of markets, the spread of corporations and production across national boundaries, the dominance of particular policy models and the homogenization of consumer taste. Proponents of globalization have argued that it represents a logical progression towards universally democratic and liberal market economies. However, such proponents are generally very much less enthusiastic about the mass movement of labour across national boundaries, an invariable by-product of the disruptions caused by the reckless imposition of neoliberal policies and climate change. Again, they are invariably silent when democratically elected governments are ousted by right-wing juntas more receptive to unrestrained marketization. Critics of globalization argue that the process has invariably been a downward one, leading to large-scale impoverishment, the destruction of secure employment, the further enrichment and accumulation of power by a tiny global elite and wholesale environmental destruction, as everything is assigned a value in terms of the immediate price with which markets are prepared to pay (Greider, 1998).

However, in reality, there is a case to be made that the world is becoming more, rather than less uniform. Global manufacturing has become increasingly concentrated in a handful of nations (most notably Germany and China), and many other countries where previously thriving manufacturing sectors have reverted to a reliance on mineral and other primary commodity exports (most notably, Australia, and also many previously diversified African countries), or on financial services driven growth (for example, the US and the UK). Again, countries vary greatly in terms of their overall economic performance, social equality and in terms of dominant work and employment relations paradigms. Institutional theories suggest that this is owing to variations in embedded (even if changing) conventions and patterns of behaviour that allow key economic players known benefits (Wilkinson et al., 2014). However, regardless of questions as to whether and how the world is becoming more uniform, other global phenomena include the large-scale movement of peoples across national boundaries, and a rising global class of impoverished workers who lack job and occupational security (Standing, 2011).

GEOFF WOOD

See also:

Coordinated market economy; Liberal market economy; Varieties of capitalism.

References and selected further readings

Greider, W. (1998), *One World, Ready Or Not: The Manic Logic of Global Capitalism*, New York: Simon and Schuster.
Lane, C. and G. Wood (eds) (2012), *Capitalist Diversity and Diversity within Capitalism*, London: Routledge.
Standing, G. (2011), *The Precariat: The New Dangerous Class*, London: Bloomsbury Publishing.
Wilkinson, A., G. Wood and R. Deeg (eds) (2014), *Oxford Handbook of Employment Relations: Comparative Employment Systems*, Oxford: Oxford University Press.

Golden handshakes

Golden handshakes are termination payments given typically to executives, whose contracts are ended, usually before their employment contract term is due to end. These payments are in effect severance pay, and as well as colloquially being called 'golden handshakes' they might also be termed 'golden parachutes' because of the often large amounts typically paid to departing executives to cushion a soft landing (especially in cases of involuntary departure).

Legally such payments are treated differently in different national regimes. In the UK, the Remuneration Committees of large companies subject to the Corporate Governance Code are charged with the role of making decisions on such payments, when directors leave their company before the end of their contract (with maximum notice periods of one year). If they can be classified as 'ex-gratia' payments, rather than severance pay specifically provided for in the contract, they may be paid tax-free (up to certain limits).

Payments may be relatively high in the USA where between two and three times annual pay are typically given (Goldman and Huang, 2011), and are typically awarded a discretionary basis by the board of directors and not according to terms of an employment agreement.

The question as to why companies offer large golden handshakes, in spite of sometimes trenchant public criticism in the media and from shareholders, may be partly explained as a form of damage control by the organization. The company may wish to maintain the confidentiality of company information and to limit the potential damage to the company not least from the departing executive. Such senior employees will have an in depth knowledge of the organization's sources of competitive advantage and its weaknesses as well as its strengths.

ANGELA WRIGHT

References and selected further readings

Goldman, E. and P. Huang (2011), *Contractual Versus Actual Severance Pay Following CEO Turnover*, Social Science Research Network, http://papers.ssrn.com/sol3/papers.cfm?abstract_id=1785798.
Yermack, D. (2006), Golden handshakes: separation pay for retired and dismissed CEOs, *Journal of Accounting and Economics*, **41**(3), pp.237–256.

Graduate recruitment

Graduate recruitment typically refers to the employment of university graduates after they complete their degrees. There are also ways of employing students while they study for their degrees, including internships, traineeships, cadetships, graduate programmes, vacation work, placements and work experience. Many organizations offer these forms of 'part-time employment' to studying students as a way of enticing good students to become part of their organization upon degree completion. The benefits are mutual: the employer gets to 'try the student out' and the student gets to 'try the organization out' before a final commitment is made by either party.

Graduate recruitment is important to organizations seeking keen minds and new ideas to complement their existing human capital. Graduate recruitment also provides security to those students successful in gaining a commitment for ongoing employment. Organizations compete for the best student talent, and the best students apply to more than one organization for employment. Employers use a number of methods to promote their graduate programmes, including their organization's website, employment websites and university careers services. However, the use of social media websites (e.g., Facebook, Twitter, YouTube, LinkedIn) is seen to be growing over time, while the use of newspaper advertising is now the least-used method. This trend is expected to continue, irrespective of employment sector.

Large organizations (with more than 500 employees and typically larger graduate intakes) are more likely to use all of the promotional methods than their smaller counterparts. Smaller organizations are more likely than their larger counterparts to use Facebook and LinkedIn to promote their graduate recruitment programme, although this is a common method for organizations regardless of size (Graduate Careers Australia, 2013). Employee referral programmes, where management asks employees to refer suitable family members, friends or other new graduates who may be qualified for a role within the organization, are becoming increasingly popular as employers seek to address particular graduate skills shortages.

Research carried out by universities and consultants is common in terms of finding the most important selection criteria used by employers. Apart from relevant qualifications, employers nominated that interpersonal and communication skills – written and oral – followed by passion/knowledge of industry/drive/commitment/attitude, and then critical reasoning and analytical skills/problem-solving/lateral thinking/ technical skills are the most important selection criteria (Graduate Careers Australia, 2013).

Kate Shacklock

See also:
Internship.

Reference list and selected further readings

Fraser, C., J. Murray and M. Dixon (2014), Apprentices and graduates — maintaining recruitment to avoid future skill shortages, *AusIMM Bulletin*, **1**, pp. 35–37.

Graduate Careers Australia (2013), *Graduate Outlook 2012: The Report of the Graduate Outlook Survey: Employers' Perspectives on Graduate Recruitment*, Melbourne: Graduate Careers Australia, www.graduate-careers.com.au.

Hanson, L. (2009), Implementing a graduate recruitment scheme, *Pharma*, **5**(6), pp. 40–41.

Schmidt, D. and N. Dmytryk (2014), Exploring a public–private partnership new-graduate physiotherapy recruitment programme: a qualitative study, *Australian Journal of Rural Health*, **22**, pp. 334–339.

Taylor, J. (2010), Graduate recruitment in the Australian public sector, *Public Management Review*, **2**(6), pp. 789–809.

Towl, M. and C. Senior (2010), Undergraduate research training and graduate recruitment, *Education and Training*, **52**(4), pp. 292–303.

Greenfield sites

'Greenfield' is a term used to describe a new workplace site for an existing employer. The term 'greenfield' came into use in the early 1980s, as these new sites were often located in areas that were previously rural areas or green fields. It can be contrasted with the term 'brownfield', which denotes an established site. The focus for management in establishing a greenfield site is to change the workplace culture and implement new processes to increase productivity. The greenfield site is associated with human resource management practices such as high-performance and high-commitment work practices, multi-skilling, job rotation and lean production. A greenfield site is a new venture of an existing company rather than a completely new firm establishment, the extent to which the new sites employment relations practices differ from the parent site is the main research interest in most studies.

Newell (1991) adopted sociologist Max Weber's notion of 'ideal-typical' to help explain work organization in greenfield workplaces. Newell suggested that an 'ideal-typical' site consisted of four dimensions: new management philosophy and HRM strategies, new employees and technology in a new site being the primary measures of typicality. Baird (2001) added to this the goal of developing an altered relationship with trade unions. This model was further developed with the evidence that there are a range of ways in which a greenfield site can be established that do not fit an ideal typical model, leading to the conception of 'shades of green' in greenfield sites.

Leopold and Hallier (1999) developed the concept of 'shades of green', demonstrating that a site could be identified as a greenfield site if only some of the five key identifiers were in place. The essential element that determined if a site was a greenfield site was the focus on changing existing workplace culture through the development of a new site, leaving behind old attitudes and behaviours.

Much of the research on greenfield sites has focused on the changing relationships with trade unions, noting the preference of employers for a single union to cover all the employees at the workplace. The selection of the greenfield site is often made with this consideration in mind; in the USA many greenfield sites were located in southern states with 'right to work' statutes that exclude unions (Kochan et al., 1994). In the UK and Australia, greenfield sites have been located in areas of high unemployment where local governments have provided subsidies and trade union bodies are willing to offer concessions. Critics of work organization in greenfield sites have noted the focus on increasing managerial control and human resource management techniques to create tight internal cultures in the organization that exclude unions.

MAGGIE MAY

See also:

High-performance work systems; Lean production; Trade unions.

References and selected further readings

Baird, M. (2001), Greenfield sites: purpose, potential and pitfalls, *Asia Pacific Journal of Human Resources*, **39**(2), pp. 66–81.
Kochan, T.A., H.C. Katz and R.B. McKersie (1994), *The Transformation of American Industrial Relations*, Ithaca, NY: ILR Press.
Leopold, J. and J. Hallier (1999), Managing the employment relationship on greenfield sites in Australia and New Zealand, *The International Journal of Human Resource Management*, **10**(4), pp. 716–736.
Newell, H. (1991), *Field of Dreams: Evidence of 'New' Employee Relations in Greenfield Sites*, PhD thesis, University of Oxford.
Richbell, S. and H.D. Watts (2001), Shades of green: the greenfield concept in HRM, *Employee Relations*, **23**(5), pp. 498–511.

Green human resource management

Green human resource management (GHRM) is defined as the HRM aspects of environmental management (EM), and GHRM practices currently include green recruitment and selection, EM training and development, green performance management/appraisal, EM pay and reward systems, green employee involvement, staff empowerment/engagement in EM, supportive green climate/culture and union roles in EM (see Renwick et al., 2013). At present, GHRM research appears somewhat diverse and piecemeal, meaning that GHRM seems a small but increasing subset of HRM. As such, literature calls include requests to integrate EM and HRM as a research subject; to expand the remit of strategic HRM (SHRM) to include sustainability concerns; and to answer the question of whether a role exists for HRM in pollution prevention.

At present, our understanding of how GHRM practices impact on employee motivation to participate in environmental activities lags behind knowledge of how organizations develop the EM abilities of staff, and also how to provide employees with opportunities to be involved in green organizational efforts. It seems that organizations are not always using the full range of available GHRM practices, and this may reduce their effectiveness when working to improve EM more generally. Another limitation is that, while acknowledging some notable exceptions (e.g. Branzei et al., 2004; Chun, 2009; Fryxell and Lo, 2003), the GHRM literature is largely a Northern and Western one. Here, due to the importance of economic development for EM in the BRIC countries (e.g., Brazil, Russia, India and China), this is an important gap that future research studies need to reduce.

For practitioners, questions in GHRM emerging include: what evidence they can see of all staff groups enacting EM-related practices in organizations; how organizations can audit their existing level of GHRM practices; what factors might encourage employees to enact eco-initiatives; how and in what ways middle managers and supervisors could embrace EM; and what role environmental regulation, law and government policy may have on shaping GHRM practices at the workplace level.

DOUGLAS W.S. RENWICK

See also:

Corporate social responsibility; Strategic HRM.

References and selected further readings

Branzei, O., T.J. Ursacki-Bryant, I. Vertinsky and W. Zhang (2004), The formation of green strategies in Chinese firms: matching corporate and individual principles, *Strategic Management Journal*, **25**, pp. 1075–1095.
Chun, R. (2009), Ethical values and environmentalism in China: comparing employees from state-owned and private firms, *Journal of Business Ethics*, **84**, pp. 341–348.
Fryxell, G.E. and C.W.H. Lo (2003), The influence of environmental knowledge and values on managerial behaviours on behalf of the environment: an empirical examination of managers in China, *Journal of Business Ethics*, **46**, pp. 45–69.
Ramus, C.A. and U. Steger (2000), The roles of supervisory support behaviours and environmental policy in employee 'eco-initiatives' at leading-edge European companies, *Academy of Management Journal*, **41**, pp. 605–626.
Renwick, D.W.S., T. Redman and S. Maguire (2013), Green HRM: a review and research agenda, *International Journal of Management Reviews*, **15**, pp. 1–14.
Rothenberg, S. (2003), Knowledge content and worker participation in environmental management at NUMMI, *Journal of Management Studies*, **40**, pp. 1783–1802.

Grievance procedure

No precise legal definition of the expression 'grievance procedure' is provided by UK law. However, the Introduction to the *Code of Practice 1 on Disciplinary and Grievance Procedures* produced by the Advisory, Conciliation and Arbitration Service (Acas, 2015) provides a helpful narrative. It provides that a grievance procedure is a procedure designed to address 'concerns, problems or complaints that employees raise with their employers'. Prior to the coming into force of the Employment Act 2008, it was a legal requirement for an employee to adhere to a statutorily prescribed grievance procedure in the UK. If the employee failed to follow the statutory grievance procedure, then this would render any claim that they subsequently raised in the courts or the employment tribunal system as incompetent and invalid. The law in the UK was modified in 2009 and such statutory grievance procedures were abolished, owing to the extent of the litigation that they had generated. Instead, the law now provides that an employee who fails to adhere to the requirements of Acas' *Code of Practice 1 on Disciplinary and Grievance*

Procedures will find that any award for compensation in their favour may be reduced by up to 25 per cent.

The basic ingredients of a grievance procedure consist of the following in sequential order:

1. A letter informing the employer of the grievance;
2. The convening of a meeting by the employer to discuss the grievance;
3. The employer should allow the employee to be accompanied at the grievance meeting;
4. The employer must take a decision regarding the employee's grievance and set out the reasons for its decision in writing; and
5. An appeal hearing.

Over the past 20 years, the prevailing theory behind the incentivization of employees to adopt pre-claim grievance procedures has been to afford an employee a measure of procedural justice. The thinking is that if employers prescribe and follow impartial and fair grievance procedures, a far greater number of employees will accept that their grievances were given sufficient consideration and that they were treated fairly. This will have the likely consequence that the tribunal and court system will have fewer disputes to resolve, since the parties will settle their disputes outside the tribunal system.

DAVID CABRELLI

See also:

Disciplinary procedure; Gross misconduct; Misconduct; Notice period.

References and selected further readings

Acas (2015), *Code of Practice 1 on Disciplinary and Grievance Procedures*, www.acas.org.uk/media/pdf/f/m/Acas-Code-of-Practice-1-on-disciplinary-and-grievance-procedures.pdf.
Collins, H. (1992), *Justice in Dismissal*, New York: Clarendon Press.
Fredman, S. (1986), Natural justice for employees: the unacceptable faith of proceduralism, *Industrial Law Journal*, **15**, pp. 15–31.
Sanders, A. (2009), Part One of the Employment Act 2008: 'better dispute resolution?' *Industrial Law Journal*, **38**, pp. 30–49.

Gross misconduct

The expression 'gross misconduct' was defined by Lord Jauncey in the case of *Neary v Dean of Westminster* [1999] IRLR 288 as conduct on the part of the employee that 'so undermines the trust and confidence which is inherent in the particular contract of employment that the [employer] should no longer be required to retain the servant in his employment.' In addition, paragraphs 23 and 24 of the *Code of Practice 1 on Disciplinary and Grievance Procedures* produced by the Advisory, Conciliation and Arbitration Service (Acas, 2015) provide that certain acts by the employee may be:

> so serious in themselves or have such serious consequences that they may call for dismissal without [giving the employee prior notice of such dismissal] for a first offence . . . [they] may

vary according to the nature of the organisation and what it does, but might include things such as theft or fraud, physical violence, gross negligence or serious insubordination.

As such, evidence of gross misconduct will empower an employer to summarily dismiss an employee on the spot without the provision of a period of notice on a lawful basis under the common law.

The primary significance of the term 'gross misconduct' lies in the fact that – as a particularly egregious form of 'misconduct' – it qualifies as one of the five available presumptively valid reasons for an employer to dismiss an employee under Part X of the ERA. If the employer can demonstrate that the employee has engaged in such gross misconduct, the end result is that the dismissal of the employee will be lawful at common law and presumed to be valid and the question for the tribunal and court to determine will be whether the employee's dismissal for the reason of misconduct was fair as a matter of substance, and procedurally fair in accordance with a disciplinary procedure.

DAVID CABRELLI

See also:

Discipline and grievance; Disciplinary procedure; Employee; Misconduct; Notice period.

References and selected further readings

Acas (2015), *Code of Practice 1 on Disciplinary and Grievance Procedures*, www.acas.org.uk/media/pdf/f/m/ Acas-Code-of-Practice-1-on-disciplinary-and-grievance-procedures.pdf.
Collins, H. (1992), *Justice in Dismissal*, New York: Clarendon Press.
Elias, P. (1978), Unravelling the concept of dismissal — I and II, *Industrial Law Journal*, 7, pp. 16–29, 100–112.

Halo effect

There are two related and prominent features of the process of people perception: the halo effect and the stereotype effect. Halo effects differ from stereotype effects. In the case of halo effects, it is a person's singular unique trait or characteristic that gives rise to unwarranted inferences. In contrast, stereotype effects occur because the generalized characteristics of a group are applied to an individual associated with that group.

The term 'halo effect', first identified and used by the psychologist Edward Thorndike in 1920, describes the basic human tendency to make specific inferences on the basis of a general impression. People often face a lot of new information about someone. It includes appearance, verbal behaviour (what is being said and how it is being said) and non-verbal behaviour (e.g., posture) and the physical and social setting. Arising from this, people become selective with respect to the information to which they pay attention, leading to what is termed the halo effect. The halo effect is a cognitive bias whereby the perception of one characteristic of a person, or trait, is influenced by information about another, often irrelevant trait. It also means that the perception or judgement of a person on one trait is favourable even when other traits, if given sufficient attention, might have led to a different evaluation. The halo effect occurs at the implicit level, bypassing conscious awareness, even in a cross-cultural context.

Halo effects have a powerful influence on assessments and impression formation, such as in job, appraisal and promotion interviews. Appraisers introduce systematic distortions into the rating process, for example, due to limited opportunities to observe the appraisee or poorly designed rating instruments. They, therefore, make judgments by relying on a single conspicuous or prominent characteristic, such as the clothes or jewellery worn, the hairstyle or the sound of the voice or accent. Studies have shown an attractive person evaluated as having a more desirable personality, and attractive-looking or smiling people are punished less severely when they commit misconduct (Dion et al., 1972). Since the halo effect is seen as a rating error, there is, therefore, the need to keep it to a minimum. It also calls for the need to have highly accurate ratings and data objectivity, robustness and especially independence. Being aware of this problem is a major step towards avoiding it. Supervisory training can also alleviate this problem.

CHRIS ROWLEY AND NAGIAH RAMASAMY

See also:
Horns effect; Interviews; Performance appraisal; Promotion.

References and selected further readings

Balzer, W.K. and L.M. Sulsky (1992), Halo and performance appraisal research: a critical examination, *Journal of Applied Psychology*, **77**, pp. 975–985.
Brown, B. and S. Perry (1994), Removing the financial performance halo from fortune's most admired companies, *Academy of Management Journal*, **37**(5), pp. 1347–1359.
Dion, K., E. Berscheid and E. Walster (1972), What is beautiful is good, *Journal of Personality and Social Psychology*, **24**(3), pp. 285–290.
Rosenzweig, P. (2007), Misunderstanding the nature of company performance: the halo effect and other business delusions, *California Management Review*, **49**(4), pp. 6–20.
Verhulst, B., M. Lodge and H. Lavine (2010), The attractiveness halo: why some candidates are perceived more favorably than others, *Journal of Nonverbal Behavior*, **34**, pp. 111–117.

Hard and soft HRM

Human resource management, defined broadly as the management of work and people, incorporates a wide range of potential options for the management of employment. While most organizations are interested in how to effectively utilize the people they employ, there are quite different views regarding how this is best achieved. An influential distinction was made by Storey (1989) between 'soft' and 'hard' forms of HRM captures these different views.

Hard HRM views workers as a factor of production or a commodity much like any other resource. The approach to managing people is therefore rational and dispassionate, and the emphasis is upon issues of control and ensuring employees comply with employer demands. Employees are thus both a cost to be minimized and a resource to be utilized. As such, it shares some of the assumptions of Taylor's scientific management and Herzberg's Theory X, and reflects the tenor of some of the corporate strategy and business policy literatures. Hard HRM stresses the need for HR tools and policies, such as performance management and training, which will ensure employees meet management expectations.

Soft HRM recognizes the importance of employee commitment and motivation, and suggests that employee attitudes and behaviours can actually make the difference between successful and unsuccessful organizations. However, employee commitment is not assumed to be automatically forthcoming; employees must be nurtured and developed in order to elicit commitment. These assumptions reflect some of the arguments made by the human relations movement and Herzberg's Theory Y, as well as more recent debates concerning best practice HRM. Soft HRM thus stresses the need for HR tools and policies such as strong leadership, extensive communication, and the development of an appropriate organizational culture in order to elicit motivation and commitment, and this is the tenor of many mainstream HRM textbooks.

Conceptually, soft and hard HRM appear to be polar opposites, and it is not always entirely clear whether they represent countervailing tendencies, a continuum of options or distinct choices. Some suggest the choice between hard and soft HRM depends on the context of the business: an organization competing on the basis of quality might favour soft HRM, while those competing on the basis of low-cost might deem hard HRM more appropriate. Even within a single organization there is the possibility for multiple employment systems to co-exist depending on the skills and perceived value of different employee groups to the organization (Lepak and Snell, 1999). This raises a moral and ethical issue as it implies that low-pay and limited voice may be deemed preferable for some groups of employees, while others benefit from more generous treatment.

Some critical commentators doubt whether HRM can ever be 'soft' and suggest that even when employers use the rhetoric of soft HRM the reality is often hard (Legge, 1995). For critics, while the language of HRM, with its grand-sounding terms such as 'empowerment' and 'high performance' may seem people-centred and liberating, the reality is often the further subjugation of workers (Keenoy, 1990; Truss et al., 1997).

STEWART JOHNSTONE

See also:

Commitment; Human relations movement; Human resource management; Scientific management; Unitarism.

References and selected further readings

Guest, D.E. (1987), Human resource management and industrial relations, *Journal of Management Studies*, **24**(5), pp. 503–521.

Keenoy, T. (1990), HRM: a case of the wolf in sheep's clothing? *Personnel Review*, **19**(2), pp. 3–9.

Legge, K. (1995), HRM: rhetoric, reality and hidden agendas. *Human Resource Management: A Critical Text*, London: Routledge, pp. 33–59.

Lepak, D.P. and S.A. Snell (1999), The human resource architecture: toward a theory of human capital allocation and development, *Academy of Management Review*, **24**(1), pp. 31–48.

Storey, J. (1989), From personnel management to human resource management, in J. Storey (ed.), *New Perspectives on Human Resource Management*, London: Routledge.

Storey, J. (1995), *Human Resource Management: A Critical Text*, London: Routledge.

Truss, C., L. Gratton, V. Hope-Hailey, P. McGovern and P. Stiles (1997), Soft and hard models of human resource management: a reappraisal, *Journal of Management Studies*, **34**(1), pp. 53–73.

Walton, R.E. (1985), From control to commitment in the workplace, *Harvard Business Review*, March–April, pp. 77–84.

Harmonization

Harmonization is the term that describes the process of bringing together the terms and conditions of groups of workers, whose current reward packages are different. There are two primary circumstances in which that is typically necessary – first, following a corporate merger and second, because of a process of merging the terms and conditions of groups which have been subject to separate pay determination processes – for example, bringing together manual workers and administrative/professional staff. In Britain some protracted processes of harmonizing different pay and benefits packages have taken place over a lengthy period of time (Russell, 1998). In spite of trends to harmonize terms and conditions for different groups of workers there remain strong differences in benefit 'single status' conditions (applying the same entitlements to different groups in a given workplace) have grown slowly. One example is in the UK local government sector, in which a national pay agreement setting out a single status framework for local implementation, agreed between employers and unions in 1997, had still to be implemented at local council level ten years later (Wright, 2011). Complex negotiations harmonizing hours of work and other terms and conditions, under the banner of modernization, were extensive in the UK public sector during the early 2000s (Perkins and White, 2010).

Harmonization of pay and conditions as a result of mergers or restructuring are covered in European Union legal regimes by regulation covering workers' right on business transfer (The EU Acquired Rights Directive and Its Impact on Business Transfers 2001/23/EC). Employees employed by the previous employer when a business changes hands automatically become employees of the new employer on the same terms and conditions. After a period of time the new employer may then decide to harmonize the terms and conditions across both the older and the more recently acquired parts of their business.

At the time of a merger the respective companies may have very different cultures and reward policies as well as different standard hours of work, pensions, sick pay and holiday entitlements resulting in a complex process of change. To level up all terms and conditions, where these are different, may entail a substantial cost, leading in some organizations to phased implementations.

Angela Wright

See also:

Human resource management in mergers and acquisitions; Terms and conditions.

References and selected further readings

Perkins, S and G. White (2010), Modernising pay in the UK public services: trends and implications, *Human Resource Management Journal*, **20**(3), pp. 244–257.

Russell, A. (1998), *The Harmonization of Employment Conditions in Britain: The Changing Workplace Divide since 1950 and the Implications for Social Structure*, Basingstoke: Macmillan.

Wright, A. (2011), 'Modernising' away gender pay inequality? Some evidence from the local government sector on using job evaluation, *Employee Relations*, **33**(2), pp. 159–178.

Headhunting

Headhunting is the colloquial term for identifying and placing managerial and executive talent into hiring organizations. The word originates from the anthropology literature and refers to taking (typically in combat) and then keeping a person's head after killing them.

In the employee selection literature, 'headhunting' is used in three contexts. Most often it refers to the executive search process overseen by executive search firms. In this case, 'headhunting' involves assessing the needs of the hiring organization, supplying the hiring organization information on suitable candidates and managing the process of matching executive candidates to organizations. The latter involves the face-to-face interviews between the client firm and the executives, the salary negotiation process and the onboarding of the newly hired executive.

The term 'headhunting' is duly used as a label for the entire executive search process, because moving employed individuals who are not looking for other job opportunities ('passive candidates') is thought to be one of the major roles of executive search firms: they add value by contacting the candidates, selling them the opportunity and getting their willingness to engage in interviews. Often, the boards of directors or the HR executives of the hiring organizations would not engage in these tasks in order not to appear as desperate to find executive talent or as failing to attract a certain candidate (Khurana, 2002). Moreover, search firms believe that they are entitled to take candidates out of firms and feel that part of their role is to help individuals change jobs (Finlay and Coverdill, 2000).

Less frequently, 'headhunting' is used to signify only a certain type of executive search activity that involves a less consultative approach than the one described above. It refers to the search firm directly approaching the competitors of the hiring organization to poach the executive candidates who are identified by the hiring firm.

Finally, the term 'headhunting' is also used to describe the activities of contingency search firms (Finlay and Coverdill, 2002). Unlike most executive search firms that work on a 'retained' basis by having an exclusive contract with the client organization, contingency search firms place candidates for mid- and lower managerial positions, work on many openings simultaneously, and are paid by organizations only if they successfully place a candidate.

MONIKA HAMORI

See also:
Executive search firms; Selection.

References and selected further readings

Beaverstock, J.V., J.R. Faulconbridge and S.J.E. Hall (2015), *The Globalization of Executive Search: Professional Services Strategy and Dynamics in the Contemporary World*, New York and London: Routledge.
Finlay, W. and J.E. Coverdill (2000), Risk, opportunism and structural holes, *Work and Occupations*, **27**(3), pp. 377–405.
Finlay, W. and J.E. Coverdill (2002), *Headhunters: Matchmaking in the Labor Market*, Ithaca, NY: ILR Press.
Hamori, M. (2010), Who gets headhunted — and who gets ahead? The impact of search firms on executive careers, *Academy of Management Perspectives*, **24**(4), pp. 46–59.
Khurana, R. (2002), *Searching for a Corporate Savior: The Irrational Quest for Charismatic CEOs*, Princeton, NJ: Princeton University Press.

Health and safety

Health and safety is sometimes termed workplace health and safety, occupational health and safety or work health and safety. In 1950, the International Labour Organization (ILO) and the World Health Organization (WHO) defined occupational health as the promotion and maintenance of the highest degree of physical, mental and social wellbeing of workers by preventing departures from health, controlling risks and adapting work to people and people to work. Preserving the health, safety and wellbeing of people at work is arguably the single most important management function in any organization.

The study of health and safety draws insights from a range of disciplines including occupational medicine, occupational hygiene, engineering, ergonomics, work psychology, industrial sociology, management, law and economics. No single perspective offers a comprehensive account of health and safety. So, a multidisciplinary perspective is essential to understand and manage the risks to health and safety of people at work.

At the organization level, the human resource management function is often responsible for managing health and safety, in cooperation with other organizational units and consulting expert advice as required. So, human resource management students and personnel need a good appreciation of the four components to managing health and safety in the workplace.

First, organizations need a health and safety management system including formal policies, demonstrated senior management commitment, adequate resourcing, health and safety infrastructure (such as a health and safety committee and worker representatives) plus a system of planning, implementing, monitoring and reviewing safety initiatives and performance. The system should be proactive with the aim of preventing injuries and illness. Where incidents do occur, investigations need to be undertaken to identify incident causation and to recommend corrective action to prevent or minimize future occurrences. The system should also include policies to assist injured workers in their transition back to work.

Second, organizations must understand and comply with the health and safety legal framework in which they operate. Legal requirements vary from country to country but invariably place upon employers a primary obligation for health and safety at workplace. The health and safety laws may include prescriptive regulations about specific hazards such as asbestos, noise exposure, working in mines and so on. To assist employers and employees, government will often produce codes of practice, guidance material or other information materials that offer practical and detailed advice about how to control specific risks. In some countries, there may also be dedicated health and safety laws regulating particular high-risk industries, occupations and workplaces.

Third, it is important to appreciate that workers can be exposed to a wide range of hazards in the workplace. Without being comprehensive, hazards include:

- Mechanical and electrical hazards (impact force, collusions, struck by objects, plant, equipment, etc.).
- Chemical hazards (acids, metals, asbestos, solvents, fumes, fire, etc.).
- Physical hazards (noise, vibration, radiation, etc.).
- Psychological hazards (stress, harassment, violence, drugs and alcohol, fatigue, etc.).
- Ergonomic hazards (prolonged stooping or crouching, repetitive movements, etc.).
- Biological hazards (infectious disease, moulds, etc.).
- Workplace environment hazards (slip, trip and fall hazards, ventilation, temperature, lighting, etc.).

To minimize the risk of injury and illness, it is essential to be able to recognize and understand the potential harm of all types of workplace hazards.

Fourth, the effective management of health and safety involves understanding risk management. Risk management is a systematic approach to assessing threats and opportunities in a situation or activity and taking action to generate the best possible outcome. For health and safety, this risk management procedure involves identifying potential hazards at work, assessing the likelihood and seriousness of an occurrence, putting in place controls to prevent harm to workers and periodically reviewing the effectiveness of the control measures.

CAMERON ALLAN

See also:

Absence; International Labour Organization and International Labour Standards; Occupational health; Stress; Wellbeing.

References and selected further readings

Students should visit the website of their local health and safety regulator for more information and advice about health and safety.

Holt, A. and H. Andrews (1993), *Principles of Health and Safety at Work*, London: IOSH Publishing.
Quinlan, M., P. Bohle and F. Lamm (2010), *Managing Occupational Health and Safety: A Multidisciplinary Approach*, Melbourne: Palgrave Macmillan.
Robinson, A.M. and C. Smallman (2013), Workplace injury and voice: a comparison of management and union perceptions, *Work, Employment & Society*, 27(4), pp. 674–693.
Taylor, P. and L. Connelly (2009), Before the disaster: health, safety and working conditions at a plastics factory, *Work, Employment & Society*, 23(1), pp. 160–168.
Taylor, P., C. Baldry, P. Bain and V. Ellis (2003), A unique working environment: health, sickness and absence management in UK call centres, *Work, Employment & Society*, 17(3), pp. 435–458.

Herzberg: motivators and hygiene factors

Frederick Herzberg was an American psychologist who is best known for developing a theory of motivation that divided up motivators and hygiene factors. He was also one of the key champions of job enrichment.

Herzberg et al.'s (1959) analysis starts with the actual characteristics of the job. His original study was on the job attitudes of 203 engineers and accountants. He asked them to describe two 'critical incidents' (extreme behaviour or event where actual behaviour is recorded) that made them feel good and bad about their jobs. The analysis of these led to the two categories motivating and hygiene factors:

- **Motivating factors** have the potential to motivate the worker and are intrinsic to the job. These include achievement, recognition, work itself, responsibility, opportunities for advancement and personal growth. These factors are at the higher end of Maslow's hierarchy of needs.
- **Hygiene factors** are aspects that have the potential to cause dissatisfaction. They are external factors such as company policy and administration, relationship with supervisors, work conditions, salary, status and security. The term 'hygiene' is from medicine, meaning preventive and environmental (organizational). These factors are at the lower end of Maslow's hierarchy of needs.

Hygiene factors are important as if they go wrong they can significantly lower the level of motivation, but having high levels of them is unlikely to significantly increase levels of motivation. For instance, having low levels of pay is likely to cause decreased motivation. However as soon as pay reaches a level considered to be normal, it quickly loses its extra motivating potential.

One of the implications of his two-factor theory is that work can be redesigned in order to minimize the negative hygiene factors and increase the positive motivating factors. Rather than simplifying jobs as seen in scientific management, which ultimately led to repetitive tasks, Herzberg (2003) argued that work should be redesigned to increase the intrinsic motivation of jobs.

One approach is *horizontal job-loading* – adding more tasks to the job but not more responsibility. This can be achieved through *job rotation* – where the worker undertakes a range of tasks than simply doing one repetitive one; and *job enlargement* – where the worker undertakes a range of tasks all at the same time.

The problem with horizontal job-loading Herzberg argues, is that it does not increase motivation as the intrinsic nature of the job has not been changed. It is simply doing a range of uninteresting jobs rather than just one. To increase motivation work should have *vertical job-loading* – where the work is made more meaningful by increasing the level of responsibility. This *job enrichment* can occur through giving teams more complex and interesting tasks to do together.

Herzberg's work is interesting in that it looks at the design of jobs themselves and how that impacts motivation. It therefore offers opportunities to design work that can be intrinsically motivating to people. His work has also been challenged. It was a relatively small and culturally specific sample of interviewees, all from similar, skilled professions. Therefore it is questionable if it is as applicable to unskilled workers, or those from other cultural contexts. The critical incident methodology has also been criticized, as people are often more likely to see things they do themselves as contributing to their motivation, and blame outside factors on aspects which demotivate them (the hygiene factors are organizational). Managers also might struggle giving over responsibility to workers and some workers, particularly in low-paid roles, might dislike increased responsibility, particularly for unskilled, part-time roles.

DANIEL KING

See also:

Job design; Job enrichment; Maslow: hierarchy of needs; McGregor; Scientific management.

References and selected further readings

Herzberg, F. (2003), One more time: how do you motivate employees? *Harvard Business Review*, **81**(1), pp. 87–96.
Herzberg, F., B. Mausner and B.B. Snyderman (1959), *The Motivation to Work*, London: Chapman and Hall.

Hierarchy

Adapted from the organization of the medieval church, the arrangement of work activities in a formal hierarchical structure, where for every office-holder there is another above licensed by enabling rules to control their activities and to whom the subordinate must report, has often been taken as a defining feature of modern, rational organization. Advocates argue that hierarchical organization creates an accountability essential for rational organization, enabling systems of centralized decision-making whether the decisions be those of the management of a capitalist enterprise or the executive of a democratic polity. The placement of individuals with the appropriate expertise in the ranks of a hierarchy adds value to the work activities of an organization as work passes from one level to another in the structure. Hierarchical structures, advocates argue, reflect the relative complexity of work activities. The complexity of the variables involved in work tasks provides a rational basis for distributing work activities in a hierarchical chain of command.

Hierarchy has been criticized by those favouring more adaptable and organic organizational structures and for its tendency to create division and damage to the social fabric of an organization as members compete for advancement and pursue their own interests. Hierarchy, critics argue, often discourages genuine accountability as organizational members pass responsibility for complex tasks from one to another. During the later years of the twentieth century, critics argued that hierarchy had lost its relevance. The growing rate of change in markets, the need for greater organizational responsiveness as well as changes in technology meant that organizations were increasingly flattening their structures and relying on the knowledge and capability of employees at lower levels, often configured in team-like structures. An alternative view suggests that where such modifications were taking place, hierarchical control remained firmly in place in the modern business enterprise. Primary organizational goals and objectives remained subject to managerial jurisdiction and management information systems were facilitating more extensive centralized forms of surveillance of the performance of individuals and teams at lower levels. Workers were being induced by their managers to exercise autonomy and discretion at work in an appropriate way.

The powers of decision invested in those at the apex of the hierarchical structures of large modern enterprises, critics also argue, deprives organizational members or other stakeholders of the ability to influence important decisions that affect their lives. Such arrangements impair the quality of organizational decision-making and stifle the creative and critical powers of organizational members. This in turn has consequences for their role in society at large, especially weakening their capacities as the citizens of a democratic state. While hierarchical control offers benefits in the control and coordination of work activities, business organizations require forms of control and surveillance of their leaders and managers, not least to guard against abuses of position and the powers of office by leaders.

EDWARD BARRATT

See also:
Bureaucracy; Empowerment; Power.

References and selected further readings

Child, J. (2011), Challenging hierarchy, in M. Alvesson, T. Bridgman and H. Willmott (eds), *Oxford Handbook of Critical Management Studies*, Oxford: Oxford University Press.
Heyderbrand, W. (1989), New organizational forms, *Work, Employment and Society*, **16**(3), pp. 323–357.
Jacques, E. (1990), In praise of hierarchy, *Harvard Business Review*, **68**(1), pp. 127–134.
Parker, M. (2009), Angelic organization: hierarchy and the tyranny of heaven, *Organization Studies*, **30**(11), 1281–1299.
Weber, M. (1978), *Economy and Society*, 2 vol., Los Angeles: University of California Press.

High-involvement management

High-involvement management is a term coined by Ed Lawler for an approach to management centred on employee involvement. It entails providing employees with opportunities to make decisions concerning the conduct of their jobs and to participate in the business as a whole. It thus includes role-involvement practices that give workers more autonomy in how and when they do their tasks, and organizational-involvement practices such as teamworking, idea-capturing schemes and functional flexibility. In addition, it involves practices that enhance the skills and knowledge of workers required for this involvement, such as training in creativity and teamworking skills, information-sharing, performance feedback, as well as motivational practices that ensure the rewards workers receive are supportive of involvement such as performance-related pay, equal opportunities policies and work–life balance practices.

High-involvement management is conceived as an alternative to a control model that is founded on job simplification, tightly defined divisions of labour, rigid allocations of individuals to narrowly defined tasks and minimal employee participation in higher-level decisions. The aspiration behind high-involvement management is the development of broader horizons among all workers so that they will think of better ways of doing their jobs, connect what they do with what others do, and take initiative in the face of novel problems.

The significance of high-involvement management is that is widely seen as increasingly consistent with the performance requirements of the modern fast-changing economy. Moreover, it offers an opportunity for employees and employers to mutually benefit in ways that were not feasible in the control model. Role involvement in particular is associated with increasing job satisfaction and workers' wellbeing, when control methods were associated with alienation, stress and excessive fatigue.

It is typically advocated that high-involvement practices should be used together and it is thought their integrated use should yield disproportionately high benefits compared with the use of low or medium levels of involvement. Research into their joint use shows that organizational involvement and skill and knowledge acquisition practices tend to be used together, but motivational supports are not necessarily used with these nor with each other. Most significantly, organizational involvement and role involvement need not go hand-in-hand (Wood et al., 2012). Indeed, many innovations in organizational involvement have been in traditional assembly-line production systems where job autonomy is low.

Studies of high-involvement management have largely centred on its performance effect to see if it justifies the 'high-performance management' label that many have given it. They have not established a causal connection, but there is sufficient evidence to suggest high-involvement management may be linked with higher rates of productivity and other key performance measures, and that in the case of role involvement this is partly explained by its positive effects on employee wellbeing and satisfaction. However, there is insufficient evidence to associate organizational involvement with such positive effects on workers' wellbeing, and in certain cases it may even increase their anxiety as it places new demands on them.

STEPHEN WOOD

See also:

Employee involvement; Managerial control; Lean production.

References and selected further readings

Appelbaum, E., T. Bailey, P. Berg and A.L. Kalleberg (2000), *Manufacturing Advantage: Why High Performance Work Systems Pay Off*, Ithaca, NY: Cornell University Press.

Lawler, E.E. (1986), *High Involvement Management*, San Francisco: Jossey-Bass.

MacDuffie, J.P. (1995), Human resource bundles and manufacturing performance: organizational logic and flexible production systems in the world auto industry, *Industrial and Labor Relations Review*, **48**(2), pp. 197–221.

Wall, T.D., S.J. Wood and D. Leach (2004), Empowerment and performance, in I. Robertson and C. Cooper (eds), *International and Organizational Psychology*, London: Wiley, pp. 1–46.

Walton, R.E. (1985), From 'control' to 'commitment' in the workplace, *Harvard Business Review*, **63**(2), pp. 77–84.

Wood, S. (2009), High involvement management and performance, in A. Wilkinson, P. Gollan, M. Marchington and D. Lewin (eds), *The Oxford Handbook of Participation in Organizations*, Oxford and New York: Oxford University Press, pp. 407–426.

Wood, S., M. van Veldhoven, M. Croon and L.M. de Menezes (2012), Enriched job design, high involvement management and organizational performance: the mediating roles of job satisfaction and well-being, *Human Relations*, **65**(4), pp. 419–446.

High-performance work systems

The emergence of the idea of high-performance work systems (HPWS) can be dated to the publication of a series of US-based studies in the mid-1990s (e.g., Huselid, 1995). The basic concern of the studies was to see whether new ways of organizing work and managing people were having an effect on the performance of organizations. A precise definition of HPWS is difficult to arrive at, but any such system is likely to involve both a degree of employee involvement in decision-making – often through the operation of semi-autonomous work teams – and a division of labour such that employees are required to perform a range of tasks. There would, in addition, be a recognition – or, at least, the hope or intention – that the management of work and people has a direct and significant effect on organizational performance.

There is a mass of evidence to support the existence of a link between HPWS and organizational performance; but, almost from the outset, the real issue has been to understand the nature of this relationship. Early work tried to establish whether the link was universal – did the same systems work in all circumstances? – or contingent – did success depend on circumstances? If it was the latter, then what was most important in an organization's circumstances? In particular, how important was an organization's overall business strategy? A second issue was whether each practice making up the HPWS had its own effect – in which case the more 'high performance' practices an organization had, the better – or whether the effect of the practices came from their interaction as part of a 'bundle'. A third distinction sometimes made was between 'best practice' and 'best fit' in work systems – a distinction in fact quite difficult to make both conceptually and in practice.

More recent work can be divided into two strands. The first of these builds on the earlier work about the nature of the HPWS–performance relationship by trying to get inside what has come to be known as the 'black box'. We can see what goes into the box – the HPWS themselves – and we can see what comes out of it – the performance of the organization. What we need to understand, it is argued, is what goes on inside the box itself. This work has given a greater and more active role in the story to employees and to line managers. Bowen and Ostroff (2004), for example, refer in this context to the importance of the 'strength' of the system of HRM. The second strand of more recent work has sought to address the HPWS–performance link at a more fundamental level. For Kaufman (2010), for example, it is not the case that the adoption of HPWS explains an organization's level of performance; rather, it is the level of performance that explains the adoption of HPWS.

STEPHEN PROCTER

See also:

Employee involvement; High-involvement management; Self-managed teams; Work organization.

References and selected further readings

Bowen, D. and C. Ostroff (2004), Understanding HRM–firm performance linkages: the role of the 'strength' of the HRM system, *Academy of Management Review*, **29**(2), pp. 203–221.

Guest, D. (2011), Human resource management and performance: still searching for some answers, *Human Resource Management Journal*, **21**(1), pp. 3–13.

Huselid, M. (1995), The impact of human resource management practices on turnover, productivity, and financial corporate performance, *Academy of Management Journal*, **38**(3), pp. 635–672.

Jiang, K., R. Takeuchi and D. Lepak (2013), Where do we go from here? New perspectives on the black box in strategic human resource management research, *Journal of Management Studies*, **50**(8), pp. 1448–1480.

Kaufman, B. (2010), SHRM theory in the post-Huselid era: why it is fundamentally misspecified, *Industrial Relations*, **49**(2), pp. 286–313.

Procter, S. (2008), New forms of work and the high performance paradigm, in P. Blyton, N.Bacon, J. Fiorito and E. Heery (eds), *Sage Handbook of Industrial Relations*, London: Sage, pp. 149–169.

Homeworking

Descriptively, homeworking is defined as 'paid work carried out at home'. However, this deceptively simple definition leaves a number of crucial conceptual issues unaddressed, such as under what conditions is the work carried out and to what extent is the work home-located. Attempts have, therefore, been made to provide greater conceptual clarity by differentiating workers according to the social relations of production under which they labour at home and what proportion of time they spend doing so (Felstead and Jewson, 2000). In this way, self-employed accountants and architects who work at home can be differentiated from machinists and Christmas cracker assemblers who are employed but carry out their work at home (Allen and Wolkowitz, 1987). Similarly, those working occasionally at home to meet a deadline can be differentiated from those who carry out all of their paid work at home. The term 'teleworking' has been used by some (e.g., Huws et al., 1990) to describe the situation where technology is crucial to this process.

Why would homeworking be of interest to practitioners and students of HRM? There are several reasons. First, its use can deliver economic benefits to organizations that no longer have to provide working space to their staff who can do at least some of their work off-site. Recently, detaching work from place has had greatest impact among office workers whose smartphones and laptops can connect them to the office wherever they are and whatever the time. This has led to the rise of working at home, working on the move and redesigning office space to cater for transient use (Felstead et al., 2005; Hislop and Axtell, 2007). Second, researchers have begun to document the rise in the numbers of workers who work in this way. Although the rate of increase does not match the heroic predictions of some futurologists, it has been sharp nonetheless. Around a quarter of workers in Europe in 2010, for example, said that they worked mainly off-site (Felstead and Jewson, 2012). Third, these developments provide a challenge to conventional modes of management control and surveillance that rely on visibility. Fourth, bringing together spheres of contemporary social life that have become increasingly differentiated during industrialization presents challenges to both workers and their managers who may be used to working but not being seen.

ALAN FELSTEAD

See also:

Flexible working; Telework and coworking.

References and selected further readings

Allen, S. and C. Wolkowitz (1987), *Homeworking: Myths and Realities*, London: Macmillan.
Felstead, A. and N. Jewson (2000), *In Work, At Home: Towards an Understanding of Homeworking*, London: Routledge.
Felstead, A. and N. Jewson (2012), New places of work, new spaces of learning, in R. Brooks, A. Fuller and J. Waters (eds), *Changing Spaces of Education: New Perspectives on the Nature of Learning*, London: Routledge.
Felstead, A., N. Jewson and S. Walters (2005), *Changing Places of Work*, Basingstoke: Palgrave Macmillan.
Hislop, D. and C. Axtell (2007), The neglect of spatial mobility in contemporary studies of work: the case telework, *New Technology, Work and Employment*, **22**(1), pp. 34–51.
Huws, U., W.B. Korte and S. Robinson (1990), *Telework: Towards the Elusive Office*, Chichester: John Wiley.

Horns effect

A performance appraisal is an evaluation of how well an individual achieves job-related duties and responsibilities. The basic purpose of conducting performance appraisals is to improve performance. However, appraiser impressions about employee performance are commonly influenced by subjectivity and their biases are often attributable to the presence of rater errors, such as contrast, recency, personal prejudices and leniency/ strictness. Such appraisal errors can lead to perceptions of unfairness. Part of this concerns the horns effect, which is the opposite of the halo effect, and refers to the process in which the appraiser's unfavourable impression of an appraisee, influences the appraiser's judgement about all other areas of performance and influences overall rating. A horns effect has the tendency to limit the overall assessment of the appraisee to a single attribute (Arnold and Pulich, 2003). This means that the appraiser might give a poor rating even though the appraisee's overall performance is commendable. Some appraisers have tendencies to view negatively all behaviours or actions of a subordinate because the appraiser dislikes a particular behaviour or action of the subordinate (Lefkowitz, 2000).

Satisfaction in the appraisal process is a key factor leading to job satisfaction (Murphy and Cleveland, 1995). If appraisees are dissatisfied with the performance appraisal system, the effectiveness of the overall appraisal and feedback process is reduced. In order for a performance system to be perceived as fair, it must be as free of bias as possible and be 'seen to be fair'. An effective performance management system must focus on diminishing the errors that occur during this appraisal process.

Furthermore, the validity of workplace decisions that are based on inaccurate appraisals would be difficult to justify if legally challenged. In addition, when performance ratings do not accurately reflect the performance levels, employees would lose their trust in the appraisal system. This would not only hinder their opportunity for career progression; it would also lead to low morale and turnover problems.

Horn effects can have serious effects on performance (Bernardin and Beatty, 2004). If an employee makes mistakes in one area the superior may think that the employee is also making them elsewhere. The result of this bias is that employees may be more concerned with not making the mistake than with striving for excellent performance thus leading to an overall lower rating than may be warranted.

CHRIS ROWLEY AND NAGIAH RAMASAMY

See also:

Halo effect; Performance appraisal.

References and selected further readings

Arnold, E. and M. Pulich (2003), Personality conflicts and objectivity in appraising performance, *Health Care Manager*, **22**(3), pp. 227–232.

Bernardin, H.J. and R. Beatty (2004), *Performance Appraisal: Assessing Human Behavior at Work*, Boston: Kent Wadsworth Publishing.

Boachie-Mensah, F.O. and P.A. Seidu (2012), Employees' perception of performance appraisal system: a case study, *International Journal of Business and Management*, **7**(2), pp. 73–88.

Lefkowitz, S.W. (2000), The role interpersonal affective regard in supervisory performance ratings: a literature review and proposed causal model, *Journal of Occupational and Organisational Psychology*, **73**(1), pp. 67–85.

MacDougall, M., S.C. Riley, H.S. Cameron and B. McKinstry (2008), Halos and horns in the assessment of undergraduate medical students: a consistency-based approach, *Journal of Applied Quantitative Methods*, **3**(2), pp. 116–128.

Murphy, K.R. and N.J. Cleveland (2005), *Understanding Performance Appraisal: Social, Organizational and Goal-Based Perspective*, Thousand Oaks: Sage Publications.

HRM process approach: attribution of HRM

About ten years ago, scholars started to criticize the one-sided focus on the HRM content-based approach where scholars examine HR practices such as recruitment and selection, pay for promotions, promotions and formal training. One of the assumptions of the HRM content-based approach is that employees perceive HRM within their organization in the same way. Scholars of the so-called HRM process approach explicitly highlight the importance of the psychological processes through which employees attach meaning to HRM and emphasized the importance of employees' perception and understanding of HRM within their organization. They developed a framework for understanding how HRM as a system can contribute to employee and organizational performance. According to attribution theory, employees should perceive HRM as being distinctive, consistent and consensual to interpret the messages conveyed by HRM in a uniform manner. In such cases, they will have a better understanding of the kinds of behaviours management expects, supports and rewards.

Although recently more studies have focused on the impact of employees' perceptions of HRM to explain the effect of HRM, only a few studies thus far have related employees' perceptions to the attribution process. The attribution theory explains how people process information to make attributions. The co-variation principle of attribution theory suggests that people try to understand the cause of situations by considering information related to those situations. According to attribution theory, people use causal explanations (*attributions*) to make sense of their surroundings, improve their ability to predict future events and attempt to (re)establish control over their lives. In addition, the attributions people make systematically influence their subsequent behaviours, motivations, cognitions and affect.

When people can perceive a situation as distinctive, consistent and consensual, they can make confident attributions about the cause–effect relationships and can better understand the situation. *Distinctiveness* refers to features that allow an object to stand out in its environment, thereby capturing attention and arousing interest. *Consistency* is the co-variation of information across time and modalities. If the information is the same for all modalities, individuals perceive this situation as consistent. *Consensus* is the co-variation of behaviour across different people. If many people perceive the situation in the same way, consensus is high.

The co-variation principle suggests that the combination of these three dimensions results in different information patterns that lead to a general class of causation. When applying the co-variation principle to HRM, we expect that where employees perceive HRM as standing out (high distinctiveness), perceive that the different HR practices are aligned with each other (high consistency) and perceive that colleagues comprehend HRM in the same way they do (high consensus), employees will attribute HRM to stimulus or entity, i.e., the management of the organization. In contrast, if employees perceive HRM as not standing out (low distinctiveness), that the different HR practices are aligned with each other (high consistency) and that colleagues comprehend HR practices in a different way (low consensus), they will attribute HRM to themselves: it is only this employee who perceives HRM in this way. Finally, if employees perceive HRM as standing out (high distinctiveness), that the different HR practices are not aligned with each other (low consistency) and that colleagues comprehend HRM in a different way (low consensus), they will attribute HRM to the current organizational circumstances (context and time) under which management makes such HR policies.

Results from experimental and field studies show that HRM is more effective in terms of employee' outcomes when employees perceive HRM as distinctive, consist and consensual. In this case they can make sense of HRM and understand HRM as it was intended by management. In this way HRM can send a clear message as to what they expect from their employees, what is rewarded and what is expected. The same results were found for different HR practices, such as performance appraisal quality and formal training. These practices are more effective under the condition that employees can understand HRM.

KARIN SANDERS

See also:

Human resource management.

References and selected further readings

Bowen, D.E. and C. Ostroff (2004), Understanding HRM–firm performance linkages: the role of the 'strength' of the HRM system, *Academy of Management Review*, **29**, pp. 203–221.

Sanders, K. and H. Yang (forthcoming), How to make sense of human resource management; employees' attribution to explain the HRM–performance relationship, *Human Resource Management*.

Sanders, K., H. Shipton and J. Gomes (2014), Is the HRM process important? past, current and future challenges, *Human Resource Management*, **53**(4), pp. 489–503.

Human capital

Human capital has its foundation in the work of Nobel Prize winner Gary Becker. He defined human capital as a stock of knowledge, comprising education, information and productive and innovative skills; that is formed through investments in education, training, health, and informal knowledge transfers (Becker, 1964). From this definition, Becker developed human capital theory, which explains how human capital can be valuable (to individuals, families, firms or societies) and how individuals make decisions regarding their investments in gaining human capital. Becker also made a distinction between general human capital, which increases the marginal productivity of labour across organizations and specific human capital, which increases the productivity of labour at a specific organization (Becker, 1964).

Building on the work of Becker, the larger management and human resource management research has tended to define human capital along the lines of individuals' knowledge, skills, abilities and other characteristics (KSAOs) used to produce a given set of outcomes (Hitt et al., 2001; Wright and McMahan, 2011). From a theoretical standpoint, the resource-based view has been combined with human capital theory. The resource-based view of the firm states that internal resources of an organization that are valuable, rare and inimitable, and non-substitutable can create a competitive advantage for organizations. Theoretical work has indicated that human capital meets the requirements of the resource-based view of the firm and may be the most important resource in organizations gaining a competitive advantage (Wright et al., 1994).

Human capital has been studied at the individual, team, and organization levels of analysis. Human capital has been measured in many ways, including but not limited to: education (level, quality and type), work experience, job tenure, organizational tenure, general cognitive ability, personality traits, job-specific KSAOs, and subjective ratings by managers. At the individual level, empirical research has shown human capital to be positively related to job performance, career success and level of income. At the team and organizational levels, human capital has been found to be positively related to performance. Some of the organizational performance outcomes include: financial performance, accounting performance and customer satisfaction. Recently, research has begun to explore the multilevel nature of human capital and the aggregation of individual-level human capital to form an organization-level construct of human capital. Overall, research has tended to find a positive relationship between human capital and performance outcomes, which demonstrates the importance of human capital to organizational performance and its potential to be a source of competitive advantage.

CHRISTOPHER M. HARRIS

See also:

Human resource strategy; Knowledge management; Resource-based view; Strategic HRM.

References and selected further readings

Becker, G. (1964), *Human Capital*, Chicago: University of Chicago Press.
Hitt, M.A., L. Bierman, K. Shimizu and R. Kochhar (2001), Direct and indirect effects of human capital on strategy and performance in professional service firms: a resource-based perspective, *Academy of Management Journal*, **44**(1), pp. 13–28.
Ployhart, R.E. and T.P. Moliterno (2011), Emergence of the human capital resource: a multilevel model, *Academy of Management Review*, **36**(1), pp. 127–150.
Wright, P.M. and G.C. McMahan (2011), Exploring human capital: putting human back into strategic human resource management, *Human Resource Management Journal*, **21**(2), pp. 93–104.
Wright, P.M., G.C. McMahan and A. McWilliams (1994), Human resources and sustained competitive advantage: a resource-based perspective, *International Journal of Human Resource Management*, **5**, pp. 301–326.

Human relations movement/Mayo

The human relations movement is a perspective that is concerned with studying human behaviour in groups. It is most closely associated with Elton Mayo and particularly the Hawthorne Studies, which it is widely credited in discovering a new way of managing people by paying attention to the 'human factor' in organizations.

The Hawthorne Studies were conducted at the Western Electric Company near Chicago, USA, between 1924 and 1932, and are one of the largest and most in depth studies in management history. The original research, which was firmly within the scientific management tradition of Taylorism, examined the link between lighting levels and productivity. A latter experiment, the 'bank wiring room' explored the link between pay and productivity (for a more in depth discussion, see King and Lawley, 2013). However, contrary to their assumptions that lighting (a physiological factor) or pay motivates, what the researchers discovered, at least as it is conventionally portrayed, is the power of the 'informal organization' and particularly 'group norms' in governing worker behaviour. While in these experiments the group would gain a bonus for producing more outputs, the researchers found the group restricted the output. Workers who made more items than was perceived by the group to be a 'fair day's work', were nicknamed 'Shrimp', 'Runt', 'Slave' and 'Speed King', excluded by the group and teased for breaking these group norms. From this observation the researchers stated the group had these informal rules:

1. You should not turn out too much work. If you do, you are a 'rate-buster'.
2. You should not turn out too little work. If you do you are a 'chiseller'.
3. You should not tell a supervisor anything that will react to the detriment of an associate. If you do, you are a 'squealer'.
4. You should not attempt to maintain social distance or act officious. If you are an inspector, for example, you should not act like one (Roethlisberger and Dickson, 1939, p. 522).

The research, particularly in Elton Mayo's hands, therefore has been credited with discovering the 'social person', that people are governed by social needs, such as belonging to a group, rather than economic self-interest (as Taylorism presupposes) (Mayo, 1949). This, supporters claim, offers a more rounded and positive view of the individual, which understands the 'relations of mutual interdependence' between people (Roethlisberger and Dickson, 1939, p. 569).

This approach also claimed that there could be harmony of interests between workers and managers, as people spontaneously want to cooperate. Supervisors and managers therefore need to work to change the group norms, rather than focusing on individuals.

However this view of the Hawthorne Studies is controversial. Mayo's involvement in the actual research was limited and was more involved in popularizing it. The researchers have been accused of downplaying or even ignoring evidence that did not fit their analysis. Also Roethlisberger and Mayo, rather than 'discovering' the concept of the 'social man' are claimed to already believe in, the idea and fitted evidence to suit their interpretation. Ultimately they offered 'a new way to control workers to accept less, while claiming that workers needed psychological counselling about their relations at work that only management could administer' (Bruce and Nyland, 2011, p. 386).

DANIEL KING

See also:

Job design; Motivation; Scientific management; Work organization.

References and selected further readings

Bruce, K. and C. Nyland (2011), Elton Mayo and the deification of human relations, *Organization Studies*, **32**(3), pp. 383–405.

King, D. and S. Lawley (2013), *Organizational Behaviour*, Oxford: Oxford University Press.

Mayo, E. (1949), *The Social Problems of an Industrial Civilisation*, London: Routledge.

Roethlisberger, F.J. and W.J. Dickson (1939), *Management and the Worker*, Cambridge, MA: Harvard University Press.

Human resource department

A human resource (HR) department is one of the functional departments of an employing organization. Its main responsibility is to organize the delivery of HR functions/services that best support the achievement of the organizational goals. A fully fledged in-house HR department may deliver the following key HR functions: strategic planning and forecasting; job design; recruitment and selection; designing and overseeing the delivery of reward, welfare, performance management and training and development systems; ensuring legal compliance of HR activities; monitoring occupational health and safety issues; addressing employees grievances; managing labour relationship (with the trade unions where unions are recognized); implementing organizational policies; managing dismissal and redundancy; and managing subcontracting relationships related to HR issues. In short, an HR department needs to play a strategic as well as an operational role to provide strategic vision and functional expertise.

In small organizations, an HR department may not exist; instead, a senior manager may be responsible for overseeing the HR function. In larger organizations, a general trend in developed countries is that the HR department has become leaner in recent decades to reduce staffing costs and also to take advantage of the growing provision of external specialist HR services. Outsourcing of part of the HR functions has become more popular (Cooke et al., 2005). In addition, organizations with multiple establishments in a country may adopt a shared services model to deliver certain HR activities (often administrative ones) in a more cost effective and professional manner (Farndale et al., 2009, 2010). HR shared services are often organized to be delivered in a shared services centre, aided by information technology. In a multinational corporation (MNC) context, the MNC may outsource part of its HR functions to local HR service providers in the host country. It may also set up regional HR headquarters to oversee the HR function of the region, supported by in-house global business partners (senior HR professionals with strategic insights), centres of excellence (providing functional expertise), and global shared services centre (Cooke and Budhwar, 2009).

The adoption of HR shared services, HR outsourcing and centre of excellence is, to a large extent, informed by Ulrich's (1998) influential thesis of the four roles of HR:

strategic partner, administrative expert, employee champion and change agent. Ulrich further argues that the in-house HR department should add value to the business by becoming a strategic partner to the organization, and outsourcing transactional HR activities will supposedly enable the in-house HR department to focus on the strategic matters. More recently, Ulrich et al. (2013) argue that, for the HR function to be taken seriously as a profession, HR professionals need to develop their competence to be: credible activist, strategic positioner, capability builder, change champion, human resource innovator and integrator, and technology proponent. A key challenge to achieving all these is: how can the HR department obtain resources needed in the first place to fulfil these roles against a context of increasing scarce organizational resources?

FANG LEE COOKE

See also:

HR function and business partnering; Human resource manager.

References and selected further readings

Cooke, F.L. and P. Budhwar (2009), HR offshoring and outsourcing: research issues for IHRM, in P. Sparrow (ed.), *Handbook of International Human Resource Management*, Chichester: John Wiley, pp. 341–361.
Cooke, F.L., J. Shen and A. McBride (2005), Outsourcing HR: implications for the role of the HR function and the workforce, *Human Resource Management*, **44**(4), pp. 413–432.
Farndale, E., J. Paauwe and L. Hoeksema (2009), In-sourcing HR: shared service centres in the Netherlands, *The International Journal of Human Resource Management*, **20**(3), pp. 544–556.
Farndale, E., J. Paauwe and P. Boselie (2010), An exploratory study of governance in the intra-firm human resources supply chain, *Human Resource Management*, **49**(5), pp. 849–868.
Ulrich, D. (1998), A new mandate for human resources, *Harvard Business Review*, January–February, pp. 124–134.
Ulrich, D., J. Younger, W. Brockbank and M. Ulrich (2013), The state of the HR profession, *Human Resource Management*, **52**(3), pp. 457–471.

Human resource development

The nature of human resource development (HRD) in organizations has changed dramatically over the past 20 years. As recently as the 1980s there was a real schism between the activities associated with human resource management and human resource development. Often operating as two separate departments, sometimes there was even little cooperation between the two.

However, more recently HRD has become an integral part of the human resource management portfolio and now encompasses the areas of talent management and development, knowledge management, coaching and career management. It has been seen to have strong links to performance and engagement and as such a strategic activity which impacts upon almost every area of people management.

The Chartered Institute of Personnel and Development (CIPD, 2015a) defines an HRD strategy as 'an organisational strategy that articulates the workforce capabilities, skills or competencies required, and how these can be developed, to ensure a sustainable, successful organisation'.

Under this definition, HRD is as much about identifying what skills and knowledge the organization needs to succeed as providing it. Indeed the new emphasis on talent management puts the emphasis on the development of potential in individuals rather than skills training.

The CIPD (2015b) describe talent management as 'the systematic attraction, identification, development, engagement, retention and deployment of those individuals who are of particular value to an organisation, either in view of their "high potential" for the future or because they are fulfilling business/operation-critical roles'. 'Talent', therefore is not necessarily job-specific. Talented individuals may be developed in a number of ways, which contributes to an organization's flexibility and agility.

Talent management links closely to workforce planning, which is an area that has proven problematic as the pace of change continues to increase. It is difficult to accurately predict the skills that are needed for the future, but if we have sufficient talent that can easily adapt and develop new skills, we can still manage our businesses effectively without having to resort to bringing in expensive scarce skills.

There are two ways of defining 'talent'. The first is to look at exclusive talent, which means identifying those individuals in the organization who have the potential to add significant value either in their current role or in a future role and who have the potential to develop further than their current position. The second is referred to as the inclusive approach, which is about recognizing that every employee has talent, which can be developed and exploited to the benefit of both the organization and the individual.

Again this is in sharp contrast to the historic role of 'training', which was essentially about equipping people to work more efficiently in current roles. HRD in contrast is about equipping people with the knowledge and skills to meet future as well as current corporate objectives.

However this shift has also brought with it a change of accountability in terms of who is responsible for training and development. Under the old training regime, this was very much the organization's responsibility and learners' participation was confined to attending and absorbing the knowledge imparted. With HRD learning is very much a partnership between the organization and the individual. Sloman (2003) calls this the 'new paradigm' of learning. Contemporary HRD puts the responsibility for learning on the learner with the organization supporting and facilitating this learning.

Contemporary HRD also recognizes that individuals learn differently and puts a much greater emphasis on adult learning styles and tailoring learning accordingly. There are many different theories of learning but all recognize that adults do not all learn in the same way.

One of the most popular typologies of learning style is that of Honey and Mumford (1982) who identify activists, pragmatists, reflectors and theorists. They define these as follows:

- Activists: thrive on challenge and continuously seek out new activities but are bored with implementation. They tackle problems by brainstorming and looking for new approaches.
- Theorists: think problems through in a logical way and assimilate factors into coherent theories. They continuously look for sense and meaning.
- Pragmatists: try out new ideas to see if they work in practice. They always look for better ways of doing things and are focused on practical solutions.
- Reflectors: like to stand back to ponder experiences and observe them from many

different perspectives. They are cautious and like to think things through before reaching a conclusion.

HRD recognizes that it is important to adapt learning to the individual's preferred style of learning rather than assume that a single training design will have the same impact for everyone.

The final important aspect of HRD is that of evaluating the learning and embedding the learning outcomes into the workplace. The transfer of learning into the workplace is sometimes more of a challenge that the learning itself. Evaluation is critical to ensure the strategic alignment of learning and that it is fulfilling its intention of building the workforce to meet current and future corporate objectives.

There are a number of evaluation models with one of the most famous being the work of Kirkpatrick (1967). Kirkpatrick proposed that learning should be evaluated on four levels: immediate reaction to the learning; immediate outcomes in terms of new knowledge or skill; intermediate outcomes in terms of the impact on job performance; and ultimately evaluation in terms of the impact on organizational performance. He subsequently added another measure: return on investment, which attempted to quantify these values.

ANGELA BARON

See also:

Management development; Strategic HRM; Training and development.

References and selected further readings

Cappelli, P. (2008), Talent management for the twenty-first century, *Harvard Business Review*, **86**(3), pp. 74–81.
CIPD (2015a), *Learning and Development Factsheet*, www.cipd.co.uk/hr-resources/factsheets/learning-talent-development-strategy.aspx.
CIPD (2015b), *Talent Management: An Overview Factsheet*, www.cipd.co.uk/hr-resources/factsheets/talent-management-overview.aspx.
Honey, P. and A. Mumford (1982), *Manual of Learning Styles*, Maidenhead: Honey.
Kirkpatrick, D. (1967), Evaluation of training, in R. Craig and L. Bittell (eds), *Training and Evaluation Handbook*, New York: McGraw-Hill.
Sheehan, M., T.N. Garavan and R. Carbery (2014), Innovation and human resource development (HRD), *European Journal of Training and Development*, **38**(1/2), pp. 2–14.
Sloman, M. (2003), *Training in the Age of the Learner*, London: CIPD.
Sparrow, P., H. Scullion and I. Tarique (eds) (2014), *Strategic Talent Management: Contemporary Issues in International Context*, Cambridge: Cambridge University Press.

Human resource function and business partnering

In the past 20 years, the term 'human resource management' (HRM) has evolved from its origins in the US, to become the preferred international discourse for modern-day people management, replacing the term 'personnel management'. While the concept of HRM, and associated notion of 'human resources' (HR), is contested, there is some consensus that it signals the importance of strategy, competitive advantage and high performance within a global economy (Armstrong, 2000). Critics of HRM have voiced concerns about the primacy given to business interests and accompanying managerial view of the employment relationship: a view that gives priority to the achievement of high levels of employee performance, flexibility and commitment underpinned by a 'unitary' framing of employment issues where all members of an organization are assumed to have mutual interests (Delbridge and Keenoy, 2010). This view marks a fundamental shift away from a 'pluralist' framing of the issues that are indicative of models of personnel management, which acknowledge the inherently contested nature of the employment relationship and articulation of different interests (Keenoy, 1990).

HR professionals are now strongly positioned as 'partners' working closely with line management, in ways that are not unlike that of the 'conformist innovator' described by Legge (1978); where dominant business values are treated as a 'given'. The term 'HR transformation' is increasingly used to denote this business-oriented positioning of HR, with special attention given to the streamlining of HR activities, the devolving of HR work to line managers and the application of information technology commonly referred to as electronic-enabled HR (e-HR). This trend is evident worldwide, and heavily influenced by Dave Ulrich's ideas launched in his 1997 book *Human Resource Champions*.

Ulrich argues that the function has concentrated too much on traditional 'activities' such as recruitment, compensation and so on, and should focus more on 'results' or outcomes, described in terms of strategy execution, administrative efficiency, employee contribution, and capacity for change (Ulrich, 1997; Ulrich and Brockbank, 2005). These deliverables were originally mapped onto four HR roles, framed as distinct but mutually interdependent and described in terms of strategy versus operations, and process versus people: strategic partner, administrative expert, employee champion and change agent. The strategic partner role involves partnering with line managers to enable effective strategy formulation and execution. The change agent is a second strategic role, supporting and leading change initiatives. The administrative expert is described as a 'transactional' role, responsible for the effective and efficient delivery of HR processes through the application of e-HR. The employee champion (later defined as the employee advocate) is defined as an operationally focused and people-oriented role concerned with listening to and responding to employee needs (Ulrich and Brockbank, 2005).

The delivery mechanisms underpinning Ulrich's modelling of HR rests on replacing the traditional, hierarchical departmental model (based on a single team with generalists, specialists and administration) with three separate components: service centres, centres of excellence and business partners. This reorganization has been referred to as the 'three legged stool' and 'shared service model' (Ulrich et al., 2009). Service centres generally concentrate on offering common service provision across business units, in routine HR administration such as recruitment, payroll and absence monitoring, provided in-house or outsourced to a third party. Business partners are typically described as 'embedded HR professionals' who remain positioned within individual business departments in order to support line managers in strategy formulation and implementation issues. Centres of excellence operate as centralized teams of HR experts, collaborating with HR business partners in the crafting of new HR policies and the provision of specialist advice around more complex HR matters.

Notwithstanding a widespread diffusion of Ulrich's ideas, there have been increasing concerns among commentators about the adoption of the shared service model. Critics point to the problematic (unitary) assumption that the four roles are mutually reinforcing, which downplays role ambiguity and role conflict associated with having to grapple with the inherent tensions in sustaining an ethos of mutuality, employee autonomy and development *and* the need to ensure staff comply with increasingly stringent organizational controls (Francis and Keegan, 2006).

The current global economic climate brings into sharp relief, competing logics underpinning reorganizing of the function. This is exemplified in the apparent discrepancy emerging between espoused HR claims that transformation is needed to enhance service provision, and the 'real' driver for change – cost reduction – resulting in various services being cut or not offered, and a reduction in HR staffing (Reilly, 2012). In this scenario business partners can be overwhelmed by transactional work, or the sheer volume of organizational change initiatives, making it difficult for the function to realize its 'strategic' ambitions.

Issues around devolving HR activities to line managers are compounded by common confusion about what is meant by 'devolution', which takes three forms: people management administration (e.g., completing leave forms); involvement in people management policymaking; exercising people management responsibilities vis-à-vis their own staff (e.g. performance management and coaching) (Reilly, 2012).

The size of the organization is another factor shaping line manager accountability for HR. A large percentage of organizations are small and medium-sized enterprises (SMEs), which are unable to support specialist in-house HR functions. More needs to be understood about what factors inhibit managers taking 'ownership' of HR duties within SMEs (Castledine and Renwick, 2012) – such as insufficient resources to fund the necessary support for line managers, organizational restructuring and pressures associated with 'short-termism' – which act to constrain managerial involvement in the softer HR activities such as appraisals and career development (Worrall and Cooper, 2012).

While the single HR function remains prevalent among SMEs, rapid growth of the shared service model within larger organizations can have significant implications for the career paths of HR professionals. Evidence suggests that moving up through the traditional departmental structure is being replaced with more 'crab-like' moves to acquire operational HR experience, and perceived as creating a significant barrier to professionals' career progression, exacerbated by outsourcing of HR services (Francis and Keegan, 2006).

Building HR capabilities within increasingly competitive and complex environments is a further key challenge facing the profession. Caldwell explains that business partners who may possess the same set of HR competencies have to deploy them *differently* depending upon the emergent context in which they are working, such as the degree of teamwork and shared learning between line managers, employees and HR professionals. He points to a growing importance being given to overarching *meta-competencies* or 'capabilities', associated with 'continuous learning', 'flexibility', 'adoption' and 'coping with ambiguity' (Caldwell, 2008, p. 289).

Closer integration of organizational development (OD) and HR disciplines may provide an important pathway to building HR capability in these areas. While critics have warned of the problems associated with increasing strategic amplification of HR roles, the HR business partnering concept does usefully afford an opportunity for HR professionals to expand their repertoire of skills in OD. In this context there is evidence of an increasing use of OD practices designed to give 'voice' to a greater number of stakeholders, and to build core capabilities in the reconciliation of competing logics about organizational effectiveness, judged in terms of the effective management of people and process, efficiency and quality, and so on (Busche and Marshak, 2009).

Arrowsmith and Parker's case example of 'New Zealand Post', usefully illustrates how the deployment of HR from an OD perspective enabled the successful crafting of an employee engagement initiative by HR business partners in ways that sought to reconcile a 'hard' focus on performance outcomes, and a 'soft', more human focus on employee needs and interests. They conclude that employee 'advocacy' may actually be bolstered by the increased status and influence that business partnering arrangements can bring to the HR function – in this scenario, however, HR has to be 'more sophisticated and politically astute in how they address employee concerns' (Arrowsmith and Parker, 2013, p. 2697; see also Francis et al., 2014).

HELEN FRANCIS

Reference list and suggested further readings

Armstrong, M. (2000), The name has changed but has the game remained the same, *Employee Relations*, **22**(6), pp. 576–593.

Arrowsmith, J. and J. Parker (2013), The meaning of 'employee' engagement for the values and roles of the HRM function, *International Journal of Human Resource Management*, **24**(14), pp. 2692–2712.

Busche, G.R. and R.J. Marshak (2009), Revisioning organization development, diagnostic and dialogic premises and patterns of practice, *The Journal of Applied Behavioural Science*, **45**(3), pp. 348–368.

Caldwell, R. (2008), HR business partner competency models: re-conceptualizing effectiveness, *Human Resource Management Journal*, **18**(3), pp. 275–294.

Castledine, J. and D.W.S. Renwick (2012), The role of line managers in HRM, learning and innovation, in H. Francis, L. Holbeche and R. Reddington (eds), *People and Organisational Development: A New Agenda For Organisational Effectiveness*, London: Chartered Institute of Personnel and Development, pp. 180–197.

Delbridge, R. and T. Keenoy (2010), Beyond managerialism, *International Journal of Human Resource Management*, **21**(4–6), pp. 799–817.

Francis, H. and A. Keegan (2006), The changing face of HR: in search of balance, *Human Resource Management Journal*, **16**(3), pp. 231–249.

Francis, H., C. Parkes and R. Reddington (2014), E-HR and international HRM: a critical perspective on the discursive framing of e-HR, *Journal of Human Resource Management*, **25**(10), pp. 1327–1350.

Keenoy, T. (1990), Human resource management: rhetoric, reality and contradiction, *International Journal of Human Resource Management*, **1**(3), pp. 363–384.

Legge, K. (1978), *Power, Innovation and Problem-Solving in Personnel Management*, London: McGraw Hill.

Reilly, J. (2012), Transforming HR to support strategic change, in H. Francis, L. Holbeche and R. Reddington (eds), *People and Organisational Development: A New Agenda for Organisational Effectiveness*, London: Chartered Institute of Personnel and Development, pp. 125–141.

Ulrich, D. (1997), *Human Resource Champions: The Next Agenda for Adding Value and Delivering Results*, Cambridge, MA: Harvard Business School Press.

Ulrich, D. and W. Brockbank (2005), *The HR Value Proposition*, Cambridge, MA: Harvard Business School Press.

Ulrich, D., J. Allen, W. Brockbank and M. Nyman (2009), *HR Transformation: Building Human Resources from the Outside*, New York: McGraw-Hill.

Worrall, L. and C. Cooper (2012), *The Quality of Working Life: Managers' Wellbeing, Motivation and Productivity*, London: Chartered Management Institute Report, in partnership with Simplyhealth, Chartered Management Institute.

Human resource information systems

The topic of human resource information systems (HRIS) entered the research podium in the early 1970s by scholars from the information systems (IS) field. However, the history of HRIS in practice goes back to the 1950s when General Electric (GE) developed a traditional transaction processing system in response to the passage of new tax legislation. During this time, terms such as computerized information systems, personnel and personnel systems were used for describing computerized HR support. Today, information technologies (IT) have dramatically changed the world of HRM research and practice. One of the latest definitions of an HRIS stresses its focus on technical support and enablement of acquiring, storing, manipulating, analysing, retrieving and distributing information to support HRM and other managerial decisions. A recent empirical survey indicates that nearly all large organizations have adopted some form of HRIS.

The term HRIS is often used simultaneously with electronic HRM (e-HRM), although there are obvious differences. HRIS research comes from the field of IS. HRIS are mostly focused on current personnel data, and their success is largely dependent on the degree with which users accept it. HRIS goals usually include cost savings, improved HR services and the strategic reorientation of the HR department. However, scholars have argued that HRIS may streamline and decrease the administrative tasks of HR professionals, while increasing the burden of the administration on to employees and line managers.

E-HRM research has more recently emerged from the HRM field and includes internet and web-based services as enablers of HRM practices. Modern research focuses on HR systems as they provide support for internal operations, enabling managers to make decisions, empowering employees to join people management processes, as well as integrating different HR-related packages (retirement benefits, sick leave administration, fringe benefits, applicant tracking). Scholarly debates are mostly located within HRM strategic discussions, new roles of HR professionals, contributions to firm performance and employee engagement. HRIS can help organizations process the personnel-related information to support HRM and business leaders in making management decisions. E-HRM is viewed as a new way of doing HRM, supported by HRIS.

Over several decades, researchers have identified various factors influencing HRIS acceptance: technology-related factors (IT architecture, digitalizing HR data, IT project management), organizational factors (users demographics, policies and HR practices, resources). In the past decade a significant increase in the relevance of so-called people factors has been observed for the successful acceptance of HRIS. Although technological and organizational factors are necessary prerequisites, people factors, organizational climate and culture, quality of communications, employee commitment, and supportive leadership determine HRIS success.

TANYA BONDAROUK

See also:
Electronic HRM; Electronic recruitment.

References and selected further readings

Bondarouk, T.V. and E. Furtmueller (2012), E-HRM research: promises, hopes, facts and path forward: reviewing four decades of empirical evidence, in *Proceedings of the Fourth International e-HRM Conference: Innovation, Creativity and e-HRM*, pp. 25–60.
Johnson, R.D., K.M. Lukaszewski and D.L. Stone (2015), The evolution of the field of human resource information systems: co-evolution of technology and HR processes, *Communications of the AIS*.
Kavanagh, M.J., M. Thite and R.D. Johnson (eds) (2015), *Human Resource Information Systems*, 3rd edn, Thousand Oaks: Sage.

Ruël, H., T. Bondarouk and J.K. Looise (2004), E-HRM: innovation or irritation? An explorative empirical study in five large companies on web-based HRM, *Management Review*, **15**(3), pp. 364–380.
Strohmeier, S. (2007), Research in e-HRM: review and implications, *Human Resource Management Review*, **17**, 19–37.

Human resource management

Human resource management (HRM) has become the predominant term to describe the theory and practices relating to the way people are managed at work. The label originated in the USA and it spread to the UK and beyond in the 1980s. In previous times, other terms have been used that, in varying degrees, broadly correspond. These other terms include personnel management, personnel administration, people management, employee relations and employment management.

The previous paragraph refers to a 'broad correspondence' rather than direct replication. It is important here to note that currently the term 'human resource management' is used in two different ways. In one usage, which we can term the generic, it is used to encompass all of the forms of employment management in its infinite variety. In this first sense, it is just a new label. But there is a second usage. In its second form the term has at times denoted a *particular* approach to employment management. Thus, the term in this second sense refers to one of the many ways of managing labour and is used to demarcate it from other ways. Not surprisingly, the existence of two different usages has caused considerable confusion in the academic literature, with commentators often talking at cross-purposes.

So, what is this second, more specific and narrow meaning? In this particular sense it has been defined as follows:

> Human resource management is a distinctive approach to employment management which seeks to achieve competitive advantage through the strategic deployment of a highly committed and capable workforce using an array of cultural, structural and personnel techniques (Storey, 2007, p. 7).

First, as noted, it is an approach that openly seeks to secure a 'competitive advantage'. This declared objective is not to every ideological taste. This element alone indicates that the approach shares a similar stance as American strategy theorists such as Michael Porter. Many critics of HRM have been, and are, uncomfortable with this first element. They posit the idea that economic activity does not to have to be quite so dedicated to free market competition. They also contend that even within a capitalist framework, collaboration as well as competition can operate and that other objectives in addition to competitive advantage such as wellbeing, equity and multiple stakeholder interests could be pursued. And they are of course correct. But some of these critics have failed to recognize that an identification and description of a movement and an idea should not be confused with an endorsement of that idea.

Second, the definition points to the distinctive means through which the objective will be sought. These include, crucially, the element of a 'strategic' approach. This means that the management of people and of the workforce in general is approached not in an ad hoc, tactical and merely reactive way but in a manner that regards this aspect of management as of central importance. As with other aspects of the definition, the interesting features are in noting what the meaning suggests HRM is not. The counterfactual is important. For the HRM debate and the emergence of HRM only makes sense when it is recognized as part of the history of its time.

HRM emerged when labour management, in broad characterization, might be described as a secondary, Cinderella, management practice. Markets were defined, finance arranged, production plans drawn up – and only then was the request for certain units of labour issued often at short notice. Similarly, as industrial conflict was of concern, the skills in subduing and 'managing conflict' were to the fore in the then field of personnel/IR management. It was into this climate when Western product markets were coming up against international competition – and often losing out – that this 'new' approach to managing labour emerged and presented a challenge to existing assumptions and practices.

Third, the definition refers to the deployment of a 'highly committed and capable workforce'. This is an important feature of the distinctive approach. As we know, very large sections of the economy operate on very different principles. The high commitment approach is relatively unusual in large swathes of the employment scene. Hire and fire, short-term contracts, even zero-hour contracts, outsourcing, agency work and many other such methods to treat labour as a mere transaction are commonplace. Recent talk of 'employee engagement' can be seen as a latter-day attempt to capture some of the high commitment agenda but in a much diluted form compared with the original formulation.

Fourth, the 'array of cultural, structural and personnel techniques' refers to the mutually reinforcing ways in which a truly thought-out strategic approach can deploy a wide range of methods that would have internal 'fit' and would complement each other (a further instance of the strategic nature of the idea). These techniques include attempts to: 'win hearts and minds' rather than merely enforce a contract; to de-emphasize custom and practice in favour of instilling values and mission; pluralism is also downplayed in favour of an implied unitary perspective where employers, managers and employees are seen to share at least one similar interest: to keep the enterprise in business. Thus, a set of beliefs and assumptions underpin this distinctive form of HRM. Other dimensions stress the role of strategy in that the business plan becomes pertinent to labour management; and an emphasis on the role of line managers as the prime front-line managers of labour (not 'personnel officers'). Then there is a set of key levers such as serious attention to selection (in place of hire and fire), performance-related pay, an attempt to move from 'temporary truces' in labour negotiations to management through culture and shared goals.

When viewed holistically, is this package to be regarded as a 'soft' 'human relations' approach with employee welfare at its core? There are facets such as an emphasis on training and development and the winning of hearts and minds that might lean in that direction. But there are also 'hard' aspects to this model of HRM. Labour is seen as a strategic resource. As such it is to be planned for, measured carefully and used as an asset. HRM sits alongside the resource-based view of the firm as strategic perspective on how to management the employment relationship.

What about practice? Ironically, while the HRM label has become so ubiquitous (contrary to expectations during its early days) employment management practice has, over the past couple of decades, predominantly shifted to a form of labour management at odds with the precepts of the distinctive model. In the wider, generic sense, human resource management continues – but with characteristics largely in sharp contrast to those of the distinctive model examined above.

JOHN STOREY

See also:

Comparative HRM; Employee engagement; Hard and soft HRM; Industrial relations; Resource-based view; Strategic HRM.

References and selected further readings

Sisson, K. (2014), *Employment Relations Matters*, University of Warwick, www2.warwick.ac.uk/fac/soc/wbs/research/irru/erm.
Storey, J. (2007), What is human resource management? in J. Storey (ed.), *Human Resource Management: A Critical Text*, London: Thomson.
Storey, J., P. Wright and D. Ulrich (eds) (2009), *Routledge Companion to Strategic Human Resource Management*, London and New York: Routledge.

Human resource management in mergers and acquisitions

Due to the continuous growing of mergers and acquisitions (M&A) as a mechanism for organizational growth, the contribution of human resource management (HRM) to their effectiveness has become an important topic within and beyond HR literature.

Given the high rate of failure of M&As, HRM comes into play to explain potential unsuccessful/successful performance, in particular in two M&A stream of research: the organizational behaviour and the process theory. The organizational behaviour stream studies the impact of acquisitions on organizational culture and employee attitudes (Buono and Bowditch, 1989; Napier, 1989). A central proposition is that the fit between the cultures of the two merged organizations will help employee satisfaction and effective integration. These conclusions on cultural issues have led to the development of the process perspective (Birkinshaw and Bresman, 2000), whose focus is that managerial action and the process of integration determine the extent to which the potential benefits of the acquisition are realized. HRM has the potential to play a significant managerial role in the integration by developing human capital, influencing motivation and communicating organizational goals in support of successful M&A strategies (Birkinshaw and Bresman, 2000; Schweiger and De Nisi, 1991).

Initial studies in the area of HRM and M&A have focused on the identification of the relevant HR activities in M&A processes: training, performance appraisal, development and compensation (Napier, 1989). More recently, researchers have examined the different HR activities in the different stages of the M&A process (Antila, 2006); the intensity and type of activities performed should vary across each stage: the pre-combination, the combination or integration and the post-combination stage. Moreover, since not all M&As are the same (Napier, 1989), it is likely to expect variation in HR activities, with a growing intensity in HR actions according to the level of the required integration in the M&A (Bagdadli et al., 2014).

SILVIA BAGDADLI

See also:
Human resource strategy; Human capital; Organizational culture.

References and selected further readings
Antila, M.A. (2006), The role of HR managers in international mergers and acquisitions: A multiple case study, *International Journal of Human Resource Management*, **17**(6), pp. 999–1020.
Bagdadli, S., J. Hayton and O. Perfido (2014), Reconsidering the role of HR in M&As: what can be learnt from practice, *Human Resource Management*, **53**(6), pp. 1005–1026.
Birkinshaw, J. and H. Bresman (2000), Managing the post-acquisition integration process: how the human integration and task integration processes interact to foster value creation, *Journal of Management Studies*, **37**(3), pp. 395–425.
Buono, A. and J.L. Bowditch (1989), *The Human Side of Mergers and Acquisitions: Managing Collisions Between People, Cultures and Organizations*, San Francisco: Jossey-Bass Publishers.
Napier, N.K. (1989), Mergers and acquisitions, human resource issues and outcomes: A review and suggested typology, *Journal of Management Studies*, **26**(3), pp. 271–290.
Schweiger, D.M. and A.S. De Nisi (1991), Communication with employees following a merger: a longitudinal field experiment, *The Academy of Management Journal*, **34**(1), pp. 110–135.

Human resource manager

A human resource manager is normally a person responsible for the management of employment issues in an organization. However, the precise job title used may vary, with alternatives including personnel manager, people manager and HR business partner. In some cases the human resource manager may be a generalist with responsibility for a variety of HR issues, perhaps as the sole specialist in the organization. In larger organizations an HR department might comprise a large team, including both generalists and specialists in particular areas such as employee relations, learning and development or reward and benefits. Organizational size is important in this respect, with 85 per cent of British workplaces with 500 or more employees having an HR specialist compared to only 9 per cent of workplaces with five to nine employees (van Wanrooy et al., 2013). Indeed in SMEs, there may no specialist human resource manager dealing with employment issues; it may be the responsibility of general or line managers. Given this heterogeneity, it is difficult to generalize regarding what HR managers do, although recent survey evidence from Britain suggests HR managers typically spent their time dealing with issues including: recruitment and selection; discipline and grievance; training; employee consultation; performance appraisals; equal opportunities; pay and pensions (Van Wanrooy et al., 2013). In some organizations, particular parts of HR, such as payroll, training and recruitment, may be outsourced to specialist providers. Many organisations have also increasingly attempted to devolve certain HR activities to line managers (Brewster et al., 2015).

In Britain, the modern human resource manager is believed to be an evolution of the welfare officer role, which evolved in the eighteenth century. Social reformers such as Robert Owen were concerned with the welfare of workers, a concern shared by the Quaker firms such as Cadbury, Rowntree and Lever Brothers, and provided a range of benefits to workers such as sick pay and subsidized housing. In the twentieth century, however, the emphasis was not only with worker welfare, but also ensuring the productivity of employees. HR thinking became increasingly influenced by broader management ideas from both the scientific management and human relations schools. In postwar Britain, the role of a personnel manager commonly included managing employment relations and collective bargaining with trade unions (Torrington and Hall, 2014). In recent decades, debates in HR circles around the world have increasingly stressed the need for HR professionals to become more 'strategic' and improve their status and influence. This had led some to question the extent to which HR professionals have abandoned traditional concerns with employee welfare in favour of a much narrower focus upon improving business performance (Kochan, 2007), and the implications this might have for worker wellbeing.

STEWART JOHNSTONE

See also:

Human resource department; Human resource function and business partnering.

References and selected further readings

www.cipd.co.uk/cipd-hr-profession
Brewster, C., M. Brookes and P. Gollan (2015), The institutional antecedents of the assignment of HRM responsibilities to line managers, *Human Resource Management*, **54**, pp. 577–597.
Kochan, T. (2007), Social legitimacy of the HR profession: a US perspective, in P. Boxall, J. Purcell and P. Wright (eds), *The Oxford Handbook of Human Resource Management*, Oxford: Oxford University Press, pp. 599–620.
Marchington, M. (2015), Human resource management (HRM): Too busy looking up to see where it is going longer term?, *Human Resource Management Review*, **25**(2), pp. 176–187.
Thompson, P. (2011), The trouble with HRM, *Human Resource Management Journal*, **21**(4), pp. 355–367.
Torrington, D. and L. Hall (2014), *Human Resource Management*, London: Pearson.
Ulrich, D. (2013), *Human resource champions: The next agenda for adding value and delivering results*, Harvard Business Press.
Van Wanrooy, B., H. Bewley, A. Bryson, J. Forth, S. Freeth, L. Stokes and S. Wood (2013), *Employment Relations in the Shadow of Recession*, Basingstoke: Palgrave Macmillan.

Human resource planning

Human resource (HR) planning is a concept that has become out of favour in the latter decade of the twentieth century, largely due to the accelerated pace of change which has made it very difficult for organizations to plan for the future. However, a lack of planning has proved to be more disastrous for some companies than inaccurate planning, and hence, in the past ten years, the ideas of HR planning has returned. Today, contemporary HR planning needs to be much more flexible to able to deal with a wide range of scenarios than in previous decades. As a result, HR planning relies heavily on good quality intelligence from both the internal and external business environment.

The CIPD factsheet on the topic describes HR planning as:

> a core process of human resource management that is shaped by organisational strategy and ensures the right number of people with the right skills are in the right place at the right time to deliver short- and long-term organisational objectives (CIPD, 2012).

It is in effect the operationalization of the business plan, ensuring the resources are in place to deliver business objectives.

Some of the activities that take place under the HR planning banner are talent management, career management, succession planning, retention strategies, labour demand

and supply forecasting and scenario planning. Talent management in particular is closely aligned to HR planning and is one of the ways that flexibility can be brought to the process. By developing 'talent pools' of labour that can be developed and directed in a number of ways, the organization increases its ability to resource itself effectively in a number of different scenarios.

HR planning is essentially about generating, analysing and using data to inform the future demand for labour and them designing a set of actions that will build or develop the existing workforce to meet demand. It can be about predicting this numerically, which is sometimes referred to as 'hard' workforce planning or about developing a framework in which such information can be considered and acted upon, sometimes called 'soft' workforce planning.

A number of issues are important to consider when designing a workforce/HR plan. First, the plan must flow from the business strategy, which will be one of the primary sources of information for the plan. Second, it is an integrated part of human resource management, which will have implications for a range of other practices such as recruitment, development and job design. Finally the plan must be organization-wide and depends on the cooperation and input from a range of stakeholders from all parts of the business.

ANGELA BARON

See also:

Careers; Recruitment; Retention; Selection; Succession planning; Talent management; Workforce intelligence planning.

References and selected further readings

CIPD (2012), *Workforce Planning Guide: Right People, Right Place, Right Time*, London: Chartered Institute of Personnel and Development.
Crush, P. (2011), Who fails to plan, *Human Resources*, August, pp. 46–49.
Incomes Data Services (2011), *Workforce Planning*, London: IDS.
Taylor, S. (2014), *Resourcing and Talent Management*, London: Chartered Institute of Personnel and Development.

Human resource strategy

Human resource (HR) strategy can be seen as one of the functional silos of an overall business strategy and incorporates the critical goals aimed at managing people and the means it adopts to reach them (Boxall and Purcell, 2011).

An important issue in the strategic HR literature concerns the theoretical debate between the 'best-fit' and 'best-practice' school about the relevance of fit (or not) between human resource management (HRM) and other aspects of the organization. The 'best-fit' school argues that HRM is more effective when it is aligned with its internal and external context. Consistent with the 'best-fit' school, HR strategies vary based on internal and external contextual factors. On the contrary the 'best-practice' school adopts a universalistic perspective. According to this approach, 'all firms will see performance improvements if they identify and implement best practices' (Boxall and Purcell, 2011, p. 85).

Looking at the definition of HR strategy, the concept of 'goals' is highly relevant. Organizations aim to achieve certain goals in order to survive or even to create sustained competitive advantage. These goals can be defined in narrow terms, like maximizing profits, or in broader terms, such as increasing efficiency (organizational goal), satisfying trade union interests (societal goal) and creating opportunities for an optimal work–life balance (employee goals) (Boselie, 2014). Paauwe (2004) developed a theoretical framework that stresses the relevance of the organizational context for designing the HR strategy. This model shows that designing the HR strategy is not an easy task, as there might be tensions between accomplishing economic goals (economic rationality) on the one hand and accomplishing employee and societal goals on the other hand (moral values). Recently, more and more attention is paid to finding a balance between economic performance and employee wellbeing.

A final issue is related to the implementation of the (HR) strategy, or put differently to translate strategic (HR) goals into an enacted strategy. If organizations want to achieve their strategic (HR) goals, then management must make sure that employees experience that these goals are relevant. Besides employees need to be able and motivated to behave and act in line with these goals (Veld et al., 2010). In other words, an HR strategy is more than a written document. It is also about implementing HR practices throughout the organization, and sending a consistent message about what is expected from employees and how they can contribute to relevant goals.

MONIQUE VELD

See also:
AMO model; Best fit; Best practice; Strategic HRM; Strategy.

References and selected further readings

Boselie, P. (2014), *Strategic Human Resource Management: A Balanced Approach*, 2nd edn, Berkshire: McGraw-Hill.
Bowen, D.E. and C. Ostroff (2004), Understanding HRM- firm performance linkages: the role of the 'strength' of the HRM system, *Academy of Management Review*, **29**(2), pp. 203–221.
Boxall, P. and J. Purcell (2011), *Strategy and Human Resource Management*, 3rd edn, Basingstoke: Palgrave Macmillan.
Paauwe, J. (2004), *HRM and Performance: Achieving Long Term Viability*, New York: Oxford University Press.
Veld, M., J. Paauwe and P. Boselie (2010), HRM & strategic climates in hospitals: does the message come across at the ward level? *Human Resource Management Journal*, **20**(4), pp. 339–356.

Immigration

Immigration refers to the process involving people from one country entering the territory of another country and typically settling on a long-term basis. It is distinct from migration, which involves the movement of people from one place to another, including within the same country. Immigration has several important implications for human resource management (HRM), particularly in terms of how the availability of migrant workers can influence employer recruitment, remuneration and retention strategies (Ruhs and Anderson, 2010). The impact of immigration on HRM practices is shaped by several factors, most importantly the skill profile and size of the immigrant population and prevailing conditions in the labour market. Employer demand for migrant labour is likely to be strongest in buoyant times, when low unemployment makes it more difficult to source workers from the local labour market. However, there are other reasons unrelated to labour market conditions that explain why employers may seek to engage migrant workers.

In many countries, particularly those with weak capacity to control immigration flows, migrants work predominantly in low-paid, lower-skilled occupations in conditions that often prove unattractive to residents. In this context, a seminal study by Michael Piore identified a desire for 'disposable labour', i.e., workers that are easy to control and to dispense with, as a key factor accounting for employer recruitment of migrant workers. According to Piore (1979), new migrants are likely to be more willing to work for inferior pay and conditions compared to resident workers because of a relative lack of knowledge about the local labour market, lower expectations if they are from a country with lower wages and weaker employment protections, or simply not being in a position to complain if mistreated due to limited rights.

Recent studies have identified a desire for more productive workers as a key reason for why employers recruit migrant workers. Employer perceptions that migrant workers are harder working, more reliable, more willing to comply with management decisions, have a better work ethic and are easier to retain than resident workers are common themes in studies of employer motivations for recruiting lower-skilled migration (Moriarty et al., 2012). Access to migrant workers can also potentially allow employers to fill vacancies without having to improve job quality or workforce training to attract a wider pool of candidates (Wright, 2012). While labour cost savings and productivity advantages help to explain why employers may recruit lower-skilled migrant workers, studies suggest that addressing skills gaps and accessing specialized skills are likely to be more important reasons for engaging higher skilled migrants (Khoo et al., 2007).

CHRIS F. WRIGHT

References and selected further readings

Khoo, S.E., P. McDonald, C. Voigt-Graf and G. Hugo (2007), A global labor market: factors motivating the sponsorship and temporary migration of skilled workers to Australia, *International Migration Review*, **41**(2), pp. 480–510.

Moriarty, E., J. Wickham, T. Krings, J. Salamonska and A. Bobek (2012), 'Taking on almost everyone?' Migrant and employer recruitment strategies in a booming labour market, *International Journal of Human Resource Management*, **23**(9), pp. 1871–1887.

Piore, M.J. (1979), *Birds of Passage: Migrant Labor and Industrial Societies*, Cambridge: Cambridge University Press.

Ruhs, M. and B. Anderson (2010), *Who Needs Migrant Workers? Labour Shortages, Immigration, and Public Policy*, Oxford: Oxford University Press.

Wright, C.F. (2012), Immigration policy and market institutions in liberal market economies, *Industrial Relations Journal*, **43**(2), pp. 110–136.

Impression management

Impression management is conscious or unconscious behaviour engaged in by an individual to create, maintain, protect or alter images others develop during social interactions. Targets of impression management can be persons on the job (e.g., supervisors), in the selection context (e.g., recruiters), or in everyday life (e.g., dating partners). By using IM, persons may influence their target's evaluations and decisions. Impression management behaviours are often divided into assertive behaviours, which aim at creating a good impression (e.g., self-promotion), and defensive behaviours, which aim at defending a good impression (e.g., excuses). In addition, there are different ways impression management can be classified. In one paradigm, typical behaviour, self-presentation, impression management and faking behaviour can be seen as a continuum ranging from honest behaviour patterns to more dishonest behaviour patterns. In another paradigm, impression management can also be seen as one of the forces that changes typical performance behaviour into maximum performance behaviour.

Studying impression management in organizations increases knowledge of how individuals try to influence others using social interactions. Research debates centre on whether impression management behaviours during evaluation processes influence decisions in an undesirable way. There is a controversy in the selection literature on whether impression management can be interpreted as socially effective behaviour or whether it must be seen as error variance that biases evaluations. Another controversy exists regarding the connection between impression management and organizational citizenship behaviour, behaviours that are by definition voluntary. The debate centres on the motive underlying organizational citizenship behaviour: do employees demonstrate organizational citizenship behaviour because they are engaged organizational members or because they want to convey a good impression on others in the organization?

Interestingly, impression management seems to have some double standards. When employment recruiters use impression management to promote a job, these behaviours are largely seen as appropriate and legitimate. Similarly, desired leadership styles such as transformational leadership can also have some behavioural overlap that is included in impression management concepts. In general, within organizations, impression management is often regarded as a legitimate or even, at times, a desired behaviour. This is also the case for using broader influence tactics in reaching relevant organizational goals. However, when applicants use impression management behaviours, these behaviours in the selection context are often seen as negative and dishonest. Therefore, a double standard exists when interpreting impression management behaviour from individuals in different roles.

MARTIN KLEINMANN, PIA INGOLD AND ANNIKA WILHELMY

See also:
Organizational citizen behaviour; Selection; Transformational leadership.

References and selected further readings
Bolino, M.C., K.M. Kacmar, W.H. Turnley and B.J. Gilstrap (2008), A multi-level review of impression management motives and behaviors, *Journal of Management*, **34**, pp. 1080–1109.
Bozeman, D.P. and K.M. Kacmar (1997), A cybernetic model of impression management processes in organizations, *Organizational Behavior and Human Decision Processes*, **69**, pp. 9–30.
Goffman, E. (1959), *The Presentation of Self in Everyday Life*, Garden City, NY: Doubleday Anchor.
Provis, C. (2010), The ethics of impression management, *Business Ethics: A European Review*, **19**, 199–212.
Rosenfeld, P., R.A. Giacalone and C.A. Riordan (1995), *Impression Management in Organizations: Theory, Measurement, and Practice*, London: Routledge.

Indirect discrimination

Indirect discrimination broadly addresses group disadvantage and is concerned with seemingly neutral practices that disproportionately affect members of a particular social group. Measures that seek to prevent indirect discrimination are informed by an acknowledgement of difference yet seek to address procedure rather than outcome as the means to tackle discrimination; as such they draw from elements of a radical and a liberal approach to equality. Within the framework of anti-discrimination law in Great Britain employers must not discriminate against job applicants or employees (Equality Act 2010, s39). Discrimination is defined with reference to certain characteristics that are designated as protected under the Equality Act 2010. The relevant characteristics for indirect discrimination are: age; disability; gender reassignment; marriage and civil partnership; race; religion or belief; sex and sexual orientation. The protected characteristic of marriage and civil partnership is not relevant for a claim of indirect discrimination.

Indirect discrimination arises where an employer applies a provision, criterion or practice that is discriminatory in relation to a relevant protected characteristic of the employee or applicant. To be considered discriminatory the provision, criterion or practice must meet the following requirements: first it must apply to persons with whom the employee or applicant does not share a relevant protected characteristic (for example, a job applicant is a woman and a selection criterion that is applied to her is also applied to men); second, it must put persons with whom the employee or applicant shares the protected characteristic at a particular disadvantage when compared with persons with whom the employee or applicant does not share it (to continue with the example the selection criterion must put women at a particular disadvantage when compared to men); finally the provision, criterion or practice must put the employee or applicant at that disadvantage (the female applicant will be put at the same disadvantage as are women as a group by the selection criterion). Employers can defend an indirect discrimination claim by showing that the provision, criterion or practice was a proportionate means of achieving a legitimate aim.

LIZ OLIVER

See also:
Equal opportunity.

References and selected further readings

Bamforth, N., M. Malik and C. O'Cinneide (2008), *Discrimination Law: Theory and Context: Text and Materials*, London: Sweet & Maxwell.

Kirton, G. and A. Greene (2010), *The Dynamics of Managing Diversity A Critical Approach*, 3rd edn, Oxford: Elsevier Butterworth-Heinemann.

Willey, B. (2012), Employment Law in Context: An Introduction for HR Professionals, 4th edn, Harlow: Pearson.

Induction

Induction programmes are learning interventions provided to new colleagues joining an organization to welcome them and begin their engagement with the organization. In some countries, induction may be referred to as orientation. Induction programmes provide insight into the organization so that new employees can get a feel for where they are working and understand what the organization does and how it operates. Usually this will include an overall introduction, market positioning and an insight into the overall organizational strategy. Senior managers or their representatives may participate in the delivery of an induction programme with a view to engaging new staff and demonstrating an open culture. The delivery of induction programmes may be led by HR professionals but due to the wide nature of materials that need to be covered there are advantages of involving other key stakeholders. Line managers can provide role-specific information and as they will work closely with new employees they can focus them on the most relevant information to their job role.

Initial induction usually covers practical details so that new employees can find their way around and function properly. There may also be statutory information to cover – for example, in relation to health and safety – as well as an introduction to key organizational policies. Introductions to new employees' departments and teams enables new employees to understand how their role contributes to the success of the organization and provides opportunities to meet the people that they will be working with and for. Role-specific induction allows new employees to make sense of information that may have previously been provided within recruitment and selection documentation such as job descriptions and person specifications. A social element to departmental/team induction can be useful in integrating new staff with their colleagues.

An induction programme may be provided in block format or spread over a longer period of time. The key benefit of spreading out the induction programme is that new employees do not receive information overload and can set the information into context. Organizations can also make use of electronically delivered resources where employees can benefit from having information at their fingertips. A further benefit of electronically provided resources is the ability to track and record the progress of new employees; this is particularly useful where statutory training is needed. It is important that induction programmes are evaluated robustly by collecting information from employees after the event and then repeated later in the year to gauge the perceived impact. The content of induction programmes needs to be updated on an ongoing basis to reflect changes in the internal and external environment.

Pre-induction is becoming increasingly popular and this is where an employee will receive information and support prior to their starting date in the organization. This may reduce the anxiety that new employees can feel in the run up to joining a new organization and may also increase their feelings of engagement.

FIONA ROBSON

See also:

Employee engagement; Recruitment; Selection; Training; Training and development.

References and selected further readings

Cable, D.M., F. Gino and B. Staats (2013), Reinventing employee onboarding, *MIT Sloan Management Review*, **54**(3), pp. 23–28.

Hendricks, K. and J. Louw-Potgieter (2012), A theory evaluation of an induction programme, *SA Journal of Human Resource Management*, **10**(3), pp. 1–9.

Lashley, C. and W. Best (2002), Employee induction in licensed retail organisations, *International Journal of Contemporary Hospitality Management*, **14**(1), pp. 6–13.

Wanous, J.P. and A.E. Reichers (2000), New employee orientation programmes, *Human Resource Management Review*, **10**(4), pp. 435–451.

Industrial action

Industrial action refers to action taken by either trade unions or employers as part of a legitimate, legal dispute. Such action occurs when there is a break-down in the management of the employment relationship. Unions then coordinate industrial action in response to the fundamental tensions present within the employment relationship (Edwards, 1986), with the aim being to improve terms and conditions of employment. There are a considerable number of institutional arrangements for regulating industrial action, which vary across different nation-states, depending on its purpose and form. The meaning attached to industrial action depends on the context in which it occurs and this in turn determines the form it takes. There are two main types of industrial action taken by unions.

First, the strike is the most visible display of industrial action and is a temporary stoppage of work undertaken by union members. Strike action is the most tightly regulated form of industrial action, in legal terms. Notwithstanding the difficulties associated with strike statistics, it can be said that strike action has declined across the globe since the high tide of the 1970s (Van Der Velden et al., 2007), with a number of causes such as the rise of neoliberalism, the changing nature of trade unionism and the alleged increase in sophistication of the HR function.

Second, action short of strike is a tactic used by trade unions and is defined as a partial withdrawal of labour. This can take many forms, including but not limited to overtime bans (refusal of employees to work overtime), work-to-rule/work-to-contract (refusal to undertake any activities not stipulated in the contract of employment) and go-slows (restriction in the speed of performance). Action short of strike can cause a considerable level of disruption to the functioning of an organization but differs from strike action by reducing the potential for loss of reward to those undertaking the action.

Action from employers in an industrial dispute can take the form of a lock-out, whereby workers are excluded from their place of work in order to put pressure on unions to end disputes. Again, the legal status of this kind of action and the extent to which it is commonplace differs according to national contexts.

Industrial action is viewed as distinct from individual manifestations of employee conflict at work, such as absenteeism, fiddles, sabotage or pilfering. Such individual forms of action, often grouped under the umbrella of organizational *mis*behaviour (Ackroyd and Thompson, 1999), are considered to be attempts to escape an employment situation rather than to induce change.

ANDY HODDER

See also:

Conflict; Organizational misbehaviour; Trade unions; Work limitation.

References and selected further readings

Ackroyd, S. and P. Thompson (1999), *Organizational Misbehaviour*, London: Sage.
Edwards, P. (1986), *Conflict at Work: A Materialist Analysis of Workplace Relations*, Oxford: Basil Blackwell.
Godard, J. (2011), What has happened to strikes? *British Journal of Industrial Relations*, **49**(2), pp. 282–305.
Hyman, R. (1989), *Strikes*, 4th edn, London: Fontana.
Kelly, J. (1998), *Rethinking Industrial Relations: Mobilization, Collectivism, and Long Waves*, London: Routledge.
Van Der Velden, S., H. Dribbusch, D. Lyddon and K. Vandaele (2007), *Strikes Around the World: Case Studies of 15 Countries*, Amsterdam: Amsterdam University Press.

Industrial relations

A classic definition of industrial relations defines the subject in relation to rule-making at work; for example, 'the making and administering of rules which regulate the employment relationship; regardless of whether these are seen as formal or informal, structured or unstructured' (Bain and Clegg, 1974, p. 95). This rules-based perspective was developed from the idea that employment relations comprises of a subsystem drawn from that in wider society, mirrored writ large in industry (Dunlop, 1958). The systems approach to industrial relations is that a set of rules govern an economic exchange between the buyers (employers) and sellers (workers) of labour. The exchange of effort for reward makes industrial relations a subject shaped by power dynamics. In this regard Edwards (1986) develops the concept of 'structured antagonism'; that is, while employers want to secure the cooperation and commitment of staff, they must also enter an effort bargain that both controls while also engaging workforce commitment (Baldamus, 1961).

The idea of tension and power informs us that the 'effort bargain' in employment is not the same as other economic transactions, such as the purchase of a pint of cider in the student bar. Employment contracts are typically of a much longer duration than the consumption of a pint of alcohol (although there are some very short-term and precarious jobs that result in highly insecure conditions for many people, including 'zero-hours' contracts).

These days, the terms 'employment relations' or 'employee relations' have eclipse the nomenclature of 'industrial'. Indeed, the most extensive survey of work and employment research since 1980s to the present now uses the term 'employment' relations (e.g., the Workplace Employment Relations Survey (WERS): see van Wanrooy et al., 2013, for the results of the sixth in the survey series). The subject area is perhaps now more electric and multidisciplinary as a field of study, linked to sociology, law, psychology, economics and broader social science perspectives (Ackers and Wilkinson, 2003). Regardless of terms, interest in employment relations and work regulation remain high on the policy agenda. Most people work for a living, and how the rules that regulate their behaviour and determine wages and terms and conditions, such as having to work on a temporary or zero-hours contract, are of central importance to some extent in all countries.

Contemporary debates have moved on from the view of employment relations as a narrow set of rules, or a miniature sub-system of wider society. For example, work by Budd (2004) reconceptualizes employment relations not as specific rules but the 'processes' that generate change and determine the way people are managed in paid employment. Budd (2004) articulates a thematic trilogy to assess the balance between the 'efficiency, equity and voice' in employment relations. Employment relations 'efficiency' is concerned with the economic rationale to best utilize resources, which in turn can shape the performance of a firm and effectiveness of labour utilization. 'Equity' is concerned with the distribution of resources and application of rules and procedures, so people can expect fair treatment with regard to the conditions of their work and the wages they receive. The final part of the trilogy is 'voice', and considers the arrangements that allow workers and managers to make a genuine contribution to participate in the decisions that affect them at work (Budd, 2004, p. 13). The point is not so much that each element of the trilogy – efficiency, equity, voice – has an equal share in the relationship or framework, but that each can differ in degree and kind. It is therefore the balance or imbalance in these that can point to the use (abuse) of power, perceptions of fair treatment (or exploitation), or indicate the way managers or governments view the importance of employment relationship policy and practice in a society. An important way to examine different approaches to employment relations practice is the perspectives of unitarism, pluralism and radical schools of thought (see 'Frames of reference', in this volume).

The principle actors (or groups) who affect employment relationships are fourfold. *Management* is both a 'function' and a group of 'actors' who control organizational decisions. *Managers* are clearly central to industrial relations and management styles are known to vary widely. For example, nineteenth-century employers such as Cadbury or Unilever preferred to manage without trade union influence, yet followed paternalist approaches by looking after employee wellbeing. Other managers are known to be exploitative, macho and reassert their right to manage by avoiding trade unions in harsh if not unethical ways (Gall and Dundon, 2013). *Trade unions* are a second group of important actors. In most countries, trade union membership has declined since the mid-1980s. In Britain, union density is less than one-third of the labour force; in the US, private sector unionization is around 10 per cent. Nonetheless, unions do protect and help improve the conditions of many workers. Indeed, it is often trade unions that campaign to improve labour standards, pay, respect and fairness at work. The third actor group is *the state*, defined as the government of the day along with all other government agencies such as the judiciary. Of all the principle employment relations actors, it is only the state who can pass and/or repeal laws, such as minimum wage or health and safety protections. These days, the state also incorporates transnational governmental agencies, such as the European Commission in passing labour standards that apply to member states (e.g., rights for employees to have a voice at work, to be treated fairly, and equality based on gender and nationality, among many other standards). A final group include what might be termed *new actors*. Recent debates argue for the recognition of a much wider set of actors in addition to managers, unions and the state. Examples include the Church and wider civil society organizations (CSOs) who shape employment relationships (Ackers, 2012; Heery et al., 2014).

Industrial relations is about the way people are managed at work. It is more than just rule-making inside a firm. As a subject it recognizes that power, authority and legitimacy to direct peoples' actions are all contentious and highly contestable. Different approaches and processes that shape important things such as equality, voice, respect, wages and general conditions for most of the population on the planet. Managers, unions and government agencies are actors who can influence these things in various ways.

TONY DUNDON

See also:

Collective bargaining; Frames of reference; Management; Pluralism; Power; Trade unions; Unitarism.

References and suggested further readings

Ackers, P. (2012), Rethinking the employment relationship: a neo-pluralist critique of British industrial relations orthodoxy, *International Journal of Human Resource Management*, **25**(18), pp. 2608–2625.
Ackers, P. and A. Wilkinson (eds) (2003), *Understanding Work and Employment: Industrial Relations in Transition*, Oxford: Oxford University Press.
Bain, G. and H. Clegg (1974), A strategy for industrial relations research in Britain, *British Journal of Industrial Relations*, **12**(1), pp. 91–113.
Bain, G.S. and R. Price (1983), Union growth: dimensions, determinants and destiny, in G.S. Bain (ed.), *Industrial Relations in Britain*, Oxford: Blackwell.
Baldamus, W. (1961), *Efficiency and Effort*, London: Tavistock.
Budd, J.W. (2004), *Employment with a Human Face: Balancing Efficiency, Equity and Voice*, Ithaca, NY: Cornell University Press.
Dunlop, J. (1958), *Industrial Relations Systems*, New York: Holt Press.
Edwards, P.K. (1986), *Conflict at Work*, Oxford: Blackwell.
Gall, G. and T. Dundon (eds) (2013), *Global Anti-Unionism: Nature, Dynamics, Trajectories and Outcomes*, London: Palgrave Macmillan.
Heery, E., B. Abbott and S. Williams (2014), Civil society organizations and employee voice, in A. Wilkinson, J. Donaghey, T. Dundon and R. Freeman (eds), *Handbook of Research on Employee Voice*, Cheltenham: Edward Elgar.
Maltby, T., B. De Vroom, M. Luisa Mirabile and E. Overbye (eds) (2004), *Ageing and the Transition to Retirement: A Comparative Analysis of European Welfare States*, Aldershot: Ashgate.
van Wanrooy, B., H. Bewley, A. Bryson, J. Forth, S. Freeth, L. Stokes and S. Wood (2013), *Employment Relations in the Shadow of Recession: Findings from the 2011 Workplace Employment Relations Study*, Basingstoke: Palgrave Macmillan.

Informal learning

Organizations and employees stress ongoing and lifelong professional learning of employees. In this way, employees can adapt to an increasingly complex and changing work environment and, as a result, increase their employability. For organizations, employees' ongoing learning is seen as a key component to organizational performance. Traditionally, employees' ongoing learning has been thought of as a top-down practice with management determining what employees' learning needs are and providing various forms of training. Although successful in enhancing employee performance, these kinds of formal learning are expensive, cumbersome, time-consuming and disconnected from day-to-day work. In contrast to formal learning, informal learning – also known as workplace learning – occurs outside a classroom or training programme; it is typically not institutionally sponsored or highly structured, and is usually directed by the learners themselves.

Informal learning can take place through different activities, such as reflection on daily activities, keeping up-to-date by reading professional journals or books, and asking for feedback from and knowledge sharing with colleagues and supervisors. Also innovative behaviour that refers to the generation of novel solutions to problems, convincing colleagues to adopt these new approaches, and ultimately implementing them within the organization is seen as an informal learning activity. While activities as reflection and keeping up-to-date are carried out autonomously without any assistance from colleagues or supervisors, feedback asking, knowledge-sharing and innovative behaviour are interactive or collaborative informal learning activities and refer to informal learning in which employees acquire knowledge and skills directly through interaction with others.

Employees may be discouraged from informal learning activities because it contains risk. Risk refers to the possibility that something unpleasant will happen, for instance reputation damage, resistance from peers, and even losing their job. Employees can be discouraged from showing these activities if they fear that they will be harshly criticized. Similarly, if employees share their creative ideas with their colleagues, they may expose their methods to criticism and risk losing their unique value or 'expert power'. In addition, proactivity is mentioned as an important characteristic of informal learning. Proactivity represents an opportunity-seeking, forward-looking perspective characterized by high awareness of external trends and events, and acting in anticipation thereof. Proactivity is associated with pioneering behaviour, initiative taking to pursue new opportunities, and attempts to lead rather than to follow.

Two separate lines of research on factors explaining employees' informal learning have been conducted. The first line of research comprises studies about organizational learning, learning organization and professional communities in which organizational conditions including leadership are considered as the main levers of an organization's capacity to change and as a prerequisite for linking employees' informal learning to organizational performance. These studies often use systems theory on change that links structural, cultural and political dimensions of organizational to professional learning. In the second line of research, the role of employees' psychological states in explaining employees' learning is examined. This line of research included studies that attempt to elucidate the influence of the psychological states of informal learning using individual factors such as personal efficacy, learning goal orientation, satisfaction, autonomy and perceived control, and sense-making.

Little is known about the influence of human resource management (HRM) on informal learning activities. There are, however, some exceptions. Performance appraisal quality (clarity, regularity and openness of feedback from the supervisor), for instance, is associated with increased participation in reflection on daily activities, knowledge-sharing with colleagues and innovative behaviour. This external provided feedback can promote more effective self-regulation of learning and can be seen as a precursor to successful self-monitoring. Feedback is also thought to encourage the setting of meaningful learning goals to build on strengths and redress weaknesses.

Also opportunities for formal learning are found to enhance employees' participation in autonomous informal learning activities (reflection and keeping up-to-date), and collaborative activities (asking for feedback, knowledge-sharing and innovative behaviour). By providing such structured opportunities to apply knowledge, organizations signal the organization's support for learning, and as a result stimulate employees to engage in informal learning activities. In addition, formal learning provides instructional support for employees to engage in follow-up informal learning activities. For example, training workshops are often accompanied by written materials and take-home exercises that are designed to help employees consolidate and apply knowledge, which may encourage greater reflection.

In addition, the relationships between performance appraisal quality and formal training, on the one hand, and informal learning activities, on the other hand, are found to be stronger when employees have an understanding of the whole HRM system, and understand the HRM system as was intended by management. In other words, high-quality performance appraisal and opportunities for formal training opportunities are much more effective in terms of informal learning activities when employees understand the whole HRM system.

KARIN SANDERS

See also:

HRM process approach: attribution of HRM; Performance appraisal; Training.

References and selected further readings

Bednall, T.C., K. Sanders and P. Runhaar (2014), Stimulating informal learning activities through perceptions of performance appraisal and human resource management system strength, *Academy of Management Learning & Education*, **13**(1), pp. 45–61.
Bowen, D.E. and C. Ostroff (2004), Understanding HRM–firm performance linkages: the role of the 'strength' of the HRM system, *Academy of Management Review*, **29**, pp. 203–221.
Eraut, M. (2004), Informal learning in the workplace, *Studies in Continuing Education*, **26**, pp. 247–273.
Schon, D.A. (1983), *The Reflective Practitioner: How Professionals Think in Action*, Aldershot: Arena.

Institutional framework

HRM exists within context and this context will vary greatly and determine the nature of its form and content to a great extent. When we speak of the institutional framework of HRM there are various meanings and there is no precise definition. The first dimension could be seen to be the political-economic context. In this respect, there are two bodies of theories that can be useful for determining this context.

A dominant stream of analysis is the varieties of capitalism debate, which has been a pivot of contemporary understanding of why systems of employment relations and regulation in general vary (Hall and Soskice, 2001). They argue that history and the role of institutions are fundamental to the development of capitalist systems of regulation, and that the different dimensions of these systems link and relate to each other in ways that create a consistent system and pattern of development. The dimensions the model refers to are the nature of corporate governance and its structure; the way relations between firms are generated, and how traditions of cooperation and competition have developed; the role of voice mechanisms, such as industrial relations processes and how they fit such relations or not; the role of vocational training and education as a key feature of the labour market's reproduction; and the nature of the workers themselves. These have been developed and linked in two different patterns of development: the liberal market economy (LME) and the coordinated market economy (CME). LMEs such as the USA tend to link a profit-driven, shareholder and low-regulation culture with a more individualized and less trade union-oriented system of industrial relations: they have a weaker state and set of regulatory structures, with an emphasis on risk-taking and a less-regulated system of firms, while CMEs have a greater state role and greater degree of regulation, whether it is joint regulation with organized labour, association-based regulation in terms of employers' associations and similar bodies, and/or a greater role for public and quasi-public bodies in areas such as training.

Similar approaches have also emerged in discussions of *national business systems* (Whitley, 2007), which also look at relations within and across organizations and broader institutions as key: in terms of ownership relations as in the means of ownership, the nature of ownership integration and production chains, ownership in relation to sector boundaries and the extent of coordination; non-ownership relations in the form of the extent of alliances and coordination or production chains, the extent of collaboration and support between competitors, the extent of alliance coordination across sectors around common interests; and employment relations and the management of work in terms of employer–employee relations and interdependence, the extent of mutual trust, and the delegation of work and decision-making to workers and local management. These systems will vary across countries and types of capitalism, as ownership may be more or less coordinated in some contexts, more or less restricted by short-term financial interests, built or not on a complex and mutually beneficial and sustained network of alliances and interests, and engaged or not with a dialogue with stakeholders, such as trade unions.

However, the institutional framework more generally speaking can vary and not always conform to a type as outlined above. There may be dimensions that are more regulated or more directive in contexts where the state is less developed. For example, in some Middle Eastern contexts you may not have advanced or highly interventionist systems of labour regulation generally speaking but have strong rules about quota systems and the use of indigenous populations. In some countries, equality legislation may be quite advanced but there may not be a strong emphasis on collective worker rights as in the USA. So different institutional dimensions are worth noting and becoming aware of as they can sometimes be more influential than one first imagines.

In general, the institutional framework covers a range of issues related to business and labour legislation, the training and education strategies of the state, the nature of public conciliation and mediation mechanisms, the role of civil society organizations such as non-governmental organizations, the role of economic and employment bodies such as trade unions, employer organizations and management institutes, and more complex and broader bodies of media or social networks that can influence the nature of HRM.

MIGUEL MARTÍNEZ LUCIO

See also:
State; Varieties of capitalism.

References and selected further readings
Hall, P.A. and D. Soskice (eds) (2001), *Varieties of Capitalism: The Institutional Foundations of Comparative Advantage*, Oxford: Oxford University Press.
Whitley, R. (2007), *Business Systems and Organizational Capabilities: The Institutional Structuring of Competitive Competences*, Oxford: Oxford University Press.

Institutional theories

Institutional theory focuses on the deeper and more resilient elements of social structure like schemes, rules, norms and routines, and the way these structures become established as authoritative guidelines for social behaviour. There are specific and well-established institutions such as family, work, religion, politics, etc. Similarly, organizational theory and management institutional approach suggest that organizations are influenced by specific socially constructed pressures. Institutional theory supports the view that there are specific external and powerful institutions that influence to a great degree the decision-making of organizations. These pressures often originate from sources such as the state and other regulatory bodies. As a result, organizations shift their structural arrangements towards these requirements – and they become 'isomorphic', as it is stated in institutional theory vocabulary.

DiMaggio and Powell (1983) identify three approaches of isomorphism:

1. **Coercive isomorphism**: refers to power relationships between organizations, in which a process or a structure is copied because of external pressures, such as the state, the legislation, culture, etc. Coercive isomorphism is also the result of formal and informal pressures applied by organizations on other organizations, which may be dependent on them.
2. **Mimetic isomorphism**: Mimetic isomorphism occurs when organizations attempt to imitate each other and especially those that are perceived successful. This form of isomorphism occurs in environments with a high degree of uncertainty. Examples of mimetic aspects can be found among organizations that apply similar performance management practices, use benchmarking and rely on consultancies.
3. **Normative isomorphism**: this type of isomorphism is the result of a standardization of professionals and executives. Resembling frameworks of education are spread by scientific elites as well as social networks, creating a global work force of experts that occupy similar positions across a range of organizations and industries. These people demonstrate similar ways of dealing with management and control of operations that, in turn, influence in a similar manner the behaviour of organizations.

According to institutional theory, there are specific predictors of isomorphic change, i.e., the level of dependence of one organization to another, the ambiguity of goal, the participation of organizational managers in professional associations and the extent of transactions with state agencies.

There are a number of different ways in which the impact of institutions on the practice of human resource management (HRM) may be understood. Developments of this tradition have taken on board the possible effects of institutions on strategic aspects of HRM, such as the extent of globalization versus localization of HR practices applied by subsidiaries of various multinational companies (MNCs). For example, there are studies suggesting that HRM tends to follow local practices, in a sense of mandated by local regulation and conventions. These local practices are: benefits, gender composition, training, executive rewards, time off and participation. Therefore, like cultural theories, institutional theories have a clear link to HRM. They suggest that HR practices do not work in the same way in all contexts, but they will be influenced strongly by various institutional drivers such as the economy, the legal environment, the political system and the financial system, as well as the educational practices.

ALEXANDROS PSYCHOGIOS

See also:

Convergence theory; Multinational companies; National culture; Varieties of capitalism.

References and selected further readings

Amable, B. (2003), *The Diversity of Modern Capitalism*, Oxford: Oxford University Press.
DiMaggio, P.J. and W.W. Powell (1983), The iron cage revisited: institutional isomorphism and collective reality in organizational fields, *American Sociological Review*, **48**, pp. 147–160.
Hall, P. and D. Soskice (2001), An introduction to the varieties of capitalism, in P. Hall and D. Soskice (eds), *Varieties of Capitalism: The Institutional Basis of Competitive Advantage*, Oxford: Oxford University Press.
Meyer, J.W. and B. Rowan (1977), Institutionalized organizations: formal structure as myth and ceremony, *American Journal of Sociology*, **83**, pp. 340–363.
Scott, W.R. (2004), Institutional theory, in G. Ritzer (ed.), *Encyclopedia of Social Theory*, Thousand Oaks, CA: Sage, pp. 408–414.
Wood, G.T., A. Psychogios, L. Szamosi and D.G. Collings (2012), Institutional perspectives on comparative human resource management, in C. Brewster (ed.), *A Handbook of Research on Comparative Human Resource Management*, Cheltenham: Edward Elgar.
Wood, G. and G. Frynas (2006), The institutional basis of economic failure: anatomy of the segmented business system, *Socio-Economic Review*, **4**(2), pp. 239–277.
Zucker, L.G. (1987), Institutional theories of organization, *Annual Review of Sociology*, **13**, pp. 443–464.

Intellectual capital

Intellectual capital (IC) has received much attention in the last few decades by both scholars and researchers. For instance, Tom Stewart (1991) adopts a dynamic view of IC by treating it as dynamic effects of the sum of intellect within an organization that gives it a competitive edge (see Sveiby, 1999). IC has been defined to comprise various forms of 'capital' such as 'structural capital', 'human capital', 'customer capital', 'organizational capital', 'innovation capital' and 'process capital'. There are an increasing number of studies that support the importance of leveraging knowledge in creating core capabilities needed for achieving a competitive advantage (e.g., Petty and Guthrie, 2000). Studies have highlighted the need for firms to develop IC, as 'stocks of knowledge' that can be leveraged as a source of competitive advantage (Kang and Snell, 2009).

While IC is an important topic in the field of strategic HRM, and despite the interest in the strategic management field in IC, it is only in the past decade where the linkage between HRM and IC has received much attention (see Kang and Snell, 2009; Subramaniam and Youndt, 2005; Reed et al., 2006). Kang and Snell (2009) argued that IC, especially in its unique of combination of human, social and organizational capital, allows organizations to adopt organizational learning needed for competitive advantage. Others studies have shown that HR practices can contribute to the creation of IC (see Subramaniam and Youndt, 2005; Reed et al., 2006). More recently, Teo et al. (2014) provided empirical evidence to show the positive contribution of an organization's HRM function in enhancing IC. Their research also showed that the involvement of an HR department together with the adoption of a collective set of strategic HR practices contributed positively to intellectual capital levels. In their study, IC acted as the mediator between HR practices and firm performance.

The research on HRM and IC has been criticized for relying on cross-sectional samples, which have a possibility of being biased due to common method variance. Additionally, the theoretical portion of prior IC studies emphasized the impact strategic HRM has on the human capital component of IC rather than the collective level of IC.

STEPHEN T.T. TEO, CHRISTINE SOO AND AMY WEI TIAN

See also:

Human capital; Knowledge management; Strategic HRM.

References and selected further readings

Davenport, T.H., L. Prusak and H.J. Wilson (2003), Who's bringing you hot ideas and how are you responding? *Harvard Business Review*, **81**(2), pp. 58–64.
Kang, S.C. and S.A. Snell (2009), Intellectual capital architectures and ambidextrous learning: a framework for human resource management, *Journal of Management Studies*, **46**(1), pp. 65–92.
Nonaka, I. (2007), The knowledge-creating company, *Harvard Business Review*, **85**(7/8), pp. 162–171.
Petty, R. and J. Guthrie (2000), Intellectual capital literature review: measurement, reporting and management, *Journal of Intellectual Capital*, **1**(2), pp. 155–176.
Reed, K.K., M. Lubatkin and N. Srinivasan (2006), Proposing and testing an intellectual capital-based view of the firm, *Journal of Management Studies*, **43**, pp. 867–893.
Stewart, T.A. (1991), Brainpower: intellectual capital is becoming corporate America's most valuable asset and can be its sharpest competitive weapon, *Fortune*, 3 June.
Subramaniam, M. and M.A. Youndt (2005), The influence of intellectual capital on the types of innovative capabilities, *Academy of Management Journal*, **48**, pp. 450–463.
Sveiby, K.E. (1999), *Intellectual Capital and Knowledge Management*, www.sveiby.com/articles/IntellectualCapital.html.
Teo, S.T.T., K. Reed and K. Le (2014), Human resource involvement in developing intellectual capital, *The Service Industries Journal*, **34**(15), pp. 1219–1233.

Intelligence tests

Intelligence tests seek to measure the differences among people in knowledge, reasoning and problem-solving that affect their performance in educational and work settings. The measurement is in terms of the difficulty level of the questions that a person can answer about their world. The questions (referred to as items) do not call for specialist knowledge but do require adequate exposure to mainstream culture. Common examples are the meanings of words, identifying the next item in a number series or completing the missing part of a pattern. People who answer more of the items, often presented with a time limit, obtain higher scores. The individual's score is usually expressed in relation to the scores obtained by people with whom they are alike (e.g., the same age level) as a percentile or standard score. The individual's score is expressed as a difference from the average score for people with whom they are alike (e.g., the same age level).

Good intelligence tests take a great deal of time and care to develop and hence are expensive to produce. The items first need to be written and checked to see that they actually distinguish among people and that they have a good deal in common with other items with which they are to be combined. The answer to one item by itself says little but aggregating across a large number of items (where large is of the order 50 to 100) provides a reasonable estimate of the person's ability. The combination of items that constitute the test then needs to be calibrated for difficulty level using representative samples from the population. Finally, the capacity of the test to predict socially important outcomes such as educational attainment or workplace performance must be demonstrated.

Intelligence tests have been subjected to a number of criticisms (e.g., that they reflect socio-economic advantage rather than innate ability; or by summing up an individual in a single number they miss the complex profile of abilities, skills, temperament and motivation that characterize the person). In reply, proponents of intelligence tests argue that, they must measure a mix of environmental and hereditary influences. In fact, intelligence tests predict socially important outcomes equally well across all groups and in that sense are not biased; and that while intelligence is only one predictor of how people will perform in work and educational settings it is in fact the best single predictor in such settings.

JOHN G. O'GORMAN AND DAVID H.K. SHUM

See also:
Psychometric testing.

References and selected further readings
Fletcher, R.B. and J. Hattie (2011), *Intelligence and Intelligence Testing*, London and New York: Routledge.
Jensen, A. (1980), *Bias in Mental Testing*, New York: Free Press.
Neisser, U., G. Boodoo, T.J. Bouchard, A.W. Boykin, N. Brody, S.J. Ceci and S. Urbina (1996), Intelligence: knowns and unknowns, *American Psychologist*, **51**, pp.77–101.
Nisbett, R.E., J. Aronson, C. Blair, W. Dickens, J. Flynn, D.F. Halpern and E. Turkheimer (2012), Intelligence: new findings and theoretical developments, *American Psychologist*, **67**(2), pp.130–159.
Shum, D., J. O'Gorman, B. Myors and P. Creed (2013), *Psychological Testing and Assessment*, 2nd edn, Melbourne: Oxford University Press.

Internal labour markets

An internal labour market refers to an organization's internal supply of labour, which is also referred to as internal recruitment or the internal labour force. Specifically, an internal labour market represents an organization's existing employees that are available for new jobs/positions (e.g., promotions and transfers) within an organization. The quality and quantity of the internal labour market is dependent on human resource practices and the successful implementation of such policies. For example, the availability of suitable internal labour will be improved when an organization invests an adequate amount in employee training and development, provide career opportunities and retains key employees. Such an approach can be further enhanced by implementing and integrating career planning and succession management. The goal is to identify employees that may be suitable for succession, future promotion or available jobs, then train and develop them, work to retain them and provide attractive career opportunities.

A well-developed internal labour market not only provides high-quality employees that have been groomed for a particular position, it can be used as a strategy to retain high-potential employees. There are also several other benefits associated with internal labour markets; for example, employees perceive a benefit from internal recruitment because the organization is providing them with personal development and career advancement opportunities. Moreover, organizations benefit because internal recruitment is typically less expensive when compared to external recruitment, it takes less time and often results in employees being hired that can hit the ground running. Due to the benefits associated with internal labour markets, many organizations will attempt to source employees from the internal labour market before proceeding with advertising to the external market. Although there are a number of advantages associated with the internal labour market, there are also a number of known limitations.

The limitations of the internal labour market are associated with the perceptions of employees and the types of employees that an organization will evidently assign to a particular position within the organization. In particular, the labour market from which to select is smaller; current employees may require training (which is both costly and time-consuming), and no new knowledge, skills and abilities are being transferred into the organization, thus contributing to the lack of diversity in organizations. Further, employees who are not selected for promotions or transfers may become disgruntled, resulting in a lack of engagement and commitment to the organization. To add to the limitations, the most suitable candidates for a job may never be selected because they are not currently employed by the organization.

MATTHEW XERRI

See also:
Recruitment.

References and selected further readings

Breaugh, J.A. (2012), Employee recruitment: current knowledge and suggestions for future research, in N. Schmitt (ed.), *The Oxford Handbook of Personnel Assessment and Selection*, Oxford: Oxford University Press, pp. 68–87.
Compton, R.L., W.J. Morrissey, A.R. Nankervis and B. Morrissey (2009), *Effective Recruitment and Selection Practices*, 5th edn, Australia: CCH Australia Limited.
Phillips, J. and S. Gully (2014), *Strategic Staffing*, London: Pearson Education.
Wilton, N. (2013), *An Introduction to Human Resource Management*, 2nd edn, London: Sage Publications.

International human resource management

Broadly speaking, international human resource management (IHRM) is about the effective management of human resources in order to efficiently achieve organizational objectives in a global context (Budhwar et al. 2009). More specifically, the field of IHRM is about understanding, researching, applying and revising all human resource activities in their external and internal contexts as they impact the processes of managing human resources in organizations worldwide in order to enhance the experience of multiple stakeholders (Schuler et al., 2009).

There are three main perspectives underpinning the field of IHRM – the multinational enterprise (MNE) perspective, cross-cultural HRM perspective and the comparative HRM perspective (e.g., Briscoe et al., 2012; Dowling, 2013). Historically, the core focus of IHRM has been on the MNE perspective, i.e., to enable the MNE to be successful globally. In this regard, globalization has been the single most significant factor due to which the field of IHRM has become substantially important, given more and more firms now compete on a worldwide basis.

Accordingly, Morgan (1986) defines 'IHRM as the interplay among three dimensions – HR activities (procurement, allocation and utilisation), types of employees (host country nationals – HCNs, parent country nationals – PCNs, and third country nationals – TCNs), and countries of operation (host, home and other)'. For example, the UK-based MNE British Airways can employ Chinese citizens for its Chinese subsidiaries (HCNs), can also send British citizens (PCNs) and recruit Japanese employees (TCNs) to work in its Chinese operations.

For a MNE to be successful globally, the HR function needs to ensure that the MNE is: (a) competitive throughout the world; (b) efficient; (c) locally responsive; (d) flexible and adaptable within the shortest of time periods; (e) capable of transferring knowledge and learning across their globally dispersed units; and (f) satisfying multiple stakeholders (Schuler et al., 2002). In order to meet such requirements, HRM for many firms is likely to be critical to their success, and effective IHRM can make the difference between survival and extinction for many MNEs (Briscoe et al., 2012).

As the field of IHRM has evolved, and over the past 15 years or so, it has been characterized by two further perspectives – cross-cultural HRM and comparative HRM (Dowling et al., 2013; Budhwar et al., 2009). Broadly speaking, cross-cultural HRM concerns the study of the behaviour of people in organizations located in cultures and nations around the world. Comparative HRM perspective helps to understand, compare, analyse and describe how HRM systems of different countries or regions of the world are different and how best to manage human resources in the same (Budhwar and Debrah, 2001; Dowling et al., 2013). It is largely based in the 'contextual' paradigm, where the emphasis is to understand the uniqueness of the particular aspect of HR, i.e., what is different between and within HRM in different contexts and why.

A combination of pressing reasons demands business and management students and practitioners to study IHRM. Broadly speaking, the present global business context informs us that we are increasingly working in an international set-up, which has made the world and organizations operating in it highly interdependent and in order to successfully operate in the same we need to better understand it. Such a context is marked by enhanced levels of globalization and internationalization, increase in the numbers of MNEs (especially from emerging markets) and their economic dominance, increasing number of consolidation through mergers and acquisitions and their failure to deliver, liberalization of economic policies by developing countries increasing both foreign direct investments via the MNEs and global transfer of work, creation of free economic trading blocs (like the European Union), underperformance or failure of international assignees (expatriates) and increasing global diversity and multiculturalism, among others.

Although the basic premise for managing human resources domestically and internationally is the same, i.e., how to contribute towards firm outcomes (e.g., performance); however, the complexity of operating in different national and international contexts and employing different nationals are key variables that differentiate domestic and international HRM (Dowling et al., 2013). Broadly speaking, in an international context, the HR manager needs to be involved in more HR activities and have a broader and diverse perspective, get more involved in the personal lives of staff and their families, consistently conduct different types of risk analysis and draw security-related plans and also understand other external influences such as currency fluctuations (see Briscoe et al., 2012; Dowling et al., 2013).

PAWAN S. BUDHWAR

See also:
Comparative HRM.

References and selected further readings
Briscoe, D., R. Schuler and I. Tarique (2012), *International Human Resource Management: Policies and Practices for the Global Enterprises*, London: Routledge.
Budhwar, P. and Y. Debrah (2001), Rethinking comparative and cross national human resource management research, *The International Journal of Human Resource Management*, **12**(3), pp. 497–515.
Budhwar, P., R. Schuler and P. Sparrow (eds) (2009), *Major Works in International Human Resource Management*, 4 vols., London: Sage.
Dowling, P.D., M. Festing and A. Engle (2013), *International Human Resource Management*, London: Prentice-Hall.
Harzing, A-W. and A. Pinnington (2014), International human resource management, in F. Horwitz and P. Budhwar (eds), *Handbook of Human Resource Management in Emerging Markets*, Cheltenham: Edward Elgar Publishing.
Morgan, P.V. (1986), International human resource management: fact or fiction? *Personnel Administrator*, **31**(9), pp. 43–47.
Schuler, R.S., P. Budhwar and G.W. Florkowski (2002), International human resource management: review and critique, *International Journal of Management Reviews*, **4**(1), pp. 41–70.
Schuler, R.S., P. Sparrow and P. Budhwar (2009), Editors' introduction: developments in IHRM — the MNE perspective (I), in P. Budhwar, R. Schuler and P. Sparrow (eds), *Major Works in International Human Resource Management — Volume 1*, London: Sage, pp. xxix–xxiv.
Sparrow, P., R.S. Schuler and P. Budhwar (2009), Editors' introduction: developments in cross-cultural HRM, in P. Budhwar, R. Schuler and P. Sparrow (eds), *Major Works in International Human Resource Management — Volume 3*, London: Sage, pp. vii–xviii.

The International Labour Organization and International Labour Standards

The International Labour Organization (ILO) is a specialist agency of the United Nations (UN) dedicated to developing and regulating international agreements on labour protection.

Established in 1919 under the Treaty of Versailles and based in Geneva, it is one of the oldest international organizations in existence and unique in the UN for its tripartite system of governance. Premised on the belief that institutionalized dialogue between employers and employees is fundamental to the development of society, each member state is represented at the annual International Labour Conference (ILC) by a delegation consisting of two government, one employer delegate and one labour delegate. Employer and labour delegates are nominated by their respective peak national organization and each has the right to speak and vote independently.

This tripartite structure is also reflected in the ILO's governing body, comprising a titular structure of 28 government, 14 employer and 14 worker members and their deputies. Ten of the government seats are permanently held by states designated as of 'chief industrial importance' (United States, China, Germany, Japan, India, United Kingdom, France, Brazil, Italy and the Russian Federation). The other government members are elected by the ILC every three years, while employer and labour delegates are appointed through a separate electoral process.

The governing body meets three times a year and takes decisions on ILO policy, the agenda of the ILC, the draft ILO's programme and budget for submission to the Conference, and elects the ILO director-general.

The ILO is most closely associated with the development and promotion of International Labour Standards, through which it has expanded labour protection into the domain of human rights, the pursuit of freedom and economic choice. At root is the acknowledgement that social problems are political and economic in nature and that economic security and equality of opportunity are basic human rights. Here, the activities of ILO tripartism and decisions of the ILC play key roles in agreeing international standards on a wide range of labour-related issues that, once adopted as legislation by member states, constitute what is broadly termed the International Labour Code.

The International Labour Code comprises two related elements; conventions, which are agreed at the ILC and become legally binding instruments through their adoption and ratification into national legislative frameworks by member states, and recommendations, which, unlike conventions, are not legal instruments but instead provide guidance to member states on legislative development, labour policy and management practice.

Proposals for conventions and recommendations arise individually or collectively from the tripartite members and are discussed at the ILC. These discussions are supported by research and analysis provided by ILO specialists. As the issue becomes clearer and its relevance to the ILC more established, a draft convention or recommendation may emerge. If this is the case, it will then be subject to further analysis and amendment until, as for a convention, for example, it is proposed and endorsed at the ILC and, ultimately, incorporated into the domestic legislation of member states.

In monitoring and enforcing compliance to ratified labour standards, the ILO has been described by critics as 'toothless' insofar that it carries no negative enforcement sanction but instead relies on moral suasion, diplomacy and annual, publically available reports on compliance. An important mechanism in this approach is the Declaration on Fundamental Principles and Rights at Work 1998, which confirms that by virtue of ILO membership and through this the endorsement of its constitution, member states are bound by principles related to four fundamental rights irrespective of their ratification of related conventions. These rights are: freedom of association and the effective recognition of the right to collective bargaining; the elimination of all forms of forced or compulsory labour; the effective abolition of child labour; and the elimination of discrimination in respect of employment and occupation.

In implementing the 1998 Declaration, a follow-up mechanism requires member states who have not ratified one of more of the conventions related to the fundamental rights to submit an annual report on their progress toward recognition, promotion and ratification. Despite a 100 per cent reporting rate there has been a downward trend in the ratification of the eight conventions related to fundamental rights with some governments simply reporting 'no change' in their progress toward ratification. Of these conventions, No. 182 Worst Forms of Child Labour Convention 1999, is the most ratified, closely followed by No. 29 on Forced Labour, while No. 87 Freedom of Association and Protection of the Right to Organise 1948 and No. 98 Right to Organise and Collective Bargaining 1949 remain those with the fewest ratifications (ILO, 2014, p. 1). Countries who have yet to ratify conventions 87 and 98 include China, India and the United States.

This is one of the challenges of relevance and delivery faced by current ILO director-general Guy Ryder. In following-up the work of his predecessor Juan Somavia in integrating ILO activities such as the Decent Work agenda into the broader structures of global governance and international decision-making, Ryder has embarked on an internal reform of the ILO in order to 'provide sound and relevant policy advice ... based on analytical work of the highest quality [and] ... be proactive in setting the global agenda on labour, social and economic policy debates (ILO, 2013, p. 1). Central to this renewed proactivity is the voice the ILO has provided in the global debate on low growth, rising unemployment and the pursuit of sustainable development. In its regular invitations to the G20 and various meetings of the International Monetary Fund and World Bank, the ILO has warned of weak employment growth, stagnant wages, widening inequality and a 'growing risk of a slide into a low growth trap' (Ryder, 2014, p. 2). It points to the challenges ahead not only for the global economy but for an organization whose focus on labour protection, social justice and shared prosperity is of acute relevance today as it was almost 100 years ago as the world emerged from the rubble of war brought about by economic depression, mass unemployment and poverty.

STEVE HUGHES

See also:
Collective bargaining; International human resource management; Labour.

References and selected further readings

Hughes, S. and N. Haworth (2010), *The International Labour Organisation (ILO): Coming In from the Cold*, New York and London: Routledge.
Hughes, S. and N. Haworth (2015), The ILO, Greece and social dialogue in the aftermath of the global financial crisis, in S. McBride, G. Boychuk and R. Mahon (eds), *Global Crisis and the Changing Prospects for Social Policy*, Vancouver: University of British Columbia Press.
ILO (2013), *Reform of the International Labour Organization's Headquarters Organizational Structure*, Geneva: International Labour Office, www.ilo.org/wcmsp5/groups/public/---dgreports/---dcomm/documents/organizationaldescription/wcms_204939.pdf.
ILO (2014), *Review of Annual Reports Under the Follow-Up to the ILO Declaration on Fundamental Principles and Rights at Work*, report to the Governing Body, 320th Session, Geneva, March 13–27.
Rodriguez, M., J. Van Daele, M. Van der Linden and G. Van Goethem (eds) (2010), *ILO Histories: Essays on the International Labour Organisation and its Impact on the World During the Twentieth Century*, Bern: Peter Lang.
Ryder, G. (2014), *The Decent Work Foundation for Shared Prosperity*, statement to the International Monetary and Financial Committee, Washington, DC, October 11.

Internships

The term 'internship' refers to the programmes in which university students as interns gain real-world career relevant work experience, in settings outside of the classroom and prior to graduation from an academic programme. The practice of internships is theoretically rooted in experiential learning theory, which has its philosophical roots in the guild and apprenticeship system of medieval times. The term internship is sometimes used interchangeably with cooperative education and work integrated learning. However, the term internship should be used when the level of structure and systematic integration with an intern's academic learning is generally low, relative to programmes such as cooperative education, which require a formal arrangement between the host organization and the educational institution, accompanied with formal structures that systematically integrate academic study with work experience.

In the 1960s the term 'internship' was almost exclusively associated with medical students in the United States. During the 1980s, internships were also undertaken by students studying for a variety of university majors and by the 2000s a majority of all university students in the United States completed internships as a component of their university education. Participation in internships is not isolated to the United States, as globally there has been an expansion of internship participation, to the point where internships are now considered a preferred entry point into a range of professional vocations across national contexts. Based on current trends in internship participation, it is likely that interns will represent a growing proportion of prospective organizational employees, and therefore a group of increasing relevance, to core HRM functions such as employee attraction, recruitment, selection and onboarding.

To date, a majority of scholarly work on internships has approached the issue from the perspective of interns rather than host organizations. However, there is a growing stream of research highlighting the importance of internships to HRM (Rose et al., 2014, Beenen and Mrousseau, 2010; Zhao and Liden, 2011; D'Abate et al., 2009). In addition, due to the growing prevalence of internships and unfavourable labour market conditions for many graduates, the topic of whether interns should be paid or unpaid has received increasing attention in the popular press (Weale, 2014). However, to date this issue has received little attention in the academic literature.

PHILIP ROSE

See also:
Experiential learning; Graduate recruitment; Young workers.

References and selected further readings

Beenen, G. and D.M. Mrousseau (2010), Getting the most from MBA internships: promoting intern learning and job acceptance, *Human Resource Management*, **49**, pp. 3–22.

Cooperative Education & Internship Association (2014), www.ceiainc.org.

D'abate, C.P., M.A. Youndt and K.E. Wenzel (2009), Making the most of an internship: an empirical study of internship satisfaction, *Academy of Management Learning & Education*, **8**, pp. 527–539.

Rose, P.S., S.T.T. Teo and J. Connell (2014), Converting interns into regular employees: the role of intern supervisor exchange, *Journal of Vocational Behavior*, **84**, pp. 153–163.

Weale, S. (2014), Unpaid work costs interns £926 a month — study, *The Guardian*, www.theguardian.com/education/2014/nov/12/unpaid-work-costs-interns-study.

Zhao, H. and R.C. Liden (2011), Internship: a recruitment and selection perspective, *Journal of Applied Psychology*, **96**, pp. 221–229.

Interpersonal skills

Interpersonal skills can be thought of as synonymous to 'social skills' and refer to the behaviours (both verbal and non-verbal) that facilitate interactions between people. Social and interpersonal skills are the means through which almost all human relationships are initiated, negotiated, maintained and ended (Spitzberg and Cupach, 2011). Interestingly, in spite of the ubiquity and importance of interpersonal skills, we tend to notice them only when they are particularly good (as in the case of an exceptional orator) or particularly bad or inappropriate (as in the case of an off-colour joke or when interacting with someone very rude or painfully shy).

The scientific enquiry of interpersonal skill as an aptitude, or form of intelligence began with Thorndike (1937, p. 275) who was the first to propose social intelligence as 'the ability to understand and manage people'. This broad area of enquiry is now dominated by the construct 'emotional intelligence' (EI). The theory of emotional intelligence proposed by Salovey and Mayer (1990) and somewhat contentiously applied to the workplace by Daniel Goleman (1998) provides a framework to examine these competencies. Emotional intelligence is the awareness of, and the ability to manage, both one's own and others' emotions. It has been found to be related to increased pro-social behaviour and positive peer relationships, and to negatively predict poor relations with friends, maladjustment and negative behaviour, particularly for males. Effective communication and interpersonal skills (i.e., competencies of emotional intelligence) are now recognized as being central to conducting successful relationships, be it a marriage (Noller et al., 1997), a workplace relationship (Goleman, 1998) or in general everyday life (Salovey and Mayer, 1990).

However, an enduring controversy in the study of interpersonal skills and emotional intelligence centres on whether they are 'innate' and related to personality (with some people simply having higher EI and better interpersonal skills than others) or whether they are a set of competencies that can be taught and learned. Another debate centres on the application of emotional intelligence theory and research (which has been primarily based in fields of psychology, physiology, education or in therapeutic contexts) to the organizational setting (Dulewicz and Higgs 2000).

RACHEL MORRISON

See also:

Communication; Emotional intelligence.

References and selected further readings

Dulewicz, V. and M. Higgs (2000), Emotional intelligence — a review and evaluation study, *Journal of Managerial Psychology*, **15**, pp. 341–372.
Goleman, D. (1998), *Working with Emotional Intelligence*, New York: Bantam Books.
Noller, P., J.A. Feeney and C.M. Ward (1997), Determinants of marital quality: a partial test of lewis and spanier's model, *Journal of Family Studies*, **3**, pp. 226–251.

Salovey, P. and J.D. Mayer (1990), Emotional intelligence, *Imagination, Cognition, and Personality*, **9**, pp.185–211.

Spitzberg, B.H. and W.R. Cupach (2011), Interpersonal skills, in M.L. Knapp and J.A. Daly (eds), *The Sage Handbook of Interpersonal Communication*, 4th edn, Thousand Oaks, CA: Sage.

Thorndike, R.L. and S. Stein (1937), An evaluation of the attempts to measure social intelligence, *The Psychological Bulletin*, **34**, pp.275–285.

Interviews

Stone (2014) defines the interview as a conversation with a purpose between an interviewer and a job applicant. Interviews can be relatively unstructured or highly structured. In a structured interview, the interviewer, using a using a predetermined outline, ensures that all relevant information on the candidate is covered systematically. The use of a structured interview yields more accurate results than an unstructured interview, that is, the candidate performance in structured interview is a good predictor of job performance (Macan, 2009). In addition, adding structure to the interview process can enhance the reliability and validity of interviewer evaluations and better direct comparisons. Since an interview is a two-way process, candidates are also evaluating the organisation.

Interviews have been perceived negatively for reasons such as being overly subjective, prone to interviewer bias and, therefore, unreliable predictors of future performance. Such criticism is aimed mainly at unstructured interviews. Interviewing problems include interviewers being unfamiliar with the job, making premature decisions, emphasis on negative information and 'similar-to-me' error. An applicant who performs poorly in the interview is likely to be eliminated regardless of test results, work experience or letters of recommendation because of the unequal amount of influence the interview process has on the selection decision.

It is the applicants who should do most of the talking and this may require the development of active listening skills in managers. Also, techniques and skills in areas such as recording information during and at the end of each interview and being aware of legal and ethical issues surrounding interviews, are required. Developments in interviewing have focused on more formally structuring the interview or supplementing the interview with less subjective selection tools such as psychometric tests and work sampling.

There are a range of types and size of interview formats, including unstructured interviews; structured interviews; mixed interviews; individual interviews; panel interviews; group interviews; telephone interviews and video interviewing. Decisions around the choice of appropriate interview method can depend on the number of interviewees to be interviewed, the seniority of the position, the ability of the interview to adequately assess the performance of the applicant, as well as time and costs.

CHRIS ROWLEY AND NAGIAH RAMASAMY

See also:

Panel interviews; Selection.

References and selected further readings

Beardwell, J. and T. Claydon (2010), *Human Resource Management: A Contemporary Approach*, 6th edn, Essex: F.T. Prentice Hall.

Chinn, V., A. Gill, L. Mackenzie, S. Young and D. Winter (2015), *How to Succeed at Interviews and Other Selection Methods*, London: The Careers Group, University of London.

Lunenburg, F.C. (2010), The interview as a selection device: problems and possibilities, *International Journal of Scholarly Academic Intellectual Diversity*, **12**(1), pp. 1–17.

Macan, T. (2009), The employment interview: a review of current studies and directions for future research, *Human Resource Management Review*, **19**, pp. 203–218.

McDaniel, M.A., D.L. Whetzel, F.L. Schmidt, and S.D. Maurer (1994), The validity of employment interviews: a comprehensive review and meta-analysis, *Journal of Applied Psychology*, **79**(4), pp. 599–616.

Stone, R.J. (2014), *Human Resource Management*, 8th edn, Milton, Queensland: Wiley.

Investors in People

Investors in People (IIP) was introduced by the UK government in 1990. It originates from the White Paper *Employment for the 1990s* and has since become part of the landscape for organizations wishing to demonstrate a clear link between people development and business objectives. It is an accreditation kitemark for which organizations are assessed and that, once approved, they may use for a period of three years before requiring reassessment. The principles upon which it was designed in the 1990s were that the accredited organization:

- is committed to develop people in order to achieve business objectives;
- regularly reviews the training and development needs of its people;
- inducts recruits and ensures development throughout employment;
- evaluates its training and development as part of continuous improvement.

Initially run through the now defunct Training and Enterprise Councils (TECs), the accreditation is now managed through Investors in People (www.investorsinpeople. co.uk). It has been through many iterations since its inception and will be launching Framework VI Standard in 2015, a new scheme with nine indicators for high-performance people management. IIP accreditation is internationally recognized with 15,000 organizations across 75 countries holding the award. IIP has also now introduced a Health and Wellbeing Award designed to improve motivation and sustainable performance by focusing upon the wellbeing of employees. Full details of the standard, how it works and the resources available to help organizations attain the accreditation may be found on the website.

The standard was originally derived through research being undertaken into successful organizations across all sectors to determine best practice in people management and development. This did lead, in the early days, to concerns around the difficulties in determining best practice, in linking best practice with business performance and the implied assumption that this could be applied and is relevant to all organizations regardless of size and sector. (Most IIP-accredited organizations in the 1990s were large corporates, well-resourced to address people management and learning and development issues.) Over the years, IIP has inevitably adopted a more flexible approach and is more focused upon outcomes rather than process. The fact that Framework VI is shortly to be launched (and that IIP has been with us for c. 25 years) suggests that it is both a strong product in the accreditations industry that is capable of evolving and adapting as organizations change.

ALISON SMITH

Reference list and selected further readings

Hoque, K. (2008), The impact of investors in people on employer-provided training, the equality of training provision and the 'training apartheid' phenomenon, *Industrial Relations Journal*, **39**(1), pp. 43–62.

Smith, S. and S. Stokes (2015), Signs and wonders: exploring the effects and impact of the investors in people logo and symbols, *European Journal of Training and Development*, **39**(4), pp. 298–314.

Smith, S.M., P. Stokes and J.F. Wilson (2014), Exploring the impact of investors in people: a focus on training and development, job satisfaction and awareness of the standard, *Employee Relations*, **36**(3), pp. 266–279.

Smith, A.J. and L.A. Collins (2007), Between a rock and a hard place? *Journal of Small Business and Enterprise Development*, **14**(4), pp. 567–581.

Rayton, B.A. and K. Georgiadis (2012), Workplace self-selection into investors in people, *Applied Economics Letters*, **19**(15), pp. 1455–1458.

Japanese management

The phenomenal success of the postwar Japanese manufacturing industry led to a global interest in 'Japanese management' practices and techniques. Over time, the term came to reflect a bundle of integrated practices involving manufacturing systems (just-in time/ lean production), industrial relations practices (enterprise unions, local bargaining, seniority pay and promotion) and employee voice arrangements (suggestion schemes, teams, quality control circles). These practices were, to a large degree, the outcome of an unwritten social contract where workers were incorporated into the efficiency culture of the firm in return for lifetime employment and employer-sponsored pension schemes. This trade-off allowed for innovation to flourish, and the acceptance of technological and organizational change directed at improving the overall performance of the firm. Underpinning this management approach was the key corporate objective of improving market share within an industrial structure based on major enterprise groupings, which usually included a major bank and allowed member firms to support each other and thereby share risk.

The question of whether this approach represented Japanese management practices more generally or the practices of a small number of well-known firms was largely neglected as Western firms searched for ways to emulate Japanese success. By this time *Japanization*, as it became to be called, was considered a universal management system and something that could be adopted elsewhere. At about this time, however, scholars began to undertake more critical research on Japanese management. First, it became clear that such approaches were generally only representative of large firms. Smaller firms, who often served as suppliers/contractors to the larger firms, faced severe cost pressures that led to inferior conditions of employment, resistance to unions and other voice mechanisms, and the implementation of traditional Taylorist-Fordist production methods. Second, debates began to arise as to whether just-in-time production systems (and other forms of Japanese management) were just another way to control work processes and intensify work, whether lifetime employment actually existed and whether enterprise unions were just another form of company unionism.

The economic decline that began in Japan in the early 1990s began to shed light on these questions. In this low-growth environment, Japanese firms were forced to restructure, resulting in the retrenchment of workers, reduced pay and bonuses, and diminished future pension benefits. Japanese management was entering a stage of transition where contingent work was becoming the norm, where workers were less likely to be represented by unions, and where management adopted a harder stance towards its employees. The social contract, based on trust and collective identity, which held the Japanese management system together during the growth years, was replaced by more legalistic and individualistic approaches to resolving the increasing number of enterprise disputes. What form Japanese management will take in the future remains to be seen. What does appear the case is that the uncritical acceptance of postwar Japanese management as a unique and integrated system overlooked to a large extent its historical, cultural and industrial context, the variability in practice and the realities of working life in Japan for the majority of workers.

JOHN BENSON

See also:

Lean production; Lifetime employment; Quality circles; Teamwork.

References and selected further readings

Benson, J. (2006), Japanese management, enterprise unions and company performance, *Industrial Relations Journal*, **37**(3), pp. 242–258.

Benson, J. (2014), Conflict management in Japan, in W. Roche, P. Teague, and A. Colvin (eds), *The Oxford Handbook of Conflict Management in Organizations*, Oxford; Oxford University Press, pp. 385–404.

Clarke, R. (1987), *The Japanese Company*, Tokyo: Charles E. Tuttle Company.

Debroux, P. (2003), *Human Resource Management in Japan: Changes and Uncertainties*, Aldershot: Ashgate.

Dore, R. (1990), *British Factory — Japanese Factory*, Berkeley: University of California Press.

Jacoby, S. (2005), *The Embedded Corporation: Corporate Governance and Employment Relations in Japan and the United States*, Princeton, NJ: Princeton University Press.

Job analysis

Job analysis is a set of procedures designed to collect information about a job to help in making human resource management decisions. There are two fundamental parts to job analysis. The first is to describe the job; that is, the tasks, duties and responsibilities of a job (job description). The second is to specify the knowledge, skills, abilities and other characteristics (KSAOs) required to be able to do the job (job specification). Some job analysis approaches go further and describe job context; that is, the organization structure in which the job is embedded, the degree to which the job is independent or integrated with other jobs and the degree to which the job is part of the strategic core of the organization. Organizations have great freedom in designing jobs, but once designed, the job specifications must be justified in terms of their relation to the tasks, duties and responsibilities chosen.

Jobs are the unit of analysis for most human resource decisions: staffing is based on the KSAOs required to perform the job, performance management focuses on how well the job has been performed, training is based on correcting person defects impacting performance of current or future jobs, and base pay is built around the value of jobs in the marketplace and to the organization. Job analysis results can also be used for career counselling, counselling the unemployed about jobs for which they may be qualified, and labour market and other government policy development.

All job analysis presupposes stable jobs held by individuals who tend to work individually, even if they are part of a team. In the industrially engineered workplace, this is a reasonable assumption, but for many workers, jobs have moved from a specified set of tasks to 'whatever it takes', and from stability to constant change. Well-integrated teams may consist of employees with the same job title who take on different roles and may interchange roles daily. Few employers have job analysts on staff anymore; what used to be a standard entry-level HR job has largely disappeared.

This does not mean that the need for job data has disappeared. Organizations have tended to seek needed job information from incumbents and managers to make specific HR decisions. There is also more reliance on occupation data banks such as O*Net. O*Net provides extensive information on the 1,100 occupations noted in the US government's System of Occupational Classification (SOC) as compared with more than 12,700 job descriptions in the Dictionary of Occupational Titles, which O*Net replaced.

Charles H. Fay

See also:

Job description; Job evaluation; Person specification.

References and selected further readings

Brannick, M.T., E.L. Levine and F.P. Morgeson (2007), *Job and Work Analysis: Methods, Research, and Applications for Human Resource Management*, Thousand Oaks, CA: Sage.
National Research Council (2010), *A Database for a Changing Economy: Review of the Occupational Information Network (O*Net)*, Washington, DC: National Academies Press.
O*NET, www.onetonline.org.
Prien, E. and L.D. Goodstein (2009), *A Practical Guide to Job Analysis*, San Francisco: Pfeiffer.
Sanchez, J.I. and E.L. Levine (2012), The rise and fall of job analysis and the future of work analysis, *Annual Review of Psychology*, **63**, pp. 397–425.
Wilson, M.A., W. Bennett, S.G. Gibson and G.M. Alliger (eds) (2012), *The Handbook of Work Analysis: Methods, Systems, Applications and Science of Work Measurement in Organizations*, New York: Routledge.

Job description

One of the outcomes of job analysis is the job description, sometimes also called position description. It is a written statement listing the job's function in the organization explaining why it exists, its relationship to other jobs, what the job-holder does and the job's working conditions.

While there is no fixed format for writing a job description, most job descriptions contain the following information (Stone, 2014):

- Job identification – includes information on employee job title, department and reporting relationships and locates the job in the organizational structure.
- Job objective – describes the primary purpose or objective of the job.
- Duties and responsibilities – the heart of the job description, it lists the major duties and responsibilities.
- Relationships – identifies the relationships with other positions, within and external to the organization, that are necessary for satisfactory job performance.
- Knowledge – concerned with the minimum levels of knowledge, skills, abilities, experience and formal qualifications required.
- Problem-solving – identifies the amount of original thinking required in decision-making and the environment in which problem-solving takes place.
- Authority – identifies the specific rights and limitations that apply to the position's decision-making authority.
- Accountability – details the financial impact of the job by identifying the quantity and value of assets, budgets, sales, etc. for which the job is accountable.
- Special circumstances – concerned with what is special, unusual or hazardous about the position and/or the environment in which it is performed.
- Performance standards – identifies the standards required for effective performance and the measures for evaluating performance.

- Professional association/trade union membership – identifies any professional association or trade union membership required.
- Other requirements – some organizations use safety clauses such as 'performs other duties and responsibilities as may be required'. Such a clause authorizes managers to allocate tasks, duties and responsibilities different from those the employee usually performs. However, such clauses are frowned upon and can become a source of employee and trade union discontent and dispute.

At lower levels in the organization, job descriptions are likely to be mainly concerned with the tasks that the job-holder is required to perform on a daily basis. However, at more senior levels, it becomes more difficult to define precisely the details of activities required. As such, job descriptions at this level are more likely to focus on the overall responsibilities or areas for which the employee is accountable.

In a dynamic and sometimes unpredictable business environment, the traditional job description is seen as archaic and therefore criticized for being a straitjacket – suitable for repetitive work (Fisher et al., 2006) and being appropriate in bureaucratic type organizations (Peters, 1989). Increasingly, computerization and automation of routine office and factory work means that work is project-based and promotes flexible work practices. Thus, job descriptions are merely a general guide, with everyone crossing job boundaries (Whitely, 1992).

CHRIS ROWLEY AND NAGIAH RAMASAMY

See also:
Job analysis.

References and selected further readings

Bergman, T.J. and V.G. Scarpello (2001), *Compensation Decision Making*, 4th edn, Orlando: Harcourt.
Dessler, G., J. Griffiths, B. Lloyd-Walker and A. Williams (1999), *Human Resource Management*, Australia: Prentice-Hall.
Fisher, C.D., L.F. Schoenfeldt and J.B. Shaw (2006), *Human Resource Management*, 6th edn, Boston: Houghton Mifflin.
Peters, T. (1989), *Thriving on Chaos*, London: Pan.
Stone, R.J. (2014), *Human Resource Management*, 8th edn, Milton: Wiley.
Whitely, W.H. (1992), *Business Systems in Asia*, London: Sage.

Job design

Job design (or work design as it is now commonly known as) concerns 'the content and organization of one's work tasks, activities, relationships and responsibilities' (Parker, 2014, p. 662). Job design research covers topics such as multi-skilling, job enrichment, self-managing teams, and virtual work. Scholars seek to understand how work design affects individual outcomes such as job satisfaction and health; team outcomes such as team adaptivity; and organizational outcomes such as organizational turnover and productivity.

As early as 1776, Adam Smith advocated the decomposition of complex jobs into simpler parts. This notion was expanded upon by Frederick Taylor's idea of 'scientific management', in which jobs were simplified into sets of narrow tasks with minimal discretion over task execution. The Industrial Revolution saw the wide-scale embedding of job simplification in many sectors. However, negative effects of job simplification on employees' mental health and job satisfaction began to be documented from the 1920s. In 1966, Herzberg published the Motivation-Hygiene Theory. Although research has not supported its core tenets, this theory stimulated a large number of job 'redesign' experiments (see, for example, job enrichment), and facilitated the development of Hackman and Oldham's (1976) Job Characteristics Model (JCM), which has become a key theory of job design.

The JCM identifies five core motivating job characteristics: skill variety (the degree to which a job requires different skills and talents); tasks identity (the extent to which an individual completes a whole piece of work); task significance (degree to which a job impacts other people in a meaningful way); autonomy (degree of freedom, independence, and discretion an individual has in completing and scheduling tasks); and job-based feedback (extent to which an individual receives clear information regarding his/her performance). These job characteristics are argued to affect individuals' sense of meaning, responsibility, and knowledge of work results (referred to as critical psychological states) that, in turn, affects outcomes such as motivation, turnover, and performance.

Although the JCM has been largely supported by research, it is rather narrow especially given contemporary changes in work (Parker et al., 2001). Morgeson and Humphrey (2006) expanded the five core job characteristics to 21 job characteristics categorized into task (or motivational, e.g., task variety), knowledge (e.g., job complexity), social (e.g., social support), and contextual (e.g., ergonomics) characteristics. A meta-analysis (Humphrey et al., 2007) demonstrated that the motivational job characteristics predict key outcomes such as performance, commitment and job satisfaction. Importantly, social characteristics predict incremental variance beyond the motivational job characteristics, especially for turnover intentions (see Grant and Parker, 2009, for an extended discussion of social and relational aspects of work design). Work context mattered too, notably for job satisfaction and stress.

A further influential theory is the demand-control model (Karasek, 1979), which particularly focuses on health and strain outcomes of work design (e.g., job strain, cardiovascular disease). Like the JCM, this model identifies the role of job autonomy (control), but it additionally focuses on the strain consequences of excess demands (such as role overload), for which there is strong support (De Lange et al., 2003). Expansions of the theory include consideration of social support and other work design 'resources' beyond control.

While the above models focus on individual work design, when jobs are interdependent it often makes sense to implement teams. Socio-technical systems theory was an early influence on the design of work teams, as manifested in the idea of self-managing teams in which the team as a whole has autonomy and variety. A further theoretical development in recent times has been greater recognition of the role of employee job crafting and other such 'bottom-up' work redesign by employees themselves (Grant and Parker, 2009).

Beyond the perspectives summarized here, job design has also been considered from biomechanical and perceptual/motor perspectives (Campion, 1988).

SHARON K. PARKER AND JOSEPH A. CARPINI

See also:

Division of labour; Job enlargement, Job enrichment; Job rotation; Motivation; Self-managed teams; Teamwork.

References and selected further readings

Campion, M.A. (1988), Interdisciplinary approaches to job design: a constructive replication with extensions, *Journal of Applied Psychology*, **73**(3), pp. 467–481.
De Lange, A.H., T.W. Taris, M.A. Kompier, I. Houtman and P.M. Bongers (2003), The very best of the millennium: longitudinal research and the demand-control-(support) model, *Journal of Occupational Health Psychology*, **8**(4), pp. 282–305.
Grant, A.M. and S.K. Parker (2009), Redesigning work design theories: the rise of relational and proactive perspectives, *Academy of Management Annals*, **3**(1), pp. 317–375.
Hackman, J.R. and G.R. Oldham (1976), Motivation through the design of work: test of a theory, *Organizational Behavior and Human Performance*, **16**(2), pp. 250–279.
Humphrey, S.E., J.D. Nahrgang and F.P. Morgeson (2007), Integrating motivational, social, and contextual work design features: A meta-analytic summary and theoretical extension of the work design literature, *Journal of Applied Psychology*, **92**(5), pp. 1332–1356.
Karasek, R.A. (1979), Job demands, job decision latitude and mental strain: implications for job redesign, *Administrative Science Quarterly*, **24**, pp. 285–308.
Morgeson, F.P. and S.E. Humphrey (2006), The work design questionnaire (WDQ): developing and validating a comprehensive measure of assessing job design and the nature of work, *Journal of Applied Psychology*, **9**(6), pp. 1321–1339.
Parker, S.K. (2014), Beyond motivation: job and work design for development, health, ambidexterity, and more, *Annual Review of Psychology*, **65**, pp. 661–691.
Parker, S.K., T.D. Wall and J.L. Cordery (2001), Future work design research and practice: toward an elaborated model of work design, *Journal of Occupational and Organizational Psychology*, **7**(4), pp. 413–440.

Job enlargement

Job enlargement is the *horizontal* expansion of jobs by increasing the number and variety of tasks an individual performs, with the intention of bolstering the motivational value of the job (Pierce and Dunham, 1976). Job enlargement is a form of job redesign (see 'Job design' in this volume) that has often been introduced as a means of counteracting monotony and boredom. It is distinct from job enrichment, which vertically expands jobs by building in autonomy and challenge.

Research shows mixed effects of job enlargement. Campion and McClelland (1991) found that enlarging jobs resulted in greater enhanced employee satisfaction, chances to catch errors/error detection, better customer service, as well as less lowered mental under-load. Enlarged jobs also had greater training requirements, basic skills (reading, writing, maths and problem-solving), compensable factors (skill, responsibility, effort and working conditions), and mental overload. In a two-year follow-up study of the same jobs, the authors identified two distinct enlargement strategies with different outcomes. *Task enlargement*, or adding additional tasks to the job that did not require more knowledge, was associated with less satisfaction and efficiency and poor customer service and greater mental overload and errors. *Knowledge enlargement*, involving the need for greater understanding of procedures, policies, and rules relating to the task, was associated with increased satisfaction, less overload and fewer errors (Campion and McClelland, 1993). In line with this finding, Axtell and Parker (2003) found that job enlargement had negative lagged effects on employees' self-efficacy (a person's confidence in performing a task), whereas job enrichment had positive effects. The authors argued that the difference might occur because enlarged jobs are a form of work intensification, whereas enriched jobs give increased feelings of personal control. It seems that, job enlargement exists along a continuum of enlargement quality, such that cognitively enhancing enlargements result in positive outcomes similar to job enrichment, which has fairly consistently been shown to predict positive attitudinal outcomes and sometimes also positive performance outcomes, whereas task enlargement can sometimes be a case of replacing one mundane task with two or three (Campion et al., 2005).

These results also draw attention to the need to consider short- and long-term benefits of job redesign. Job enlargement might prove a useful technique in addressing immediate issues but may not be a sustainable redesign strategy. Additionally, it is also difficult to predict how employees will perceive job redesign. Tombaugh and White (1990) showed that job enlargement initiated from the 'top-down' was seen by employees as job enlargement, whereas bottom-up job enlargement was more often perceived as job enrichment. The bottom-up enlargement of a job is consistent with the concept of job crafting, which occurs when employees actively redesign their jobs by choosing tasks, negotiating work content, and assigning meaning to tasks (Grant and Parker, 2009). Nevertheless, regardless of the motivational consequences, it is likely that job enlargement will increase employees' knowledge and skills (Campion and McClelland, 1991), and can potentially play an important role in alleviating physical strain if the enlarged tasks are distinct from each other.

JOSEPH A. CARPINI AND SHARON K. PARKER

See also:

Empowerment; Job design; Job enrichment; Job rotation; Job satisfaction; Motivation.

References and selected further readings

Axtell, C.M. and S.K. Parker (2003), Promoting role breadth self-efficacy through involvement, work redesign and training, *Human Relations*, **56**(1), pp.113–131.
Campion, M.A. and C.L. McClelland (1991), Interdisciplinary examination of the costs and benefits of enlarged jobs: a job design quasi-experiment, *Journal of Applied Psychology*, **76**(2), pp. 186–198.
Campion, M.A. and C.L. McClelland (1993), Follow-up and extension of the interdisciplinary costs and benefits of enlarged jobs, *Journal of Applied Psychology*, **78**(3), pp. 339–351.
Campion, M.A., T.V. Mumford, F.P. Morgeson and J.D. Nahrgang (2005), Work redesign: eight obstacles and opportunities, *Human Resource Management*, **44**(4), pp. 367–390.
Grant, A.M and S.K. Parker (2009), Redesigning work design theories: the rise of relational and proactive perspectives, *Academy of Management Annals*, **3**(1), pp. 317–375.
Pierce, J.L. and R.B. Dunham (1976), Task design: a literature review, *The Academy of Management Review*, **1**(4), pp. 83–97.
Tombaugh, J.R. and L.P. White (1990), Downsizing: an empirical assessment of survivors' perceptions in a postlayoff environment, *Organization Development Journal*, **8**(2), pp. 32–43.

Job enrichment

Job enrichment is a type of job 'redesign' (see 'Job design' in this volume) initially derived from Herzberg's Motivation-Hygiene Theory. It refers to building into jobs 'greater scope for personal achievement and its recognition, more challenging and responsible work, and more opportunity for individual advancement and growth' (Paul et al., 1969,

p. 835). Job enrichment involves the *vertical* expansion of jobs and especially includes greater job autonomy, whereas job enlargement involves the *horizontal* expansion of jobs in which the range of tasks is broadened.

The Job Characteristics Model is the main theory that underpins job enrichment. This theory suggests that, by increasing skill variety, task identity and task significance, feelings of meaningfulness are fostered; while augmented perceptions of responsibility are achieved by increasing employee autonomy, and an increase in job-related feedback promotes employees' knowledge of the results of work, thus increasing the motivational potential of the job.

Research on job enrichment as a form of job redesign was highly prevalent in the 1970s. Although there is meta-analytic evidence that enriching (or motivating) work characteristics such as autonomy positively predict many outcomes, mostly through enhancing meaningfulness, research is more mixed when it comes to demonstrating positive change as a result of job enrichment interventions. The evidence is most consistent for attitudes like job satisfaction and commitment and beliefs like self-efficacy (Parker, 1998), but is inconsistent when it comes to performance (Kelly, 1992; Yan et al., 2011).

In part, inconsistent outcomes might reflect the challenges involved in implementing work redesign (Locke et al., 1976). Performance effects might also depend on contingencies such as job incumbent personality (e.g., their growth need strength), task and job type, and organizational and national culture. For example, in a Chinese high-tech organization, job enrichment increased job satisfaction and task performance for knowledge workers but this was not so for manual workers (Yan et al., 2011). The authors argued that manual workers might perceive enrichment as an obstacle or additional stressor.

Time lags might also play a role in explaining mixed performance effects. In a study of fundraising callers, the amount of pledges earned more than doubled following a task significance intervention (see Grant et al., 2011); whereas the positive performance effects of a more multifaceted job enrichment initiative involving bank tellers were only evident after several months (Griffin, 1991).

Job enrichment can apply at the group level in the form of self-managed teams or autonomous work groups. As with individual job enrichment, organizational/occupational context can mitigate the effects. For example, the introduction of self-managed teams had a positive effect on performance, attitudes and behaviours in government administrative staff; however, these results were not fully replicated and in some cases were negative in a military sample (Langfred, 2000).

There is evidence that an optimal level of job enrichment exists. For example, Xie and Johns (1995) demonstrated that jobs can be 'too rich', with associated role overload and strain, while Fried and colleagues (2013) demonstrated that jobs that are both 'not rich enough' or 'too rich' increased obesity rates, which the authors argue is due to employee experiences of stress. Job enrichment can also support professional and skill development.

Sharon K. Parker and Joseph A. Carpini

See also:

Empowerment; Job design; Job enlargement; Job rotation; Job satisfaction; Lean production; Quality circles; Scientific management; Teamwork.

References and selected further readings

Fried, Y., G.A. Laurence, A. Shirom, S. Melamed, S. Toker, S. Berliner and I. Shapira (2013), The relationship between job enrichment and abdominal obesity: a longitudinal field study of apparently healthy individuals, *Journal of Occupational Health Psychology*, **18**(4), pp. 458–468.
Grant, A.M., Y. Fried and T. Juillerat (2011), Work matters: job design in classic and contemporary perspectives, in S. Zedeck (ed.), *APA Handbook of Industrial and Organizational Psychology, Vol. 1*, Washington, DC: American Psychological Association, pp. 417–453.
Griffin, R.W. (1991), Effects of work redesign on employee perceptions, attitudes, and behaviors: a long-term investigation, *The Academy of Management Journal*, **34**(2), pp. 425–435.
Kelly, J. (1992), Does job re-design theory explain job re-design outcomes? *Human Relations*, **45**(9), pp. 753–774.
Langfred, C.W. (2000), The paradox of self-management: individual and group autonomy in work groups, *Journal of Organizational Behavior*, **21**(5), pp. 563–585.
Locke, E.A., D. Sirota and A.D. Wolfson (1976), An experimental case study of the successes and failures of job enrichment in a government agency, *Journal of Applied Psychology*, **61**(6), pp. 701–711.
Parker, S.K. (1998), Enhancing role breadth self-efficacy: the roles of job enrichment and other organizational interventions, *Journal of Applied Psychology*, **83**(6), pp. 835–852.
Paul, W.J., K.B. Robertson and F. Herzberg (1969), Job enrichment pays off, *Harvard Business Review*, **47**(2), pp. 67–78.
Xie, J.L. and G. Johns (1995), Job scope and stress: can job scope be too high? *Academy of Management Journal*, **38**(5), pp. 1288–1309.
Yan, M., K.Z. Peng and A.M. Francesco (2011), The differential effects of job design on knowledge workers and manual workers: a quasi-experimental field study in China, *Human Resource Management*, **50**(3), pp. 407–424.

Job evaluation

Job evaluation is a procedure used in organizations to assign relative value to the different jobs that exist in the organization. It is sometimes referred to as 'building the internal hierarchy.' Job evaluation does not assign a specific wage or salary amount to a job, but instead assigns 'points', which can then be used to assign a job to a grade in a salary structure. Job evaluation is a judgemental process, giving rise to all the shortcomings of any judgemental process. Job evaluation is common in larger organizations, although many organizations have dropped it in favour of 'whole-job slotting' or the market pricing of jobs.

There are three forms of job evaluation that are common today. The simplest is whole-job ranking. In its simplest form, ranking is done by managers or other subject matter experts placing the jobs in an ordered list, from most valuable to least valuable. The problems typical in ranking include a lack of agreement across raters and the inability of the procedure to allow for ties. Ranking can work in a small organization but is becoming less common.

A second form of job evaluation, 'classification', is common in government organisations, especially in the US. Classification systems begin with a desired salary structure containing the number of grades desired by the organization. Each grade/class is defined by a series of job characteristics. Jobs are compared to the class definitions and placed in the grade with the definition that fits the job most closely. Classification systems are relatively easy to construct but most jobs can justifiably fit into two or more grades/ classes, resulting in employee appeals and strong employee perceptions of inequity.

The most common form of job evaluation in place today is point-factor job evaluation. In this system a series of four to ten scales are created that are believed to capture job characteristics lending value to jobs from the organization's perspective, with the total value of each scale weighted by the strategic importance of the job characteristic to the organization. Common scales include experience required (by the job), education required, responsibility for people, responsibility for process and working conditions. A typical scale would contain the scale title, a short description of the meaning of the job characteristic and three to nine interval-scale levels, each defined by different (and increasingly valued) levels of the job characteristic. A job evaluation committee – composed of managers and other job-knowledgeable employees – rates each job on all scales, resulting in a point score that increases with perceived job value. Scale scores are summed to get a job score and jobs are then ranked (from high to low) by the total points awarded, resulting in the internal hierarchy of value. These value hierarchies are then used as the basis of a wage/salary structure.

CHARLES H. FAY

See also:

Job analysis; Labour market.

References and selected further readings

Gilbert, K. (2012), Promises and practices: job evaluation and equal pay forty years on, *Industrial Relations Journal*, **43**(2), pp. 137–151.
Heneman, R.L. (2003), Job and work evaluation: a literature review, *Public Personnel Management*, **32**(1), pp. 47–70.
Quaid, M. (1993), *Job Evaluation: The Myth of Equitable Assessment*, Toronto: University of Toronto Press.
Treiman, D. (1979), *Job Evaluation*, Washington, DC: National Academy of Science.
WorldatWork (2013), *Job Evaluation and Market Pricing Practices*, Arizona: Scottsdale.

Job quality

Job quality is a broad and multidimensional concept encompassing the intrinsic nature of work (such as skills, pace, discretion and autonomy), the employment or contractual arrangements within which work takes place (including pay, contractual status, benefits, work-life balance and opportunities for progression) and aspects of work relations (perceptions of fairness and trust, voice and due process/procedural justice).

The study of job quality – by sociologists, psychologists and economists – has a long history spanning the Tavistock Institute of Human Relations studies of the 1950s, the quality of working life movement and research on job enlargement in the 1970s. Following a two-decade lull, interest in job quality by scholars, policymakers and practitioners has undergone a resurgence over the past decade and a new lexicon of job quality has emerged with the ILO's emphasis on *decent work*, the EU's discussion of *better jobs* and *good work* and country-specific debates on *fair work* (for example, in Scotland and Australia).

Job quality matters – to individuals, organizations and societies. For individuals, job quality can impact on health, wealth and wellbeing. For organizations, good jobs are associated with positive organizational outcomes, eliciting discretionary effort and commitment from employees that drives productivity and performance. At a societal level, job quality can impact on health and welfare spending (including in-work benefits), inclusion, competitiveness and growth.

There is no one accepted measure of job quality. Some researchers use only objective or subjective indicators and others use a mixture of both. While some studies utilize a single measure, such as pay, others use multiple measures. A number of job quality indices exist comprising different job quality components and differing weightings attached to these components (see, for example, Muñoz de Bustillo et al., 2011). Moreover, 'job quality is a contextual phenomenon, differing among persons, occupations and labour market segments, societies and historical periods' (Findlay et al., 2013, p. 441). Taken together, the lack of an accepted conceptualization of job quality and its inherently contextual nature creates a number of challenges. First, it is difficult to produce reliable job quality comparisons across occupations, industries, sectors and countries. Second, trajectories of change in job quality are difficult to measure. Third, competing conceptualizations hinder interventions to improve job quality and evaluating the effectiveness of any such interventions.

PATRICIA FINDLAY

See also:

Job design; Job enlargement; Skill; Work.

References and selected further readings

Eurofound (2012), *Trends in Job Quality in Europe*, Luxembourg: Publications Office of the European Union.
Findlay, P., A.L. Kalleberg and C. Warhurst (2013), The challenge of job quality, *Human Relations*, **66**(4), pp. 441–451.
Gallie, D. (ed.) (2007), *Employment Regimes and the Quality of Work*, Oxford: Oxford University Press.
Holman, D. (2013), Job types and job quality in Europe, *Human Relations*, **66**(4), pp. 475–502.
Muñoz de Bustillo, R., E. Fernández-Macías, J.I. Antón and F. Esteve (2011), *Measuring More than Money*, Cheltenham: Edward Elgar.
Warhurst, C., F. Carre, P. Findlay and C. Tilly (2012), *Are Bad Jobs Inevitable? Trends, Determinants and Responses to Job Quality*, Basingstoke: Palgrave Macmillan.

Job rotation

Job rotation is the *lateral* shifting of employees between jobs with similar levels of responsibility, work complexity and decision-making latitude. Job rotation emerged in the 1920s as a means of addressing the negative effects of job simplification. While this technique first became popular to combat boredom due to repetition, recent research has identified further important outcomes. For example, job rotation has been linked with increased employee satisfaction and health, as well as organizational outcomes such as increased product quality, firm learning and growth (Eriksson and Ortega, 2006). Job rotation has become pervasive, with 55.5 per cent of American for-profit organizations using this technique, the greatest proportion of which is in manufacturing (Osterman, 2000).

Job rotation can be used in orienting and placing new employees as well as a strategy for career development. Empirical evidence suggests that job rotation, moving laterally within and between functional groups, is positively related to promotion, salary growth, work satisfaction, organizational integration, involvement, commitment, networking, development of technical, administrative and business knowledge as well as personal development (Campion et al., 1994). With this said, the same research found that job rotation was associated with higher employee workloads, higher costs of organizational learning and perceptions of reduced productivity, potentially explained due to disruptions in workflow and processes. Additionally, non-rotated employees reported lower job satisfaction and motivation at work, potentially due to resentment or animosity for not being included in the rotations.

Job rotation can also be a means of dealing with ergonomic issues. Job rotation can reduce the overall physical workload of employees, muscle fatigue, as well as exposure to harmful working conditions such as sound levels (Tharmmaphornphilas et al., 2003). Job rotation can decrease diastolic blood pressure and muscle activity in service industry workers engaged in highly repetitive work, which the authors explained in terms of increased overall job satisfaction and greater variation in required postures and movements, although stress levels remained constant (Rissén et al., 2002). Indeed, it appears that research agrees that 'a change is as good as a rest' (Winston S. Churchill).

The positive effects of job rotation on the physical wellbeing of employees are important in light of changing worker demographics. As the average age of the workforce increases, so do issues related to workplace strain and injury, particularly in physically demanding roles. Faced with the challenges associated with an aging workforce, BMW's Dingolfing manufacturing plant adopted job rotation as a means of reducing musculoskeletal strain (Loch et al., 2010). Job rotation may also prove a useful tool when addressing organizational knowledge loss. As Baby Boomers transition into retirement, they take with them significant organizational knowledge that may be lost if not properly managed. As such, job rotation may be leveraged as a means of capturing and transmitting knowledge to the next generation of workers. Job rotation may prove useful for the training and development of employees.

Finally, while there can be benefits of job rotation, there are limitations. It is likely that the positive outcomes associated with job rotation are at least partially dependent on the quality of the tasks through which the employee is being rotated. Shifting between boring or low-skill tasks means that employees do not gain greater autonomy, responsibility, or more meaning from their work.

JOSEPH A. CARPINI AND SHARON K. PARKER

See also:

Ageing workforce; Job design; Job enlargement; Job enrichment.

References and selected further readings

Campion, M.A., L. Cheraskin and M.J. Stevens (1994), Career-related antecedents and outcomes of job rotation, *The Academy of Management Journal*, 37(6), pp. 1518–1542.
Eriksson, T. and J. Ortega (2006), The adoption of job rotation: testing the theories, *Industrial and Labor Relations Review*, 59(4), pp. 653–666.
Loch, C.H., F.J. Sting, N. Bauer and H. Mauermann (2010), How BMW is defusing the demographic time bomb, *Harvard Business Review*, 88(3), pp. 99–102.

Osterman, P. (2000), Work reorganization in an era of restructuring: trends in diffusion and effects on employee welfare, *Industrial and Labour Relations Review*, **53**(2), pp. 179–196.

Rissén, D., B. Melin, L. Sandsjö, I. Dohns and U. Lundberg (2002), Psychophysiological stress reactions, trapezius muscle activity, and neck and shoulder pain among female cashiers before and after introduction of job rotation, *Work & Stress*, **16**(2), pp. 127–137.

Tharmmaphornphilas, W., B. Green, B.J. Carnahan and B.A. Norman (2003), Applying mathematical modelling to create job rotation schedules for minimizing occupational noise exposure, *American Industrial Hygiene Association Journal*, **64**(3), pp. 401–405.

Job satisfaction

Job satisfaction is often defined as 'a pleasurable or positive emotional state resulting from the appraisal of one's job or job experiences' (Locke, 1976, p. 1300). Job satisfaction can be assessed at a general level (satisfaction with the job in general), as well as with regard to different aspects of the job, such as the nature of the job, co-workers or working conditions.

Organizations are interested in job satisfaction for two reasons. On the one hand they are interested in the psychological wellbeing of their employees, and on the other because it is often assumed that job satisfaction affects employees' behaviours (such as organizational citizenship behaviour, absenteeism and turnover) and ultimately their performance (the happy-productive worker thesis). The relationship between job satisfaction and job performance is very well-studied. Research evidence indicates that job satisfaction is, at least weakly, related to job performance. However, the causal mechanisms linking job satisfaction and job performance remain unclear. Does job satisfaction cause job performance, is it the other way around, or are there other factors influencing the relationship? In other words, this relationship is not as clear as often assumed.

There are two types of antecedents of job satisfaction: job and individual characteristics. Examples of job characteristics that can contribute to job satisfaction are communication, job autonomy, task variety and the feedback employees receive from supervisors or co-workers. Individual characteristics that are regarded as important antecedents of job satisfaction are personality and previous job experience.

There are a wide range of job satisfaction measures and most of these are employee self-report scales. These vary largely in the number of items. The most extensive scale consists of 100 items. However, research by Wanous and colleagues (1997) has shown that single-item measures of job satisfaction correlate significantly with scale measures of job satisfaction. Therefore, many researchers use a single-item measure of job satisfaction ('overall, I am satisfied with my job'), as this takes less time to complete and may contain more face validity.

Eva Knies

See also:

Absenteeism; Employee turnover; OCB; Organizational commitment.

References and selected further readings

Judge, T.A., C.J. Thoresen, J.E. Bono and G.K. Patton (2001), The job satisfaction–job performance relationship: a qualitative and quantitative review, *Psychological Bulletin*, **127**(3), pp. 376–407.

Judge, T.A., D. Heller and M.K. Mount (2002), Five-factor model of personality and job satisfaction: a meta-analysis, *Journal of Applied Psychology*, **87**(30), pp. 530–541.

Locke, E.A. (1976), Nature and causes of job satisfaction, in M.D. Dunnette (ed.), *Handbook of Industrial and Organizational Psychology*, Chicago: Rand McNally.

Loher, B.T., R.A. Noe, N.L. Moeller and M.P. Fitzgerald (1985), A meta-analysis of the relation of job characteristics to job satisfaction, *Journal of Applied Psychology*, **70**(2), pp. 280–289.

Spector, P.E. (1997), *Job Satisfaction: Application, Assessment, Causes, and Consequences*, Thousand Oaks, CA: Sage.

Wanous, J.P., A.E. Reichers and M.J. Hudy (1997), Overall job satisfaction: how good are single-item measures? *Journal of Applied Psychology*, **82**(2), pp. 247–252.

Job security

Job security is an extremely subjective concept and its meaning can differ from one individual to another. Nevertheless, it can be broadly conceptualized as the degree of permanency an individual is able to associate with employment, in terms of both tenure and mobility. Job security comprises an individual's expectations of their employment future and is influenced by a number of factors both internal and external to the firm. Thus job security can be calculated in different ways. One internal factor involves a consideration of the probability and cost of potentially being subject to redundancy or threat of redundancy. The reasons for this consideration may be linked to the financial performance of the firm or the extent to which employees are subject to stringent human resource management practices and policies. Secondary to this is the extent to which an individual is confident that they would quickly be able to get another job (at comparable rates of pay and location) if they were to leave their current position for whatever reason. This is, of course, determined by the state of the external labour market and levels of unemployment.

There are numerous benefits to both the employee and the employer in having a workforce with a high degree of job security. For employers, promotion of job security is likely to lead to increased organizational effectiveness, with associated benefits of improved employee commitment and productivity. There has also been a considerable amount of research that links job security with the notion of the psychological contract in terms of trust and mutual obligation (Guest, 2000). For employees, job security is associated with a stable, adequate income, reasonable human resource practices, provision of training and development, as well as opportunities for career progression.

The perceived nature of job security has changed over time with the growth in non-standard forms of employment across the world. The relationship between non-standard jobs and feelings of insecurity has been subject to debate, although it can be said that as non-standard forms of employment have increased, the concept of the *job for life* has declined, leading to a decrease in overall feelings of job security. Therefore implicit in an understanding of job insecurity are issues of high stress, low levels of commitment and motivation, all of which can impact upon an individual's performance. However, job security can be managed through progressive human resource management practices, which seek to improve employment relations in organizations.

ANDY HODDER

See also:

Downsizing; Flexible working; Lifetime employment; Precarious employment.

References and selected further readings

Beck, U. (1992), *Risk Society: Towards a New Modernity*, London: Sage.
Guest, D. (2000), Management and the insecure workforce, in E. Heery and J. Salmon (eds), *The Insecure Workforce*, London: Routledge.
Heery, E. and J. Salmon (2000), The insecurity thesis, in E. Heery and J. Salmon (eds), *The Insecure Workforce*, London: Routledge.
Kalleberg, A. (2000), Nonstandard employment relations: part-time, temporary and contract work, *Annual Review of Sociology*, **26**, pp. 341–365.
Maurin, E. and F. Postel-Vinay (2005), The European job security, *Work and Occupations*, **32**(2), pp. 229–252.
Standing, G. (2009), *Work after Globalization: Building Occupational Citizenship*, Cheltenham: Edward Elgar Publishing.

Joint consultation

Joint consultation is a process whereby an employer seeks the views, feelings and ideas from workers and their representatives prior to making an organizational decision. In this process, trade unions can be informed of management plans and possibly come up with useful suggestions as to how these might be modified to better secure management objectives. It is important to emphasize that under this process the ultimate decision rests with the management. Issues dealt with by joint consultation vary from social matters to issues relating to production.

Consultation requires a free exchange of ideas and views affecting the interests of workers, consequently, any workplace issue should be an appropriate subject for discussion. However, both employers and workers may wish to place some limits on the range of subjects open to consultation, this might be because of commercial sensitivity or where it is more appropriate to discuss a subject matter within a negotiating forum, what issues are agreed upon as appropriate for discussion should involve all the parties.

Within the European Community there is a legal requirement to consult with workers in relation to fundamental decisions that affect their employment. In the United Kingdom up until the entry into European Community, joint consultation had been on a voluntary basis in line with the voluntarist tradition adopted within British industrial relations. However, over the past 40 years, the law both domestically and through the European Union has seen joint consultation becoming enshrined within the law. From the 1974 Health and Safety at Work Act, the Transfer of Undertakings (Protection of Employment) Regulations, and the Trade Union and Labour Relations (Consolidation) Act (1992), which put a legal obligation on employers to consult with trade unions; and since the millennium, the introduction of the Transnational Information and Consultation Regulations (2000), which permits employee representatives the right to meet central management at least once a year for information and consultation about the progress and prospects of the organization on a pan-European basis. The Information and Consultation Regulations (2004) established a general framework setting out the minimum requirements for the rights to information and consultation of employees employed in organizations employing 50 or more employees. These regulations crystalized within the law that employees have a right to be informed and consulted on employment prospects and decisions likely to substantially change in how work is organized and on contractual relations.

PETER F. BESZTER

See also:

Collective bargaining; Pluralism; Regulation; Unitarism.

References and selected further reading

Bain, G.S. (ed.) (1983), *Industrial Relations in Britain*, Oxford: Basil Blackwell.
Blyton, P. and P. Turnbull (2004), *The Dynamics of Employee Relations*, 3rd edn, Basingstoke: Palgrave Macmillan.
Burchill, F. (1992), *Labour Relations*, Basingstoke: Macmillan.
Rose, E. (2008), *Employment Relations*, 3rd edn, New York: Prentice Hall.
Van Wanrooy, B., H. Bewley, A. Bryson, J. Forth, S. Freeth, L. Stokes and S. Wood (2013), *The Workplace Employment Relations Study — First Findings*, London: Department of Business, Innovation, and Skills.

Knowledge management

Knowledge management can be formally defined as, 'any deliberate efforts to manage the knowledge of an organization's workforce' (Hislop, 2013, p. 56). This can involve managing the participation of workers in a diverse range of activities including the sharing, codification or creation of knowledge. Organizations have become interested in managing employee knowledge as it is assumed that doing so can provide them with a source of competitive advantage; for example, via increasing levels of creativity or increasing the speed of innovation processes. Knowledge management is thus seen as providing a means of dealing with capitalist pressures for perpetual innovation via the effective utilization of employee knowledge. Organizational interest in this topic, as well as academic analysis of such processes, is relatively recent, with the contemporary growth of interest emerging around the mid-1990s. The assumption that managing employee knowledge can facilitate organizational performance is linked to the closely interrelated ideas that economies have evolved to become knowledge-based, that an increasing proportion of organizations can be thought of as knowledge-intensive firms, and that there has been a significant transformation in the nature of work, such that more and more work has a significant intellectual component. The role of knowledge as a source of competitive advantage is crystallized in the theory of the knowledge-based view of the firm, a variant of the resource-based view.

However, the management of employee knowledge is by no mean simple or straightforward, due in large part to its characteristics. Fundamentally, much of the most valuable knowledge that employees possess is highly tacit, specific and personal in character, having been developed experientially over time, through the particular work activities that people have engaged in. This means the success of knowledge management activities is ultimately dependent on workers being willing and motivated to actively engage in organizational knowledge management activities. A crucial challenge for organizations is that due to a heterogeneous range of factors, workers are often not willing to fully engage in these activities. For example, employee concerns about engaging in such activities may be related to fears about 'giving up' a resource that is deemed to be a personal source of power and status, that doing so is likely to be time-consuming and a distraction from 'core' work activities, that levels of interpersonal trust may be limited, or that conflicts of interest between employees and their colleagues or employers may exist regarding how individual knowledge is utilized. A further organizational challenge related to the tacit nature of much employee knowledge is that when employees leave their jobs they take their (tacit) knowledge with them, and their employer thus loses access to it. If this happens with workers who possess what is regarded as valuable knowledge, such departures can have a significant detrimental effect on the organizational knowledge base.

Due to workers' questionable willingness to engage in organizational knowledge management activities, organizations typically need to motivate and reward them for engaging with such activities. This can be done via a range of mechanisms including the adoption of particular leadership styles, the development of strong, community-based organizational cultures, and the use of a range of HRM practices, including recruitment and selection, training, reward and mentoring. Such means can also be utilized to develop levels of employee commitment and loyalty in order to reduce the likelihood of employees leaving their organization.

Donald Hislop

See also:

Knowledge worker; Learning organization; Resource-based view.

References and selected further readings

Cushen, J. and P. Thompson (2012), Doing the right thing? HRM and the angry knowledge worker, *New Technology, Work and Employment*, **27**(2), pp. 79–92.

Giauque, D., F. Resenterra and M. Siggen (2011), The relationship between HRM practices and organizational commitment of knowledge workers: facts obtained from Swiss SMEs, *Human Resource Development International*, **13**(2), pp. 185–205.

Hislop, D. (2013), *Knowledge Management in Organizations: A Critical Introduction*, Oxford: Oxford University Press.

Minbaeva, D., K. Mäkelä and L. Rabbiosi (2012), Linking HRM and knowledge transfer via individual-level mechanisms, *Human Resource Management*, **51**(3), pp. 387–405.

Knowledge, skills and abilities

Knowledge refers to learning concepts, principles and information regarding a particular subject. Skill refers to the ability of using that information and applying it in context, and it is an aspect of behaviour necessary for satisfactory job performance. Knowledge refers to theory and the skill required to successfully apply theory in to practice to achieve the expected results. There are two types of skills and knowledge. These include tacit (sometimes termed implicit or soft skills) and explicit skills (sometimes termed hard skills). Tacit skills and knowledge are difficult to describe and document. Tacit skills and knowledge refers to the skills and knowledge gained by an individual through education and experience of which they are not explicitly aware. These may include emotional skills, interpersonal skills or communication skills, all of which are difficult to quantify and assess. Explicit skills and knowledge are when skills and knowledge can be easily communicated (verbal or written) from one person to another. These may include a person's intellectual quotient (IQ), which can be assessed and tested more easily. Abilities relate to the skills an individual possess that enable them to act effectively. Exceptional ability means that the individual is proficient and/or talented at a particular skill.

The identification of individual knowledge, skills and abilities (KSA) are fundamental to role of the human resource (HR) administrator and are central to the four HR functions. First, KSA's need to be determined in the job analysis stage of the staffing process. KSA are critical in determining the job and person specifications and to ultimately find the right person for the job. Second, KSA form the basis of the performance appraisal process, whereby employees will be evaluated and development plans are formed on the basis of an employee's KSA. Third, the type and level of KSA are important for determining the learning, training and development needs of employees. Finally, KSA will also determine the type and level of rewards deemed appropriate for each individual employee.

Amie Southcombe

See also:

Competence; Skill.

References and selected further readings

Cannon-Bowers, J.A., S.I. Tannenbaum, E. Salas and C.E. Volpe (1995), Defining competencies and establishing team training requirements, in R. Guzzo and E. Salas (eds), *Team Effectiveness and Decision Making in Organizations*, New York: Pfeiffer, pp. 333–380.

Evans, K. and N. Kersh (2004), Recognition of tacit skills and knowledge: sustaining learning outcomes in workplace environments, *Journal of Workplace Learning*, **16**(1/2), pp. 63–74.

Garavan, T.N. and D. McGuire (2001), Competencies and workplace learning: some reflections on the rhetoric and the reality, *Journal of Workplace Learning*, **13**(4), pp. 144–164.

Guest, D.E. (1997), Human resource management and performance: a review and research agenda, *International Journal of Human Resource Management*, **8**(3), pp. 263–276.

Stevens, M.J. and M.A. Campion (1994), The knowledge, skill, and ability requirements for teamwork: implications for human resource management, *Journal of Management*, **20**(2), pp. 503–530.

Knowledge worker

The term 'knowledge worker' first entered the managerial lexicon in 1959 via the work of Peter Drucker. Generally understood as having to 'think for a living', the knowledge worker is typically an educated professional who has access to bodies of theoretical, specialized and abstract knowledge and comes to work with their tools in their heads, not in their hands. Knowledge workers draw upon their knowledge under conditions of relative work autonomy and knowledge is an 'input, medium and output of their work' (Newell et al., 2002, p. xii). The emergence of the knowledge worker is thought to coincide with the rise of the 'knowledge economy' in which the trading of 'smart', 'expert', 'knowledge-based' systems and services form the bedrock of economic activity; although this claim has been challenged.

Two broad categories of knowledge worker can be identified (Cushen, 2013). Generative knowledge workers undertake work that is future-oriented and involves generating change such as creating a new product, service or process. Generative knowledge workers deploy their knowledge to research, analyse, provide new ideas, proposals, business cases, project plans and undertake project work. Operational knowledge workers undertake work that is oriented in the present and involves executing the ongoing but complex processes and activities central to the effective operation of the organization. Operational knowledge workers deploy their knowledge to complete known yet complex work processes, achieving performance standards and resolving complexities arising along the way.

Much of the scholarship focuses on the simultaneous importance and difficulty of maximizing the inherently undefinable full potential of a knowledge worker. In particular, an individual's tacit knowledge is deemed to be a critical source of organizational competitive advantage as well as the most difficult type of knowledge to extract, verbalize and transfer. Tacit knowledge involves both the act of knowing and the awareness and insights that accumulate through experience. Tacit knowledge is understood to reside within the knowledge worker and the goal for organizations is to create a work environment that prompts the knowledge worker to continuously develop, share and deploy their knowledge for the purposes of creating a valuable organizational resource that cannot be imitated by a competitor. The other type of knowledge, often referred to as explicit knowledge, is articulated, codified, formal knowledge, such as rules or manuals and routine workplace standard operating procedures.

JEAN CUSHEN

See also:

Knowledge management; Learning organization; Organizational citizenship behaviour.

References and selected further readings

Cushen, J. (2013), Financialization in the workplace: hegemonic narratives, performative interventions and the angry knowledge worker, *Accounting, Organizations and Society*, **38**(4), pp. 314–331.

Davenport, T.H. (2013), *Thinking for a Living: How to Get Better Performances and Results from Knowledge Workers*, Cambridge, MA: Harvard Business Press.

Drucker, P. (1959), *Landmarks of Tomorrow*, New York: Harper & Bros.

Newell, S., M. Robertson, H. Scarbrough and J. Swan (2002), *Managing Knowledge Work*, Basingstoke: Palgrave.

Polanyi, M. (1967), *The Tacit Dimension*, London: Routledge.

Thompson, P. and B. Harley (2012), Beneath the radar? A critical realist analysis of 'the knowledge economy' and 'shareholder value' as competing discourses, *Organization Studies*, **33**(10), pp. 1363–1381.

Labour

In the field of industrial relations (IR), labour has always been associated with and opposed to capital. It represents capital's conceptual antithesis, labour as the source of capital's value and the concept that expresses the constant conflict and opposition of workers to management in workplaces and of workers as a social class to capitalism. Pluralist and Marxist views of IR have traditionally agreed on this basic contraposition between labour and capital, although disagreed on the extent and pervasiveness of it. Mainstream IR textbooks highlight the mutual interdependence of labour with capital but insist on the idea of the existence of a 'structured antagonism'. Others consider the opposition between labour and capital as a far too narrow view of social realities and call for a more partnership/collaborative relation.

Independently from the theoretical and political point of views, in the field of IR and overlapping disciplines, labour has always been intended, however, as 'organized labour'. Trade unions have personified labour in society and workplaces forging the system of rules and participating in the institutions that regulate the labour and capital relationship. Presupposed to the organization of labour and its participation in the system was the existence of employment contracts and rights and thus of work in formal economy settings.

This particular conceptualization of labour has been criticized within many disciplines concerned with labour and workers for its one-sidedness. By focusing on one specific category of worker (male/collectively employed on a stable basis in industrial context/protected by collective bargaining and represented by trade unions) it excluded all those workers whose work was considered unproductive, unregulated, unrepresented; making particularly invisible women, reproductive work and the work in informal economies. It restricted the analysis to just one particular form of exploitation, that of the wage labourer, without considering how different labour regimes co-exist and contribute to the development of capitalism as a system. It was rooted in a theoretical framework whose primacy was that of analysing workers' reactions to the political economy of capital rather than understanding labour as an independent agent. Geographically it concentrated on struggles at the workplace without considering the linkages of these with broader struggles over workers' daily lives. Methodologically it was Eurocentric in so far as it conceptualized labour by using categories proper of the social realities, economic arrangements and historical developments of the West.

In the context of globalization, labour is no longer synonymous for work, trade unions no longer synonymous with workers' collective organization, and the West no longer synonymous with the world. We are called to broader and redefine conceptual categories, as that of labour, which while keeping their analytical relevance, are still deeply rooted in the twentieth-century idealization of societies and social structures.

MAURIZIO ATZENI

See also:
Alienation; Division of labour.

References and selected further readings
Ackers, P. (2014), Rethinking the employment relationship: a neo-pluralist critique of British industrial relations orthodoxy, *International Journal of HRM*, **25**(18), pp. 2608–2625.
Atzeni, M. (ed.) (2014), *Workers and Labour in a Globalised Capitalism: Contemporary Themes and Theoretical Issues*, Basingstoke: Palgrave Macmillan.
Blyton, P. and P. Turnbull (2004), *The Dynamics of Employees Relations*, Basingstoke: Palgrave Macmillan.
Federici, S. (2013), *Revolution at Point Zero: Housework, Reproduction, and Feminist Struggle*, Oakland: PM Press.
Van der Linden, M. (2008), *Workers of the World: Essays Towards a Global Labour History*, Leiden: Brill.

Labour law

Laws (such as legislation and cases) along with voluntary forms of social regulation (such as collective bargaining, custom and practice and self-regulatory codes of conduct) determine how employment relationships are constituted and regulated. The subject matter of labour law narrowly defined encompasses the individual and collective aspects of the employment relationship and broadly defined covers the existence and operation of the institutions of the labour market (Deakin and Morris, 2012). The purpose and scope of labour law is contested and often at the heart of political debate (Collins et al., 2012). Two key roles for labour law can be identified within models of employment regulation developed in Western economies in the post-World War II period. The first is a protective role whereby labour law ought to protect workers from the vulnerabilities that are associated with their weak bargaining position. The second role is a productive one whereby labour law ought to ensure that employment relationships function as market transactions (Fudge, 2011). The problem addressed by labour law requires responses serving both of these competing ends and has been characterized as a 'complex dual one' (Collins, 2010, p. 5). Any resolution will be complex and contested; moreover the settlement reached will continue to evolve over time (Collins, 2010).

Labour law does not stand alone as a category of law; instead it draws on various other conceptually distinct categories of law (such as contract law, tort law and public law). Moreover labour law is derived from a range of sources that in Great Britain encompass international and national legislation, the common law (judge made law) and non-formal sources such as collective bargaining and workplace custom and practice (Deakin and Morris, 2012).

Labour law has become recognized as a distinct area of scholarship (Collins, 2010; Deakin and Morris 2012). Nevertheless the discipline of labour law faces internal challenges concerning its conceptual coherence and more broadly its normative salience in a changing world of work (Longille and Davidov, 2011). Debates around the future of labour law have raised questions about what its central purpose ought to be. These questions are intensified by external challenges such as globalization, which threatens state-based models of regulation (Hepple, 2005; Blanpain et al., 2013). Labour law continues to evolve in light of changing political, economic and social demands.

Liz Oliver

See also:
Collective bargaining; Contract of employment; Employment relationship.

References and selected further readings

Blanpain, R., S. Bisom-Rapp, W.R. Corbett, H.K. Josephs and M.J. Zimmer (2013), *The Global Workplace: International and Comparative Employment Law: Cases and Materials*, Cambridge: Cambridge University Press.
Collins, H. (2010), *Employment Law*, 2nd edn, Oxford: Oxford University Press.
Collins, H., K.D. Ewing and A. McColgan (2012), *Labour Law*, Cambridge: Cambridge University Press.
Deakin, S. and G. Morris (2012), *Labour Law*, 6th edn, Oxford: Hart.
Fudge, J. (2011), Labour as a 'fictive commodity': radically reconceptualizing labour law, in B. Longille and G. Davidov (eds) (2011), *The Idea of Labour Law*, Oxford: Oxford University Press, pp. 120–137.
Hepple, B. (2005), *Labour Laws and Global Trade*, Oxford: Hart.
Longille, B. and G. Davidov (2011), Introduction, in B. Longille and G. Davidov (eds), *The Idea of Labour Law*, Oxford: Oxford University Press, pp. 1–13.

Labour market

The labour market is the arena of exchange between the buyers (employers) and sellers (workers) of labour. While typically conceived as a national entity, a multitude of discrete (although often overlapping) labour markets distinguished by geographical location, industry, skill and occupation exist within a given territory. Labour markets are becoming increasingly internationalized, with technological advancements allowing employers and workers to recruit and apply for jobs across national borders to a growing extent.

The dynamics of supply and demand within the labour market influence outcomes of central importance to human resource management, such as wage rates, working conditions and the availability of jobs. Economic conditions play a central role in shaping these outcomes. For instance, low rates of unemployment have the effect of reducing the supply of available labour, thus making it more difficult for employers to recruit the workers that they need. However, labour market institutions – such as government laws and regulations, the decisions of industrial tribunals and negotiations between trade unions and employer associations – are also important in determining outcomes such as the wage rate for a given occupation. Population demographics and sociological forces such as changes in the extent and nature of workforce participation among workers of different gender, race and age may also influence outcomes in the labour market. For example, in many countries, increased female participation has coincided with a structural shift towards more flexible employment arrangements (Kaufman and Hotchkiss, 2005).

The labour market is unlike the markets that exist for the exchange of goods and services. In contrast with other tradeable commodities, labour cannot be separated from its producer, i.e., the worker. While goods and services are typically 'sold', workers essentially 'rent' their labour to employers for a defined period of time. This requires employers to develop a personal relationship with the workers that they engage, often on a longer-term basis than those formed between buyers and sellers in other markets. Within the employment relationship, the inclination of workers to utilize their labour productively is likely to be influenced by pay, the conditions of work and the nature of the work environment. Workers also need to be motivated and directed in order to be productive. The unique features of labour are therefore fundamentally different from other goods, services and commodities exchanged in the marketplace. In particular, these features require employers to adopt certain human resource management practices in order to ensure that the labour power 'purchased' from workers in the labour market is sufficiently productive and performs according to expectations.

CHRIS F. WRIGHT

See also:

Employment relationship; Labour.

References and selected further readings

Freeman, R.B. (1973), *Labor Economics*, Englewood Cliffs: Prentice-Hall.
Gahan, P. and T. Harcourt (1998), Labour markets, firms and institutions: labour economics and industrial relations, *Journal of Industrial Relations*, **40**(4), pp. 508–532.
Jacobsen, J.P. and G.L. Skillman (2004), *Labor Markets and Employment Relationships*, Oxford: Blackwell.
Kaufman, B.E. and J.L. Hotchkiss (2005), *The Economics of Labor Markets*, 7th edn, Boston: South-Western.
Solow, R.M. (1990), *The Labor Market as a Social Institution*, Cambridge, MA: Blackwell.

Labour mobility

Labour mobility is the movement of workers across geographical, organizational and professional boundaries to places where they can utilize their skills and talents. While labour mobility can refer to career mobility, such as movement across occupational fields, geographical mobility, such as movement across borders, has been the main focus of scholarship.

'The importance of mobility stems from its contribution to the creation and diffusion of knowledge,' according to the Organisation for Economic Co-operation and Development (OECD, 2008, p. 9). In particular, the mobility of 'talent' or highly skilled labour can act a source of dynamism and entrepreneurship, bringing new ideas into organizations and national economies. For organizations, labour mobility can facilitate linkages and information flows with other organizations including across national borders. These linkages can contribute to the emergence of networks and clusters of knowledge and innovation at the local level, and can expand opportunities for trade and investment at the international level. Labour mobility can also help to make labour markets more flexible and rectify imbalances between supply and demand.

It is important to consider the dynamics of labour mobility within as well as between countries and regions. While countries such as the United States have traditionally had high rates of internal mobility, this has generally not been the case in Europe. However, this scenario has changed recently through the enlargement of the European Union to include several Central and Eastern European member states, with the effect of facilitating greater intra-European labour mobility.

There are various factors that encourage labour mobility, including global cities and knowledge clusters that attract workers with diverse talents, multinational corporations with large and transnational workforces, networks of firms that engage in personnel transfer and policies that facilitate cultural and educational exchange, such as international student programmes. Wealth and development disparities, particularly the prospect of higher earnings and better job and life opportunities, are also key factors motivating labour mobility. Conversely, immigration controls preventing workers from moving across borders, problems gaining formal recognition of skills acquired elsewhere, language barriers and social and family attachments that deter workers from moving are common factors constraining labour mobility.

Labour mobility is often painted as a 'win-win' scenario. However, there are the potential costs such as brain drain for regions and countries that lose talent, as well as diversity management challenges if the potentially varied needs of new talent from different backgrounds are not sufficiently accommodated.

CHRIS F. WRIGHT

See also:

Immigration; Labour market.

References and selected further readings

Bauder, H. (2012), The international mobility of academics: a labour market perspective, *International Migration*, **53**(1), pp. 83–96.

Favell, A. (2008), *Eurostars and Eurocities: Free Movement and Mobility in an Integrating Europe*, Blackwell: Oxford.

Harvey, W.S. and D. Groutsis (2015), Reputation and talent mobility in the Asia Pacific, *Asia Pacific Journal of Human Resources*, **53**(1), pp. 22–40.

OECD (2008), *The Global Competition for Talent: Mobility of the Highly Skilled*, Paris: Organisation for Economic Co-operation and Development.

Solimano, A. (2008), *The International Mobility of Talent: Types, Causes, and Development Impact*, Oxford: Oxford University Press.

Labour process/theory

The labour process is the term given by Marx to denote the terrain in which human labour transforms raw materials with technology to produce first products for use and then under capitalism, commodities with exchange value on the market. Labour process *theory* (LPT) is a post-Marxist framework for analysing those transformations in the context of contemporary capitalism. With a focus on skills, effort bargaining and the regulation of the employment relationship, LPT shares many of the concerns of HRM, but takes capitalism much more seriously as a source of constraint, change and conflict (Thompson and Harley, 2007).

Although a key part of Marx's framework, it remained relatively unexplored and updated until Braverman's *Labor and Monopoly Capital* was published in 1974. Subtitled *The Degradation of Work in the Twentieth Century*, the book's critical commentary sparked significant and successive waves of research into issues such as deskilling, managerial control and worker resistance. This body of concepts and research is known as labour process theory. The development of such a theory-building project can be understood as a series of 'waves'.

The first wave focused on applying Braverman's claims concerning work degradation linked to Taylorism and deskilling, while the second used broadly the same framework to establish alternative models of the relationship between the development of capitalism and outcomes in terms of skill, managerial control strategies, consent and conflict. At the end of the 1980s a third wave attempted to pull together these threads into a 'core theory' that set out some basic features of the capitalist labour process (such as a control imperative and a structured antagonism between capital and labour) that shaped work and employment relations at a general level.

This broad approach has continued to act as a guide for research into the workplace and its economic context for a substantial body of researchers in the UK and beyond (Ackroyd, 2009). This contemporary 'fourth wave' has focused on deepening and updating research into traditional issues such as skill, control, technology, resistance and misbehaviour; while extending the coverage to the newer territories of emotional and aesthetic labour, identity, global value chains and production networks, financialization of the economy (Thompson and Smith, 2010). The diffusion of labour process research and theory is facilitated by an annual conference and book series (www.ilpc.org.uk).

PAUL THOMPSON

See also:
Disconnected capitalism; Managerial control; Resistance.

References and selected further readings

Ackroyd, S. (2009), Labor process theory as normal science, *Employee Rights and Responsibilities*, **21**, pp. 263–272.
Braverman, H. (1974), *Labor and Monopoly Capital*, New York, Monthly Review Press.
Smith, C. (2015), Rediscovery of the labour process, in S. Edgell, H. Gottfried and E. Granter (eds), *The Sage Handbook of the Sociology of Work and Employment*, London, Sage.
Thompson, P. (1989), *The Nature of Work*, 2nd edn, Basingstoke: Macmillan.
Thompson, P. and B. Harley (2007), HRM and the worker: labor process perspectives, in P. Boxall, J. Purcell and P. Wright (eds), *The Oxford Handbook of Human Resource Management*, Oxford, Oxford University Press.
Thompson, P. and C. Smith (2010), *Working Life: Renewing Labour Process Analysis*, Basingstoke: Palgrave.

Labour turnover

According to Banfield and Kay (2008), labour turnover refers to employees who leave an organization and are replaced. Different sectors and industries have significantly different turnover rates. For example, in the UK, retailing and catering have the highest turnover levels, averaging more than 40 per cent in recent years. The CIPD (2008, in Beardwell and Claydon, 2010) reported that the average labour turnover rate was 17.3 per cent but this varied between different industries (e.g., 41 per cent in hotels, catering and leisure, and 7.9 per cent in electricity, gas and water) and sectors (e.g., 20.4 per cent in private sector services and 13.5 per cent in public services).

The method for calculating labour turnover involves taking the average number employed during the period. For example, in an organization employing 235 people at the start of the period and 275 at the end, with 25 leavers, the calculation would be:

$$\frac{25}{(235 + 275) / 2} \times 100\%$$
$$= 9.8 \text{ per cent}$$

A detailed turnover analysis of why people leave the organization is essential if meaningful information is to be obtained. Exit interviews giving information on employee reasons for leaving and labour turnover rates from past years are the best sources of information. Turnover for each job classification and department should also be calculated because turnover can vary dramatically among various work activities and departments.

High labour turnover is not necessarily problematic and might even prove useful if an organization is seeking to resolve a situation of labour surplus. It can result in the loss of poor performers and their replacement with more effective employees. Low labour turnover can cause problems as a lack of people with new ideas, fresh ways of looking at things and different skills and experiences can cause organizations to become stale and stunted. New faces, or 'fresh blood', bring new ideas and experiences that help make organizations more dynamic. Furthermore, it can also be difficult to create promotion and development opportunities for existing employees.

Labour turnover in an organization may result from employee retirement, death, illness or disability, resignation, retrenchment or termination. The reasons why employers resign may be avoidable (e.g., unfair treatment, poor supervision, dissatisfaction with working conditions and lack of challenging work) or unavoidable (e.g., relocation, serious illness). Employees may also choose to leave and either pursue careers elsewhere take a career break or return to education.

Persistently high rates of labour turnover are usually a cause for concern to managers who face disruption to production and service standards arising from the time and costs of having to recruit, select, induct and train new employees, who are usually less experienced and productive compared to those they replace.

CHRIS ROWLEY AND NAGIAH RAMASAMY

See also:

Exit interview; Resignation; Retention; Succession planning.

References and selected further readings

Banfield, P. and R. Kay (2008), *Introduction to Human Resource Management*, Oxford: Oxford University Press.
Beardwell, J. and T. Claydon (2010), *Human Resource Management: A Contemporary Approach*, 6th edn, Essex: FT Prentice Hall.
Morrell, K., J. Loan-Clark and A. Wilkinson (2001), Unweaving leaving: the use of models in the management of employment turnover, *International Journal of Management Reviews*, **3**(3), pp. 219–244.
Stone, R.J. (2014), *Human Resource Management*, 8th edn, Milton: Wiley.
Torrington, D., L. Hall, S. Taylor and C. Atkinson (2011), *Human Resource Management*, 8th edn, Essex: Pearson.

Leadership and leader–member exchange (LMX)*

Leader–member exchange theory (LMX) is a dyadic leadership theory proposing that leaders develop differential relationships with subordinates within a work group (e.g., Dansereau et al., 1975). This definition was derived from vertical dyad linkage (VDL) theory, which assumes that leaders treat each subordinate differently because the subordinate is unique with different needs, personalities, attitudes, and behaviours (Dansereau et al., 1973). LMX theory focuses on the way leaders and subordinates form unique relationships over time as they influence each other and negotiate their roles in the relationship (Yukl, 2002). According to the theory, supervisor–subordinate relationships are reciprocal exchanges and involve a continuous role making process, influenced by leaders' and subordinates' expectations (Dansereau et al., 1973, 1975; Graen, 1976).

LMX theory also suggests that leaders have difficulties forming high-quality relationships with every member within a workgroup because of limited resources, time and abilities. Thus, leaders tend to develop high-quality relationships with a few employees who in turn can act as 'trusted assistants' (they are the in-group members), and they form low-quality relationships with others. These other subordinates, in effect, act as 'hired hands', and are considered to be members of the out-group. The relationship quality between a leader and his or her subordinates has strong implications for both parties. A high-quality LMX relationship is characterized by mutual trust, respect and influence that go beyond the formal employment contract. Both parties in this high-quality exchange relationship report higher job satisfaction and better work performance (e.g., Gerstner and Day, 1997; Graen and Uhl-Bien, 1995). It is argued that leaders focus on developing, challenging, supporting and satisfying employees in high-quality relationships by delegating more interesting tasks, providing access to important resources, and giving them increased autonomy and responsibilities (Gerstner and Day, 1997). On the other hand, a low-quality relationship develops based on the terms and conditions of a formal employment contact. Subordinates in this form of relationship often receive less supervisory attention, less accessibility to organizational resources, and less opportunity to be empowered; potentially leading to job dissatisfaction and lower organizational commitment (Gerstner and Day, 1997). It is argued that in such relationships, leaders emphasize the use of formal authority and power to assign job responsibilities to their subordinates based on their formal job descriptions. The differential quality of LMX relationships thus results in different employees' work attitudes and behaviours (Gerstner and Day, 1997; Graen and Uhl-Bien, 1995).

LMX theory builds on, and extends, two key theoretical foundations: social exchange theory and role theory. First, Blau (1964, p. 91) defines social exchange as 'voluntary actions of individuals that are motivated by the return they are expected to bring and typically do in fact bring from others'. This exchange process is reciprocal in nature, and when reciprocations do not occur as expected, the other member may withdraw his or her services (Blau, 1964). Therefore, social interactions based on these exchanges are guided by norms of reciprocity (Gouldner, 1960) that help create an obligation for an individual to return a favour when he/she receives a benefit. In the LMX context, leaders and subordinates engage in a give-and-take process where they exchange resources, information and work-related benefits. If both leaders and subordinates value what they receive from each other, then the leader will offer more organizational resources to increase the likelihood that subordinates would also return favours that are expected by the leaders.

The second theoretical foundation of LMX, is role theory. According to Katz and Kahn (1978), roles are a patterned sequence of learned actions performed by individuals in an interaction situation. Role-playing in a formal organization requires an actor and a functionally interdependent other to negotiate, through reciprocal reinforcement, an agreed set of behaviours against certain norms, standards or expectations. Graen and Cashman (1975) suggest that the interdependence between a person in a leadership position and one in a follower position is a special type of relationship based on roles. The development of roles within leader–member exchange relationships proceeds in three phases: role-taking, when members are initially evaluated; role-making, when relationships begin to formalize; and role-routinization, when LMX relationships become stabilized (Graen and Scandura, 1987). Specifically, role-taking is described as the first or initial dyadic exchange whereby the relationship between leaders and subordinates is based on economic and contractual transactions (Graen and Scandura, 1987). As the term implies, leaders and subordinates focus on relevant resources and responsibilities to complete tasks. Rewards and task involvements are specific and clear, and both supervisors and subordinates understand what they will receive and return within the transactions (Graen and Scandura, 1987; Graen and Uhl-Bien, 1995). The role-taking process also serves as a platform for supervisors and subordinates to test each other in terms of their commitment and motivation. For example, supervisors attempt to identify abilities, competencies, and personalities of subordinates through the ongoing exchanges, whereas subordinates also observe the behaviours and the resources given by the supervisors.

The second stage is role-making, whereby supervisors describe and communicate role expectations to members, who in turn receive these expectations and decide how to respond to them (Graen and Scandura, 1987; Graen and Uhl-Bien, 1995). It is here that members are sorted into in-groups and out-groups. After several repeated exchanges, for those members of the in-group, the high-quality exchange relationship between the supervisor and subordinate will become stronger and more stable than before.

Finally, after the supervisors and subordinates have negotiated their respective roles and have developed a shared understanding of the relationship, the final stage of role-routinization is reached. This stage is characterized by the stabilization of the relationship. This occurs when the relationship is determined to be interdependent and interlocked. In high-quality LMX relationships, the exchanges in this stage go beyond the expected roles, and supervisors and subordinates engage in exchanging personal resources and performing discretionary behaviours (Graen and Scandura, 1987).

Most workplace investigations testing LMX theory have been at the individual level, from either the leaders' or the subordinates' perspective, or at the dyadic level of analysis (leader and subordinate agreement). In recent years, attention has now turned to the group level of analysis, with LMX relationships being considered within the context of all other LMX relationships within a team. The quality of relationship between a leader and subordinate may be impacted by the average LMX relationship quality within the team, or by relationship quality relative to other relationships within the team, as perceived by the subordinate (see Tse et al., 2008, 2012).

HERMAN H.M. TSE AND MARIE T. DASBOROUGH

* This entry is adapted from Tse et al. (2005).

References and selected further readings

Blau, P.M. (1964), *Exchange and Power in Social Life*, New York: John Wiley.
Dansereau, F., J. Cashman and G. Graen (1973), Instrumentality theory and equity theory as complementary approaches in predicting the relationship of leadership and turnover among managers, *Organizational Behavior and Human Performance*, **10**, pp. 184–200.
Dansereau, F., G.B. Graen and W.J. Haga (1975), A vertical dyad linkage approach to leadership within formal organizations, *Organizational Behavior and Human Performance*, **13**, pp. 46–78.
Gerstner, C.R. and D.V. Day (1997), Meta-analytic review of leader–member exchange theory: correlates and construct issues, *Journal of Applied Psychology*, **82**(6), pp. 827–844.
Gouldner, D.L. (1960), The norm of reciprocity, *American Sociological Review*, **25**, 165–167.

Graen, G.B. (1976), Role-making process within complex organizations, in M.D. Dunnette (ed.), *Handbook of Industrial and Organizational Psychology*, Chicago: Rand McNally, pp.1201–1245.

Graen, G.B. and J.F. Cashman (1975), A role-making model of leadership in formal organizations: a developmental approach, in J.G. Hunt and L.L. Larson (eds), *Leadership Frontiers*, Kent, OH: Kent State University Press, pp.143–165.

Graen, G.B. and T.A. Scandura (1987), Toward a psychology of dyadic organizing, *Research in Organizational Behavior*, **9**, pp.175–208.

Graen, G.B. and M. Uhl-Bien (1995), Relationship-based approach to leadership: development of leader-member exchange (LMX) theory of leadership over 25 years: applying a multi-level multi-domain perspective, *The Leadership Quarterly*, **6**, pp.219–247.

Katz, D. and R.L. Kahn (1978), *The Social Psychology of Organizations*, New York: John Wiley.

Tse, H.H.M. and N.M. Ashkanasy (2008), The role of affect in vertical and lateral exchange work relationships in teams, in N.M. Ashkanasy and C.L Cooper (eds), *Research Companion to Emotions in Organizations*, Cheltenham: Edwin Elgar, pp.499–512.

Tse, H.H.M., M.T. Dasborough and N.M. Ashkanasy (2005), The role of affect, fairness and social perception in team member exchange, in N.M. Ashkanasy., C.E.J. Hartel and W.J. Zerbe (eds), *Research on Emotion in Organizations: The Effect of Affect in Organizational Settings*, Oxford: Elsevier, pp.143–171.

Tse, H.H.M., M.T. Dasborough and N.M. Ashkanasy (2008), A multi-level analysis of team climate and interpersonal exchange relationships at work, *The Leadership Quarterly*, **19**(2), pp.195–211.

Tse, H.H.M., N.M. Ashkanasy and M.T. Dasborough (2012), Relative leader–member exchange, negative affectivity and social identification: a moderated-mediation examination, *The Leadership Quarterly*, **23**(3), pp.354–366.

Yukl, G. (2002), *Leadership in Organizations*, Delhi: Pearson Education.

Lean production

The term 'lean production' was coined by the authors of the 1990 book, *The Machine that Changed the World* (Womack et al., 1990). It referred to the just-in-time (JIT) principles of operations management that appeared to account for the superiority of Japanese automotive manufacturers over their American and European competitors. Despite claims that workers' decision-making responsibilities would be enhanced, and that work teams lay at its 'heart', the implications of lean production for the management of employees were not always made clear.

Lean production re-emerged – now as just 'lean' – in the early years of the new century. The setting out of the 'five principles' of 'lean thinking' (Womack and Jones, 2003) represented an attempt to show that these ideas could be successfully applied outside the confines of the manufacturing sector. Again, however, the question of what lean implied for the management of employees was not a central concern.

As part of this 'second wave', the principles of lean have been taken up and applied in a variety of settings, particularly health services and the public sector. The widespread adoption of lean ideas has allowed their implications for employees to be studied at first-hand. Critics have focused on the idea that 'lean is mean.' The implementation of lean is thus associated with the deskilling of work and the intensification of effort (e.g., Carter et al., 2011).

Other research has gone back to the issue of how teams might operate as part of lean. Although conceptually different from self-managed teams, lean teams might be said to operate an indirect, Japanese-style form of autonomy through their input into the way that work is organized (Benders and Van Hootegem, 2000). Their operation at a workplace level, moreover, might also need to take account of the situation into which they are introduced (Procter and Radnor, 2014). Particular issues here are the nature of the service an organization provides, and the nature of the market in which it operates.

STEPHEN PROCTER

See also:

Japanese management; Self-managed teams; Work organization.

References and selected further readings

Benders, J. and G. Van Hootegem (2000), How the Japanese got teams, in S. Procter and F. Mueller (eds), *Teamworking*, London: Macmillan, pp. 43–59.

Carter, B., A. Danford, D. Howcroft, H. Richardson, A. Smith and P. Taylor (2011), Lean and mean in the civil service: the case of processing in HMRC, *Public Money and Management*, **31**(2), pp. 115–122.

Holweg, M. (2007), The genealogy of lean production, *Journal of Operations Management*, **25**(2), pp. 420–437.

Procter, S. and Z. Radnor (2014), Teamworking under lean in UK public services: lean teams and team targets in Her Majesty's Revenue & Customs (HMRC), *International Journal of Human Resource Management*, **25**(21), pp. 2978–2995.

Womack, J. and D. Jones (2003), *Lean Thinking*, New York: Simon & Schuster.

Womack, J., D. Jones and D. Roos (1990), *The Machine That Changed the World*, New York: Rawson Associates.

Learning cycle

Kolb's (1984) definition of the experiential learning cycle is the process whereby knowledge is created through the transformation of experience. The experiential learning cycle is holistic and includes affective, perceptual, behavioural and cognitive strategies. The learning cycle also emphasizes the central role that experience plays in the learning process, an emphasis that distinguishes the experiential learning from cognitive learning. Kolb's model of experiential learning has been widely used as a basis for helping individuals identify the kinds of learning activities that are the most satisfying and will improve an individual's learning achievement.

In Kolb's (1984) model, learning is a circular process that begins with the acquisition of concrete experience (feeling), followed by reflection and observation (watching), the formulation of abstract concepts and generalizations (thinking), and active experimentation (doing). A fundamental notion of the experiential learning model is that, because of generic qualities and environmental demands, the learning process is not the same for everybody. As the experiential learning process moves through time, the implicit assumption is that the learner is operating on the basis of previous accumulated knowledge.

The experiential learning cycle is dynamic at two levels. The first level defines the learning process as an oscillation cycle between tacit and explicit knowing. The second level is the movement through the cycle, a transaction of productive inquiry, which means that learning is a transaction between a conscious agent and the knowledge embedded in the social context. Furthermore, the experiential learning is the epistemic work that develops practices that allow the generative dance between knowing and what is known. Within the experiential learning cycle, Kolb (1984) defines learning styles as distinctive individual differences in the learning process that arise from consistent patterns of transactions between the individual and their environment.

AMIE SOUTHCOMBE

See also:
Experiential learning.

References and selected further readings
Dixon, N.M. (1999), *The Organizational Learning Cycle: How We Can Learn Collectively*, Hampshire: Gower Publishing Ltd.
Easterby-Smith, M. (1997), Disciplines of organizational learning: contributions and critiques, *Human Relations*, **50**(9), pp. 1085–1113.
Kolb, D.A. (1984), *Experiential Learning: Experience as the Source of Learning and Development*, New York: Prentice Hall.
Kolb, D.A. and R.E. Boyatzis (2000), Experiential learning theory: previous research and new directions, in R.J. Sternberg and L.F. Zhang (eds), *Perspectives on Cognitive, Learning and Thinking Styles*, New Jersey: Lawrence Erlbaum.
Murray, P. (2002), Cycles of organisational learning: a conceptual approach, *Management Decision*, **40**(3), pp. 239–248.
Vince, R. (1998), Behind and beyond Kolb's learning cycle, *Journal of Management Education*, **22**(3), pp. 304–319.

Learning organization

Pedler et al. (1989) and Senge (1990) were the first to introduce the concept of learning organization to the management literature. It can be defined as the organization in which employees are empowered to continuously learn and develop in a way that promotes collective capacity and therefore helps the organization incessantly reinvent itself. The underlying rationale lies in that through continuous individual and collective learning, an organization may achieve sustainable competitive advantage.

According to Senge (1990), those interested in transforming their institution into a learning organization need to abide by five key disciplines. Specifically, employees in a learning organization are interested to keep their skills and knowledge up-to-date and be willingly involved in self-development (personal mastery). In addition, they share the same vision, which infuses trust and triggers constructive creative tension (shared vision). The basic assumptions upon which employees behave and interact are appreciated, assessed and challenged (mental models), while teams form the cradle in which individual learning transforms into collective learning through positive interaction and exchange between the members (team learning). Finally, an understanding exists that any action taken within the organization forms part of an integrated whole and thus, it affects multiple organizational aspects (systems thinking).

The concept of the learning organization has received much criticism, mainly because past literature assumed a rather positive, prescriptive perspective describing an idealized notion of organizations. In addition, the majority of research on learning organizations adopted an action learning design examining solely successful cases. As a result, the theoretical underpinning of the concept not only lacks generalization but also the acknowledgement of important organizational processes, including politics, ethics, power dynamics and individual differences. Indeed, several processes may hinder the effective transformation of an organization. For example, employees in a learning organization are willingly involved in continuing professional development. Yet, it is highly unlikely that all employees in an organization that aspires to become a learning organization are eager to constantly enhance their knowledge and competencies. Hence, the transformation may take substantial time and may even be considered unsuccessful in the short-term.

Contemporary literature moves away from the idealistic concept of learning organization and focuses more on the existence of a 'learning culture' within an organization. Indeed, the term 'learning culture' seems not only to highlight the efforts of an organization to facilitate learning, but also to imply a long-term endeavour as well as the existence of groups with different views (subcultures).

MARGARITA NYFOUDI

See also:

Continuing professional development; Knowledge management; Training and development.

References and selected further readings

Garvin, D.A., A.C. Edmondson and F. Gino (2008), Is yours a learning organization? *Harvard Business Review*, **86**(3), pp.109–116.

Pedler, M., T. Boydell and J.G. Burgoyne (1989), Towards the learning company, *Management Education and Development*, **20**(1), pp.1–8.

Senge, P.M. (1990), *The Fifth Discipline: The Art and Practice of the Learning Organization*, London: Century Business.

Learning style

Learning style involves the investigation of individual differences: people perceive and gain knowledge differently; they form ideas and think differently and they act differently (Duff and Duffy, 2002). The conceptual definitions in the literature that constitute a 'learning style' are confusing due to the multiplicity of terms and definitions. Different disciplines have different interpretations of the term. For example, management development specialists view 'style' in association with the various stages in the learning cycle, as exemplified in the work of Kolb (1984) and Honey and Mumford (1992). In contrast, a psychologist is likely to view 'style' as an individual's habitual way of representing and processing information in memory, such as cognitive style. One of the principal debates in the field of individual differences in learning styles is the level of relatedness between cognitive style and learning style.

Within the experiential learning framework, Kolb (1984) defines learning styles as distinctive individual differences in the learning process that arise from consistent patterns of transaction between the individual and their environment. Furthermore, according to Kolb, learning style differs from personality traits, which focus on specific attributes particular to each individual. Thus, a learning style is much broader and focuses on how individuals deal with ideas and day-to-day situations. People vary in their preferences for information perception, along an abstract–concrete dimension, as well as in their preferences for information processing, along an active–reflective dimension. The combination of preferences along these two dimensions results in four learning styles labelled as converger, diverger, assimilator and accommodator.

Learning style differences are relevant to the diversity of employees in organizations today. There are many simple quizzes and questionnaires available to help determine employee learning styles. This information can help people see the correct type of learning that a particular task and environment demands. Researchers acknowledge that the learning style of individuals must be matched with the conditions that bring out the best in them, rather than conditions that oppress and pacify. Differences between learners in terms of their learning style are important in the learning process and have been adopted and developed by many training and development specialists.

AMIE SOUTHCOMBE

References and selected further readings

Berings, M.G.M.C., R.F. Poell and P.R.J. Simons (2005), Conceptualizing on-the-job learning styles, *Human Resource Development Review*, **4**(4), pp. 373–399.

Buch, K. and S. Bartley (2002), Learning style and training delivery mode preference, *Journal of Workplace Learning*, **14**(1), pp. 5–10.

Duff, A. and T. Duffy (2002), Psychometric properties of Honey and Mumford's Learning Style Questionnaire (LSQ), *Personality and Individual Differences*, **33**(1), pp. 147–163.

Honey, P. and A. Mumford (1992), *The Manual of Learning Styles*, Berkshire: Peter Honey.

Kolb, D.A. (1984), *Experiential Learning: Experience as the Source of Learning and Development*, New York: Prentice Hall.

Sadler-Smith, E. (1996), Learning styles: a holistic approach, *Journal of European Industrial Training*, **20**(7), pp. 29–36.

Liberal market economy

The term 'liberal market economy' came into widespread usage following on from Hall and Soskice's (2001) collection denoting the developed economies of the Anglo-Saxon world, Ireland and possibly Estonia. Other terms to denote some or all liberal market economies (LMEs) include shareholder capitalism (Dore), Anglo-Saxon capitalism and compartmentalized business systems (Whitley, 1999). Such economies are characterized by weak ties between key actors and adversarial competition (Hall and Soskice, 2001; Whitley, 1999). In practical terms, this is associated with the dominance of short-term investors, a relatively weak emphasis on stakeholder and environmental well-being, deregulated labour markets and poor social protection. Within the workplace, LMEs are associated with relatively weak worker rights and voice, and managerial unilateralism in the organization of work. Implicit (and indeed, at times, explicit) in the literature on comparative capitalism is the assumption that LMEs are inferior in terms of generating sustainable growth and societal wellbeing than is the case in coordinated market economies (CMEs). Inequality is higher, while many workers on low wages make it difficult to secure consumer demand without unsustainable levels of debt. Although LME firms often spend a great deal on training, this tends to be induction training, necessitated by high staff turnover. Proponents of the liberal market model claim it generates superior growth and job creation. However, claims around the former are normally buttressed by very selective usage of data (choosing time periods when liberal markets were doing particularly well), and characterized by vulgar lip-smacking at any misfortunes suffered by coordinated markets (even if, in objective terms, LMEs are doing much worse). Although on the surface, the job creation record of LMEs has been impressive in the 1990s and 2000s, many of the jobs were insecure, poorly paid and often part-time through no choice of the incumbent. This continues to be the case.

A key feature of LMEs is the dominance of financial intermediaries, prone to excessive short-termism and speculation. This has made for great speculative bubbles, but also the hollowing out of manufacturing, as accumulated assets are liquidated and production outsourced and/or offshored to the cheapest possible provider. A similar trend has been notable in retailing, with premises being sold off, or used as a vehicle to leverage debt. In this process, the possibilities of liquidation and debt leverage assume greater importance than the original aims of making or selling products or services, leaving all stakeholders in the firm, including workers in a precarious position.

GEOFF WOOD

See also:
Comparative HRM; Coordinated market economy; Varieties of capitalism.

References and selected further readings

Hall, P. and D. Soskice (2001), An introduction to the varieties of capitalism, in P. Hall and D. Soskice (eds), *Varieties of Capitalism: The Institutional Basis of Competitive Advantage*, Oxford: Oxford University Press.
Lane, C. and G. Wood (eds) (2012), *Capitalist Diversity and Diversity within Capitalism*, London: Routledge.
Whitley, R. (1999), *Divergent Capitalisms: The Social Structuring and Change of Business Systems*, Oxford: Oxford University Press.
Wilkinson, A., G. Wood and R. Deeg (eds) (2014), *Oxford Handbook of Employment Relations: Comparative Employment Systems*, Oxford: Oxford University Press.
Wood, G., P. Dibben and S. Ogden (2014), Comparative capitalism without capitalism, and production without workers: the limits and possibilities of contemporary institutional analysis, *International Journal of Management Reviews*, early online at http://onlinelibrary.wiley.com/doi/10.1111/ijmr.12025/abstract.

Lifetime employment

Lifetime employment is an employment system that has been a distinguishing characteristic of large Japanese companies, particularly in the high economic growth period in Japan. It is said that James C. Abegglen (1958) first introduced this concept to an English-speaking audience. Under this system, new graduates are employed by a company as regular employees at the beginning of April on a contract of employment without term. The regular employees can stay with the company until the age of retirement and Japanese companies do not make their regular employees redundant except for some extraordinary reason, while non-regular employees are used for employment adjustment associated with economic downturns.

The practice of lifetime employment is considered to be closely tied with seniority wages. New employees in a large Japanese company start their carrier with a relatively low wage, which subsequently increases in accordance with the number of service years. In many cases *shokuno-shikaku-seido* (ability-based grade system) is linked to the wage increase and promotion, whereby upgrading does not always involve position advancement but can be limited to pay. This system grades employees according to their ability to perform a job, and includes factors such as experience, knowledge, personality and motivation. Each grade has its own eligibility requirements, and employees move to a higher grade in a step-by-step manner while broadening their scope of experience and knowledge accordingly. Through this grade system, Japanese employees develop their job skills within a company over time. The prevalence of lifetime employment allows employees to have a long-term view of their skill development within a company, while the grade system provides them with an incentive to develop their job skills (Koike, 1996).

The practice of lifetime employment contributed to Japan's high economic growth by developing high-quality workers for its manufacturing industries. However, as the Japanese economy went through a process of maturation and crisis, it became difficult for Japanese companies to maintain this employment practice, particularly in the period after the burst of the Japanese bubble economy in 1991. There are two new trends in Japanese employment during this period. One is the increasing use of non-regular employees in almost all sectors. This movement has been promoted by the Japanese government's deregulation policies, such as the amendments of the Worker Dispatch Law and the Labour Standards Law. The other one is the introduction of *seika-shugi* (performance-related-pay), mainly among large companies. However, recent studies such as Keizer (2010) and Olcott (2009), suggest that the introduction of *seika-shugi* does not lead to a drastic change in Japanese employment and pay practices, but rather is used for maintaining lifetime employment for regular employees.

KATSUKI AOKI

See also:
Internal labour markets; Lean production; Performance-related pay; Varieties of capitalism.

References and selected further readings

Abegglen, J.C. (1958), *The Japanese Factory: Aspects of its Social Organization*, Glencoe: Free Press.
Dore, R. (1973), *British Factory, Japanese Factory: The Origins of National Diversity in Industrial Relations*, Berkeley, CA: University of California Press.
Keizer, A.B. (2010), *Changes in Japanese Employment Practices: Beyond the Japanese Model*, London: Routledge.
Koike, K. (1996), *The Economics of Work in Japan*, Tokyo: LTCB International Library Foundation.
Olcott, J. (2009), *Conflict and Change: Foreign Ownership and the Japanese Firm*, Cambridge: Cambridge University Press.

Line managers

As involving line managers (LMs) in human resource management (HRM) now appears such a commonplace development in work organizations, it could arguably be viewed as a key element of an HRM-based approach to managing people at work, for practitioners at least. In the related literature, commentators define LMs as implementing 'general management work' rather than being functional management specialists and differentiate between management levels, such as middle managers that have direct responsibility for subordinates, front-line managers (FLMs) and supervisors. The reasons why LMs seem useful in HRM appear clear, namely that LMs occupy a leading role in the staff-related aspects of general management work, such as motivating, communicating, rewarding, disciplining and releasing employees. As such, LMs may be viewed as day-to-day people managers and key agents in enacting workplace HRM policies and procedures. Moreover, HR managers 'devolving' or 'assigning' HR work to LMs may also release HR specialists to undertake complex HR work, such as strategy and employment law, thus enabling HR to take a holistic, longer-term and rigorous approach to staff management.

However, challenges and concerns seem to be linked to involving LMs in HRM, which include LMs' reluctance to undertaking HR work; confusion about current developments in HRM; lacking support and/or training in HRM; having role conflict/ambiguity; and lacking commitment, competence, consistency and credibility in HRM. As LMs may have to manage organizational costs, to take increasing levels of accountability in managing people and also make key choices on how to manage their staff subordinates, coping with such demands may see LMs come under huge work pressure, anxiety and stress. However, LMs seem to need to practice HRM more professionally and consistently, as their expediency when it comes to dealing with HR work is long known in the literature, and arguably needs tackling if LMs are to become more credible people managers overall.

DOUGLAS W.S. RENWICK

See also:

Human resource manager; Management.

References and selected further readings

Brandl, J., M.T. Madsen and H. Madsen (2009), The perceived importance of HR duties to Danish line managers, *Human Resource Management Journal*, **19**(2), pp. 194–210.
Mishra, S.K. and D. Bhatnagar (2010), Linking emotional dissonance and organizational identification to turnover intention and emotional well being: a study of medical representatives in India, *Human Resource Management*, **49**, pp. 401–419.
Purcell, J. and S. Hutchinson (2007), Front-line managers as agents in the HRM–performance causal chain: theory, analysis and evidence, *Human Resource Management Journal*, **17**(1), pp. 3–20.
Renwick, D. (2013), Line managers and HRM, in T. Redman and A. Wilkinson (eds), *Contemporary Human Resource Management*, 4th edn, Harlow: Pearson Education, pp. 264–289.
Sanders, K. and S. Frenkel (2011), HR–line management relations: characteristics and effects, *International Journal of Human Resource Management*, **22**(8), pp. 1611–1617.
Townsend, K., A. Wilkinson, C. Allan and G. Bamber (2012), Mixed signals in HRM: the HRM role of hospital line managers, *Human Resource Management Journal*, **22**(3), pp. 267–282.

Living wage

The term 'living wage' has been used for hundreds of years, possibly as far back as Plato and Aristotle, but particularly since the emergence of capitalism when workers had to sell their labour for a wage. The basic concept reflects the wage necessary for a worker to cover basic costs of living as well as reproduction. In many uses, the term also includes a moral dimension, as advocates assert that workers should live in dignity and be treated with respect.

The precise definition of living wage varies. Most methodologies include shelter, food, clothing, utilities, transportation and healthcare, but some also include items such as childcare, savings for emergencies and children's education. The wage needed will also vary depending on the level of social services available in that country. The methodologies also tend to account for workers with different family types and sizes, as a worker with children will need a higher living wage than one without. In most cases, the definition assumes a worker with full-time work. In the United States, a 'living wage' has also been defined as the hourly wage necessary to bring a worker up to the federal poverty line for a family of four.

In addition to a specific wage level or methodology, 'living wage' can also refer to specific campaigns initiated by activists, or policies adopted by employers or governments. In the United States, trade unions and community organizations have pressured municipal governments to adopt 'living wage' ordinances that mandate firms receiving public service contracts or economic development subsidies to pay their workers a living wage. In the UK and Canada, living wage campaigns pressure specific employers to voluntarily agree to pay the higher wage.

The living wage has also been a focus of the international movement to end sweatshops. Labour non-governmental organizations, social responsibility monitors and transnational corporations have explored approaches to establishing living wage mandates for contractors producing garments and other goods for export. The International Labour Organization has noted the increased interest in living wage and attempted to refine a standard methodology.

While views vary somewhat about the best way to define a living wage, the controversies surrounding the idea lie more in the critiques of living wage policies. As with similar debates about minimum wage laws, neoclassical economists asserted that when firms are mandated to pay higher wages, they will be forced to cut jobs or raise prices, creating more harm than good. Yet a growing body of empirical literature finds the reality appears to contradict the theory, and there is little evidence of negative impacts on employment or prices. At the same time, living wage ordinances do not always reduce poverty levels, as many low-wage workers do not have access to full time work. Furthermore, there is often weak implementation and monitoring, particularly in the context of sweatshops but even in municipal ordinances. This suggests that the living wage may be only one component of a larger policy platform to assure workers earn enough to cover their basic needs.

STEPHANIE LUCE

See also:

International Labour Organization and International Labour Standards; Minimum wage; Wages.

References and selected further readings

Anker, R. (2011), *Estimating a Living Wage: A Methodological Review*, Conditions of Work and Employment Series No. 29, Geneva: International Labour Organization.
Card, D. and A.B. Krueger (1995), *Myth and Measurement: The New Economics of the Minimum Wage*, Princeton: Princeton University Press.
Figart, D.M. (2004), *Living Wage Movements: Global Perspectives*, New York: Routledge.
Luce, S. (2004), *Fighting for a Living Wage*, Ithaca, NY: Cornell University Press.
Pollin, R. and S. Luce (1998), *The Living Wage: Building a Fair Economy*, New York: New Press.
Stabile, D. (2009), *The Living Wage: Lessons from the History of Economic Thought*, Cheltenham: Edward Elgar Publishing.

Long hours culture

The term 'long hours culture' refers to the routine and systematic working of relatively long hours. There is no consensus around what constitutes long hours in absolute terms but it is typically seen as at least an average of 45 or 48 hours or more per week.

Patterns of long working hours vary significantly across countries, sectors and occupations. There is also a strong gender component, with men tending to work longer hours than women. There are various explanations for why a long hours culture might be sustained despite evidence that is potentially harmful to individuals and less productive for employers. First, low basic pay means that long hours are needed for workers to earn a reasonable income. Low productivity (which is linked to low pay) also encourages long hours to maximize output. In 'blue-collar' occupations, overtime can become institutionalized at workplace level as a means to reward and control workers as well as respond flexibly to changes in demand.

Second, extensive 'unpaid overtime' is common for managers and professionals (and the self-employed). These workers have task-driven jobs that might not readily be delegated or duplicated. Those on relatively high salaries may also see long hours as an implicit expectation of their employer, compared to those on hourly pay, or may choose to work long hours in order to advance (or protect) their careers. In Europe, half of those working more than 48 hours a week are in the top three income deciles. Full-time managers and senior officials in the UK typically work 7.6 hours of unpaid overtime on top of their average formal weekly commitment of 38.5 paid hours, compared to 0.9 hours for skilled trades. Third, for both groups, long hours might be linked to shortages of skilled workers.

There are also more general social, fiscal and regulatory considerations. A fourth factor in patterns of long hours might relate to national cultural dimensions. For example, Asian concepts of collective team loyalty and hierarchical commitment might help explain the relatively extreme working hours of South Korea and Japan, whereas high hours in the US might be linked to individualism and enterprise. In both the US and Japan there is also a culture of not taking available annual leave, with workers in the latter typically using only nine of their 18.5 days average entitlement. A fifth consideration is the rate of marginal taxation and the 'tax wedge' (the difference between labour costs and take-home pay due to social security contributions and taxes). Relatively high marginal tax rates and tax wedge serve as a disincentive to paid long hours.

Finally, long hours are facilitated by weak employment regulation, whether by law or collective bargaining. In Europe, for example, the longest hours are found in the post-communist 'new' member states, where trade unions are weak, and the UK, which retains an 'individual opt out' provision from the 48-hours maximum weekly limit under the European Working Time Directive. According to the European Labour Force Survey, male workers in the UK work an average of 5.6 hours a week more than their counterparts in Denmark, and more than one in five (23 per cent) of Polish workers usually work 48 hours or more a week. This is similar to Japan (22 per cent) but double that of France and Germany. The figure in South Korea is 35 per cent. In addition, there is enormous variation in paid leave. The combined total of agreed annual leave and public holidays in the European Union varies from 40 days in Germany and France to 29 days in Belgium – a difference of more than two working weeks.

Long working hours can be a sign of poor productivity and management and represent a substantial health and safety risk for staff through stress and fatigue. In Japan, hundreds of people each year are officially recognized as ultimately having died from overwork (*karoshi*), usually through brain aneurisms, strokes, heart attack or suicide. A law was introduced in 2014 compelling the government to conduct active research and education around the phenomenon, which is also recognized in Korea and developing countries such as China and Bangladesh.

JAMES ARROWSMITH

See also:

Annualized hours; Overtime; Shift work; Unsocial hours; Working time; Work–life balance.

References and selected further readings:

Burke, R.J. and C.L. Cooper (eds) (2008), *The Long Work Hours Culture: Causes, Consequences and Choices*, Bingley: Emerald.
Johnson, J.V. and J. Lipscomb (2006), Long working hours, occupational health and the changing nature of work organization, *American Journal of Industrial Medicine*, **49**(11), pp. 921–929.
Messenger, J.C. (2011), Working time trends and developments in Europe, *Cambridge Journal of Economics*, **35**(2), pp. 295–316.

Low pay

Low pay is a characteristic of labour markets in all regions of the world, developed and less developed, wealthy and poor. There are alternative definitions. Low pay may be defined in relation to an *absolute* level of pay, chosen, for example, to reflect the income a household requires to escape poverty – as illustrated by estimates of 'living wages'. Low pay can also be defined by a *relative* measure – by setting the upper threshold in relation to a fixed proportion of average or median pay. The most commonly used definition defines low pay as less than two-thirds of the median wage for all employees.

Mainstream economic theory argues that in a perfectly competitive labour market, a worker's wage is the result of a market exchange that reflects the skill potential of the worker, labour demand conditions and the productivity of the work done. To combat low pay, policy should therefore focus on either the supply side (raise education and skill levels) or the demand side (incentivize more high-productivity workplaces). Minimum wages, living wages or trade union pressures are, in this view, unnecessary restrictions.

However, many empirical studies suggest low pay is shaped by a more complex interplay of factors. First, employer strategy matters. Some employers may be unable to distribute income so that pay aligns with productivity, perhaps because strategies to boost market share or win a contract for an outsourcing service have squeezed profit margins Others may simply be unwilling to distribute profits because they prioritize shareholders' or owner/manager interests over those of low-paid workers.

Second, labour market and welfare institutions matter. A low incidence of low-wage work is more likely in a country with a high-value minimum wage, wide collective bargaining coverage and generous unemployment benefits. The challenge for policymakers is to appreciate the interconnections between different institutional rules.

But why are women overrepresented in low paid jobs? Sex discrimination means women face lower pay offers at recruitment and promotion than men. Moreover, women are often crowded into jobs that are *undervalued* – pay is low because the employer does not recognize the level of skill required. Women may also be less likely than men to meet eligibility criteria for unemployment benefits (e.g., hours or earnings thresholds) and therefore more willing to accept a low-paid job.

Finally, it is important to balance low pay against other job quality factors. Taking on a low-paid job for a temporary period presents a different scenario for policymakers than a dead-end job. Also, in some jobs low pay may be compensated by other conditions such as high-quality training, health benefits or control over working hours.

DAMIAN GRIMSHAW

See also:

Equal pay; Living wage; Minimum wage; Sex discrimination.

References and selected further readings

Gautié, J. and J. Schmitt (eds) (2010), *Low-Wage Work in the Wealthy World*, New York: Russell Sage Foundation.

Grimshaw, D. (2011), *What Do We Know About Low Wage Work and Low Wage Workers?* ILO Conditions of Work and Employment Series No. 28, Geneva: International Labour Organization, www.ilo.org/travail/whatwedo/publications/WCMS_157253/lang--en/index.htm.

Lucifora, C. and W. Salverda (2009), Low pay, in W. Salverda, B. Nolan and T. Smeeding (eds), *The Oxford Handbook of Economic Inequality*, Oxford: Oxford University Press.

OECD data on the incidence of low pay by gender, www.oecd-ilibrary.org/sites/factbook-2013-en/13/02/02/index.html?itemId=/content/chapter/factbook-2013-106-en.

Management

Although there are no universally agreed definitions of management, the term usually refers to the control and coordination of organizations in order to ensure that they meet their desired ends. The English word 'manager' first appears in an official document in 1589, referring to someone who had been entrusted with the management of a landed estate. However, people carrying out functions very similar to those of the modern manager have existed for millennia, often bearing job titles such as 'factor' or 'steward'. Management as a set of activities is far older than the word itself.

Attempts to define management usually follow one of two lines of thinking: agency theory, which postulates that managers are agents of the owners of the business, the shareholders, and that management is largely an economic function; and process theory, which focuses on what managers do and who they are. The agency theory approach is relatively new, and grew partly out of the notion of the separation of ownership and control in the late 1920s. Agency theory reminds us that managers are not automatons; they have an agenda, whether it is the agenda of the owners or is rooted in their own self-interest. This has led to a number of theories of organizations as political systems, wherein management is seen as a series of coalitions, sometimes working together, sometimes in conflict as each tries to achieve their own goal. While this undoubtedly happens, however, agency theory does not always tell us much about what managers actually do.

Process theory is rather older. Attempts to identify what makes a good manager can be traced back to St Bernardino in the fifteenth century, who noted that good managers should be efficient, accept responsibility, be hard-working and be able to accept and manage risk. The advent of the scientific management movement saw renewed attention paid to the process theory of management. A notable contribution was made by the French positivist Henri Fayol, who set out five key tasks of a manager: planning, organization, coordination, leadership and control. Fayol saw these activities as essential to organizational success.

At the heart of process theory lies the notion that management is essential for an organization to be greater than the sum of its parts. The controlling and coordinating aspects of management receive particular stress. Without management, everyone would simply go their own way. Not only would there be no synergies, but the organization might actually pull apart as people worked against each other. One weakness of process theory, however, is that despite Fayol's original insistence, leadership has become gradually detached from management. The focus of management is increasingly on getting things done, rather than on considering what things *should* be done.

Another weakness of process theory is that it tends to focus on goals and targets and not on people. The hiving off of human resource management into a separate discipline has, in the eyes of some managers, absolved them of responsibility for managing people. This is a weakness that current management thinking needs to correct.

MORGEN WITZEL

See also:
Human resource management; Management style.

Management consultancy

Management consultancy is the business of providing management and related advice to a wide variety of organizations ('clients') and, increasingly, the implementation of that advice. Most definitions tend to exclude the undertaking of operations for the client. The latter would more properly be called 'interim management' in the case of individuals, and 'outsourced services' in the case of managed business processes. However, such definitions are not uncontested, as some 'strategy' consultancies would insist that the *implementation* of advice is not consultancy.

Modern analyses tend to assume 'management' was a nineteenth-century invention, but the provision of management advice can be traced back to wherever there were complex coordination problems: biblical kings had prophets, Persian sultans had viziers, and the Mafia had consiglieres. However, the dedicated *business* of management advice grew out of the increasing complexity and scale of organizations after the Industrial Revolution, focusing initially on achieving efficiencies through 'scientific management' but subsequently responding to a variety of challenges that clients were facing, from personality testing and recruitment, through to e-business and corporate social responsibility. The resulting sustained growth of consulting has caused it to be of interest to analysts both interested in its success and concerned by its power.

This recent attention to the power of management consultancy has been driven by four concerns. The first, is the conflict of interest between audit and consultancy, which, although banned in many countries after it contributed to the collapse of Enron and Arthur Andersen, is still alive and well in the US and the UK (albeit subject to greater regulation). The second is the growth of management consultancy in all aspects of government, where commentators perceive a conflict of interest between advice provided to government decision-makers and the interests of other consultancy clients, who can benefit from government decisions. Third, a number of academics point to the involvement of management consultancy, together with banks and the World Trade Organization (WTO), in imposing neoliberalism on developing countries. Highlighted consequences of this involvement have included higher utility prices following privatizations and lower levels of job security following deregulation of labour markets. Finally, more widely, there have been consistent arguments in the critical literature that consultants are 'witch-doctors' or 'snake-oil salesmen' who sell clients overpriced and ineffective (repackaged) solutions. However, there is also considerable evidence of clients becoming significantly more sophisticated and adept in their purchasing and use of consultancy, making their characterization as 'victims' less credible.

Ethical considerations aside, the consulting industry reflects and contributes to a number of wider sociological and management themes. Consultancies are, for example, central in the development and dissemination of management ideas, and thus provide fertile ground for those interested in understanding knowledge dynamics. Consultants themselves not only manifest an ambiguous and dynamic skill-set, but are also increasingly the model for managers in non-consulting organizations. This makes the industry useful to those interested in the changing boundaries between consultants and clients. Finally, as management consultancies can be described as professional service firms, knowledge-intensive firms and also a 'weak' profession, they provide an interesting arena for a number of academics examining the changing structures which constrain and enable modern work.

JOE O'MAHONEY

See also:

Knowledge worker; Management; Professionalism.

References and selected further readings

Kipping, M. and T. Clark (eds), *The Oxford Handbook of Management Consulting*, Oxford: Oxford University Press.
O'Mahoney, J. and C. Markham (2013), *Management Consulting*, Oxford: Oxford University Press.
Saint-Martin, D. (2004), *Building the New Managerialist State: Consultants and the Politics of Public Sector Reform in Comparative Perspective*, Oxford: Oxford University Press.
Sturdy, A., K. Handley, T. Clark and R. Fincham (2009), *Management Consultancy: Boundaries and Knowledge in Action*, Oxford: Oxford University Press.

Management development

Management development is a contested term in both practitioner and academic worlds and an ambiguous concept that is variously defined. How it is defined depends on whether one assumes that it exists in an objective sense or whether it is viewed as a concept shaped by context (Lees, 1992). It is also a term that is more frequently used in Anglo-Saxon countries such as the UK, Ireland, Australia and New Zealand. Outside of these countries the more frequently used term is 'leadership development'.

In general, definitions of management development emphasize a number of dimensions:

- It is concerned with enhancing the effectiveness of managers to contribute to organizational performance.
- It is a future-oriented activity that is used to grow an organization's managerial expertise.
- It encompasses both formal and informal learning experiences, structured and unstructured experiences and learning derived from the role, from relationships and formal classroom development.
- It is a process that continually shapes and is shaped by the organizational context in which it is enacted.

Management development is typically presented as a value-free activity with very little exploration or understanding of how it contributes to individual and organizational effectiveness. Lees (1992) proposed that management development has as its core three intersecting variables: individual career, organizational succession and organizational performance. There is considerable difficulty in achieving alignment between these concepts. In reality, it is very difficult to achieve all of these purposes. Furthermore, organizations invest in management development for an assortment of reasons, many of which are in conflict with each other. Storey (1990) suggested that management development is provided to achieve five broad objectives: (a) engineer and manage organizational cultural change; (b) pursue quality improvement, cost reduction and profitability; (c) structure and change attitudes and embed organizational values; (d) develop a common identity and approach and (e) broaden the roles of line managers. These purposes or objectives emphasize a functional performance perspective. Functionalist perspectives assume a strong alignment between management development and performance; however, research demonstrating the performance link is scarce. Management development operates at the individual manager level with the assumption that the managerial competencies developed translate into team and organizational performance.

Most definitions view management development as an activity that is driven by organizational rather than individual manager needs. It is assumed that organizations can identify in a mechanistic fashion the priority development needs and match these against appropriate development strategies to result in performance improvement that can be evaluated in an objective way. As a result, management development operates in a closed loop with organizations investing in development activities that are perceived to enhance performance. The primacy of organizational needs reflects the strong unitarist underpinnings of many conceptualizations of management development. Definitions have traditionally given priority to the formal, planned and deliberate dimensions of management. Managers are typically viewed as resources that can be developed and who can contribute to business performance. Rigg (2007) calls this the 'technocrat perspective', whereby management development is viewed as an activity or process that enhances managerial capabilities.

Definitions of management development have traditionally ignored issues of power and policies and given little emphasis to the reality that managers are 'individuals with power to generate meanings or make significant contributions to how learning happens in organisations' (Cullen and Turnbull, 2005, p. 337). Recent scholarship has started to engage with the inherent tensions in management development and the blurring of the lines with related concepts such as management learning and management education. However, many consider the emphasis on the delineation between these concepts not to be a very fruitful line of investigation. Therefore, conceptions of management development may include education and learning components.

THOMAS GARAVAN

See also:

Human resource development; Personal development plan.

References and selected further readings

Cullen J. and S. Turnbull (2005), A meta-review of the management development literature, *Human Resource Development Review*, **4**(3), pp. 335–355.

Garavan, T.N., B. Barnicle and T. O'Suilleabhain (1999), Management development: contemporary trends, issues and strategies, *Journal of European Industrial Training*, **23**(4), pp. 191–207.

Garavan, T.N., C. Hogan and A. Cahir-O'Donnell (2009), *Developing Managers and Leaders; Perspectives, Debates and Practices in Ireland*, Dublin: Gill & Macmillan.

Lees, S. (1992), Ten faces of management development, *Management Education and Development*, **23**(2), pp. 89–105.

Rigg, C. (2007), Corporate technocrats or world stewards? What's the point of management development? in R. Hill and J. Stewart (eds), *Management Development: Perspectives from Research and Practice*, London: Routledge.

Storey, J. (1990), Management development: a literature review and implications for future research – part ii: profiles and contexts, *Personnel Review*, **19**(1), pp. 3–11.

Management style

Management style is essentially the way in which a manager exercises authority and power in the workplace. The idea of management style began with the work of Lewin (Lewin et al., 1939). For Lewin, management style tended to distil into three main types: autocratic, democratic and laissez-faire. The autocrat practised top-down decision-making, allowing little or no involvement by subordinates. The democrat tended towards involving subordinates in a participative form of decision-making, and the laissez-faire approach allowed more freedom for subordinates to make their own decisions.

Following Lewin, the discussion and debate about management styles has gone through several phases. In the 1950s, management thinking centred on interpretations of human nature. There were those managers who believed workers to be indolent and to dislike work. Such workers needed to be controlled and directed, if the business was to be successful. Managers with a more optimistic view of human nature viewed workers as willing partners in a cooperative enterprise. These workers were seen as creative and enthusiastic participants in an enterprise that afforded them respect and recognition. This encouraged a more consultative and participative management style.

By the 1970s the issue of trust in the workplace was assuming increasing importance. The idea that there were 'high-trust' and 'low-trust' relationships in the workplace helped throw a further insight into the troubled world of employee relations. It was realized that high-trust workplaces tended to be linked with levels of high-discretion for the worker – allowing the worker choice in how the task was completed. Low-trust relations were linked with workplaces where low-discretion was the norm, and workers were subject to control and direction on the job.

These notions were used as the basis for the ideas that emerged initially in the work of Purcell and Sisson (1983). There were five styles that helped explain the approaches and behaviours managers might employ: the *traditionalist* who tended to exploit workers and avoid engagement with trade unions, the *sophisticated paternalist* who still avoided trade unions, but nevertheless treated workers with a degree of benevolence, the *sophisticated modern (constitutionalist)* who engaged with trade unions through forms of collective bargaining, the *sophisticated modern (consultative)* who again recognized trade unions, but preferred more consultative forms of engagement, and the *standard modern* who engaged with trade unions reluctantly, and in a fire-fighting fashion.

Later, it was suggested that these ideas could be viewed through the prism of two dimensions. *Individualism* focused on the worker as an individual, and the ways in which his or her capacity to work could be fulfilled. The *collectivist* dimension recognized the essentially social nature of the workplace, and sought ways of engaging with the work group through their trade unions or in other ways.

Today, HRM thinking on management style prefers consultative and participative approaches. Traditional approaches based on 'command and control' appear less persuasive, with more democratic approaches much more appealing. Nevertheless, practices will always vary, dependent to a large extent on the current climate, organisational environment and individual circumstance.

JOHN KIMBERLEY

See also:

Collectivism; Industrial relations; Power.

References and selected further readings

Fox, A. (1974), *Beyond Contract: Work, Power and Trust Relations*, London: Faber and Faber.
Lewin, K., R. Lippit and R.K. White (1939), Patterns of aggressive behavior in experimentally created social climates, *Journal of Social Psychology*, **10**, pp. 271–301.
McGregor, D. (1960), *The Human Side of Enterprise*, New York: McGraw-Hill.
Purcell, J. (1987), Mapping management styles in employee relations, *Journal of Management Studies*, **24**, pp. 533–548.
Purcell, J. and K. Sisson (1983), Strategies and practice in the management of industrial relations, in G. Bain (ed.), *Industrial Relations in Britain*, Oxford: Blackwell.

Managerial control

Control in the context of the employment relationship refers both to the requirement for management to secure profitable or otherwise productive outcomes from the labour it hires and sets to work, and the various methods and strategies for doing so. With its unitarist bias towards assumptions of common goals and interests, control is not a prominent feature in HRM. Yet it is implicit within discussion of issues such as performance management or managerial styles.

The conceptual vocabulary and associated research with respect to control tends to come from labour process theory (LPT). To emphasize that it is a structural pressure on management to ensure the purchase of labour power is converted to profitable labour, LPT refers to a control imperative. However, that is qualified in two ways. First the imperative does not specify the type, means or level of control. Second, it is never complete as the assertion of worker interests or identities in forms of negotiation or resistance results in a 'frontier' of control.

To take account of such variations and their causes, LPT and other commentators distinguishes between direct and detailed controls (over work tasks, enforced by supervisors), and general or indirect controls (for example, over who is recruited or by achieving targets irrespective of how). In his book *Contested Terrain*, Richard Edwards (1979) identified two of the most significant and innovative managerial strategies. Technical control refers to the design of work embedded in the physical apparatus of production to pace, sequence and monitor the work, such as through the assembly line or automatic call distribution systems in customer contact centres. Meanwhile, bureaucratic control focuses on accountability within the chain of command and the exercise of authority through depersonalized rules through the rules, procedures, codes or service scripts.

As market conditions have changed in recent decades, employment relations researchers have tried to understand how control practices have evolved. Some of the sharpest debates have been between LPT and followers of Foucault or poststructuralists. The latter (for example, Sewell 1998) have argued that there has been a shift in the locus of control towards combinations of electronic surveillance and normative or identity-based managerial interventions. LPT has disputed the extent and effectiveness of such practices and highlighted the pervasiveness of traditional target-driven methods associated with performance management. There is, however, some common ground. It is widely accepted that managerial controls have expanding their scope and coverage, whether this is the kinds of rules and scripts underpinning emotional and aesthetic labour or audits of professional employees.

PAUL THOMPSON

See also:

Labour process/theory; Performance management; Resistance.

References and selected further reading

Edwards, R. (1979), *Contested Terrain: The Transformation of the Workplace in the Twentieth Century*, London: Heinemann.
Reed, M. (2010), Control in contemporary work organizations, in P. Blyton, E. Heery and P. Turnbull (eds), *Reassessing the Employment Relationship*, Basingstoke: Palgrave Macmillan, pp.41–70.
Ritzer, G. (1993), *The McDonaldization of Society*, London: Pine Forge Press.
Sewell, G. (1998), The discipline of teams: the control of team-based industrial work through electronic and peer surveillance, *Administrative Science Quarterly*, **43**(2), pp.406–469.
Thompson, P. and D. van den Broek (2010), Managerial control and workplace regimes: an introduction, *Work Employment and Society*, **24**(3), pp.1–12.

Maslow: hierarchy of needs

Abraham Maslow's hierarchy of needs is possibly one of the most recognized concepts in management training and development, and continues to be popular some 70 years after its original publication. This theory, usually presented as a triangle, offers a seemingly intuitive concept makes it one of the most enduring – but also potentially misunderstood – concepts in management theory.

Maslow (1943) claimed that there are five basic needs:

- Physiological – these are the basic needs for survival such as food and drink, particularly those that bring comfort.
- Safety needs – feeling physically safe and secure.
- Love needs – feeling love, affection and belonging – missing friends or family.
- Esteem needs – desire for self-respect and for the esteem of others.
- Self-actualization – self-fulfilment – doing what the person is fitted for.

For Maslow these needs exist in a hierarchy, where one needs to satisfy the lowest need before the next one emerges. For instance the person who is really hungry will be completely conscious of this need and will put all their efforts into satisfying their hunger and therefore anything that does not fulfil this need is dormant. Maslow claims the desire to write poetry, or buy new shoes would be forgotten or of secondary importance for someone who is hungry. Once one level of needs is met then the next level emerges. They unfold sequentially until the top layer, self-actualization, is met.

They were first applied to the workplace by Davis (1957), who sought to connect these layers to how workers would be motivated. Therefore a worker would need to be paid enough to be able to eat and pay rent, so might take on any job (physiological need). Once these basic needs are met, they might want job security (safety needs). When a level of safety is reached, they might be move motivated by belonging to the organization and being part of a team (social needs). As the social needs are met, a positive word from the boss or undertaking a personal project might boost esteem (esteem needs). Finally, achieving ones potential at work might achieve self-fulfilment (self-actualization).

Maslow's work does reveal that people might be motivated by different factors, depending on their circumstances. It also shows that motivation is not fixed and that a purely transactional approach (you only work for money) is not sufficient to understand motivation. It also helped to pave the way for a more people-centred approach to management.

However, Maslow's concepts, and particularly how they are applied to management, have also been heavily criticized. Self-actualization has often been misunderstood as linked to promotion in an organization rather than achieving self-fulfilment as Maslow presented it. It is not proved by experience; many artists might be working for self-actualization while at the same time struggling to pay their rent.

The theoretical foundations are also questioned. Cullen and Gotell (2002) argue Maslow's research was based on interviewing young college women's sexual behaviour, and asserts the naturalness of female submission. Cullen (1997) also argues Maslow's early work on monkeys and apes reinforces hierarchy, by claiming that an individual's ability to dominate others was due to their superiority, thereby justifying management power.

DANIEL KING

See also:
Herzberg: motivators and hygiene factors; McGregor; Motivation.

References and selected further readings
Cullen, D. (1997), Maslow, monkeys and motivation theory, *Organization*, **4**(3), pp. 355–373.
Cullen, D. and L. Gotell (2002), From orgasms to organizations: Maslow, women's sexuality and the gendered foundations of the needs hierarchy, *Gender, Work & Organization*, **9**(5), pp. 537–555.
Davis, K. (1957), *Human Relations in Business*, New York: McGraw-Hill.
Maslow, A.H. (1943), A theory of human motivation, *Psychological Review*, **50**(4), pp. 370–396.

Master of Business Administration

The Master of Business Administration (MBA) arose in the nineteenth century in the USA (see Khurana, 2007). At that time, the joint-stock corporation had emerged as a device to raise funding for major infrastructure projects that were beyond the scope of the owner-managed firm. These corporations employed thousands of people across multiple locations, and in so doing required a new type of employee, the corporate administrator. These administrators had the power to guide a company towards increased revenues and profits, while also serving workers by helping to create increased employment and wealth opportunities (see Cummings, 2005; Khurana, 2007). However, these administrators could also make ill-informed decisions creating adverse impacts on societal, business, and personal welfare. Thus their administrative and managerial competence was critical. Given this power and responsibility, a challenge was to ensure these individuals become professionalized, and in response the MBA emerged as an offering in universities. MBAs were conceived as general management degrees that would provide an understanding of key business functions to individuals that may not have studied business at undergraduate level in a university; in turn enabling them to become effective leaders. To deliver the general understanding, MBAs typically cover standard business functions such as marketing, accounting, finance, people management (or HRM), strategy and operations.

During the latter half of the twentieth century, MBAs were lamented as having too overt a focus on profit maximization and ignoring the concomitant risks this focus has on society (see Datar et al., 2010; Mintzberg and Gosling, 2002; Pierson, 1959; Whitney, 1970). Given this criticism, MBAs began changing to include subjects on business ethics, leadership, responsibility and the consideration of human wellbeing, in order to fully recognize that the welfare of an organization is linked to the welfare of society. While this move is positive, a challenge with this approach is that it can still treat ethics, human and societal impacts as if they are just another category to deal with after making money, as opposed to being foundational. Given this and the challenges of the twenty-first century (rising population, climate change and environmental stresses) truly progressive programmes are ensuring a human and societal focus is understood as the fundamental context. Further programmes are now becoming accessible digitally, to recognize the changing delivery landscape for education and the requirements from students that their studies fit their working lives.

NICK BARTER

Reference list and selected further readings

Cummings, S. (2005), *Recreating Strategy*, London: Sage.
Datar, S.M., D.A. Garvin and P.G. Cullen (2010), *Rethinking the MBA: Business Education at a Crossroads*, Cambridge, MA: Harvard Business Press.
Khurana, R. (2007), *From Higher Aims to Hired Hands*, Princeton: Princeton University Press.
Mintzberg, H. and J. Gosling (2002), Educating managers beyond borders, *Academy of Management Learning & Education*, **1**(1), pp. 64–76.
Pierson, F.C. (1959), *The Education of American Businessmen: A Study of University-College Programs in Business Administration*, New York: McGraw-Hill.
Whitney, E.P. (1970), Business education at the crossroads, *The Journal of Business Education*, **45**(8), pp. 312–313.

Maternity, paternity and parental leave

The terms 'maternity leave', 'paternity leave' and 'parental leave' refer to either a statutory entitlement, a company policy or a union-negotiated provision to enable a mother or father to be absent from work for a period of time when a child is born. (Adoption leave is also often covered by the same terms.) In most cases, it is assumed that the leave is accompanied by a job guarantee. Countries and companies differ in relation to whether or not the name of the leave is gender-specific, that is, whether it is referred to as maternity leave (for mothers only), paternity leave (for fathers only) or parental leave (for either parent).

In almost all countries, legislation providing leave from employment for mothers at and around childbirth was introduced first. In some cases this was followed by a more gender-neutral policy and nomenclature, such as 'parental leave'. The term 'primary carer leave' is now also being adopted. In many countries, specific leave for fathers, 'paternity leave', followed the introduction of maternity leave. The early objective of maternity leave was to encourage procreation, to promote and protect maternal and infant health and to allow for the establishment and continuation of breast-feeding. Paternity leave is typically available exclusively to fathers and is intended to enable the father to spend time with his new child and partner. More recent policy debates have given greater attention to two other objectives of maternity, paternity and parental leave (a) to increase women's labour force participation and (b) to improve gender equity by providing men with more opportunity and incentive to share with childrearing.

Around the globe, there is significant variation in the architecture of maternity, paternity and parental leave schemes, but two key characteristics of all schemes are the duration of leave and the level of payment. The total duration of maternity leave tends to range from 12 weeks to 12 months. Paternity leave periods are generally shorter, from two weeks to 12 weeks. However, in some contexts, parental leave is considered separate to maternity and paternity leaves and generally refers to periods of leave from work to enable time off to care during the child's pre-school years. Funding is usually derived from government revenue or social insurance systems. Pay levels vary widely from flat payments, to percentage payments or combinations of percentage and flat payments. Greater gender equality is achieved if the maternity or parental leave payment is at full income replacement levels.

Employers and organizations may also introduce their own specific parental leave policies, either through managerial prerogative or as a result of union collective bargaining. These often co-exist with or supplement government schemes. The aims of these organizationally specific policies are to increase the attraction and retention of skilled female employees, to assist working parents to achieve better work and family balance and to differentiate the organization in the market place as an 'employer of choice'. Overall, in the past few decades there has been considerable development of maternity, paternity and parental leave policies at both national and organizational levels, reflecting the change in workforce demographics and social norms around parenting and work.

MARIAN BAIRD

See also:

Absence; Benefits; Collective bargaining.

References and selected further readings

Baird, M. and M. O'Brien (2015), Dynamics of parental leave in Anglophone countries: the paradox of state expansion in liberal welfare regimes, *Community, Work and Family*.
Kamerman, S. and P. Moss (eds) (2009), *The Politics of Parental Leave Policies*, Bristol: Policy Press.
Moss, P. (ed.) (2014), *International Review of Leave Policies and Research 2014*, www.leavenetwork.org/lp_and_r_reports.
Ray, R., J.C. Gornick and J. Schmitt (2010), Who cares? Assessing generosity and gender equality in parental leave policy designs in 21 countries, *Journal of European Social Policy*, **20**, pp.196–216.

McGregor

Douglas McGregor is best known for his concept of human motivation embedded within his 'Theory X and Theory Y' view of employees. His classic text was *The Human Side of Enterprise*.

McGregor puts forward two competing views of how to manage organizations and the underlying beliefs of human nature. The first is Theory X, and is based on the belief that management is responsible for controlling the organization to work towards economic ends; management direct, motivate and control and modify employees behaviour to fit the needs of the organization; and without the active intervention of management, most people would not serve the organization's needs. Management's role is getting things done through people. The underlying assumptions of human nature are that people dislike work, are lazy, need to be told what to do, lack ambition and see money as the prime motivation for work. This view of people is common in classical views of management, particularly as epitomized by theorists such as Frederick Taylor. As such it creates a management style of reward or punishment, close supervision of the workforce and using money as the central form of motivation. This 'carrot and stick' approach, McGregor states, only works when a worker is seeking to fulfil his/her lower needs (on Maslow's hierarchy of needs), but is inadequate when a person is seeking to reach the higher needs.

The opposite assumption is what he called Theory Y. This perspective still sees the management role as organizing production for achieving profit but it has different attitudes to human nature. Theory Y view sees work as natural as rest or play, that people want to be self-directing, enjoy taking responsibility, have imagination and creativity. This view of managing people, McGregor states, is about creating opportunities, removing barriers and providing guidance to allow people to grow. Theory Y is therefore more about coaching and supporting individuals in their development. Individuals should therefore achieve their own personal growth and meet the organization's ends.

Which view of human nature is correct? McGregor states that at the time he was writing (the early 1960s), Theory X is probably right. This is not because this is how people have to be, but, McGregor argues because people have been managed in a Theory X way, particularly through Frederick Taylor's scientific management, which resulted in workers learning to act and behave in particular ways. Theory X management style has resulted in people not wanting to take responsibility, to have become passive and have not utilized their capacities. In other words they have learnt to act, behave and think in passive ways because they have been managed in a Theory X manner. However, given the right help and support, and changes in management style, McGregor argued people can become Theory Y. However it will not be easy and require changes in attitudes by both workers and managers alike.

McGregor's opposition between Theory X and Y might be a little simplistic but it does have some important implications. First, it challenges some of the Taylorist assumptions about management, arguing for a Theory Y perspective, particularly by arguing it results in a substantial loss in human potential. Second, it argues that human nature is not fixed but is conditioned by the environment they are in. Finally McGregor's view of management anticipated many of the ways of organizing (particularly through decentralized organization and consultative management style), which have become more popular in recent years.

DANIEL KING

See also:

Management style; Maslow: hierarchy of needs; Motivation; Scientific management.

References and selected further readings

McGregor, D. (1960), *The Human Side of Enterprise*, New York: McGraw-Hill.

Mediation

Mediation is an alternative dispute resolution process in which an independent third party assists 'interacting parties' (Wall and Dunne, 2012). Various models exist, although the dominant approach in the workplace context is 'facilitative', where the mediator helps parties in conflict identify and explore issues and consider options for settlement. In this guise it has strong similarities with conciliation. In contrast, Bush and Folger's (1994) 'transformative' model – most famously used in the US Postal Service – emphasizes equipping parties to manage conflict through 'empowerment' and 'recognition' shifts, with resolution largely a by-product. While flexible, mediation is typically a structured process, often conducted in a single day, with individual meetings followed by a joint meeting.

Evidence suggests mediation provision is almost ubiquitous in larger US organizations, and has gained significant traction elsewhere. Among its benefits in the workplace context, proponents point to high settlement and satisfaction rates (with process, mediator(s) and outcomes), and advantages in terms of speed, cost, confidentiality and preservation of relationships compared with more adversarial processes such as grievances or litigation. However, such claims are subject to caveats around the potential for (self-) selection effects and the absence of any counterfactual. There are also challenges for practice including the potential for employees to feel obliged to participate, the resilience of outcomes, resistance from both managers and employees, reputational fragility, and for conflict to be viewed as a transactional rather than strategic issue (Saundry et al., 2014).

Current research continues to focus on quantifying the benefits of mediation, a challenge being the absence of a single, accepted measure of success and the more retrospective and often descriptive nature of much of the evidence. The last is at least partly a function of small numbers of mediations in all but the very largest organizations. There remains ongoing debate too about notions of (im)partiality, neutrality and power (linked to whether mediation is provided in-house or by external providers), fairness and justice, mediator styles and values and how these might shape practice, as well as the relative merits of particular techniques and approaches and how mediators draw on and potentially combine/integrate these.

PAUL LATREILLE

See also:

Alternative dispute resolution; Arbitration; Conciliation; Employment tribunal.

References and selected further readings

Bingham, L.B. (2003), Mediation at work: transforming workplace conflict at the United States Postal Service, *Washington, DC IBM Centre for the Business of Government*, pp. 1–46.

Bush, R. and J. Folger (1994), *The Promise of Mediation: Responding to Conflict Through Empowerment and Recognition*, San Francisco: Jossey-Bass.

Coben, J.R. (2004), Gollum, meet Smeagol: a schizophrenic rumination on mediator values beyond self-determination and neutrality, *Cardozo Journal of Conflict Resolution*, **5**, pp. 65–86.
Saundry, R., T. Bennett and G. Wibberley (2013), *Workplace Mediation: The Participant Experience*, Advisory, Conciliation and Arbitration Service Research Papers, no. 02/13.
Saundry, R., P. Latreille, L. Dickens, C. Irvine, P. Teague, P. Urwin and G. Wibberley (2014), *Reframing Resolution — Managing Conflict and Resolving Individual Employment Disputes in the Contemporary Workplace*, Advisory, Conciliation and Arbitration Service Policy Series.
Wall, J.A. and T.C. Dunne (2012), Mediation research: a current review, *Negotiation Journal*, **28**(2), pp. 217–244.

Mentoring

Mentoring originates in ancient Greek and specifically in Homer's Odyssey. In the sizable epic poem, Mentor was the elder tutor of young Telemachus, acting as a wise advisor and responsible for the latter's education and guidance. At present, mentoring is used in a similar vein in diverse settings, including education and business. In the workplace, it may be defined as the practice whereby an experienced employee partners up with a more junior employee (protégé or mentee) in order to offer guidance, advice and access to networking opportunities with the aim to support the protégé's personal development and career progression. When entering a mentoring relationship, no specific developmental targets are set, but the objectives are broad and general. In this regard, mentoring has a rather medium to long-term timeframe.

Mentoring as a developmental practice is used to help high-flyer employees identify a long-term career development plan within the organization and thus it facilitates talent retention. In addition, it enables effective transfer of implicit and explicit knowledge, while it helps in promoting a culture of trust and understanding. Further still, mentoring is beneficial for both individuals involved. The protégé not only receives honest advice and guidance from an experienced member, but also develops a better understanding of the business and self. The mentor may give the protégé access to a pool of key contacts and thus constructive exposure to other senior practitioners. Moreover, the mentor could act as a role model, inspiring the employee to follow a similar career trajectory. In return, the mentor draws satisfaction from passing on knowledge and experiences to newer members of the organization, while gaining a great understanding of the organizational environment in junior positions. Working with a protégé may also help a mentor improve their people skills.

Despite the benefits, mentoring is not panacea. Effective implementation of the practice necessitates thorough assessment of the mentor–protégé compatibility as well as discretionary participation of both members. Furthermore, substantial consideration should be given to budget and other resource allocation, as they may hinder the successful implementation of the practice. For instance, when there is no time allowance for mentoring in the work schedule of either the mentor or protégé, they will feel pressurized and may eventually have to cancel or withdraw from the mentoring relationship.

Since the seminal work of Kram (1985) on workplace mentoring, research has found that mentoring is linked to diverse employee outcomes, such as job satisfaction, career promotion, salary and career expectations. However, a holistic appreciation of the practice necessitates research that expands beyond employee outcomes and examines cross-cultural differences, longitudinal designs and the linkages of mentoring with psychosocial properties.

MARGARITA NYFOUDI

See also:
Careers; Continuing professional development; Retention; Succession planning; Talent management.

References and selected further readings

Kram, K.E. (1985), *Mentoring at Work: Developmental Relationships in Organisational Life*, Glenview: Scott Foresman.
Lankau, M.J. and T.A. Scandura (2002), An investigation of personal learning in mentoring relationships: content, antecedents, and consequences, *Academy of Management Journal*, **45**(4), pp. 779–790.

Migrant worker

Migrant workers are people who have migrated to another country in search of better job opportunities and lifestyle. Migrant workers may enter foreign countries through formal immigration programmes (e.g., skilled, humanitarian) or illegally. Many countries are faced with significant issues regarding migrant workers due to the increasing numbers of people moving from their home country. International migration has increased from approximately 75 million people spread over 30 different countries in 1960, to around 191 million people spread across 64 countries in 2005 (McGovern, 2007). Today, around 232 million people are living away from their country of origin, totalling just over 3 per cent of the global population.

While many migrants migrate in the hope of seeking better employment prospects, many – particularly those from non-English-speaking background (NESB) countries – do not find comparable employment in their new home labour market. They experience a lack of recognition of their qualifications and their pre-migration work experience by employers and can also experience language barriers. Such problems can lead migrants towards experiencing social inequality, marginalization and exclusion within local labour markets (Ressia, 2010). Pioch (2004) argues that occupational segregation is evident between national and migrant workers. In European labour markets, migrants are overrepresented within vulnerable and low-paid sectors. Such examples can be found in the hospitality sector, as well as in occupations such as manufacturing and construction. Many argue that migrant workers are more likely to be excluded from occupations such as agriculture and fishing, education, health and community services, wholesale and retail trade, and public administration (Hopkins, 2012; Pioch, 2004). The growth of service-based industries and the decline of the manufacturing sector has also directly impacted workers from more vulnerable backgrounds, particularly in the case of NESB migrants living in western countries. In addition, migrant women tend to experience higher unemployment levels than migrant men due to a range of social factors.

SUSAN RESSIA

See also:
Expatriate; Immigration; Labour mobility.

References and selected further readings

Chiswick, B.R., Y.L. Lee and P.W. Miller (2005), A longitudinal analysis of immigrant occupational mobility: a test of the immigrant assimilation hypothesis, *International Migration Review*, **2**, pp. 332–353.

Hopkins, B. (2012), Inclusion of a diverse workforce in the UK: the case of the EU expansion, *Equality, Diversity and Inclusion: An International Journal*, **31**(4), pp. 379–390.

Liversage, A. (2009), Vital conjunctures, shifting horizons: high-skilled female immigrants looking for work, *Work, Employment & Society*, **23**(1), pp. 120–141.

McGovern, P. (2007), Immigration, labour markets and employment relations: problems and prospects, *British Journal of Industrial Relations*, **45**(2), pp. 217–235.

Pioch, R. (2004), Transnational labour markets, citizenship and welfare state reforms, in P. Littlewood, I. Glorieux and I. Jonsson (eds), *The Future of Work in Europe*, Aldershot: Ashgate Publishing, pp. 49–63.

Ressia, S. (2010), Starting from scratch: skilled dual-career migrant couples and their search for employment in Southeast Queensland, *International Journal of Employment Studies*, **18**(1), pp. 63–88.

Minimum wage

A minimum wage is generally defined as the wage floor applying to all workers to ensure they receive a minimum level of pay protection. It is a core labour market institution used in the majority of countries in the world and is an important instrument of both economic and social policy.

Minimum wages are implemented in a variety of forms distinguished by (a) statutory rule or collective bargaining and (b) single or multiple rates (Eyraud and Saget 2005). The most common form is a single (national) statutory rate where the state is the key decision-maker, although trade unions and employer associations may be consulted. Many countries set lower rates for young workers. Governments may also set multiple rates that vary by sector, occupation or region. Regional minima in China, for example, reflect a tradition of regional autonomy as well as differences in living standards.

Some countries set minimum wages through collective bargaining rather than legislation – including Sweden and Italy, as well as Germany until 2015. While raising the political status of social dialogue, to be effective this institutional form relies upon wide coverage of collective bargaining agreements. Problems of coverage caused unions in Germany to call for a new statutory national minimum wage (from 2015) as a better way to protect workers in very low-paid jobs outside collective agreement protection.

The operationalization of a minimum wage is often a source of conflict among employers, unions and governments. Employers may oppose a minimum wage rise because it interferes with autonomous wage-setting, but equally may welcome it as part of a quality-enhancing approach to work organization. Unions are likely to support a minimum wage as a core labour standard protecting against exploitative pay. However, pitched too low, they may worry it might pull down wages in low paid sectors and pitched too high that it interferes with collective bargaining. Finally, governments face competing pressures with respect to minimum wages ranging from inflation and job growth targets to efforts to combat 'parasitic employers' and poverty among workers.

Most academic studies of the minimum wage have focused on its employment effects. Until the mid-1990s, most economics research claimed minimum wages caused unemployment. With improved statistical methods, better computer technology and revised theoretical models, a new wave of analyses show that minimum wage rises have insignificant effects on employment – whether measured as the number of jobs, hours or people working.

Fewer studies have investigated what is arguably the primary purpose of a minimum wage – its distributive effects. Most evidence shows that the higher the value of a country's minimum wage, the lower the incidence of low-paid work. However, the complementarity of minimum wages with other wage-setting institutions (especially collective bargaining) shapes the results; for example, a high-value minimum wage alongside weak collective bargaining may compress the bottom half of the wage distribution and sustain a high incidence of workers paid at or just above the minimum wage as has occurred in the UK. Finally, because women are overrepresented in low-paid employment, higher minimum wages tend to have a positive effect on gender pay equity.

DAMIAN GRIMSHAW

See also:

Collective bargaining; Low pay; State.

References and selected further readings

Brown, W. (2009), The process of fixing the British national minimum wage, 1997–2007, *British Journal of Industrial Relations*, **47**(2), pp. 429–443.

Eyraud, F. and C. Saget (2005), *The Fundamentals of Minimum Wage Fixing*, Geneva: International Labour Organization.

Grimshaw, D. (ed.) (2013), *Minimum Wages, Pay Equity and Comparative Industrial Relations*, London: Routledge.

OECD minimum wage database — includes international data on minimum wage levels relative to average wages, http://stats.oecd.org/Index.aspx?DataSetCode=RMW.

Webb, S. (1912), The economic theory of a legal minimum wage, *Journal of Political Economy*, **20**(10), pp. 973–998.

Misconduct

The expression 'conduct' is found in section 98 of the Employment Rights Act 1996 (ERA). The word 'conduct' is taken to be interchangeable with the term 'misconduct' in this context, but is not defined in the ERA. As such, case law has filled the void. For instance, the courts have held that 'conduct' covers a multitude of sins on the part of the employee. Criminal convictions will fall within its remit, as will incompetence, poor performance and breaches of the employment contract or indiscipline and wilful disobedience of a managerial order. Where an employer suspects that an employee has committed a crime within the workplace and this is the motivation for a dismissal, it must demonstrate that it believed that the employee was guilty of the relevant misconduct at the time it took the decision to dismiss. A genuine, even if mistaken, belief on the part of the employer as to the conduct of the employee relied upon will be sufficient to discharge the burden of establishing misconduct as a reason for dismissal. It should be stressed that evidence of misconduct will not empower an employer to summarily dismiss an employee on the spot on a lawful basis under the common law: it will only be where the employee is guilty of 'gross misconduct' that an employer will be entitled to do so.

The primary significance of the term 'conduct' and 'misconduct' lies in the fact that it qualifies as one of the five available presumptively valid reasons for an employer to dismiss an employee under Part X of the ERA. If the employer can demonstrate that the employee has engaged in bad behaviour, carelessness or poor performance/incompetence, this will satisfy the test of misconduct. The end result is that the dismissal of the employee will be presumed to be valid and the question for the tribunal and court to determine will be whether the employee's dismissal for the reason of misconduct was fair as a matter of substance, and procedurally fair in accordance with a disciplinary procedure.

DAVID CABRELLI

See also:
Disciplinary procedure; Employee; Gross misconduct; Notice period.

References and selected further readings
Collins, H. (1992), *Justice in Dismissal*, London: Clarendon Press.
Elias, P. (1978), Unravelling the concept of dismissal — I and II, *Industrial Law Journal*, 7, pp. 16–29, 100–112.

Motivation

Job performance = ability × motivation. This equation shows that despite an employee's high level of knowledge and skill, job performance will be low if the person has little or no motivation to use it.

A taxonomy of motivation includes seven variables. First, there are needs for physical and psychological wellbeing. Second, there are individual difference variables, such as desire for autonomy, that are rooted in needs. Third, values determine what one considers beneficial and acts to gain or keep. Fourth, the environment including the organizational and job context affects the extent to which needs are met and values are fulfilled. Thus, (a) societal culture, (b) job characteristics and (c) person–job fit must be examined. The fifth is cognition, particularly goals. Goals are situationally specific values, the specific object or aim of an action. Sixth is affect, the form in which one experiences value appraisals. Typically, goal attainment leads to positive affect. Seventh, are rewards. Rewards affect performance to the extent they lead to the setting of, and commitment to, a specific high goal.

Theory in the behavioural sciences provides a framework for HR managers to predict, understand and influence the behaviour of others and themselves. The most frequently used theory of motivation in human resource management is goal-setting theory. This theory was developed from the results of more than 400 studies. Today, there are more than 1,000. The theory states and the data show that a goal is the immediate regulator of behaviour. Moreover, the theory and the data indicate that a specific, high goal leads to higher performance than an easy goal, a vague goal to do one's best or no goal. Given ability, commitment, feedback and the necessary resources, the higher the goal, the higher an employee's or a team's performance. This is because a specific, high goal results in the choice as to where to focus effort and to persist in doing so until the goal is attained. Finally, a specific, high goal cues an employee or team to draw on extant strategies or search for new ones that will result in goal attainment.

As is the case with most HRM practices, there have been arguments as to the optimum method for setting goals. Below are some of the key debates.

1. Should goals be assigned or set participatively with employees? Goals that are assigned with a rationale are as effective for increasing performance as those set participatively given that they are equal in difficulty level. However, employee participation can lead to the setting of goals that are more difficult than those that are assigned unilaterally by a supervisor, and hence higher performance. Participatively set goals can also increase understanding as to optimal ways of performing a task and increase self-efficacy for doing so. Self-set goals have been found to be particularly effective for increasing job attendance. A drawback of self-set goals is that they are often lower than goals assigned or set participatively.

2. Do employees tend to rest on their laurels when the goal is attained? Employees as well as athletes with high self-efficacy typically raise the goal once they attain it.

3. What happens if the goal set is too high? Supervisors who perceive the goals they receive from upper management are too high tend to abuse their subordinates. Ability and adequate resources are critical to the goal-performance relationship. The goal set must be challenging yet attainable.

4. How long do the effects of goal-setting last? Goal setting and feedback on goal progress has been shown to have a positive effect on an individual's and an organization's performance for years.

5. Is a goal for a specific performance outcome always appropriate? No. In the early stages of learning, when ability to perform the task is lacking, urging people to do their best leads to higher performance than the setting of a specific, high performance goal. Even better than a do-best goal is to set a specific, high learning goal where the emphasis is shifted from a performance outcome to discovering a specific number of strategies, processes, or procedures for performing the task effectively.

6. To what extent does personality play a role in goal setting? People who score high on need for achievement tend to set high goals. Similarly, people who score high on conscientiousness tend to set and commit to high goals. That being said, setting goals is an effective motivation strategy for everyone, regardless of their personality.

GARY LATHAM AND JELENA BRCIC

See also:

AMO model; Maslow: hierarchy of needs; McGregor; Reward management.

References and selected further readings

Latham, G.P. (2012), *Work Motivation: History, Theory, Research, and Practice*, 2nd edn, Thousand Oaks, CA: Sage.

Latham, G.P. and E.A. Locke (forthcoming), Goal setting theory: controversies and resolutions, in D. Ones, N. Anderson, C. Viswesvaran and H. Sinangil (eds), *Handbook of Industrial, Work & Organizational Psychology, Vol. 1*, Thousand Oaks, CA: Sage.

Latham, G.P. and C.C. Pinder (2005), Work motivation theory and research at the dawn of the twenty-first century, *Annual Review of Psychology*, **56**, pp. 485–516.

Locke, E.A. and G.P. Latham (eds) (2013), *New Developments in Goal Setting And Task Performance*, New York: Routledge.

Multinational companies

A multinational company or a multinational corporation (MNC) or a multinational enterprise (MNE) is an organization that operates in several countries. It is mainly managed from its headquarters based in the parent country, but there are cases where strategic decisions can be delegated to head offices in other countries. There are mainly four categories of MNCs: (1) a multinational, decentralized organization with strong home country presence; (2) a global, centralized organization that acquires centralized production in order to reduce operational costs; (3) an international company that is based on its knowledge capabilities and technology; and (4) a transnational organization that combines all the aforementioned features.

International human resource management (IHRM) theory suggests a specific four-fold typology to explain the relationship between the headquarters of a MNC and its subsidiaries:

- **The ethnocentric MNC**: these corporations are home-country-oriented. Their managers believe that home-country nationals are more intelligent, reliable and trustworthy than foreign nationals.
- **The polycentric MNC**: these are host-country-oriented corporations. Profit potential is seen in a foreign country, but the foreign market is too hard to understand.
- **The region-centric MNC**: these organizations capitalize on the synergistic benefits of sharing common functions across regions. A region-centric corporation believes that only regional insiders can effectively co-ordinate functions within the region.
- **The geocentric MNC**: these are world-oriented, geocentric corporations. Their ultimate goal is to create an integrated system with a worldwide approach. Subsidiaries are no longer satellites, but independent city-states.

MNCs have become global economic actors and influence drastically the economic, social and political environments. As global actors, MNCs have various advantages, such as promotion of employment opportunities, transfer of expertise and knowledge across countries and formation of economies of scale. Despite these advantages, MNCs have accepted a lot of criticism mainly related to their practices applied in developing countries. In particular, they have been accused of exploiting the workforce and/or the environment. For example, the jobs they create are repetitive assembly-line type jobs described as low-paid (below minimum wage) and demanding (long hours). Moreover, they have been accused of trying to influence national governments in order to avoid taxes, get deals on workforce (wages) or overheads (land, rent and rates) and pollution/clean-up deals and consequently to gain competitive advantage over small and medium-sized enterprises (SMEs).

ALEXANDROS PSYCHOGIOS

See also:

Globalization; International human resource management; National culture.

References and selected further readings

Edwards, T. and C. Rees (2011), *International Human Resource Management: Globalization, National Systems and Multinational Companies*, 2nd edn, Harlow: Pearson.

Farndale, E., J. Paauwe, S.S. Morris, G.K. Stahl, P. Stiles, J. Trevor, and P.M. Wright (2010), Context-bound configurations of corporate HR functions in multinational corporations, *Human Resource Management*, **49**(1), pp.45–66.

Ferner, A. and J. Quintanilla (1998), Multinationals, national business systems and HRM: the enduring influence of national identity or a process of Anglo-Saxonisation, *The International Journal of Human Resource Management*, **9**(4), pp.710–731.

Ferner, A., J. Quintanilla and M.Z. Varul (2001), Country-of-origin effects, host-country effects, and the management of HR in multinationals: German companies in Britain and Spain, *Journal of World Business*, **36**(2), pp.107–127.

Schmitt, M. and D. Sadowski (2003), A cost-minimization approach to the international transfer of HRM/IR practices: Anglo-Saxon multinationals in the Federal Republic of Germany, *International Journal of Human Resource Management*, **14**(3), pp.409–430.

Multi-skilling

'Multi-skilling' is a workforce strategy based on worker flexibility. It is defined as the acquisition of knowledge, skills, abilities and other personal characteristics (KSAOs), which enable employees to perform tasks outside their initial job description. Multi-skilling allows employees to undertake a number of different jobs and it facilitates covering for each other which results in increased workplace flexibility. The concept of multi-skilling is based on the emergence of skill-based human resource management (Lawler and Ledford, 1992). Environmental, economic and organizational drivers were at the origin of the competency approach largely introduced, for example, in French organizations in the 1990s (MEDEF, 1998). Managing employability and employees' careers became a priority for human resource (HR) professionals.

Different categories of labour flexibility can be identified (Chen and Wallace, 2011). Functional flexibility covers to what extent employees can be shifted to different activities and tasks within an organization. Job rotation is an example of this form of flexibility. Numerical flexibility helps organizations to cope with seasonal peaks or large orders. The use of a contingent workforce – such as temporary workers, seasonal workers, freelancers and fixed-term contracts – helps to overcome an important influx of work. Some industries, such as construction or the hospitality industry, are well-known for adopting multi-skilling as a workforce strategy (Gomar et al., 2002). Labour flexibility via multi-skilling allows organizations to match labour demand and supply more efficiently.

Multi-skilling has several advantages and disadvantages. Benefits of multi-skilling for organizations are a reduction in terms of cost and time. Multi-skilling can be further a strategic human resource development tool that contributes to an alignment of HR processes with the business strategy and to a sustainable and competitive organizational advantage. Other benefits include increased employee retention, decreased employee absenteeism and lower employee turnover (Lucas, 2004). Better-trained employees are less likely to have accidents at the workplace and studies also show improved service quality (Williamson, 1992). Multi-skilling does not only have benefits for organizations but also for individuals. Multi-skilling leads to higher job satisfaction, remuneration and promotion.

CHRISTINE NASCHBERGER

See also:

Competence; Employability; Human resource development; Knowledge, skills and abilities; Skill.

References and selected further readings

Chen, L.C. and M. Wallace (2011), Multiskilling of frontline managers in the five star hotel industry in Taiwan, *Research and Practice in Human Resource Management*, **19**(1), pp. 25–37.

Gomar, J.D., C.T. Haas and D.P. Morton (2002), Assignment and allocation optimization of partially multi-skilled workforce, *Journal of Construction Engineering and Management*, **128**(2), pp. 103–109.

Lawler, E.E. and G.E. Ledford (1992), *A Skill-Based Approach to Human Resource Management*, Los Angeles: Center for Effective Organizations.

Lucas, R. (2004), *Employment Relations in the Hospitability and Tourism Industry*, London: Routledge.

MEDEF (1998), *Deauville 1998: Objective Competencies*, working paper, La Revue des Entreprises, No. 606.

Williamson, R.M. (1992), Optimum performance through multi-skill maintenance, *AIPE Facilities*, **2**, pp. 34–42.

National culture

National culture (NC) is a set of norms, beliefs, values, customs and behaviours that exist within a population of a sovereign nation. It is a pattern of basic, socially derived and, to an extent, dogmatic assumptions about how people within a nation think and act. Although NC grows with generations, it stabilizes in patterns across generations using some mechanisms, such as language, religion, education, social organization, politics, law, technology, etc. There are three main NC models. The first is the single-dimensional model, where countries are classified according to a single cultural dimension. The second is the multidimensional model, where countries are categorized on the basis of various cultural dimensions. The third is the historical-social models, where countries are classified according to historical-social events. NCs differ from each other in numerous ways. For example, in the way that they perceive time, verbal and non-verbal communication, etc. In a global and transnational world, NC is very important for many reasons. It gives people a sense of identity and uniqueness; it provides the legal framework within which international trade is carried out and international projects are conducted.

At the same time, the NC is a very significant issue for managers and organizations. Organizations and their cultures are embedded into NC. Organizations in particular countries favour particular ways of doing business because of their *national cultural background*. Employees in particular countries display particular behaviour patterns and preferences in the work organization because of their NC. The awareness of cultural similarities and dissimilarities assist managers to deal with the diversified market dynamics and to achieve higher level of intercultural organizations. There are examples of failed global ventures because of poor understanding of how national cultures differ. Trompenaars (1993) explained why NC mattered in organizations and argued that organizations and their cultures are embedded into NC. The latter defines how organizations in particular countries favour particular ways of doing business as well as why employees display particular behaviour patterns and preferences in the organization of work.

The most well-known theorist on NC and management is Geert Hofstede (1991). He distinguished five dimensions of NC that can influence management attitudes:

- **Power distance:** the extent to which people within a social context accept that power is distributed unequally.
- **Individualism/collectivism:** the extent to which the ties between individuals within a social context are loose (individualism) or strong (collectivism).
- **Masculinity/femininity:** the extent to which a NC focus on values of competition, achievement and material reward (masculinity) or on values like cooperation, affiliation and perception of material reward as less important (femininity).
- **Uncertainty avoidance:** the extent to which the members of a social context feel threatened by uncertain or unknown situations and they try to avoid them.
- **Short and long-term orientation:** the cultures that use long-term orientation refer to tolerance, determination, and long-term results. Short-term orientation possesses the exact opposite qualities.

These five dimensions of NC seem to determine the operation of various management practices like human resources management (HRM), total quality management (TQM), etc. For instance, the influence of NC on HRM is most visible in the motivation to work, risk-taking, communication, consensus, etc.

ALEXANDROS PSYCHOGIOS

See also:
Globalization; International human resource management; Organizational culture.

Reference and selected further readings
French, R. (2010), *Cross-Cultural management in Work Organisations*, 2nd edn, London: Chartered Institute of Personnel and Development.
Gannon, M.J. (2004), *Understanding Global Cultures: Metaphorical Journeys Through 28 Nations, Clusters of Nations, and Continents*, 3rd edn, Thousand Oaks, CA: Sage.
Hofstede, G. (1991), *Cultures and Organizations: Software of the Mind*, London: McGraw-Hill International.
Hope, C.A. and A.P. Mühlemann (2001), The impact of culture on best-practice production/operations management, *International Journal of Management Review*, 3(3), pp. 199–217.
Maude, B. (2011), *Managing Cross-Cultural Communication*, Basingstoke: Palgrave Macmillan.
Nakata, C. (2009), *Beyond Hofstede: Culture Frameworks for Global Marketing and Management*, Basingstoke: Palgrave Macmillan.
Trompenaars, F. (1993), *Riding the Waves of Culture*. London: Brealey.

Negotiation

Negotiation is the basic form of interaction people and organizations use to establish or change the terms of a relationship or to settle a dispute short of litigation. If one party has all the power in the relationship, the interaction may be more akin to dictation than negotiation. But otherwise, negotiation is the process used more often than any other to interact with parents, partners, children, suppliers, buyers, bankers, agents, hostage-takers and foreign powers, as well as employers and employees.

Negotiation is a basic language of HRM. It is most evident in the industrial or employment relations part of HR – negotiating collective contracts with unions or negotiating a resolution to an unfair dismissal claim. But negotiation skills feature in a wide variety of HR functions – hiring people, negotiating salaries, resolving conflicts between employees, conducting performance interviews and other 'difficult conversations', managing organization change and negotiating exits from the organization, among others. Some of these functions involve HR managers exercising negotiation skills as third-party mediators.

Much of the research and writing on negotiation comes out of the study of labour relations, so it is no coincidence that Richard Walton and Robert McKersie's classic *Behavioral Theory of Labor Negotiations* (1991) still provides the ideal model for adopting a strategic approach to negotiation in HR practice. Walton and McKersie's thesis was that, while the negotiation process was just a single, cohesive process, for strategic and analytical purposes it could be seen as four sub-processes operating simultaneously. To be truly effective, a negotiator needs to be alert to what is happening in each sub-process and to act purposefully and strategically in each, recognizing that actions taken in one sub-process could well have implications for the negotiator's ability to move in the other sub-processes.

Two of the sub-processes – distributive bargaining and integrative bargaining – dealt with the substantive issues arising in negotiation. It is important to identify whether or not the parties have a conflict of interests over the issues under negotiation and to adopt competitive (distributive) or collaborative (integrative) approaches accordingly. A compensation claim by a dismissed employee may not offer much opportunity for collaboration, but negotiation over restructuring might.

The other two sub-processes have to do with relationships. Managing the relationship between bargaining parties may be as important to successful outcomes as negotiating the issues themselves. Whatever the subject, your agenda is more likely to be served if you, rather than the other party, are leading the process.

Finally, Walton and McKersie highlighted the importance to reaching successful outcomes of effective 'intra-organizational' negotiations. HR managers are often negotiating as agents for others in the organization. It is important that, as those negotiations proceed, the HR manager's principals be kept informed in such a way that their expectations are consistent with what is shaping up as the likely outcome. Further, sometimes there will be competing expectations within the constituency or clientele, and those too have to be reconciled for an acceptable outcome. All four of these areas demand attention for successful negotiations across the HR portfolio.

IAN MCANDREW

See also:
Conflict; Employment relationship; Mediation.

References and selected further readings
Fisher, R. and W. Ury (2011), *Getting to Yes: Negotiating Agreement without Giving In*, revised edition, London: Penguin.
Kolb, D. and J. Williams (2003), *Everyday Negotiation: Navigating the Hidden Agendas in Bargaining*, San Francisco: Jossey-Bass.
Walton, R.E. and R.B. McKersie (1991), *A Behavioral Theory of Labor Negotiations*, 2nd edn, Ithaca, NY: ILR Press.

Neoliberalism

Neoliberalism is an approach to economic and social organization that assumes that human prosperity and wellbeing is best served by optimizing the freedom of capitalist enterprise and the operation of the private sphere of the market. From the reform of organized labour to the welfare state and macroeconomic state intervention, neoliberals have sought to rectify what they see as impediments to freedom. Friedrich Hayek and Chicago School economists have been a decisive influence. Writing in the 1940s in response to the expanding powers of the state in liberal societies, Hayek argued that the local knowledge of market actors was a surer guide to the satisfaction of human wants than decisions taken by state planners. Departing from the principles of the rule of law and imposing a particular morality on society, the welfare state possessed its own totalitarian tendencies. Yet Hayek assumed that an active state, promoting free markets and free trade through supportive law and institutions, was an essential support in establishing the private sphere of the market.

Supporters of neoliberalism have also sought to extend the principles, values and practices of the market to other fields. Markets or market-like forms and entrepreneurial qualities are commonly assumed to have wider benefits for social and economic organization. An obvious example here would be the organization of the public sector in nation-states favouring the privatization of state assets, deregulation and management techniques borrowed from the private sector. Influential theories of human resources management (HRM), excellence and total quality management (TQM) can be seen as elements in a broader neoliberal project in so far as they justify their priorities and aims with reference to the market and assume qualities of enterprise and self-reliance on the part of the ideal employee.

Today, although varied in the detail of its operation and the extent of its influence, neoliberalism can be said to have global reach in the sense that few nation-states are untouched by its central assumptions. Neoliberalism has emerged in different local circumstances following a variety of different trajectories. Military force played a direct role in the implementation of reform in the case of Chile after the military coup in 1973, as it did in Iraq after the American occupation. For less developed states, neoliberal reform has been a condition of securing credit from international economic institutions. In yet other cases, neoliberal measures have been the chosen course of countless elected governments.

If neoliberalism now occupies a pre-eminent position in the way that effective social and economic organization is conceived, it is vulnerable to an array of criticism. Measures favoured by neoliberals encouraged the expansion and collapse of deregulated finance. Neoliberalism is associated with a marked growth in material inequality and with growing insecurity at work. The material wealth of members of the business elites has grown disproportionately, in part as a result of the privatization of the state. At the same time, employees increasingly carry responsibility for the fate of the enterprise in which they work. The integrity of the state is at risk with neoliberal reform undermining an alternative 'tradition' of bureaucratic impartiality, fairness and accountability. The cultural change sought by neoliberals has encouraged a petty acquisitiveness and delegitimized public provision. There would nonetheless seem to be little prospect of neoliberalism losing its dominance at this time.

EDWARD BARRATT

See also:
Public sector; Regulation.

References and selected further readings

Boltanski, L. and E. Chiapello (2007), *The New Spirit of Capitalism*, London: Verso.
Harvey, D. (2007), *A Brief History of Neoliberalism*, Oxford: Oxford University Press.
Rose, N. (1999), *Powers of Freedom*, Cambridge: Cambridge University Press.

Non-union workplace

A non-union workplace is identified by nil or minimal union membership and an absence of trade union recognition and representation. Over the past three decades non-union workplaces are increasingly commonplace in most western economies due to a confluence of factors such as the significant decrease in union density, rise of high performance work practices, desire of employers and employees for a more direct and collaborative relationship and union avoidance of management (Gollan, Kaufman, Taras and Wilkinson, 2015). This trend of non-unionism is echoed in the literature in the way of how non-union workplaces are classified. Earlier classification schemes were typically based on why being non-union, and the tendency to unionise, which clearly demonstrates its roots in an era when trade unions were more prevalent, whereas later developments in its classification has shifted focus through incorporating the dimensions of strategic HRM and the nature of HRM policy and practice (Guest and Hoque, 1994).

The findings are mixed in determining whether non-union workplaces are, as compared to their unionised counterparts, more innovative in HRM practices and comparable in employment relations measures (Deery, Walsh and Knox 2001). It is clear that across different types of non-union workplaces, HRM practices and outcomes of employment relations and business performance can vary substantially (Guest, 2001; Dundon, Wilkinson, Marchington and Ackers, 2005). A valid evaluation needs to take into account the specific context such as the legal system in which a workplace is operating, market competitiveness, industry and workplace IR climate, managerial preference and attitudes (Dundon and Gollan, 2007).

YING XU AND PAUL J. GOLLAN

See also:

Employee voice; Non-unionism; Representation gap.

References and suggested further readings

Deery, S., J. Walsh and A. Knox (2001), The non-union workplace in Australia: bleak house or human resource innovator? *The International Journal of Human Resource Management*, **12**(4), pp. 669–683.

Dundon, T. and P.J. Gollan (2007), Re-conceptualizing voice in the non-union workplace, *International Journal of Human Resource Management*, **18**(7), pp. 1182–1198.

Dundon, T., A. Wilkinson, M. Marchington and P. Ackers (2005), The management of voice in non-union organisations: managers' perspectives, *Employee Relations*, **27**(3), pp. 307–319.

Gollan, P.J., G. Patmore and Y. Xu (2014), Regulation of employee voice, in A. Wilkinson, T. Dundon, J. Donaghey and R. Freeman (eds), *Handbook of Research on Employee Voice*, Cheltenham: Edward Elgar Publishing, pp. 363–380.

Gollan, P.J., B. Kaufman, D. Taras and A. Wilkinson (2015), Voice and involvement at work: an overview of the experience with non-union representation in Anglo-American countries, in P.J. Gollan, B. Kaufman, D. Taras and A. Wilkinson (eds), *Voice and Involvement at Work: Experience with Non-Union Representation*, New York: Routledge, pp. 1–41.

Guest, D. (2001), Industrial relations and human resource management, in J. Storey (ed.), *HRM: A Critical Text*, London: Thompson Learning.

Guest, D. and K. Hoque (1994), The good, the bad and the ugly: employment relations in new non-union workplaces, *Human Resource Management Journal*, **5**(1), pp. 1–14.

Kaufman, B. and D.G. Taras (2010), Employee participation through non-union forms of employee representation, in A. Wilkinson, P.J. Gollan, M. Marchington and D. Lewin (eds), *The Oxford Handbook of Participation in Organizations*, Oxford: Oxford University Press, pp. 258–285.

Non-unionism

The concept of non-unionism refers to the lack of support for and an absence of trade union recognition and representation in collective bargaining, as opposed to simply having no or minimal union membership within an organization (Dundon and Rollinson, 2004). Despite the policy support and recent debate on union revival, the employee relations landscape has significantly changed in many Western countries over the past few decades due to a continuous decline in union density, especially within the private sectors of the economy (Gollan et al., 2015).

Much of the research on non-unionism has focused on the motives and strategies of management and the subsequent implications for organizations and individuals. Many employers (and employees) believe unions bring negative issues to workplaces, such as adversarial labour-management relationships, non-competitive costs and inflexible HR practices. Employers or management typically engage with non-unionism for a multiplicity of overlapping motives, including preference for a more direct and collaborative employer–employee relationship, preserving managerial prerogatives and the control over labour, and the competitive pressure from the marketplace. Management have used various strategies to marginalize union representation, such as through superior terms and conditions in employment contracts, participative work practices (Dundon and Gollan, 2007), support for non-union employee representation (NER) (Campolieti et al., 2013), and union suppression mechanisms (McLoughlin and Gourlay, 1994).

Nonetheless, a firm's adoption of strategic HRM, high-involvement and high-performance working systems, and/or NER is not necessarily targeted to avoid union representation (Kaufman and Miller, 2011). HRM and NER may co-exist with union representation depending on management choice and labour legislations (Pyman et al., 2010). In fact, there has been a growing interest from academics and practitioners for realistic new models of employment relations underpinned by workplace cooperation such as the approach of sustainable HRM (Gollan and Xu, 2014).

YING XU AND PAUL J. GOLLAN

See also:

Employee voice; Non-union workplace; Representation gap.

References and selected further readings

Campolieti, M., R. Gomez and M. Gunderson (2013), Does non-union employee representation act as a complement or substitute to union voice? Evidence from Canada and the United States, *Industrial Relations: A Journal of Economy and Society*, **52**, pp. 378–396.

Dundon, T. and P.J. Gollan (2007), Re-conceptualizing voice in the non-union workplace, *International Journal of Human Resource Management*, **18**(7), pp. 1182–1198.

Dundon, T. and D. Rollinson, D. (2004), *Employment Relations in Non-Union Firms*, London: Routledge.

Gollan, P.J. and Y. Xu (2014), Re-engagement with the employee participation debate: beyond the case of contested and captured terrain, *Work, Employment and Society*, **62**, pp. 1–13.

Gollan, P.J., B. Kaufman, D. Taras and A. Wilkinson (2015), Voice and involvement at work: an overview of the experience with non-union representation in Anglo-American countries, in P.J. Gollan, B. Kaufman, D. Taras and A. Wilkinson (eds), *Voice and Involvement at Work: Experience with Non-Union Representation*, New York: Routledge, pp. 1–41.

Kaufman, B.E. and B.I. Miller (2011), The firm's choice of HRM practices: economics meets strategic human resource management, *Industrial & Labor Relations Review*, **64**(3), pp. 526–557.

McLoughlin, I. and S. Gourlay (1994), *Enterprise without Unions: Industrial Relations in the Non-Union Firm*, Buckingham: Open University Press.
Pyman, A., P. Holland, J. Teicher and B.K. Cooper (2010), Industrial relations climate, employee voice and managerial attitudes to unions: an Australian study, *British Journal of Industrial Relations*, **48**(2), pp. 460–480.

Notice period

According to UK law, it is a legal requirement for an employee to be given a period of notice of termination of his/her contract of employment. As for the requisite period of notice, Section 86 of the Employment Rights Act 1996 (ERA) prescribes a minimum, namely one week's notice where the employee has been continuously employed for a period between one month and two years, which increases by a week for each year of continuous employment beyond two years, subject to a maximum of 12 weeks' notice. The common law-implied period of reasonable notice or the parties by agreement may derogate *in melius*, i.e., upwards from the statutory minimum. The calculation of the 'reasonable' period of notice under the common law is not a scientific process and is dependent on three factors, namely the custom of the employee's trade, the standing of the individual's job (i.e., professional or otherwise), and the frequency of the payment of the wage or salary (e.g., one week's notice where payment is weekly or one month's notice in the case of a monthly salary).

The legal significance of the notice period lies in the fact that a failure to tender the correct period will constitute a wrongful dismissal of an employee, entitling such employee to the payment of damages in respect of his/her financial losses. As an alternative to the service of prior notice, it is lawful for an employer to tender a payment in lieu of notice where the employment contract of the employee concerned empowers the employer to do so. The payment in lieu must correspond to the gross pay of the employee for the period of notice in question. For example, if the employment contract provides for eight weeks' notice of termination and the employer pays the employee eight weeks' salary in lieu, then such a practice will be lawful.

DAVID CABRELLI

See also:

Contract of employment; Employee; Temporary worker; Worker; Wrongful dismissal.

References and selected further readings

Ford, M. (1998), Re-thinking the notice rule, *Industrial Law Journal*, **27**, pp. 220–233.
Freedland, M. (2003), *The Personal Employment Contract*, Oxford: Oxford University Press, pp. 329–332.

Occupational health

Occupational health's modern development began with the Industrial Revolution when heavy engineering, mining and manufacturing became dominant industries. Concerns about work-related accidents and diseases were dealt with under the banner of 'industrial health'. Some employers, such as Coleman's Mustard, developed a paternalistic approach to employee relations during the late nineteenth century providing, housing and healthcare to their workers (Thornbory, 2014, p. 5).

During the twentieth century, workers in factories, coal mines, etc. began to have access to on-site medical services for emergency and specialist treatment. Since the 1970s, more regulation and statutes have developed, a cornerstone of the legislation being the Health and Safety at Work Act, which was followed by more and more legislation, often linked to European directives.

Today business is dominated by non-manufacturing enterprises including the financial services sector, leisure industries and IT. A definition of occupational health (OH) is provided by the CIPD: 'a specialist branch of medicine focusing on health in the workplace. It is concerned with the physical and mental well-being of employees'.

Fewer OH services now offer treatment and many are outsourced by employers. OH offers advice on a range of health-related issues to both workers and employers: risk assessments, health surveillance, absence, rehabilitation, reasonable adjustments that an employer may consider as a means of enabling people with a disability or significant long-term health problem to fulfil their working role. The duty to make these adjustments is equally important whether a person's disability relates to physical or mental health.

Absence is disruptive and costly. An holistic approach to absence management, by the involvement of OH, HR and management, can provide significant improvement in the health of workers, their morale and attendance levels.

Employers must comply with anti-discrimination legislation, therefore OH advice on health, rehabilitation, prognosis, workplace adjustments, etc. can be an integral part of achieving best practice and statutory compliance. Guidance and codes of practice are available from ACAS, the HSE, and other government bodies. These cover all areas of good practice including workers' health, absence management, risk assessment, hazards, reporting obligations, etc. Confidentiality is a regulatory obligation of the qualified professionals in OH (GMC, 2009). There is also a general duty on the organization to respect employee privacy: guidance is available from the overseeing body, the Information Commissioner's Office (ICO).

As global business competition increases so cost drivers become ever more important. An ethical dilemma is emerging with regard to the conscience of consumers and the health of workers in unregulated societies whose goods and services we use.

JOAN LEWIS

See also:

Absence; Direct discrimination; Paternalism; Welfare.

References and selected further readings

Acas (2012), *Health, Work and Wellbeing Advisory Booklet*, www.acas.org.uk/media/pdf/3/t/Health-work-and-wellbeing-accessible-version.pdf.

CIPD (2013), *Occupational Health Factsheet*, www.cipd.co.uk/hr-resources/factsheets/occupational-health.aspx.

GMC (2009), *Confidentiality: Disclosing Information for Insurance, Employment and Similar Purposes*, London: General Medical Council, www.gmc-uk.org/confidentiality.

Griffiths, E. (2010), Managing for health, *Occupational Health*, **62**(5), pp. 14–15.

Thornbory, G. (2014), *Contemporary Occupational Health Nursing*, London: Routledge.

Off-the-job learning

Off-the-job learning refers to a class of methods generally used in the formal training and development of individuals. These methods are used by employers to develop occupational and work-related skills among employees. Methods can be subdivided into two categories; those that are applied *at* the workplace and those that are applied *away* from the workplace. A formal course of learning can be delivered in premises at the workplace, often in a designated area such as a training room or training workshop. Sometimes, and especially for sales, professional or management development, off-the-job learning is provided at an employer owned and operated training centre. In some cases, such learning spaces are associated with what is termed a corporate university. It is debatable whether these spaces are included in the category of *at work* or *away from work*. What is less debatable is formal learning provided by an organization other than the employer. The obvious example is where an employer sponsors and funds employees on educational/qualification courses delivered at a university or college. This example is clearly in the category of *away* from the workplace.

Secondments to a project team or different department in the employing organization can also be examples of off-the-job learning *at work.* They are within the definition of off-the-job learning as the individual employee is not performing their substantive job. Similar examples include job swaps, job rotation and shadowing (Glaister et al., 2013). Whatever the degree of formality of any particular method, there are two related problems associated with off-the-job learning. First is a general principle that the further away from the job that learning occurs, the less effective in improving job performance it is likely to be (Stewart, 2014). The second problem is known as the 'transfer of learning problem' (Grossman and Salas, 2011), where estimates suggest that as little as between 5 per cent and 20 per cent of off-the-job learning is applied back in the job at the workplace. This range is accounted for by the varying spatial and temporal distance from the job of varying methods that, in turn, has some association with the degree of formality of the method. The available research and evidence is clear that the general principle suggested by Stewart (2014) holds true in most circumstances. For that reason, solutions to the transfer of training problem have been the subject of much research (Holton and Baldwin 2003).

JIM STEWART

See also:

Experiential learning; Human resource development; On-the-job learning; Skill; Systematic training cycle; Training; Training needs analysis.

References and selected further readings

Glaister, C., R. Holden, V. Griggs, P. McCauley and M. Blackburn (2013), The design and delivery of training, in J. Gold, R. Holden, J. Stewart, P. Iles and J. Beardwell (eds), *Human Resource Development: Theory and Practice*, Basingstoke: Palgrave Macmillan.

Grossman, R. and E. Salas (2011), The transfer of training: what really matters, *International Journal of Training and Development*, **15**(2), pp. 103–120.

Holton, E.F. and T.T. Baldwin (eds) (2003), *Improving Learning Transfer in Organizations*, San Francisco: Jossey-Bass.

Stewart, J. (2014), Developing employees and managers, in G. Rees and P. Smith (eds), *Strategic Human Resource Management: An International Perspective*, London: Sage.

Older worker

As populations around the world age, governments, especially those in the West, have taken a growing interest in measures to raise real retirement ages through a combination of 'sticks' (such as raising the age at which the state pension could be drawn) and 'carrots', such as encouraging employers to introduce HRM policies conducive toward longer working lives such as phased retirement options (OECD, 2006). Efforts by both governments and employers to raise real retirement ages have brought into focus the working conditions and career management of older workers (Naegele and Walker, 2006). The definition of 'older worker' varies across national context, industry, gender and social class. Generally, an older worker is defined as being in between mid-career and retirement age, although these two points of time can vary. For example, 'retirement age' can mean the age at which the individual can start to draw her/his pension (and it is important to remember that state and occupational pensions can differ); the age at which an employer can lawfully dismiss an employee for reasons of age (also known as a mandatory retirement age); or the average age at which people leave the workforce. As part of the 2001 Lisbon Agenda (European Commission, 2005), the European Union has defined the older workforce as those between 55 and 64, although since then, state pension ages have risen in several countries including Australia (set to rise to 67 by 2023); the UK (set to rise to 69 by 2028); Portugal (66 by 2023) and Spain (67 by 2023) (OECD, 2011). It is important to remember that while public policies have primarily focused on retirement or pension ages as the end point of the older workforce, there has also been a steady increase in the number of people who are staying in work beyond retirement age. In Norway, older workers have the right to extend working life for an extra two years after the State Pension Age (Maltby et al., 2005), while in the UK, mandatory retirement has been abolished in most circumstances (Acas, 2011).

Defining the age at which the 'older workforce' begins has drawn less attention. However, now that governments are seeking to extend working life, some state programmes have been introduced to provide career planning for people at mid-career so as to help people prepare for longer working lives (Damman et al., 2011). In the UK, for example, the Department for Business, Industry and Skills has piloted and is committed to rolling out universal career advice for people at or around the age of 50 (McNair, 2015), while the French government provides financial support for training for people 45 and over who are transitioning to a new job (Caser, 2014).

MATT FLYNN

See also:

Ageing workforce; Retirement.

References and selected further readings

Acas (2011), *Working without the DRA*, London: Acas.
Caser, F. (2014), *The Mid Career Review in France*, Paris: ANACT.
Damman, M., K. Henkens and M. Kalmijn (2011), The impact of midlife educational, work, health, and family experiences on men's early retirement, *Journals of Gerontology. Series B: Psychological Sciences and Social Sciences*, **66**(5), pp. 617–627.
European Commission (2005), Lisbon Action Plan Incorporating EU Lisbon Programme and Recommendations for Actions to Member States for Inclusion in their National Lisbon Programmes, Brussels: European Commission.
McNair, S. (2015), *Mid-Career Review: The Pilot Study*, Leicester: NIACE.
OECD (2006), *Live Longer, Work Longer*, Paris: Organisation for Economic Co-operation and Development.
OECD (2011), *Pensions at a Glance*, Paris: Organisation for Economic Co-operation and Development.

On-the-job learning

On-the-job learning has gained relevance in the postmodern society where globalized markets and technological advancements require individuals and organizations to continuously learn and adapt to constantly changing environments. While traditional education and vocational training continue to play an important role equipping individuals with core knowledge and skills, the workplace has been recognized as a prolific site for learning (Illeris, 2011).

As learning and working are interdependent (Billett, 2001), on-the-job learning is embedded in the processes, tasks and social relations of the workplace. As such, learning in the workplace is situated, occurring as participation in social practices (Lave and Wenger, 1991), and is strongly dependent on access and exposure to sources of knowledge in the form of social partners and artefacts (Billett, 2004).

Given the participatory nature of on-the-job learning, high-impact learning activities include work shadowing, allowing observation of more experienced workers providing insight into new practices and perspectives (Eraut, 2007), and challenging tasks, such as roles involving processes of decision-making, problem-solving, supervisory and managerial responsibilities (Brown, 2009), stretching individuals' practical, cognitive, emotional and relational capabilities.

On-the-job learning is highly dependent on the qualities of the workplace as a supportive learning environment. Job design, in terms of the allocation and structuring of work, is a central contextual factor influencing the extent to which the job presents challenging features, the degree of individuality or collaboration, and the opportunities to work in contact with other actors (Eraut, 2007). The configuration of work is thus central for providing individuals with opportunities to stretch their capabilities in a variety of tasks presenting novel challenges, and to secure access to a support network of experts and peers for interaction and regular feedback.

Despite the centrality of the qualities of the workplace as an environment conducive to learning, it has been argued that learning is an inter-psychological process, entailing a dual and reciprocal relationship between the individual and the social sources of knowledge (Billett, 2004). As such, the quality of learning experiences is mediated by both workplace affordances, in the form of opportunities for participation and interaction, and the level of guidance provided, and by an individual's agency and intention to engage in such activities and interactions (Billett, 2004). This assumption represents a shift towards the learner's ownership of the process, as individuals act as autonomous and self-directed agents, who engage in learning when this is perceived as relevant for their job and of value when the required support and guidance are in place and, consequently, organizations are thus able to enhance informal learning as a resource for their human capital and their competitive advantage.

SILVIA PIRRIONI, HELEN SHIPTON AND NING WU

See also:

Informal learning; Organizational learning.

References and selected further readings

Billett, S. (2001), *Learning in the Workplace: Strategies for Effective Practice*, Sydney: Allen & Unwin.
Billett, S. (2004), *Learning Through Work: Workplace Participatory Practices*, in H. Rainbird, A. Fuller and A. Munro (eds), *Workplace Learning in Context*, London: Routledge, pp. 109–125.
Brown, A. (2009), *Higher Skills Development at Work: A Commentary by the Teaching and Learning Research Programme*, London: ESRC, TLRP.
Eraut, M. (2007), Learning from other people in the workplace, *Oxford Review of Education*, 33(4), pp. 403–422.
Illeris, K. (2011), *Learning in Working Life*, Copenhagen: Roskilde University Press.
Lave, J. and E. Wenger (1991), *Situated Learning: Legitimate Peripheral Participation*, Cambridge: Cambridge University Press.

Online learning

While there are several definitions of online learning (OL), our review of the literature suggests a common theme wherein it involves the design and delivery of learning that is fully or partially mediated through the internet and related technologies. Some have preferred to use the terms e-learning, web-based learning or forms of technology-mediated instruction to describe the broader domain of OL. The underlying principles for designing and delivering OL have overlaps with the key tenets of the three dominant schools of learning: behaviourist, cognitive and constructivist theories. Each has a role to play in delivering effective online learning (Ally, 2004). Poor attention to elements of each of the learning schools and lack of appropriate instructional design tools and technologies can adversely impact OL's effectiveness.

OL is one of the fastest growing approaches to designing and delivering learning and education and it covers a range of learning contexts (school, higher education and industry). While a number of researchers opine that OL and education is a direct offshoot of distance education, there are distinctive features that characterize it. For example, OL personifies multimedia richness, high levels of access and reach, and allows synchronous and asynchronous communities of leaners to engage with and learn from each other. OL also significantly reduces the cost of instruction and its redevelopment and has potential for high interactivity due to its media richness.

The differences between the effectiveness of online versus traditional approaches has attracted a lot of attention among policymakers. Some studies claim that OL is particularly effective not because of the use of advanced technology and internet tools that the learners are familiar with, but it is more to do with the instructional design technologies embedded in such learning. It goes without saying how disengaging it can be for learners to continuously scroll down screeds of information on webpages without any embedded activities, breaks, or organizing the learning around large chunks without clear objectives (Clark, 1983; Schramm, 1977). Advancing a theory of OL, Anderson (2008) suggests that the challenge for designers and deliverers of OL is to facilitate three key forms of interaction: learner–facilitator/instructor, learner–content, and learner–learner as well as create a learning environment that is centred around the learner, content, community and assessment.

CHRIS ROWLEY AND ASHISH MALIK

See also:
Blended learning; Distance learning; E-learning; Organization development; Organizational learning.

References and selected further readings
Ally, M. (2004), Foundations of educational theory for online learning, *Theory and Practice of Online Learning*, **2**, pp. 15–44.
Anderson, T. (2008), Towards a theory of online learning, in T. Anderson (ed.), *Theory and Practice of Online Learning*, Edmonton: Athabasca University Press, pp. 45–74.
Clark, R.E. (1983), Reconsidering research on learning from media, *Review of Educational Research*, **53**(4), pp. 445–459.
Moore, M.G. (ed.) (2013), *Handbook of Distance Education*, 3rd edn, New York: Routledge.
Ruderstam, K.E. and J. Schoenholtz-Read (eds) (2010), *Handbook of Online Learning*, 2nd edn, Thousand Oaks, CA: Sage.
Schramm, W. (1977), *Big Media, Little Media*, Thousand Oaks, CA: Sage.

Organization development

Reviewing a multitude of definitions surrounding the study and practice of organization development (OD), we can conclude that it is a long-term behavioural approach, involving senior management commitment and support for improving an organization's effectiveness and adaptability towards change is approached via multiple levels. This is often achieved through planned interventions by employing a combination of internal and/or external change agents and through active involvement and collaboration of employees (Burnes and Cooke, 2012; Hinckley, 2006). In today's dynamic and turbulent business environment, OD, through a range of interventions at the individual, group and systems levels helps businesses in adapting and renewing their product and service offerings to cater to changing customer needs by responding with new technologies while also effectively exploiting emerging market opportunities.

Some have argued that recent academic discourse on human resource development (HRD) and organizational learning are treading on what has traditionally been the profession of OD consultants and the organizational behaviour field. This is evident in lively debates that suggest HRD 'is living the shadow of OD' (Grieves and Redman, 1999, p. 81) and that a learning organization approach is ideally placed to articulate 'the goals and values of OD' (Stewart, 2005, p. 90). One of the sharpest criticisms of OD has been the prescriptive nature of its approaches and the inability of Western OD practitioners to deal with the issues impacting multinational organizations. This is evident in the repetitive steps such as goal clarity, planned approaches, action-research methodology, force-field theory, and consultative approaches applied in culturally different contexts. The approach often undermines context, organizational politics and the choices regarding the balance between internal and external change agents. Consequently, numerous unethical issues associated with OD interventions remain unattended. The overtly economic and rational focus of OD is not surprising due to clients' increasing focus on efficiency outcomes and an extremely low focus on emotional content in the decisions (George, 2015; Malik and Rowley, 2015).

CHRIS ROWLEY AND ASHISH MALIK

See also:

Change management; Human resource development; Organizational learning.

References and selected further readings

Burnes, B. and B. Cooke (2012), Review article: the past, present and future of organization development: taking the long view, *Human Relations*, **65**(11), pp. 1395–1429.

George, J. (2015), Process consulting and adaptations of organisation development in the Indian IT industry, in A. Malik and C. Rowley (eds), *Business Models and People Management in the Indian IT Industry: From People to Profits*, London: Routledge.

Grieves, J. and T. Redman (1999), Living in the shadow of OD: HRD and the search for identity, *Human Resource Development International*, **2**(2), pp. 81–102.

Hinckley, S.R. (2006), A history of organisation development, in B.B. Jones and M. Brazzel (eds), *The NTL Handbook of Organization Development and Change: Principles, Practices, and Perspectives*, San Francisco, CA: Pfeiffer.

Malik, A. and C. Rowley (2015), *Business Models and People Management in the Indian IT Industry: From People to Profits*, London: Routledge, London.

Stewart, J. (2005), The current state and status of HRD research, *The Learning Organization*, **12**(1), pp. 90–95.

Organizational career systems

Organizational career system (OCS) is the combined effort that organizations, in particular the HRM unit, put into managing and developing its human talent. OCS is rooted in career studies, and relates to HRM and its associated fields, like strategic HRM, where organizations manage their human resources in line with the business strategy, or international HRM, where people are managed across geographies. This entry approaches career planning and management from a managerial rather than from an individual perspective.

OCS comprises the development and utilization of a set of practices for the purpose of retaining talent and managing it effectively. Practices vary according to their level of sophistication, time span, target population, how developmental they are (versus how far they are used for decision-making such as promotion, appointments to different roles and redundancy) and their fit with the overall strategy. Some examples of career practices are: induction, to introduce new recruits to the organization; mentoring, to develop employees (and benefit both mentors and protégés); performance appraisal to identify talent, point out training needs and apply performance-related payment; and succession planning, to explore possible future career moves and identify who may replace whom (typically done for the higher echelons). Yet, the true value of OCS is in integrating a set of specific career practices into a coherent and comprehensive system that answers the needs of the organization and the individuals employed.

While much of the career literature explores individual perspectives, the planning and management of careers is shared, sometime led by the organization. The contemporary view considers the individual as the major stakeholder in the career – the choice, the planning, progress, and the ability to change trajectory, follow a calling or open a totally new direction (or withdrawal from working life). Yet, organizations offer positions, roles and activities. Organizations select people, induce them to work, take care of their needs, appoint mentors, offer career consultancy, or use performance appraisal systems to determine training and other needs.

The debate here is who is taking a lead role or how the planning and managing of the career is to be shared between individuals and employers. Managing diversity at the organizational level, managing careers across borders, such as expatriation and repatriation, operating HR and career systems in different countries pose challenges to employers. The organization should also decide on how to enable employees to gain work–life balance and still be competitive and challenged.

YEHUDA BARUCH

See also:
Careers; Talent management; Training and development.

References and selected further readings

Baruch, Y. (1999), Integrated career systems for the 2000s, *International Journal of Manpower*, **20**(7), pp. 432–457.

Baruch Y. (2003), Career systems in transition: a normative model for career practices, *Personnel Review*, **32**(2), pp. 231–251.

Baruch, Y. (2004), *Managing Careers: Theory and Practice*, Harlow: FT-Prentice Hall/Pearson.

Baruch, Y. and M.A. Peiperl (2000), Career management practices: an empirical survey and theoretical implications, *Human Resource Management*, **39**(4), pp. 347–366.

Boxall, P. and J. Purcell (2008), *Strategy and Human Resource Management*, Basingstoke: Palgrave.

Dickmann, M. and Y. Baruch (2011), *Global Career*, New York: Routledge.

Organizational citizenship behaviour

The concept of organizational citizenship behaviour (OCB) was introduced by Organ in the 1980s. Organ (1988, p. 4) defined OCB as 'individual behavior that is discretionary, not directly or explicitly recognized by the formal reward system, and that in the aggregate promotes the effective functioning of the organization'. In other words, OCB is behaviour that employees show voluntarily, which goes beyond their formal job description. OCB is considered to improve organizational effectiveness. Examples of OCBs are assisting co-workers, working extra hours to get the job done and volunteering for tasks that are not part of the job description. Constructs that are closely related to, but also distinct from OCB are: contextual performance, extra-role behaviour and prosocial behaviour.

There is a discussion about the composition of OCB. Some authors (e.g., Organ, 1988) have argued that OCB is a multidimensional construct, composed of the following five dimensions: altruism, courtesy, conscientiousness, civic virtue and sportsmanship.

Others (e.g., Williams and Anderson, 1991) have made a distinction between two types of OCB: behaviours directed at other individuals in the organization (OCBI) and behaviours directed at the organization as a whole (OCBO). However, research has shown that these five dimensions are highly correlated, indicating that there is significant overlap in the dimensions.

The antecedents and consequences of OCB are well-researched. Important predictors of OCB are job satisfaction, organizational commitment, fairness and leader supportiveness. These positive attitudes and supportive context contribute positively to OCB. In terms of outcomes, research has shown that OCB has a positive effect on both individual level and unit level outcomes. OCB results in better employee performance and lower levels of turnover and absenteeism. Moreover, at the unit level it contributes to productivity, efficiency and customer satisfaction. Longitudinal studies indicate that OCB is causally related to these outcome measures.

An ongoing discussion is whether OCB is distinct from task performance. Research evidence shows that the two concepts are significantly related, but that OCB is more strongly correlated with employee attitudes than task performance. This indicates that OCB mediates the relationship between employee attitudes and task performance.

EVA KNIES

See also:
Absence; Commitment; Job satisfaction; Labour turnover.

References and selected further readings

LePine, J.A., A. Erez and D.E. Johnson (2002), The nature and dimensionality of organizational citizenship behavior: a critical review and meta-analysis, *Journal of Applied Psychology*, **87**(1), pp. 52–65.
Organ, D.W. (1988), *Organizational Citizenship Behavior: The Good Soldier Syndrome*, New York: Lexington Books.
Organ, D.W. and K. Ryan (1995), A meta-analytic review of attitudinal and dispositional predictors of organizational citizenship behavior, *Personnel Psychology*, **48**(4), pp. 775–802.
Organ, D.W., P.M. Podsakoff and S.P. MacKenzie (2006), *Organizational Citizenship Behavior: Its Nature, Antecedents, and Consequences*, London: Sage.
Podsakoff, N.P., S.W. Whiting, P.M. Podsakoff and B.D. Blume (2009), Individual-and organizational-level consequences of organizational citizenship behaviors: a meta-analysis, *Journal of Applied Psychology*, **94**(1), pp. 122–141.
Williams, L.J. and S.E. Anderson (1991), Job satisfaction and organizational commitment as predictors of organizational citizenship and in-role behaviors, *Journal of Management*, **17**(3), pp. 601–617.

Organizational culture

The importance of the concept of culture for organizations stems from the notion that it provides a dynamic and interactive model of organizing and can help explain how organizational environments might be characterized, assessed and ultimately controlled (Deal and Kennedy, 1982). An important aspect here is the longstanding belief that successful organizations have a strong or positive corporate culture (Deal and Kennedy, 1982; Peters and Waterman, 1982), and that an understanding of culture can provide a way of explaining how and why particular organizations enjoy differing levels of success. Peters and Waterman (1982, p. 75) found that 'the dominance and coherence of culture proved to be an essential quality of the excellent companies. Moreover the stronger the culture . . . the less the need there was for policy manuals, organization charts or detailed procedures and rules.' Consequently, organizational culture is often held to be a key factor in understanding the modern working environment.

Schein (1985) has defined organizational culture in terms of employees shared values and perceptions of the organization, beliefs about it, and common ways of solving problems within the organization. In short, culture helps an organization's members to make sense of and accept their world. Rousseau (1990) found that various authors have defined organizational culture in different ways; however, a number of salient points emerge when considering its overall meaning. Emphasis, in many cases, is on values, beliefs and expectations that are shared within the group and/or organization, and which, in turn, can help the members interpret their environment.

It may be that the use of culture as a concept can be seen to be too embracing, and some writers (Rousseau, 1990; Schein, 1985) describe culture as having a series of different layers. Schein (1985) suggests that there are three levels of culture: artefacts, values and basic assumptions. Rousseau (1990) describes these layers of culture, organized from readily accessible, and therefore more easily studied, to difficult to access. At the most accessible level are visible artefacts, or products of cultural activity. Next are patterns of behaviour or the structures that reflect patterns of activity. Both of these layers are observable to those outside the culture. The third layer relates to group behavioural norms, or beliefs about what is acceptable and unacceptable behaviour within the organization. Values and priorities assigned to organizational outcomes are found on the next layer. The third and fourth layers can be learned about through interaction with, and questioning of group members. Patterns of unconscious assumptions are the deepest of the layers of culture, and these may not be directly known by the organization's members and therefore require a period of intensive interaction to uncover. Identifying different levels of culture is an important step in understanding how culture may be managed, influenced and changed. However, advocates of cultural change programmes tend to focus only on the more accessible surface level elements, whereas those who argue culture change is difficult concentrate on the deeper levels.

In addition to being layered, culture may also have different effects at different levels in the organization. Subcultures might develop which can be associated with different roles, functions and levels in the organization. Subcultures within an organization will depend on its type and nature. It may be that certain types of organizations are more likely to have a single, unitarist culture, whereas others are more likely to be pluralistic.

The assessment of organizational culture is an essential prerequisite for the design and implementation of intervention programmes. While both quantitative and qualitative methods persist in the study of organizational culture, Schein (1984) suggests that, since each organization is unique, it is difficult for an outside researcher to form *a priori* questions or measures to tap into its culture, and that the use of quantitative methods is unethical in its use of aggregated data and not the participants' own words. Despite the complex multidimensional and multilevel nature of the construct many attempts have been made to assess and characterize culture, usually based on an evaluation of its 'surface' or manifest elements and using a variety of methods including interview schedules and questionnaires. These types of study have focused on behavioural norms, organizational values and processes and on individual perceptions or climate.

Cultural assessment aimed at behaviours, values and norms have been used to test the assumption that culture can impact on organizational effectiveness (Peters and Waterman, 1982). Several attempts have been made to define and assess the link between culture and various organizational outcomes, often in the hope of identifying or nurturing the 'best' culture associated with those outcomes. For example, Petty and colleagues (1995) have attempted to link the assessment of organizational culture with broader performance measures. Their study found evidence of associations between the measures of performance and organizational culture, with the strongest indication of the link being evident in the correlations between 'teamwork' and performance. Similar evidence exists across various studies of the impact of shared views of culture on attitudes and behaviour and ultimately on performance giving weight to attempt to manage performance through understanding culture.

ALISTAIR CHEYNE

See also:

Change management; Teamwork.

References and selected further readings

Ashkanasy, N.M, C.P.M. Wilderom and M.F. Peterson (eds) (2011), *The Handbook of Organizational Culture and Climate*, 2nd edn, Thousand Oaks, CA: Sage.

Deal, T.E. and A.A. Kennedy (1982), *Corporate Cultures: The Rites and Rituals of Organisational Life*, Reading MA: Addison-Wesley.

Peters, T.J. and R.H. Waterman (1982), *In Search of Excellence: Lessons from America's Best Run Companies*. New York: Harper and Row.

Petty, M.M., N.A. Beadles, C.M. Lowery, D.F. Chapman and D.W. Connell (1995), Relationships between organizational culture and organizational performance, *Psychological Reports*, **76**, pp.483–492.

Rousseau, D.M. (1990), Assessing organizational culture: the case for multiple methods, in B. Schneider (ed.), *Organizational Climate and Culture*, San Francisco: Jossey-Bass.

Schein, E.H. (1984), Coming to a new awareness of organizational culture, *Sloan Management Review*, **25**, pp.3–16.

Schein, E.H. (1985), *Organizational Culture and Leadership*, San Francisco: Jossey-Bass.

Organizational learning

Organizational learning is defined as the process by which the organization increases the knowledge created by individuals in an organized way and transforms this knowledge into the organization's knowledge systems (Crossan et al., 1999). Organizational learning helps in building the knowledge base required to achieve strategic renewal by drawing on tacit and explicit knowledge from internal and external sources (Shipton et al., 2013). It also inspires people to persistently and collectively expand their capability to generate the results they truly desire (Senge, 1990).

Little empirical analysis is available concerning the mechanisms that transform organizational learning into performance. The time lag between organizational learning and performance improvement makes it difficult to study the phenomenon empirically. In general, that organizational learning positively influences performance is more evident in technological companies and manufacturing firms. Learning organizations sacrifice today's performance to achieve future performance because the efforts employed in learning activities causes delays to some extent to immediate performance, furthermore, the return on investment of learning activities is not immediately visible (Jiménez-Jiménez and Sanz-Valle, 2011).

Several theories can predict the relationship between organizational learning and performance: marketing theory (organizations that concentrate on speed of innovation gain a greater market share); strategic theories (stress that organizations that adopt an innovation first are able to create isolation mechanisms); and theory of resources and capabilities (maintains that capabilities, resources and technologies needed to adopt the innovation make external imitation more difficult and allow firms to sustain their competitive advantages and obtain greater organizational performance).

Flores et al. (2012) developed a measure of organizational learning. They identified six sub-processes to capture the organizational learning cycle. The cycle starts with 'information acquisition', which is a process by which the company obtains new knowledge and information for the purpose of developing or creating skills, insights, and relationships. Active participation in training, seminars and conferences are examples of information acquisition. New information is then 'distributed' throughout the organization and is shared by employees within the firm. The third and fourth sub-processes are 'interpretation' and 'integration' of the new information that happens when individuals give meaning and transform information into new common knowledge to suite organizational goals. Finally, this information is stored in 'organizational memory' for future use as well as making it broadly available to new situations as 'institutionalized knowledge'.

MAHA ALFARHAN, HELEN SHIPTON AND TIM CAMPBELL

See also:

Informal learning; On-the-job learning.

References and selected further readings

Crossan, M.M., H.W. Lane and R.E. White (1999), An organizational learning framework: from intuition to institution, *The Academy of Management Review*, **24**(3), pp. 522–537.
Flores, L.G., W. Zheng, D. Rau and C.H. Thomas (2012), Organizational learning: subprocess identification, construct validation, and an empirical test of cultural antecedents, *Journal of Management*, **38**(2), pp. 640–667.
Jiménez-Jiménez, D. and R. Sanz-Valle (2011), Innovation, organizational learning, and performance, *Journal of Business Research*, **64**(4), pp. 408–417.
Senge, P.M. (1990), *The Fifth Discipline: The Art and Practice of the Learning Organization*, New York: Doubleday.
Shipton, H., Q. Zhou and E. Mooi (2013), Is there a global model of learning organizations? An empirical, cross-nation study, *International Journal of Human Resource Management*, **24**(12), pp. 2278–2298.

Organizational misbehaviour

Organizational misbehaviour is the most frequently used term to designate behaviour in organizations that does not conform to managerial or other expectations and which, although discouraged, is not entirely prevented (Ackroyd and Thompson, 1999; Vardi and Weitz, 2004). Misbehaviour is of interest today is because it is apparently becoming more frequent, varied and troublesome (Fleming and Spicer, 2007). Whether misbehaviour is really more prevalent or simply more salient for managers and because of new technology is more quantifiable is questionable, however.

It is useful to distinguish between misbehaviour *in* organizations and misbehaviour *by* organizations. The latter considers the failure of organizations to comply with the law and or moral codes and is often overlooked by researchers into misbehaviour. However, misbehaviour *by* organizations is actually the traceable to those who act on behalf of their organization. This misbehaviour, then, is part of the misbehaviour of privileged groups, which also may be becoming more common (Sayles and Smith, 2006) and should be included in the subject.

Knowledge of organizational misbehaviour was first assembled by examining the findings from research in the sociology of work (Ackroyd and Thompson, 1999). From this it was found that there were some standard forms of misbehaviour – absenteeism, effort limitation, fiddling and pilferage. In all areas of misbehaviour, a similar pattern of causation was found. Efforts to control behaviour were never entirely successful. Thus incentives and controls of working effort were not entirely effective. Similarly, some degree of time indiscipline was usually disregarded, and some access to the products of work allowed. Thus, misbehaviour is behaviour that is not officially allowed, but for which there is nonetheless some degree of toleration. Special language is typically developed to describe it: 'absenteeism' for unauthorized absence; 'soldiering', 'loafing' and other terms for effort limitation; 'pilferage' and 'wastage' for theft. Misbehaviour is thus both allowed and not allowed, and constitutes a precarious, liminal territory under constant renegotiation.

Most of the research considered in studies of misbehaviour was undertaken in factories and plants, and evidence from other of organizations was patchy. Nevertheless, there is every indication that some misbehaviour is found almost everywhere. Current work on misbehaviour, which draws on studies of a wider range of organizations, suggests there is a range of new forms of misbehaviour that research has yet fully to uncover. It is a common finding, for example, that, despite attempts to engage employees in work, there is nonetheless widespread psychological disengagement and distancing by employees. Dissent, the spoken or written failure to approve official views (Collinson and Ackroyd, 2005), combined with cynicism about employers' motives and intentions, are common findings from the ethnographic study of organizations today (Fleming and Spicer, 2007). Thus, there are new forms of misbehaviour in contemporary organizations that have not yet been very fully considered by social scientists or acknowledged by human resource professionals.

STEPHEN ACKROYD

See also:

Conflict; Organizational politics; Resistance.

References and selected further readings

Ackroyd, S and P. Thompson (1999), *Organisational Misbehaviour*, London: Sage.
Collinson, D.L. and S. Ackroyd (2005), Resistance, misbehaviour and dissent, in S. Ackroyd, R. Batt, P. Thompson and P.S. Tolbert (eds), *The Oxford Handbook of Work and Organisation*, Oxford: Oxford University Press.
Fleming, P and A. Spicer (2007), *Contesting the Corporation: Struggle, Power and Resistance in Organisations*, Cambridge: Cambridge University Press.
Sayles, L. and C. Smith (2006), *The Rise of the Rogue Executive: How Good Companies Go Bad and How to Stop the Destruction*, New York: Pearson Education/Prentice Hall.
Vardi, Y and E. Weitz (2004), *Misbehavior in Organisations*, Mahwah, NJ: Lawrence Erlbaum.

Organizational politics

From the beginnings of research into work and work organizations, contestation and negotiation between groups, which is the basic stuff of politics, have been noticed. Often, of course, much of this political activity in the workplace becomes formalized and channelled through industrial relations arrangements and systems. This entry mainly considers informal workplace politics and systems, of which there is a rich variety. It has long been known, for example, that the culture of an organization including its internal politics, will vary according to its formal purposes (Blau and Scott, 1962). But because almost all organizations are hierarchies or heterarchies, in which power is concentrated in the hands of owners and/or the controllers of key resources, there is invariably some sort of informal politics in which issues are mobilized and decisions and their consequences are contested.

The hierarchical nature of most organizations virtually guarantees that, in larger organizations especially, political issues are not organization-wide. Business strategy is likely to feature in the politics of the upper levels of an organization, but more mundane issues such as rates of pay, promotion criteria, and conditions of work are typical issues lower down. Researchers have described such phenomena as organizational 'coups d'état' in which an organization is taken over much as states can be, while 'organizational insurgency' involving larger sections of the membership is not unknown (Zald and Berger, 1978). However, the majority of organizational politics is low-key and concerned with limited issues. At the lower levels of an organization, particularly, employees are usually able only to negotiate about a few of the details of their work, but this they usually try to do. That much organizational politics is about seemingly small issues does not mean it is unimportant. Organizational politics often centrally features chronic issues that are not resolved but are the source of continuing problems. The negotiation of piecework rates in industry is an important historical case in point. Employees' dislike and subversion of piecework payments continued for decades; that is, as long as the payment system existed, and eventually contributed to its abolition. This is true despite the fact that, legally speaking, there was no reason for managers to take the views of employees on this into account. Today the issue of the lack of employee engagement in work is a similar area of chronic contestation: employers see the value of high levels of commitment by employees, but often at best find cynicism and at worst active dissent endemic in the workforce.

Organizational theorists and students of work vary in their attitude to informal politics in organizations. Traditional thinking has disregarded it, finding no place for it or reason for it to exist. For functionalist and contingency theorists, whose ideas were dominant for several decades after World War II, any resistance to change by individuals and groups was assumed to be both dysfunctional and unlikely. Contingency researchers in particular were seemingly unable to see the extent to which organizations – particularly large ones – are political actors and the extent to which their leaders may be motivated by short-term gains. For many subsequent writers, however, organizational politics has been accepted as not only existing but an unavoidable feature of organizations and workplaces that is best taken seriously. It is widely held and taught today that, although organizations have elements of rational design, they are also held together by essentially political relationships and projects

(Jackall, 2008). Any changes that are introduced are seen not simply to be functionally necessary, but have political dimensions as well. Those who seek to develop their organizations will have to mobilize the consent of many other people, giving rise to political processes. Accordingly, teaching about workplace politics is now often a part of executive education. Buchanan and Badham (2008) for example argue that factions and alliances backing different policies and activities are ubiquitous in organizations and so it is advisable that employees recognize this, and consider their place in these political relationships. If executives in particular wish to survive and thrive in modern business, to do what these authors call 'win the turf game', then they must understand the politics that accompanies organizational change. More generally, a similar kind of realism has pervaded the public sphere and the nature of work has become a political issue in its own right. What is happening to such matters as employment levels, the quality of jobs and the work–life balance are now public issues and enter national politics (Edwards and Wajcman, 2005).

A key question with which many social theorists have been historically concerned is not, of course, confined to the politics within organizations. For social theorists, what is important is how conflict in organizations and workplaces mediates conflict in society (Clegg et al., 2006). Marx, for example, influentially thought that conflict – originating in capitalist organizations – would build up tensions that would eventually spill over into insurrectionary politics on the streets, leading to the revolutionary transformation of society. The view of many contemporary theorists is the opposite of this. They suggest that, by various essentially managerial mechanisms, including sustained surveillance and the internalization of work discipline, conflict in society has been reduced, contained and normalized. In this view the politics between groups in society is now largely managed as opposed to being controlled by threat or the use of force. Certainly, societies constituted with many organizations have a much higher relational density than those which do not, making it difficult for clear lines of social cleavage (essential for confrontational politics) to be sustained. An organizational society is more likely to absorb and diffuse political confrontation than it is to amplify it (Ackroyd, 2009).

STEPHEN ACKROYD

See also:
Industrial relations; Organizational misbehaviour; Resistance.

References and selected further readings

Ackroyd, S. (2009), Organisational conflict, in S.R. Clegg and C.L. Cooper (eds), *The Sage Handbook of Organizational Behaviour, Vol 2: Macro Approaches*, London: Sage, pp. 192–208.
Blau, P.M. and W.R. Scott (1962), *Formal Organizations: A Comparative Approach*, San Francisco: Chandler.
Buchanan, D. and R. Badham (2008), *Power, Politics and Organizational Change: Winning the Turf Game*, London: Sage.
Clegg, S.R., D. Courpasson and N. Phillips (2006), *Power and Organisations*, London: Sage.
Edwards, P. and J. Wajcman (2005), *The Politics of Working Life*, Oxford: Oxford University Press.
Jackall, R. (2008), *Moral Mazes: The World of Corporate Managers*, 20th anniversary edition, Oxford: Oxford University Press.
Zald, M.N. and M. Berger (1978), Social movements in organisations: coup d'etat, insurgency and mass movements, *American Journal of Sociology*, **83**(4), pp. 823–861.

Outsourcing

Outsourcing involves the contracting out of a business activity, including some of the human resource functions, which used to be carried out in-house to an external party. Outsourcing may involve the transfer of staff and assets from one business entity to a new party that is to perform the outsourced activity as part of the changeover process. In principle, an organization can outsource any part of its functions/activities, such as production, administration, business process management, and service provisions. An outsourcing contract arrangement may take place on a permanent basis but is often on a fixed duration that may be renewed. Outsourcing can take place domestically as well as internationally, also known as offshoring (offshore outsourcing).

In general, organizations consider using outsourcing for a number of (overlapping) perceived benefits. First, it allows them to concentrate resources on their 'core' business activities where they have expertise and are likely to do best. Second, it enables firms to profit from the rising comparative advantage of specialized producers and service providers who may have expertise in the areas concerned. Third, it provides firms with greater flexibility and productivity by using temporary subcontractors to cover fluctuating demands for labour. The 'just-in-time' deployment of resources also brings other advantages of saving direct costs (e.g., reducing headcount and overtime working) and indirect costs (e.g., cutting administration and backup cost, saving recruitment and training costs, saving absence cost and reduced industrial relations problems). Fourth, outsourcing creates opportunities for firms to shift the burden of risk and uncertainty associated with the business (Williamson, 1985) to someone else. In addition, outsourcing enables firms to keep future costs down by selecting the most competitive tender for renewing the contract (Domberger, 1998). Critics of outsourcing, however, are sceptical about the added value of outsourcing to sustaining a firm's competitive advantage that is built on people-embodied skills (e.g., Prahalad and Hamel, 1990). Other pitfalls of outsourcing include, for example, the loss of quality and control, which may end up costing the firm more to outsource.

The decision-making process as to whether to 'make or buy' (goods) or 'supply or buy' (services) has been conceptualized by Williamson's (1985) transaction cost economic model. According to this model, firms should decide whether to provide goods and services internally or to outsource based on the relative costs of production and transaction. Other scholars have used the 'core' and 'periphery' concepts to explain and explore the outsourcing of company functions (e.g., Atkinson, 1985). It is argued that core activities are those that the firm does best and/or are crucial to the firm's competitive advantage and therefore must be kept internally; whereas 'non-core' activities are considered to have a lower impact on the overall performance of the organization and can therefore be outsourced to external providers. In the context of accelerating global competitive pressures, organizations are being advised to concentrate on their core competencies and utilize outsourcing to capitalize on others' expertise (Domberger, 1998). However, what constitutes core activities and competencies is not static. Moreover, advocates of the resource-based view of the firm (e.g., Barney, 1991) believe that outsourcing can be a valuable learning process to help organizations develop their core competence.

Fang Lee Cooke

See also:
Global supply chains; Strategic HRM; Subcontracting.

References and selected further readings
Atkinson, J. (1985), *Flexibility, Uncertainty and Manpower Management*, Brighton: Institute of Manpower Studies.
Barney, J. (1991), Firm resources and sustained competitive advantage, *Journal of Management*, **17**(1), pp. 99–120.
Domberger, S. (1998), *The Contracting Organisation: A Strategic Guide to Outsourcing*, Oxford: Oxford University Press.
Marchington, M., D. Grimshaw, J. Rubery and H. Willmott (eds) (2005), *Fragmenting Work: Blurring Boundaries and Disordering Hierarchies*, Oxford: Oxford University Press.
Prahalad, C.K. and G. Hamel (1990), The core competence of the corporation, *Harvard Business Review*, May–June, pp. 79–91.
Williamson, O.E. (1985), *The Economic Institutions of Capitalism*, New York: Free Press.

Overtime

Overtime involves the purchase of additional hours from staff, usually at premium rates. It provides a simple and cost-effective form of flexibility for employers as it responds immediately to upwards and downwards fluctuations in demand without labour hiring or dismissal. The use of overtime is sometimes a contractual requirement but is normally agreed on a voluntary and individual basis. Rules governing the overall framework of rates and usage may be subject to collective agreement, especially in countries with strong systems of industrial relations.

Overtime pay typically applies only to hourly paid or 'blue-collar' staff. Salaried workers may be offered 'time of in lieu' in the event of working additional hours, or receive no compensation at all. This 'unpaid overtime' may be a product of (a) a higher degree of job autonomy and employee choice to work extra hours; (b) employment contracts that specify 'reasonable' recourse to additional hours; or (c) implicit mutual expectations of what is required by a given remuneration package and to advance in a career.

A fundamental problem of paid overtime is the perverse incentive that it provides to 'spin out' work. This can contribute to a 'long hours culture' where employees come to depend on the earnings it provides, and is more likely where basic rates of pay are low. Overtime can also become institutionalized because firms are unwilling or unable to hire new staff, or because managers rely on it as a form of control. However, the ability to select workers for overtime can lead to dysfunctional management practices such as favouritism and discrimination. The extensive use of overtime can also be dysfunctional because organizations end up paying premium rates for what may well be less productive work. Another downside is the dependency that employers come to have on a volunteer labour force. For example, informal 'overtime bans' can be an effective form of industrial action amounting to partial strike without falling foul of labour legislation.

Overtime is thus a cost-effective and efficient means to vary labour inputs so long as it is a more or less exceptional practice. Alternatives to overtime include shift-work, which extends basic operating time, and arrangements known variously as 'hours banks', 'working time accounts' or 'annualized hours' systems, which effectively obligate and incorporate overtime into routine labour scheduling.

JAMES ARROWSMITH

See also:

Annualized hours; Long hours culture; Low pay; Shift work; Work–life balance; Working time.

Panel interviews

Panel interviews, also referred to as board or team interviews, consist of two or more interviewers who together interview one candidate and combine their evaluations into an overall score. This allows all interviewers to evaluate the applicant on the same questions and answers at the one time. It also overcomes idiosyncratic biases that individual interviewers might have as well as guarding against possible infringements of legal requirements. These interviews can help better ensure the candidate is acceptable to the whole organization and allow the candidate to get a good feel for the business and its culture.

Studies, with regard to race and its effects on interview scores, have found that the racial composition of the interview panel affect judgements in ways consistent with similarity-attraction and social identity theories. In general, interviewer ratings showed a same-race bias and difference between panels dependent upon the racial composition of the panel, but the size of the effects were small. As such, it appears important to consider not only the interviewer and applicant's race, but also the race of interview panel members.

Research shows, however, that in racially mixed panels where there is a lone white or black interviewer, that interviewers identify more with other panel members than with their own racial group. This suggests that it is important that the membership of racially mixed panels be balanced (Prewett-Livingstone et al., 1996). Provided thorough preparation is undertaken by panel members before the interview, the same panel members ask the same questions of each candidate and there is discussion of the candidates between interviews (Cascio, 1998).

The problem with panel interviews lies in the tribunal nature of the panel. They are not having a conversation with the candidates; they are sitting in judgement upon them and assessing the evidence they are able to present in response to the panel's requests. There is little prospect of building rapport and developing discussion and there is likely to be as much interplay between members of the panel as there is between the panel and the candidate. Panel interviews tend towards over-rigidity. They are dubious as a useful preliminary to employment (Torrington et al., 2011). However, the benefits of the panel interview can be increased, and the disadvantages reduced, if interviewers are properly trained and the interview is well-organized, thoroughly planned and made part of a structured selection process.

Although a thorough questioning of the applicant is likely, the experience can be quite stressful for the interviewee. Another disadvantage can be the time and cost of involving senior managers as panel members. The panel interview is widely used in universities, the military and the public sector.

CHRIS ROWLEY AND NAGIAH RAMASAMY

See also:
Interviews; Selection.

References and selected further readings

Cascio, W.F. (1998), *Applied Psychology in Human Resource Management*, New Jersey: Prentice Hall.
Macan, T. (2009), The employment interview: a review of current studies and directions for future research, *Human Resource Management Review*, **19**, pp. 203–218.

Prewett-Livingstone, A.J., H.S. Field, J.G. Veres and P.M. Lewis (1996), Effects of race on interview ratings in a situational panel interview, *Journal of Applied Psychology*, **81**, pp.178–186.
Stone, R.J. (2014), *Human Resource Management*, 8th edn, Milton: Wiley.
Torrington, D., L. Hall, S. Taylor and C. Atkinson (2011), *Human Resource Management*, 8th edn, Essex: Pearson.

Part-time working

Work is generally considered to be part-time when employees are contracted to work anything less than the standard normal full-time hours. This may be by working fewer days in the week or fewer hours per day. Definitions of part-time working, however, differ from country to country, thus making cross-country comparisons difficult. In the UK, for example, there is no specific number of hours that makes someone part-time (and full-time) although it is commonly defined as working 30 hours or less a week. In the Netherlands it is defined as working less than 35 hours and in France and Belgium it is categorized as four-fifths or less of collectively agreed working time.

Part-time work is the most widely used form of flexible working arrangement. In the UK, official figures indicate that in 2013 just over a quarter of employees worked part-time and around three-quarters of these were female, although it is anticipated than more men will work part-time in the future. Part-time working is more likely to be undertaken in lower-level jobs, and is common in wholesale, retail and motor trades, hotels and restaurants (Lyonette et al., 2010).

Part-time work is generally considered to be demand-led, with most people who work part-time stating they chose to do so because they do not want a full-time job. The benefits to employees are that part-time working allows them to combine work with other responsibilities such as caring for dependents and it provides a better work–life balance, less stress and exhaustion. Studies, however, reveal a more a more ambiguous picture of part-time working for the employee. There can be less access to training, development and promotion opportunities, and part-time work is often associated with lower pro rata pay and lower quality jobs. Part-timers are less likely to perform complex tasks compared to full-timers and research in the UK found that the majority of male and female part-time workers considered they were working below their potential. There is also evidence of occupational downgrading when moving to part-time work, which affects more females than males.

For employers it is a means of attracting and retaining staff, provides flexibility to deal with cyclical demand and allows employers to pay only the most productive hours of an employees' time (on the basis that the longer one works, the less productive per hour one becomes). There is also evidence that work-related illness absences are reduced by means of part-time work. However, there are disadvantages to employing part-time workers. Overall labour costs may increase due to fixed costs such as training, administration and recruitment, particularly where two part-timers are employed instead of one. Providing continuous cover may also be more difficult. Part-timers are sometimes inflexible, choosing to work hours around personal commitments, and this can create resentment among full-time workers. Also certain jobs may not be designed or suited to part-time hours.

Sue Hutchinson

See also:

Absence; Family-friendly policies; Flexible working; Work–life balance.

References and selected further readings

BIS (2014), *Costings and Benefits to Business of Adopting Work Life Balance Working Practices: A Literature Review*, London: Policy Studies Institute, BIS, www.gov.uk/government/uploads/system/uploads/attachment_data/file/323290/bis-14-903-costs-and-benefits-to-business-of-adopting-work-life-balance-working-practices-a-literature-review.pdf.

Eurofound (2011), *Part Time Work in Europe: European Company Survey 2009*, www.eurofound.europa.eu/pubdocs/2010/86/en/3/EF1086EN.pdf.

Kalleberg, A. (2000), Nonstandard employment relations: part-time, temporary and contract work, *Annual Review of Sociology*, **26**, pp. 341–365.

Lyonette, C., B. Baldauf and H. Behle (2010), *'Quality' Part-Time Work: The Evidence Review*, London: Government Equalities Office.

Walsh, J. (2007), Experiencing part-time work: temporal tensions, social relations and the work family interface, *British Journal of Industrial Relations*, **45**(1), pp. 155–177.

Partnership

The notion of 'partnership at work' – also referred to as 'labour management partnership', 'workplace partnership', 'enterprise partnership' and 'social partnership' – has been one of the most topical in employment relations in the past two decades. Although the core ideas have a long history, the term has primarily been used to describe the development of collaborative rather than adversarial relationships between employers and trade unions, as well as a loose term for cooperative workplace relations in both union and non-union workplaces. More precise definitions suggest partnership is concerned with establishing certain principles and commitments between employers, employees and trade unions regarding the conduct of workplace relations. These typically include making joint commitments to organizational success, employment security, improving working life, information-sharing, as well as sharing the fruits of success. Employee voice, and in particular collective employee representation, is also normally a central pillar of partnership, distinguishing it from other concepts such as employee involvement and employee engagement. Usually, employee representation is assumed to be through trade unions, and in the late 1990s many large British employers including Tesco and Barclays signed partnership agreements with their recognized trade unions. There have also been experiments with partnership at the workplace level in other liberal market economies including the United States, Ireland, Australia and New Zealand (Johnstone and Wilkinson, 2016).

However, partnership has proved controversial (Johnstone et al., 2009). On the one hand, advocates suggest that partnership provides trade unions with an opportunity to regain legitimacy and reposition themselves as part of the solution to the development of positive employment relations, successful organizations and ultimately successful social democratic societies (Johnstone, 2015). Employees are said to benefit from higher levels of satisfaction, greater voice and improved work–life balance, while employers gain from greater employee commitment, less conflict and improved productivity. However, the extent to which such mutual gains can be realized has been hotly contested. Some believe that while partnership is not inherently flawed, developing sustainable partnerships likely to result in the benefits proposed above is very difficult. The argument is that, while not quite impossible, effective partnership is likely to be both rare and fragile in lightly regulated liberal market economies such as the UK and US. From this perspective, financialization and an increasingly disconnected capitalism mean even the most good-willed and committed employers cannot necessarily keep their promises (Simms, 2015; Thompson, 2013). Others suggest that the dynamics of capitalism render any notion of partnership at the workplace level fundamentally contradictory, serving only to further the interests of employers (Danford and Richardson, 2016). Critics of partnership prefer alternative trade union strategies such as union organizing, as well as more oppositional and militant forms of unionism.

STEWART JOHNSTONE

See also:

Disconnected capitalism; Financialization; Trade unions; Union organizing.

References and selected further readings

Danford, A. and M. Richardson (2015), Why partnership cannot work and militant alternatives can: historical and contemporary evidence, in S. Johnstone and A. Wilkinson (eds), *Developing Positive Employment Relations: International Experiences of Labour Management Partnership*, Basingstoke: Palgrave.

Johnstone, S., P. Ackers and A. Wilkinson (2009), The British partnership phenomenon: a ten-year review, *Human Resource Management Journal*, **19**(3), pp. 260–279.

Johnstone, S. (2014), Workplace partnership, in A. Wilkinson, J. Donaghey, T. Dundon and R.B. Freeman (eds), *Handbook of Research on Employee Voice*, Cheltenham: Edward Elgar Publishing.

Johnstone, S. (2015), The case for workplace partnership, in S. Johnstone and P. Ackers (eds), *Finding a Voice at Work: New Perspectives on Employment Relations*, Oxford: Oxford University Press.

Johnstone, S. and A. Wilkinson (2016), *Developing Positive Employment Relations: International Experiences of Labour Management Partnership*, Basingstoke: Palgrave.

Simms, M. (2015), Union organizing as an alternative to partnership. Or what to do when employers can't keep their side of the bargain, in S. Johnstone and P. Ackers (eds), *Finding a Voice at Work: New Perspectives on Employment Relations*, Oxford: Oxford University Press.

Thompson, P. (2013), Financialization and the workplace: extending and applying the disconnected capitalism thesis, *Work, Employment & Society*, **27**(3), pp. 472–488.

Paternalism

Paternalism in the field of people management has a history going back to the nineteenth century, but its origins go back further. Thornton identified paternalism as being the history of a certain tradition and practice of governance, particularly in England (Thornton, 1966). Although paternalism continues as an important explanatory term in the field of management, it remains something of a contested concept.

Paternalism has been described as a large and loose term, without any clear definition. This is because the idea itself can be divided into weak and strong definitions. The weak version is seen as simply the benign and benevolent behaviour of the good employer. A stronger version would identify a power nexus at the heart of the employment relationship. The subordinate in the relationship would be unable to recognize his or her 'real' interests, but would instead submit him or herself to the care and protection of the superior in return for acts of service. It is a reciprocal relationship that can develop into one of excessive control by the superior of the subordinate.

The idea, or versions of it, like 'welfare capitalism' in the USA, has taken hold, and is normally associated with a company that provides a range of welfare services to employees in return for a relatively compliant workforce. Cadbury of Bourneville is the example most often cited in the UK, but there were others such as Lever Brothers at Port Sunlight and Rowntree's of York. All three were heavily influenced by their strong Christian convictions.

In the workplace, the employment relationship remains an economic one between employer and employee. But the sharpness of this relationship can be significantly ameliorated by a range of benefits supplied wholly or partially by the company. The Cadbury company in the early part of the twentieth century epitomized this tradition, and provided its workers with a range of benefits unsurpassed at the time. Beginning with medical care, it expanded to encompass pensions, sickness benefits, convalescent provision and sports and recreational facilities.

Less attention has been given to paternalism in more recent times, and the idea still awaits detailed analysis and evaluation. Until then, Ackers (1998) supplies a framework that is perhaps most helpful in providing a set of propositions by which to judge the applicability or otherwise of using the term 'paternalism' in the contemporary workplace. We are reminded that in the workplace coercion and consent almost always sit alongside each other, but the overriding guide is that of the human impulse. Early pioneers of paternalism were often driven by a spiritual influence, and ethical questions still lie at the heart of understanding and applying paternalism in the workplace.

JOHN KIMBERLEY

See also:
Employment relationship; Ethics; Management style.

References and selected further readings

Ackers, P. (1998), On paternalism: seven observations on the uses and abuses of the concept in industrial relations, past and present, *Historical Studies in Industrial Relations*, **6**, pp. 173–193.
Ackers, P. (2001), Paternalism, participation and partnership: rethinking the employment relationship, *Human Relations*, **54**(3), pp. 373–384.
Fitzgerald, R. (1988), *British Labour Management & Industrial Welfare*, London: Croom Helm.
Fox, A. (1986), *History and Heritage: The Social Origins of the British Industrial Relations System*, New York: Allen and Unwin.
Melling, J. (1983), Employers, industrial welfare and the struggle for work-place control in British industry, 1880–1920, in H. Gospel and C. Littler (eds), *Managerial Strategies and Industrial Relations: An Historical and Comparative Study*, London: Heinemann Educational Books.
Thornton, A.P. (1966), *The Habit of Authority: Paternalism in British History*, New York: Allen and Unwin.

Payment by results

Payment by results is a type of payment system sometimes used in a strict sense to indicate a system in which there is a direct relationship between pay and output (e.g., piecework). At other times, the term may be taken to refer to any system in which an element of pay is related to employee performance, and thus could include such items as attendance bonus. Piecework is a payment system in which an agreed sum of money is paid in exchange for a specified unit of work. There are two basic types:

money piecework, which attaches a price to each piece of work, and time piecework, in which a worker is given a fixed time to do a job but is paid the same amount if the job is finished early. The term piecework is sometimes, incorrectly, used more generally as a synonym for payment by results. Systems of payment by results were the most common form of payment for manual workers in British manufacturing. Evidence now points to a shift away from strict output-based systems especially for manual workers (Drucker, 2009).

MARK GILMAN

See also:

Bonuses/incentives; Payment system.

References and selected further readings

Armstrong, M. (2012), *Armstrong's Handbook of Reward Management*, London: Kogan Page.
Gilman, M. (2013), Reward management, in T. Redman and A. Wilkinson (eds), *Contemporary Human Resource Management: Text and Cases*, New York; Pearson.
Perkins S.J. and G. White (2008), *Employee Reward: Alternatives, Consequences and Contexts*, London: Chartered Institute of Personnel and Development.
White, G. and J. Drucker (2009), *Reward Management: A Critical Text*, London, Routledge.

Payment system

Payment systems are methods of rewarding people for their contribution to the organization. There are many different kinds of payment systems, ranging from payment by results, time-related pay, individual and group bonuses, profit-related, etc. There are also systems based in part on the worker gaining and using additional skills or competencies. So pay systems provide the basis on which an organization rewards workers for their individual contribution, skill and performance. They are not to be confused with pay structures, which are used to determine specific pay rates for particular jobs, usually based on the nature of the job, its content and requirements. A pay structure provides the framework within which the organization places the pay rates for its various jobs or groups of jobs.

Pay systems fall into two main categories: (a) those where pay does not vary in relation to achievements or performance, (basic rate systems); and (b) those where pay, or part pay, does vary in relation to results/profits/performance (including the acquisition of skills). There are also systems where pay – and any enhancement – is related to the gaining of extra skills or competencies.

Factors that need to be taken into account when considering a payment system may include product market, labour market, technology and employee expectations.

Identifying the objectives of the payment system is also important especially in attempting to link to the organization's overall objectives. Examples might include:

- Increase productivity.
- Control unit labour costs.
- Recruit, retain and motivate suitably qualified workers.
- Improve quality.

- Move towards or encourage teamwork.
- Change organizational culture and attitudes.
- Simplify the existing system.
- Reduce conflict arising from the existing system.
- Comply with the law on equal pay.

MARK GILMAN

See also:
Bonuses and incentives; Payment by results; Performance-related pay.

References and selected further readings
Acas (2015), *Payment Systems*, Acas advisory booklet.
Beacham, R.H.S. (1979), *Pay Systems: Principles and Techniques*, London: Heinemann.
White, G. and J. Drucker (2009), *Reward Management: A Critical Text*, London, Routledge.

Peer appraisal

Peer appraisal is a performance assessment conducted by an employee's colleagues or peers. The performance appraisal had been originally conducted by supervisors and now involves a variety of individuals, including peers. Changes to the traditional performance appraisal is due to changes in the work environment, such as autonomous work groups, team-based structures, downsizing, total quality management, employee empowerment and reengineering (Barclay and Harland, 1995). In addition, research has also suggested that there are a variety of negative outcomes with the use of single-source performance appraisals. Although research is relatively scarce on peer appraisals, the main argument supporting peer appraisals is that peers may provide more accurate information and offer higher quality feedback relating to their colleagues' performance than from their supervisors. Peers can offer unique perspectives about the quality and consistency of performance that occurs on a daily basis and this information can help to control for confounding factors that may contribute to the rating variation, as peer raters are on the same organizational level as the ratee (Valle and Davis, 1999).

A peer appraisal is a valuable tool towards increasing employee participation, giving employees a sense of importance and value, and is linked to empowerment and a range of positive employee attitudes and behaviours (satisfaction, motivation, self-efficacy and performance). However, some negative perceptions on peer appraisals mean that organizations may be reluctant to include them within their performance management systems. For example, some employees may become defensive with this process and believe it is outside the scope of their job responsibilities. Peers may feel vulnerable depending on the training and support provided to guide them through the process and may be afraid to deliver an honest appraisal. In addition, organizational politics, procedural fairness and individual ethical values and personality traits (extrovert versus introvert) may influence the validity and integrity of the peer appraisal process (Bamberger et al., 2005). Furthermore, some authors have argued that in some team-based work environments, peer appraisals are particularly critical, as supervisors are considered not to have direct and valid performance information.

AMIE SOUTHCOMBE

See also:
Performance appraisal; 360-degree appraisal.

References and selected further readings

Bamberger, P.A., I. Erev, M. Kimmel and T. Oref-Chen (2005), Peer assessment, individual performance, and contribution to group processes: the impact of rater anonymity, *Group & Organization Management*, **30**(4), pp. 344–377.

Barclay, J.H. and L.K. Harland (1995), Peer performance appraisals: the impact of rater competence, rater location, and rating correctability on fairness perceptions, *Group & Organization Management*, **20**, pp. 39–60.

Dominick, P.G., R.R. Reilly and J.W. Mcgourty (1997), The effects of peer feedback on team member behavior, *Group & Organization Management*, **22**(4), pp. 508–520.

Drexler, J.A., T.A. Beehr and T.A. Stetz (2001), Peer appraisals: differentiation of individual performance on group tasks, *Human Resource Management*, **40**(4), pp. 333–345.

Fedor, D.B., K.L. Bettenhausen and W. Davis (1999), Peer reviews employees' dual roles as raters and recipients, *Group & Organization Management*, **24**(1), pp. 92–120.

Valle, M. and K. Davis (1999), Teams and performance appraisal: using metrics to increase reliability and validity, *Team Performance Management*, **5**(8), pp. 238–244.

Pensions

A pension is a regular payment to those who have retired from work due to age or ill-health paid by the state or an employer (Heery and Noon, 2001). There are two main types of pension – state pension and occupational pensions, and they are available to everyone as long as they are in employment. The UK state pension is made up of the basic state pension and additional state pension. All UK citizens are entitled to the full basic state pension (£115.95 per week for a single person and £185.45 per week for a married couple, as at April 2015) if they have built enough qualifying years during their working life (Perkins and White, 2011). The state pension age (SPA) is currently 65 for men and it is in the process of being increased from 62 to 65 for women. The Pensions Act 2007 will raise the SPA to 66 for both men and women by April 2020 and the government is considering future increases in SPA from 66 to 68. The state pension provides a minimum level of entitlement for all citizens but many employers also provide occupational pension schemes. Many people take out a pension with their employer to top up their retirement income.

In occupational pension schemes, the employee and employer contribute to a pension fund. There are two types of occupational pension schemes – defined benefits (DB) and defined contributions (DC). In a DB scheme, the benefit provided on retirement is determined by a set formula. The pension is typically proportional to service and salary and the employee will be able to project exactly the amount of final benefit to be received. The employee contributions are fixed and those of the employer vary based on specialist advice to guarantee the level of the final benefit paid to the employee. In this case, the employer bears the risk, since salaries grow faster than expected and the fund investments managed by the employer may perform less well than expected (Armstrong and Murlis, 2007). In a DC scheme, contributions are paid into an individual account for each employee. The contributions are invested, for example in the stock market, and the returns on the investment are credited to the individual's account. Under a DC scheme, the benefit provided to the employee on retirement depends on investment returns paid on the pension fund. In this case the employee bears the risk, since the fund investments may perform poorly either in the long term or in the period preceding retirement (Armstrong and Murlis, 2007).

In the past several years, the UK has seen a shift from DB schemes to DC schemes as a response to a combination of factors such as: the increasing cost of employer pension scheme contributions; poor return on pension fund investments and an increase in life expectancy, meaning that pensions have to provide for a much longer period of retirement. Moreover there has been a decline in the number of employers offering occupational pension schemes. The first Turner Report (Pensions Commission, 2004) provided an analysis of the problems faced in the UK and suggested that people will have to save more and work longer in order to provide a sufficient retirement income. In response to these concerns, new legislation has been introduced, making the enrolment of employees to a private pension scheme and mandatory minimum contributions from employers compulsory.

BETHANIA ANTUNES

See also:
Benefits; Retirement; Reward management.

References and selected further readings

Armstrong, M. and H. Murlis (2007), *Reward Management: A Handbook of Remuneration Strategy and Practice*, 5th edn, London: Kogan Page.
CIPD (2015), Occupational Pensions: A Strategic Overview, www.cipd.co.uk/hr-resources/factsheets/occupational-pensions-strategic-overview.aspx.
Heery, E. and M. Noon (2001), *A Dictionary of Human Resource Management*, Oxford: Oxford University Press.
Pensions Commission (2004), *Pensions: Challenges and Choices. The First Report of the Pensions Commission*, London: The Stationary Office.
Perkins, S. and G. White (2011), *Reward Management: Alternatives, Consequences and Contexts*, 2nd edn, London: Chartered Institute of Personnel and Development.

Performance appraisal

A performance appraisal is a formal review and evaluation of an employee's job performance and productivity in relation to goals that have been agreed upon. Appraisals may also contain general criteria related to the employee's position within the organization. The formal performance appraisal process should be supported by more informal monitoring and support, which can be provided on an ongoing basis as required or appropriate.

A performance appraisal is an opportunity for an employee to reflect on their performance and productivity normally over the previous year, or other specified period. The primary objectives of the performance appraisal are to (a) support the continued high performance of staff, their career development and the advancement of the organization's strategic objectives, and (b) set specific annual objectives and outcomes in the context of the organization's strategic objectives and to review progress towards previously established employee objectives and outcomes. For new employees, the performance appraisal process begins during orientation. It is normally during this time that their performance is appraised to determine whether they will successfully complete their probationary period. Once this occurs, an employee's performance objectives can be set for an agreed period of time. Performance appraisals are an important strategic tool that aligns the goals of the organization to that of the individual (Gruman, 2011).

The benefits of a formal appraisal process include increased communication and clear guidelines for employees to achieve and progress their careers and for the organization to achieve their strategic goals such as increasing performance and productivity as well as providing feedback on important future needs. One common concern raised by employees and managers is the possibility that performance appraisals may be misused as a control or punishment method. In organizations where such beliefs exist, it is often that the implementation and communication of the purpose and importance of the process is not communicated clearly (Gurbur and Dikmenli, 2007). Furthermore, supervisors who lack the required skills and receive little or no training in conducting performance appraisals may be reluctant, avoid, or in some cases misuse the process.

AMIE SOUTHCOMBE

See also:

Performance appraisal interview.

References and selected further readings

Chiang, F. and T. Birtch (2010), Appraising performance across borders: examinations of the purposes and practices of performance appraisal in a multi-country context, *Journal of Management Studies*, **47**(7), pp. 1365–1393.
Fletcher, C. (2001), Performance appraisal and management: the developing research agenda, *Journal of Occupational and Organizational Psychology*, **74**(4), pp. 473–487.
Gruman, J.S. (2011), Preformance management and employee engagment, *Human Resource Management Review*, **21**, pp. 123–136.
Gurbur, S. and O. Dikmenli (2007), Performance appraisal biases in a public organization: an emprical study, *Journal of Social Sciences*, **13**(1), pp. 108–138.
Kavanagh, P., J. Benson and M. Brown (2007), Understanding performance appraisal fairness, *Asia Pacific Journal of Human Resources*, **45**(2), pp. 132–150.
Prowse, P. and J. Prowse (2009), The dilemma of performance appraisal, *Measuring Business Excellence*, **13**(4), pp. 69–77.

Performance appraisal interview

The appraisal interview is a time where the staff member and their supervisor review performance documentation. There has been growing interest in the importance of performance appraisal interviews for employee performance and development. There are three main groups of studies in this area. First, research has found that what happens during the actual appraisal interview has an impact on organizational value. Second, studies have found that the interview itself, employee rating systems and interpersonal relations all play a crucial role in job satisfaction. Third, studies have investigated the 'best practice' of performance appraisal interviews and established guidelines from analysing personal experience, interviews with supervisors and employees, and analysis of preparation forms or the performance appraisal interview and evaluation sheets (Asmuß, 2008).

The supervisor should prepare for the appraisal interview by reviewing the documentation, any additional supporting material and having a discussion with the staff member concerned. The interview should focus on achievements and progress made over the last review period against previously established objectives and actions and the required expectations of the level of the position and person (Gurbur, 2007). During the appraisal interview and upon its completion, it is important to consider where the information gathered can be fed back into the organization. This may be through informing better job design, initiating further job analysis, determining training and development needs, informing succession planning and career development, as well as remuneration and rewards plans and programmes.

AMIE SOUTHCOMBE

See also:

Performance appraisal.

References and selected further readings

Asmuß, B. (2008), Performance appraisal interviews: preference organization in assessment sequences, *Journal of Business Communication*, **45**(4), pp. 408–429.

Cederblom, D. (1982), The performance appraisal interview: a review, implications, and suggestions, *Academy of Management Review*, **7**(2), pp. 219–227.

Erdogan, B. (2003), Antecedents and consequences of justice perceptions in performance appraisals, *Human Resource Management Review*, **12**(4), pp. 555–578.

Gurbur, S. and O. Dikmenli (2007), Performance appraisal biases in a public organization: an emprical study, *Journal of Social Sciences*, **13**(1), pp. 108–138.

Holbrook, R.L. (2002), Contact points and flash points: conceptualizing the use of justice mechanisms in the performance appraisal interview, *Human Resource Management Review*, **12**(1), pp. 101–123.

Silverman, S.B. and K.N. Wexley (1984), Reaction of employees to performance appraisal interviews as a function of their participation in rating scale development, *Personnel Psychology*, **37**(4), pp. 703–710.

Performance management

Performance management (PM) describes the system of HRM activities within the workplace that is designed to motivate employees to perform in line with corporate goals. Often used interchangeably in practice with the term 'performance appraisal', PM is a broader set of practices, of which performance appraisal is one element. The full range of activities includes: setting employee performance goals; regularly monitoring performance against expectations; providing ongoing feedback to employees; conducting periodic formal performance appraisals; identifying high-performers and high-potentials; linking the reward system with appraisal results; and providing developmental and career opportunities.

Performance appraisal (or evaluation) used to be the primary concern of organizations, with great emphasis placed on the accuracy of ratings. Appraisal is an event during which an employee's performance is assessed, usually observed over a specified period of time. This requires the application of reliable and valid methods of evaluation (either at individual or team level), resulting in ratings through systems such as forced distribution. The role of the assessor (usually the supervisor) is critical in the process of applying such rating systems effectively, and avoiding bias in the process. To combat this potential bias, 360-degree performance appraisal was introduced, which includes the input of the supervisor along with peers, subordinates, customers and the employee him or herself.

PM is, however, more than just the appraisal process. It also involves goal-setting and continuous feedback for employees. For PM to be effective, the goals of individuals need to be aligned with the goals of the organization. Importantly, if employees lack a clear view of how their daily activities contribute to the organization as a whole, PM is unlikely to have its intended motivating effect. Similarly, all the practices that make up the PM system need to be aligned to ensure they are complementary. The whole PM system is therefore often managed through information technology systems to control the process and ensure alignment. This often results in a standardized PM system being rolled out across an organization, producing performance data that can be benchmarked between organizational units.

It is noteworthy that a standard PM system may not always be most effective in every organizational setting. More contingent PM systems take into account not only the organizational goals, but also the institutional and cultural factors that affect what motivates a person to perform well. These factors vary within organizations and across countries. Within organizations, the extent of union involvement may determine whether or not PM systems are in place, and what activities they might include. Comparing across countries, in less-developed economies, for example, performance management is a relatively new phenomenon in the HRM field, as organizations become more performance-oriented. The idea of performance being managed is therefore relatively new to both employees and supervisors, so a complex system of 360-degree appraisals with forced distribution is unlikely to be effective. The PM field has most recently focused on global PM, considering how multinational corporations manage performance across organizational and national boundaries (Hellqvist, 2011).

Alongside the strategic objectives of PM systems to support organizational goals, PM is primarily designed for one of two operational functions: administrative decisions or development (Biron et al., 2011). An administrative system focuses on facilitating the linkage between individual performance and rewards. As such, the system is being used as an input mechanism to measure, assess change and benchmark employee performance. PM for developmental purposes, in contrast, is an output mechanism that focuses on the continuous improvement of performance through training and development opportunities (Gravina and Siers, 2011). In talent management, the use of PM to identify high-performers and high-potentials in an organization combines both an administrative decision (labelling an individual as 'talent') and development (providing continuous feedback and improvement activities as part of a defined talent programme).

Ultimately, the aim of PM is to have a positive effect on employee attitudes and behaviours, which in turn is expected to improve the organization's overall performance (De Nisi and Smith, 2014). To this end, we have witnessed the emergence of high-performance work systems (HPWS), bundles of HRM practices expected to deliver high performance outcomes. These can be considered an extension of PM systems, in that they incorporate a range of HRM activities, including PM, which are expected to have a positive effect on employee performance.

Whether part of a HPWS or not, the implemented PM system requires interaction between employees and their supervisors. How the employee reacts to the PM process is important in determining its outcomes. Perceptions of fairness that emerge from the employee experience of the PM process are critical in this respect. If an employee considers the PM process and/or outcome to be fair, they are more likely do demonstrate high levels of engagement, commitment, and job satisfaction, as well as reduced absenteeism and turnover.

ELAINE FARNDALE

See also:

High-performance work systems; Performance appraisal; Performance appraisal interview; Reward management; Strategic HRM; Talent management; Training and development.

References and selected further readings

Biron, M., E. Farndale and J. Paauwe (2011), Performance management: lessons from world-leading firms, *International Journal of Human Resource Management*, **22**(6), pp. 1294–1311.
Den Hartog, D.N., P. Boselie and J. Paauwe (2004), Performance management: a model and research agenda, *Applied Psychology: An International Review*, **53**(4), pp. 556–569.
De Nisi, A. and C.E. Smith (2014), Performance appraisal, performance management, and firm-level performance: a review, a proposed model, and new directions for future research, *The Academy of Management Annals*, **8**(1), pp. 127–179.
Gravina, N.E. and B.P. Siers (2011), Square pegs and round holes: ruminations on the relationship between performance appraisal and performance management, *Journal of Organizational Behavior Management*, **31**(4), pp. 277–287.
Hellqvist, N. (2011), Global performance management: a research agenda, *Management Research Review*, **34**(8), pp. 927–946.

Performance-related pay

There is no accepted single definition of performance-related pay (PRP). It is described as both a form of pay progression within the grade or scale, based on an individual performance appraisal or review (often referred to as appraisal-related or merit pay), and as any form of payment system that relates pay in some way to a measure(s) of work performance. This broader definition would encompass most forms of variable pay (see 'Variable pay' in this volume). As a form of pay progression, any increase in salary level is normally consolidated into base pay. There are several forms of performance-related pay progression – some organizations increase pay up a fixed salary scale while others use movement through a band or range.

There is a substantial literature on performance-related pay, both academic and practitioner, and the debate about its effectiveness as a means to manage employee performance continues (see, for example, Kohn, 1993; Pfeffer, 1998; Gerhart and Fang, 2014). In both the USA and the UK there has been conflicting research evidence about the impact of such payment systems. The psychological literature places much more emphasis upon individual differences in performance than economic theory and psychologists have found many more variables to consider, such as personality, the need for personal achievement and self-esteem. Gerhart and Rynes (2003) argue that economists and managers may find this complexity inconvenient but that ignoring the individual and contextual differences may lead to problems in managing organizational performance.

While the content theories of motivation (e.g., Maslow, Herzberg, MacGregor) indicate that pay is not a motivator, the concept of linking pay to performance is strongly embedded in management culture and appears to be supported by several process theories of motivation (e.g. goal theory, expectancy theory, equity theory, attribution theory and tournament theory).

Kessler (2005) argues that any typology of performance management must address three issues:

1. What is assessed?
2. How is it measured?
3. How is it rewarded?

A major issue in the design of PRP systems is whether there are adequate measures of individual performance available to employers to ensure a fair evaluation of the employee. For many lower-level jobs, it is hard to distinguish the contribution of individuals (on a production line, for example) and team- or organization-level rewards might make more sense. There are also debates about the efficacy of using PRP in some public sector professional roles (e.g., school teachers, police, doctors and nurses) and also concerns about the creation of perverse incentives that reward financial targets but may conflict with quality objectives or customer needs. The role of large bonuses in the collapse of the banks in the economic recession is one example.

While most of the literature on PRP focuses on whether such systems motivate employees or not, Marsden (2009) argues that there is a paradox in that, while there is little evidence that PRP motivates employees, it clearly has had an effect on organizational performance. According to Marsden, this is because the introduction of PRP has been more about renegotiating the effort bargain than its motivational effect.

GEOFF WHITE

See also:
Motivation; Reward management; Variable pay.

References and selected further reading

Gerhart, B. and M. Fang (2014), Pay for (individual) performance: issues, claims, evidence and the role of sorting effects, *Human Resource Management Review*, **24**, pp. 41–52.
Gerhart, B. and S.L. Rynes (2003), *Compensation: Theory, Evidence and Strategic Implications*, Thousand Oaks, CA: Sage.
Kessler, I. (2005), Remuneration systems, in S. Bach (ed.), *Managing Human Resources: Personnel Management in Transition*, Oxford: Blackwell.
Kohn, A. (1993), Why incentive plans cannot work, *Harvard Business Review*, **71**, pp. 54–63.
Marsden, D. (2009), *The Paradox of Performance Related Pay Systems: Why Do We Keep Adopting Them in the Face of Evidence that they Fail to Motivate?* CEP Discussion Paper No 946, London: London School of Economics and Political Science.
Pfeffer, J. (1998), Six dangerous myths about pay, *Harvard Business Review*, **76**, pp. 108–119.

Peripheral worker

Peripheral workers, also referred to as contingent workers, are typically those engaged in temporary part-time, fixed-term contracts, zero-hour contracts or casual employment. They may also include interns and temporary workers dispatched from employment agencies. According to the core-peripheral model, the deployment of peripheral workers offers employers staffing flexibility and helps reduce labour cost. Compared to the core workers, peripheral workers typically receive inferior employment terms and conditions, with negligible employment security and career prospect, limited workplace benefits and a reduced level of social security. In comparison, peripheral workers are much less unionized or represented than core workers. They also enjoy less protection from employment regulations.

Peripheral workers often engage in non-core activities with a lower level of human capital requirement, and are therefore treated as an expense with limited human resource investment. However, increasingly peripheral workers may be deployed to carry out core tasks as firms try to contain labour cost and, for some, try to avoid legal responsibilities by employing only a very small core workforce. While traditionally peripheral workers in the Anglo-Saxon context may consist of primarily women, older men and semi-skilled labour, peripheral workers today may comprise young and relatively well-educated workers. They may be performing similar tasks alongside their counterparts in permanent employment, such as contract nurses and university graduate agency workers in banks in China and production workers in Indian–Japanese joint venture automotive plants in India (Cooke, 2015). In some cases, peripheral workers may even perform more knowledge-intensive work with greater value to the business than their counterparts in the core workforce (e.g., Gamble and Huang, 2009).

The rise of contingent employment reflects a shift from an internal labour market towards an external labour market as employers' human resource strategy becomes more sophisticated in order to remain competitive. The transactional approach to managing the employment relationship with the peripheral workers may undermine their commitment and create conflicts between the core and the peripheral group of the workforce. A broader social consequence of the adoption of contingent employment, it is argued, is the creation of a new social underclass through the withdrawal of job security and social welfare to contingent workers (Beck, 2000). Research evidence has largely pointed to the fact that the job quality of peripheral workers is inferior to that of their counterparts with a permanent contract, measured by the nature of work, pay and conditions, training and development opportunities, intrinsic value of the work and job/career prospect (e.g., Bolton et al., 2012). Arguably, the adoption of contingent employment enables firms to transfer risks and insecurity from the organization to individuals (Bolton et al., 2012). And the weak bargaining power of the workers in the labour market, often with the absence of trade unions as a traditional source of institutional protections, is one of the main causes that accounts for the collective experience of disenchantment of the disadvantaged workers.

FANG LEE COOKE

See also:

Core worker; Fixed-term contract; Flexible firm; Temporary work; Zero-hours contract.

References and selected further readings

Beck, U. (2000), *The Brave New World of Work*, Malden: Blackwell.
Bolton, S., M. Houlihan and K. Laaser (2012), Contingent work and its contradictions: towards a moral economy framework, *Journal of Business Ethics*, **11**(1), pp. 121–132.
Cooke, F.L. (2015), The role of international HRM in offshoring and managing contingent workers, in D. Collings, G. Wood and P. Caligiuri (eds), *The Routledge Companion to International Human Resource Management*, London: Routledge, pp. 496–510.
Gamble, J. and Q.H. Huang (2009), One store, two employment systems: core, periphery and flexibility in China's retail sector, *British Journal of Industrial Relations*, **47**(1), pp. 1–26.
Liden, R.C., S.J. Wayne, M.L. Kraimer and R.T. Sparrowe (2003), The dual commitments of contingent workers: an examination of contingents' commitment to the agency and the organisation, *Journal of Organisational Behavior*, **24**(5), pp. 609–625.
Way, S.A., D.P. Lepak, C.H. Fay and J.W. Thacker (2010), Contingent workers' impact on standard employee withdrawal behaviors: does what you use them for matter? *Human Resource Management*, **49**(1), pp. 109–138.

Person–environment fit

It has long been argued that behaviour is a function of the person and the environment (Lewin, 1951); employees in the same organization do not behave identically, nor does one employee act the same across different organizational contexts. Simply put, individuals and situations influence one another. This means we can expect that the interaction between workers and the organizations in which they operate will influence both individual and collective outcomes. These assumptions lay the groundwork for the person–environment (P–E) fit literature, which proposes that outcomes are more positive when there is congruence between individual characteristics (e.g., personality, values, needs, abilities) and environmental characteristics (e.g., demands, supplies, norms, values).

P–E fit is a broad term that encompasses distinct dimensions of fit within the general area of work including employees' fit with their job, group, vocation, organization and supervisor. Of these five categories, person–organization (P–O) fit and person–job (P–J) fit have achieved the most scholarly interest in HRM. P–O fit is a topic that concerns antecedents and consequences of compatibility between people and the organizations in which they work (Chatman, 1989). P–J fit is defined as the compatibility between individuals and the jobs or tasks that they perform in the workplace (Kristof-Brown, 2007). Both P–O and P–J fit have a significant impact on individual outcomes.

P–E scholars have defined compatibility in different ways, which has caused debate in the field (Kristof, 1996). In P–O fit, a dominant distinction has been between supplementary and complementary fit. Supplementary fit looks at whether a person achieves congruence because they supplement, embellish or possess similar characteristics to others already in the organization. On the other hand, complementary fit focuses on whether the person adds to the organization by providing what was previously missing (Muchinsky and Monahan, 1987). In the P–J literature, researchers have distinguished between fit, resulting from a job that satisfies individuals' needs or preferences (needs–supplies perspective), and compatibility, occurring when employees' abilities meet organizational or job demands (demands–abilities perspective) (Edwards, 1991).

Positive outcomes of both P–J and P–O fit include positive job attitudes such as satisfaction, commitment and turnover, as well as motivation and behaviours such as extra-role behaviour and reduced turnover intentions (Kristof-Brown et al., 2005).

Antecedents of P–J fit have mainly focused on personality characteristics. P–O fit ante-cedents have been a bit broader, focusing on organizational selection and socialization practices. P–O fit can be achieved through hiring and socialization. Selection (the set of procedures though which an organization chooses its members) is a strong determi-nant of fit for a new employee, whereas socialization has been shown to have a strong influence on P–O fit for more tenured employees (Kristof-Brown, 2007).

In empirical studies, fit has been assessed both subjectively (perceived fit) and objec-tively (actual fit). Perceived fit examines how congruent an individual and his/her organi-zational or job values are from the employee's perspective. Researchers have created actual fit indices by using objective measures that compare the person to the environ-ment using separate sources, and then compute an index to mathematically represent the degree of fit. The closer the match between the two measures, the better the fit.

Notably, recent research is focusing on trying to understand the dynamic nature of perceived and actual P–E fit. For instance, there is evidence that P–E fit evolves over time, as people's perceptions and experiences change. Additionally, recent studies using interpretive perceptions of fit have been able to complement and extend earlier models that were based on more positivistic assumptions (e.g., Shipp and Jensen, 2011).

BRIANNA BARKER CAZA

References and selected further readings

Cable, D.M. and T.A. Judge (1996), Person–organization fit, job choice decisions, and organizational entry, *Organizational Behavior and Human Decision Processes*, **67**, pp. 294–311.

Chatman, J.A. (1989), Improving interactional organizational research: a model of person organization fit, *Academy of Management Review*, **14**, pp. 333–349.

Chatman, J.A. (1991), Matching people and organizations: selection and socialization in public accounting firms, *Administrative Sciences Quarterly*, **36**, pp. 459–484.

Edwards, J.R. (1991), Person–job fit: a conceptual integration, literature review, and methodological critique, in C.L. Cooper and I.T. Robertson (eds), *International Review of Industrial and Organizational Psychology, Vol. 6*, New York: Wiley, pp. 283–357.

Kristof, A.L. (1996), Person–organization fit: an integrative review of its conceptualization, measurement, and implications, *Personnel Psychology*, **49**, pp. 1–49.

Kristof-Brown, A. (2007), Person–job fit, in S. Rogelberg (ed.), *Encyclopedia of Industrial and Organizational Psychology*, Thousand Oaks, CA: Sage, pp. 619–621.

Kristof-Brown, A.L., R.D. Zimmerman and E.C. Johnson (2005), Consequences of individuals' fit at work: a meta-analysis of person–job, person–organization, person group, and person–supervisor fit, *Personnel Psychology*, **58**, pp. 281–342.

Lewin, K. (1951), *Field Theory in Social Science: Selected Theoretical Papers*, Westport, CT: Greenwood Press.

Muchinsky, P.M. and C.J. Monahan (1987), What is person–environment congruence? Supplementary versus complementary models of fit, *Journal of Vocational Behavior*, **31**, pp. 268–277.

Shipp, A.J. and K.J. Jensen (2011), Reinterpreting time in fit theory: crafting and re-crafting narratives of fit in medias res, *Academy of Management Review*, **36**(1), pp. 76–101.

Person specification

A person specification, also referred to as job specification, forms one of two parts of job analysis. The first part of job analysis involves the development of a formal job descrip-tion to list and describe the position's tasks and duties detailing the type of work to be performed, the responsibilities of the position, the working conditions and job hazards, as well as information about the equipment that would be used in order to carry out a job's tasks. The second part of the job analysis is the person specification. Person specification is concerned with defining the human attributes required by an employee to perform in the position. Traditionally, person specification stems from two well-known attribute classification systems – the seven-point plan (Rodger, 1952) and the five-point plan (Fraser, 1966), which were developed to describe and categorize the principal features of any job type.

Person specification details the knowledge, skills and abilities (KSAs) required for the job, including the level of education, previous work experience, qualifications and in some cases, the physical skills required. Often, the person specification is split into two distinct parts; essential criteria and desirable criteria. The essential criteria details the attributes that a candidate must have in order to successfully carry out the job. The desirable criteria lists KSAs that are considered non-essential; however, a candidate would be considered more favourably if they have experience with some or all of the listed criteria. Desirable criteria is particularly useful when discriminating between job applicants in the selection process.

As person specification is important for forming the basis of the selection criteria, it is important that it provides objective criteria to be used for selection purposes. Such attention will then assist in guarding against subjective or impressionistic assessment of an applicant's suitability for the job. However, person specification is often seen as a bureaucratic process, considered time-consuming in their development as well as in keeping them up-to-date in accordance with the changing requirements of the organization.

SUSAN RESSIA

See also:
Job analysis; Job description; Knowledge, skills and abilities; Recruitment; Selection.

References and suggested cross-references

Fraser, M. (1966), *Employment Interviewing*, London: McDonald & Evans.
Kramer, R., T. Bartram, H. De Cieri, R.A. Noe, J.R. Hollenbeck, B. Gerhart and P.M. Wright (2014), *Human Resource Management in Australia: Strategy, People, Performance*, 5th edn, North Ryde: McGraw Hill.
Rodger, A. (1952), *The Seven Point Plan*, London: National Institute for Industrial Psychology.
Taylor, S. (1998), *Employee Resourcing*, London: IPD.
Wilton, N. (2012), *An Introduction to Human Resource Management*, 2nd edn, London: Sage.

Personal development plan

A personal development plan (PDP) is a tool utilized by an individual to plan, organize, monitor, review and evaluate their personal and professional development. The focus can be exclusively work, job and/or career related. In that case, a PDP is often associated with the individual's employing organization's performance management process. A PDP in that context is one outcome of an annual or more frequent performance appraisal meeting with the individual employee's manager (Gold, 2013). While a PDP can be and often is also used in assessment of the employee, where PDPs are used, the focus of appraisals is commonly development as well as performance. The role of the manager has been found to be significant in the organization use of PDPs (Beausaert et al., 2013). In some cases, managers have to agree the content of the PDP. In all cases, the manager can support the employee in identifying development needs, provide resources to achieve learning goals, support employees' reflections to aid learning and give feedback on achievements.

Whether in an organization context or not, PDPs are associated with the broader concepts of self-development, or self-managed development (Pedler et al., 2013). For that reason, a PDP can and often does include a focus on broader life goals as well as work and career goals. The starting point, therefore, in formulating a PDP is to decide the breadth of the focus. Once that is done, goals and objectives can be decided. The latter should focus on learning that is needed to achieve the goals set. In other words, this stage of the process involves identifying learning needs. When learning needs are identified, the next stage is to decide which methods will best meet them. The full range of learning methods can be considered. A possible limiting factor is that of resources available. So, the next stage is to identify resources required and to the support required to meet each learning need. In the context of an organization-based PDP, the topic of resources will be discussed and agreed with the individual's manager in an appraisal meeting. Timescales for achieving each learning need, as well as processes for monitoring progress and assessment of achievement are then decided. These stages in formulating a PDP also constitute the content of a PDP. Headings such as 'Goal', 'Objective', 'Method', 'Resources', 'Target Date' and 'Evaluation' are commonly found on standard PDP formats used in organizations or provided/recommended by professional bodies. Professional bodies are concerned with continuing professional development (CPD), which is a concept and process with strong links to PDP (Gold, 2013).

JIM STEWART

See also:

Competence; Continuing professional development; Experiential learning; Learning cycle; Learning style; Training needs analysis.

References and selected further readings

Beausaert, S., M. Segers, A. van den Berge, J. Hommes and W. Gijselaers (2013), The crucial role of the supervisor in supporting employees' use of a personal development plan: an exploratory intervention study, in P. Van den Bossche, W.H. Gijselaers and R.G. Milter (eds), *Facilitating Learning in the 21st Century: Leading Through Technology, Diversity and Authenticity*, Dordrecht: Springer.
Gold, J. (2013), Lifelong learning and continuing professional development, in J. Gold, R. Holden, J. Stewart, P. Iles and J. Beardwell (eds), *Human Resource Development: Theory and Practice*, Basingstoke: Palgrave Macmillan.
Pedler, M., J. Burgoyne and T. Boydell (2013), *A Manager's Guide to Self-Development*, 6th edn, Maidenhead: McGraw-Hill.

Personality test

Personality tests can form part of the selection process after shortlisting has been completed and may be used with other selection methods such as résumés/CVs, structured interviews, references and other performance ability measures. Personality tests can often be used in assessment centres when recruiting for managerial level positions. Some examples of personality tests include the Myers-Briggs Type Indicator (MBTI) instrument and the Five-Factor Model or Big-Five Personality Test. The Five-Factor

Model suggests that differences in the personalities of people can be explained via five dimensions: extraversion, conscientiousness, agreeableness, neuroticism or emotional stability, and openness to experience (Costa and McCrae, 1992).

Personality is a non-cognitive characteristic, and relates more so to a set of 'traits' or 'types' on which the personalities of individuals may differ. Such 'traits' or 'types' tend to be consistent in the behaviour of individuals. For example, an individual with the extraversion trait would be extraverted much of the time, in most social settings. Conscientiousness has been found to be the most reliable of the five dimensions in predicting work performance, predicting performance in aspects including hard work, thoroughness, self-control and dependability.

However the use of personality testing in the selection process is not without issue. Personality tests are not considered to be a good predictor when the correlation between the factors and performance is not strong. For example, a personality trait that is significantly related to performance in one job might not work at all in another job. Problems can also arise when the wrong trait is assessed or an incorrect questionnaire is used. Another issue of debate is the 'fakeability' of tests by individuals. To overcome this, personality tests should be used in conjunction with more accurate selection methods such as well-structured behavioural dimension interview questions, and followed up with reference checks.

Caution should be exercised in terms of selecting personality tests. There are multiple personality test instruments that claim to be accurate available on the market. It is important that a reputable test is selected and administered by a trained professional (such as an occupational or industrial psychologist). We can turn to meta-analysis of personality testing in various job contexts that will provide insight into the correlation between personality traits and job performance, and how accurately certain tests can predict performance.

Susan Ressia

See also:

Assessment centres; Big Five; Interviews; Recruitment; Selection.

References and selected further readings

Costa, P.T. and R.R. McCrae (1992), Normal personality assessment in clinical practice: the NEO Personality Inventory, *Psychological Assessment*, **4**, pp. 5–13.

Guion, R.M. and R.F. Gottier (1965), Validity of personality measures in personnel selection, *Personnel Psychology*, **18**, pp. 135–164.

Kramer, R., T. Bartram, H. De Cieri, R.A. Noe, J.R. Hollenbeck, B. Gerhart and P.M. Wright (2014), *Human Resource Management in Australia: Strategy, People, Performance*, 5th edn, North Ryde: McGraw Hill.

McCrae, R.R. and P.T. Costa (1989), The structure of interpersonal traits: Wiggins's circumplex and the five-factor model, *Journal of Personality & Social Psychology*, **56**(4), pp. 586–559.

Robertson, I. and M. Smith (2001), Personnel selection, *Journal of Occupational and Organizational Psychology*, **74**(4), pp. 441–472.

Taylor, S. (1998), *Employee Resourcing*, London: IPD.

Personality traits

Traits are relatively stable, dimensional characteristics of people, which influence – or are descriptions of – habitual thoughts, feelings and behaviours. Since the beginning of personality psychology, traits have been an important component of personality research, and are often seen as the dominant unifying concept within the field, despite continued debate about their ontological status (e.g., Bandura, 2012).

The dimensionality of traits imply that an individual will occupy a specific position with respect to others on a trait, such as when a person is assessed as being above-average on a specific trait. Individual assessment on traits is distinct from the type-based approach to personality, which instead assumes that there are distinct, discrete, categories of people. Type-based approaches have the advantage of being conceptually simple, but empirical evidence for personality typologies is unreliable or lacking (Haslam et al., 2012), especially within the normal ranges of personality encountered within HRM. Nonetheless, many researchers and practitioners choose to use types to summarize scores on traits for purposes of simplicity (in effect, the Myers-Briggs Type Indicator is an example of this: see McCrae and Costa, 1989). The major problem with such an approach is that it collapses continuous constructs into a dichotomy, which loses most of the information obtained from personality assessments. To date, the evidence supporting dimensional rather than typological assessment of personality is compelling (Haslam et al., 2012).

The implications of the reality of personality traits for HRM are several, but most important is that it allows a degree of confidence that properly measured personality traits will have reliable effects upon workplace behaviours. A corollary of this is that the intra-individual causes of personality traits impose limits upon individual change. However, there is growing evidence from educational research that personality can be effectively altered by training programmes (e.g., Poropat, 2015), so HRM practitioners should exercise caution in attributing limits to personal change to underlying personality traits.

Personality traits have been established as reliable measures of individual differences in behaviour, both generally and within work settings. Thoughtful assessment of personality traits is often justified for making choices about current and potential employees, but provides a poor guide for employee development. The capacity for employees to grow and develop creates further requirements for HRM practitioners to show care in the interpretation and application of personality trait assessment within organisations.

DANIEL J. CUMMINGS AND ARTHUR POROPAT

See also:

Big Five; Personality test.

References and selected further readings

Bandura, A. (2012), On the functional properties of perceived self-efficacy revisited, *Journal of Management*, **38**(1), pp. 9–44.

Fleeson, W. and P. Gallagher (2009), The implications of Big Five standing for the distribution of trait manifestation in behavior: Fifteen experience-sampling studies and a meta-analysis, *Journal of Personality and Social Psychology*, **97**(6), pp. 1097–1114.

Haslam, N., E. Holland and P. Kuppens (2012), Categories versus dimensions in personality and psychopathology: a quantitative review of taxometric research, *Psychological Medicine*, **42**, pp. 903–920.

McCrae, R.R. and P.T. Costa (1989), The structure of interpersonal traits: Wiggins's circumplex and the five-factor model, *Journal of Personality & Social Psychology*, **56**(4), pp. 586–559.

Poropat, A.E. (2015), Beyond the shadow: The role of personality and temperament in learning, in L. Corno and E. Anderman (eds), *Handbook of Educational Psychology*, Washington DC: American Psychological Association, Division 15 – Educational Psychology, pp. 172–185.

Poropat, A. (2015), Other-related personality and academic performance: evidence and implications, *Learning and Individual Differences*.

Picketing

Traditionally, picketing is the act of strikers (and their supporters) seeking to stop the movement of goods and people in and out of strike-bound workplaces. This is done by the strikers assembling outside the workplace and seeking by persuasion or force to prevent goods (components, finished goods) and people (workers, customers) entering or leaving. However, more recently (and especially in the case of public-sector strikes), picketing is undertaken to highlight to the public that a strike is taking place in order to gain publicity and awareness. To accentuate this, picketing is often complemented by demonstrations and rallies out the strike-bound workplaces.

Picketing is often necessary to win a strike because there are stockpiles of parts or finished goods that could be moved out of the workplace in order to be used or sold and because not all employees may be union members and union members that agree to strike. Thus, managers, supervisors, non-union workers and replacement workers from outside the company or organization are among those that can undermine a strike if not persuaded or compelled not to cross the picket line. The same is true of lorry/truck drivers delivering supplies or collecting goods. Consequently, union activists often say the eleventh commandment is 'thou shalt not cross a picket line'.

However, legal restrictions often prevent picketing from being effective for the most effective pickets are those that physically bar such movements by dint of sheer force of numbers. One of the most contentious forms of picketing is the flying picket, when workers from one company or workplace picket out other workers at other workplaces or companies. In Britain, lawful picketing is limited to six persons while in the United States, static picketing is not permitted so that pickets must continually walk around the gate. Whether the laws are enforced to prevent effective picketing is a matter of politics and police discretion.

The application of picketing to contemporary workplaces faces challenges because so much work and servicing is now carried out electronically. Nonetheless, with the application of 'just-in-time' production techniques, picketing for a very limited period can be very effective and two new types of picketing have been developed recently.

The first is 'informational picketing' where information is given out to those going into, leaving or passing by the workplace about the industrial dispute. The second is the 'leverage' tactic of targeting suppliers to and buyers (such as retailers) of the company in dispute with pickets, which is part of a strategy to damage its brand and reputation. Both allow unions to augment the number of pickets with supporters and because the pickets do not seek to blockade the workplace, policing is fairly 'soft-touch'.

Developments in technology have also allowed pickets to film those that break their strike and seek to embarrass or intimidate them into desisting from doing so. This then counters employer attempts to film pickets in an attempt to intimidate them and possibly victimize them after a return to work (given than pickets are the more active union members, that is, the activists).

GREGOR GALL

See also:

Conflict; Strikes; Trade unions.

References and selected further readings

Baker, D. (2014), *Police, Picket-Lines and Fatalities: Lessons from the Past*, Basingstoke: Palgrave.
Schwartz, R. (2006), *Strikes, Picketing and Inside Campaigns: A Legal Guide for Unions*, Cambridge, MA: Work Rights Press.

Pluralism

Alongside unitarism and radicalism, pluralism offers another influential frame of reference in human resource management (HRM). Its origins lie in a rejection of unitarism, particularly the latter's prejudices towards harmony and consensus within the firm. For pluralists, employers and employees hold many opposing interests on various aspects of the employment relationship. Consequently, employers should not demand, or expect, absolute deference to their authority, but accept that conflict is a legitimate and inevitable feature of work. Conflicting interests between employers and employees should not be suppressed, but reconciled to accommodate differing demands of business efficiency, equity and employee voice. Negotiation and compromise, not blunt appeals to rights and coercion, is the preferred route to managing conflict (Budd et al., 2004). The acceptance of inevitable clashes at work and the preference for negotiation prompts pluralists towards favouring formal means of institutionalizing conflict management. Trade unionism and collective bargaining were historically the preferred mechanisms, but as these have declined in coverage across many industrialized economies, pluralists have looked to other instruments such as legal regulation, mandated consultation rights and alternative dispute resolution systems. Such institutional mechanisms are considered by pluralists to potentially offer a fairer and more viable way in which conflicts of interests at work can be identified, debated and resolved in a mutually agreed fashion. From such agreements 'rules' can be derived that act as signposts in guiding further reconciliations of difference between employers and employees.

The pluralist ethos is typically embedded in a social democratic conception of capitalism, scepticism of neoliberal labour market policy and a desire to shield the weak from exploitation by the strong. Yet a customary criticism of pluralism from radical quarters is that it does little to counter the wider structures of inequality within capitalism, leaving intact the dominant social and economic power of capitalist business. This is held to weaken pluralists' favoured means of institutional rule-making insofar as capitalists, through various instruments, can circumvent regulatory constraint and largely secure their preferred arrangements. A pluralist would not necessarily deny such possibilities, but maintain that the radical's solution to such problems, if indeed one is offered, is no real solution at all: an 'unrealistic' preference for a post-capitalist society. As one leading pluralist has argued: 'to talk about power, loudly, incessantly and abstractly, as many radicals do, is not the same as doing something practical about it' (Ackers, 2002, p. 17). For a pluralist, 'practical' change to ensure equity and fairness at work would not entail radical social transformation, but rather piecemeal reform and regulatory experimentation through the joint efforts of the state, unions, public opinion and progressive employers.

NIALL CULLINANE

See also:
Employment relationship; Equity; Frames of reference; Radicalism; Unitarism.

References and selected further readings
Ackers, P. (2002), Re-framing employee relations: the case for neo-pluralism, *Industrial Relations Journal*, 33(1), pp. 2–19.
Budd, J., R. Gomez and N.M. Meltz (2004), Why a balance is best: the pluralist industrial relations paradigm of balancing competing interests, in B. Kaufman (ed.), *Theoretical Perspectives on Work and the Employment Relationship*, Illinois: Industrial Relations Research Association.

Polycentric management

Polycentric management refers to a way of managing employees in international firms, which gives primacy to the 'local' values or host country values where subsidiaries of multinational enterprises (MNEs) are located. Polycentric management recognizes the differences in the values held by people in different countries and in turn considers the most effective way for MNEs to manage businesses through adopting the organizational culture, structures and process that reflect 'local' values.

Polycentric management originates from the work of Perlmutter (1969), where he proposed a taxonomy for understanding the organization of MNEs that shifted the emphasis from the formal structure of organizations towards a focus on managerial culture. He distinguished between four types of attitudes, or mindsets, about international management held by senior managers, which he referred to as ethnocentric (home-country mindset), polycentric (host-country mindset), geocentric (world mindset) and regiocentric (regional mindset). This geocentric mindset was developed further by Bartlett and Ghoshal (1990) as the transnational mindset.

Building from managerial mindset to organizational types, polycentric firms are described as those that have a local identity, are integrated through financial controls, but from an organizational cultural and structural perspective they operate as loosely coupled groups akin to a federation structure.

As the concept of polycentrism has relevance to how staff are organized, it has been applied extensively in the international human resource management (IHRM) literature:

1. To develop frameworks of IHRM strategy, which identify the MNEs overall strategic IHRM approach and how this determines its subsidiaries' HRM system. The polycentric mindset promotes decentralization and relative autonomy from the parent allowing subsidiary HRM systems (e.g. appraisals, training, recruitment, performance management) to largely follow local norms.
2. To explain the approach MNEs take to the use of expatriates. MNEs with a

polycentric orientation will use limited expatriate managers in their overseas operations, instead opting to promote local managers to senior managerial appointments locally.

Limitations of polycentric management are: first, local talent can be overlooked for use within the wider global firm. Second, local growth and market success may be achieved at the expense of growth in global markets. With the complexity of global value chains, which require a degree of coordination and where standardization aids the flow of resources, then the polycentric approach could be counterproductive. Third, where local HRM processes fall below the parent company's expectations in terms of ethics, equality, diversity or a broader agenda of corporate social responsibility, then a MNE has fewer control mechanisms for addressing the shortfall.

The benefit, however, is that local talent can secure senior appointments providing them career opportunities and is critical for the retention of talent. Business success can also be strong because local employees are often better informed about local market demands and resources and additionally there can be less management–employee conflict as the managerial systems meet the norms and expectations of local employees.

OLGA TREGASKIS

See also:

Expatriate; Ethnocentric management; Geocentric management; International human resource management.

References and selected further readings

Bartlett, C.A. and S. Ghoshal (1990), The multinational corporation as an interorganisational network, *Academy of Management Review*, **15**(4), pp. 603–625.
Perlmutter, H.V. (1969), The tortuous evolution of the multi-national corporation, *Columbia Journal of World Business*, pp. 8–18.
Taylor, S., S. Beechler and N. Napier (1996), Toward an integrative model of strategic international human resource management, *Academy of Management Review*, **21**(4), pp. 959–985.

Positive action

Positive action involves the steps employers can take in areas such as recruitment, selection, promotion and training to encourage more people from disadvantaged or low participation groups. These groups were traditionally based on ethnicity/race and gender, but have spread to include age and other characteristics. There is some agreement that positive action consists of specific measures to redress discrimination experienced by particular groups within society. Such measures are undertaken to achieve effective equality for members of groups who are socially or economically disadvantaged, or otherwise face the consequences of past or present discrimination or disadvantage (European Commission, 2009). Positive action is often seen as necessary as some discrimination in employment is so entrenched that mere prohibition is insufficient.

We can locate positive action within linked approaches. First, 'equal opportunities', with its underpinning rationale to treat everyone the same, has a legislative and compliance focus and is concerned with equality of status, opportunities and rights, stressing the importance of treating people equally irrespective of differences. The objective is that individuals should be treated on the basis of job-related criteria and that differences should not be considered relevant criteria in either their favour or disadvantage. This suggests that individuals can be stripped of their differences for the purposes of organizational decision-making. Second, managing diversity, with its raison d'être of recognizing and using people's differences, goes further in an explicit strategy of valuing people's differences driven by organizational needs.

In contrast to the above, 'positive discrimination' allows discrimination in defined terms. This approach explicitly recognizes certain characteristics and actions to encourage greater participation from people with them. In non-European countries, the term 'affirmative action' is widely used. In the US, affirmative action tends to be associated with preferential treatment, such as quotas in the allocation of jobs. In Europe, the term 'positive action' is more commonly employed as a means of avoiding the stereotypes in connection with affirmative action (Bacchi, 2004). However, positive action is not the same as positive discrimination.

The key practical drivers for positive action include state direction and legislation, corporate social responsibility, moral/ethical considerations, leadership and organizational policy and the business case. In some countries, where there is no direct legislation, the moral case has been identified as the principal driving force. In many situations, the legal frameworks lag behind social policy (European Commission 2009).

CHRIS ROWLEY AND VIMOLWAN YUKONGDI

See also:

Direct discrimination; Diversity management; Equal opportunity; Gender; Indirect discrimination.

References and selected further readings

Anderson, T. (2004), *The Pursuit of Fairness: A History of Affirmative Action*, Oxford: Oxford University Press.
Bacchi, C. (2004), Policy and discourse: challenging the construction of affirmative action as preferential treatment, *Journal of European Public Policy*, 11(1), pp. 128–146.
European Commission (2009), *International Perspectives on Positive Action Measures: A Comparative Analysis in the European Union, Canada, the United States and South Africa*, Luxembourg: The Research Consortium, University of Bradford, European Communities.
Sowell, T. (2004), *Affirmative Action Around the World: An Empirical Study*, Connecticut: Yale University Press.
Waddington, L. and M. Bell (2011), Exploring the boundaries of positive action under EU law: a search for conceptual clarity, *Common Market Law Review*, **48**, pp. 1503–1526.

Positive discrimination

Certain policies and practices are designed to take a more proactive approach to the advancement of equality or the removal of discrimination than the complaints-led approach that dominates anti-discrimination law. The terms used to describe these positive forms of intervention are imprecise and vary by national context and according to the conceptual underpinning of the policy. It is important to clarify the precise nature of any particular policy because a wide range of different techniques with different effects might fall under a particular heading.

In Britain the term 'positive action' does not have a precise definition but is commonly used to describe forms of proactive intervention designed to reduce obstacles to the free operation of the labour market that are experienced by disadvantaged groups. It often refers to those measures that do not confer direct preferences on members of disadvantaged groups in access to activities such as employment. 'Positive discrimination' is attributed a narrower meaning and commonly refers to interventions that are designed to achieve a representative distribution of members of disadvantaged groups often by conferring a direct preference on members of that group. Positive discrimination is a particularly controversial form of positive intervention, as it may involve deliberate direct or indirect discrimination in favour of members of underrepresented groups and may subvert orthodox notions of merit. Some see this as necessary to overcome historical and structural disadvantage, while others emphasize the problematic use of categories such as gender and race in decision-making concerning recruitment and employment. Only certain forms of positive action are lawful in Britain.

The Equality Act 2010 contains provisions that allow employers to make positive interventions (labelled 'positive action') if they choose to (it is not mandatory). Here the anti-discrimination provisions of the Equality Act become suspended and do not prevent the employer from intervening where certain circumstances are present. Where an employer reasonably believes that one of three equality issues are at play (a disadvantage suffered by those sharing a protected characteristic, different needs among those sharing a protected characteristic and disproportionately low participation by those sharing a protected characteristic) they are not prevented from taking proportionate action to address the issue (section 158) (even if that action might ordinarily amount to direct or indirect discrimination). In the employment context, this form of positive action is designed to take place before or at the application stage; for example, an employer might provide training to members of a disadvantaged group to better enable them to compete within recruitment processes. Additionally, and specifically in the area of recruitment and promotion, the Equality Act allows employers to select a candidate on the basis of a protected characteristic in very narrowly defined 'tie-breaker' situations, where the candidates are equally qualified (section 159). This is a harder form of positive action, arguably positive discrimination. The selection of a candidate on the basis of a protected characteristic will only be permitted where one of two equality issues are reasonably thought to be present (a disadvantage suffered by those sharing a protected characteristic or disproportionately low participation by those sharing a protected characteristic). The effect of the tie-breaker is that the employer is not prohibited from treating a candidate more favourably than another person on the basis of the candidate's protected characteristic (this would ordinarily amount to direct discrimination). The use of this tie-break provision is only permitted where the action is a proportionate way of addressing the equality issue and where the employer does not have a routine policy of recruiting or promoting those sharing a protected characteristic over those who do not.

LIZ OLIVER

See also:
Equal opportunity.

References and selected further readings

Bamforth, N., M. Malik and C. O'Cinneide (2008), *Discrimination Law: Theory and Context: Text and Materials*, London: Sweet & Maxwell.

Kirton, G. and A. Greene (2010), *The Dynamics of Managing Diversity a Critical Approach*, 3rd edn, Oxford: Elsevier Butterworth-Heinemann.

Noon, M. (2010), The shackled runner: time to rethink positive discrimination? *Work Employment & Society*, 24(4), pp. 728–739.

Willey, B. (2012), *Employment Law in Context: An Introduction for HR Professionals*, 4th edn, Harlow: Pearson.

Power

The contested concept of power relates both to the shaping and control of human action but also suggests a more positive notion of the capacity to act or do something. Views of power often assume a relation of immediate and direct causation: actor or actors being able, by virtue of the resources or capacities they possess, to induce or control the actions of others. The reliance of the human resource practitioner on the specific resources of expertise, if he or she is to have power at the highest levels of an enterprise, has been a familiar theme in the literature. Other influential variants of this causal and possessive view of power foreground power differences on a vertical plain. Neo-Marxist labour process theorizing assigns a controlling presence to the owners of capital or their workplace managerial representatives in the capitalist mode of production. Crucially power lies in part in the capacity to influence the beliefs of others; human resource managers become key agents in promoting practices that secure not only the control but the consent of labour, occluding the truth of a fundamentally exploitative employment relationship. Theory of this kind has sought to explore not only the changing strategies for the extraction of surplus value but the dynamics of power and resistance at work, charting the varied ways in which labour refuses systems of management control. And yet everyday practices of resistance in the contemporary workplace are shown to preserve, rather than displace the fundamental relations of domination and exploitation.

For scholars influenced by the French philosopher and historian Michel Foucault, rather than focusing only a singular class power, we should recognize the multiple sites in which power is at work in the employment relationship; the various practices and techniques of human resource management that unobtrusively order the thought and actions of human subjects at work. And where neo-Marxist theorizing associates power with attempts to disguise the facts of subordination and exploitation, Foucauldians – sceptical of the appeal to a definitive truth – construe the relations between power and knowledge in other ways. Interest turns to the historical formation and consequences of the specific 'truths' or rationalities concerning work organization and relationships that human resource practices presuppose or instantiate, the identities that human resource techniques and practices define for and enforce upon individuals at work, albeit in ways that are invariably contested and resisted. We should think less about who 'holds power' and more about power relationships; recognizing that no human subject, including those who aspire to lead an organization, ever exists outside or beyond power relations and that power, through diverse skills and capacities we acquire, has enabling (as well as constraining) aspects. The diverse agencies in a liberal society that shape the contemporary orthodox truths of human resource management, from the state to those laying claim to efficacious competence – management gurus, consultants and business academics – become central objects of enquiry. Foucauldians have commonly highlighted the increasing intensification and sophistication of practices of surveillance and self-discipline in the employment relationship. But in this respect, they often appear vulnerable to the criticism that they exaggerate the degree of integration and effectiveness of management controls.

EDWARD BARRATT

See also:

Labour process/theory; Managerial control; Resistance.

References and selected further readings

Barratt, E. (2003), Foucault, HRM and the ethos of the critical management scholar, *Journal of Management Studies*, **40**(5), pp. 1069–1087.
Clegg, S., D. Courpasson and N. Phillips (2006), *Power and Organization*, London: Sage.
Legge, K. (1978), *Power, Innovation and Problem Solving at Work*, Maidenhead: McGraw-Hill.
Thompson, P. and C. Smith (2009), Labour power and labour process; contesting the marginality of the sociology of work, *Sociology*, **43**(5), pp. 913–930.
Townley, B. (1994), *Reframing Human Resource Management: Reframing the Subject at Work*, London: Sage.

Precarious employment

Precarious employment is described as low-wage, insecure, non-standard employment, from the perspective of the worker (Kalleberg, 2009, p. 2). Issues of precarity and job security were previously only associated with low-skilled, labour-intensive work in the private sector. However, as a result of public-sector restructuring, governments around the world have contracted out (non-core) services and increasingly used agency staff to carry out such work, which has contributed to the rise of precarious employment across the public sector (Standing, 2009). It has therefore been suggested that precarious employment is now much more prevalent across the wider economy. Thus, structural changes led by neoliberal government policies, accompanied by the rise in globalization and the decline in trade unionism have contributed to the decline in the number of workers in full-time, permanent employment (Kalleberg, 2011), and with it, the changing nature of employment relations has led to the growth of precarious employment. Precarious employment is often undertaken by young workers (Tailby and Pollert, 2011; Standing, 2009) and it has been argued that young people experience considerably more difficulties in entering stable employment than older workers.

Standing has analysed the growth in precarious employment and has suggested that it has resulted in the emergence of a new, dangerous class of workers, labelled 'the precariat', described as a 'disparate group in non-regular statuses, including casual workers, outworkers and agency workers' (Standing, 2009, p. 110). However, there is much debate as to whether a new class of worker has actually emerged or whether precarious employment has now become standard employment.

There are several categories of precarious employment. Temporary employment is the most obvious form of insecure work and this can take many forms, such as the use of fixed-term contracts (work for a specified period of time, or completion of a specific task) and zero-hours contracts (whereby workers are given contracts that do not stipulate guaranteed hours of work). Such numerical flexibility can be good for organizations in terms of cost reduction and an additional indicator of precarious work has been the shifting of risk from the employer to the worker.

Unsurprisingly, employees tend to express dissatisfaction with precarious employment, and experience low-wages, feelings of job insecurity (which can have implications for commitment and productivity at work), limited chance of gaining alternative work, restricted opportunities for training and development at work, and are rarely able to access collective representation through trade unions.

ANDY HODDER

See also:

Fixed-term contracts; Flexible working; Young workers; Zero-hours contracts.

References and selected further readings

Heery, E. and J. Salmon (eds) (2000), *The Insecure Workforce*, London: Routledge.
Kalleberg, A. (2009), Precarious work, insecure workers: employment relations in transition, *American Sociological Review*, **74**, pp.1–22.
Kalleberg, A. (2011), *Good Jobs, Bad Jobs: The Rise of Polarized and Precarious Employment Systems in the United States, 1970s–2000s*, New York: Russell Sage Foundation.
Standing, G. (2009), *Work after Globalization: Building Occupational Citizenship*, Cheltenham: Edward Elgar Publishing.
Standing, G. (2011), *The Precariat: The New Dangerous Class*, London: Bloomsbury Academic.
Tailby, S. and A. Pollert (2011), Non-unionised young workers and organising the unorganised, *Economic and Industrial Democracy*, **32**(3), pp.499–522.

Prejudice

Prejudiced people may fall victim to errors in the processing and recall of information regarding the objects of their negative feeling: Such individuals will, over time come to think of their 'targets' in a certain way, and effectively will filter out or ignore information inconsistent with or contrary to what they have come to believe about those targets.

Prejudice is defined as a preconceived attitude or feeling, driven by emotion, towards an outgroup; that is, a group that is from a different racial, ethnic, religious or socioeconomic group from one's own (Steel et al., 2004). It is based on faulty, incorrect and invalid generalizations. As such, having negative thoughts about people solely because they belong to a certain group is considered prejudice. While positive attitudes are harmless, negative attitudes in terms of nationality, gender, sexual orientation, social status, race/ethnicity, religious affiliation, age and disability lead to individuals being the enduring victims of prejudice.

In addition, groups based on features such as hair colour and style, accent, beards, turbans, height, weight, tattoos and body piercings, and clothes are also frequently a source of prejudice. All forms of prejudice, whether intentional or unintentional, would leave the targeted employees feeling they have been discriminated and reduce their ability to work effectively. Prejudice is an attitude, whereas discrimination is a behaviour.

Discrimination is an unfair act or series of acts taken toward an entire group of people or individual members of that group, often on the basis of prejudicial attitude.

The process of appraising employees is an area of human resource management in which the potential for error, bias and prejudice is high. The appraiser may actually be prejudiced against the appraisee, or be anxious not to be prejudiced; either could distort the appraiser's judgement. Prejudices include older employees receiving lower performance ratings than younger employees or high-performance female employees rated significantly lower than male employees.

When people of Latin American extraction make statements such as 'all whites behave badly,' the prejudice towards whites is revealed in the stereotype statement (Andersen and Taylor, 2006). While prejudice is the belief or perception that people of different cultures are inferior or have negative characteristics merely because of their colour, religion or cultural background, discrimination is the act of using prejudice against someone in order to refuse to hire someone, work with someone, socialize with someone, fire someone or some other act that is imposed on someone due to a prejudicial opinion or perception.

CHRIS ROWLEY AND NAGIAH RAMASAMY

See also:
Direct discrimination; Positive action.

References and selected further readings
Andersen, M.L. and H.F. Taylor (2006), *Sociology: Understanding a Diverse Society*, 4th edn, New York: Wadsworth.
Jones, J. (1997), *Prejudice and Racism*, 2nd edn, New York: McGraw-Hill.
Pettigrew, T.F. (1971), *Racially Separate or Together?* New York: McGraw-Hill.
Steel, J., S.J. Choi and N. Ambady (2004), Stereotyping, prejudice and discrimination: the effect of group based expectations on moral functioning, in T.A. Thorkildsen, J. Manning and H.J. Walberg (eds), *Nurturing Morality, Children and Youth Series*, New York: Kluwer Academic.
Whitley, B.E. and M.E. Kite (2010), *The Psychology of Prejudice and Discrimination*, Belmont: Wadsworth.

Presenteeism

The term 'presenteeism' refers to employees coming into work when they are genuinely ill and should be at home recovering. It is usually discussed alongside absenteeism, being considered its opposite. The term has, in the past, been used to refer to instances when people stay at work longer than they are contracted to. For example, not leaving work in the evening before your boss to demonstrate dedication. However, this meaning has largely been superseded by the issue of coming to work ill, which we will focus on here.

Presenteeism has negative effects for both the employee and the employer. People coming to work ill tend to be less productive and more likely to make costly mistakes, and may spread their germs to colleagues. A study by Ashby and Mahdon (2010) found that presenteeism can be more costly to the business than absence, accounting for up to 50 per cent more working time lost. Presenteeism can also be a sign of anxiety, with the 2013 CIPD/*Simplyhealth* Absence Management survey finding that those organizations reporting an increase in presenteeism were significantly more likely than those who have not to also say they have seen an increase in stress and mental health problems.

Research by the CIPD (2013) has uncovered various reasons why employees come into work ill. A survey of 2,200 UK employees found the most common reason is not wanting to let your team down (45 per cent), followed by having deadlines to meet (30 per cent). Looming deadlines is more of an issue for senior managers (54 per cent) and middle managers (46 per cent) than for team leaders (32 per cent) or those with no management responsibility (25 per cent). Around a quarter of employees surveyed said they came into work when they were ill because they were worried their colleagues would have to pick up their work as well as their own and they weren't sure if they were ill enough to stay off work. Other studies have found that people in certain occupations may be more likely to demonstrate presenteeism. For example, those working with vulnerable people or in healthcare, where there was a concern the service user may suffer if they didn't go into work.

Presenteeism trends tend to echo the economic context, with people more likely to come to work ill when unemployment is high or when there is a threat of redundancy. In these circumstances, employees may be worried that taking time off may be seen as a lack of commitment to their job or employer. Not being entitled to sick pay can also be a reason people go into work ill, as well as not wanting to put extra work on your colleagues. To discourage presenteeism, employers need to send a message to the workforce that it is ok to stay at home when they are ill. Serious thought should also be given to whether it is appropriate to be working from home when ill.

JILL MILLER

See also:
Absence; Wellbeing; Working time.

References and selected further readings

Ashby, K. and M. Mahdon (2010), *Why Do Employees Come to Work When Ill? An Investigation into Sickness Presence in the Workplace*, London: Work Foundation and AXA PPP Healthcare.
Australian Public Service Commission (2012), Managing presenteeism, *APS Human Capital Matters*, June.
CIPD (2013), *Employee Outlook: Focus on Employee Well-Being*, London: Chartered Institute of Personnel and Development.

Probation

The probationary period serves to establish whether an appropriate match exists between new staff, the job and the work environment. The probationary period is particularly useful when the company wishes to hire non-traditional employees whose credentials are difficult to establish (Baron and Kreps, 1999). Probationary periods are useful as the information available at the time of application may be inadequate to make an informed decision on the applicant's suitability for the job, but once on the job, they provide initial feedback to evaluate probationers against performance and behavioural standards. The desired outcome of this process is to confirm the probationers under a new contract of employment and integrate them as new employees into the organization.

There is no fixed duration for the probation and it varies from job to job, the job position as well as the company's policy. However, the probation provides the probationer with an opportunity to be exposed to a new work environment and be trained up and become familiar with the work processes while on the job. It allows them to become better aware of their own strengths and weaknesses. The probationer is given the opportunity to decide whether the job and the organization are what they are looking for.

The success of the probationary process is dependent on the principles of equity, effectiveness and accountability (Banfield and Kay, 2008). Generally, a probationer has the benefit of similar rights as a confirmed employee. As such, the services of a probationer cannot be terminated without just cause or excuse. Although it is the prerogative of the employer to confirm or not to confirm a probationer, there must also be valid reasons for the decision. To avoid claims of wrongful dismissal, it is pertinent at the outset to inform potential candidates at the selection stage that the job has a probationary period attached.

Where the performance of a probationer is unsatisfactory, it should be discussed with the probationer. The discussions should be acknowledged by the probationer and kept in the probationer's records. Probationers would need the support of their superior or manager for successful completion of the probationary period and this would entail supporting the probationers with coaching, training and development as well as providing them with regular feedback. The manager must also monitor the probationers' performance, and evaluate them on areas such as work performance, teamwork and conduct. Probationers who do not meet the required standard will need to know that their employment will be terminated.

CHRIS ROWLEY AND NAGIAH RAMASAMY

See also:
Performance appraisal; Selection; Training and development.

References and selected further readings

Banfield, P. and R. Kay (2008), *Introduction to Human Resource Management*, Oxford: Oxford University Press.
Baron, J.N. and D.M. Kreps (1999), *Strategic Human Resources: Frameworks For General Managers*, New York: John Wiley.
Chandran, R. (1993), The probationary employee, *Singapore Academy of Law Journal*, **5**, pp. 245–253.
Ezekiel, R.B. (2013), Terminating a probationary employee: debunking some myths about the Tanzanian labour legislation, *Open University Law Journal*, **4**(1), pp. 140–148.
Riphahn, R.T. and B.A. Thalmaier (1999), *Behavioral Effects of Probation Periods: An Analysis of Worker Absenteeism*, Institute for the Study of Labor (IZA) Discussion Paper No. 67.
Stone, R.J. (2014), *Human Resource Management*, 8th edn, Milton: Wiley.

Professionalism

Profession, professional and professionalism are somewhat overused terms. This is because they have unarguably positive connotations such as quality, status and a public orientation. As such, defining these terms is somewhat of a contested exercise. The literature in this area can be distinguished in two perspectives: a dominant approach that views professionalisms as a distinctive occupational category and a more recent one that treats it as a discursive resource.

The first approach starts from the assumption that professions can be analytically distinguished from other occupations. This work originally stresses the distinctive functional contribution that professions make to the effective operation of society (Parsons, 1954; Durkheim, 1957) and is often characterized by hagiographic tones. Later work in the 1950s and 1960s assumes a more analytical stance as it sets out to identify lists of 'traits' that can be used to empirically distinguish professions from other occupations (Goode, 1957; Greenwood, 1957; Etzioni, 1969). Under this approach, we have had the production of several taxonomies but little consensus over the core characteristics of professionalism (Millerson, 1964). What agreement there was tended to reproduce the idealized features of showcase professions such as nineteenth-century law and medicine.

A more critical approach became dominant in the 1970s (Freidson, 1970; Johnson, 1972; Larson, 1977). This redefined professionalism from a particular type of occupation to a specific method of controlling and organizing an occupation. This was predicated on conscious political project designed to advance the interests of an occupational group by translating 'a scarce set of cultural and technical resources into a secure and institutionalised system of social and financial rewards' (Larson, 1977, p. xvii). At the heart of this is the concept of occupational closure or the ability to restrict the ability to perform specific tasks to a limited circle of eligibles (Parkin, 1979). While this literature emphasizes the self-interest rather than the public orientation of the professions, like the previous work it treats professionalism as a distinctive work organization method. Specifically, professionalism places in an occupation itself, through its own professional association, the ability to control the definition, execution, organization and evaluation of its own work (Freidson, 2001). This contrasts with alternative occupational principles such as managerialism or entrepreneurship, where work is organized through imperative coordination and market exchanges respectively.

More recently an alternative body of work (Grey, 1998; Anderson-Gough et al., 1999; Fournier, 1999; Evetts, 2006) relaxes these definitional requirements by treating professionalism as a discursive rather than an analytical category. This discursive turn decouples professional status from its underlying practices and structures and is rooted in the recognition that 'profession', 'professional' or 'professionalism' are valuable labels that confer on the beholder significant symbolic and material advantages. As such professionalism is claimed by semi-professions (Witz, 1992) or new occupations such as project management or management consulting (Muzio et al, 2011; Paton et al, 2013) to signal their equivalence to high status groups such as law or accountancy. More recently, there is a growing recognition (Anderson-Gough et al., 1999; Fournier, 1999) of the performative value of professionalism, which is deployed by management as a normative tool to motivate and discipline individuals, often in contexts beyond the traditional professions.

DANIEL MUZIO

See also:

Knowledge worker; Management consultancy.

References and selected further readings

Abbott, A. (1988), *The System of Professions: An Essay on the Division of Expert Labor*, Chicago: University of Chicago Press.
Anderson-Gough, F., C. Grey and K. Robson (1999), *Making Up Accountants*, Aldershot: Ashgate.

Brock, D., M. Powell and C.R. Hinings (1999), *Restructuring the Professional Organization. Accounting, Healthcare and Law*, London and New York: Routledge.

Brock, D., H. Leblebici and D. Muzio (2014), Understanding professionals and their workplaces: the mission of the Journal of Professions and Organization, *Journal of Professions and Organization*, 1(1), pp. 1–15.

Burrage, M. and R. Torstendahl (eds) (1990), *Professions in Theory and History: Rethinking the Study of the Professions*, London: Sage.

Durkheim, E. (1957), *Professional Ethics and Civic Morals*, London: Routledge and Kegan Paul.

Empson, L., D. Muzio, J. Broschak and B. Hinings (eds) (2015), *Oxford Handbook of Professional Service Firms*, Oxford: Oxford University Press.

Etzioni, A. (1969), *The Semi-Professions and their Organization: Teachers, Nurses, Social Workers*, New York: Free Press.

Evetts, J. (2006), Short note: the sociology of professional groups: new directions, *Current Sociology*, 54(1), pp. 133–143.

Fournier, V. (1999), The appeal to 'professionalism' as a disciplinary mechanism, *The Sociological Review*, 47(2), pp. 280–307.

Freidson, E. (1970), *Profession of Medicine: A Study of the Sociology of Applied Knowledge*, New York: Dodd, Mead & Co.

Freidson, E. (2001), *Professionalism: The Third Logic*, Chicago: University of Chicago Press.

Goode, W.J. (1957), Community within a community: the professions, *American Sociological Review*, 22(2), pp. 194–200.

Greenwood, E. (1957), Attributes of a profession, *Social Work*, 2, pp. 45–55.

Grey, C. (1998), On being a professional in a Big Six firm, *Accounting, Organizations and Society*, 23, pp. 569–587.

Johnson, T.J. (1972), *Professions and Power*, London: Macmillan.

Larson, M.S. (1977), *The Rise of Professionalism: A Sociological Analysis*, Berkeley: University of California Press.

Macdonald, K.M. (1995), *The Sociology of the Professions*, London: Sage.

Millerson, G. (1964), *The Qualifying Associations: A Study in Professionalization*, London: Routledge and Kegan Paul.

Muzio, D., D. Hodgson, J. Faulconbridge, J. Beaverstock and S. Hall (2011), New and old professionalism: the case of management consultancy and project management, *Current Sociology*, 59(4), pp. 443–464.

Parkin, F. (1979), *Marxism and Class Theory: A Bourgeois Critique*, New York: Columbia University Press.

Parsons, T. (1954), Professional and social structure, in *Essays in Sociological Theory*, Glencoe, IL: Free Press.

Paton, S., D. Hodgson and D. Muzio (2013), The price of corporate professionalisation: analysing the corporate capture of professions in the UK, *New Technology, Work and Employment*, 28(3), pp. 227–240.

Witz, A. (1992), *Professions and Patriarchy*, London: Routledge.

Profit-related pay/gainsharing

Profit-related pay refers to an element of the total pay package that is related by some formula to the profitability of the company (or a unit thereof). As with profit-sharing, there were tax advantages for employees where the scheme was approved by the Inland Revenue. The intention of a profit-related pay scheme is that part of the employees' pay will move up or down according to the profits made by the company, thus making pay more responsive to company performance. As well as being seen as a way of improving individual performance and motivation through giving employees a direct interest in the success of the business, and as a means of fostering commitment to the company, profit-related pay is argued by its supporters to have employment implications in that labour costs will be automatically reduced when the company runs into difficulties (through the profit-related element), thus minimizing the risk of layoff and redundancy. These claimed advantages of profit-related pay have yet to be substantiated by research findings.

Companies that have introduced profit-related pay generally express relatively long-term objectives, such as making employees feel they are part of the company, increasing employee commitment and making employees profit-conscious. Conversely, arguments against profit-related pay are: the double risk it involves for employees in tying their jobs and savings to the success of the same organization; the recruitment inhibiting effects that may result from existing employees attempting to maximize their proportion of the profits; and the fear that employees, through their representatives rather than as shareholders, may demand a greater say than management is prepared to concede in the strategic decisions that can affect the company's profitability and consequently their pay. With gainsharing, employees share financially in the gain, as performance improves through greater involvement and participation

MARK GILMAN

See also:
Payment system; Profit-sharing; Variable pay.

References and selected further readings
Armstrong, M. (2012), *Armstrong's Handbook of Reward Management*, London: Kogan Page.
Gilman, M. (2013), Reward management, in T. Redman and A. Wilkinson (eds), *Contemporary Human Resource Management: Text and Cases*, New York: Pearson.
Perkins, S.J. and G. White (2008), *Employee Reward: Alternatives, Consequences and Contexts*, London.
White, G. and J. Drucker (2009), *Reward Management: A Critical Text*, London, Routledge.

Profit-sharing

Profit-sharing means giving employees, in addition to a fixed wage, a variable part of income directly linked to profits or some other measure of enterprise results. Contrary to traditional bonuses linked to individual performance (e.g., piece rates), profit-sharing is a collective scheme applied to all, or a large group of employees. Employers establish these for reasons of productivity, commitment and identification with the company. Some of these outcomes are supported by research.

Profit-sharing can take various forms. It can provide employees with immediate or deferred benefits; it can be paid in cash, enterprise shares or other securities; or it can be allocated to specific funds invested for the benefit of employees.

Although deferred profit-sharing and cash-based profit-sharing have some common features, the differences are more significant than the similarities. The most important difference from the point of view of the employee participant is that the reward from a cash-based profit-sharing plan is paid much closer in time (and in immediate cash) to the performance being rewarded than it is with deferred profit-sharing. Cash-based profit-sharing is easily mixed up with gain-sharing. Gain-sharing is usually considered as a productivity-improving or cost-reducing activity not directly related to company profit levels.

Deferred profit-sharing is a form of deferred compensation under which the allocated profit share is held (most commonly) in trust and is not immediately available to the employee. A deferred scheme allocates a certain percentage of profits to enterprise funds, which are then invested in the name of employees. Investment can be made in the company of the employees but under the heading of DPS also investments in other assets are developed (the Finnish Personnel Funds is an example). Or alternatively it is allocated to an employee account with a certain minimum retention period before the amount is made available.

Share-based profit-sharing consists of giving employees, in relation to company performance, a number of shares in the company where they work. Deferred share-based profit-sharing comes close to asset savings plans and employee share ownership. Asset accumulation and savings plans provide for employees to set aside a portion of their pay, and perhaps to receive contributions from their employer, in an account that is in most cases invested in stocks, bonds or other investment choices for a period of time before being made available to the employee. The most common examples are savings plans in the United States, France and Germany. These are mainly so-called defined contribution plans, which try to follow tax provisions of governments.

Government regulation mainly consists of regulation of the amount of contributions by employees and employers, eligibility criteria to prevent discrimination, and retention periods for tax exemption.

ERIK POUTSMA

See also:

Employee share ownership plans; Financial participation; Profit-related pay and gainsharing.

References and selected further readings

Pendleton, A. and E. Poutsma (2013), Financial participation, in C. Brewster and W. Mayrhofer (eds), *Handbook of Research in Comparative Human Resource Management*, Cheltenham: Edward Elgar Publishing, pp. 345–368.
Poutsma, E. and E. Kaarsemaker (2015), Added value of employee financial participation, in M. Andresen and C. Nowak (eds), *Human Resource Management Practices, Management for Professionals*, New York: Springer, pp. 181–196.
Poutsma, E., P.E.M. Ligthart, A. Pendleton and C. Brewster (2013), The development of employee financial participation in Europe, in E. Parry, E. Stravrou and M. Lazarove (eds), *Global Trends in Human Resource Management*, Basingstoke: Palgrave Macmillan.

Promotion

Promotion is the movement of employees into a higher position with a higher job classification, which brings with its more responsibility, and higher internal and external status. Generally, it also attracts higher pay and benefits, more challenges, greater autonomy, greater power and greater levels of authority (Stone, 2014).

When a job vacancy exists, the first source to consider for replacement with a suitable candidate is within the organization; that is, through internal transfer and promotion. Filling vacancies through promotions assumes that employees have the potential to develop to the point where they are promotable. Organizations benefit from the returns on their investment in recruiting, selecting and training their current employees.

Not only does a promotion serve as an incentive to employees arising from their past performance; employers hope that it will continue to motivate employees. Promotions convey a positive message to other employees that similar efforts by them will also be recognized, with possibly a promotion as well. Nevertheless, the organization's promotion policy and reward system must be made known to all employees; for example, in employee handbooks and by way of inductions and career workshops.

Beyond the motivational value that promotion brings to those promoted, the organization has to ensure that the movement of employees aims to achieve alignment between its strategic needs and human resources. Promoting employees, either within the same function or across units, is one way to ensure that competent and knowledgeable people are placed in key positions within the organization. Promotions should serve to build competitiveness of the organization. In addition, it should be focused on future business needs. In well-managed organizations, succession planning necessitates that performance be the key factor in determining promotions.

Internal promotion does have its shortcomings. When employees who applied for vacancies get rejected, they can become discontented with the processes and the organization. The pool of candidates available within the organization may be limited. Focusing only on internal promotions can stifle creativity as a result of 'the way we do it is the best way' views.

Further, not all employees desire to be promoted. They would be more contented being at the level where they are, particularly if they believe that they are being adequately remunerated. In addition, they can continue performing the duties they like or to avoid duties that they would not find particularly interesting. Excessive concerns on promotion can lead to behaviour that is focused more by career concerns than on achieving organizational objectives.

CHRIS ROWLEY AND NAGIAH RAMASAMY

See also:

Careers; Performance appraisal; Succession planning; Training and development.

References and selected further readings

Beardwell, J. and T. Claydon (2010), *Human Resource Management: A Contemporary Approach*, 6th edn, Essex: Financial Times Prentice Hall.
Dessler, G., J. Griffiths, B. Lloyd-Walker and A. Williams (1999), *Human Resource Management*, Australia: Prentice-Hall.
Furnham, A. and K.V. Petrides (2006), Deciding on promotions and redundancies: promoting people by ability, experience, gender and motivation, *Journal of Managerial Psychology*, 21(1), pp. 6–18.
Greenhaues, J.H., G.A. Callanan and V.M. Godshalk (2000), *Career Management*, 3rd edn, Orlando: Harcourt.
Perlmutter, D.D. (2010), *Promotion and Tenure Confidential*, Cambridge, MA: Harvard University Press.
Stone, R.J. (2014), *Human Resource Management*, 8th edn, Milton: Wiley.

Psychological capital

Psychological capital (PsyCap) is a higher-order construct defined as an 'individual's positive psychological state of development', demonstrated by the psychological assets of efficacy (having confidence); hope (persevering towards goals and where needed, redirecting the path needed to reach the goal); optimism (positive future expectations and attributions) and resiliency (bouncing back and beyond from adversity) (Luthans et al., 2015). Research clearly demonstrates that when the four psychological resources are combined, they not only form one higher-order, core construct, but PsyCap is a stronger predictor of attitudes and behaviour than any one of the four components by itself. PsyCap is considered 'state-like' in nature. As such, PsyCap is differentiated from both fixed traits (e.g., Big Five personality dimensions, core-self evaluations) and transient states (e.g., moods and emotions). Research supports the state-like nature of PsyCap and its overall construct validity including convergent and discriminant validity in relation to other constructs (see Dawkins et al., 2013 for a detailed psychometric review of the PsyCap construct). The subject of three meta-analysis (see Avey et al., 2011; Dawkins et al. 2013; Newman et al., 2014) finds PsyCap has a strong positive relationship with a vast array of desirable attitudes, behaviours and performance and, similarly, a strong and negative relationship with a wide range of dysfunctional outcomes such as cynicism, intentions to quit, counterproductive behaviours and stress (see also Luthans et al., 2010, 2015). Furthermore PsyCap has a positive relationship with leadership, enhancing leadership effectiveness and resultant employee wellbeing and behaviour (Luthans et al., 2015).

In addition to the meta analyses, there are more than 67 published papers on PsyCap. However, research in PsyCap has been examined predominately at the individual level, and team and organizational level PsyCap has largely been missing from analysis (Dawkins et al. 2013; Newman et al. 2014). Similarly many more studies have been undertaken on the outcomes of PsyCap, such as wellbeing, than the antecedents of PsyCap such as supportive organizations and workplace security (see Newman et al. 2014). Furthermore the boundary conditions, such as the interaction of job-demands and resources that attenuate or diminish PsyCap are less explored (Luthans et al., 2015). The role of PsyCap as a mediator is still very much in its infancy, and more research is needed to help us understand the underlying mechanisms through which PsyCap influences workplace outcomes (Roche, 2014) and at different levels of analysis. Finally, PsyCap research is dominated by self-report research, and although implicit and biological/physiological measures are alluded to (see Newman et al., 2014), the development of PsyCap research would benefit from research that is objective (i.e., physiological) or other rated (i.e., partner or team member). Notwithstanding the above, in nearly ten years of research, individuals, leaders and organizations that cultivate PsyCap clearly display many benefits in terms of wellbeing, productivity, and commitment. Thus PsyCap is expected to continue to be a dominant research topic as it is clearly beneficial to individual and workplace success (Luthans et al., 2015).

MAREE ROCHE

See also:
Resilience; Wellbeing.

References and selected further readings

Avey, J.B., R.J. Reichard, F. Luthans and K.H. Mhatre (2011), Meta-analysis of the impact of positive psychological capital on employee attitudes, behaviors, and performance, *Human Resource Development Quarterly*, **22**(2), pp. 127–152.
Dawkins, S., A. Martin, J. Scott and K. Sanderson (2013), Building on the positives: a psychometric review and critical analysis of the construct of psychological capital, *Journal of Occupational and Organizational Psychology*, **86**(3), pp. 348–370.
Luthans, F., J.B. Avey, B.J. Avolio and S.J. Peterson (2010), The development and resulting performance impact of positive psychological capital, *Human Resource Development Quarterly*, **21**(1), pp. 41–67.

Luthans, F., C.M. Youssef and B.J. Avolio (2015), *Psychological Capital and Beyond*, New York: Oxford University Press.

Newman, A., D. Ucbasaran, F. Zhu and G. Hirst (2014), Psychological capital: a review and synthesis, *Journal of Organizational Behavior*, **35**(S1), pp. S120–S138.

Roche, M., J.M. Haar and F. Luthans (2014), The role of mindfulness and psychological capital on the well-being of leaders, *Journal of Occupational Health Psychology*, **19**(4), pp. 476–489.

Psychological contract

The psychological contract is commonly defined as 'individual beliefs, shaped by the organization, regarding terms of an exchange agreement between the individual and their organization' (Rousseau, 1995, p. 9). Since Rousseau's (1989) seminal reconceptualizing of the psychological contract, its key defining features include beliefs that refer to explicit and implicit promises. Explicit promises are employee perceptions of verbal and written agreements, whereas implicit promises are where employees perceive consistent patterns of exchange behaviour between themselves and the organization. Since Rousseau, psychological contract research has largely focused on the employee's perspective, rather than the employer's perspectives, and psychological contracts are highly subjective held in 'the eye of the beholder'. The exchange underpinning psychological contracts refers to the perceived links between employee contributions (e.g., effort, skills, flexibility) in return for organizational offerings (e.g., pay, promotion, support).

There have been two main areas of research inquiry. The first is research into the *contents* of psychological contracts, which refers to the promised exchanges (explicit and implicit) between an employee and their organization. A common approach has been to categorize contents into transactional and relational psychological contracts, which are similar in meaning to classic ideas of economic and social exchange. The content of a psychological contracts is important because it establishes the deal between employee and organization; that is, what each party promises to do for each other.

The second area of inquiry is research into psychological contract *breach*, defined as when a party to a psychological contract perceives the other to have failed to fulfil promises (Conway and Briner 2005). Related to breach is the idea of psychological contract *violation*, which are the intense emotional reactions following breach under certain conditions. Several meta-analyses (based on largely cross-sectional studies) find breach associated with a wide range of attitudinal and behavioural withdrawal from the organization (e.g., Conway and Briner, 2005). For example, psychological contract breach negatively associates with employment relationship outcomes such as job satisfaction, organizational commitment, in-role and extra-role performance, and intentions to quit.

The psychological contract is important because it is a major construct for understanding employee attitudes and behaviour (Conway and Briner, 2005; Levinson et al., 1962; Rousseau, 1995), where breach is the key theoretical concept linking the psychological contract to attitudinal and behavioural outcomes (Conway and Briner, 2005). From an HRM perspective, human resource practices and line manager behaviour are found to have a major influence on shaping the contents of psychological contracts (via communicating psychological contract content), and human resources policies and practices, when delivered effectively, are a major factor in ensuring psychological contracts are fulfilled (i.e., not breached), which in turn relates positively to employee attitudes, behaviour and performance. Some researchers propose the psychological contract as a framework to explain how HRM relates to workplace performance (Guest, 1998). In other words, if organizations deliver high-quality HRM, this will lead to fulfilled psychological contracts, which leads to positive employee attitudes and high employee performance.

The psychological contract is a potentially useful practitioner tool because it offers a framework for employees and managers to negotiate deals that meet each other's needs, as well as concepts to understand how HR policies and practices communicate the organization's side of the psychological contract (Guest, 1998). Organizations must manage human resource practices to ensure promises are fulfilled (e.g., making sure human resource policies are consistent with practice), thereby preventing breach.

There are several major critiques of the psychological contract (Conway and Briner, 2005; Guest, 1998). One controversy is that key terms within the psychological contract definition are defined unclearly. For example, there is a longstanding debate as to whether the beliefs that constitute psychological contracts should refer to promises, obligations and/or expectations (Conway and Briner, 2005). A second controversy is whether organizations can hold psychological contracts and, if so, how should the organization be conceptualized (as a network of individuals, as organizational culture, as HRM practices, as an anthropomorphized entity)? A third controversy is where researchers dispute the importance of psychological contract breach, arguing that it is what employees actually get that matters, rather than any discrepancy with promises made.

NEIL CONWAY

See also:
Employment relationship; Equity; Job satisfaction.

References and selected further readings

Conway, N. and R. Briner (2005), *Understanding Psychological Contracts at Work: A Critical Evaluation of Theory and Research*, Oxford: Oxford University Press.
Guest, D. (1998), Is the psychological contract worth taking seriously? *Journal of Organizational Behavior*, **19**, pp. 649–664.
Levinson, H., C.R. Price, K.J. Munden and C.M. Solley (1962), *Men, Management, and Mental Health*, Cambridge, MA: Harvard University Press.
Rousseau, D.M. (1989), Psychological and implied contracts in organizations, *Employee Responsibilities and Rights Journal*, **2**, pp. 121–139.
Rousseau, D.M. (1995), *Psychological Contracts in Organizations: Understanding Written and Unwritten Agreements*, Thousand Oaks, CA: Sage.

Psychometric testing

Psychometric testing refers to the use of standardized processes and tools to collect information about individual psychological differences. The term is commonly used to refer to measures of intelligence, cognitive ability or personality and to the standardized measurement of any psychological construct (e.g., work attitudes such as job satisfaction and psychological states such as work engagement). Psychometric tests are widely used in work settings as they can offer a way of quantifying psychological differences between workers with possible implications for worker behaviour, performance, satisfaction and wellbeing.

Modern psychometric testing has its origins in the late nineteenth-century work of Francis Galton and James McKeen Cattell. Working in controlled laboratory conditions, they showed that measurable differences existed in people's problem-solving abilities. Since then tests have been developed to measure general cognitive problem-solving ability (often referred to 'g'), separate and specific aspects of cognitive ability (e.g., the abilities that help us to work quickly and accurately with numbers, words, diagrams, mechanical problems, etc.) and work-related clusters of abilities (aptitudes). These maximal performance tests have correct or incorrect answers and may have a time limit to measure speed of reasoning. Other tests without stringent time limits examine power and quality of reasoning (e.g., Raven's Progressive Matrices). Typical performance tests include self-report measures of personality, attitudes, values, integrity and interests. In these tests there are no predetermined right or wrong answers as these are used to collect data about preferences or consistency of thought and behaviour. The purpose of testing must be carefully considered before an appropriate test is selected.

Results from good psychometric tests have three properties:

1. High reliability: results are a sufficiently accurate indication of the construct being measured.
2. Good validity: results predict subsequent behaviour/performance.
3. Fairness: results provide reliable and valid data for all test takers regardless of factors such as age, gender and ethnicity.

Details of extensive research examining these properties are included in the user manuals that accompany high-quality psychometric tests. Tests must be administered in a carefully controlled environment by suitably qualified administrators and feedback needs to be provided by appropriately trained individuals.

There is considerable debate about the utility of psychometric tests. Research has identified that tests of intelligence and ability can be used to make reasonable predictions about work performance, but that users need to be alert to the potential for problems with test fairness. The use of self-report measures of typical performance to predict work behaviour remains highly controversial.

RAYMOND RANDALL

See also:

Aptitude test; Intelligence tests; Personality test; Selection.

References and selected further readings

Kline, P. (1990), *Intelligence: The Psychometric View*, London: Routledge.
Kline, P. (1999), *The Handbook of Psychological Testing*, 2nd edn, London: Routledge.
Morgeson, F.P., M.A. Campion, R.L. Dipboye, J.R. Hollenbeck, K. Murphy and N. Schmitt (2007), Reconsidering the use of personality tests in personnel selection contexts, *Personnel Psychology*, **60**, pp. 683–729.
Ones, D.S., S. Dilchert, C. Viswesvaran and T.A. Judge (2007a), In support of personality assessment in organizational settings, *Personnel Psychology*, **60**, pp. 995–1027.
Ones, D.S., C. Viswesvaran and S. Dilchert (2007b), Cognitive ability in personnel selection decisions, in A. Evers, O. Voskuijl and N. Anderson (eds), *Handbook of Selection*, Oxford: Blackwell.

Rust, J. and S. Golombok (2008), Modern Psychometrics: The Science of Psychological Assessment, 3rd edn, London: Routledge.

Public sector

The public sector can be defined as those parts of the economy that are either in state ownership or under contract to the state, plus those parts that are regulated and/or subsidized in the public interest. The main organizations that make up the public sector are in the following subsectors: central and local government, healthcare, education, the emergency services and the armed forces.

In the past 35 years, across Western economies where a neoliberalist agenda has been adopted by governments, the public sector has undergone major reform. The marketization of the public sector has seen a blurring of the public and private sectors in the provision of public services. However, despite the changes that have occurred and have affected the boundaries of the public sector there remains a distinctiveness. This distinctiveness lies in the political dimension.

There are a number of key features relating to the political power of the state, which distinguishes employment in the public sector from private-sector employment. First, governments have the ability to create legislation and take executive action, which impacts directly on employment policy within the public sector. Second, the state raises revenue for the public sector through taxation rather than through the generation of profit from the activities carried out within the sector. As a consequence, governments can prioritize political and macroeconomic considerations rather than commercial ones. Third, governments – unlike private sector employers – can justify employment policy on grounds of national or public interest. Fourth, within Western economies, the state is subject to constraint through the executive, legislature and the judiciary and ultimately the electorate.

Summing up, the public sector can be characterized in general, as having institutional goals that are more numerous, intangible, and conflicting than those in the private sector. Whereas the private sector is concerned with profit and loss, the public sector has to consider a number of diverse and competing objectives. These are based on its role as a political, legal and administrative entity that is responsible for the provision of public services that transcends commercial and economic considerations and is shaped by social utility that benefits all and excludes none.

PETER F. BESZTER

See also:
Neoliberalism; State.

References and selected further readings
Bach, S. and I. Kessler (2012), *The Modernisation of the Public Services and Employee Relations Targeted Change*, Basingstoke: Palgrave Macmillan.
Corby, S. and G. Symon (2011), *Working for the State: Employment Relations in the Public Services*, Basingstoke: Palgrave Macmillan.
Flynn, N. (2007), *Public Sector Management*, 5th edn, London: Sage.

Purpose-driven leadership

In an organizational context, purpose-driven leadership is related to bringing meaning to work through an overarching organizational purpose so that employee work activities are meaningful and rewarding. Purpose-driven leadership involves creating a clarity of purpose to ignite, embed and sustain employee engagement, motivation and discretionary effort. Purpose-driven leaders align values and beliefs to their organizational purpose. This alignment creates an opportunity to develop value driven behaviours that guide employee behaviour towards achieving the organizational mission and objectives.

Purpose-driven leadership has existed from the earliest days of human evolution and played out over history across tribes, armies, religions and governments. In business there have been many examples including Walt Disney, who summed up his mantra in four words: 'To make people happy.' Yet while purpose-driven leadership is deemed to be important to business success by some leaders, it's ignored by others (Turner, 2014).

Shareholder value has placed emphasis on short-term objectives and a reduced focus on long-term sustainability. Purpose-driven leaders aim to re-balance this equation through employing transformational leadership behaviours as well as transactional management behaviours (Bass and Riggio, 2006). The transactional task-driven approach is often driven by situational factors including environment, culture, market positioning and leadership potential. Advocates believe that purpose provides a powerful driver of transformational change and performance. A research study found that purpose is seen by employees as second to pay as a motivator (Woods, 2012).

A sense of purpose is increasingly recognized as essential for both business and personal success. Research studies indicate that companies with a core purpose and a values based culture outperform general market and comparison companies, for example by 15:1 and 6:1 respectively (Collins and Poras, 1994).

Organizational purpose generally relates to discovery, excellence, heroism and/or altruism (Mourkkogiannis, 2006) and is driven by past legacy or future aspirations showing up in brand, products, services and customer experiences. To be impactful, purpose must be understood by employees and it often grows in importance at times of organizational change. This is possibly due to the fact that change forces leaders to make hard decisions about what the organization stands for and the difference it makes to employees, customers and wider communities. Creating a core purpose enables organizations to communicate not just what they do and how they do it but why they're doing it.

PAUL S. TURNER

See also:

Employee engagement; Transformational leadership.

References and selected further readings

Bass, B.M. and R.E. Riggio (2006), *Transformational Leadership*, 2nd edn, New Jersey: Lawrence Erlbaum Associates.
Collins, J.C. and J.I. Poras (1994), *Built to Last*, New York: Harper Business.

Mourkkogiannis, N. (2006), *Purpose: The Starting Point for Great Companies*, New York: Palgrave Macmillan.
Turner, P.S. (2014), *My Job is to Put a Man on the Moon*, White Paper, Georgia Group Consulting UK and
    Australia, http://us8.campaign-archive1.com/?u=4193263c2c0e8dc9eff160304&id=62b5649377; www.hrma-
    gazine.co.uk/hro/news/1073337/two-thirds-staff-extra-mile-organisation-purpose-commercial-gain-survey.
Woods, D. (2012), *Crunch Time: The Power of Purpose*, YouGov Report.

Qualifications

In an educational context, a qualification refers to the official completion of a course where a recognized standard of assessment has been attained, either through examination or by assessment of coursework. Qualifications begin, mostly, in the latter stages of schooling, where school students are required to be examined in a number of subjects before leaving. They are of course assessed both formally and informally throughout their school years, but (in the UK at least) it is only at the age of 16 that formal assessment resulting in qualifications such as GCSEs take place. These enable the student to demonstrate to employers or further education providers that they have reached a specified standard of education. Further qualifications may be added to these initial awards throughout life, which are intended to open doors to career development.

Post-16 awards at school and college are typically, in the UK, subject-based AS- and A-levels, which can lead to university entrance. Many schools are now providing additional awards such as the Baccalaureate and more vocationally based awards such as BTEC. Colleges now provide university entry courses (A-levels) and technical courses, often linked to apprenticeships, which will qualify students to embark upon trades such as catering, hairdressing, carpentry, plumbing, etc. These trades will all have vocational awards that qualify the college leaver to practise and they may be added to as careers develop.

Post-18 education in the UK continues in colleges and universities. The number of students studying at university continues to rise but the qualification of an honours degree is no longer perceived as being any more than an entry qualification to a job. Indeed, the number of students applying for 'graduate-level' jobs far outstrips the number of jobs available, although there has been some recent improvement in graduate prospects Most twenty-first-century graduates will need additional qualifications, which they may undertake as full time postgraduate study or 'on the job'. Other work-based qualifications include National Vocational Qualifications (NVQ or SVQ in Scotland). These have sought to assess on-the-job competence for many who have left school without or with few qualifications. Critics of NVQs have argued they are not developmental since they assess competence and do not encourage engagement with theory or learning.

Finally, to maintain professional accreditation to practise, members of the professional bodies are required to undertake continual professional development (CPD) in the form of course attendance or development of a portfolio of reflective practice that can be checked at any time. Human resource professionals, for example, will be required by the Chartered Institute of Personnel and Development (CIPD) to provide evidence that their personal development is up-to-date – a form of maintaining the qualification.

ALISON SMITH

References and selected further readings

Hodgson, A., K. Spours and A. Hodgson (2014), *Dearing and Beyond: 14–19 Qualifications, Frameworks and Systems*, London: Routledge.
Misko, J. (2015), *Developing, Approving and Maintaining Qualifications: Selected International Approaches*, National Vocational Education and Training Research Program research report, NCVER, Adelaide, www.ncver.edu.au/publications/2775.html.
Raffe, D. (2015), First count to five: some principles for the reform of vocational qualifications in England, *Journal of Education and Work*, **28**(2), pp. 1–18.

Skubic, E.K. and E. Keep (2015), Implementing national qualifications frameworks across five continents, *Journal of Education and Work*, **28**(1), pp. 106–115.

Quality circles

The emergence of quality circles (QCs) dates back to the early 1960s by Kaoru Ishikawa who put stress on the idea of 'organization-wide employee training and development programmes' as a means to help Japanese's organizations recover post World War II, with a national training programme launched in 1962 placing emphasis on creating a problem-solving culture through offering training programmes to the individual foreman in quality control techniques. This led to the development of QCs and thus gave equal weight to the importance of employee training and dissemination of quality control knowledge to the shop floor level.

By definition, a QC is a volunteer group of three to 12 employees in the same or related department who are usually led by a departmental supervisor or a senior worker and are trained and organized as a work unit to discuss and solve work-related problems during regular weekly meetings. The emphasis of QC is not so much 'employee control' but the compelling idea of 'employee empowerment' in the sense that the circles really become managers at their own level. A QC thus fosters the participatory approach to managing human resources through encouraging a measure of direct employee involvement and participation in identifying and solving quality and operations-related problems.

In order to help for QCs to make a meaningful contribution to the improvement of company-wide QC programmes, employees are expected to understand and be capable of acting in accordance with several key principles. Chief among these is the view that QCs are integral to the improvement, development and core performance of individual employees and consequently the enterprise as a whole and that the performance impact and contribution of QCs hinges upon the existence of an organizational climate that fulfils the following dual objectives: (a) to promote an organization-wide respect for basic employee rights, which in turn makes the organization favourable to work in, and (b) to develop employee abilities, competencies and capabilities fully, which in the long run have the potential to bring about infinite possibilities.

Ebrahim Soltani

References and suggested further readings

Hill, S. (2009), Why quality circles failed but total quality management might succeed, *British Journal of Industrial Relations*, **29**(4), pp. 541–568.
Hutchins, D. (1985), *The Quality Circles Handbook*, New York: Pitman Press.
Ishikawa, K. (1980), *QC Circle Koryo: General Principles of the QC Circle*, Tokyo: QC Circle Headquarters, Union of Japanese Scientists and Engineers.
Storey, J. (1992), *Developments in the Management of Human Resources*, Oxford: Blackwell Publishers.
Wilkinson, A., T. Redman, E. Snape and M. Marchington (1998), *Managing with Total Quality Management: Theory and Practice*, Basingstoke: Palgrave Macmillan.
Wood, R., F. Hull and K. Azumi (1983), Evaluating quality circles: the American application, *California Management Review*, **26**(1), pp. 37–53.

Race discrimination

In Britain, legislation addressing race discrimination dates back to the 1960s. At the EU level, the introduction in 1998 of a treaty article allowing for action to prevent discrimination based on racial or ethnic origin (now found in Article 19 of the Treaty on the Functioning of the European Union) was later followed by Directive 2000/43/EC implementing the principle of equal treatment between persons irrespective of racial or ethnic origin. From 2003, the national legislation was amended to implement EU legislation in areas relating to race, ethnic and national origins. All of the previous legislation has now been consolidated into the Equality Act 2010.

Employers must not discriminate against job applicants or employees (Equality Act 2010, section 39). Discrimination is defined with reference to certain characteristics that are designated as protected under the Equality Act 2010. Race is a protected characteristic (section 4). The definition of race encompasses colour, nationality and ethnic or national origins (section 9).

Direct race discrimination occurs where, because of race an employer treats an employee or applicant less favourably then they treat or would treat others (see section 13). Direct discrimination encompasses associative discrimination and this means that the less favourable treatment does not have to be because of the race of the employee or applicant themselves, but can be because of the race of another. Direct discrimination also encompasses perceptive discrimination here the less favourable treatment would be because the employer perceives the employee or applicant to be of particular racial group when in fact they are not of that group. Direct race discrimination includes segregating the employee or applicant from others (section 13(5)).

Indirect race discrimination occurs where an employer applies a provision, criterion or practice to an employee or applicant that is discriminatory in relation to the employee or applicant's race. A provision criterion or practice will be discriminatory in relation to an employee or applicant's race if it applies to persons of a different racial group, it puts or would put persons of the same racial group as the employee or applicant at a particular disadvantage and it puts or would put the employee or applicant themselves at that disadvantage. Employers can defend an indirect race discrimination claim by showing that the provision, criterion or practice was a proportionate means of meeting a legitimate aim.

LIZ OLIVER

See also:
Direct discrimination; Indirect discrimination.

References and selected further readings

Deitch, E.A., A. Barsky, R.M. Butz, S. Chan, A.P. Brief and J. Bradley (2003), Subtle yet significant: the existence and impact of everyday racial discrimination in the workplace, *Human Relations*, **56**(11), pp. 1299–1324.
Willey, B. (2012), Employment Law in Context: An Introduction for HR Professionals, 4th edn, Harlow: Pearson.

Radicalism

Radicalism as a frame of reference in human resource management (HRM) is broad and can refer to several perspectives derived from sociological theory and radical political economy. As an approach it tends to integrate an analysis of HRM with a wider appreciation of the social structure of capitalism and the various features that are held to characterize this structure: class power, exploitation, ideology and alienation. The perspective is characterized by a general scepticism over the capacity of HRM to empower workers or eradicate the strains of workplace conflict. Radicals will tend to emphasize the uneven, exploitative and dehumanizing nature of the relationship between employers and employees. Radicals are likely to see the relationship as uneven due to the wide disparity of power in favour of the employer, based on their ownership of the means of production. The relationship is exploitative insofar as the product of labour is seen to be appropriated and controlled, not by the direct producers (employees), but by the employer. Finally, the relationship is dehumanizing in that employees' labour is commodified and alienated within a production process geared to private profit and not social needs.

A significant body of radical analysis stems from a Marxian tradition, often exemplified in labour process theory (Thompson and Smith, 2010). Labour process radicals are interested in the way employers erect control structures to realize productive labour and how such structures engender consent and resistance on the part of workers. Radicals in this tradition have also emphasized the dynamics of capital accumulation in shaping outcomes at the level of the employment relationship. There is also a branch of radicalism that focuses less on structural relations between capital and labour, and more on the contested nature of human identity and subjectivity at work (Bolton and Houlihan, 2007). Foucauldian concepts of surveillance, discipline and resistance often take centre-stage in this perspective. In applying their particular strain of analysis, there is a longstanding tradition of radicals (alongside many pluralists) debunking unitary accounts of practices such as 'corporate culture' or 'high-performance management' that claimed to deliver employee empowerment and job enrichment. Radicals have also clashed with pluralists: the latter are seen to promote a 'partnership' between capital and labour, thereby perpetuating social structures of inequality, exploitation and subordination. While some radicals may be disinclined to offer policy prescription, many are nonetheless likely to favour democratic forms of worker control or mobilization which empowers labour in the workplace and society at large (Gall, 2003).

NIALL CULLINANE

See also:

Alienation; Frames of reference; Labour process/theory; Pluralism; Unitarism.

References and selected further readings

Bolton, C. and M. Houlihan (eds) (2007), *Searching for the Human in Human Resource Management*, Basingstoke: Palgrave Macmillan.
Gall, G. (2003), Marxism and industrial relations, in P. Ackers and A. Wilkinson (eds), *Understanding Work and Employment: Industrial Relations in Transition*, Oxford: Oxford University Press.
Thompson, P. and C. Smith (eds) (2010), *Working Life: Renewing Labour Process Analysis*, Basingstoke: Palgrave Macmillan.

Recognition

From a psychological perspective, recognition may be seen an intrinsic reward that might be connected with meaningful work and achievement in a total reward approach. Recognition might be viewed conceptually as distinct from extrinsic rewards (pay and benefits) (Latham, 2007) since it is more symbolic than tangible. More subtly, Long and Shields (2010) argue that the symbolic and instrumental role of rewards are linked – so that cash may be both tangible and symbolic and that recognition or praise as non-cash rewards have a similar function to the symbolic role of cash.

In practice as well as theory, reward and recognition have been seen as both linked and not linked. On the one hand, Hansen et al. (2002) argue they are fundamentally different, because reward schemes are essentially instrumental in nature, and perceived as such by employees, In contrast they argue recognition is about 'honoring and noticing' (Hansen et al., 2002, p. 65) and lacks the instrumentality of cash reward systems. On the other hand in less cash-rich environments, Rose (2011) argues that non-cash rewards are a method of recognition because employers are thinking about what they can do to recognize extra effort even though they may not have so much in the way of cash rewards to disperse. Perhaps because of limits on performance pay and lower inflation, recognition schemes have been developed by reward and HR practitioners. Such schemes offer small symbolic gifts as a recognition of good service or performance in the organization – traditionally they may have been be 'employee of the month' or similar awards, but practice is very varied (Suff, 2004).

Long and Shields (2010) in a study conducted in Australia and Canada found evidence that organizations use cash and non-cash recognition rewards in a complementary way, rather than substituting less expensive non-cash recognition for cash in straightened times. They say that such non-cash recognition rewards include a range of *social reinforcers*, such as mentions in company newsletters, plaques or letters of commendation, learning and development opportunities, merchandise or travel prizes, or extra time off. Both individual and group-based schemes were evident in both countries but Australian organizations were more likely to use combinations of group and individual schemes (and to link cash with non-cash rewards) than those in Canada. The difference seems to be related to the extent to which, more generally, pay determination is individualized (more individualization connected with greater linkages of recognition with cash and link of group with individual approaches).

Angela Wright

See also:

Motivation; Reward management; Total reward.

References and selected further readings

Hansen, F., M. Smith and R. Hansen (2002), Rewards and recognition in employee motivation, *Compensation and Benefits Review*, September/October, pp. 64–72.
Latham, G.P. (2007), *Work Motivation: History, Theory, Research, and Practice*, London: Sage.
Long, R. and J. Shields (2010), From pay to praise, *International Journal of Human Resource Management*, **21**(8), pp. 1145–1172.

Rose, M. (2011), *A Guide to Non-Cash Reward: Learn the Value of Recognition Reward Staff at Virtually No Cost Improve Organizational Performance*, London, Kogan Page.
Suff, R. (2004), Thank you goes a long way, *IRS Employment Review*, **792**, pp. 32–36.

Recruitment

Recruitment is one of the most important activities of HR specialists, defined by Barber (1989, p. 5) as 'practices and activities carried out by the organisation with the primary purpose of identifying and attracting potential employees'. Although often conflated, recruitment is distinct from *selection*, which is the process that follows recruitment. Recruitment is the process of generating a pool of suitable applicants to apply for a particular position. Selection is then the process whereby organizations decide, from within that pool, which applicants are the best people for the vacant positions, using contextually relevant methods. The ultimate success of the selection stage, however, depends upon the quality of applicants generated during recruitment. Despite these differences the term 'recruitment' is still sometimes used as a catch-all phrase.

There are many methods of recruitment, including: various forms of advertising; more 'informal' methods (e.g., word of mouth and employee referrals); apprenticeships; the use of headhunters; and links with intermediaries (such as government job centres, employment/temporary agencies and educational institutions). Of particular growing interest is 'e-recruitment' whereby employers use their own websites, specialist recruitment websites and/or social media to try and attract desired recruits. The choice of method(s) depends upon the nature of the job vacancy, the resources of the organization, and the potential pool of labour an employer wishes to attract. Consistent with utility considerations (Boudreau and Rynes, 1985) organizations may choose to use more expensive and/or targeted methods for those employees in more 'critical' positions; for example, the use of executive headhunters for senior management positions.

Although some recruitment activity is internal within organizations, recruitment is normally outward-facing, requiring interaction with the external environment. The labour market is thus a key factor enabling or inhibiting recruitment. External labour markets may or may not contain applicants with the desired skills and if especially scarce or specialist skills are required, then the recruitment net may need to be cast wider. Government education and skills policies and the supply of appropriate skills thus impact upon organizations' recruitment practices. Changing demographic trends in wider society (such as immigration and an ageing population) also affect the availability of suitable labour within particular locales. Demographic changes also affect the kind of job and organizational factors that applicants consider to be attractive with, for example, work-life-balance increasingly important in attracting new staff (Iles, 2007). The wider economy also impacts upon recruitment activities with recession and levels of unemployment affecting employers' ability to recruit. Economic pressures may be contradictory as when there is most available labour (e.g., during a recession) employers may face the most financial constraints in their recruitment activities. Employers thus need to balance exogenous contingencies and constraints with their own recruitment preferences.

Traditional pre-recruitment activities include HR planning and the development of job descriptions and person specifications, although not all recruitment processes may follow this approach. Planning determines the need for labour and should ideally be strategic and anticipatory rather than reactive. Succession planning and future demand are thus key factors. The use of job descriptions and person specifications is consistent with the rational 'psychometric-objective' model of staffing which aims to 'match the "right" people with the "right" jobs and to *attract candidates who possess the required skills* (while putting off those who do not)' (Iles, 2007, p.99, emphasis added). Job descriptions identify the 'tasks, duties and responsibilities' within a particular job (Iles, 2007, p.99), while the person specification details the personal qualities needed to perform the job description. The person specification may include elements such as education, skills, knowledge and personal traits. Job descriptions and person specifications can then feed into recruitment materials. There is a risk, however, that recruitment activities based upon rigid job descriptions ignore the role of future change and the individual's potential future career within the organization. Many recruitment processes thus now also focus upon 'fit' with the organization and/or team. To facilitate fit more informal recruitment processes (such as employee referrals) may prove to be just as valuable as more resource intensive methods (Hurrell and Scholarios, 2014), counter to the psychometric-objective model. Informal methods, if not strategically integrated with organizations' skills needs, may, however, run the risk of idiosyncratic or prejudiced recruitment and should thus be used with care.

A key current trend in recruitment is a shift in emphasis away from the psychometric-objective model to consider applicant perspectives and what attracts applicants to organizations. This is, in part, to facilitate fit. The applicant perspective emphasizes not just how applicants apply for jobs that suit their skills but also how they are attracted to other aspects of organizations, such as brands and values (Hurrell and Scholarios, 2014). Such a concern is becoming particularly acute due to the perceived preferences of Generation Y job candidates. Such candidates are seen as more value driven than their predecessors and also as having more varied demands of their jobs and employers. There is a risk, however, of an organization concentrating too much on 'impression management' (Iles, 2007, p.100) to attract the best candidates during recruitment. Adapting Schneider's (1987) attraction selection attrition (ASA) framework, candidates may exit the organization if they are selected but later discover that the organizational reality (as painted during recruitment) does not meet their needs. Recruitment is thus frequently seen as the first stage in developing the psychological contract. Clear and honest 'realistic job previews' during recruitment (and subsequently selection) may alleviate the risk of later attrition (Iles, 2007), showing how the applicant perspective and the use of more traditional job descriptions may coincide.

SCOTT A. HURRELL

See also:

External labour markets; Generations; Internal labour markets; Job analysis; Labour market; Person–environment fit; Psychological contract; Resourcing; Selection; Skill; Succession planning; Talent management.

References and selected further readings

Barber, A. (1989), *Recruiting Employees: Individual and Organisational Perspectives*, London: Sage.
Boudreau, J.W. and S.L. Rynes (1985), Role of recruitment in staffing utility analysis, *Journal of Applied Psychology*, **70**(2), pp.354–366.

Hurrell, S.A. and D. Scholarios (2013), Recruitment, in A. Wilkinson and T. Redman (eds), *Contemporary Human Resource Management*, 4th edn, Harlow: Pearson Education.

Hurrell, S.A. and D. Scholarios (2014), 'The people make the brand': reducing social skills gaps through person-brand fit and human resource management practices, *Journal of Service Research*, **17**(1), pp. 54–67.

Iles, P. (2007), Employee resourcing and talent management, in J. Storey (ed.), *Human Resource Management: A Critical Text*, 3rd edn, London: Thomson Learning.

Schneider, B. (1987), The people make the place, *Personnel Psychology*, **40**(3), pp. 437–453.

Red-circling

The term 'red-circling' describes the action that reward practitioners may take with respect to jobs, which after a new pay structure are paid more than the maximum of their newly set pay range. This typically follows the implementation of a new job evaluation scheme leading to a new grading structure (Acas, 2010).

The individuals whose jobs have been red-circled may have their pay protected for a certain period of time, in order that the job-holders do not suffer an immediate loss of income. The amount of pay protection and the time span over which it is protected are controversial, since this is intended as a temporary arrangement to help the red-circled individuals. Protecting the pay of those in red-circled jobs over extended periods of time can become (as in the UK) an equal pay issue if most of the individuals whose pay is protected are men as this could mean that their pay is higher than women now in the same grade or pay range.

A report by the Office of Manpower Economics (OME, 2013) said that many organizations find it difficult to gain employee commitment to embarking on job evaluation without an element of pay protection since this will offer reassurance to those employees who fear their pay may fall when the job evaluation scheme is implemented. In the UK local government sector, some protected negotiations and disputes arose when new job evaluation schemes, with an emphasis on equal pay for work of equal value between men and women, were used as a basis for new pay and grading structures. Extensive litigation concerning the pay protection of red-circled employees took place on equal pay grounds (Wright, 2011) since while there is no prescribed time limit on the use of red-circling, there is a general legal principle that pay protection should only be used by employers as a transitional tool to cushion the blow of pay cuts rather than an arrangement to maintain pay differentials permanently.

ANGELA WRIGHT

See also:

Equal pay: Job evaluation.

References and selected further readings

Acas (2010), *Job Evaluation: Considerations and Risks*, London: Acas.

OME (2013), *Discrimination Law and Pay Systems*, London: Office of Manpower Economics.

Wright, A (2011), 'Modernising' away gender pay inequality? Some evidence from the local government sector on using job evaluation, *Employee Relations*, **33**(2), pp. 159–178.

Redeployment

Redeployment is defined as the process of transferring or relocating employees from their current jobs to jobs in other parts of the organization where they are needed. It may be undertaken either to pursue growth and development or to solve financial and operational difficulties. Therefore, when the organization has surplus employees, it does not automatically mean that all of these employees have to be made redundant. Alternative courses of action to retain them could include redeployment, reduction in working time and wages, and temporary lay-offs.

Greenhaues et al. (2000) identify two basic reasons for the use of redeployment. First, as a planned development technique, it can be used to improve the level of skills and broaden the experiences of identified employees. For example, a multinational organization may want its high-performing employees to gain international exposure and, therefore, international redeployment becomes inevitable. Second, redeployment is used as a strategic response to a change in business conditions, for example, offshoring to take advantage of better business opportunities in another geographical location. Globalization of business activities may require the redeployment of employees, and sometimes makes the sending of the key employees abroad inevitable.

Other reasons motivating the redeployment of employees overseas is not just the transfer of knowledge from the parent organization to its subsidiary abroad, but also training employees in areas such as research and development, production processes, finance and marketing. In addition, redeployment is linked to career development. It is a means to gain international experience, an opportunity for career growth and increased compensation and benefits (Kupfer, 2008).

To be effective in the new positions, redeployed employees should undergo retraining, providing them the skills and the knowledge required. Having multi-tasked employees would generally enable the process of redeployment to be made easier. The redeployment may be complemented by generic job descriptions. It may also be appropriate to consider flexibility clauses in job descriptions (Rees and Porter, 2009).

Using redeployment as an alternative to redundancy has its problems (Gilmore and Williams, 2009). Organizations may not necessarily want to retain employees during an economic downturn. Further, when vacancies arise within their own business units, managers would be expected to give priority to redeployed employees, who are under the threat of redundancy elsewhere in the organization. Even then, there may not be many redeployment opportunities in the organization. As such, redeployments can lead to a sense of uncertainty and insecurity as well as disruptions of social life.

CHRIS ROWLEY AND NAGIAH RAMASAMY

See also:

Downsizing; Globalization; Job analysis; Psychological contract.

References and selected further readings

Clarke, M. (2007), Choices and constraints: individual perceptions of the voluntary redundancy experience, *Human Resource Management Journal*, **17**(1), pp. 6–93.

Ferres, N., J. Connell and A. Travaglione (2005), The effect of future redeployment on organizational trust, *Strategic Change*, **14**, pp. 77–91.

Gilmore, S. and S. Williams (eds) (2009), *Human Resource Management*, Oxford: Oxford University Press.

Greenhaues, J.H., G.A. Callanan and V.M. Godshalk (2000), *Career Management*, 3rd edn, Orlando: Harcourt.

Kupfer, H. (2008), International redeployment of management personnel, *International Journal of Business Insights & Transformation*, 1(2), p. 1.

London, M. (1989), *Managing the Training Enterprise*, San Francisco: Jossey Bass.

Rees, W.D. and C. Porter (2009), Redundancy handling — a key training need, *Industrial and Commercial Training*, 41(4), pp. 175–180.

References

As a selection method, references are used to obtain additional information about candidates from third parties such as former employers, lecturers or colleagues. Not only is it a straightforward way of verifying information about the applicant, it is also a low-cost method.

It seeks to verify the truthfulness of factual information submitted by the applicant, such as dates of employment, current and previous job titles and educational background. In addition, reference-checking seeks an appraisal of the applicant's character and an assessment of the applicant's job performance capabilities. It also serves to uncover any negative information.

Reference-checking can help employers match candidates with vacant positions and with the organization's overall needs. By getting candidates into the right jobs, it reduces employee turnover and disciplinary problems. Employers may use reference-checking at different stages in the selection process, that is, either to confirm details of the chosen candidate after the position has been offered, or to request references for shortlisted candidates prior to interview.

While many employers would not want to reduce a former employee's chances of a job, others might prefer giving an incompetent employee good reviews if it will get rid of that employee, which often leads to recommendation inflation (Kasambira, 1984), rendering such references invalid. Some employers, fearful of being sued, hesitate to give objective references, particularly if the references are negative. As such, the accuracy of the information about the character and suitability of the applicant can be questionable and unreliable.

The issue of references is always a controversial one, for it involves balancing concerns of fairness to former employees, providing appropriate information to prospective employers, and employers' fears of legal liability. Employers have a duty of care when providing a reference which is accurate and honest, not malicious or retaliatory, and must conform to statutory limitations if any.

In the UK, while employers are under no statutory duty (other than those in the finance sector) to provide a reference, the House of Lords held that employers have 'at least a moral obligation' to do so (*Spring v Guardian Assurance plc* [1994] IRLR 460). The Court of Appeal in the case stated that although there is a duty on the employer to ensure that references are true, accurate and fair in substance, they must also mention any relevant negative issues.

CHRIS ROWLEY AND NAGIAH RAMASAMY

See also:

Recruitment; Selection.

References and selected further readings

Anderson, N. and V. Shackleton (1993), *Successful Selection Interviewing*, Oxford: Blackwell.
Beardwell, J. and T. Claydon (2010), *Human Resource Management: A Contemporary Approach*, 6th edn, Essex: Prentice Hall.
Emmott, M. (2014), *Lies, Damn Lies, and Employee References*, London: Chartered Institute of Personnel and Development, www.cipd.co.uk/blogs/cipdbloggers/b/policy_at_work/archive/2014/05/07/lies-damn-lies-and-employee-references.aspx.
Evuleocha, S.U., S.D. Ugbah and S. Law (2009), Recruiter perceptions of information that employment references should provide to assist in making selection decisions, *Journal of Employment Counseling*, **46**, pp.98–106.
Kasambira, K.P. (1984), Recommendation inflation, *The Teacher Educator*, **20**(2), pp.26–29.
Muir, C. (2009), Rethinking job references: a networking challenge, *Business Communication Quarterly*, **72**(3), pp.304–317.

Regulation

The question of regulation is important to HRM and labour and employment relations whether the national context is heavily or lightly regulated. The notion of regulation is usually meant to refer the role of legislation and rights/responsibilities in work and in employment. The role of governments in developing the rights of workers and the responsibilities of workers and employers – and of the state itself – can determine and shape the way people work and the way they are employed. We could call such regulation 'formal regulation' as it is normally backed by some type of sanction – although how heavy this sanction is or whether it is applied effectively is another matter. This may vary according to the extent of autonomy a state has from dominant economic interests. In addition, there are also informal regulations, which are rules or customs that may not even be written down but that are important to the way expectations and behaviours are shaped at work. There may be customs related to time off or job rotation that may be unwritten, for example. Regulation therefore varies greatly (see Martínez Lucio and MacKenzie, 2015, for an introduction to the literature). Some contexts are more heavily regulated due to a greater social tradition and a greater role for the state and law. These may be systems with a more coordinated and less liberal or market-oriented approach to work, employment and economic relations in general (Hall and Soskice, 2001; Whitley, 2007).

In addition, in terms of international human resource management and employment relations we are seeing a discussion about *hard* and *soft* regulation. There is an increasingly level of concern as to how to regulate companies that operate between different national systems and therefore different legal systems. The issue here is that we need to comprehend that hard regulation based on laws that can be more effectively implemented – as there are sanctions and punishments – does not always extend beyond the national context. While there are international bodies that try to develop codes of conduct and advisory processes and rules for MNCS and national governments (such as the International Labour Organization), these may not be implemented due to a lack of resources and ability in terms of coercion or compulsion (see the question of

Transnational Collective Agreements). So there is a debate about *hard* and *soft* law too that is relevant to this discussion (see Abbott and Snidal, 2000).

There is much discussion about deregulation and the emergence of management prerogative but this is an ideological argument that does not take into account that it is the nature of regulation and the actors of regulation that need to be discussed and not solely the extent of any presence of regulation (MacKenzie and Martínez Lucio, 2005). Regulation is a process that involves various bodies in its design and development as well as different organizations and processes in terms of its implementation and enforcement. It is therefore important to acknowledge that we need to be aware of the ways rules are constructed in relation to work and employment as we are seeing more regulations on questions of individual rights and matters such as equality as well health and safety.

MIGUEL MARTÍNEZ LUCIO

See also:

Custom and practice; International Labour Organization and International Labour Standards; Labour law; State; Varieties of capitalism.

References and selected further readings

Abbott, K.W. and D. Snidal (2000), Hard and soft law in international governance, *International organization*, **54**(3), pp. 421–456.

Hall, P.A. and D. Soskice (eds) (2001), *Varieties of Capitalism: The Institutional Foundations of Comparative Advantage*, Oxford: Oxford University Press.

MacKenzie, R. and M. Martínez Lucio (2005), The realities of regulatory change: beyond the fetish of deregulation, *Sociology*, **39**, 3.

Martínez Lucio, M. and R. MacKenzie (2015), Regulation and multinational corporations: the changing context of global employment relations, in A.-W. Harzing and A. Pinnington (eds), *International Human Resource Management*, London. Sage.

Trubek, D.M. and L.G. Trubek (2005), Hard and soft law in the construction of social Europe: the role of the open method of co-ordination, *European Law Journal*, **11**(3), pp. 343–364.

Whitley, R. (2007), *Business Systems and Organizational Capabilities: The Institutional Structuring of Competitive Competences*, Oxford: Oxford University Press.

Religious discrimination

Legal provision specifically addressing discrimination on the basis of religion or belief came into force in Britain when the Employment Equality (Religion or Belief) Regulations 2003 implemented the provisions of an the EU Directive 2000/78/EC Establishing a general framework for equal treatment in employment and occupation. This legislation has now been consolidated by the Equality Act 2010.

Employers must not discriminate against job applicants or employees (Equality Act 2010, section 39). Discrimination is defined with reference to certain characteristics that are designated as protected under the Equality Act 2010. Religion or belief is a protected characteristic (section 4). For the purposes of the Equality Act 2010 religion means any religion and belief means any religious or philosophical belief (section 10). Reference to religion or to belief includes a reference to lack of religion or to a lack of belief (section 10). The definition of religion or belief under the Equality Act 2010 is widely drafted and allows for interpretation in line with the European Convention of Human Rights which, within Article 9, sets out the right to freedom of thought, conscience and religion. The guidance notes issued with the Equality Act 2010 suggest that the religion must have a clear structure and belief system. The guidance notes suggest that denominations or sects within a religion could be considered to be a religion or belief (such as Protestants and Catholics within Christianity). Examples of relevant religions given within the guidance notes include: the Baha'i faith, Buddhism, Christianity, Hinduism, Islam, Jainism, Judaism, Rastafarianism, Sikhism and Zoroastrianism and examples of belief include humanism and atheism. The case law of the European Court of Human Rights would suggest that for a belief to qualify for protection it must have sufficient cogency, seriousness, cohesion and importance, in addition to being worthy of respect in a civilised society (*Campbell v UK*). The Employment Appeal Tribunal case of *Grainger plc v Nicholson* gave guidance on the definition of philosophical belief and identified some criteria for a philosophical belief to be protected: (a) the belief must be genuinely held, (b) it must be a belief and not an opinion or viewpoint based on the present state of information available, (c) it must be a belief as to a weighty and substantial aspect of human life and behaviour, (d) it must attain a certain level of cogency, seriousness, cohesion and importance and (e) it must be worthy of respect in a democratic society, be not incompatible with human dignity and not conflict with the fundamental rights of others. In that case it was held that Nicholson's belief that climate change was man-made could, if genuinely held, constitute a philosophical belief.

Direct religion or belief discrimination occurs where, because of religion or belief an employer treats an employee or applicant less favourably then they treat or would treat others (see section 13). Indirect religion or belief discrimination occurs where an employer applies a provision, criterion or practice to an employee or applicant which is discriminatory in relation to the employee or applicant's religion or belief. A provision criterion or practice will be discriminatory in relation to an employee or applicant's religion or belief if it applies to persons of a different religion or belief, it puts or would put persons of the same religion or belief as the employee or applicant at a particular disadvantage and it puts or would put the employee or applicant themselves at that disadvantage. Employers can defend an indirect religion or belief discrimination claim by showing that the provision, criterion or practice was a proportionate means of meeting a legitimate aim. An example of potential indirect discrimination on the basis of religion or belief would be an appearance policy that prevents employees from wearing jewellery. Some religions require people to wear symbolic jewellery; furthermore, even where not required to, some individuals choose to wear religious symbols as an expression of their belief. A ban on jewellery might put people of a particular religion or belief at a particular disadvantage compared to others. An employer would therefore need to show that the ban on jewellery is a proportionate means of achieving a legitimate aim.

LIZ OLIVER

See also:

Direct discrimination; Equal opportunity; Indirect discrimination.

References and selected further readings

Pitt, G. (2013), Taking religion seriously, *Industrial Law Journal*, **42**(4), pp. 398–408.
Willey, B. (2012), *Employment Law in Context: An Introduction for HR Professionals*, 4th edn, Harlow: Pearson.

Repatriation

Repatriation represents a critically important, if somewhat understudied phase of the international assignment cycle comprising pre-expatriation, expatriation and repatriation. The repatriation phase can be defined as the period of time following completion of the international assignment within which the returnee readjusts and becomes assimilated back into the work and socio-cultural domains of the home environment. Repatriation in a broader sense may also entail a subsequent posting to either a different cultural environment or to a different organizational context than the one the individual was in prior to the assignment. Repatriation research lines of enquiry dealing with readjustment can be classified into two major streams: one focusing on objective aspects relating to the explanatory power of post-assignment work and organizational experiences; the other dealing with more subjective aspects referring to psychosomatic wellbeing and psychosocial aspects of the repatriate's adjustment arising from transition uncertainty, disorientation, anomie and reverse culture shock all of which can be experienced in response to individual level changes to attitudes and values while abroad and to an altered home environment as a result of changes that have occurred during the assignment period. While the expatriate adjustment experience has been modelled as a U-shaped curve, the repatriate adjustment process has been characterized as a 'W'.

The retention of expatriate employees during repatriation and beyond remains a talent management challenge for many organizations. Chief among factors identified in empirical studies as determinants of whether an expatriate is likely to remain with the home organization on repatriation are issues encompassing the experiencing of status loss on returning, a perceived diminution in autonomy, identity strain, a decrease in job satisfaction and a concomitant rise in perceived job misfit from being placed in non-challenging work roles that do not stretch the repatriate in terms of using the knowledge and skills acquired while abroad. This failure on the part of the organization to capitalize and value the international experience gained by the repatriate can represent a significant missed opportunity. Concomitantly a failure by the repatriate to secure the career trajectory that may have been anticipated as a result of taking the assignment in the first instance, along with a loss of income and lifestyle and family readjustment problems have also been identified as holding significant explanatory power in accounting for repatriation outcomes.

MICHAEL J. MORLEY

See also:

Cross-cultural training; Expatriate; International human resource management.

References and selected further readings

Black, J.S., H.B. Gregersen and M.E. Mendenhall (1992), Toward a theoretical framework of repatriation adjustment, *Journal of International Business Studies*, **23**(4), pp. 737–761.
Gullahorn, J.T. and J.E. Gullahorn (1963), An extension of the U-curve hypothesis, *Journal of Social Issues*, **19**, pp. 33–47.
Kraimer, M.L., M.A. Shaffer, D.A. Harrison and H. Ren (2012), No place like home? An identity strain perspective on repatriate turnover, *Academy of Management Journal*, **55**(2), pp. 399–420.
Lazarova, M.B. and J.L. Cerdin (2007), Revisiting repatriation concerns: organizational support versus career and contextual influences, *Journal of International Business Studies*, **38**(3), pp. 404–429.
Reiche, B.S., M.L. Kraimer and A.-W. Harzing (2011), Why do international assignees

stay? An organizational embeddedness perspective, *Journal of International Business Studies*, **42**(4), pp. 521–544.

Stroh, L.K. (1995), Predicting turnover among repatriates: can organizations affect retention rates? *The International Journal of Human Resource Management*, **6**(2), pp. 443–456.

Representation gap

The use of employee participation schemes have changed dramatically over the last few decades, both in terms of the collective (indirect) and individualistic (direct) types of practices (Wilkinson et al., 2014). As a result, there remains concern that a gap exists between what employees want, in terms of having a voice at work, how they articulate that voice and whether it is actually heard and acted upon by managers (Towers, 1997). A *representation gap* need not be the simple absence of a policy or practice, but the underlying utility (or value and impact) of the voice practice on shared decision-making outcomes. A representation gap can therefore be defined as the 'difference between how much influence employees say they have over management decisions, and how much influence they say they would like' (Dundon and Rollinson, 2011, p. 282).

Debate surrounding a representation gap relates to the lack of, or weak utilization of voice practices at the workplace (Marchington, 2008). The focus of academic and policy interest tends to consider the type of issues upon which employees may express a view or offer an option to management, and this requires a consideration of the *forms* of employee involvement and participation (Wilkinson et al., 2013). When assessing the forms of employee representation, it is evident that there has been a distinctive shift away from the power-centred union or collective systems of voice to direct and individual channels. For example, there is a greater propensity for managers to use individual face-to-face meetings with employees, rely on problem-solving forums than collective negotiations, and to communicate through the likes of newsletters, emails or team briefings (Kersley et al., 2006; van Wanrooy et al., 2013). An argument can be made that direct or individual forms of voice could lead to a wider representation gap because managers control and shape the issues on which workers may have a say. While it is always difficult to generalize, evidence does point to less influence through representation, with employee influence confined more so to trivial matters.

TONY DUNDON

See also:

Employee involvement; Employee voice; Representative participation.

References and selected further readings

Dundon T. and D. Rollinson (2011), *Understanding Employment Relations*, 2nd edn, London: McGraw Hill.

Kersley, B., C. Alpin, J. Forth, A. Bryson, H. Bewley, J. Dix and S. Oxenbridge (2006), *Inside the Workplace: Findings from the 2004 Workplace Employment Relations Survey*, London: Routledge.

Marchington, M. (2008), Employee voice systems, in P. Boxall, J. Purcell and P. Wright (eds), *The Oxford Handbook of Human Resource Management*, Oxford: Oxford University Press.

Towers, B. (1997), *The Representation Gap: Change and Reform in the British and American Workplace*, Oxford: Oxford University Press.

van Wanrooy, B., H. Bewley, A. Bryson, J. Forth, S. Freeth, L. Stokes and S. Wood (2013), *Employment Relations in the Shadow of Recession: Findings from the 2011 Workplace Employment Relations Study*, Basingstoke: Palgrave.

Wilkinson, A., T. Dundon and M. Marchington (2013), Employee involvement and voice, in S. Bach and M. Edwards (eds), *Managing Human Resources*, 5th edn, Chichester: Wiley-Blackwell.

Wilkinson, A., T. Dundon, J. Donaghey and R. Freeman (2014), Employee voice: charting new terrain, in A. Wilkinson, J. Donaghey, T. Dundon and R. Freeman (eds), *Handbook of Research on Employee Voice*, Cheltenham: Edward Elgar.

Representative participation

'Representative participation' is defined as an indirect form of worker voice that allows employees to have a say and participate in described work-related decisions through elected or appointed employee representatives (Marchington, 2008). By definition, 'representative participation' is collective and indirect in nature; whereas 'employee involvement' is often direct and individualistic (Wilkinson et al., 2013). Employee representatives can be elected trade union shop stewards, full-time union officials or non-union employee representatives.

As a general trend, representative participation has declined across most Western economies, largely because of the accompanying decline in trade union membership as the main form of indirect representation. For example, in the US, less than 12 per cent of establishments recognize a trade union (Dixon and Fiorito, 2009). In the UK, about one-third of workplaces recognize a union for bargaining or representative purposes (van Wanrooy et al., 2011). The types of mechanisms that fall under the representative participation rubric include collective negotiating committees, joint consultative forums, workers councils or European works councils. With the decline in union membership, non-union employee representation (NER) is another form of representative worker voice in organizations where unions are absent (Gollan et al., 2014).

Debates about representative participation concern the extent (or depth) of power and decision-making influence workers may have regarding work and HR issues. It is perhaps this aspect of power that explains why collective voice is contentious. For example, the Workplace Employment Relations Study data from Britain consistently points out that around 80 per cent of all managers would prefer to involve employees without union influence (van Wanrooy et al., 2013). Indeed, as union membership has declined, alternative NER structures have evolved. Non-union employee representatives are evident in about 7 per cent of all UK workplaces, and are slightly more common (in about 10 per cent) among larger private sector employers (van Wanrooy et al., 2013).

Tony Dundon

See also:

Collective bargaining; Employee involvement; Employee voice.

References and selected further readings

Cullinane, N., J. Donaghey, T. Dundon, T. Dobbins and E. Hickland (2014), Regulating for mutual gains: non-union employee representation and the information and consultation directive, *International Journal of Human Resource Management*, **25**(6), pp. 810–828.

Dixon, M. and J. Fiorito (2009), Can unions rebound? Decline and renewal in the US labour movement, in G. Gall (ed.), *Union Revitalization in Advanced Economies*, Basingstoke: Palgrave.

Gollan, P., B. Kaufman, D. Taras and A. Wilkinson (2014) (eds), *Voice and Involvement at Work: Experience with Non-Union Representation Across Three Continents*, New York: Routledge.

Marchington, M. (2008), Employee voice systems, in P. Boxall, J. Purcell and P. Wright (eds), *The Oxford Handbook of Human Resource Management*, Oxford: Oxford University Press.

van Wanrooy, B., H. Bewley, A. Bryson, J. Forth, S. Freeth, L. Stokes and S. Wood (2013), *Employment Relations in the Shadow of Recession: Findings from the 2011 Workplace Employment Relations Study*, Basingstoke: Palgrave.

Wilkinson, A., T. Dundon and M. Marchington (2013), Employee involvement and voice, in S. Bach and M. Edwards (eds), *Managing Human Resources*, 5th edn, Chichester: Wiley-Blackwell, pp. 268–289.

Resignation

'Quit' means to resign from one's job voluntarily (Heery and Noon, 2008; Shearer, 1990). The words 'quit' and 'resign' have been used interchangeably, to mean the same thing. Similarly, the expression 'voluntary turnover' has been defined as any employee-initiated separation (Davis et al., 2015). Often, the most commonly cited reasons of employee turnover are change of career, promotion outside the organization, level of pay, lack of development or career opportunities, and leaving to have or look after children (CIPD, 2008).

The rate of resignation is a percentage of the number of employees leaving divided by the total number of employees in the organization. High rates of resignation are a considerable cost, both because they increase labour costs and because they lower organizational performance (Batt et al., 2002). Resignations of experienced employees reduce organizational effectiveness, impact on continuity of projects and increase operational costs due to recruitment and training of new employees.

Research on 'high commitment' or high performance work practices has shown that coherent sets of human resource (HR) practices lead to lower turnover rates and better organizational performance. These practices include those that invest in the skills of the work force and provide the opportunity and incentives for employees to use those skills effectively. Research has also found that employees with 'enhanced or enriched jobs', such as those with greater autonomy, variety or ability to complete a whole task, have higher job satisfaction and lower turnover. In addition, performance-based pay enhances employee commitment and reduces resignation rates. Lower turnover is found among employees who are satisfied with promotion opportunities, perceive their employment to be secure or have higher relative pay or pay satisfaction.

The use of cost-reduction practices, such as downsizing, outsourcing, use of contingent workers and contingent pay, are likely to decrease employee commitment to the firm. These practices convey a message to core employees that future employment is insecure. Ongoing downsizing creates uncertainty and disheartenment. The more qualified or skilled employees who have alternative employment opportunities are more likely to resign.

Some employee resignations involve employees the organization would prefer not to retain. Losing such employees through resignations may be viewed merely as a convenient substitute for termination. In lieu of discharge, employers often allow – and indeed encourage – negotiated resignations that ostensibly permit the employee to circumvent the stigma of having been fired.

CHRIS ROWLEY AND NAGIAH RAMASAMY

See also:

Flexible firm; Retention.

References and selected further readings

Batt, R. and A.J.S. Colvin (2011), An employment systems approach to turnover: human resources practices, quits, dismissals, and performance, *Academy of Management Journal*, **54**(4), pp. 695–717.
Batt, R., A.J.S. Colvin and J. Keefe (2002), Employee voice, human resource practices, and quit rates: evidence from the telecommunications industry, *Industrial and Labor Relations Review*, **55**(4), pp. 573–594.
CIPD (2008), *Recruitment, Retention and Labour Turnover, Survey Report*, London: Chartered Institute of Personnel and Development.
Davis, P.R., C.O. Trevor and J. Feng (2015), Creating a more quit-friendly national workforce? Individual layoff history and voluntary turnover, *Journal of Applied Psychology*, **23**, pp. 1–22.
Heery, E. and M. Noon (2008), *A Dictionary of Human Resource Management*, 2nd edn, Oxford: Oxford University Press, www.oxfordreference.com/view/10.1093/acref/9780199298761.001.0001/acref-9780199298761-e-1773?rskey=54y9Lu&result=1315.
Shearer, R.A. (1990), Quit or be fired: when is resignation involuntary? *The Journal of Applied Business Research*, **6**(1), pp. 87–92.

Resistance

Resistance is a concept used to describe a recurrent stance of employees towards work. It is obviously applicable when work activity is coerced, which many analysts think is actually much of the time in a wide range of occupations. The view is that, when work is imposed and work performance is the subject of control, then resistance is an expected feature of the response. Hence also, resistance is usually coupled with the idea of control (Thompson, 1989, pp. 122–152).

Resistance can be thought of as a natural but passive phenomenon. The model here would be a component in a circuit board (which offers resistance to the flow of current) or a rock in a stream (which holds back the flow of water). In this conception, resistance is simply a minor, expected and unchanging feature of the properties of things. This is not what is found in resistance to work, however. In human relations generally, resistance is usually reactive. Certainly the use of the ideas of resistance at work is dominated by analysts who have an active and dynamic conception of resistance. Thus resistance is liable to change its character: to become stronger or weaker, to become more or less focused on specific issues and to be targeted in its behaviour responses. The idea of resistance features centrally in the labour process analysis of work, for example. This approach, which has for long time been a very important way of thinking in the sociology of work, has its origins in Marxian ideas (Braverman, 1974). In this perspective, resistance is a widespread feature of the response to work, and much more so than many realize. Research in this tradition has shown the relevance of the control and resistance concepts in traditional factory settings in the past, but contemporary analysts have updated and applied the same perspective to a range of new forms of work and workplaces. To these analysts, given favourable changes of circumstances, there can be sudden increases in the scale of resistance by employees. Resistance, once self-consciously discovered and activated, can be a potent feature of the response to work in the contemporary workplace.

Controversy surrounds the use of the concept of resistance today. While it has been has been applied to a surprising range of work and work-related activities, there is little consensus over the appropriate conclusions. For some analysts (especially those using a neo-Foucaultian perspective), the resistance of employees to management had been effectively terminated. This had been achieved through a combination of techniques and procedures such as increased surveillance and internal discipline. Others argue that the response had not disappeared so much as proliferated and taken many forms (Thomas et al., 2011), gone underground. However, many still accept the applicability of the orthodox control resistance paradigm.

STEPHEN ACKROYD

See also:
Labour process/theory; Managerial control.

References and selected further readings:

Braverman, H. (1974), *Labour and Monopoly Capital*, New York: Monthly Review Press.
Thomas, R., L.D. Sargent and C. Hardy (2011), Managing organizational change: negotiating meaning and power-resistance relations, *Organization Science*, **22**(1), pp. 22–41.
Thompson, P. (1989), *The Nature of Work*, London: Macmillan.

Resource-based view

The resource-based view (RBV) gained mainstream recognition in the early 1990s with the argument that the essence of competitive advantage resides internally within the firm. In so doing, the RBV serves as a counter to externally focused models that focus on positioning in a given market. The underlying premise of the RBV is that the performance differential between firms is directly attributable to the way a firm develops and manages its tangible and intangible resources. The focus is on *how* a firm conducts its activities and the human factors underpinning firm behaviour. The initial foundation for RBV arguments was laid by Edith Penrose who criticized dominant economic approaches for ignoring the 'collection of productive resources' that made up the black-box of the firm. Overtime authors associated with the RBV have developed a clearer sense of the conditions that make resources advantageous. Most notably, work by Barney (1991) denoted critical characteristics of resources as the extent to which they are valuable, rare, inimitable and the appropriately exploited by the organization.

By emphasizing a firm's distinctive resources and capabilities the RBV has provided a theoretical rationale for much HRM research and interventions. The RBV sheds light on management processes, culture and the nature of knowledge use and sharing within firms. The logic of RBV also accommodates important temporal dimensions including path dependency and economies of experience, while also allowing for informality and process. In HRM terms, the unit of analysis and precise mechanisms through which RBV explains competitive advantage range from a focus on human capital, to HR practices, through to HR processes or broader HR philosophy. Beyond this the RBV has been applied to consider the entire human capital pool of an organization or to an elite grouping such as senior management or core employees.

A key difficulty that plagues the RBV is that beyond its attractive ideas rests some confusion and uncertainty. Debate abounds over whether the resource-based view is in fact a view, perspective or a theory. There are also considerable difficulties in operationalizing key concepts such as inimitability and causal ambiguity and whether these can be appropriately captured as empirical regularities of the type mandated by survey research. Some have taken the criticism further to argue that RBV logic is conceptually impenetrable, tautological and biased in its exclusive internal emphasis. RBV logic has a tendency to stress the positive aspects of resources to the neglect of prospective resource limitations, negative path dependency or the costs of developing resources in the first instance. A very benign view of organizations is presented absent of consideration of political factors or power differentials that may influence resource deployment decisions. Nonetheless, the RBV has served to elevate internal factors while also pointing to critical domains for future exploration including implementation and leveraging social capital.

BRIAN HARNEY AND JOHN TREHY

See also:

Competitive advantage; Knowledge management; Strategic HRM.

References and selected further readings

Barney, J. (1991), Firm resources and sustained competitive advantage, *Journal of Management*, **17**(1), pp. 99–120.
Barney, J., D. Ketchen and M. Wright (2011), The future of resource-based theory: revitalization or decline? *Journal of Management*, **37**(1), pp. 1299–1315.
Boxall, P. (1996), The strategic HRM debate and the resource based view of the firm, *Human Resource Management Journal*, **6**(3), pp. 59–75.
Penrose, E. (1959), *Theory of the Growth of the Firm*, Oxford: Blackwell.

Resourcing

The terms 'employee resourcing' and more recently 'people resourcing' have commonly been used over the past 30 years to describe that part of a human resource (HR) function's activity that is concerned with staffing an organization. The aim can be neatly summed up as seeking to ensure that an organization has at its disposal sufficient numbers of people with the 'right skills in the right places at the right time'. Resourcing activity is thus focused on mobilizing a workforce that is able to perform well. Others take primary responsibility for subsequently motivating employees, engaging them and developing their capabilities.

Larger employers with sizeable HR departments typically employ specialists to undertake resourcing activities, the major areas of work being long-term and short-term workforce planning, the recruitment, selection and induction of new staff, employee retention and the management of redundancy and retirement procedures. Such activities, along with the development of long-term resourcing strategies, are commonly overseen by heads of resourcing (Sparrow et al., 2015, p. 179). Since the turn of the century, it has become increasingly fashionable for organizations to use the term 'talent management' instead of 'resourcing'. While it is possible to differentiate the field of talent management from that of resourcing, in practical terms there is considerable overlap in terms of the types of activity that specialists working in the two fields carry out.

The term 'resourcing' is also widely used in the teaching of human resource management (HRM) in business schools. This is particularly the case in the UK and Eire where it is usual for students who aspire to develop an HR career to complete qualifications accredited by the Chartered Institute of Personnel and Development (CIPD) – the major professional body to which HR professionals belong. The CIPD has long made extensive use of the term 'resourcing' in its professional standards, its educational syllabi and more recently, in its 'profession map'. As a result, the term is commonly used in book titles and as the heading to a significant section within the most widely read texts.

One of the major ways that resourcing specialists add value for organizations is through their planning activities. Some of these are wide in terms of their scope and encompass the whole workforce. They typically involve looking forward two to five years and estimating what skills the organization is likely to need in the future and the number and types of people it will employ in different places. Plans are then put in place and regularly adjusted with a view to minimizing the impact of any likely skills short-ages. In an increasingly unpredictable business environment this type of workforce planning activity involves preparing for a variety of possible future scenarios. It requires resourcing managers to gather labour market intelligence while also making projec-tions for labour turnover and patterns of career development within the organization. By contrast, succession planning activities tend to be a great deal more focused on an organization's senior managers and professionals. The primary aim here is to manage the individual careers of people who have the potential at some stage to occupy the most significant jobs in the organization. To that end, resourcing managers maintain records of people's individual performance and development, planning future career moves and opportunities so as to establish a 'talent pipeline' filled with people who have the required knowledge and experience to succeed in a senior job should it come avail-able. In larger global corporations, succession planning involves keeping track of many hundreds of people working on a range of international assignments.

Recruitment activities also vary considerably in terms of their scope and nature. At one level they are largely administrative and involve drawing up job descriptions and person specifications, dealing with enquiries from would-be employees, dealing with their applications, corresponding with them through the subsequent selection process, checking references and then providing them with written contracts of employment, staff handbooks and other documentation. Resourcing specialists are also involved in the design of the recruitment literature and webpages that are designed to attract appli-cations from well-qualified people. They may also liaise with recruitment agents and educational institutions or undertake headhunting activities via network-building with a view to securing high-quality applications when posts need to be filled.

In recent years, we have seen organizations adopt a more strategic approach to both their recruitment and retention activities as they have sought to develop their standing vis-à-vis other employers. Instead of simply allowing labour market reputations to form of their own accord, employers are increasingly seeking to manage them proactively. Hence, for example, we see the development of compelling 'employee value propositions' (EVPs) and the fostering of 'employer brands' that are both distinct and attractive. The aim is to differentiate the employment experience on offer in a bid to attract and retain superior performers.

A second major contemporary development in resourcing is the steady movement towards employing people on a wider variety of contractual terms. The extent of this trend is sometimes exaggerated by commentators who have a tendency wrongly to imply that full-time, permanent employment is no longer offered to more than a privileged few. Nonetheless, in many industries we see a growing inclination on the part of employers to resource the skills that they require in a greater variety of ways. Part-time and fixed-term employment are a great deal more prevalent than they were in the past, as are agency working, self-employment, outsourcing and employment on a casual or zero-hours basis. Other forms of flexible working such as flexitime, annual hours contracts and term-time working are also becoming more common over time.

STEPHEN TAYLOR

See also:

Employer branding; Flexible working; Induction; Outsourcing; Recruitment; Retention; Selection.

References and selected further readings

Pilbeam, S. and M. Corbridge (2010), *People Resourcing and Talent Planning: HRM in Practice*, 4th edn, Harlow: Financial Times/Prentice Hall.
Sparrow, P., M. Hird and C. Cooper (2015), *Do We Need HR?* Basingstoke: Palgrave Macmillan.
Taylor, S. (2014), *Resourcing and Talent Management*, 6th edn, London: Chartered Institute of Personnel and Development.

Retention

The ability to attract and retain employees can be essential to organizational competitiveness. Therefore, managing retention is an important fundamental means of achieving competitive advantage. Employee retention has been defined by the Workforce Planning for Wisconsin State Government (2006) as 'a systematic effort to create and foster an environment that encourages employees to remain employed by having policies and practices in place that address their diverse needs'. For many, the process of hiring new employees is far difficult and costlier than keeping current employees in the organization (Baker, 2006). That is why a core issue should be the continuous efforts by managers to identify and try to keep performers, irrespective of their age.

A strategic approach to employee retention may include adopting effective methods of engagement, safe and healthy workplaces and creating flexible work arrangements. Retention practices help create an inclusive and diverse workforce where barriers are reduced and individuals can participate in the workplace. Various strategies that go beyond pay and benefits can be employed to retain employees. Walker (2001) identified six factors that can boost employee retention: (1) compensation and appreciation of the work done, (2) challenging work, (3) opportunities for promotion, (4) positive relations with colleagues, (5) a healthy work–life balance, and (6) good communications. Other factors found to have a direct influence on employee retention include the individual's sense of loyalty, trust, commitment and identification and attachment with the organization. Indirect influences include rewards, leadership style, career opportunities, training and development, physical working conditions and work–life balance (Hytter, 2007).

Losing even a single high-performing employee could have a negative impact on creativity, innovation and productivity. Consistency in providing products and services may be jeopardized and major delays in the delivery of services to customers may occur

(Abbasi and Hollman, 2000). High levels of employee turnover may jeopardize efforts to attain organizational objectives. The costs associated with employee turnover can include lost customers and business as well as damaged morale. In addition, there are costs incurred in screening, verifying credentials and references, interviewing, hiring and training a new employee.

CHRIS ROWLEY AND NAGIAH RAMASAMY

See also:

Labour turnover; Promotion; Recruitment; Redeployment; Secondment.

References and selected further readings

Abbasi, S.M. and K.W. Holmer (2000), Turnover: the real bottom line, *Public Personnel Management*, **29**(3), pp. 333–342.

Baker, E. (2006), The human factor, *CIO Insight*, **73**, pp. 40–50.

Hutchings, K., H. De Cieri and T. Shea (2011), Employee attraction and retention in the Australian resources sector, *Journal of Industrial Relations*, **53**(1), pp. 83–101.

Hytter, A. (2007), Retention strategies in France and Sweden, *The Irish Journal of Management*, **28**(1), pp. 59–79.

Kevin, M.M., L.C. Joan and J.W. Adrian (2004), Organizational change and employee turnover, *Personnel Review*, **33**(2), pp. 161–166.

Ramlall, S. (2003), Managing employee retention as a strategy for increasing organizational competitiveness, *Applied Human Resource Management Research*, **8**(2), pp. 63–72.

Walker, J.W. (2001), Perspectives, *Human Resource Planning*, **24**(1), pp. 6–10.

Workforce Planning for Wisconsin State Government (2006), *Retention*, http://workforceplanning.wi.gov/category.asp?linkcatid=1506&linkid=17.

Retirement

For most people, retirement is a major transition from one's career since it is a signal that their years of employment are coming to an end. However, with increasing lifespans of people, it is difficult to justify retirement ages. As such, employees may want to continue to work either for a certain period or indefinitely. It can become difficult to establish when an employee has in fact retired when the employer provides employees with either extended annual contracts or part-time employment as a substitute to complete retirement.

Work and personal factors explain why employees may or may not prefer retirement. While some employees may have pleasant memories to take with them, others may have bitter episodes, or bittersweet experiences. Many employees look forward to retirement, at the height of their careers and take delight in thinking about it. For some it is the time to enjoy the fruits of their labour. There will be no more stresses from having to meet deadlines, long working hours, difficult colleagues and bosses, and the money and long hours spent on travelling to and from work.

How an employee views retirement is dependent on the employee's attitude towards work. Work may be so important, for it performs so many human functions. One derives an income, and possibly status and control over others. Over time, employees develop a sense of solidarity with, and attachment to, their work groups and their organization. Their work environment takes on a central role in their lives. From being a busy and productive employee to becoming a 'non-productive' retiree, staying at home with little or nothing to do, may not be a pleasant experience. They may face a loss of a sense of identity and self-worth.

Some organizations provide retirement preparation programmes directed at those approaching retirement. These programmes can vary in duration, providing a few days' workshop where participants would be exposed to financial matters such as pension and tax regulations. Better programmes may take place a few months prior to retirement and take into consideration the psycho-social needs of the employee upon retirement, with a focus on adjustment to life after retirement.

Early retirement, that is retirement before the normal retirement age, may also be advantageous to employees, particularly older ones, who may have fewer financial commitments, such as personal loans, mortgages and children pursuing higher education, or for those who can draw their pension after moving on to other employment, offering some financial advantage. Early retirement is also an expedient way of ensuring that downsizing is achieved without the need to go through formal redundancy steps. However, this may result in skill shortages when employees decide to accept the incentives and retire early.

CHRIS ROWLEY AND NAGIAH RAMASAMY

See also:
Downsizing; Resignation.

References and selected further readings

Baruch, Y. (2004), *Managing Careers: Theory and Practice*, Essex: Prentice-Hall.
Dobson, C. and P.C. Morrow (1984), Effects of career orientation on retirement attitudes and retirement planning, *Journal of Vocational Behavior*, **24**(1), pp. 73–83.
Feldman, D.C. (1994), The decision to retire early: a review and conceptualization, *Academy of Management Review*, **19**(2), pp. 285–311.
Greenhaues, J.H., G.A. Callanan and V.M. Godshalk (2000), *Career Management*, 3rd edn, Orlando: Harcourt.
Hanisch, K.A. (1994), Reasons people retire and their relations to attitudinal and behavioural correlates in retirement, *Journal of Vocational Behavior*, **45**(1), pp. 1–16.
Stone, R.J. (2014), *Human Resource Management*, 8th edn, Milton: Wiley.

Reward management

The term 'reward management' refers to the area of human resource management concerned with the ways in which employees are remunerated and motivated to improve performance or productivity. Its definition has been widened over time to embrace other elements of employee reward, including intrinsic factors such as non-financial rewards, work satisfaction and employee wellbeing and engagement (see 'Total reward' in this volume). The term's origins can be found in the seminal book of this title by Michael Armstrong and Helen Murlis in 1988 – *Reward Management: A Handbook of Remuneration Strategy and Practice* – which set out a new strategic approach to managing remuneration, although John Child had earlier coined the term 'reward policies' in his book *Organization: A Guide to Problems and Practice* (1984). The distinguishing characteristic of the new term 'reward management' was that it envisaged the active management of remuneration policies and practices, rather than the traditional 'pay administration' that had existed before. In this respect, reward management has much in common with the American 'New Pay' paradigm (Lawler, 1990; Schuster and Zingheim, 1992). However, the concept of remuneration being contingent on business circumstances and needs was not new in the UK. As early as 1969 Lupton and Gowler had envisaged the concept of actively 'designing' remuneration systems to meet business needs in their book *Selecting a Wage Payment System* (1969). Armstrong and Murlis (2011, p. 3) define reward management as 'the formulation and implementation of reward strategies and policies that aim to reward people fairly, equitably and consistently in accordance with their value to the organisation'.

The terms 'compensation', 'remuneration' and 'reward' tend to be used interchangeably in the HR literature, and in the USA the term 'compensation' tends to be used more than 'reward'. The concept of remuneration being dependent on business strategy reflects the shift from a world where the management of remuneration was primarily an outcome of collectively bargained agreements or, in the case of large corporations in the USA, strong internal labour markets where job evaluation and external pay referencing fixed the pay structures for most staff. The core message of the US New Pay writers – such as Lawler (1990), Schuster and Zingheim (1992) and Gomez-Mejia and Balkin (1993) – was that the pay design process should start with business strategy and organizational design, rather than being based on some external reference such as a collective agreement or job evaluation. It argued against the assumption that there were certain 'best practices' that all employers should adopt. Heery (1996) identified three important aspects about the New Pay. First the ratio of variable to fixed remuneration should be shifted in favour of the former, reducing the amount of guaranteed pay to the employee. There was also a view that indirect remuneration (i.e. benefits) should be reduced in favour of more direct forms of reward. Second, the scope of variable pay should be expanded to reflect a number of different measures of performance. Third, the New Pay emphasized the importance of the individual employee's performance, rather than the level of job done. Hence the New Pay writers saw job evaluation, collective agreements, external pay referencing and narrow-banded grading structures as inimical to more strategic forms of reward.

Reward management draws on two main theoretical sources – economics and psychology – but sociology and employee relations also have important insights into the linkage between employee behaviour and reward (see Perkins and White, 2011). Reward systems consists of both policies and practices and in general three determinants of reward have been identified (Mahoney, 1992) – job, person and performance. The job is the essential element for designing reward systems as they are the major way in which value is attributed to particular skills and attributes. The job has become key to the creation of grading structures and is at the centre of job evaluation techniques. However, as Kessler (2005, p. 320) has argued: 'If the job is the basis for establishing the grading structure, a pay system is the mechanism used to drive pay movements once the post and the individual filling it have been placed in the structure' and that the relationship between business strategy and remuneration appears to equate more to person and performance than to job. For this reason, the New Pay writers have argued that issues of internal equity are secondary to the business objectives of the organization (Gomez-Mejia and Balkin 1993).

The concepts of reward management and New Pay have not been unchallenged in both the practitioner and academic literatures. Pfeffer (1998) suggested that an over-reliance on pay to secure the motivation of employees may be at the cost of more powerful motivators such as meaningful work, job satisfaction and a trusting and friendly employment environment (although the widening of the definition of reward to encompass intrinsic elements has to some extent addressed this issue). Lewis (2001) argued that, while the concept of strategic reward seems highly rational, it makes significant assumptions about both business strategy and human behaviour. Heery (1996) provided a cogent critique of the New Pay from the perspective of business ethics, arguing that the shift in the balance of risk born by employees under the new approach to remuneration was not just unfair to workers but unethical.

In recent times the term reward management has to some extent been replaced by the terms 'strategic reward' and 'total reward', which reflect a rather wider conception of managing employee motivation and performance, including both extrinsic and intrinsic motivators.

GEOFF WHITE

See also:

Employee benefits; Total reward; Variable pay.

References and selected further reading

Armstrong, M. and H. Murlis (2011), *Reward Management: A Handbook of Remuneration Strategy and Practice*, 5th edn, London: Kogan Page.

CIPD (2013), *Reward Management Annual Survey Report 2013*, London: Chartered Institute of Personnel and Development.

Gomez-Mejia, L.R. and D.B. Balkin (1993), *Compensation, Organizational Strategy, and Firm Performance*, Cincinnati, OH: Southwestern Publishing.

Heery, E. (1996), Risk, reputation and the new pay, *Personnel Review*, 25(6), pp. 54–65.

Kessler, I. (2005), Remuneration systems, in S. Bach (ed.), *Managing Human Resources: Personnel Management in Transition*, Oxford: Blackwell.

Lawler, E.E. (1990), *Strategic Pay: Aligning Organizational Strategy and Pay Systems*, New York: Jossey-Bass.

Lewis, P. (2001), Resource management, in T. Redman and A. Wilkinson, *Contemporary Human Resource Management*, New York: Prentice Hall, pp. 98–127.

Mahoney, T.A. (1992), Multiple pay contingencies: strategic pay contingencies, in G. Salamon (ed.), *Human Resource Strategies*, Thousand Oaks, CA: Sage.

Perkins, S.J. and G. White (2011), *Reward Management: Alternatives, Consequences and Contexts*, London: Chartered Institute of Personnel and Development.

Pfeffer, J. (1998), Six dangerous myths about pay, *Harvard Business Review*, **76**, pp. 108–119.

Schuster, J. and P. Zingheim (1992), *The New Pay: Linking Employee and Organisational Performance*, New York: Lexington Books.

Sabotage

Generally sabotage is any deliberate action aimed at weakening a country or an occupying power by the destruction of property or other act of commission or omission aimed at having such effects. It can obviously be extended to apply to destructive actions against corporations and workplaces. Today in the UK, destructiveness at work does take place, but the description of it as sabotage is not common. At other times and places, sabotage at work and against organizations has been thought of as a very important concept.

Among several notions about possible sources for the origin of the word (and the idea) of sabotage is the alleged practice of sixteenth-century French textile workers, who supposedly put their clogs (called *sabots*) in the workings of their looms to disable them. Whether such acts were very destructive is not clear. There are other examples – many from the modern study of work – that could be similar and that only involve the temporary disablement of machinery. It was a widespread practice in British industry for machine tool workers, for example, to remove some parts from their machines, and claim they had broken down. The operatives would then take a break. Such acts appear to involve destruction of property but, on closer examination, are actually practical or utilitarian ways of limiting work. Usually the word 'sabotage' is reserved for more destructive events than these, and there certainly are examples in which there has been the widespread deliberate destruction of property where the label 'sabotage' more obviously applies. Luddism is a case in point. In this example, unemployed workers destroyed the machines that were replacing their work (Hobsbawm and Rude, 1969). More recently examples of wholesale destruction are less numerous but do occur. Taylor and Walton (1971) quote the case of the arsonist worker who, in his defence when on trial, stated that he usually set only small fires, and the one for which he was being tried got out of hand.

The meaning of sabotage as destruction has powerful symbolism and considerable potential propaganda value, which has been recognized from time to time. Using the idea of sabotage as an organizing metaphor, allows almost any act that is not in conformity with the expectations of owners and managers to be thought of as destructive. In this view, it is the essence of sabotage that it undermines, compromises and potentially destroys the employer's economic project of producing goods or services and of making profits. Accordingly, in some periods, groups of militant workers, anarchists and syndicalists being the most important, used the idea of sabotage as a basic description of their activities and project (Brown, 1977; Dubois, 1979). According to this view, any act of non-conformity or defiance from going slow at work (*ca'canny*) to giving away trade secrets (*sabotage a la bouche ouvert*) up to the outright destruction of property may be thought of as sabotage because of the threat they offer to the interests of business owners. This is an alternative way of thinking about grassroots responses to work. The idea had a brief vogue in the 1970s.

STEPHEN ACKROYD

See also:
Conflict; Organizational misbehaviour.

References and selected further readings
Brown, G. (1977), *Sabotage: A Study in Industrial Conflict*, London: Spokesman Books.

Dubois, P. (1979), *Sabotage in Industry*, Harmondsworth: Penguin.
Hobsbawm, E. and G. Rude (1969), *Captain Swing*, London; Phoenix Press.
Taylor, L. and P. Walton (1971), Industrial sabotage: motives and meanings, in I. Taylor and P. Walton (eds), *Images of Deviance*, Harmondsworth: Penguin.

Salary

A fixed weekly or monthly wage is usually called a salary. Payment by wage contrasts with salaried work, in which the employer pays an arranged amount at steady intervals (such as a week or month) regardless of hours worked. The salary is normally expressed in an overall annual figure and as such, a salaried worker would not expect to get paid for hours worked over and above (e.g., overtime pay).

Salary is also traditionally associated with professional and white-collar work. In the past, a big difference between salaried and waged workers is that the former would have more secure and guaranteed incomes but little in the way of incentive pay. In contrast, waged work tend to have less security of income and is often associated with incentive pay, overtime or shift pay on top of lower hourly rates.

More recently, the lines between salaried work and waged work have become increasingly blurred, especially with the growth of performance-related pay schemes and a lessening distinction between blue-collar and white-collar workers.

MARK GILMAN

See also:

Payment system; Performance-related pay; Shift work; Wages.

References and selected further readings

Armstrong, M. (2012), *Armstrong's Handbook of Reward Management*, London: Kogan Page.
Gilman, M. (2013), Reward management, in T. Redman and A. Wilkinson (eds), *Contemporary Human Resource Management: Text and Cases*, London: Pearson.
Perkins, S.J. and G. White (2008), *Employee Reward: Alternatives, Consequences and Contexts*, London: Chartered Institute of Personnel and Development.
White, G. and J. Drucker (2009), *Reward Management: A Critical Text*, London: Routledge.

Scientific management

Frederick Taylor is widely credited as the founder of scientific management, an approach to designing work using scientific principles. These ideas were laid out in his book the *Principles of Scientific Management* (1911) based on his work in the Philadelphia steel industry and is often given the shorthand 'Taylorism'.

The core belief in Taylor's approach is that there is a science to managing. This is largely conducted by redesigning work, breaking it down into its smallest constituent components, which are measured in precise ways and designed to be completed as efficiently as possible. This work design is completed using *time and motion studies*, where work activities are closely observed and measured. They are then redesigned in ways that eliminate unnecessary movements and tasks. Therefore each task has one best way, where workers are trained to follow often exacting procedures to complete the task. This scientific approach also focused on employee selection.

This approach to work design had profound consequences. It shifted knowledge, and therefore control, away from the hands of workers towards that of management. Within a *craft* approach, workers acquired skill through years of training, and thus had more knowledge of the work process than managers, meaning they could control their own work better as managers had little knowledge to go against them. However, through Taylor's scientific approach, not only did managers know how long a task should take, but they also designed the work into small parts so no worker could know the whole process. For Taylor, managers were the head and did the design and thinking, whereas the workers were like bodies and only did what they were told. Workers, by only doing small, repetitive and simple tasks were, in Harry Braverman's words 'deskilled' (Braverman, 1974) and thus easily replaceable. Work was designed so that with very little training a new worker could be put in place. Power therefore was firmly placed in the hands of management. Work was also individualized, allowing managers to closely monitor and control individuals.

Taylor was not the only person to undertake such approach. Frank and Lillian Gilbreth pioneered time and motion studies, and Henry Ford used many of the same principles within his car factories.

While Taylor's approach, coupled with increased use of mechanization within factories, led to an increase in efficiency it was not without its critics. Taylorist jobs have been widely claimed as boring, repetitive and dehumanizing. Marxist theorist Harry Braverman (1974), drawing on his own experience in the print industry, argues overall knowledge of the production process rests in the heads of the management and the deskilling ultimately leads to the replacement of jobs with technology. Taylor was even subject to a US Congress inquiry and declared Taylorism a failure (King and Lawley, 2013). However, despite these reservations, these principles continue to be important to organizations today in the form of lean management and the design of many jobs, from McDonald's to university teaching (Parker and Jary, 1995).

DANIEL KING

See also:
Division of labour; Job design; Work organization.

References and selected further readings

Braverman, H. (1974), *Labor and Monopoly Capital: The Degradation of Work in the Twentieth Century*, New York: Monthly Review.
King, D. and S. Lawley (2013), *Organizational Behaviour*, Oxford: Oxford University Press.
Parker, M. and D. Jary (1995), The McUniversity: organization, management and academic subjectivity, *Organization*, **2**(2), pp. 319 338.
Taylor, F.W. (1911), *The Principles of Scientific Management*, New York: Harper.

Secondment

Secondment is broadly referred to as a temporary movement or 'loan' of an employee to another part of an organization (internal secondment) or to a completely different organization (external secondment) (CIPD, 2009), for an agreed period of time on a full-time or part-time basis. External secondments can range from a staff member being seconded to another organization to enable them to gain the experience of a different organization, to a technical staff member being seconded to suppliers or customers to gain experience of the supply chain. The implication of the word 'temporary' in the definition is that the employee (secondee) will return to their original business unit or organization.

Eligibility for secondments is a policy decision. Organizations may decide that opportunities for secondments may be open to all. On the other hand, secondments may be limited to managers, technical and professional employees and those on talent management programmes.

There are many reasons for secondments. In the face of challenging business environments, organizations adopt ever flatter management structures. In doing so, traditional opportunities for promotion through a succession of line management positions are more limited. Secondments offer employees the opportunity to expand their skills base. Used increasingly for manager development, secondments provide for the secondee to attain diverse perspectives within the organizational boundaries, help build interactions with colleagues and increase communication after. Further, by serving a period of time in another organization, the secondees share knowledge, broaden experience, develop skills and gain insight in return. This approach also encourages the cross-fertilization of ideas (Baruch, 2004).

When implemented effectively, all parties in this relationship, that is the secondee, the secondee's employer and the host organization, gain. The secondee gains valuable experience in project management and new skills and experiences in challenging areas thus improving their career. The secondee's organization also benefits when secondees apply the acquired transferable skills once they return to their substantive post. The employer also gains improved employee morale. The host organization, too, benefits from taking on secondments when it receives assistance with projects and gains an external perspective.

However, some key challenges need to be dealt with. Dissatisfied staff members, from among those who are not selected, may have to be dealt with. Others include the secondee's failure to adapt to the organizational culture of the host organization and difficulty in settling back in the parent organization on completion of the assignment. Another cause of dissatisfaction may be the unfulfilled expectation of promotion at the end of the secondment period.

CHRIS ROWLEY AND NAGIAH RAMASAMY

See also:

Careers.

References and selected further readings

Baruch, Y. (2004), *Managing Careers: Theory and Practice*, Essex: Prentice-Hall.

CIPD (2009), *CIPD Secondment Factsheet*, London: Chartered Institute of Personnel and Development, www.cipd.co.uk/hr-resources/factsheets/secondment.aspx.

Ellis, D.W. (2011), A second look at secondments, *Benefits and Compensation International*, **40**(8), pp. 3–8.

Gerrish, K. and H. Piercy (2014), Capacity development for knowledge translation: evaluation of an experiential approach through secondment opportunities, *Worldviews on Evidence-Based Nursing*, **11**(3), pp. 209–216.

Hayward, M. (2005), Cross border employee secondments — the tax implications, *Ottawa Business Journal*, www.obj.ca/Other/Archives/2005-07-22/article-2138073/Cross-Border-Employee-Secondments---The-Tax-Implications/1.

Renshaw, P. and D. Holland (2013), *A White Paper: Secondments Missed Opportunity?* London: Centre for Progressive Leadership, London Metropolitan University.

Security of employment

Employment security has been linked positively to skill level and is regarded as an important factor in determining job quality. Employment security has been found to be greater among skilled employees than unskilled employees (Beardwell and Claydon, 2010). Its use and prevalence has also traditionally varied across organizations by size, sector and location. For example, exemplars were the large conglomerates of Japan and Korea, with their battalions of 'salarymen' spending their whole working lives in the company.

During the market-oriented policies and the subsequent financial crises of the 1980s and 1990s, organizational restructuring brought about reduced demand for human resources (HR) (Heery and Salmon, 2000). The early 1990s saw significant change in the nature and notion of the psychological contract, with freezes in recruitment, lay-offs, plant closures and even plant relocations. It also witnessed a substantial increase in non-standard employment forms. Organizations restructured to meet cost reduction and workplace flexibility strategies by employing a variety of non-standard work arrangements, the most common being part-time and temporary or casual jobs.

The psychological contract is the set of unspoken expectations or promises, not written in the contract of employment. This implicit dialogue between the individual employee and the employer specifies what each expects to give and receive in the working relationship. Appearing in an environment of continuous and sometimes turbulent change, and with employers seeking greater flexibility in managing their operations, employees began to be rewarded based on work performance but where tenure is not guaranteed.

In a typical traditional arrangement where the relationship is based on mutual trust, employees offer their conformity, commitment and loyalty to their employers. In this reciprocal relationship, employers offer employment security, training and development, and career growth. However, the new psychological contract has altered the way that organizations and their employees relate to each other. Employees provide a broader range of skills, assume additional responsibility, offer extended working hours and tolerate change and ambiguity. Here there are no long-term contracts. Instead, employers offer high pay, performance-based pay (Baruch, 2004), flexibility and the prospect for lifelong training and development. The organization's commitment to provide the training and development is in order to develop a 'portable portfolio' of skills, which will facilitate the employees' search for alternative employment if the organization no longer requires their services (Handy, 1989).

While employers demand wider deregulation in order to cope with global competition and seek more flexible use of HRs to increase productivity and competitiveness, employees seek security of employment, a series of promotions and pay increases within the organization.

CHRIS ROWLEY AND NAGIAH RAMASAMY

See also:
Flexible firm; Job security; Psychological contract.

References and selected further readings
Baruch, Y. (2004), *Managing Careers: Theory and Practice*, Essex: Prentice-Hall.
Beardwell, J. and T. Claydon (2010), *Human Resource Management: A Contemporary Approach*, 6th edn, Essex: Prentice Hall.
Handy, C. (1989), *The Age of Unreason*, London: Hutchinson.
Heery, E. and J. Salmon (2000), The insecurity thesis, in E. Heery and J. Salmon (eds), *The Insecure Workforce*, London: Routledge.
Herriot, P. and C. Pemberton (1995), *New Deals*, Chichester: John Wiley.
Zeytinoglu, I.U. (ed.) (2005), *Flexibility in Workplaces: Effects on Workers, Work Environment and the Unions*, Geneva: IIRA/ILO.

Selection

Selection is a two-way process in which employers make job offers to selected prospective employees who have chosen to enter the selection process. The premise of selection is that the assessment of candidates reveals individual differences that have implications for future work motivation and performance. Selection consists of several linked activities from attracting candidates through to the evaluation of selection decisions designed to produce a good fit between the worker and the content and context of the work. There are many evidence-based techniques that can improve the effectiveness of selection processes. Widely used and well-researched selection methods include the scrutiny of candidates' biographical data, interviews, work samples (work-related tasks), psychometric tests of cognitive ability and job aptitude and measures of personality.

In order to make good selection decisions, employers need selection processes to yield reliable and accurate information. Without such data, there is little chance that the performance of candidates during selection will be linked to their future work performance (i.e., the process will lack predictive validity). In addition, ethical and fair processes are robust to legal challenges, enhance employers' reputations and improve the chances that the most able candidates will accept offers of employment. Selection decisions should not be influenced by factors irrelevant to performance in the work role (e.g. gender or race) even if this is unintentional (this is called adverse impact).

Selection should be based on the assessment of the knowledge, skills, abilities and other characteristics that are required for successful performance in the work role. Rigorous job analysis needs to be carried out to identify job-related competencies (e.g. drive and determination, interpersonal skills, numerical ability etc.). The content of recruitment materials should be based on the results of the job analysis in order to attract a suitably qualified and motivated pool of candidates. Information about job-related competencies should be used to identify selection methods that detect relevant signs of candidates' potential and samples of their existing capabilities. These methods may include existing 'off-the-shelf' tools (such as psychometric tests) and bespoke instruments designed using the information gathered from the job analysis (e.g., structured interviews).

Candidate performance in selection tasks needs to be carefully recorded and interpreted as evidence of their job-related competencies. This is often done by translating the evidence collected into numerical scores of their competencies that summarize the quality and quantity of evidence. After successful candidates have been employed for some time (usually at least 6–12 months) their scores during selection can also be linked to information collected about the work performance to determine the reliability, fairness and predictive validity of the process. The results of this evaluation can be used to enhance future iterations of the selection process (e.g., by removing or redesigning elements that are not working well).

Each method used during selection should offer some unique insight into the candidate's suitability. The inclusion of different methods that assess similar competencies also helps to improve the reliability of the process (e.g., it shows a candidate can demonstrate similar competencies in different situations). Academic research and industry examples have highlighted the strengths and weaknesses of various widely used methods. Assessment centres combine various selection methods in order to capture large amounts of data about candidates in a way that offsets the various advantages and disadvantages of each method. This is a labour-intensive and relatively costly approach to selection but one that tends to work well.

Biographical and interview data are widely used. Analysis of candidates' biographical data (on an application form or CV) can help to reduce the size of the applicant pool (e.g., by 'selecting out' those with insufficient educational qualifications). This can be done when threshold levels of experience or specific formal qualifications are required for effective job performance. Research shows that biographical data are not consistently strong predictors of work performance and social inequalities such as differences in educational opportunities can place some groups in society at an unfair disadvantage. Selection interviews are well-liked by employers because they facilitate direct interaction with prospective employees. The interview is a flexible enough method to capture information about various competencies (e.g., from technical knowledge to interpersonal skills). Candidates also tend to expect an interview as they feel it gives them a good opportunity to demonstrate their suitability for the role and allows them to evaluate the employer. Research shows that structured interviews containing competency-based questions and performance evaluation frameworks can have good reliability, validity and fairness. Without standardized interview protocols and in the absence of sufficient interviewer training, there is a risk that interviewers may ask irrelevant or unfair questions or form biased judgements based on factors such as gender, race or appearance that are unrelated to the performance in the work role.

Work sample tests require candidates to perform part of the work role during selection and have good predictive validity. Candidates usually see these as a fair test of their suitability and as a good insight into the nature of the job. High design and administration costs mean they are often only used to assess a small pool of candidates near the end of a selection process. Online ability testing has proved increasingly popular because individual differences in cognitive ability can be easily measured in large applicant populations. Extensive research shows that these differences tend to be good predictors of job performance especially for complex work roles. Psychometric tests offer a standardized and 'mechanical' way of collecting evidence about work-related abilities with objective scoring methods. However, such measures offer little insight into competencies such as interpersonal or communication skills.

Personality questionnaires can provide information about candidates preferred thinking styles and typical ways of interacting with others. There are significant concerns about the opportunities for candidates to manipulate or fake their responses to suit the requirements of the job role (although many measures do contain checks for deliberate manipulation). There is some evidence that self-reported extraversion and conscientiousness are linked to job performance but the predictive validity of personality measures is fiercely debated in the academic literature.

RAYMOND RANDALL

See also:

Aptitude test; Assessment centres; Competence; Interviews; Psychometric testing; Selection method; Selection test.

References and selected further readings

Chamorro-Premuzic, T. and A. Furnham (2010), *The Psychology of Personnel Selection*, Cambridge: Cambridge University Press.
Cook, M. (2009), *Personnel Selection: Adding Value Through People*, 5th edn, Chichester: Wiley-Blackwell.
Huffcut, A.I. (2010), From science to practice: seven principles for conducting employment interviews, *Applied Human Resource Management Research*, **12**, pp. 121–136.
Sackett, P. and F. Lievens (2008), Personnel selection, *Annual Review of Psychology*, **59**, pp. 419–445.

Selection method

A 'selection method' is the part of an organization's selection process that comprises the structured application of multiple assessment tests designed to gather a body of information about applicants for employment; this information can be predictive or criterion-based in form and is used to evaluate individuals on a comparative basis, in order to select one (or more) individual(s) to whom an offer of employment will be made. The aim of the selection method is to identify the applicant(s) who is (are) most likely to represent the best person–job fit and/or person–organization fit available using the organization's criteria for employment.

In designing a selection method, the likelihood of a successful outcome to an organization's selection process can be related to the following design criteria: maximizing person–job fit and/or person–organization fit; avoiding negative applicant reactions to specific assessment tests; minimizing the possibility of adverse impact on an applicant's opportunity to demonstrate suitability for appointment against the employment criteria; the importance of gathering information that is both valid and reliable as a basis for predicting an applicant's future job performance; and the usability and cost-effectiveness of the assessment tests, both separately and combined, chosen to form the selection method.

WAYNE O'DONOHUE

See also:

Aptitude test; Big Five; Intelligence tests; Interviews; Job analysis; Personality test; Person–environment fit; Psychometric testing; Selection; Selection test.

References and selected further readings

Huffcutt, A. (2011), An empirical review of the employment interview construct literature, *International Journal of Selection and Assessment*, **19**(5), pp. 62–81.

Huo, Y.P., H.J. Huang and N.K. Napier (2002), Divergence or convergence: a cross national comparison of personnel selection practices, *Human Resource Management*, **41**, pp. 31–44.

Phillips, J. and S. Gully (2014), *Strategic Staffing*, Harlow: Pearson.

Ryan, A.M. and R.E. Ployhart (2014), A century of selection, *Annual Review of Psychology*, **65**, pp. 693–717.

Singh, P. (2008), Job analysis for a changing workplace, *Human Resource Management Review*, **18**(2), pp. 87–99.

Wilk, S.L. and P. Cappelli (2003), Understanding the determinants of employer use of selection methods, *Personnel Psychology*, **56**, pp. 103–124.

Selection test

'Selection' is the part of an organization's staffing process that commences once the closing date for applications for employment has passed, and continues until a decision has been reached as to which one (or more) of the applicants will be offered employment. Defined in process terms, selection is that set of activities, shaped by strategic, legal and environmental factors, and through which information is gathered from individual applicants for employment; this information is evaluated, on a comparative basis and against criteria for employment, to select one (or more) individual(s) to whom an offer of employment will be made. A successful applicant may be either new to an organization or an existing employee. Strategically, the outcomes of a selection process should support effective implementation of the organization's business strategy through acquisition of the best talent with the required knowledge, skills, attributes and competencies to meet the organization's short- and long-term interests.

Examples of specific assessment tests that are commonly used include interviews of various types (behavioural/situational, structured/unstructured, individual/group), personality tests, situational judgement tests, job knowledge tests, work samples, cognitive ability tests, integrity tests, assessment centres and references; to name but a few. Assessment tests have been traditionally conducted on a face-to-face basis; however, the advent of internet technology has seen the development of online delivery of testing adopted by many organizations where possible and suitable.

The sequencing of the various assessment tests that form a selection method will usually commence with an initial screening process, utilizing information gathered through some but not all of the assessment tests. The aim of initial screening is to determine which applicants do not satisfy the minimum acceptable standards in relation to those criteria for employment which are considered as essential. This activity is then followed in sequence by a more intensive and extensive assessment that commences after a 'shortlisting' process.

WAYNE O'DONOHUE

See also:

Aptitude test; Big Five; Intelligence tests; Interviews; Job analysis; Personality test; Person–environment fit; Psychometric testing; Selection; Selection method; Shortlisting.

References and selected further readings

Donovan, J.J., S.A. Dwight and D. Schneider (2014), The impact of applicant faking on selection measures, hiring decisions, and employee performance, *Journal of Business and Psychology*, **29**(3), pp. 1–15.

Huffcutt, A. (2011), An empirical review of the employment interview construct literature, *International Journal of Selection and Assessment*, **19**(5), pp. 62–81.

Lievens, F. and F. Patterson (2011), The validity and incremental validity of knowledge tests, low-fidelity simulations, and high-fidelity simulations for predicting job performance in advanced-level high-stakes selection, *Journal of Applied Psychology*, **96**(5), pp. 927–940.

Risavy, S.D. and P.A. Hausdorf (2011), Personality testing in personnel selection: adverse impact and differential hiring rates, *International Journal of Selection and Assessment*, **19**, pp. 18–30.

Ryan, A.M. and R.E. Ployhart (2014), A century of selection, *Annual Review of Psychology*, **65**, pp. 693–717.

Van Iddekinge, C.H., P.L. Roth, P.H. Raymark and H.N. Odle-Dusseau (2012), The criterion-related validity of integrity tests: an updated meta-analysis, *Journal of Applied Psychology*, **97**(3), pp. 499–530.

Self-appraisal

Self-appraisal involves asking an employee to evaluate their own job performance. Self-appraisals are a powerful and effective tool to start the performance appraisal process. Typically, employees will be asked to rate their own performance prior to meeting formally with their supervisor. Employees will either use the same rating form as their supervisors or they may use an independent form of self-ranking. Self-appraisal results will generally be discussed in the formal appraisal interview, along with the supervisor's thoughts, comments and final evaluations. Self-appraisals can help employees prepare for the performance appraisal conversation with their supervisor and also forms the discussion basis about the employee's current roles and responsibilities, their performance contributions and future career interests and needs. Self-appraisals are also an important tool in the professional development and career planning process.

Self-appraisals offer a number of benefits, including increased job performance, employee development and empowerment, perceived accuracy, fairness and acceptance of the performance appraisal process. Research has found that when employees were given assertiveness training and the opportunity to self-appraise, they reported greater trust in the supervisor and organization, and experienced more positive attitudes toward the appraisal process. However, leniency problems exist as employees generally rate themselves more positively in comparison to their supervisor's ratings. Furthermore, self-appraisals may also influence supervisor perceptions and ratings, as self-appraisals are normally completed prior to the formal performance appraisal (Shore and Tashchian, 2002).

AMIE SOUTHCOMBE

See also:

Performance appraisal; 360-degree appraisal.

References and selected further readings

Bobocel, D.R., R.L. McCline and R. Folger (1997), Letting them down gently: conceptual advances in explaining controversial organizational policies, *Trends in Organizational Behavior*, **4**, pp. 73–88.

Conway, J.M. and A.I. Huffcutt (1997), Psychometric properties of multisource performance ratings: a meta analysis of subordinate, supervisor, peer, and self-ratings, *Human Performance*, **10**(4), pp. 331–360.

Longenecker, C.O. and S.J. Goff (1992), Performance appraisal effectiveness: a matter of perspective, *SAM Advanced Management Journal*, **57**, pp. 17–23.

Roberson, L., S. Torkel, A. Korsgaard, D. Klein, M. Diddams and M. Cayer (1993), Self-appraisal and perceptions of the appraisal discussion: a field experiment, *Journal of Organizational Behavior*, **14**(2), pp. 129–142.

Shore, T.H. and A. Tashchian (2002), Accountability forces in performance appraisal: effects of self-appraisal information, normative information, and task performance, *Journal of Business and Psychology*, **17**(2), pp. 261–274.

Self-employment

An individual is in self-employment if they work for themselves and have responsibility for the success or failure of their business (see, for example, UK Government, 2015). Self-employment constitutes a large proportion of paid work in many countries. For example, according to the Organisation for Economic Co-operation and Development (OECD, 2014), in 2012, self-employment accounted for more than 30 per cent of those employed in countries including Greece and Turkey, although in some countries, generally those with high per capita income rates such as the USA, rates can be as low as 6.8 per cent.

An interesting strand of research relates to self-employment as an alternative to being an employee. For example, Guerra and Patuelli (2014) confirm a relation between dissatisfaction with paid employment and the transition into self-employment but, as opposed to those who change jobs instead, those choosing self-employment have lower levels of financial satisfaction. This is an interesting finding given the experiences of many self-employed workers, which can involve forms of self-exploitation owing to intense competition and low returns (MacDonald, 1996). Those remaining in self-employment may therefore draw non-financial satisfactions from their work such as being their own boss and a sense of autonomy.

However, becoming self-employed is not always a positive choice from a range of viable potential options. As, perhaps, in the case of the high rates of self-employed women (up to 50 per cent of women in paid work in some countries; OECD, 2014), self-employment also can also reflect a lack of alternatives; for example, owing to social exclusion, discrimination and limited opportunities in the labour market. Self-employment is suggested by many governments and charities as a means of overcoming these problems of disadvantage. However, becoming self-employed out of necessity may provide few answers given the relatively lower levels of satisfaction reported when compared with other entrepreneurs (Block and Koellinger, 2009) and the risks associated with generally high rates of new business mortality. Hence, while self-employment can be a positive and rewarding experience, it can also be a precarious and risky form of paid labour.

ROBERT WAPSHOTT AND OLIVER MALLETT

See also:

Employee; Freelance work; Labor market; Worker.

References and selected further readings

Block, J. and P. Koellinger (2009), I can't get no satisfaction – necessity entrepreneurship and procedural utility, *KYKLOS*, **62**(2), pp. 191–209.
Guerra, G. and R. Patuelli (2014), The role of job satisfaction in transitions into self-employment, *Entrepreneurship Theory and Practice*, Early View September 2014 DOI: 10.1111/etap.12133.
MacDonald, R. (1996), 'Welfare dependency, the enterprise culture and self-employed survival', *Work, Employment & Society*.
OECD (2014), *OECD Factbook 2014: Economic, Environmental and Social Statistics*, Paris: Organisation for Economic Co-operation and Development, http://dx.doi.org/10.1787/factbook-2014-en.

Saridakis, G., S. Marlow and D.J. Storey (2014), Do different factors explain male and female self-employment rates? *Journal of Business Venturing*, **29**(3), pp. 345–362.

UK Government (2015), *Employment Status*, www.gov.uk/employment-status/selfemployed-contractor.

Self-managed teams

A self-managed work team is an identifiable group of employees who have a degree of control over a designated area of an organization's operations. Such teams can also be called autonomous work groups (AWGs) or semi-autonomous work groups (SAWGs). The use of self-managed teams in an organization is based broadly on the idea that giving employees a greater degree of involvement in deciding how their work is done will have the effect of aligning their attitudes and actions more closely with the interests of the organization as a whole.

The emergence of self-managed teams is often associated with socio-technical systems (STS) theory (Trist and Bamforth, 1951), although we can identify a number of different theoretical and practical influences on the development of the idea. Most recently, self-managed teams have been seen as an integral part of high-performance work systems (HPWS).

The idea of self-managed teams continues to generate a large amount of discussion. One key issue is the nature and degree of the self-management that teams are or should be given. Teams are often associated with lean production, for example, but other aspects of lean production would seem to place severe limits on the autonomy or discretion that employees are able to exercise. A related issue is what the self-management of teams implies for management more generally in an organization. If self-management is extended but not made absolute, then the question is: how should the teams be managed (Manz and Sims, 1986)?

More recently we have seen increased attention paid to the relationship between the autonomy of the team and the autonomy enjoyed by its individual members. It cannot simply be assumed that the two things will go hand-in-hand (Jonsson and Jeppesen, 2013). Indeed, a distinct body of work has emerged that highlights what are seen as the negative aspects of self-managed teams. Barker (1993), for example, developed the idea of 'concertive control' as a way of understanding of how employees might feel more controlled as a result of the introduction of self-managed teams.

From an organizational point of view, there is also the question of the precise means by which self-managed teams might contribute to improved performance (Delarue et al., 2008). Any contribution might come not from the efforts of more highly motivated individual employees but from the structural changes associated with the redesign of work. In this view, the effects of greater individual and team self-management have to be considered in conjunction with the degree of interdependence between the work of team members (Procter and Currie, 2004).

STEPHEN PROCTER

See also:

Employee involvement; High-involvement management; High-performance work systems; Work organization.

References and selected further readings

Barker, J. (1993), Tightening the iron cage: concertive control in self-managing teams, *Administrative Science Quarterly*, **38**(3), pp. 408–437.

Delarue, A., G. Van Hootegem, S. Procter and M. Burridge (2008), Teamworking and organizational performance: a review of survey-based research, *International Journal of Management Reviews*, **10**(2), pp. 127–148.

Jonsson, T. and H. Jeppesen (2013), Under the influence of the team? An investigation of the relationships between team autonomy, individual autonomy and social influence within teams, *International Journal of Human Resource Management*, **24**(1), pp. 78–93.

Manz, C. and H. Sims (1986), Leading self-managed groups: a conceptual analysis of a paradox, *Economic and Industrial Democracy*, **7**(2), pp. 141–165.

Procter, S. and G. Currie (2004), Target-based teamworking: groups, work and interdependence in the UK civil service, *Human Relations*, **57**(12), pp. 1547–1572.

Trist, E. and K. Bamforth (1951), Some social and psychological consequences of the longwall method of coal-getting, *Human Relations*, **4**(1), pp. 3–38.

Self-management

Self-management, workers' democratic decision-making power on production and administration, is a radical alternative to traditional business organization. It is radical in standing directly opposite the authoritarian, alienating, profit-driven reality of a capitalist work organization and in contesting 'management right to manage', a cardinal principle within capitalism that it is so common-sense that it has been assumed by workers themselves as the natural state of things. It is alternative in proposing in its practices a model of organization based on democracy in the decision-making process, on workers' autonomy in the management of the labour process, on solidarity and equality among producers, on the idea of work as purposive and creative activity, and on production as socially rather than market determined. In this sense workers' self-management, or workers' control as it has also been historically known, is a form of work organization and management of production and distribution prefigurative of a different, more equalitarian democratic and participative society.

What is particularly striking about self-management is that in all its historical manifestations it has been the result not of a blueprint for a future organization and society imposed from above, but an alternative that has often emerged as a grassroots workers' response to the contradictions generated within workplaces by capitalist socio-economic and productive crises. Self-management is thus a prefigurative alternative, a historically recurrent phenomenon rooted at the very core of capitalist dynamics.

Historically, experiments with self-management have been associated worldwide with cooperatives, the legal form that, through the collectivization of property rights, allows workers to set their own productive organization autonomously and independently, and with the broader cooperative movement. This association has been, on the one hand, a powerful vehicle in the diffusion of alternative ideas and practices about people management, helping to nurture participatory system of management. But on the other hand, cooperatives have often been criticized for curbing the transformative potential of self-management. Democratic decision-making and widespread participation, horizontal processes of work organization, income equality policies and broader issues about the social use and distribution of production, all aspects that have characterized the first organizing stages in many cases and experiences, have often been distorted and transformed in practice by cooperatives need to play within the rules of market competition.

While it is true that capitalism strongly distorts or eliminates any serious attempts at changing the organization of work, all experiences of self-management have represented an advance in terms of workers' emancipation and empowerment. This is the starting point if we aim to make the search for an alternative and more democratic organization of work central to the social science and policy agenda.

MAURIZIO ATZENI

See also:

Alienation; Deskilling; Division of labour.

References and selected further readings

Atzeni, M. (ed.) (2012), *Alternative Work Organisations*, Basingstoke: Palgrave Macmillan.
Atzeni, M. and Ghigliani, P. (2007), Labour process and decision making in factories under workers' self-managment: empirical evidence from Argentina, *Work, Employment and Society*, **21**(4), pp. 653–672.
Ness, I. and D. Azzellini (2011), *Ours to Master and to Own: Workers' Control from the Commune to the Present*, Chicago: Haymarket Books.
Vieta, M. (2014), The stream of self-determination and *autogestión*: prefiguring alternative economic realities, *Ephemera: Theory and Politics in Organisations*, **14**(4), pp. 781–809.

Sex discrimination

The right to equal treatment for men and women in the workplace in Britain was initially introduced by the Sex Discrimination Act in 1975. European Union law has been influential in this area, where the pursuit of sex equality has had a long history beginning with the signing of the Treaty of Rome in 1957. The Equality Act 2010 now addresses sex discrimination in Britain.

Employers must not discriminate against job applicants or employees (Equality Act 2010, section 39). Discrimination is defined with reference to certain characteristics that are designated as protected under the Equality Act 2010. Sex is a protected characteristic (section 4). Reference to a person who has a particular protected characteristic is a reference to a man or a woman (section 11).

Direct sex discrimination occurs where, because of sex an employer treats an employee or applicant less favourably then they treat or would treat others (see section 13). Indirect sex discrimination occurs where an employer applies a provision, criterion or practice to an employee or applicant which is discriminatory in relation to the employee or applicant's sex. A provision criterion or practice will be discriminatory in relation to an employee or applicant's sex if it applies to persons of the opposite sex, it puts or would put persons of the same sex as the employee or applicant at a particular disadvantage and it puts or would put the employee or applicant themselves at that disadvantage. Employers can defend an indirect sex discrimination claim by showing that the provision, criterion or practice was a proportionate means of meeting a legitimate aim.

LIZ OLIVER

See also:

Direct discrimination; Equal opportunity; Indirect discrimination.

References and selected further readings

Fredman, S. (2014), Reversing roles: bringing men into the frame, *International Journal of Law in Context*, **10**(4), pp. 442–459.

Tomlinson, J. (2011), Gender equality and the state: a review of objectives, policies and progress in the European Union, *International Journal of Human Resource Management*, **22**(18), pp. 3755–3774.

Willey, B. (2012), Employment law in context: an introduction for HR professionals, 4th edn, Harlow: Pearson.

Sexual harassment

Harassment is a type of prohibited conduct under the Equality Act 2010 (section 26). In the context of employment, employers must not harass employees and applicants (section 40). A distinction can be drawn between sex-related harassment and sexual harassment. Harassment is defined as unwanted conduct related to a relevant protected characteristic (age, disability, gender reassignment, race, religion or belief, sex, sexual orientation), where that conduct has the purpose of effect of violating the claimant's dignity or creating an intimidating, hostile, degrading, humiliating or offensive environment for him or her (section 26(1)). In order to decide whether the conduct has that effect, an employment tribunal would take into account the following subjective and objective aspects of the context: the perception of the claimant, the other circumstances of the case and whether it is reasonable for the conduct to have that effect (section 26(4)). Unwanted conduct related to sex that aims to or does create one of the prohibited environments for an employee or applicant would be unlawful in the context of work.

Another form of harassment addresses specifically the matter of unwanted conduct of a sexual nature. This is often referred to as sexual harassment. Here harassment occurs where a person engages in unwanted conduct of a sexual nature and that conduct has the purpose or effect referred to above (section 26(2)). Guidance from the Equality and Human Rights Commission suggests that conduct of a sexual nature might include unwelcome sexual advances, touching, forms of sexual assault, sexual jokes, displaying pornographic photographs or drawings or sending emails with material of a sexual nature (EHRC, 2014).

Harassment will also occur when, there is unwanted conduct of a sexual nature or unwanted conduct related to sex or to gender reassignment, and the claimant is treated less favourably because of his or her rejection of, or submission to the conduct (section 26(3)).

Liz Oliver

See also:

Bullying; Discipline and grievance.

References and selected further readings

EHRC (2014), *Your Rights to Equality at Work: How You Are Managed: Equality Act 2010 Guidance for Employees, Vol. 5*, London: EHRC, www.equalityhumanrights.com/sites/default/files/publication_pdf/Your%20Rights%20to%20equality%20at%20work%20-%20how%20you%20are%20managed.pdf.

Willey, B. (2012), *Employment Law in Context: An Introduction for HR Professionals*, 4th edn, Harlow: Pearson.

Shared services

Shared services are generally referred to as a hybrid organizational model that integrates centralization and decentralization models (Maatman et al., 2010). Most organizations use the shared services model for HRM by establishing a shared service provider that offers HRM services from a central one-stop-shop that is controlled by their clients: the local business units and their employees. In doing so, organizations anticipate to reap the benefits of centralization and decentralization models, while reducing their drawbacks. As such, reasons for using shared services for HRM range from cost-cutting and improving service quality to strengthening the strategic role of HR professionals.

In practice, shared service providers can be distinguished into two groups: service centres and expertise centres. Service centres are traditionally implemented to centralize personnel administration and payroll services against low costs, whereas expertise centres were reserved for creating strategic value through bundling transformational HRM services such as training and development. However, service centres nowadays also create value and have strategic impact as they find new ways of leveraging their central position and resources for expanding service portfolios and bring about changes in the human capital of their clients.

To decentralize control over their operations to the business units and their employees, shared service providers rely on various mechanisms which can be classified into three categories: input controls (e.g., steer groups), throughput controls (e.g., process tracking) and output controls (e.g., service level agreements). Although the concept holds that control over shared services is fully decentralized, only a few (public) organizations adopt this ideal type structure. Instead, the majority adopts a hybrid structure where corporate headquarters and local business units jointly control shared services operations (Meijerink et al., 2013). However, this hybrid nature creates some challenges (e.g., conflicting interests among stakeholders) for realizing the benefits of HRM shared services. Further, the extent to which HR shared services add value to the organization depends on how well employees, line managers, HR business partners or corporate HR headquarters enact their HR responsibilities.

Jeroen Meijerink and Marco Maatman

See also:
Capability procedure; Outsourcing.

References and selected further readings
Farndale, E., J. Paauwe and P. Boselie (2010), An exploratory study of governance in the intra-firm human resources supply chain, *Human Resource Management*, **49**(5), pp. 849–868.
Hofman, E. and J. Meijerink (2015), Platform thinking for services: the case of human resources, *The Service Industries Journal*, **35**(3), pp. 115–132.
Maatman, M. and T. Bondarouk (2014), Value creation by transactional shared service centers: mapping capabilities, in T. Bondarouk (ed.), *Shared Services as a New Organizational Form*, New York: Emerald Group Publishing Limited.
Maatman, M., T. Bondarouk and J.C. Looise (2010), Conceptualizing the capabilities and value creation of HRM shared service models, *Human Resource Management Review*, **20**(4), pp. 327–339.
Meijerink, J., T. Bondarouk and D. Lepak (forthcoming), Employees as active consumers of HRM: linking employees' HRM competences with their perceptions of HRM service value, *Human Resource Management*.
Meijerink, J., T. Bondarouk and M. Maatman (2013), Exploring and comparing HR shared services in

subsidiaries of multinational corporations and indigenous organisations in the Netherlands: a strategic response analysis, *European Journal of International Management*, **7**(4), pp. 469–492.

Shift work

Shift work is the practice of using multiple work rotas of succeeding teams to maximize productive (operational or opening) hours. For example, in any 24-hour period there may be three eight-hour shifts of mornings, afternoons and nights. Alternatively, there may be two 12-hour 'days' and night shifts, with workers usually rostered over a 'compressed work week' of three days. Shift working originated in capital-intensive manufacturing sectors but is also a common feature of service work (e.g., in the health, leisure and retail sectors) and thus is now extensive. Almost one in five people in employment in the UK works shifts, for example.

Workers can be allocated to a particular shift or 'rotate' shifts, which may overlap in order to accommodate team briefings. There are various patterns:

- Double day/two shift: this is the most common arrangement and involves two successive shifts (e.g. 6am–2pm and 2pm–10pm) of 'earlies' and 'lates'. These may be alternated weekly or over longer intervals.
- Three shift: a night shift is added to the double-day system providing three shifts (e.g., 6am–2pm, 2pm–10pm and 10pm–6am). Some employees work nights as part of a rotating arrangement while others may work permanent nights.
- Continental shift: a type of continuous shift-working characterized by fast rotation, commonly a 'three-two-two' pattern so that no shift is worked for more than three days. Rest days are worked into the cycle.
- Evening/twilight shift: a short shift worked in the evenings (typically 5pm–9pm).

Shift working might have some positive implications for work–life balance, for example, where it enables 'shift parenting' or permits greater overall time off work. However it also generally diminishes the degree and quality of family and social life. Shift work is thus normally compensated for by additional payments to acknowledge the problems for workers associated with 'atypical hours'. However, in sectors such as cleaning, where inconvenient 'split shifts' of early and evening work are common, there may be no extra payment at all. Shift working is also known to have a negative impact on health. Night work in particular disrupts the body's daily natural cycle or 'circadian rhythms'.

JAMES ARROWSMITH

See also:

Annualized hours; Overtime; Unsocial hours; Working time; Work–life balance.

References and selected further reading

Berryman, P., E. Lukes and S.M. Keller (2009), Effects of extended work shifts and shift work on patient safety, productivity, and employee health, *Workplace Health and Safety*, **57**(12), pp. 497–502.
Caruso, C.C. (2014), Negative impacts of shiftwork and long work hours, *Rehabilitation Nursing*, **39**(1), pp. 16–25.

Dhande, K.K. and S. Sharma (2011), Influence of shift work in process industry on workers' occupational health, productivity, and family and social life: an ergonomic approach, *Human Factors and Ergonomics in Manufacturing and Service Industries*, **21**(3), pp. 260–268.

Shop steward

A shop steward is an employee of an organization who is elected by a group of employees who are members of a particular trade union to be their representative. Depending on the nature of the work, this may be all of the employees in the organization or a certain group of employees. For instance, cleaners in any company may be members of a general union such as the GMB or Unison, whereas other types of jobs such as nurses will likely be members of the Royal College of Nursing, a trade union that represents only nurses.

As the elected representative of the employees of a particular trade union – that is recognized by their employer – they will be the voice of the employees in any discussions with management, as well as the voice for the trade union members in communications with their trade union. They provide a vital link between the national and regional trade unions and their members.

Shop stewards differ from trade union officials in that union officials are not normally elected by the workers but are normally appointed by, employed by and paid by the trade union. The shop steward's role is unpaid and voluntary. 'Shop steward' is often viewed as an out-of-date term and associated more with manufacturing and masculine work. It also comes under the guise of many other titles depending on the type of work including: union representative, lay workplace union representative, workplace representative, father of the chapel (the male representative of a group of trade union members, especially in the newspaper or publishing industries, a female is referred to as mother of the chapel).

The role of a shop steward is to be the union members' voice, recruit new members to the trade union, take up workers' grievances with management, negotiate on issues that concern union members at work, take the decisions of management and/or trade union to workers. They also provide members with guidance and direction about their work and their employment. In order to do this, they receive training from the trade union and have a legal right to time off to undertake this training. Other rights to time off relate to negotiating pay and/or terms and conditions of employment, helping union members with disciplinary or grievance procedures including meetings to hear their cases, attending meetings with union members with their line manager to discuss working requests, discussing issues that affect union members such as redundancies. However, since the 1980s and the changed industrial structure from manufacturing to services has brought a dramatic decline in the role and duties of shop stewards and in their numbers (see, e.g., Van Wanrooy et al., 2013).

Workplace representatives now spend less time on collective bargaining and negotiating at the workplace and more time on grievance and disciplinary issues. There has also more recently been the development of 'union learning representatives' and their role is predominantly related to promoting training, learning and development in the workplace.

This has led to a debate as to whether the role of the shop steward has become less influential in the employment relationship (Cohen, 2006; Darlington, 1994, 2002; Gall, 2000; McBride, 2004).

Jo McBride

See also:

Representative participation; Trade unions.

References and selected further readings

Cohen, S. (2006), *Ramparts of Resistance: Why Workers Lost their Power and How to Get it Back*, London and Ann Arbour, MI: Pluto Press.

Darlington, R. (1994), *The Dynamics of Workplace Unionism: Shop Stewards' Organization in Three Merseyside Plants*, London and New York: Mansell.

Darlington, R. (2002), Shop Stewards' leadership, left wing activism and collective workplace union organization, *Capital & Class*, **26**(1), pp. 95–126.

Gall, G. (2000), What is to be done with organised labour? *Historical Materialism*, **5**, pp. 327–343.

McBride, J. (2004), Renewal or resilience? The persistence of shop steward organisation in the Tyneside maritime construction industry, *Capital & Class*, **82**, pp. 115–141.

Van Wanrooy, B., H. Bewley, A. Bryson, J. Forth, S. Freeth, L. Stokes and S. Wood (2013), *Employment Relations in the Shadow of Recession: Findings from the 2011 Employment Relations Study*, Basingstoke: Palgrave Macmillan.

Shortlisting

'Shortlisting' is a process by which a subset of applicants, consisting of a sufficient number of the best-qualified applicants who have progressed through the initial screening phase, are selected to participate in the substantive evaluation phase of the selection method. The number of applicants shortlisted will reflect not only the overall quality and size of the applicant pool as measured against the employment criteria for the specific position to be filled, but will also reflect the organization's staffing and hiring yields for similar employees, i.e., the organization's historical staffing process effectiveness measured as transition ratios from one staffing phase to the next; from sourcing and attracting quality applicants, identifying and progressing the best talent through each stage of evaluation, and to the acceptance of offers of employment by the best-qualified applicant(s).

Wayne O'Donohue

See also:

Aptitude test; Big Five; Intelligence tests; Interviews; Job analysis; Personality test; Person–environment fit; Psychometric testing; Selection; Selection method; Selection test.

References and selected further readings

Phillips, J. and S. Gully (2014), *Strategic staffing*, Essex: Pearson.

Roth, P.L., P. Bobko, C.H. Van Iddekinge and J.B. Thatcher (2013), Social media in employee-selection-related decisions: a research agenda for uncharted territory, *Journal of Management*.

Ryan, A.M. and R.E. Ployhart (2014), A century of selection, *Annual Review of Psychology*, **65**, pp. 693–717.

Singh, P. (2008), Job analysis for a changing workplace, *Human Resource Management Review*, **18**(2), pp. 87–99.

Taylor, S. (2010), *Resourcing and Talent Management*, 5th edn, London: Chartered Institute of Personnel and Development.

Single pay spine

A single pay spine is a form of pay structure that groups similar roles or jobs together and applies a range of pay or band of pay from a minimum to a maximum. There is typically a nationally or centrally set pay scale, onto which each organization locally may map its own pay grades or pay ranges. Single pay spines are in use, for example, in parts the UK public sector where there are two level of bargaining on pay – the national level that agrees the national pay spine and the locally agreed pay and grading system, which then applies its pay ranges or grades onto the pay spine, Perkins and White (2011) comment that pay spines provide the backbone to local grading structures.

The use of such an approach allows for pay negotiating machinery that engages in a form of national-level pay setting, while at the same time giving local flexibility to set pay ranges for jobs – thereby enabling a more flexible response to local pay or labour market factors.

ANGELA WRIGHT

See also:
Collective bargaining.

References and selected further readings
Perkins, S. and G. White (2011), *Reward Management: Alternatives, Consequences and Contexts*, 2nd edn, London: Chartered Institute of Personnel Development.

Single-table bargaining

Single-table bargaining is the process where all trade unions recognized by an employer come together to discuss and agree their position before sending a single team representing all the trade unions' interests to the bargaining table to meet with the employer. Pay and conditions of employment for all eligible workers making up the organizational bargaining unit are determined around the table in a single set of negotiations. Bargaining arrangements are harmonized, usually within a single status context, covering both manual and non-manual workers.

Single-table bargaining shortens the communications chain and can help to harmonize conditions of employment and aid in introducing new working practices. The 2011 Workplace Employment Relations Survey found that single-table bargaining took place in 60 per cent of the workplaces surveyed that recognized more than one trade union.

Trade unions generally prefer single-table bargaining to single-union agreements as they do not pose the same threat to trade unions' representational and recognition interests. Some of the perceived benefits of single-table bargaining are: the process is cost- and time-effective; bargaining outcomes are achieved more efficiently; it facilitates workplace change; and it allows the potential to discuss workplace issues at a strategic level.

Single-table bargaining has been viewed as potentially problematic because: it may be inappropriate for organizations that do not have harmonized conditions of employment for its workers; unions must have a united position, which means putting aside historical interests borne out of occupational/status differences, which can be difficult; and the question of trade union representation around the single table – the potential dominance of a trade union in the negotiating process over other unions with an interest in the bargaining process and outcome can create a degree of inter union tension.

In the United Kingdom, single-table bargaining arrangements are more than three times more likely to be in the public sector rather than in the private sector.

PETER F. BESZTER

See also:

Collective bargaining; Greenfield sites; Single-union agreements.

References and selected further reading

Blyton, P. and P. Turnbull (2004), *The Dynamics of Employee Relations*, 3rd edn, Basingstoke: Palgrave Macmillan.
Colling, T. and M. Terry (eds) (2010), *Industrial Relations Theory & Practice*, 3rd edn, Oxford: Blackwell.
Rose, E. (2008), *Employment Relations*, 3rd edn, London: Prentice Hall.
Van Wanrooy, B., H. Bewley, A. Bryson, J. Forth, S. Freeth, L. Stokes and S. Wood (2013), *The Workplace Employment Relations Study — First Findings*, London: Department of Business, Innovation, and Skills.

Single-union agreements

Single-union arrangements come about through an employer's wish to recognize only one trade union for collective bargaining purposes. In workplaces that recognize only one trade union, this has normally come about through a formal single-union agreement. The 2011 Workplace Employment Relations Survey reported that among the 30 per cent of workplaces that recognized trade unions, around half (49 per cent) recognized a single trade union. Within the United Kingdom, the recognition of a single trade union is more likely to be in the private sector than in the public sector.

Since the 1980s single-union agreements have grown, particularly, on greenfield sites, where multinational companies, primarily from the United States and Japan, have come to the United Kingdom and Europe. During this period, their growth was controversial, as these overseas employers, in many cases sought to achieve single-union bargaining arrangements by de-recognizing existing trade unions and selecting a trade union by a 'union beauty contest', where trade unions vied for selection to be the sole collective representative body within these organizations. These 'beauty contests' resulted in some trade unions being selected where they had no tradition of membership in the particular industry.

The claimed advantages of single-union agreements are: they simplify the bargaining machinery, benefiting both employers and trade unions; they increase worker commitment to organizational objectives and help to promote less resistance to change among the workforce; they reduce the potential for conflict over demarcation; allow full-time trade union representatives the opportunity to develop expert knowledge in organizational operations; and having single-union agreements is better than having no trade union representation in workplaces.

The claimed disadvantages of single-union agreements are: where such agreements exist, a trade union relinquishes a degree of independence and is more likely to be under the influence of managerial control, therefore, losing it bargaining edge with the employer; a single trade union might not have the capacity to represent the different occupational interests in the organization; a trade union's ability to defend and promote their members is weakened where there is a perception that it lacks the means of imposing sanctions on the employer; and the use of single-union agreements increases competition and conflict between trade unions and the quest for recognition.

Single-union agreements have proven attractive to organizations that promote human resources strategies based on total quality management, teamworking and flexibility among the workforce, since the presence of one trade union reduces the likelihood of employee opposition to the introduction of new working practices.

PETER F. BESZTER

See also:

Collective bargaining; Greenfield sites; Regulation.

References and selected further readings

Blyton, P. and P. Turnbull (2004), *The Dynamics of Employee Relations*, 3rd edn, Basingstoke: Palgrave Macmillan.
Colling, T. and M. Terry (eds) (2010), *Industrial Relations Theory & Practice*, 3rd edn, Oxford: Blackwell.
Rose, E. (2008), *Employment Relations*, 3rd edn, London: Prentice Hall.
Van Wanrooy, B., H. Bewley, A. Bryson, J. Forth, S. Freeth, L. Stokes and S. Wood (2013), *The Workplace Employment Relations Study — First Findings*, London: Department of Business, Innovation, and Skills.

Skill

Skill is a contentious concept, and one that is difficult to define unequivocally. Different disciplines understand skill differently. There are also social preconceptions as to what skill is and how it can be established and measured.

Skill has three dimensions (Cockburn, 1983): the individual (skill in the person), the job design (skill in the job) and the social (skill in the social setting). Skill in the person is the traditional understanding of skill as an individual quality, aptitude or capacity to do something. It is the ability to perform a task, the manual dexterity or spatial awareness a person has. These are usually acquired through training, education or experience, and reside with the individual. In the past decades, these skills were extended to include a wide range of individual qualities, attitudes and behaviours known as 'soft' skills. The second dimension, skill in the job, refers to the space a job gives an individual to apply (and develop) their individual skills. It is the scope for application of the skills individuals have depending on the structure and nature of the job they perform. Narrowly defined jobs can lead to deskilling. The third dimension, skill in the social setting, concerns the historically developed understanding in the society of whether something is a skill, and how advanced a skill. This is usually manifested through institutional means and codified through formal qualifications and licences to practice. High skills status is achieved through the process of 'social closure' whereby through ideological, political and material processes certain occupational groups achieve and protect high skilled status. Skills are important as they confer pay, material, and status-related benefits to the individual. Therefore defining a person as skilled has direct implications for their status and earnings.

By their nature skills are socially constructed. They reflect societal values and are subject to power relationships. As there is no objective understanding of what constitutes high or low skill, there is also no objective measure of them. Attempts to provide an evaluation of skill levels can include tests, observations and job analysis. In trying to establish a measure of skill it is common to use proxies, such as formal qualifications and training.

Skills are also gendered: defining jobs or people as skilled is linked to the gender of those performing the tasks. Traditionally skills have been associated with technical, physical and generally male properties. With the later entry of women into the labour market, their skills were assigned lower status. In addition, certain skills related to domestic roles women have traditionally performed are perceived as 'natural' and therefore are invisible in the labour market. Since few of them are developed formally, proxies cannot be used to render them visible. They are therefore associated with lower status and lower material premium in the labour market.

DIMITRINKA STOYANOVA RUSSELL

See also:

Competence; Deskilling; Training and development.

References and suggested further readings

Cockburn, C. (1983), *Brothers: Male Dominance and Technological Change*, London: Pluto Press.
Grugulis, I. (2007), *Skills, Training and Human Resource Development*, Basingstoke: Palgrave Macmillan.
Noon, M., P. Blyton and K. Morrell (2013), *The Realities of Work*, Basingstoke: Macmillan.

Skills-based pay

Skill-based pay (SBP), also known as 'knowledge-based pay' is a form of performance-related pay that rewards the acquisition of skills or knowledge. Skills refer to specific expertise whereas knowledge is acquired information, both focused on the inputs required to do the job effectively. SBP is related, but slightly different, to competency-based pay, which focuses on general traits or skills that are less job-specific.

SBP is widely acknowledged to have originated in Procter & Gamble in the USA in the 1960s but has increased in popularity since, particularly in USA and Europe. SBP is most widely used in manual or service work. For example, apprentices are commonly rewarded with a pay increase at points during their apprenticeship for achieving certain levels of skills and knowledge. SBP can also be seen in some professional careers. For example, it is adopted for university academic staff, where lecturers (known as professors in the USA) will typically receive a grade promotion within their job to recognize knowledge acquisition, without the job itself fundamentally changing. SBP is also used in the USA and some European countries in the teaching and medical professions.

Whilst SBP most commonly refers to base pay progression, there is also a growing prevalence of skills-based bonus schemes. Skills-based bonuses may be more appropriate where the required skills and knowledge change quickly. The bonuses therefore provide short-term rewards for skills that may soon be out of date. These can be seen in, for example, high-tech engineering jobs and are also used in the US military.

The skills to be rewarded are categorized into 'skills blocks'. These blocks are then accredited with specific qualifications, through tests or an evaluation of job performance. An important distinction can be made between the types of skills that are being rewarded. Recardo and Priccone (1996) identify five types of SBP: vertical skills plans recognize the skills acquired within one job, whereas horizontal plans recognize the acquisition of skills across multiple jobs. Depth skills plans recognize the development of specialist skills, whereas basic skills plans recognize skills such as reading or spoken English. Finally, combination plans combine multiple approaches.

In reality, most SBP schemes incorporate factors other than skills or knowledge into account, such as individual or group performance, or job-based factors. This combined approach may in some circumstances be what Brown and Armstrong (1999) refer to as 'pay for contribution'. Such schemes adopt a 'best fit' approach to HR strategy in that they take into account organizational characteristics and priorities in designing pay structures to achieve specific strategic outcomes. These schemes may recognize skills or competence, but are also likely to take into account the nature of the job.

SBPs can be effective in encouraging more flexibility, investment in training, and promoting self-directed learning. However, SBPs are potentially costly to administer because of the need to develop and assess skills levels, so organizations must be certain that the investment is worthwhile. More successful SBPs seem to be those which are more in line with organizational characteristics (for example, in manufacturing firms), and where employees were involved in the design of the scheme, which can increase perceptions of fairness (Shaw et al., 2005).

REBECCA HEWETT

See also:

Payment system; Performance-related pay; Team pay.

References and selected further readings

Brown, D. and M. Armstrong (1999), *Paying for Contribution: Real Performance-Related Pay Strategies*, London: Kogan Page.
Heneman, R.L. (2000), *Strategic Reward Management: Design, Implementation, and Evaluation*, Greenwich, CT: IAP.
Lawler, E. (2000), *Rewarding Excellent: Pay Strategies for the New Economy*, San Francisco: Jossey-Bass.
Ledford, G.E. and H.G. Heneman (2011), *Skill Based Pay*, Alexandria, VA: Society for Human Resource Management.
Perkins, S.J. and G. White (2011), *Reward Management: Alternatives, Consequences and Contexts*, 2nd edn, London: Chartered Institute for Personnel Development.
Recardo, R.J. and D. Pricone (1996), Is skills-based pay for you? *SAM Advanced Management Journal*, 6(4), pp. 16–22.
Shaw, J.D., N. Gupta, A. Mitra and G.E. Ledford (2005), Success and survival of skills-based pay plans, *Journal of Management*, 31, pp. 28–49.

Small and medium-sized enterprises

SMES are a key part of many national economies. While precise definitions differ internationally, the EU defines SMEs in terms of ceilings for staff headcount (250) and turnover (€50 million) or balance sheet total (€43 million). There are around 23 million SMEs in the EU, representing 99% of all EU companies, and employing around 75 million people (European Commission, 2005).

Employment in SMEs is often presented in polarized terms, ranging from 'small is beautiful' on the one hand to a 'bleak house' on the other (Wilkinson, 1999). Beautiful firms are portrayed as good employers, offering varied work opportunities, with employees encouraged to express their views within a supportive and familial environment. Bleak houses, on the other hand, suggest that the opposite may be actually be true, and that small firms may be characterized by autocratic management regimes, limited employee voice, poor working conditions, low pay, few benefits, and arbitrary treatment (Rainnie, 1989). The empirical evidence has proved inconclusive.

It is noteworthy, however, that employees in smaller firms often report higher levels of job satisfaction compared to their counterparts in large firms (Forth et al., 2006), but it is unclear why this is. It may reflect, for example, different expectations, prior experiences, perceptions of 'fairness' or better relationships. However, other studies highlight a range of less positive HR outcomes in small firms including job insecurity, skills shortages, few career development opportunities, and high levels of applications to employment tribunals (Hoque and Bacon, 2006). This would seem to suggest that the reality of employment in SMEs is much more complex than either of the positive and negative views outlined above. While it is likely that size is an important factor in understanding approaches to HR, other variables are also potentially relevant including ownership structure, management strategy, sector, technology, labour conditions and product markets.

Despite the heterogeneity of HR approaches found in SMEs, a recurring theme that seems to distinguish smaller enterprises from larger organizations is a greater reliance upon more informal approaches to managing key HR issues such as recruitment, training and employee performance. This informality might reflect a more informal approach to business generally, management preference, or the lack of a perceived need for more formalized HR processes and systems.

An informal approach to HR can be double-edged. On the one hand, informality may allow rapid decision-making and enable changes to be implemented relatively rapidly. Formal processes may be viewed as bureaucratic, slow, and unnecessary in a smaller organization. However, informality may be problematic in areas such as employment law, where specific procedures and processes are often required. Some SMEs may decide to 'professionalize' their approach to HR, especially as they grow or feel informality is no longer effective. Of course formality and informality are not mutually exclusive; they are better thought of as countervailing tendencies rather than distinct choices. In understanding HRM in SMEs there is therefore both a need to understand the various contextual factors that influence the specific HR approaches adopted, in addition to organizational size, as well as a need to explore the realities of pursuing a more informal approach to HRM which contrasts with the formality implicit in much mainstream HR thinking.

STEWART JOHNSTONE

See also:

Hard and soft HRM; Management style.

References and selected further readings

European Commission (2005), The new SME definition: User guide and model declaration, Enterprise and Industry Publications, Brussels.

Forth J., H. Bewley and A. Bryson (2006), *Small and Medium-sized Enterprises: Findings from the 2004 Workplace Employment Relations Survey*, London: Department of Trade and Industry.

Hoque, K. and N. Bacon (2006), The antecedents of training activity in British small and medium-sized enterprises, *Work, Employment & Society*, **20**(3), pp. 531–552.

Rainnie, A. (1989), *Industrial Relations in Small Firms*, London: Routledge.

Saridakis, G., R. Muñoz Torres and S. Johnstone (2013), Do human resource practices enhance organizational commitment in SMEs with low employee satisfaction? *British Journal of Management*, **24**, pp. 445–458.

Wilkinson, A. (1999), Employment relations in SMEs, *Employee Relations*, **21**, pp. 206–217.

Social capital

The concept of social capital has received increasing attention from researchers in various disciplines such as sociology, political science, organizational psychology and economics. Many studies have confirmed that effective knowledge transfer occurs when there are close relationships or strong social ties between senders and receivers. These network ties and relationships generate a degree of goodwill that forms the foundation of social capital, which in turn facilitates access to broader sources of knowledge as well as improving its relevance, quality and timeliness (Adler and Kwon, 2002). Social capital, defined as 'the sum of the actual and potential resources embedded within, available through, and derived from the network of relationships possessed by an individual or social unit' (Nahapiet and Ghoshal, 1998, p. 243), has been examined and found to play a crucial role in facilitating both intra-organizational and inter-organizational linkages and knowledge exchange. In addition to the impact on knowledge-sharing, studies have also found a direct relationship between the social capital and firm performance. For example, Florin et al.'s (2003) longitudinal study on high growth ventures, and Zahra's (2010) study of family firms revealed the important role of social capital as a means of accumulating and leveraging the resources necessary to generate long-term sustainability. The findings from these studies clearly indicate the importance of nurturing social networks and relationships as a means of gaining access to valuable (often knowledge-based) resources crucial to a firm's long-term performance.

The development of social capital in organizations can be attributed to its strategy and policies. As Snell et al. (2000, p. 16) argue that 'HR strategy and practices transcend the development of knowledge, skills and behaviors alone to also incorporate the development of relationships and exchanges inside and outside the organization'. Strategic HRM researchers have established an empirical link between specific HR practices and the development of social capital. For example, Kaše et al. (2009) found that work design and training and development directly contributed to the intensity of face-to-face interaction between co-workers (i.e., structural relations). Cabello-Medina et al. (2011) found that a firm's social capital can be directly enhanced by the selection of individuals with learning potential and interpersonal skills, as well as through job design that promotes participation in decision-making.

Christine Soo, Amy Wei Tian and Stephen T.T. Teo

See also:

Human capital; Knowledge management; Strategic HRM.

References and selected further readings

Adler, P.S. and S.W. Kwon (2002), Social capital: prospects for a new concept, *Academy of Management Review*, **27**(1), pp. 17–40.

Cabello-Medina, C., L. Lopez-Cabrales and R. Valle-Cabreraa (2011), Leveraging the innovative performance of human capital through HRM and social capital in Spanish firms, *The International Journal of Human Resource Management*, **22**(4), pp. 807–828.

Florin, J., M. Lubatkin and W. Schulze (2003), A social capital model of high-growth ventures, *Academy of Management Journal*, **46**(3), pp. 374–384.

Kaše, R., J. Paauwe and N. Zupan (2009), HR practices, interpersonal relations, and intrafirm knowledge transfer in knowledge-intensive firms: a social network perspective, *Human Resource Management*, **48**(4), pp. 615–639.

Nahapiet, J. and S. Ghoshal (1998), Social capital, intellectual capital, and the organizational advantage, *Academy of Management Review*, **23**(2), pp. 242–266.

Snell, S.A., M.A. Shadur and P.M. Wright (2000), *Human Resources Strategy: The Era of Our Ways*, CAHRS Working Paper #00-17, Ithaca, NY: Cornell University, School of Industrial and Labor Relations, Center for Advanced Human Resource Studies.

Zahra, S.A. (2010), Harvesting family firms' organizational social capital: a relational perspective, *Journal of Management Studies*, **47**(2), pp. 345–366.

Staff association

A staff association is a representative body that exists to represent the interests of employees. However, unlike a conventional trade union, which usually represents employees working for a wide range of employers in the same sector or within a particular occupation, staff associations normally only represent employees working for a single employer. Many of the first formal staff associations in Britain originated in banks and building societies, typically as an evolution of existing non-union company councils, or were created by employers as an alternative to trade unions as a form of union avoidance/substitution.

A key debate is the extent to which enterprise-based staff associations are essentially non-union systems of employee representation (NER), or whether they perform the same role and activities as an independent external trade union. Answering this question depends partly upon the extent to which a staff association can be considered to be 'independent' of the employer. In the case of Britain, independence is defined by Acas as 'not under the domination or control of an employer and independent from the employer financially'. The Certification Officer (CO, 2015) maintains a list of trade unions and determines whether or not they can reasonably be regarded as 'independent'. Where this is the case, the CO can issue a 'Certificate of Independence' to confirm that an in-house staff association meets the criteria of independence in the same way as a trade union. However, even where a staff association does meet official independence criteria, they still generally represent a distinctive form of employee representation: enterprise-based; often representing white-collar workers, and in favour of developing and maintaining cooperative rather than adversarial relationships with employers.

It is noteworthy, however, that use of the term 'staff association' has declined. Following the award of a Certificate of Independence, many former staff associations rebranded as 'staff unions' or simply 'unions', and in non-union contexts the terms staff councils, staff forums or staff committees may be used. Irrespective of the name, it is the internal and enterprise – rather than external or occupational/sectoral – form of representation, which continues to distinguish staff associations and former staff associations from most conventional trade unions, and can also make them difficult to distinguish from other non-union representative bodies.

STEWART JOHNSTONE

See also:

Employee voice; Trade unions; Non-union employee representation; Union avoidance: substitution and suppression.

References and selected further readings

Acas (2005), *Trade Union Recognition*, www.acas.org.uk/media/b/j/A02_1.pdf.
CO (2015), *Certification Officer*, www.gov.uk/government/organisations/certification-officer.
Gall, G. (1997), Developments in trade unionism in the financial sector in Britain, *Work, Employment & Society*, **11**(2), pp. 219–235.
Purcell, J. (1984), Industrial relations in building societies, *Employee Relations*, **6**(1), pp. 12–16.
Swabe, A and P. Price (1984), Building a permanent association? The development of staff associations in the building societies, *British Journal of Industrial Relations*, **22**, pp. 195–204.
Swabe, A. and P. Price (1984), White-collar unionism in the building societies, *Employee Relations*, **6**(3), pp. 8–12.
Winterton, J. and R. Winterton (1982), Employee representation in building societies, *Employee Relations*, **4**(2), pp. 11–16.

Staff poaching

Staff poaching is defined as the process of persuading employees of another company to become your employees instead. To put it simply, staff poaching is what takes place when a company hires an employee from a competing company. Employee poaching is very popular phenomenon in the small business context, particularly in high-growth, specialized and technology industries. Hiring an employee from a rival firm can mean bringing on someone who already knows your industry, your business and can bring valuable new knowledge and clients to you. This is supposed to happen in a cost-effective manner, since the hiring firm avoids the cost of training provision. From a free market perspective, poaching can also help society put assets to their very best use. On the negative side of poaching, external hires often have a longer adjustment period and orientation costs are higher.

The danger of training employees in small and large organizations is the high probability of poaching by competitors. Many organizations may perceive training as a costly activity, with the benefits being reaped elsewhere. In the small business context specifically, the type of skills that are needed in the multi-skilled environment in which small firm employees operate are mainly generic skills that can be used across all occupational sectors, and therefore moves to another company are easy to accomplish.

The probability of poaching is reduced when skills are not valued outside the training firm either due to their inherent nature or the characteristics of the labour market. As Acemoglu and Pischke (1998) explain, firms invest in general training when labour markets are highly non-competitive. In such cases, general skills become specific because they cannot receive value in other employment positions. Under such conditions, firms can be expected to train because they are relatively certain that trained workers will not quit. Other studies have pointed to the relationship between internal labour markets and training showing that poaching can be reduced in cases where firms provide incentives (e.g., promotional opportunities) to trained workers to stay after training is completed. Further studies have revealed that the risk of poaching can be reduced by lowering the cost of poaching to training firms. Such cost reductions can occur when training is regulated or subsidized. In this context, firms manage to reduce the risk of poaching by establishing industry-wide standards to which firms are expected to train and have developed monitoring mechanisms to ensure sufficient numbers of workers are trained.

ANTONIOS PANAGIOTAKOPOULOS

See also:
Retention; Talent Management.

References and selected further readings

Acemoglu, D. and J. Pischke (1998), Why do firms train? Theory and evidence, *Quarterly Journal of Economics*, **113**, pp. 79–118.
Panagiotakopoulos, A. (2012), Staff poaching in the small business context: overcoming this key barrier to training, *Industrial and Commercial Training*, **44**(6), pp. 326–333.

State

When discussing the state we need to appreciate that this is an important feature of the context of HRM. The state consists of an ensemble of institutions that represent various interests within the economy and in society (bodies such as parliaments) and various forms of intervention within these as well (e.g., public education, the courts) (Jessop, 1982). The state is important for HRM because, for example, it influences the development of the quality of labour and management through public training and education structures, intervenes in disputes between labour and capital through forms of mediation bodies (normally linked to a ministry of labour) and through the police and other coercive mechanisms in the case of disputes that raise public order issues, and sets the legal context of rights and obligations both employers and workers must adhere to (see 'Regulation' in this volume). In this respect, the state influences the abilities of actors in HRM such as management and trade unions, as well as influencing the framework of rules and relations between them. In some cases, the state will be more interventionist and play a range of roles in terms of the kinds of issues outlined above, while in others it may be less important or less able to intervene due to its lack of resources. Some states may be more developed and integral to the conduct of HRM, while in others they may be more withdrawn and play a more supportive or distant role. The state is also an employer as it consists of departments or agencies that directly employs individuals in large numbers, such as civil servants, teachers, medical staff, police officers and others. This allows it to send signals and set standards for other employers in terms of working practices. It also indirectly employs staff through outsourcing, which can allow it to influence employment practices in a specific national context. The state also plays a role in signalling changes and providing training to employers and workers on a range of ideas and processes through its various departments and learning bodies (Martínez Lucio and Stuart, 2011). There are various views on the state. There is a neo-liberal view that argues the state should influence matters as little as possible and allow employers and workers (normally the former) to conduct matters independently. This view argues that regulation and the state undermine the role of management prerogative: some in fact argue that with the greater globalization we are seeing a weakening of the state anyway as the national level at which it operates cannot easily control the increasing development of transnational corporations. The second view is that the state is an actor that can do much to stabilize the negative features of the employment relationship and create greater balance between employers and workers through the development of rules and regulations, as well as being a mediator. This is known as the pluralist view of the state. It is a very common view in the study of labour and employment relations. The role of the state is a third actor between the 'two sides of industry'. The third view – normally associated with a Marxist approach or labelled a conflict approach – argues that the state is normally dominated by employer elites and its interests and that it tends to side with them on most matters. Rights that are provided to workers are normally minimal with very little content in terms of their ability to control affairs within work and employment. Finally, the state is normally an important feature of the HRM context and environment and provides a series of resources and rules which shape its conduct in one form or another.

MIGUEL MARTÍNEZ LUCIO

See also:

Pluralism; Public sector; Radicalism; Regulation.

References and selected further readings

Blyton, P.R. and P.J. Turnbull (2004), *The Dynamics of Employee Relations*, Basingstoke: Palgrave Macmillan.
Howell, C. (2011), *Regulating Labor: The State and Industrial Relations Reform in Postwar France*, Princeton: Princeton University Press.
Jessop, B. (1982), *The Capitalist State: Marxist Theories and Methods*, Oxford: Martin Robertson.
Martínez Lucio, M. and M. Stuart (2011), The state, public policy and the renewal of HRM, *The International Journal of Human Resource Management*, **22**(18), pp. 3661–3671.

Strategic choice

The concept of strategic choice is associated with the work of John Child (1972) and continues to have a significant influence on the study of organizations and management. Up until the emergence of the concept in the early 1970s, understanding of organizations was largely deterministic and functional in nature. Essentially, varying environmental conditions (e.g., whether an environment was dynamic or static) and/or organizational contingencies (e.g., whether the focus was on batch or mass manufacturing) were seen to automatically mandate a specific type of organizational response. This contingency approach served the objective of offering prescriptive insights for what management should do. However, in so doing, it inadvertently relegated the agency of management to a non-significant role.

The utility of strategic choice is that it brings managerial agency and decision-making more directly into the equation. For Child (1997, p. 45), strategic choice refers to 'the process whereby power holders within organizations decide upon courses of strategic action'. While an appreciation of the role of management has a historical legacy the concept of strategic choice in its contemporary guise came to the fore with the work of Kochan and colleagues (1984). Here, managerial discretion via strategic choice was highlighted as a key dimension explaining variation in the diffusion and operation of industrial relations mechanisms and HRM practices. Moreover, the role of management was not necessarily objective or rational but rather was informed by underlying values and beliefs. The logic that management had agency in determining the nature of HRM that best served their organizational objectives ultimately provided a conceptual underpinning to early models of HRM. Research in turn examined internal factors related to strategic choice, including management styles and the strategic influence of the HR function, while also examining external factors framing the extent of strategic choice such as institutional contexts and, more recently, the role of networks.

The significance of strategic choice stems from the more voluntaristic and social explanations it affords to understanding HRM. That said, more recent attempts at exploring HRM including models of best fit and best practice are relatively silent on the strategic choice available to HR managers. As a result, they risk falling back to the type of determinism that Child's concept initially set out to avoid. By contrast there is a healthy stream of research examining the fragility of the HR function and its quest for strategic influence (Guest and King, 2004), coupled with work that has reintroduced a focus on discretionary behaviour by examining leadership styles and the role of critical intermediaries such as line managers (Harney and Jordan, 2008). Understanding of strategic choice itself has also evolved with earlier conceptions criticized for ignoring power, path dependency and the role of emotion and identity in framing decision-making. Nonetheless, strategic choice remains a concept of management, for management.

BRIAN HARNEY

See also:
Best fit; Management style; Non-unionism; Strategic HRM; Strategy.

References and selected further readings

Child, J. (1972), Organizational structure, environment and performance: the role of strategic choice, *Sociology*, **6**, pp. 1–22.

Child, J. (1997), Strategic choice in the analysis of action, structure, organizations and environment: retrospect and prospect, *Organization Studies*, **18**(1), pp. 43–76.

Guest, D. and Z. King (2004), Power, innovation and problem-solving: the personnel managers' three steps to heaven? *Journal of Management Studies*, **41**(3), pp. 401–423.

Harney, B. and C. Jordan (2008), Unlocking the black box: line managers and HRM performance in a call centre context, *International Journal of Productivity and Performance Management*, **57**(4), pp. 275–296.

Kochan, T., R. McKersie and P. Cappelli (1984), Strategic choice and industrial relations theory, *Industrial Relations*, **23**(1), pp. 16–39.

Strategic HRM

Strategic human resource management (SHRM) involves management decisions in different organizational contexts related to policies and practices that shape the employment relationship and are aimed at achieving individual employee, organizational and/or societal goals (Boselie, 2014). SHRM is a sub-discipline of human resource management. The 'strategic' dimension in SHRM refers to strategy, strategic decision-making and notions of alignment of decision-making with the internal and external organizational context (Wright and McMahan, 1992). The 'human' dimension refers to the key subject of SHRM: employees and employment relationships (Paauwe, 2004). 'Resource' represents the potential value of workers for achieving goals and gaining organizational success in line with the resource-based view (RBV) of the firm (Barney, 1991). Finally, the 'management' component refers to decision-making, actual implementation and taking actions aimed at employee attitudes and behaviours for organizational goal achievement. SHRM is mainly focused on organization-level analysis and heavily influenced by other disciplines such as strategic management, industrial relations and organizational behaviour.

In addition to the RBV, other popular theories in SHRM include the strategic contingency approaches with an emphasis on different types of fit (Schuler and Jackson, 1987), the AMO model focused on employee abilities, employee motivation and employee opportunity to participate (Bailey, 1993) and new institutionalism focused on coercive, normative and mimetic mechanisms affecting the shaping of the employment relationship and HRM in general (Paauwe, 2004). Wright and McMahan (1992) provide an extensive overview of potential relevant theories for SHRM research also including power and behavioural theories.

Delery and Doty (1996) make an important distinction between three modes of theorizing in SHRM. First, the universalistic mode of theorizing in SHRM builds on 'best practices' assumptions that particular HRM policies and practices can be applied successfully in all organizational contexts. Second, the contingency mode of theorizing in SHRM builds on 'best fit' notions with regard to internal fit (or horizontal fit) and external fit (or vertical fit). Internal fit is the coherent and consistent alignment of different individual HRM practices into HRM systems and HRM bundles. External fit is the alignment of the HRM system as a whole to the organization strategy. Finally, the configurational mode of theorizing is the most complex form, also building on 'best-fit' notions and taking into account internal and external fit in combination with potential unique organizational contexts linked to the administrative cultural heritage of an organization (Paauwe, 2004). The debate with regard to 'best practice' versus 'best-fit' approaches is one of the most important debates in contemporary SHRM (Boxall and Purcell, 2011). The key question is whether organizations can apply universalistic HRM practices for gaining (long-term) organizational success or not.

A further debate in SHRM concerns the meaning of performance. SHRM is relevant for linking human resource management (HRM) to different types of outcomes and performance. Narrow SHRM approaches tend to focus on organizational performance in terms of financial indicators (for example, sales, profits and market value), while broad SHRM approaches define performance, for example, in terms of organizational effectiveness (productivity, quality, etc.), employee wellbeing (satisfaction, motivation, commitment, trust, vitality, etc.) and societal wellbeing (employment, social legitimacy, fair pay, etc.) (Beer et al., 1984). The broad SHRM approaches often build on stakeholder notions.

A recent SHRM debate concerns the degree of HRM differentiation towards different employee groups in an organization (Lepak and Snell, 2007). In the HR Architect model by Lepak and Snell (2007), for example, a distinction is made between four employee groups depending on the strategic value and the uniqueness of employee groups. Knowledge workers are unique and have strategic value to the organization, while contract workers (often externalized) are not. The HRM differentiation approaches in SHRM can be linked to themes such as outsourcing, offshoring, flexibility, core employees and peripheral workers. Both transaction cost theory and human capital theory have influenced the HRM differentiation debates.

Paul Boselie

See also:

AMO model; Best fit; Best practice; Human resource management; Resource-based view.

References and selected further readings

Bailey, T. (1993), Organizational innovation in the apparel industry, *Industrial Relations*, **32**, pp. 30–48.
Barney, J.B. (1991), Firm resources and sustainable competitive advantage, *Journal of Management*, **17**, pp. 99–120.
Beer, M., B. Spector, P. Lawrence, D.Q. Mills and R. Walton (1984), *Human Resource Management: A General Manager's Perspective*, New York: Free Press.
Boselie, P. (2014), *Strategic Human Resource Management: A Balanced Approach*, 2nd edn, Berkshire: McGraw-Hill.
Boxall, P. and J. Purcell (2011), *Strategy and Human Resource Management*, 3rd edn, Hampshire: Palgrave Macmillan.
Delery, J.E. and D.H. Doty (1996), Modes of theorizing in strategic human resource management: tests of universalistic, contingency, and configurational performance predictions, *Academy of Management Journal*, **39**, pp. 802–835.
Lepak, D.P. and S.A. Snell (2007), Employment subsystems and the 'HR architecture', in P. Boxall, J. Purcell and P.M. Wright (eds), *The Oxford Handbook of Human Resource Management*, Oxford: Oxford University Press, pp. 210–230.
Paauwe, J. (2004), *HRM and Performance: Achieving Long-Term Viability*, Oxford: Oxford University Press.
Schuler, R.S. and S.E. Jackson (1987), Linking competitive strategies with human resource management practices, *Academy of Management Executive*, **1**(3), pp. 209–213.
Wright, P.M. and C.G. MacMahan (1992), Theoretical perspectives for strategic human resource management, *Journal of Management*, **18**, 295–321.

Strategy

In its most basic form, strategy can be defined as the long-term direction and scope of an organization. The origins of the term can be traced back to early military warfare via the work of army generals like Sun Tzu and his treatise *The Art of War*, which appeared around 500 BC. This legacy is reflected in understanding of strategy as the desire to achieve victory by defeating the enemy or competition. In modern parlance, the ultimate purpose of strategy is to secure and sustain a competitive advantage; that is, a proven value proposition that is sustained even despite competitor's constant attempts at replication. Understanding the means to achieve this goal has evolved over time.

Early work on strategy in a corporate context emerged in the 1950s in the form of business policy and strategic planning. Here, strategy constituted formal, annual planning conducted by top management or a designated planning department. Strategic planning was necessitated as corporations were becoming more diverse both geographically and in the scope of their activities. Chandler's extensive research into growing multidivisional organizations formed the basis of the thesis that 'structure followed strategy'. Chandler's (1962, p. 13) definition of strategy as 'the determination of basic long-term goals and objectives of an enterprise, and the adoption of courses of action and allocation of resources necessary for carrying out those goals' is still frequently cited. Reflecting the military origins of the concept these early definitions inherited an emphasis on strategy as the formulation of ideas by top commanders, with implementation and translation of goals into action assumed unproblematic.

As strategy gained ground as an academic discipline it required a more rigorous and scientific underpinning. This was largely provided through the work of Michael Porter, who drew on the economic theory of industrial organization to examine the competitive conditions faced by a firm. This not only provided rigour but also pragmatic tools like the five forces model to assess industry attractiveness and, by consequence, the alternative ways a firm could position itself in terms of a value proposition to customers (e.g., cost, differentiation). A number of strategy consultancies also emerged, offering their own models to assess the diversity and growth potential of various business units in the corporate portfolio (e.g., the BCG matrix). By the 1980s, strategy was a mainstream academic discipline delivered widely in business schools, with ideas and research diffused through specialist outlets, including the *Strategic Management Journal*. However, the key ideas underpinning what Whittington (1993) terms 'classic' strategy, such as rational, top-down planning and an exclusive profit focus, were not immune to criticism.

The viability of long-term planning was questioned in light of environmental changes such as those brought about by the oil crisis in the early 1970s and recessionary conditions in the 1980s. Increasingly planning departments were viewed as isolated from competitive realities. Strategic positioning of the type advocated by Porter, was judged uni-linear and static, with an inability to accommodate change and blurring industry boundaries. Partly in reaction to these circumstances, understanding progressed from a market-driven logic inwards to the resource endowment of the firm. Peters and Waterman's hugely successful *In Search of Excellence: Lessons from America's Best-Run Companies* highlighted the role of culture and human capital in arguing that 'the crucial problems in strategy are most often those of execution and continuous adaptation; getting it done and staying flexible' (Peters and Waterman, 1982: 4). This logic was ultimately theoretically manifest through the resource-based view of the firm, which argued that in dynamic and unpredictable environments, building a foundational base of capabilities that fostered innovation, flexibility, adaptability and organization learning was a much more secure basis on which to gain competitive advantage. This internal emphasis served to accommodate not only strategy formulation, but critically, strategy implementation. Moreover, a human dimension was recognized whereby strategy was formed rather than formulated so that its development was fluid, iterative and shaped by learning and intuition as much as by clipboards and formal meetings. The title of Mintzberg's contribution in the mid-1990s – *The Rise and Fall of Strategic Planning* – aptly captures the extent of the shift in thinking. More recently strategy understanding has evolved further to accommodate the reconfigured boundaries of the firm and the logic of co-opetition where firms may work with direct competitors. This reflects an era of more open innovation and networked organizations. From this perspective strategy loses some of its military win-win mentality and instead embraces the logic of a win-win relational perspective (Chen and Miller, 2014).

While the evolution of understanding of strategy is not as neat as presented and meaning of the term remains contested, this consideration does serve to identify the key fault lines of debate. These include whether strategy is formulaic and designed as per classical definitions or is more emergent and fluid; whether strategy is the remit of an exclusive few at the top of the firm or an organization-wide phenomenon; whether understanding a given market takes precedence or whether it is the resource endowment of the firm that matters. Drawing on the lens of 'strategy as practice' more recent contributions have further accommodated the process of strategy and the activities of people involved. This has helped surfacing some hidden voices and perspectives, although it remains the case that 'no one can much agree what strategy as people actually means' (Kiechel, 2010, p. 288). In an attempt to counter simplistic depictions and current dogma Richard Rumelt (2011) suggests that strategy is best understood as a cohesive response to a challenge. This reflects that strategy is not about a fixed solution but an ongoing process. Moreover, the existence of strategy does not imply success but merely reflects the firm's own theory about how to compete. Of course, according to more critical accounts, the dominance of a more classical perspective is not surprising as it serves to reinforce and legitimize the current order, with strategy operating as a discourse which legitimizes and justifies managerial action while silencing alternative or dissenting voices. It remains the case that strategy is still largely understood in a simplistic fashion, with power, conflict or disorder ignored in favour of a rational portrayal. Arguably there is much to be gained from opening up a greater diversity of understanding and ensuring the term is diffused into related fields in a pluralistic manner, else enhanced understanding becomes victim to premature conceptual foreclosure.

BRIAN HARNEY

See also:
Competitive advantage; Resource-based view; Strategic choice; Strategic HRM.

References and selected further readings

Chandler, A.D. (1962), *Strategy and Structure*, Cambridge, MA: MIT Press.
Chen, M.J. and D. Miller (2014), Reconceptualizing competitive dynamics: a multidimensional framework, *Strategic Management Journal*, **36**(5), pp. 758–775.
Cunningham, J. and B. Harney (2012), *Strategy and Strategists*, Oxford: Oxford University Press.
Kiechel, W.I. (2010), *The Lords of Strategy: The Secret Intellectual History of the New Corporate World*, Cambridge, MA: Harvard Business School Publishing.
Peters, T.J. and R.H. Waterman (1982), *In Search of Excellence: Lessons from America's Best-Run Companies*, London: Harper & Row.
Rumelt, R. (2011), *Good Strategy/Bad Strategy*, London: Profile Books.
Whittington, R. (1993), *What is Strategy and Does it Matter?* London: Routledge.

Stress

The term 'stress' is used for different purposes in different sciences, but in the context of human resource management (HRM) this term is used mostly to refer to psychological stress and it indicates the range of responses that people experience when in acute, severe circumstances and/or when they are chronically overtaxed. This use of the word 'stress' goes back to the pioneering work of early psycho-physiologists such as Walter Cannon and Hans Selye, who tried to uncover how the body responds to external threats (Cooper and Dewe, 2008). In the context of HRM, it is common to limit the perspective to work-related stress; for example, the responses in workers to acute severe circumstances at work and/or chronic overtaxing by work. Examples of acute work stressors are threats or acts of aggression by customers and conflicts with colleagues. Examples of chronic stressors are too much work and too complicated work. The term 'work-related strain' is often used as a synonym for work-related stress. It is common to describe stress in terms of a range of different responses including physical responses (e.g., high blood pressure, increased heart rate, muscle tension, headaches), emotional responses (e.g., nervousness, irritability, instability), cognitive responses (e.g., difficulty concentrating, proneness to making errors), as well as behavioural responses (e.g., mood-related drinking and eating, use of medication).

A large recent study among more than 40,000 workers in 34 European countries investigated to what extent workers experience the stress responses mentioned above. It was found that 20 per cent of the workers can be classified as experiencing stress responses to the extent that their mental health is considered at risk. As such it is one of the largest health-related problems in the modern European workforce (Parent-Thirion et al., 2012). It is not the stress at work per se that is problematic, although severe work-related stress indicates a serious reduction in quality of working life. The problematic part lies more in the fact that stress is causing accidents, performance failures, absenteeism, permanent disability to work and other negative effects for workers and organizations alike (Jex, 1998). Preventing serious negative consequences of stress at work is important in all jobs, but it is especially relevant in critical jobs, such as those that perform critical tasks for society and/or organizations. Examples of such jobs are flight controllers and control room operators in a nuclear plant. For this reason it is important to design (critical) jobs in ways that prohibit stress from building up.

Several theories exist that are used to explain how and why stress is caused at work. Some of these theories emphasize factors in the work environment as the main causes of stress at work, like the Demand-Control-Support Model by Karasek and Theorell (1990), and the Job Demands-Resources Model by Demerouti et al. (2001). Both models share the idea that high job demands use the resources that are available in a job. If demands outweigh resources, over time this may result in health impairment, and stress-related symptoms are an early indicator that this may be happening. Other theories emphasize how environmental and worker factors interact in the development of stress at work, like the so-called Michigan Model of stress (Caplan et al., 1975). In the Michigan Model, employee factors such as abilities and needs are highlighted. Evidence shows that such factors play a role in the resilience of employees in stress at work.

A term that is linked to dealing with stress by individual people is that of 'coping'. Lazarus and Folkman (1984) have – in their influential transactional approach to stress – described coping as 'cognitive and behavioural efforts to master, reduce or tolerate internal and/or external demands'. This work has paved the way for all kinds of training programmes and counselling approaches aimed at providing workers with better skills for coping with work demands and helping them with current stress symptoms, an industry known as 'stress management'. In addition, it is more and more customary to monitor psychosocial job conditions and stress levels in groups of workers using national, sectoral and/or organizational surveys. The purpose for such surveys is to signal departments, job groups, etc. with high stress levels, and to indicate these groups for intervention in order to diminish stress levels/prevent stress levels from becoming dangerously high. In some European countries, employers are obliged by law to provide such risk assessments of workplace psychosocial factors causing stress. The development of effective approaches for preventing stress at work and the effective treatment of burnout is a priority for occupational health and safety in many countries across the globe.

MARC VAN VELDHOVEN AND KARINA VAN DE VOORDE

See also:
Burnout; Occupational health; Wellbeing.

References and selected further readings
Caplan, R.D., S. Cobb, J.R. French, R.V. Harrison and S.R. Pinneau (1975), *Job Demands and Worker Health: Main Effects and Occupational Differences*, Ann Arbor: Institute for Social Research.
Cooper, C.L. and P.J. Dewe (2008), *Stress: A Brief History*, Chichester: John Wiley & Sons.
Demerouti, E., A.B. Bakker, F. Nachreiner and W.B. Schaufeli (2001), The Job Demands-Resources Model of burnout, *Journal of Applied Psychology*, **86**(3), pp. 499–511.
Jex, S.M. (1998), *Stress and Job Performance: Theory, Research, and Implications for Managerial Practice*, Thousand Oaks, CA: Sage.
Karasek, R. and T. Theorell (1990), *Healthy Work: Stress, Productivity, and the Reconstruction of Working Life*, New York: Basic Books.
Lazarus, R.S. and S. Folkman (1984), *Stress, Appraisal, and Coping*, New York: Springer.
Parent-Thirion, A., G. Vermeylen, G. Van Houten, M. Lyly-Yrjänäinen, I. Biletta, J. Cabrita and I. Niedhammer (2012), *Fifth European Working Conditions Survey*, Luxembourg, Eurofound.

Strikes

Strikes are a temporary withdrawal of labour – a temporary cessation of the willingness to work for the employer. No matter how long strikes last, they are full withdrawals of labour (compared to industrial action short of striking such as overtime bans, work-to-rules and go-slows, and lockouts where employers refuse to allow employees to work). The reason strikes are temporary actions is that their purpose is to alter the terms and conditions of work in favour of the strikers, upon which time they resume their work. Strikes are collective actions so that when more than a single worker withdraws their willingness to work, a strike is created. The importance of the collective nature of the strike is that without banding together, individual workers have little or no power over their employers.

Strikes can be either defensive or offensive in terms of whether workers are trying to defend or advance their interests. But because employers and managers hold the initiative in employment, strikes are normally against something that management has done. This is crystallized into a grievance. Because strikes require prior collective organization in order to come into being, nearly all are organized by unions. Most strikes are undertaken during collective bargaining, with the strike being a weapon of last resort. The object of the bargaining is for the employer and the union to come to an agreement over wages, benefits and working conditions.

The onset of mass industrialization brought about by capitalism created the conditions for the widespread potential for strikes, namely workers working together in large numbers and under a capitalist employment relationship. The first mass (or general) strike in modern times was the 1842 Chartist strike in Britain. It fused together economic and political demands, indicating that some types of strikes seek to not only influence immediate employers but also governments.

Strikes are normally characterized by those withdrawing their labour leaving the employers' premises. Hence, strikes are often known as 'walk-outs' even if the walking out is only to the perimeter of the premises for picketing. Occasionally, the strike takes the form of occupations of premises because this puts the strikers in a more powerful position. In the USA, these are known as 'sit down' strikes.

Most private sector strikes are economic strikes – aimed at causing economic loss to the employer – while most public sector strikes are political strikes – aimed at causing disruption of government and society. With the decline in private sector union membership, a larger proportion of strikes are political strikes (in the public sector). Most strikes, regardless of their sectoral location, are now short strikes of one or two days. This reflects that, even in the private sector, strikes are of declining effectiveness and increased cost to workers.

The right to strike exists in international law but how this is manifest in individual countries varies considerably. Correlations between strike levels and strength of individual labour movements also vary. Some countries like Germany and Sweden have had relatively low levels of strikes and powerful union movements, while others like Greece, Spain and Italy relatively high levels and powerful union movements. Nonetheless, in many parts of the world, striking has been in decline for several decades.

One unusual type of strike is a 'sickout' or 'sickie' where workers en masse call in sick when they are not sick, thus, in effect, striking. This tactic is used to get around restrictions on striking by some public servants or to stop loss of pay as a result of striking.

GREGOR GALL

See also:
Collective bargaining; Conflict; Picketing; Work limitation.

References and selected further readings

Brecher, J. (2014), *Strike!* Oakland, CA: PM Press.
Gall, G. (2013), Quiescence continued? Recent strike activity in nine Western European economies, *Economic and Industrial Democracy*, **34**(4), pp. 667–691.
Silver, B. (2003), *Forces of Labor: Workers' Movements and Globalization since 1870*, New York: Cambridge University Press.

Subcontracting

Subcontracting refers to contracting out (part of) the production or service activities from the main contractor to another party (subcontractor) lower down the production or value chain. It is usually a temporary arrangement and often project-based, although the main contractor and the subcontractor may have developed a long-term relationship. In many ways, reasons for subcontracting may be similar to those for outsourcing. That is, to reduce cost, to take advantage of the specialist expertise possessed by the subcontractor, to deliver the whole project on time and to increase production or service capacity. Subcontractors may be self-employed or a team of (semi-) self-employed individuals. In less developed countries like China, subcontracting arrangements are quite common in industrial businesses such as construction and shipbuilding. Those who work for the subcontractor may have little employment and social security protection. Exploitation may be common, so may be wage arrears.

In large projects, subcontracting may take place more than once. In other words, a subcontractor may further subcontract part of the business further down the supply chain. This kind of subcontracting arrangement tends to weaken the control of the main contractor over the quality and on-time delivery of the project. In a supply chain involving multiple layers of subcontracting arrangements, communication, goal alignment and coordination are critical to ensure successful delivery of products/services. The failure of one subcontractor may have a domino effect and lead to the failure of the whole project. A project manager or liaison manager may be deployed to oversee the relationship.

There may be a number of pitfalls in using subcontracting as an operation strategy. One is the loss of brand. This problem may be twofold: the subcontractor's performance not reflecting the client firm's brand; and the subcontractor using the client's brand for their other activities. Trust and confidentiality are two other important issues to manage in subcontracting relationships to maintain competitive advantage.

FANG LEE COOKE

See also:
Outsourcing.

References and selected further readings
Domberger, S. (1998), *The Contracting Organisation: a Strategic Guide to Outsourcing*, Oxford: Oxford University Press.
Smitka, M. (1991), *Competitive Ties: Subcontracting in the Japanese Automotive Industry*, New York: Columbia University Press.
Tam, V.W.Y., L.Y. Shen and J.S.Y. Kong (2011), Impacts of multi-layer chain subcontracting on project management performance, *International Journal of Project Management*, **29**(1), pp.108–116.
Williamson, O.E. (1985), *The Economic Institutions of Capitalism*, New York: Free Press.

Succession planning

Succession planning refers to the plans an organization makes to fill its key executive positions. This deliberate and systematic effort by the organization is to ensure leadership continuity by establishing a talent pipeline, a process to develop and replace key staff arising from promotions, retirements, serious illnesses, death and any new positions which may be created in future organization plans.

While succession planning can be used to motivate and retain members of the organization, without 'new blood' there is a risk that the organization can become 'stale'. In addition, it is necessary to recruit employees with different skills and experiences and to improve employee diversity. Therefore, there is the need to balance recruitment from the internal and external labour markets.

In stable economic environments, the traditional approach to succession planning relied on identifying an individual or a few key individuals who would be ready to take on the key executive positions at certain points in time. However, businesses operate in an increasingly complex and rapidly changing environment. The key challenge is to identify the competencies that will contribute to organizational performance in a future that is uncertain. The focus is on developing talent for groups of jobs as well as planning for jobs that do not yet exist, rather than those that have been valued in the past (Beardwell and Claydon, 2010).

Key elements of a succession plan identified by Larcker and Saslow (2014) include a shared vision of the future direction of the organization, identification of high-level development plans for each potential successor, coaching and mentoring promising senior executives, developing a skills and experience profile for the future chief executive officer as well as for key senior executive positions, nurturing a culture of management development and identification of high-performing external candidates.

Selecting potential successors is more challenging in small family organizations when compared to large organizations. Some of the issues include the reluctance of founders to withdraw from the business and the lack of grooming of the next generation within the family and managing the transition (Ibrahim et al., 2003). The direct consequence of the lack of proper succession planning can cause the failure of these organizations. When implemented well, succession planning ensures stability and continuity of leadership, providing confidence to investors and the organizational preparedness to thrust the business to the next level.

Chris Rowley and Nagiah Ramasamy

See also:

Careers; Human resource planning; Management development; Mentoring; Talent management; Training and development; Workforce intelligence planning.

References and selected further readings

Beardwell, J. and T. Claydon (2010), *Human Resource Management: A Contemporary Approach*, 6th edn, Essex: Prentice Hall.

Burack, E.H. (1998), *Creative Human Resource Planning and Applications: A Strategic Approach*, New Jersey: Prentice Hall.

Garg, A.K. and E. Van Weele (2012), Succession planning and its impact on the performance of small micro medium enterprises within the manufacturing sector in Johannesburg, *International Journal of Business and Management*, 7(9), pp.96–107.

Ibrahim, A.B., K. Soufani and J. Lam (2003), Family business training: a Canadian perspective, *Education and Training*, 45(8/9), pp.474–482.

Larcker, D.F. and S. Saslow (2014), *Report on Senior Executive Succession Planning and Talent Development*, Stanford: Stanford University, the Institute of Executive Development, Rock Center for Corporate Governance and Stanford Graduate School of Business.

Stadler, K. (2011), Talent reviews: the key to effective succession management, *Business Strategy Series*, **12**(5), pp. 264–271.

Suggestion scheme

A suggestion scheme is a formal mechanism that enables employees to voice their concerns and encourages employees to contribute constructive ideas and recommendations for improving their organization. Suggestions may range from employee concerns, such as workplace conditions, through to suggestions on improving organizational processes and systems. The first documented employee suggestion scheme was established by the Eastman Kodak Co in 1898 (Matthes, 1992) and empirical studies (Dundon et al., 2005) suggest that suggestion schemes are still a popular tool used for employee participation and involvement in organizations.

Suggestion schemes can take a number of forms, from the traditional box on the wall, where employees may anonymously post their suggestions, through to electronic filing and the use of more innovative technological systems, such as a purpose-built intranet. The suggestion will typically be reviewed by a person or committee within the organization to evaluate its value or merit. Organizations will often provide rewards or compensation for suggestions made, particularly those related to innovation and improving productivity and efficiency.

Suggestion schemes serve a number of purposes. First, they provide employees with an opportunity to participate within the organization. Second, they encourage organizational learning through the transfer of employees' tacit knowledge. Third, they are a source of capturing innovative ideas and identifying concerns and potential issues that may harm the organization. Thus, they are an effective means of facilitating continuous improvement.

The successful implementation of a suggestion scheme relies on several factors. In its start-up, a champion within the organization is needed to create and implement the suggestion scheme. Once established, the process for submitting and monitoring the suggestions should be relatively simple and not be time-consuming. To ensure its longevity, the support and commitment of management is essential, along with ongoing feedback to employees (Rapp and Eklund, 2002). Key to its success is trust in management, as employees are more likely to engage in using the suggestion scheme when they believe their ideas are being listened to and rewarded (Clegg et al., 2002).

PAULA K. MOWBRAY

See also:

Communication; Consultation; Employee involvement; Employee voice; Grievance procedure.

References and selected further readings

Clegg, C., K. Unsworth, O. Epitropaki and G. Parker (2002), Implicating trust in the innovation process, *Journal of Occupational and Organizational Psychology*, **75**(4), pp. 409–422.
Dundon, T., A. Wilkinson, M. Marchington and P. Ackers (2005), The management of voice in non-union organisations: managers' perspectives, *Employee Relations*, **27**(3), pp. 307–319.
Matthes, K. (1992), What's the big idea? Empower employees through suggestion, *HR Focus*, **69**(10), p. 17.

Rapp, C. and J. Eklund (2002), Sustainable development of improvement activities – the long-term operation of a suggestion scheme in a Swedish company, *Total Quality Management*, **13**(7), pp. 945–969.
Schuring, R.W. and H. Luijten (2001), Reinventing suggestion systems for continuous improvement, *International Journal of Technology Management*, **22**(4), pp. 359–372.

Summary dismissal

Summary dismissal occurs where an employer dismisses an employee or worker 'on the spot' without notice. A summary dismissal will only be lawful in certain circumstances. According to contract law, the breach of a fundamental contract term repudiates the contract. A fundamental breach of contract gives the innocent party (here the employer) a choice as to whether to accept the other party's (employee or worker) repudiation and rescind the contract or to affirm and continue the contract. It should be noted that not all contract terms will be considered fundamental terms such that a breach would repudiate the contract, only those terms that are central or 'go to the root of the contract' are fundamental. A key issue in determining the lawfulness of a summary dismissal at contract law is whether the employee or worker's actions amounted to a fundamental breach of contract. If the summary dismissal is unlawful, then the employee or worker will have a claim of wrongful dismissal.

For a summary dismissal to be considered fair for the purposes of the statutory right not to be unfairly dismissed (Employment Rights Act 1996, section 94), the employer would need to show that the dismissal was for a fair reason (these are listed in section 98(2)) and an employment tribunal would need to surmise that the employer had acted reasonably in treating that as sufficient reason to dismiss the employee (section 98(4)). A key factor in establishing reasonableness is the question of procedural fairness. While a failure to follow a procedure will not automatically render a dismissal unfair (*Polkey v A E Dayton (Services) Ltd*), procedure is one of the factors to be weighed by an employment tribunal in deciding whether or not the decision to dismiss was reasonable. The Acas code of practice on disciplinary and grievance procedures (Acas, 2015) sets out good practice guidance to help employers, employees and their representatives to deal with disciplinary situations within the workplace. Although the code is not legally binding, it can be admitted as evidence in an employment tribunal and employment tribunals have the discretion to increase or decrease compensation awarded by up to 25 per cent where there has been an unreasonable failure to comply with the code (Trade Union and Labour Relations (Consolidation) Act 1992, section 207A). The code notes that some acts (gross misconduct) are so serious that they may warrant a dismissal without notice for a first offence (paragraph 23). However, it goes on to state that a fair disciplinary process should always be followed before dismissing for gross misconduct. The code suggests that disciplinary rules should give examples of actions that the employer regards as gross misconduct (paragraph 24). There may be circumstances, therefore, where a summary dismissal would be lawful at common law and yet would be considered an unfair dismissal under the statutory provisions.

LIZ OLIVER

See also:

Discipline and grievance; Dismissal.

References and selected further readings

Acas (2015), *Code of Practice 1—Disciplinary and Grievance Procedures (Revised 2015)*, London: Acas, www. acas.org.uk/dgcode.

Emir, A. (2014), *Selwyn's Law of Employment*, 18th edn, Oxford: Oxford University Press.

Willey, B. (2012), *Employment Law in Context: An Introduction for HR Professionals*, 4th edn, Harlow: Pearson.

Systematic training cycle

The systematic training cycle is the recurring process of determining training needs, designing appropriate training programmes and resources, implementing the training programs and evaluating the effectiveness of the training. The methodology most used to develop systematic training programmes is the instructional systems design (ISD), which originated soon after WWII (Swanson and Holton, 2001). ISD is the methodical process of converting principles of learning and training into plans for instructional materials, activities, resources and evaluation (Smith and Ragan, 1999).

Contemporary systematic and systemic training is believed to have originated from Training Within Industry (TWI), a project applied by the military in the United States during World War II (Ruona, 2001). Training requirements post-World War II were the motivation for the development of the systematic training stages used for military personnel. The training was based on the 'analysis, design, develop, implement and evaluate' (ADDIE) model (Gagne et al., 2005). Most of the systematic training models developed, and there are more than 100 variations, have their foundation in the ADDIE model (Gagne et al., 2005).

While the ADDIE model provided a systematic approach to design and development well-suited to the military at the time, it was deemed too rigid in other contexts. Consequently it has been continually developed to suit organizational and contextual differences. For example, one model considers ADDIE as an interactive training process with a flexible starting point chosen to fit the current situation, rather than a fixed cycle beginning with 'analysis' and terminating with 'evaluation'.

Current developments in technology, diversity and organizational competitiveness have posed continual challenges to the training industry. It is evident that a move to flexibility within the training context is required in the modern organizational environment. More importantly, it is vital that professionals understand and know how to use the systematic training cycle effectively as simply enhancing the ADDIE methodology will not suffice. The systematic training cycle has proven to provide long-lasting results with learners developing the required expertise and ultimately contributing to organizational objectives and performance (Gagne et al., 2005).

KATHRYN MOURA

See also:

Training; Training evaluation.

References and selected further readings

Allen, W.C. (2006), Overview and evolution of the ADDIE training system, *Advances in Developing Human Resources*, **8**(4), pp. 430–441.

Gagne, R.M., W.W. Wager, K.C. Golas and J.M. Keller (2005), *Principles of Instructional Design*, Belmont: Wadsworth/Thompson Learning.

Ruona, W.E.A. (2001), The foundational impact of the Training within Industry project on the human resource development profession: origins of contemporary human resource development, *Advances in Developing Human Resources*, **3**(2), pp. 119–126.

Smith, P.L. and T.J. Ragan (1999), *Instructional Design*, 2nd edn, Columbus, OH: Merrill/Prentice Hall.

Swanson, R.A. (ed.) (2001), Origins of contemporary human resource development, *Advances in Developing Human Resources*, **3**(2), pp. 115–290.

Swanson, R.A. and E.F. Holton (2001), *Foundations of Human Resource Development*, San Francisco: Berrett-Koehler.

Talent management

Talent management is broadly defined as the identification, development and retention of talent. Talent management, however, varies in meaning and conceptualization in terms of to whom talent refers and the practices incorporated in managing such individuals. Its emergence is primarily attributed to the McKinsey consultancy group when it suggested that a war for talent was emerging. Since this point there has been substantial interest in the topic in the both the practitioner and academic lexicons. Much of the early attention has focused on whether talent management was a fad and if it referred to anything more than a rebranding of HRM or employee development. It appears some decades later that such accusations are less commonly made as the field has developed at an impressive rate.

Why has talent management emerged as an important concept? The interest in 'talented' or 'star' employees is not necessarily a new feature of organizational life. What, however, appears to be new is the far greater acknowledgement and appreciation of the importance of human capital in delivering organizational strategy and the concerns organizations have in attracting, motivating and retaining staff. External business conditions now encompass much greater competition than previously, the continual advancement of information technologies continues apace, globalization pressures are leading to increasing internationalization of small and medium-sized enterprises and the emerging countries of China and India are now powerful forces, meaning that more organizations, industries and countries are competing for talent. Further, the working population has never been as diverse and the demographical profile of countries continues to change, while the knowledge worker has strongly emerged in the burgeoning global services industry. It is the combination of these factors that primarily lie behind the emergence of the talent management phenomenon.

One of the most pertinent issues in the talent management literature is the question of what, or who, is talent? This traditionally has been overlooked, with the term 'talent' being used without clearly setting out or defining as to what it means or to whom it refers. Talent is often viewed from the perspective of someone possessing natural ability or innateness, mastering a particular skill or competence, and commitment to the job and organization. In considering what talent is, one is inevitably drawn to the question of inclusiveness or exclusiveness. For some, talent management refers to realizing the full potential of each individual, thus a very inclusive, encompassing approach. In other words, each individual has talent that can and should be fostered in order to be fully realized. The other approach, which appears as the most commonly viewed, calls for a more exclusive or elitist focus on a small segment. This perspective is very focused on some people possessing greater skills, ability and/or potential than others, which can benefit the organization.

The inclusive approach can stand accused of being little more than a rebranding exercise for HRM and employee development. The more exclusive approach tends to be much more focused on methodically identifying the pivotal positions in an organization, and placing the highest-performing staff in such roles, developing talent pools of high potentials (i.e., those individuals with the ability to move into key positions) and managing these through appropriate HR practices. The key differentiator to HRM appears to be the call for a systematic identification of pivotal positions, or in other words, the most strategically important positions, which may vary from organizational context to context. It is these roles that disproportionally impact the success or otherwise of an organization, and where the performance of an individual can have a significantly positive or negative impact. The identification of truly strategic roles, i.e., those roles where changes in talent can lead to the greatest impact on executing corporate strategy, is a significant challenge for organizations.

A key area of concern in a more exclusive talent management approach is the decision on whether individuals are informed of their status. There seems to be considerable differences in the performance levels, commitment and turnover intentions between employees that are identified as 'talent' and those who are not. There certainly appears to be some sort of positive motivational aspect for those identified as talent but there is concern of the impact on those who are not. Where more exclusive approaches are adopted and individuals are informed, the perceived fairness of the system of talent identification will be vital to reducing the potential negative fallout from staff that do not 'make the cut'. In addition, any approach needs to be counterbalanced with providing each individual with support and development opportunities and that they may be included in the future. Thus, talent management needs to be a dynamic process. To turn to a sports analogy, you want to incorporate the potential 'late developer'. There is a need for greater scholarship in these areas.

Talent management is intrinsically linked to workforce segmentation and differentiated HR architectures or systems. Not all employees are the same in terms of their expectations and organizational contribution. Consequently, a monolithic approach to people management is unlikely to be the optimum approach. The argument proposed is that different HR systems should be applied to different groups or talent pools depending on their strategic value. Consequently, HR practices (e.g., rewards systems, development activities) should be targeted to particular groups.

ANTHONY MCDONNELL

See also:
Knowledge worker.

References and selected further readings

Bjorkman, I., M. Ehrnrooth, K. Makela, A. Smale and J. Sumelius (2013), Talent or not? Employee reactions to talent identification, *Human Resource Management*, **52**, pp. 195–214.
Chambers, E.G, M. Foulon, H. Handfield-Jones and E. Michaels (1998), The war for talent, *McKinsey Quarterly*, **3**, pp. 44–57.
Collings, D.G. and K. Mellahi (2009), Strategic talent management: a review and research agenda, *Human Resource Management Review*, **19**, pp. 304–313.
Lewis, R.E. and R.J. Heckman (2006), Talent management: a critical review, *Human Resource Management Review*, **16**, pp. 139–154.
McDonnell, A. (2011), Still fighting the 'war for talent': bridging the science versus practice gap, *Journal of Business and Psychology*, **26**, pp. 169–173.

Team-based appraisal

Team-based appraisal assesses the performance of teamwork on organization performance. Team-based appraisals can range from recognition of individual performance and its contribution to group outcomes to an assessment of overall group performance. When only an organization's performance is evaluated, no individual appraisals are completed and individuals do not receive performance ratings. Complications exist for team-based appraisals due to the importance of balancing both the individual and the team performance. Also, the appraisal must include non-traditional performance criteria such as teamwork or cooperation (Levy and Williams, 2004). Effective team-based appraisals should include a multi-source rating of both individual and team performance (e.g., quality, knowledge), objective measures of individual and team performance (e.g., quantity, defects) as well as measures of teamwork (communication, conflict resolution skills). Legal challenges are an important consideration for team-based appraisal systems, with increasing issues of accuracy and fairness, especially with multi-rater systems. Accuracy and fairness can be enhanced through organizations ensuring that their instruments are highly reliable and content valid (Valle and Davis, 1999).

Team members are often an effective way to evaluate team members' performance due to the personal knowledge and experience that they have working with them. It is argued that team members know each other's performance better than managers or supervisors and can evaluate their peers more accurately. Since teams will often work together through various appraisal cycles, there is also the opportunity for members to reflect and make improvements. Team member evaluation supports the development of assessment skills among team members who function as evaluators. Team members also become more aware of performance standards and behaviour requirements because they are accountable for maintaining them.

Team-based appraisals should be customized for different types of teams within the organization. For example, work teams that are fairly stable should focus on the competencies, behaviours and outcomes of the team. However, teams that are more dynamic and undefined may need to focus more on the actual competencies and behaviours of the individual team members. The alignment of team characteristics, target outcomes, rating source and purpose is critical for effective team-based performance appraisals (Scott and Einstein, 2001).

AMIE SOUTHCOMBE

See also:

Performance appraisal.

References and selected further readings

Farr, J.L. and P.E. Levy (2007), Performance appraisal, in L.L. Koppes (ed.), *Historical Perspectives in Industrial and Organizational Psychology*, New York: Psychology Press, pp. 311–327.

Levy, P.E. and L.A. Steelman (1997), Performance appraisal for team-based organizations: a prototypical multiple rater system, in M. Beyerlein, D. Johnson and S. Beyerlein (eds), *Advances in Interdisciplinary Studies of Work Teams: Team Implementation Issues*, Greenwich: JAI Press, pp. 141–165.

Levy, P.E. and J.R. Williams (2004), The social context of performance appraisal: a review and framework for the future, *Journal of Management*, **30**(6), pp. 881–905.

Reilly, R.R. and J. McGourty (1998), Performance appraisal in team settings, in J.W. Smither (ed.), *Performance Appraisal: State of the Art in Practice*, New York: Wiley, pp. 244–277.

Scott, S.G. and W.O. Einstein (2001), Strategic performance appraisal in team-based organizations: one size does not fit all, *The Academy of Management Executive*, **15**(2), pp. 107–116.

Valle, M. and K. Davis (1999), Teams and performance appraisal: using metrics to increase reliability and validity, *Team Performance Management*, **5**(8), pp. 238–244.

Team briefing

Team briefing is a form of one-way communication as information is given and 'cascaded' down through organizational levels. It is seen as an important means to communicate downwards to groups of managers and employees throughout an organization (Rose, 2008). Often part of the team brief has core information relating to corporate issues, supplemented by more local news at each stage. It may concern general information on goals and performance and explain reasons for decisions concerning aspects of change.

Team briefing evolved from the ideas of briefing groups (Adair and Thomas, 2003), first promoted in the UK by the Industrial Society from the 1960s. It has been recognized as an important tool for organizations to communicate internally since the end of 1970s (Farrant, 2003). The management principles underlying team briefing is that good communications are an essential part of organizational effectiveness because team briefing enables regular face-to-face meetings of small groups that are relevant to their work to be planned and conducted systematically by team leaders and provides opportunities for questions. Therefore, team briefing as a system is designed to reflect the unitarist approach to human resource management and employee involvement, which ensures that all employees from executive management down to the shop or office floor are fully informed of matters that affect their work (Gennard and Judge, 1997).

However, the benefits of team briefing may not be easily achieved in reality because it can have a number of problems and pitfalls. Often it can be difficult to set up team briefing meetings within a workplace that operates on a continuous shift-working basis or when organizations are widely dispersed geographically (Marchington and Parker, 1990). The content of briefs is the other most common issue as employees may get irrelevant content when the agenda is driven from the top rather than by demand, or when managers do not have sufficient skill to present material in a manner that makes it relevant (Marchington et al., 1989). Also, there are issues when many people are involved in leading the briefing meetings. Briefings can also be irregular, dispensable in terms of pressure and variable in coverage. In short, team briefings are not the panacea that too many managers think they are because they are too often simply top-down, one-way communications giving information of limited utility about decisions already made with no opportunity for influence or feedback.

QI WEI AND CHRIS ROWLEY

See also:

Communication; Employee involvement; Employee voice.

References and selected further readings

Adair, J. and N. Thomas (2003), Briefings, in N. Thomas (ed.), *Concise Adair on Communication & Presentation Skills*, London: Thorogood, pp. 55–66.
Farrant, J. (2003), Face-to-face communication, in J. Farrant (ed.) *Internal Communications*, London: Thorogood, pp. 50–61.
Gennard, J. and G. Judge (1997), *Employee Relations*, London: IPD.
Marchington, M. and P. Parker (1990), *Changing Patterns of Employee Relations*, Hemel Hempstead: Harvester Wheatsheaf.

Marchington, M., P. Parker, P. and A. Prestwich (1989), Problems with team briefing in practice, *Employee Relations*, 11(4), pp. 21–30.
Rose, E. (2008), *Employment Relations*, 3rd edn, Essex: Pearson Education.

Team pay

In team-based reward schemes, performance-related bonuses are distributed among the members of the team to recognize the overall performance of the group. Team pay relates to small work groups, and can be distinguished from large group incentives such as gainsharing or profit-sharing.

Team pay has increased in popularity since the 1990s as teamworking has become a more prevalent form of working, identified as a so-called 'high-performance work practice' or 'best practice' approach to HR. Team pay aims to recognize the interdependence between jobs in teams, thereby acknowledging that it is difficult to isolate individual team members' contributions to team outcomes. One aim of team pay is to overcome some of the issues relating to individual performance-related pay. In particular, individual incentives might create within-group competition and be a risk to team cohesion.

There are many factors that might influence the approach to the design of team pay taken by an organization. Two particularly important factors are the types of work teams present in the organization, and the distribution of rewards within the team.

Gross (1995) suggests three main categories of teams: In 'process teams' (also known as work teams), workers are structured into permanent team structures with interdependent tasks. Such teams are more common in manufacturing or service industries. Second, 'project teams' focus on a finite package of work, which could be short or long-term, with individual team members holding different specialities, which are interdependent. Finally in 'parallel teams' team members are likely to be drawn from different functional areas and meet to focus on solving particular problems. Quality circles and health and safety groups are common forms of parallel teams. The level of team interdependence and cohesiveness in these types of teamworking is likely to impact on the effectiveness of team pay. Balkin and Montemayor (2000) suggest that team-based pay is more appropriate for process and project teams than parallel teams because the former types are more interdependent and autonomous. Incentives for project teams are more likely to be paid at the completion of the project whereas process teams may be more periodic and based on the organization's performance evaluation cycle.

With respect to the organization's philosophy towards pay distribution, team-based pay schemes can be distributed according to four main methods (Shields, 2007). First, they can take an equality approach, in which incentives are divided equally among team members, regardless of individual contribution. This is, therefore, more effective when team members are doing similar jobs, at the same level, and making comparable contributions to team performance. Second, team-pay might be distributed based on a percentage of individuals' base pay. This may be more effective when team members are doing different jobs, or are on different pay grades. The third approach, based on the principle of equity, distributes the reward amongst the team based on individual performance rating, thereby recognizing individual contributions to the team. This might be seen as a more strategic approach to team pay, and aims to combat 'freeloading' which is a potential risk with teamworking (Heneman and von Hipple, 1995). In the final approach, teams can be rewarded with non-cash rewards that aim to recognize both individual and team performance. The decision of which type of scheme to operate is likely to be influenced by organizational culture and philosophy and what the organization aims to achieve with the team pay.

REBECCA HEWETT

See also:
Performance-related pay; Profit-related pay and gainsharing; Profit-sharing; Teamwork.

References and selected further readings

Balkin, D.B. and E.F. Montemayor (2000), Explaining team-based pay: a contingency perspective based on the organizational life cycle, team design, and organizational learning literatures, *Human Resource Management Review*, **10**(3), pp. 249–269.
DeMatteo, J.S., L.T. Eby and E. Sundstrom (1998), Team based rewards: current empirical evidence and directions for future research, *Research in Organizational Behavior*, **20**, pp. 141–183.
Gross, S. (1995), *Compensation in Teams*, New York: American Management Association.
Heneman, R.L. and C. von Hipple (1995), Balancing group and individual rewards: rewarding individual contributions to the team, *Compensation and Benefits Review*, **27**(4), pp. 63–68.
Perkins, S.J. and G. White (2011), *Reward Management: Alternatives, Consequences and Contexts*, 2nd edn, London: Chartered Institute of Personnel Development.
Shields, J. (2007), *Managing Employee Performance and Reward: Concepts, Practices and Strategies*, Cambridge: Cambridge University Press.

Teamwork

By 'teamwork' here we refer to the internal dynamics of a team of employees. Our focus is thus on the operation and the development of the team itself, rather than on the organization of which the team is a part. The two levels are, of course, intimately connected with each other, but from the point of view of analysis it makes sense to consider them separately – at least in the first instance.

A first set of issues concerns the composition of a team. Some research, for example, has examined whether a team operates better if its members are all alike in some way, or whether there are benefits to be gained – in such areas as innovation and creativity – from having a more dissimilar or heterogeneous membership. A particularly influential approach in the area of team composition has been developed by Meredith Belbin (1981, 1993), who identified a certain number of team roles (e.g., implementer, completer-finisher) that a successful team was likely to include. This model is widely used, but its assumptions and its implications have also been called into question on a number of different grounds (Aritzeta et al., 2007).

A second set of issues covers how teams might develop over time. Tuckman's (1965) model of the 'stages of group development' had four stages: forming, storming, norming and performing. Like Belbin's, this model has been widely used in organization; also like Belbin's, its underpinnings have been called into question. Other work has identified different kinds of trajectories for teams. Gersick (e.g., 1988) has used the idea of 'punctuated equilibrium' to argue that teams, rather than moving smoothly between different stages of development, instead experience change through a series of more abrupt jumps.

A third, more recent concern of work on teams has been to put their internal dynamics in a much more direct relationship with performance. Important here is the work of Katzenbach and Smith (1993). Their book, *The Wisdom of Teams*, described team development in terms of the 'team performance curve', along which a team might start as a 'working group' and go through various stages before emerging as a 'high performing team'.

STEPHEN PROCTER

See also:

High-involvement management; Self-managed teams.

References and selected further readings

Aritzeta, A., S. Swailes and B. Senior (2007), Belbin's team role model: development, validity and applications for team building, *Journal of Management Studies*, **44**(1), pp. 96–118.
Belbin, R.M. (1981), *Management Teams: Why They Succeed or Fail*, London: Heinemann (3rd edn, 2010).
Belbin, R.M. (1993), *Team Roles at Work*, Oxford: Butterworth-Heinemann (2nd edn, 2010).
Gersick, C. (1988), Time and transition in work teams: toward a new model of group development, *Academy of Management Journal*, **31**(1), pp. 9–41.
Katzenbach, J. and D. Smith (1993), *The Wisdom of Teams*, Cambridge, MA: Harvard Business School Press.
Tuckman, B. (1965), Developmental sequence in small groups, *Psychological Bulletin*, **63**(6), pp. 384–399.

Telework and coworking

Telework, or telecommuting is 'work performed within the home or from a satellite office space' (Shin et al., 2000, p. 85) where an employee has access to technologies that enable them to work from such locations. This form of working can have numerous benefits for employees, with improvements such as increases in job satisfaction by providing flexible work options to enable a better work–life balance, reduced commute times and a reduction in employee stress. Telework is somewhat different to 'homeworking' where people are primarily employed to perform work solely within their own homes (e.g., renowned in the textile and clothing industry), as opposed to teleworkers who may have the choice or opportunity to work from home due to an organization implementing and supporting policies and practices that allow workers to complete set tasks at home and/ or to provide flexibility to support work–family needs.

Coworking is a more recent phenomenon emerging from traditional forms of teleworking, and has recently gained attention in the academic literature. There is also emerging interest from business and government in the usage of coworking space by employees that has implications for the development of organizational teleworking policies. Coworking centres provide technologically equipped offices resulting from the benefits of 'cloud computing' technologies and provide the opportunity for social interaction and collaboration with other, often unaffiliated coworking centre users. Such arrangements can offer additional benefits for employees and business for collaboration and innovation rather than working from home or within a traditional office environment. Coworking centres have become popular for small start-up firms and entrepreneurs, enabling them to move out of the home office and/or save on costs of renting traditional office space. These centres also provide flexibility around the needs of the user or business. Space can be rented from a couple of hours per week for a 'hot desk' space, to daily, weekly or monthly usage that may incorporate a variety of additional services provided (e.g., mail service and boardroom and meeting spaces) depending upon the price structure selected.

SUSAN RESSIA AND PETER ROSS

See also:

Homeworking.

References and selected further readings

Bosua, R., M. Gloet, S. Kurnia, A. Mendoza and J. Yong (2013), Telework, productivity and wellbeing: an Australian perspective, *Telecommunications Journal of Australia*, **63**(1), pp. 11.1–11.12.

De Jong, A. and E. Mante-Meijer (2008), Teleworking behind the front door: the patterns and meaning of telework in the everyday lives of workers, in E. Loos, E. Mante-Meijer and L. Haddon (eds), *The Social Dynamics of Information and Communication Technology*, Burlington: Ashgate, pp. 171–187.

Ellison, N.B. (2004), *Telework and Social Change*, Westport, CT: Praeger.

Ross, P.K. and S. Ressia (2015), Neither office nor home: coworking as an emerging workplace choice, *Employment Relations Record*, **15**(1), pp. 42–57.

Shin, B., O.R. Sheng and K. Higa (2000), Telework: existing research and future directions, *Journal of Organizational Computing and Electronic Commerce*, **10**(2), pp. 85–101.

Spinuzzi, C. (2012), Working alone together: coworking as emergent collaborative activity, *Journal of Business and Technical Communication*, **26**(4), pp. 399–441.

Temporary work

Temporary work covers a wide range of contractual arrangements. It is typically taken to comprise casual, seasonal, fixed-term contract and temporary agency working arrangements. It is important to note that the meaning and nature of temporary work varies markedly across countries, shaped by institutional and cultural norms, and labour market regulation. Temporary work is usually contrasted with more permanent, ongoing employment relationships, although the boundaries between temporary and permanent work are often blurred. In reality, there are more differences than similarities between the individual forms of temporary work listed above.

There has been much academic interest in temporary work, with attention focusing on the reasons why employers seek recourse to such arrangements, the implications of temporary work for those who undertake it, and the regulation of temporary employment. Temporary employment was a key feature of the much-debated flexible firm model, for example, with some temporary forms of employment identified as part of a 'periphery' used by employers to provide a numerical buffer for a 'core' workforce. As critics pointed out however, temporary workers were increasingly likely to be part of a core workforce, particularly in sectors where the use of temporary work was commonplace (Pollert, 1991). Other 'demand-focused' models, such as the 'resource based view' of the firm have sought to identify the circumstances where temporary workers may provide strategic value to firms.

There has also been an increasing interest in understanding the reasons why workers undertake temporary work and their experiences. Many forms of temporary employment, particularly seasonal, casual and temporary agency employment appear to be of lower quality, on average, to permanent employment, when judged in terms of pay levels and subjective indicators of job quality (see Conley, 2008; Forde and Slater, 2005; Green, 2008). Regulation of temporary work in different countries reflects quite varying traditions and norms of use of individual forms of temporary employment. In Europe, equal treatment directives have sought to provide a base level of protection for temporary workers, although differences in national level implementation have resulted in gaps in protection, and scope for employers to move towards less regulated forms of temporary contracts. The scope and varying nature of temporary work has also posed challenges to trade unions in the development of effective organizing and mobilization strategies (see Heery, 2009).

CHRIS FORDE AND GARY SLATER

See also:

Employment agency; Fixed-term contract; Flexible firm; Temporary worker.

References and selected further readings

Conley, H. (2008), The nightmare of temporary work: a comment on Fevre, *Work, Employment and Society*, **22**(4), pp. 731–736.
Forde, C. and G. Slater (2005), Agency working in Britain, character, consequence and regulation, *British Journal of Industrial Relations*, **43**(2), pp. 249–271.
Green, F. (2008), *Demanding Work: The Paradox of Job Quality in the Affluent Economy*, Princeton: Princeton University Press.
Heery, E. (2009), Trade unions and contingent labour: scale and method, *Cambridge Journal of Regions, Economy and Society*, **2**(3), pp. 429–442.
Pollert, A. (1991), *Farewell to Flexibility*, London: Wiley Blackwell.

Temporary worker

There is no standard legal definition of the expression 'temporary worker'. As such, it is a term of art, rather than a legal concept. However, European law and domestic UK law both recognise the concept of the 'part-time' 'employee' or 'worker'; for example, Clause 3 of the Agreement annexed to the European Directive on Part-time Work 97/81/EC (OJ 1998 L14/9) (PTWD) and Regulation 2(2) of the Part-Time Workers Regulations (SI 2000/1551) (PTWR). The latter prescribes that a 'part-time worker' is a worker who 'is paid wholly or in part by reference to the time he works and, having regard to the custom and practice of the employer in relation to workers employed by the worker's employer under the same type of contract, is not identifiable as a full-time worker'. As such, whether a 'worker' or 'employee' is engaged on a 'part-time' basis hangs on the definition of 'full-time' in Regulation 2(1) of the PTWR, which provides that an individual is working 'full-time' 'if he is paid wholly or in part by reference to the time he works and, having regard to the custom and practice of the employer in relation to workers employed by the worker's employer under the same type of contract, is identifiable as a full-time worker'.

The significance of the concept of temporary worker and part-time worker or employee is attributable to the statutory protection afforded to such individuals by the PTWD and PTWR. For instance, Regulation 5 of the PTWR stipulates that it is unlawful for an employer to treat a part-time worker less favourably than a comparable full-time worker in two particular contexts. First, in respect of the contractual terms of the part-time worker's contract, such as pay, remuneration and conditions conferring contractual benefits. Second, it is also a breach of the legislation for an employer to subject the part-time worker to a detriment because he/she is a part-time worker. However, the employer has a defence to such allegations of disparity of treatment vis-à-vis its part-time and full-time workers or employees, namely that it is justifiable on objective grounds.

The majority of the scholarship addressing the regulation of temporary workers and part-time workers focuses on the social and economic justifiability of the use of such contracts, whether restrictions ought to be placed on the use of such contracts by employers and, most importantly, whether the terms of the PTWD and PTWR provide sufficiently robust employment protection for such individuals (McColgan, 2000; Bell, 2011). In particular, the main criticism of the PTWD and PTWR is that they fail to facilitate transitions in working patterns; for example, from full-time work to part-time work, or vice versa (McCann, 2008). Furthermore, it is argued that such temporary work or part-time work arrangements do not necessarily serve as a stepping stone to more permanent full-time (Booth et al., 2002).

DAVID CABRELLI

See also:

Employee; Employment agency; Part-time working; Temporary work; Worker.

References and selected further readings

Bell, M. (2011), Achieving the objectives of the part-time work directive? Revisiting the part-time workers regulations, *Industrial Law Journal*, **40**, pp. 254–279.
Booth, A., M. Francesconi and J. Frank (2002), Temporary jobs: stepping stones or dead ends? *Economic Journal*, **112**, pp. F189–F213.
McCann, D. (2008), *Regulating Flexible Work*, Oxford: Oxford University Press.
McColgan, A. (2000), 'Missing the point? The Part-Time Workers (Prevention of Less Favourable Treatment) Regulations 2000, *Industrial Law Journal*, **29**, pp. 260–267.

Term-time working

Under a term-time only working arrangement, a person is contracted to work only during the school term times. The employee remains on a permanent contract and, although working fewer than 52 weeks a year, they will normally have their pay averaged over 12 months. Many organizations stipulate that term-time only staff are only allowed to take holiday in weeks when their attendance is not required.

This working arrangement is obviously attractive to parents with younger children and gives employers the opportunity to tap into a labour market of people who are unwilling to work throughout the year. The fact that the time off is planned ahead also gives employers plenty of time to schedule cover for the absence/s. However the long absences during peak holiday times can present cover problems and there may be pressure on other work colleagues who are unable to take time off during the school holidays and resentment may build up. There is also evidence that term-time working is significantly associated with higher levels of absence (BIS 2014b).

The Work–Life Balance (WLB) Employer Survey (BIS 2014a) of workplaces in

Great Britain shows that although the availability of term-time working has increased over the past decade, the proportion of employees taking up these contracts has reduced: 38 per cent of employers reported that term-time only working was available in their establishment compared to 31 per cent in 2003, but 13 per cent of employees worked on this basis in comparison to 16 per cent of employees in 2003. According to the WLB Employee Survey (BIS 2012), employees most likely to take up this arrangement were women, those with caring responsibilities, and those working in the public administration, education and health industry.

SUE HUTCHINSON

See also:

Absence; Family-friendly policies; Flexible working; Flexitime; Work–life balance.

References and selected further readings

BIS (2012), *The Fourth Work–Life Balance Employee Survey*, Employment Relations Research Series 122, www.gov.uk/government/uploads/system/uploads/attachment_data/file/32153/12-p151-fourth-work-life-balance-employee-survey.pdf.

BIS (2014a), *The Fourth Work–Life Balance Employer Survey (2013)*, Research Paper No. 184, www.gov.uk/government/uploads/system/uploads/attachment_data/file/398557/bis-14-1027-fourth-work-life-balance-employer-survey-2013.pdf.

BIS (2014b), *Costings and Benefits to Business of Adopting Work–Life Balance Working Practices: A Literature Review*, Policy Studies Institute, BIS, www.gov.uk/government/uploads/system/uploads/attachment_data/file/323290/bis-14-903-costs-and-benefits-to-business-of-adopting-work-life-balance-working-practices-a-literature-review.pdf.

CIPD (2012), *Flexible Work Provision and Uptake*, London: Chartered Institute of Personnel and Development.

Terms and conditions

Terms are the binding promises exchanged by the parties when a contract is formed. If a contract term is breached, the innocent party will have a remedy in contract law. Commonly this would take the form of damages; a money payment to put the party in the position s/he would have been in had the contract been properly performed. Where a term is central to the contract ('goes to the root of the contact'), a breach of that term would give rise to a fundamental breach of contract. This would allow the innocent party to choose either to accept the repudiation and rescind the contract or to affirm and continue the contract. A decision to rescind the contract would terminate the contact and might be deemed to be a constructive dismissal or summary dismissal depending on whether it was the employer or the worker who was in fundamental breach (see 'Constructive dismissal' and 'Summary dismissal' in this volume). To lawfully change the terms of a contract, agreement of both parties must be obtained and fresh consideration (the element of exchange in a contract) provided.

Contract terms can be expressly agreed (whether oral or in writing) or implied. Terms may be implied by fact (to reflect the unspoken intentions of the parties to a particular contract or to make a contract workable) or by law (by the common law or statute). A set of generic terms are implied by the common law into 'contracts of service' (employment contracts) by virtue of the form that the contract takes (see 'contract of employment'). As a general rule, express terms outweigh implied terms and this makes it possible for the parties to a contract to agree to exclude or to modify the generic implied terms. Terms can be incorporated into a contract from other sources; for example, parts of a collective agreement or employer handbook may be incorporated by a reference within the contract.

Generally the phrase 'terms and conditions' is taken together to mean the binding obligations contained within the contract (the terms). However, sometimes the word 'conditions' is used as a standalone, non-technical term to describe those non-binding, unilateral policies, rules or instructions that determine how the workplace functions. A breach of these would not directly give rise to a remedy in contract law but may, depending on the circumstances, amount to a breach of one of the generic implied terms (such as the duty of the employee to follow reasonable instruction or the duty of the employer to maintain mutual trust and confidence).

LIZ OLIVER

See also:
Contract of employment; Constructive dismissal; Dismissal; Summary dismissal.

References and selected further readings

Collins, H. (2007), Legal responses to the standard form contract of employment', *Industrial Law Journal*, **36**(1), pp. 2–18.
Dolding, L. and C. Fawlk (1992), Judicial understanding of the contract of employment, *The Modern Law Review*, **55**(4), pp. 562–569.
Willey, B. (2012), *Employment Law in Context: An Introduction for HR Professionals*, 4th edn, Harlow: Pearson.

360-degree appraisal

The 360-degree appraisal or multi-source appraisal is a performance appraisal tool that requires the obtainment of feedback from two or more members in the organization. The 360-degree appraisal provides a holistic picture of employee performance and involves seeking performance input from a variety of perspectives, including, subordinates, peers, supervisors and customers. Research argues that the 360-degree appraisal data should only be used for development (personal development plans), rather than evaluative purposes. Traditional job performance ratings are derived from a job analysis of identifiable task or behaviours; however, the 360-degree appraisal rating identifies higher order competencies that include behaviours that are crucial to the organization's success. These competencies are normally broader than job performance ratings (Beehr et al., 2001).

The 360-degree appraisal systems have been implemented in organizations largely as a means to provide developmental feedback for employees. The benefits of a 360-degree appraisal system means that each of the rating sources can provide unique information about the target, multiple ratings provide incremental validity over individual sources, and the feedback from multiple sources will increase the target's self-awareness and lead to behavioural change. Authors have found that the social context (knowledge and experience of the system, individual's self-efficacy, supportive work environment), is important to the success of 360-degree appraisal system (Levy and Williams, 2004). However, often 360-degree appraisals are time-consuming and difficult to coordinate, hence the common reliance upon the immediate supervisor conducting the appraisal in most organizations. In situations, where performance data is reliant upon the immediate supervisor, it is important that various sources of information be sought to better inform and provide evidence in support of decisions made.

AMIE SOUTHCOMBE

See also:

Performance appraisal.

References and selected further readings

Beehr, T.A., L. Ivanitskaya, C.P. Hansen, D. Erofeev and D.M. Gudanowski (2001), Evaluation of 360 degree feedback ratings: relationships with each other and with performance and selection predictors, *Journal of Organizational Behavior*, **22**(7), pp. 775–788.
Ghorpade, J. (2000), Managing five paradoxes of 360-degree feedback, *The Academy of Management Executive*, **14**(1), pp. 140–150.
Lepsinger, R. and A.D. Lucia (2009), *The Art and Science of 360 Degree Feedback*, New Jersey: John Wiley & Sons.
Levy, P.E. and J.R. Williams (2004), The social context of performance appraisal: a review and framework for the future, *Journal of Management*, **30**(6), pp. 881–905.
Mabey, C. (2001), Closing the circle: participant views of a 360 degree feedback programme, *Human Resource Management Journal*, **11**(1), pp. 41–53.
Tornow, W.W. and M. London (1998), *Maximizing the Value of 360-Degree Feedback: A Process for Successful Individual and Organizational Development*, San Francisco: Jossey-Bass Publishers.

Time-based pay

Time-based pay is a system where payment is related to the time you spend at work (e.g., a 40-hour week) rather than the number of things that you do or produce. Employees on similar grades receive the same pay, expressed in either hourly (waged) or salaried terms. Pay is distinguished by an hourly rate of pay, with a specified working week in terms of the normal expected hours. Under wage systems, earnings may consist of many elements, including a basic rate, shift or overtime payments, bonuses and allowances (White and Drucker, 2009).

Under time-based payment systems, employers control over pace and performance is reliant on either direct supervision or the willingness of employees to engage with the task. Time-based pay often provides a baseline from which other wage systems are developed. In comparison, within time-based pay arrangements, salaries are calculated on an annual basis and are normally paid monthly. Although traditionally blue-collar workers have been waged and white-collar worker salaried, there is no clear occupational classification that determines which categories of employees receive wages or salaries.

The main advantages of time-rate pay are said to be: they are simpler for a business to calculate and administer; they are suitable for businesses where employee productivity is not easy to measure; they are easy to understand from an employee's perspective; and they make it easier to plan and budget for employee costs

The main disadvantages of time-rate pay are: does little to encourage greater productivity – there is no incentive to achieve greater output; time-rate payroll costs have a tendency to creep upwards (e.g., due to inflation-related pay rises and employee promotion.

MARK GILMAN

See also:
Payment system; Salary; Wages.

References and selected further readings
Armstrong, M. (2012), *Armstrong's Handbook of Reward Management*, London: Kogan Page.
Gilman, M. (2013), Reward management, in T. Redman and A. Wilkinson (eds), *Contemporary Human Resource Management: Text and Cases*, New York: Pearson.
Perkins, S.J. and G. White (2008), *Employee Reward: Alternatives, Consequences and Contexts*, London: Chartered Institute of Personnel and Development.
White, G. and J. Drucker (2009), *Reward Management: A Critical Text*, London: Routledge.

Total reward

The term 'total reward' implies a holistic approach to the concept of reward management by including both extrinsic elements (to which an explicit monetary value can be allocated) and intrinsic elements (with perceived added value to employees) within the reward package. There is, however, no agreed definition of the term and in some cases it is used to describe simply the total remuneration received by employees (pay and benefits) but not the wider intangible rewards of employment. As Davis (2007, p. 2) suggests: 'It is easy to see how people can use the term . . . only to find that they are referring to very different notions.' The total reward concept can be traced back to theories of high-investment work systems, mutual gains, high-involvement work practices, employee involvement, employee voice, employee wellbeing and the psychological contract. Corby and Lindop (2009) view total reward as everything that is rewarding about working for a particular employer or everything employees receive as a result of their employment. The Chartered Institute of Personnel and Development (CIPD) views total reward as having the possibility of 'being a powerful management tool' but, while fairly easy to understand as a concept, views it as very complex in operation (Richards and Hogg, 2007). The CIPD definition of total reward is: 'A term . . . adopted to describe a reward strategy that brings additional components such as learning and development, together with aspects of the working environment into the benefits package. It goes beyond standard remuneration by embracing the company culture and is aimed at giving all employees a voice in the organisation, with the employer in return receiving an engaged employee performance' (Richards and Hogg 2007, p. 1).

In the wider definition of total reward, the Hay Group divides reward between extrinsic and intrinsic rewards. The extrinsic rewards will include base cash, short-term variable pay (e.g., annual bonuses, commission), long-term incentives (e.g., share ownership or profit-share schemes), passive benefits (e.g., pensions, holidays) and active benefits (e.g., company cars or corporate discounts). The intrinsic elements include engagement factors such as quality of working life and emotional alignment such as leadership, values and organisational reputation. Thompson (2002) argues that total reward combines the following features: holistic, best fit, integrative, strategic, people-centred, customised, distinctive and evolutionary.

Given the importance of non-financial rewards in the psychological literature, the key distinguishing characteristic of total reward is the inclusion of the non-financial elements in the reward proposition to employees. These include the workplace environment and working conditions, learning and development opportunities and intrinsic psychological rewards such as a sense of meaningfulness, choice, growth and community (Heneman, 2007). The working environment will include job design, work–life balance measures and recognition.

The operation of the concept of total reward remains, however, elusive for many employers. According to Brown (2014), the rhetoric has not matched the reality of reward practice over the post-recession period since 2008, at least in the UK, with many employers freezing base pay, reducing pension entitlement and placing more employees on insecure temporary employment contracts.

GEOFF WHITE

See also:

Employee benefits; Employee engagement; Reward management; Wellbeing.

References and selected further reading

Brown, D. (2014), The future of reward management: from total reward strategies to smart rewards, *Compensation and Benefits Review*, **236**(3), pp. 147–151.
Corby, S. and E. Lindop (2009), *Rethinking Reward*, Basingstoke: Palgrave Macmillan.
Davis, M.L. (2007), Total rewards: everything that employees value in the employment relationship, in *WorldatWork Handbook of Compensation, Benefits, and Total Rewards*, New York: John Wiley & Sons.
Heneman, R.L. (2007), *Implementing Total Rewards Strategies*, Alexandria, VA: SHRM Foundation.
Richards, J. and C. Hogg (2007), *Total Reward*, London: Chartered Institute of Personnel and Development.
Thompson, P. (2002), *Total Reward: Executive Briefing*, London: Chartered Institute of Personnel and Development.

Trade union recognition

Trade union recognition can be defined as 'an arrangement that exists where an employer agrees that one or more trade unions will be recognised to represent the interests of some or all of the employees in an organisation' (Dundon and Rollinson, 2011, p. 153). The purposes for which recognition may exist can vary, including both individual types of representation (e.g., grievance or mediation over a complaint) as well for collective bargaining (e.g., about pay or contractual terms, and wages and conditions).

While trade union recognition may be a straightforward definition, it is far from a simple or uncontested concept. It can be controversial because when an employer is asked (or agrees) to meet and bargain with a trade union, considerations invariably involve issues of power, authority and who has legitimacy to agree to rules and regulations affecting human resource practice and policy. Since the emergence of trade unions in the eighteenth century, employers have tended to contest the idea of having to recognize a union for bargaining with workers. Many employers have what can be termed an ideological view, in that the idea of recognizing a trade union interferes with managements' right to manage, or the managerial prerogative (Moore et al., 2013). The latter is often predicated on a somewhat misguided application of the notion of property rights: that is an employer can feel that decisions to determine the rules of employment in a firm are akin to the rights of property ownership (Wedderburn, 2001). However, the regulation of employment and what managers can (and cannot) instruct workers to do is not quite the same as owing a piece of property. Working rules and constitutions can and do affect the health, welfare, pay and overall wellbeing of people. As such there is considerable legislation surrounding employment rights. So too is there protections for trade union recognition.

Although many employers still dislike the idea of having to recognize a trade union, it is now viewed as a Western democratic principle. That is to say, the right to collective bargaining and union representation is regarded in many parts of the world as a defined human right, supported in United Nations Conventions. Yet such protections and rights are only relatively recent (Moore et al., 2013) and the effect of legislation for trade union recognition is debatable (Bogg, 2012).

TONY DUNDON

See also:

Collective bargaining; Managerial control; Representation gap; Union avoidance: substitution and suppression.

References and suggested further readings

Bogg, A.L. (2012), The death of statutory union recognition in the United Kingdom, *Journal of Industrial Relations*, **54**(3), pp. 409–425.
Dundon, T and R. Rollinson (2011), *Understanding Employment Relations*, 2nd edn, London: McGraw-Hill.
Gall, G. and T. Dundon (2013) (eds), *Global Anti-Unionism: Nature, Dynamics, Trajectories and Outcomes*, London: Palgrave Macmillan.
Moore, S., S. McKay and S. Veale (2013), *Statutory Regulation and Employment Relations: The Impact of Statutory Trade Union Recognition*, London: Palgrave Macmillan.
Wedderburn, B. (2001), Collective bargaining or legal enactment: the 1999 Act and union recognition, *Industrial Law Journal*, **29**, pp. 1–42.

Trade unions

A trade union is 'a continuous association of wage [and salary]-earners for the purpose of maintaining or improving the conditions of their working lives' (an early definition by Webb and Webb (1920), updated). Just as a corporation is a collective of capital, so too a union is a collective of labour. Workers come together to form unions to increase their bargaining power. In the absence of this, most workers would have little bargaining power as individuals when negotiating with a corporation. Unions achieve gains for their members by obtaining and exercising power in the workplace and elsewhere. They are recognized as generally reducing inequality in societies.

There are various union personnel. A *union delegate* is an employee chosen to represent the union in dealings with management; s/he may also be known as a 'shop steward', 'workplace union representative', or sometimes by industry-specific terms such as 'mother/father of the chapel'. Delegates are volunteers, usually elected by workplace members, who perform their union duties on an unpaid basis in addition to their normal job. Paid union *officials*, as salaried employees of the union, work solely on union business. Terms used to describe them include 'full-time official', 'organizer' and 'industrial officer', while leaders are usually 'secretaries' or 'presidents'.

Union *density* is the ratio of the number of members to the number of employees in an industry, workplace or country. For most of the twentieth century, unions were at the heart of the industrial relations system. In most industrialized countries, union density declined from the 1980s or 1990s. In some countries, especially some developing countries, unions face hostile governments and active suppression. It can be dangerous work: in 2011, 76 people were killed for union activities around the world. In some countries, only government-approved union federations are officially sanctioned, so competing, more militant and grassroots-based union federations emerge. Sometimes, the difficulties for unions of organizing precarious workers (those in casual jobs or the 'informal' economy) mean that non-government organizations represent such workers.

Union density varies substantially between countries, industries and workplaces. While in most countries only a minor proportion of workplaces are unionized, this is in part because most workplaces are, themselves, very small and therefore difficult to unionize. Many large workplaces have a union presence. At the national level, legal and institutional differences and economic structures are important in explaining differing densities. Below that level, a range of factors beyond size influence union membership, including: employer approaches to unions; unions' ability to find and organize workplaces; union security arrangements; the perceived instrumentality of union membership; employee satisfaction with the union; perceptions of union infighting or relations with management; workplace change; employee involvement in decision-making, and trust of management. In countries with relevant data, unions normally enjoy high levels of membership approval, and a significant minority of non-members would often prefer to belong, if given the opportunity. While union density is considerably lower among young workers, this often reflects low awareness and opportunity (exacerbated by declining parental union membership). Over time, economic forces affect union density, and institutional changes have had a major negative impact, but there is little evidence that changes in employee attitudes explain the decline in density.

Several studies have shown job satisfaction is negatively related to union membership. Three non-exclusive explanations are provided by: frustration-aggression theory (employees join a union because they are frustrated with their job); exit-voice theory (dissatisfied members will stay in a job because the union gives them a voice, while dissatisfied non-members will leave) and adaptive expectations theory (members are more dissatisfied because they have higher expectations of management than do non-members).

Unions mobilize workplace campaigns but campaigns are not confined there. The legal framework substantially affects their ability to deliver gains. Often, unions must combine political lobbying and wide-scale mobilization of other groups with workplace activism. In some countries unions have affiliated with, or created, political parties ('labour parties'). As market liberalism has spread among policymakers since the 1980s, unions have found the political process less beneficial, organizing more difficult and faced more obstacles from employers.

As bargaining has become more decentralized and density has declined, unions in several countries, most notably industrialized English-speaking ones, shifted towards 'organizing' approaches from the 1990s, although with considerable unevenness between countries, and between and within unions. At its core is the idea of workplace activism, developed through support and training for workplace delegates; members are empowered to solve problems themselves, instead of paid union officials solving them on their behalf. Critics argue unions that stop servicing members will fail to meet member expectations and lose support. In practice, 'organizing' unions engage in both 'organizing' and 'servicing' activities, in varying ways. Organizing approaches differ between countries, due to varying institutional arrangements.

Union power is widely discussed. A classic observation was Hyman's (1975) on the significance of both the *power of* a union's members – its ability to advance their interests – and a union's *power over* its members – without which it would not have *power for* its members. Thus unions rely on promoting solidarity and enforcing discipline. Unions also need to be democratic; hence a union cannot have *power for* its members 'unless [the members] have *power in* the union' (Peetz and Pocock, 2009, emphasis in original). Lévesque and Murray (2010) point to the importance of both the resources available to unions and their strategic capabilities in using those resources in explaining union power.

One of the oldest issues facing collectives of any type is the problem of the 'free-rider' or 'cheat', someone who obtains the benefits of group membership without contributing towards the costs. For trade unions, free-riders dilute bargaining strength, reducing the impact on an employer of any collective action and the power resources available to union members. Hence several jurisdictions have permitted 'union security' arrangements ('closed shops', the 'Rand formula' and so on) enabling the costs as well as the benefits to be applied to those who would otherwise not be in a union. Overwhelmingly, however, unions are voluntary organizations – typically the largest in civil society.

DAVID PEETZ

See also:

Industrial relations; Trade union recognition; Union density; Union organizing.

References and selected further readings

Hyman, R. (1975), *Industrial Relations: A Marxist Introduction*, London: Macmillan.
Lévesque, C. and G. Murray (2010), Understanding union power: resources and capabilities for renewing union capacity, *Transfer: European Review of Labour and Research*, **16**(3), pp. 333–350.
Peetz, D. and B. Pocock (2009), An analysis of workplace representatives, union power and democracy in Australia, *British Journal of Industrial Relations*, **47**(4), pp. 623–652.
Webb, S. and B. Webb (1920), *The History of Trade Unionism*, London: Longmans.

Training

Training is a process comprised of the methodical assessment, application and evaluation of information and aptitudes essential to an organizational task or job performance (Goldstein, 1980). Training aims to provide employees with the skills and abilities to meet industry requirements and performance benchmarks or build upon existing ones. It plays an important role in organizational legal compliance and can greatly contribute to employee development, motivation, retention and organizational competitive advantage. It also addresses employee and organizational needs, consequently adding to the realization of business objectives and organizational performance (Salas and Cannon-Bowers, 2001).

Training can be implemented throughout organizations in both formal and informal ways. Formally through accredited and non-accredited courses and workshops such as apprenticeships, traineeships and diplomas, and informally through on-the-job experience such as coaching, mentoring, job rotation and behaviour modelling. Both of these approaches are used in the training process to build on both hard and soft skills. Hard skills are tangible and measurable, such as operating a bobcat. Soft skills, on the other hand, are not as tangible and relate to an individual's ability to deal effectively with people in diverse situations.

Adequate planning, design, delivery and measurement of training processes play an important role in current organizational strategic human resource management. Key involvement of stakeholders (individual, organizational) in the training process can contribute to greater training effectiveness, as clearer links can be set from training to business outcomes. As the training investment is costly, 'training transfer' is paramount. Training transfer is defined as the level of knowledge and abilities implemented in the job and sustained over time (Holton and Baldwin 2003). Ensuring training transfer occurs can be complex, as individuals and organizations differ significantly. Organizational objectives and individual learner characteristics such as learning styles, motivation, cognitive ability and personality should be considered within the training process and design.

The training process faces several current challenges, such as continuous technological upgrades and a growing cultural diversity within organizations. Organizations tend to be cautious when investing in the training process as they attempt to minimize overspending, and aim for a return on their investment.

KATHRYN MOURA

See also:

Human resource management; Systematic training cycle; Training evaluation; Training needs analysis.

References and selected further readings

Goldstein, I.L. (1980), Training in work organizations, *Annual Review of Psychology*, **31**(1), pp. 229–272.
Holton, E.F. and T.T. Baldwin (2003), Making transfer happen: an action perspective on learning transfer systems, in E.F. Holton and T.T. Baldwin (ed.), *Improving Learning Transfer in Organizations*, San Francisco: Jossey-Bass, pp. 3–15.
Kraiger, K., D. McLinden and W.J. Casper (2004), Collaborative planning for training impact, *Human Resource Management*, **43**(4), pp. 337–351.
Salas, E. and J.A. Cannon-Bowers (2001), The science of training: a decade of progress, *Annual Review of Psychology*, **52**, pp. 471–499.

Training and development

Training is a structured, relatively formalized intervention aimed at developing skills and knowledge. Development is the process of enhancing an individual's skills, knowledge and expertise. Training can include a range of activities such as education, experience and on-the-job instruction. The processes of development include structured initiatives, such as training, as well as workplace (on-the-job) learning practices such as mentoring, coaching, shadowing, reflexive practice and observation. Certain development techniques involve job redesign practices such as job enrichment, job rotation or job enlargement. Training and development are often (inaccurately) used as synonyms, although they do both involve processes of learning. Development is also related to individual career advancement. Within companies training and development resides with the HR department and can be a dedicated function within it.

Training is a broad term covering a wide variety of structured interventions. These can vary significantly in length, purpose and content. For example, training can involve a rather brief health and safety instruction, or a few years of study towards obtaining a qualification. These have different purposes and outcomes, and result in development of different types and levels of skill and expertise. Such differences are important in judging which training is developmental, and need to be interrogated, as 'training' is often written about and used by policymakers and practitioners in generic terms.

Training and development can be internal (in-house) or external to an organization (e.g., at an educational institution or outsourced). Training and development can be on-the-job or off-the-job depending on whether they are integrated with performing work tasks or involve instruction away from the workplace. Training can be company-specific or aimed at developing generic skills. In recent years, companies are increasingly using information technology and online courses to train and develop their workforce (e.g., e-learning). The process of training commonly involves needs analysis, design, delivery and evaluation.

Training can also have a non-developmental function. It can send messages to employees and to stakeholders outside the organization. It can have a motivational effect on the workforce, serve a social function and improve employees' work experience. Externally, it can improve the employer brand, especially through certificates such as Investors in People in the UK.

There are a number of individual and organizational benefits of training and development. For the individual, training generates higher skills, knowledge, increased power in the labour market, higher pay and better career prospects. There are numerous benefits from training for companies, too. It can enable the smooth and safe performance of work, and result in better quantity and quality of output. It can insulate the company from skills shortages in the labour market and provide functional flexibility. It can also lead to increased productivity and competitiveness, resulting in superior organizational performance.

Training and development constitute elements of contemporary performance-enhancement human resource management practices. It is argued that in the face of changed and increased competition, companies must invest in training and development activities in order to gain competitive advantage. There is a major debate whether increased training and development contributes to better performance: a proposition with some empirical support but no unequivocal conclusion due to the difficulties of 'singling out' the role of training and development in performance-enhancement HRM strategies such as high performance work practices.

Training is sometimes considered in relation to recruitment as two alternative ways for companies to secure a skilled workforce. Training is related to the size of the company – small and medium-sized enterprises have less resources and interest in investing in training and development. The level, degree and scope of training within companies is also related to the nature of the product and the competitive strategy a company adopts (Keep and Mayhew, 1999). Thus, high-quality complex products and non-standardized methods of production may require high skills and training, while cost-based competitive strategy and Taylorized production practices will not.

Training, especially vocational training, takes place within national systems with different institutional settings. There are two main approaches to training: voluntarist and regulated. Under the voluntarist system (for example, US and UK) training is market-based and led by the demand from business. There is little regulation, as it is assumed that the market (through companies) will demand and develop the right type and level of skills and expertise required. The system can be effective but there is a danger that companies may not provide substantive training: for example, by investing in narrow firm-specific training, or by acquiring the skills from the labour market through recruitment. They may also standardize their production systems and job design to reduce discretion, which might eliminate the need for advanced skills.

By contrast, regulated systems (e.g., Germany, France) provide extensive training, which is considered a public good and is funded by the state. This can happen in different ways: for example, through a system of apprenticeships endorsed by stakeholders such as employers' associations, trade unions and regional governments, as is the case in Germany. A main criticism of such systems has been the limited flexibility of training to respond to changing business needs. A key issue in discussing national training systems is where and how training is funded, and where the responsibility for the skills development lies. Importantly, training and development is also systemic (Grugulis, 2007) and therefore should not be looked at in isolation from other aspects of work and employment.

DIMITRINKA STOYANOVA RUSSELL

See also:

Apprenticeship; Coaching; Experiential learning; High-performance work systems; Human resource development; Mentoring; Off-the-job learning; On-the-Job learning; Online learning; Qualifications; Training evaluation; Training needs analysis; Varieties of capitalism.

References and suggested further readings

Brown, P., A. Green and H. Lauder (2001), *High Skills: Globalization, Competitiveness and Skill Formation*, Oxford: Oxford University Press.
Finegold, D. (1999), Creating self-sustaining, high-skills ecosystems, *Oxford Review of Economic Policy*, 15(1), pp. 60–81.
Grugulis, I. (2007), *Skills, Training and Human Resource Development: A Critical Text*, Basingstoke: Palgrave Macmillan.
Grugulis, I. and D. Stoyanova (2011), Skills and performance, *British Journal of Industrial Relations*, 49(3), pp. 515–536.
Keep, E. and K. Mayhew (1999), The assessment: knowledge, skills and competitiveness, *Oxford Review of Economic Policy*, 4(3), pp. i–iv.

Training evaluation

Training evaluation is the systematic process of gathering descriptive and critical information on training. It is necessary for making informed decisions concerning the implementation, modification or value of organizational training. Evaluation provides a means of measuring whether training is meeting employee needs and organizational requirements in a cost-effective way. This is vital in the current economic climate as organizations endeavour to cut costs without affecting their competitiveness and cutting edge.

Training evaluation involves analysing the programme both pre- and post-training. Pre-training evaluation should begin early on in the training process by outlining the requirements and reasons for training. When essential information is established, clear results and objectives expected from the training should be demarcated in relation to organizational goals. These can then be used to develop a training evaluation strategy taking aspects such as cost, timing and organizational culture into account.

Planning the evaluation involves formative evaluation and the assessment of training outcomes. Outcomes should be evaluated at individual, group and organizational levels. When designing the training evaluation, the best possible measurement should be chosen. Measurements vary extensively and include questionnaires, tests, performance observations, statistics, cost-benefit analysis and focus groups. Only when clear measurements are set can training be adequately evaluated.

The starting point for most evaluations is Kirkpatrick's hierarchical model of training outcomes (Kirkpatrick, 1998). According to Kirkpatrick, outcomes used when evaluating training programmes post training are (a) responses, (b) knowledge and attitudes, (c) behaviour and (d) organizational outcomes. The ideal would be to evaluate training at multiple levels; however, evaluations are often restricted to whether an individual enjoyed the training or not and this does not provide evidence of any training transfer (the level of knowledge and ability applied to the job and over time; Holton and Baldwin, 2003).

Unclear or non-existent training evaluation can lead to the misuse of training funds and to the notion that training is a waste of time and money. Providing an adequate training evaluation is one of the ways to demonstrate its value to the organization. Adequate evaluation enables an organization to determine whether the training programme has reached its objectives, whether it was suitable or not and establishes areas to be adjusted, improved, replaced or made redundant.

KATHRYN MOURA

See also:

Systematic training cycle; Training; Training needs analysis.

References and selected further readings

Goldstein, I. and J.K. Ford (2002), *Training in Organizations*, 4th edn, Belmont: Wadsworth.
Holton, E.F. and T.T. Baldwin (2003), Making transfer happen: an action perspective on learning transfer systems, in E.F. Holton and T.T. Baldwin (eds), *Improving Learning Transfer in Organizations*, San Francisco: Jossey-Bass, pp. 3–15.
Kirkpatrick, D.L. (1998), *Evaluating Training Programs: The Four Levels*, 2nd edn, San Francisco: Berrett-Koehler Publishers.
O'Connor, J. and B. Little (2012), Evaluation – training's ignored leverage point, *Industrial and Commercial Training*, **44**(5), pp. 273–280.
Salas, E., K.A. Wilson, H.A. Priest and J.W. Guthrie (2006), Design, delivery, and evaluation of training systems, in G. Salvendy (ed.), *Handbook of Human Factors and Ergonomics*, Hoboken: Wiley, pp. 472–512.

Training needs analysis

Training needs analysis (TNA) is the first step in the recurring training process and is essential for developing relevant training programmes. It is a systematic process through which organizations gather data to determine: (a) whether training is needed, (b) who needs to be trained and (c) the type of training content required (Goldstein, 1993). The information collected may reveal disparities between what exists and what is desired and thus becomes the rationale for developing and implementing training programmes.

TNA is broadly mentioned as the foundation for training decisions within organizations. It has been used in business and education for more than half a century and remains current in organizations today. The information gained from a comprehensive TNA benefits both individuals and groups, providing the mechanism through which successful training programmes can be designed to more effectively achieve predetermined objectives.

The TNA process begins with a consultation to identify learning needs, followed by course planning, design, delivery and evaluation. Implementing certain measures within the TNA process can contribute to its effectiveness, namely: (a) identify clear, focused business objectives and (b) appoint a specific person, such as a manager or supervisor, to gather information on what needs to be done, what is being done, and how well individuals are performing in their current job/task. The information gathered from a comprehensive analysis should be correlated and organized to create the training needs report.

McGehee and Thayer (1961) in their seminal text on TNA, outline three interrelated training analysis components: (1) organization, (2) operations and (3) man analysis. First, organization analysis determines where training is needed within the organization and the impact further training will have on organizational performance. Second, operations analysis is the collection of information related to specific jobs and requirements attached to these and how training will increase or contribute further to job outcomes. Third, man analysis (now known as people analysis) provides information on employee performance. Other areas can be added to TNA as required such as analysis of environmental and structural needs.

TNA can be conducted at a micro (single organization) or macro (multiple organization) level.

KATHRYN MOURA

See also:

Human resource management; Systematic training cycle; Training; Training evaluation.

References and selected further readings

Clark, N. (2003), The politics of training needs analysis, *Journal of Workplace Learning*, **15**(4), pp. 141–153.
Goldstein, I.L. (1993), *Training in Organizations: Needs Assessment, Development, and Evaluation*, 3rd edn, Pacific Grove: Brooks/Cole.
McGehee, W. and P.W. Thayer (1961), *Training in Business and Industry*, New York: Wiley.
Surface, E. and E. Dierdorff (2007), Assessing training needs: do work experience and capability matter? *Human Performance*, **21**(1), pp. 28–48.
Taylor, P.J. and M.P. O'Driscoll (1998), A new integrated framework for training needs analysis, *Human Resource Management Journal*, **8**(2), pp. 29–50.

Transferable skills

Transferable skills refer to skills that are learned and developed by working in one context or domain and applying a significant proportion of such skills to other contexts, sometimes with minor adaptations and enhancements. Skills, in essence, are portable and flexible in nature and are critical for supporting an individual's employability and career development needs because an individual may change jobs several times during their lifetime and can carry the skills learned in one job/context to another. Examples of such skills include: interpersonal, communication, research and analysis, organizing and project planning skills etc. (ESF, 2009). For example, the research training skills that a doctoral student acquires for their doctoral research project are highly transferable to other research projects that are subsequently undertaken in one's academic career. Such skills are highly portable and can be applied in academic, business, market research firms and government's policy analysis roles across geographical borders (OECD, 2012).

One of the earliest references to transferable skills was made by Becker (1964) in his human capital theory. This compared and contrasted generic and transferable skills training with non-transferable firm-specific training. It argued that organizations will invest more in firm-specific skills, as these skills are directly relevant to an employee's job and usually not transferable to other employers, allowing the organization to recoup its investments in training during the an employee's tenure. In the case of transferable skills training, organizations should limit their investment in such training, as these skills are of equal value to other employers and can lead to poaching, thus limiting the organization's ability to recoup its investment in transferable skills. This topic has attracted numerous debates and raised questions as to whose responsibility it is to develop transferable skills and ideas for the benefits of internal versus external labour markets. A further debate focuses on the inextricable nature of both firm-specific and transferable skills, as often there are elements of both in each type of skill. This blurred distinction often results in employers investing in transferable skills as well due to the need for effective implementation of workplace change (Smith et al., 2004), or the inability of firms to observe the true potential of their employees due to asymmetrical market information (Acemoglu and Pischke, 1998a, 1998b).

CHRIS ROWLEY AND ASHISH MALIK

See also:

Employability; Human capital; Skill.

References and selected further readings

Acemoglu, D. and J. Pischke (1998a), Why do firms train? Theory and evidence, *Quarterly Journal of Economics*, **113**, pp. 79–119.
Acemoglu, D. and J. Pischke (1998b), Beyond Becker: training in imperfect markets, *The Economic Journal*, **109**, pp. 112–142.
Becker, G. (1964), *Human Capital: A Theoretical and Empirical Analysis*, Princeton: Princeton University Press.
ESF (2009), *Research Careers in Europe: Landscape and Horizons*, Strasbourg: Forum on Research Careers, European Science Foundation.
OECD (2012), Issues in transferable skills training for researchers, in *Transferable Skills Training for Researchers: Supporting Career Development and Research*, Paris: Organisation for Economic Co-ordination and Development.
Smith, A., E. Oczkowksi, R. Macklin and C. Noble (2004), The impact of organisational change on the nature and extent of training in Australian enterprises, *International Journal of Training and Development*, **8**(2), pp. 2–15.

Transformational leadership

Transformational leadership is grounded on a leadership–management paradigm in which leadership is focused on creating a desired future state, whereas management aims to effectively maintain the current state. Transformational leadership was developed from contrasting the differences between management and leadership, linking these terms to transformational and transactional leadership respectively (MacGregor Burns, 1978). The discussion on transformational leadership gained pace when Bass (1985) set out a theory proposing that optimum performance was facilitated by a balanced mix of transformational and transactional leadership behaviours focused on the task to be achieved and the way in which the team and organization delivered.

Transformational leadership behaviours facilitate extra discretionary effort from team members, thus achieving higher performance levels. These transformational leadership behaviours centre on charismatic leadership (role modelling to create respect and trust), intellectual stimulation (encouraging creativity and ideas generation), inspirational motivation (adapting an enthusiastic and optimistic attitude to challenges) and individualized consideration (recognizing individual differences). These four behavioural elements form the transformational leadership part of the Full Range Leadership Model (FRLM), a leadership framework that is underpinned by transformational leadership theory (Bass and Avolio, 1993).

Transformational leadership seeks to achieve a step-change in culture and performance through encouraging employee personal responsibility and ownership, whereas transactional management encompasses traditional managerial styles aimed at gaining performance through compliance by offering reward (or punishment) and is generally suited to maintaining stable situations. Transactional management behaviours are therefore less effective for organizations wishing to achieve cultural change where transformational styles have been found to be more effective when connected to a compelling vision aimed at generating high employee commitment through personal involvement.

Research studies have shown that transformational leadership behaviours encourage employees to perform beyond expected levels of performance as a consequence of their leaders' influence in inspiring them to transcend self-interest for a higher purpose, vision and mission. Transformational leadership behaviours change the perception of employees to produce extra discretionary effort and have been shown to augment most traditional management behaviours by upwards of 40 per cent in impact strength on the same measurable outcomes (Avolio and Bass, 2004).

The Multi-Level Leadership Questionnaire (MLQ) is a 360-degree feedback tool developed to measure, evaluate and develop transformational leadership behaviours within the FRLM, evaluating leadership strengths and weaknesses to enable leaders to develop personal leadership development interventions. Research indicates that when using 360-degree feedback, organizations should use well-constructed survey models and skilled facilitators to provide feedback to participants (Coates, 1996). Over the past decade, the FRLM (including the MLQ) is reported to be the most researched leadership model and has become an accurate guide for developing exemplary leadership in diverse cultures, organizations, and leadership positions (Avolio, 2010).

Paul S. Turner

See also:

Purpose-driven leadership; 360-degree appraisal.

References and selected further readings

Avolio, B.J. (2010), *Full Range Leadership Development*, 2nd edn, Thousand Oaks, CA: Sage.
Avolio, B.J. and B.M. Bass (2004), *Technical Research Manual: The Multifactor Leadership Questionnaire*, 3rd edn, Redwood: Mind Garden, Inc.
Bass, B.M. (1985), *Leadership and Performance Beyond Expectation*, New York: Free Press.
Bass, B.M. and B.J. Avolio (1993), Transformational leadership: a response to critics, in M.M. Chemers and R. Ayman (eds), *Leadership Theory and Research: Perspectives and Directions*, Sydney: Academic Press Inc.
Coates, D. (1996), Multi-source feedback: seven recommendations, *Career Development International*, 1 (3), pp. 32–36.
MacGregor Burns, J. (1978), *Leadership*, New York: HarperCollins.

Transnational collective agreements

Increasingly many multinational corporations (MNCs) are under pressure to implement labour standards and regulations nationally and internationally in a more coherent and cogent manner (see 'Regulation' in this volume). The growing awareness of labour rights and the increasing political and media interest in the employment activities of MNCs has meant that these organizations are increasingly being discussed and criticized for aspects of their international operations. Issues such as health and safety or child labour have led to a range of campaigns and high-profile cases. There are international labour standards MNCs normally relate to, but these are usually voluntary and come in the form of general codes of conduct from various international private and public agencies. In addition, the implementation of national legislation by a MNC within any one national context varies according to the ability or desire of those national governments to enforce their regulations on a range of issues. In recent years, we have seen some MNCs begin to develop with their workforce representations agreements on how their staff should be treated on a range of issues such as representation, equality, health and safety and others. International framework agreements have been signed with trade union organizations as a way of ensuring a basic platform of rights. These are attempts to integrate the general codes of conduct that are developed externally but in some cases there have been very specific transnational collective agreements within MNCS signed on a range of issues such as the use of temporary staff or agency staff, the development of equality strategies and others (see Dehnen and Pries, 2014, on such types of agreements). As a consequence of this, we are seeing a specific set of high-profile MNCs recreate an industrial relations-type system of bargaining and negotiations at its headquarter levels and not just at the local national level. The idea is that local subsidiaries within MNCs use these agreements as frameworks for the development of their own industrial relations activity on the specific issues signed in them. Some observers see these as further step towards a transnational system of regulation and industrial relations. However, some are critical because the number of MNCs involved in such agreements remains relatively low. In addition, they are not always fully implemented and understood at all levels of the MNC (see Hammer, 2005, for a review and evaluation). Yet these are a new development that begins to create a new set of transnational activities in the sphere of HRM, which are related to labour rights and regulation. Along with European works councils, global works councils and other representatives bodies in MNCs they form the basis of a new set of developments and influences.

MIGUEL MARTÍNEZ LUCIO

See also:

European works councils; International Labour Organization and International Labour Standards; Multinational companies; Trade unions.

References and selected further readings

Dehnen, V. and L. Pries (2014), International Framework Agreements: a thread in the web of transnational labour regulation, *European Journal of Industrial Relations*, **20**(4), pp. 335–350.

Gollbach, J. and T. Schulten (2000), Cross-border collective bargaining networks in Europe, *European Journal of Industrial Relations*, **6**(2), pp. 161–179.

Hammer, N. (2005), International framework agreements: global industrial relations between rights and bargaining, *Transfer*, **15**(1), pp. 511–530.

Keune, M. and V. Schmidt (2009), Global capital strategies and trade union responses: towards transnational collective bargaining? *International Journal of Labour Research*, **1**(2), pp. 9–26.

TUPE

TUPE is an acronym for the Transfer of Undertakings (Protection of Employment) Regulations 2006. These implement a European Union directive and deal with employees' rights in the event of a business transfer. The TUPE Regulations define relevant transfers. These include business transfers (Regulation 3(1)(a)) and service provision changes (Regulation 3(1)(b)). The inclusion of service provision changes as a relevant transfer goes beyond the strict requirements of the EU directive but creates clarity and legal certainty at the national level (within Great Britain and Northern Ireland where equivalent provisions apply).

The TUPE Regulations protect the contract of employment. Where a relevant transfer takes place the TUPE Regulations ensure that the contract of employment continues following the transfer (Regulation 4). This means that all of the rights powers, duties and liabilities of the 'original employer' (transferor) towards an employee move over to the 'new employer' (the transferee) and the employment contract continues as if it had been originally made between the employee and the transferee. Variations to the contract will be void if the sole or principle reason is the transfer (Regulation 4(4)). Where a contract of employment incorporates the provisions of a collective agreement, the rights powers, duties and liabilities contained within the collective agreement will transfer over to the transferee. Terms incorporated from collective agreements can be varied if more than a year has passed since the transfer, provided that, taken as a whole, the rights and obligations are no less favourable to the employee (Regulation 5B). If the collective agreement contains a 'dynamic clause' that allows the content of the agreement to be renegotiated 'from time to time' then if the transferee is not a participant in the collective bargaining, changes to the provisions of a collective agreement made after the transfer will not affect the transferee and will not amend the terms and conditions of the employee's contract (Regulation 4A).

The TUPE Regulations provide protection from dismissal. If an employee is dismissed and the sole or principle reason for the dismissal is the transfer, then the employee will be deemed to have been unfairly dismissed within the meaning of the Employment Rights Act 1996 (an automatically unfair dismissal). Where a relevant transfer would involve a substantial change in working conditions to an employee's detriment, then the employee can treat the contract as having been terminated and this will be classed as a dismissal for the purposes of the statutory right not to be unfairly dismissed (section 94 Employment Rights Act 1996).

The TUPE regulations provide for information and consultation. Transferors (the 'original employer') must provide transferees (the 'new employer') with certain employee liability information (Regulation 11). There is also a duty to inform and consult employee representatives (Regulation 13).

LIZ OLIVER

See also:

Collective agreements; Contract of employment; Terms and conditions.

References and selected further readings

McMullen, J. (2006), An analysis of the Transfer of Undertakings (Protection of Employment) Regulations 2006, *Industrial Law Journal*, **35**(2), pp. 113–139.

McMullen, J. (2007), TUPE: ringing the (wrong) changes: The Collective Redundancies and Transfer of Undertakings (Protection of Employment) (Amendment) Regulations 2014, *Industrial Law Journal*, **43**(2), pp. 149–169.

Willey, B. (2012), Employment Law in Context: An Introduction for HR Professionals, 4th edn, Harlow: Pearson.

Undocumented immigrant worker

An undocumented immigrant worker is a non-citizen who works without authorization from a country's immigration authority. This occurs when a person enters a country without authorization, their visa expires or they work contrary to the conditions of their visa.

This entry does not use the term 'illegal worker' that is popular among media and immigration authorities. The term carries much negative meaning, is legally inaccurate and there are many other reasons not to use it (PICUM, n.d.).

Many people are working without authorization in a variety of countries. For instance, it is estimated there are eight million undocumented immigrant workers in the United States (Pasel and Cohn, 2011), and several hundred thousand in the United Kingdom. Issues arise with undocumented immigrant work, occurring mainly at the intersection of immigration and employment laws, the most notable of which are identified here.

Those engaging in unauthorized work face heavy penalties under country-specific migration laws. For employers there can be fines and, in some cases, criminal sanctions and workers can be fined, detained and deported. Employment laws of only some countries apply to undocumented immigrant workers. Australian and United Kingdom courts have found that employment contracts for undocumented work are void for illegality. That is, the employment contracts have no effect and workers cannot benefit from legislated minimum employment rights. In contrast, in the United States, undocumented workers are entitled to almost all of the same minimum employment rights enjoyed by citizens (Dewhurst, 2014).

The optimum form of regulation remains a live issue in many countries. For instance, in the US in 2014, President Obama announced executive action including revising deportation priorities so that undocumented immigrants who had not disobeyed a prior order for removal nor committed a serious criminal offence would be considered a lower priority for deportation. This action reduces relatively the priority of discovering, detaining and deporting other undocumented immigrant workers.

Undocumented immigrant workers are vulnerable to exploitation by unscrupulous employers. Due to their precarious immigration status, financial dependence and often lack of local language skills and support network they are commonly underpaid, harassed and work in unsafe conditions (Cunningham-Parmeter, 2008; Bernhardt et al., 2009).

STEPHEN CLIBBORN

See also:

Immigration; Labour mobility.

References and selected further readings

Berg, L. (2016), *Migrant Rights at Work: Law's precariousness at the intersection of migration and labour*, London: Routledge.
Bernhardt, A., R. Milkman, N. Theodore, D. Heckathorn, M. Auer, J. DeFilippis, A. González, V. Narro, J. Perelshteyn, D. Polson and M. Spiller (2009), *Broken Laws, Unprotected Workers*, Chicago, IL: Center for Urban Economic Development; National Employment Law Project; UCLA Institute for Research on Labor and Employment.

Clibborn, S. (2015), Why undocumented immigrant workers should have workplace rights, *The Economic and Labour Relations Review.*

Cunningham-Parmeter, K. (2008), Fear of discovery: immigrant workers and the fifth amendment, *Cornell International Law Journal,* **41**(1), pp. 27–82.

Dewhurst, E. (2014), Models of protection of the right of irregular immigrants to back pay: the impact of the interconnection between immigration law and labor law, *Comparative Labor Law and Policy Journal,* **35**(2), p. 217.

Pasel, J. and D. Cohn (2011), *Unauthorized Immigrant Population: National and State Trends,* Washington, DC. Pew Research Center, www.pewhispanic.org/files/reports/133.pdf.

PICUM (n.d.), *Why 'Undocumented' or 'Irregular'?* http://picum.org/picum.org/uploads/file_/Terminology Leaflet_reprint_FINAL.pdf.

Unfair dismissal

The Employment Rights Act 1996 gives qualifying employees in Britain a right not to be unfairly dismissed (section 94). This is a major employment right in Britain, but to qualify for the right an individual must be an employee (see 'Contract of employment' in this volume) and must have been continuously employed for a minimum of two years (section 108). Relevant dismissals for the purposes of the provisions on unfair dismissal include: termination of the contract by the employer (whether with or without notice), the expiry and non-renewal of a limited-term contract and the termination of the contract by the employee in circumstances in which she or he is entitled to terminate it by reason of the employer's conduct (see 'Constructive dismissal' in this volume). The first step to establishing whether a dismissal was fair or unfair involves scrutiny of the reason for the dismissal. The employer must establish the reason for the dismissal and show that the reason either falls within one of the potentially fair reasons listed within the statute or is some other substantial reason of a kind such as to justify a dismissal (section 98(1)). The potentially fair reasons include: capability, conduct, redundancy or that the employee could not continue to work in their job without contravening a legal restriction (section 98(2)). The second step to establishing whether a dismissal is fair or unfair entails an assessment of whether the employer acted reasonably or unreasonably in treating the reason as a sufficient reason for dismissing the employee (section 98(4)). The statute prescribes that the determination of reasonableness should take into account the circumstances (including the size and administrative resources of the employer) and should be established in accordance with equity and the substantial merits of the case (section 98(4)(a)-(b). The Employment Appeal Tribunal and the appellate courts have established authoritative case law on the interpretation of the concept of reasonableness and this is a source of guidance on the broad expectations on employers in the context of different reasons for dismissal and on how employment tribunals should assess reasonableness. Employment tribunals should not substitute their own opinion for that of the employer but should consider whether the employer's decision to dismiss fell within a range of reasonable responses (*Iceland Frozen Foods v Jones*). This range of 'reasonable responses test' gives greater scope for managerial discretion in decision making around dismissal.

A key factor in establishing reasonableness is whether a fair procedure was followed. While a failure to follow a procedure will not automatically render a dismissal unfair (*Polkey v A.E. Dayton (Services) Ltd*), procedure is one of the factors to be weighed by an employment tribunal in deciding whether or not the decision to dismiss was reasonable. The Acas code of practice on disciplinary and grievance procedures (Acas, 2015) sets out good practice guidance to help employers, employees and their representatives to deal with disciplinary issues within the workplace and contains a series of steps that are key. Although the code is not legally binding, it can be admitted as evidence in an employment tribunal and employment tribunals have the discretion to increase or decrease the compensation awarded for an unfair dismissal by up to 25 per cent where there has been an unreasonable failure to comply with the code (Trade Union and Labour Relations (Consolidation) Act 1992, section 207A).

In certain situations, a dismissal will be 'automatically unfair'; for example, where an employee is dismissed for asserting a statutory right (section 104), here the reasonableness test is not applied and the two-year qualifying period has no effect (section 108(3)).

LIZ OLIVER

See also:
Constructive dismissal; Contract of employment; Discipline and grievance.

References and selected further readings

Acas (2015), *Code of Practice 1 – Disciplinary and Grievance Procedures (Revised 2015)*. London: Acas, www.acas.org.uk/dgcode.
Brodtkorb, T. (2010), Employee misconduct and UK unfair dismissal law: Does the range of reasonable responses test require reform? *International Journal of Law and Management*, **52**(6), pp. 429–450.
Collins, H. (1992), Justice in Dismissal: The Law of Termination of Employment, Oxford: Clarendon Press.
Ewing, K.D. and J. Hendy (2012), Unfair dismissal law changes – unfair? *Industrial Law Journal*, **41**(1), pp. 115–121.
Harcourt, M., M. Hannay and H. Lam (2013), Distributive justice, employment-at-will and just-cause, *Journal of Business Ethics*, **115**(2), pp. 311–325.
Willey, B. (2012), *Employment Law in Context: An Introduction for HR Professionals*, 4th edn, Harlow: Pearson.

Union avoidance: substitution and suppression

'Union avoidance' is a broad term that described a range of tactics and strategies used by an employer to actively avoid trade union recognition (Gall and Dundon, 2013). Two approaches to union avoidance are 'union substitution' and 'union suppression'. Union substitution is an approach where management seek to substitute the triggers (or conditions) that would prompt workers to seek to join a trade union (Foulkes, 1980). For example, paternalist employers in nineteenth-century Britain – such as Cadbury whose management were influenced by a Quaker religion with a strong sense of ethical community – sought to look after workers and their families with social welfare, health and housing supports as a way to discourage unionization. In more recent times, employers such as the computer giant IBM and the retailer Marks & Spencer have been regarded as more sophisticated non-union employers (Guest and Hoque, 1994). Regarded as so-called 'good' non-union employers, the HR strategy seeks to 'substitute' the conditions that would encourage unionization among workers. The substitution practices vary and tend to include extensive non-union employee voice opportunities so workers feel they have a say and are involved in management decision-making. Substitutive employers tend to offer above average pay, with extensive fringe benefits and generally more attractive employment packages. The idea is that management create a climate that means a trade union is felt to be unnecessary because of internal personnel arrangement. In the 1960s and 1970s, Charles Hughes, a leading managerial psychologist working for IBM and Texas Instruments, pioneered a determined opposition to unions using a substitutive approach (Logan, 2006, p. 661).

If a union substitution employer engenders a climate so a union is felt to be unnecessary, the opposite is union suppression, whereby management insist, often aggressively, that workers won't be allowed to have a union. In such a situation, management actively resist unionization using hostile tactics, including victimization and intimidation (Gall, 2013). Literature around small firms or those companies that resemble 'sweatshop' working conditions conjure up the image of a union suppression employer (Sisson, 1993). The American sociologist, Donald Roy (1980), eloquently referred to the hostility of union suppression as the 'fear' and 'evil' stuff of anti-union employers. Fear stuff is the tactics that threaten workers' jobs, or pose unions as reds-under-the-beds who will make a firm unprofitable. The evil stuff is outright intimidation and victimization: unfair and unpleasant treatment or outright sackings (Dundon and Rollinson, 2004). It has been claimed that the largest private-sector employer in America, Walmart, has violated US labour rights without much concern for its brand, reputation or indeed the feeling of employees (Greenhouse, 2007).

However, there are debates about the extent to which union suppression and substitution are very different in reality (Dundon, 2002). It is not unknown for so-called good employers who appear to resemble the softer substitutive type, who engage and involve employees, to also utilize anti-union tactics. Gall (2004) points out that there is no definitive 'Chinese wall' separating suppressive and substitutive strategies as either/or alternatives. For example, in Britain, the retail giant Tesco, known for its leading-edge union-management collaborative partnership arrangements, advertised in America for a US-based chief executive with specific union avoidance expertise (Dundon et al., 2006).

In other so-called good employers, hostility to unionism can be hidden beneath a velvet glove of soft HRM, or an above average employment package serves to create an illusion that employee–employer relations are harmonious (Moody, 2013). In short, there is a body of analysis indicating that so-called good employers may in fact simultaneously adopt hostile union avoidance tactics. There is recent analysis which points to a burgeoning disdain for collective (unionized) systems of representation among governments and businesses, which in turn serves to legitimatize an anti-union ideology as normal among managers, politicians and business group lobbyists (Cooper and Ellem, 2013; Friedman, 2013).

TONY DUNDON

See also

Collective bargaining; Hard and soft HRM; Trade unions.

References and selected further readings

Cooper, R. and B. Ellem (2013), The state against the unions: Australia's neo-liberalism, 1996–2007, in G. Gall and T. Dundon (eds), *Global Anti-Unionism: Nature, Dynamics, Trajectories and Outcomes*, London: Palgrave Macmillan.

Dundon, T. (2002), Employer opposition and union avoidance in the UK, *Industrial Relations Journal*, **33**(3), pp. 234–245.

Dundon, T. and D. Rollinson (2004), *Employment Relations in Non-Union Firms*, London: Routledge.

Dundon, T., N. Cullinane and B. Harney (2006), The ideology of union-busting, *International Union Rights Journal*, **13**(2), pp. 5–6.

Friedman, G. (2013), The economists turn against the unions: from historical institutionalism to neoclassical individualism after the American century, in G. Gall and T. Dundon (eds), *Global Anti-Unionism: Nature, Dynamics, Trajectories and Outcomes*, London: Palgrave Macmillan.

Foulkes, F. (1980), *Personnel Policies in Large Non-Union Companies*, New York: Prentice Hall.

Gall, G. (2004), British employer resistance to trade union recognition, *Human Resource Management Journal*, **14**(2), pp. 36–53.

Gall, G. (2013), Employers against union recognition: the British experience, in G. Gall and T. Dundon (eds), *Global Anti-Unionism: Nature, Dynamics, Trajectories and Outcomes*, London: Palgrave Macmillan.

Gall, G. and T. Dundon (2013) (eds), *Global Anti-Unionism: Nature, Dynamics, Trajectories and Outcomes*, London: Palgrave Macmillan.

Greenhouse, S. (2007), Report assails Wal-Mart over unions, *New York Times*, 1 May 1.

Guest, D. and K. Hoque (1994), The good, the bad and the ugly: employment relations in new non-union workplaces, *Human Resource Management Journal*, **5**(1), pp. 1–14.

Logan, J. (2006), The union avoidance industry in the United States, *British Journal of Industrial Relations*, **44**(4), pp. 651–675.

Moody, K. (2013), Contemporary employer aggression and state complicity: resistance to unionisation in the US, in G. Gall and T. Dundon (eds), *Global Anti-Unionism: Nature, Dynamics, Trajectories and Outcomes*, London: Palgrave Macmillan.

Roy, D. (1980), Repression and incorporation: fear stuff, sweet stuff and evil stuff: management's defenses against unionization in the south, in T. Nichols (ed.), *Capital and Labour: A Marxist Primer*, Glasgow: Fontana.

Sisson, K. (1993), In search of HRM, *British Journal of Industrial Relations*, **32**(2), pp. 201–210.

Union busting

Union busting is a strategy to either degrade the capacity of an existing union to the point that it no longer exists or operates in any meaningful or effective way or to prevent one from getting to the point where it can exist and operate in a meaningful way. In this sense, union busting has far more in common with anti-unionism than non-unionism because deliberate and conscious reactive and proactive, preventative steps are taken become or remain 'union free'. The term 'union busting' is one used by unions and their supporters and sympathizers while 'union avoidance' or 'proactive' HRM measures would be terms more commonly used by employers and managers.

Historically, the first well-known case of union busting took place in Britain in 1834 when six Dorset farm labourers – known as the Tolpuddle Martyrs – were deported to Australia for seven years for organizing a union. More contemporaneously, the sacking of more than 11,000 members of the Professional Air Traffic Controllers' Organization (PATCO) in 1981 by President Reagan for not ending a strike is the obvious case, given that this lead to the dissolution of the union.

The techniques by which to operationalize the strategy and goal of union busting are many and varied, ranging from lawful and unlawful, implicit and explicit, and subtle and violent. Despite the existence of international law and international labour standards, varying nation-state regulation and political cultures have a bearing on what is deemed to be acceptable and unacceptable employer behaviour in these regards.

In countries with less regulated labour markets, such as the United States and Britain, individual dismissals using spurious reasons to decapitate the union are common as are threats to shut down or relocate production facilities if workers unionize. Provoking strikes in order to be able to dismiss union workers or sign a 'sweetheart' no-strike deal with a tame union are others. In developing economies, threats and use of violence are common. Disappearances are not unheard of.

However, in the United States the extent and sophistication of union busting is the most advanced and has been pioneered and practised by a range of anti-union management consultants, industrial psychologists and lawyers known as 'union busters'. This has been in spite of the National Labor Relations Act (1935), which introduced various rights to organize and means by which to gain union recognition from an employer.

In the United States, an ideological war is mounted upon the idea of union by union busters with attempts at inoculation by unions most often unsuccessful. Among the messages used are that unions are a divisive third party between workers and managers; that unions are run by communists; and that the payment of subscriptions to unions benefits union bureaucrats and spurious left-wing causes and not the dues-paying members.

In most countries, union busting is a high-risk and often high-cost strategy. This is because of the possibility of the issue becoming a political 'hot potato', which damages the company's reputation, and because of the time and financial resources that can be needed to mount an effective union busting operation. However, the financial rewards can be great and, often, permanent.

GREGOR GALL

See also:

International Labour Organization and International Labour Standards; Non-unionism; Strikes; Trade unions.

References and selected further readings

Gall, G. and T. Dundon (eds) (2013), *Global Anti-Unionism – Nature, Dynamics, Trajectories and Outcomes*, Basingstoke: Palgrave.
Levitt, M. with T. Conrow (1993), *Confessions of a Union Buster*, New York: Crown Publishers.
Logan, J. (2006), The union avoidance industry in the United States, *British Journal of Industrial Relations*, **44**(4), pp.651–675.

Union density

Union density is the proportion of employees who are union members. It is one of the most-used measures of union power, along with collective bargaining coverage and strike frequency. It is only a proxy measurement but it provides useful information, although that data must be triangulated with other sources.

Union membership statistics needed to measure density are not unproblematic and are subject to error, including sampling error. Surveys of unions themselves, and household surveys or censuses, are the two most common methods. Union counts may or may not include retired and unemployed members, and censuses have differing methodologies. In addition, there are significant differences between countries in the way data is collected.

However, despite the measure being a proxy and subject to various kinds of measuring error, union density figures have been used to chart the growth and decline of unions.

Density is a comparative measure of union fortunes with respect to organizations, social groups (e.g., gender or race), industry sectors, and countries. Union density figures are used to provide cross-sectional estimates (e.g., between countries at one point in time) or longitudinal information over time regarding trends.

In many countries (although not all), density rates have traditionally been higher among men than women, although that is rapidly changing and in some industries and countries there is little or no difference. With respect to age, density in most countries follows an inverted U-shaped pattern, often maximizing in the mid-40s to mid-50s. Typically, union density is declining among young employees at a faster rate than among older workers. Black workers in countries like the UK and US have higher density rates than whites, although this is not true for other racial groups. Union density is higher than in the public than the private sector. It is often, although not universally, much higher among full-time employees than part-timers.

The general fall in density globally has a number of overlapping causes, one or more of which may be more significant in a particular case than others. Reasons include changing labour market institutions, shifting economic and labour market configurations, the declining success of social democratic parties, reduced public sympathy for unions, organizations adopting neoliberal ideologies and strategies, and the erosion of class as an organizing principle (Peetz, 1998; Western, 1995). Various strategies labelled revitalization or renewal have been attempted, including the 'organizing model' used by union movements for the past 20 years in most Anglophone countries.

JANIS BAILEY

See also:

Bargaining levels; Bargaining scope; Industrial relations; Union organizing; Trade unions.

References and selected further readings

Bain, G.S. and R. Price (1983), Union growth: dimensions, determinants, and destiny, in G.S. Bain (ed.), *Industrial Relations in Britain*, Oxford: Basil Blackwell.
Peetz, D. (1998), *Unions in a Contrary World*, Melbourne: Cambridge University Press.
Schnabel, C. (2003), Determinants of union membership, in J.T. Addison and C. Schnabel (eds), *International Handbook of Trade Unions*, Cheltenham: Edward Elgar Publishing.
Visser, J. (2002), Why fewer workers join unions in Europe: a social custom explanation of membership trends, *British Journal of Industrial Relations*, **40**(3), pp. 403–430.
Visser, J. (2006), Union membership statistics in 24 countries, *Monthly Labor Review*, **129**, pp. 38–49.
Western, B. (1995), A comparative study of working-class disorganization: union decline in eighteen advanced capitalist countries, *American Sociological Review*, **60**(2), pp. 179–201.

Union organizing

Union organising refers to activities undertaken by trade unions to expand and strengthen their membership. Trade unions are independent organisations that represent the interests of workers who are their members. One of the main mechanisms to do that is through collective bargaining with employers.

Union organising is a commonly used term in many Anglo-Saxon countries including the USA, UK, Australia, New Zealand and the Republic of Ireland. It's usage is now spreading to other settings. As the ideas of organising spread, they come to mean slightly different things in different settings. This is not especially surprising, but it does make it difficult to pin down exactly what we mean by 'union organising'.

Underpinning ideas are that trade unions build collective interests amongst members. This contrasts with using union power to influence government policy and law, or to speak primarily to employers. In some settings, organising can be associated with quite radical objectives that challenge existing union structures; perhaps where members try to develop autonomy to pursue their own agenda rather than follow the agenda of the central union. In other settings, it simply means that unions are interested in working on issues that appeal to a wide range of workers in the hope those campaigns will help boost membership in a workplace.

One of the challenges of thinking about union organising rests on whether it is seen as a separate, specialist activity or whether it is integral to what a union does across its activities. Where it is a specialist activity, there is a danger that newly organised workers will not have the skills to integrate into the wider objectives and activities of the union. Where it is integral to the work of everyone within the union, it is important that there are mechanisms to make sure it doesn't slip down the agenda in the busy workload of professional union officers.

Union organising is a risky activity. It can be expensive because time and effort has to be put aside to explore the issues affecting particular groups of workers and to help them build the skills and expertise to make sure those issues are addressed. If the union is working with a group of workers who do not yet have formal bargaining rights with their employer (often called 'union recognition') it is probable that it will take a lot of time and effort to get that recognition – and the outcome is by no means a guaranteed success as employers may countermobilise to avoid having to bargain with the union.

It is less risky for unions to try to expand and deepen membership in workplaces where they already have bargaining rights. However, in most industrialised countries, union membership has been declining for decades and this approach has the danger of failing to make unions relevant in new and expanding sectors. Focusing on organising across geographical areas, sectors and between different employers has therefore become more important to unions as they seek to rebuild their influence.

MELANIE SIMMS

See also:

Collective bargaining; Trade union recognition; Trade unions; Union density.

References and selected further readings

Bronfenbrenner, K., S. Friedman, R.W. Hurd, R.A. Oswald, R.A. and R.L. Seeber (1998), *Organizing to Win: New Research on Union Strategies*, Ithaca, NY: Cornell University Press.
Heery, E. (2002), Partnership versus organising: alternative futures for British trade unionism, *Industrial Relations Journal*, 33(1), pp. 20–35.
Simms, M., J. Holgate and E. Heery (2013), *Union Voices – Tactics and Tensions in UK Organizing*, Ithaca, NY: Cornell University Press.
Wills, J. (2008), Making class politics possible: organizing contract cleaners in London, *International Journal of Urban and Regional Research*, 32(2), pp. 305–323.

Unitarism

Unitarism refers to a frame of reference that almost exclusively portrays the employment relationship in harmonious terms: a site of shared interests between employers and employees. A unitarist assumes that the company will, or should have, a single source of authority, wholly exercised by management and accepted by all employees. As a consequence, unitarists will view challenges to employer decisions as illegitimate. Conflict will be regarded as lacking validity, irrational or unnecessary. Where conflict occurs, a unitarist will be inclined to explain it in psychological terms (ignoring the social, economic and class structure of the employment relationship) or reduce it to poor communications, 'agitators' or misunderstandings among the workforce. The unitary approval of unquestioned employer authority offers little room for trade unions, which are viewed as illegitimate or unnecessary intrusions into the workplace. Unions are seen to disrupt harmony and undermine rational managerial authority and should be avoided or suppressed. Indeed, other interventions into the realm of the private firm, like legal regulations, are also viewed negatively by unitarists insofar as they are perceived to undermine managerial flexibility and prerogative.

The above description is an ideal type and in practice unitary assumptions will be expressed in different ways. Variations of unitarism are likely to exist between those that are simply apologetics for crass authoritarianism and those that emphasize, more benignly, the value of employee loyalty and commitment in a union-free milieu. Such variance should not distract from what is common to all flavours of unitarism, however: a general preference to control employees; to limit or delegitimize their capacity for independent 'employee voice'; to avoid outside intervention into labour relations and to see workplace conflict as entirely unacceptable, as something that can, and should be, eradicated. Despite pluralist and radical critics frequently dismissing unitarism as undemocratic, its assumptions prevail within many sections of society. One will typically find a body of business leaders, managers and human resource management (HRM) professionals who purvey unitarist sentiment. It is not uncommon to find elements within conservative media outlets and political circles propagate unitary assumptions too. Within certain realms of management theory, the spectre of unitarism also looms large: some formulations of HRM are underpinned by a distinctly unitarist ethos that provide little scope for independent employee voice (Marchington and Grugulis, 2000, p. 1119). The apparent prevalence of unitarism might derive simply from bias and prejudice, but also from its ability to legitimate the position of those in formal authority and justifying their preferred arrangement of social relations (Fox, 1966).

NIALL CULLINANE

See also:

Conflict; Employee voice; Frames of reference; Pluralism; Radicalism.

References and selected further readings

Cullinane, N. and T. Dundon (2014), Unitarism and employer opposition to trade unionism, *International Journal of Human Resource Management*, **25**(18), pp. 2573–2590.

Fox, A. (1966), Managerial ideology and labour relations, *British Journal of Industrial Relations*, **4**(3), pp. 366–378.
Marchington, M. and I. Grugulis (2000), Best practice human resource management: perfect opportunity or dangerous illusion? *International Journal of Human Resource Management*, **11**(6), pp. 1004–1124.

Universalistic theory

Universalistic theory argues that certain human resource practices have a direct and positive impact on organizational performance irrespective of the context in question. For HRM researchers and practitioners, this logic has intuitive appeal and helps demonstrate the strategic significance of HRM. Empirically, universalistic theory has underpinned research that has attempted to statistically demonstrate the direct relationship of HRM to organizational performance. Initially, the universalistic focus was on single HR practices such as pay and staffing. Over time, research evolved to examine how mutually reinforcing bundles of HRM practices could have a synergistic impact on financial performance. Typical HR practices advocated as part of such bundles include sophisticated recruitment tests, internal promotions, job security, extensive training and performance-related pay schemes. An exemplar is research by Mark Huselid (1995, p. 644), which concluded that 'the use of high-performance work practices and good internal fit should lead to positive outcomes for all types of firms'. The various labels attached to HRM are indicative of the universal emphasis; for example, best practice HRM, high-performance work practices/systems (HPWS) and high commitment management.

Universalistic theory has played a huge role in legitimizing the significance of HRM and enabling HR managers to demonstrate bottom-line impact. A steady stream of research has deployed increasingly sophisticated statistical techniques to demonstrate, and later offer greater precision, on the magnitude of the HRM–performance relationship. Yet the simplistic and uni-linear logic of universal theory has also been criticized. Most obviously, if such HRM practices are so beneficial, what explains their limited diffusion? More contingency-based arguments point to the inevitable cost considerations of introducing practices, while industry context and the nature of organizational strategy are likely to have a role to play in determining which form of HRM is likely to be most effective. Universalistic arguments are largely founded on certain types of firms (large, private sector) from certain regions (Anglo-Saxon) and so the significance of institutional context is not given due acknowledgement. With respect to methodology, there is still some debate over the precise mix of practices that should be included as part of a universal bundle, how these are best measured, what the appropriate outcomes is (financial performance, productivity, employee outcomes) and whether the impact needs to be captured over time.

However, research has also evolved from a focus on examining the content of HR practices per se, to explaining how the universal impact takes effect, including via mediators such as organizational climate and, increasingly, employee responses. Multi-level research brings together both managerial and employee perspectives to offer a more rounded understanding of the impact of HRM. Conceptually, some have suggested universal logic resides at the level of general principles (e.g., how we treat our staff), whereas contingency explanations then look to context specific operation of HR for this task. The longstanding paradox at the heart of universalistic theory is that it neatly captures the benefits of HRM but does so at the risk of simplistically glossing over organizational realities.

BRIAN HARNEY

See also:

Best practice; Competitive advantage; Context; Contingency theory; Strategic HRM.

References and selected further readings

Godard, J. (2004), A critical assessment of the high-performance paradigm, *British Journal of Industrial Relations*, **42**(2), pp. 349–378.

Guest, D. (2011), Human resource management and performance: still searching for some answers, *Human Resource Management Journal*, **21**(1), pp. 3–13.

Huselid, M.A. (1995), The impact of human resource practices on turnover, productivity, and corporate financial performance, *Academy of Management Journal*, **38**(4), pp. 635–672.

Unofficial strikes

An unofficial strike is a strike action undertaken by members of a union without their leadership's authorization, support or approval. The strikes are, thus, taken outside of and in contravention to the union's rulebook. For this reason, they pose a challenge to the authority of a union and its national leadership in particular (especially in terms of being taken as a credible bargaining partner by an employer). Yet seldom are unofficial strikes completely unofficial (called 'unofficial unofficial' strikes), because there will usually be some level of support for them on the lower runs of the union hierarchy. Equally too, seldom are unofficial strikes aimed at the members' union (although there have been some cases when members strike unofficially against an agreement that was signed on their behalf by their union).

Unofficial strikes can often be an extremely potent weapon for workers because they are taken with the element of surprise, disavowing the employer of the opportunity to make counter-preparations to limit the impact of the strike (as is the case with official and, thus, notified strikes). For this reason, these are often called 'wildcat' strikes, meaning they are unpredictable. The element of surprise is particularly important when the grievance at hand is a perishable one. Thus, if action is not taken to challenge a change to work practices or the dismissal of a worker, by default the change or dismissal will become permanent. It is for these reasons – in regard of unions, employers and government – that unofficial strikes are also deemed irresponsible and deviant. Consequently, they have little legitimacy in society at large.

Unofficial strikes are more frequent in several circumstances. The first is where there is a non-independent union, either sanctioned or controlled by an employer or state. Strikes in China, Vietnam and Indonesia are taken in contravention of the official unions. The second is where strikes have an immediate and major impact because there are no available substitutes and the good or service is of a time-fixed nature such as transport (air, sea, rail), prisons, communications (newspapers, postal delivery). The third is where official strike action is heavily regulated in terms of procedures for mandatory balloting and notification or subject matter (as in Britain, Germany and the United States). The fourth is where lawful strike action is proscribed (as in a number of 'essential services' such as transport, fire service, postal service, police). The fifth is where small groups of workers are strategically well placed in a work system and can exercise a disproportionate amount of leverage. Finally, there is the situation in manufacturing where 'just-in-time' production techniques are used because these are very susceptible to disruption given the lack of back-up supplies.

The duration of unofficial strikes is normally short because there is an absence of total, full union support. Therefore, unofficial strikes are usually short and sharp actions. Recent examples of large unofficial strikes include workers at the Jeffboat shipyard (Indiana, 2001), Dhaka garment workers (Bangladesh, 2006), Toronto Transit Commission (Canada, 2006), Freightliner Trucks (North Carolina, 2007), Lindsey Oil Refinery (Britain, 2009), Marikana miners (South Africa, 2012) and Alberta Union of Provincial Employees (Canada, 2013).

GREGOR GALL

See also:

Conflict; Strikes; Trade unions.

References and selected further readings

Eldridge, J. and G. Cameron, G. (1964), Unofficial strikes: some objections considered, *British Journal of Sociology*, **15**(1), pp. 19–37.

Gall, G. and S. Cohen (2013), Britain – ballots, industrial action short of a strike and unofficial strikes, in G. Gall (ed.), *New Forms and Expressions of Conflict at Work*, Basingstoke: Palgrave, pp. 86–107.

Unsocial hours

Unsocial (or 'atypical') hours refers to working time scheduled outside of traditional daily and weekly norms (e.g., 9am–5pm, Monday to Friday), or on public holidays. It is a feature of many shift systems and often attracts an enhancement to pay to compensate for the disruption to family life and leisure as well as to incentivize its use.

The practice of unsocial hours increased with the expansion of the service sector (such as retail, healthcare and hospitality) and concomitant shift working and declining trade union density. In the UK alone, more than 1.3 million people regularly work night shifts and around 2 per cent of all workers work exclusively between Friday and Sunday. It has become more disruptive of the quality of family life with the rise of dual earner families, especially where schedules are not fixed (Barnes et al., 2006).

However, workers are increasingly not compensated for unsocial hours, or are having their enhancements and allowances reduced. Research in Australia suggests that most employees (54 per cent) do not receive additional pay for working outside normal hours, notwithstanding extensive regulation in that country (Daly, 2014). One of the biggest schemes is in the UK National Health Service (NHS) (see Table 1), which has higher premia for the lowest paid staff. The Department of Health launched a review of these unsocial hours payments in 2014 in order to cut costs and enable more efficient rostering across a '24/7' service.

Table 1   NHS unsocial hours payments

Pay band	All time on Saturday (midnight to midnight) and any weekday after 8pm and before 6am	All time on Sundays and public holidays (midnight to midnight)
1	Time plus 50%	Double time
2	Time plus 44%	Time plus 88%
3	Time plus 37%	Time plus 74%
4–9	Time plus 30%	Time plus 60%

Source: NHS Employers.

JAMES ARROWSMITH

See also:
Annualized hours; Overtime; Shift work; Work–life balance; Working time.

References and selected further readings
Barnes, M., C. Bryson and R. Smith (2006), *Working Atypical Hours: What Happens to Family Life?* London: National Centre for Social Research.
Daly, T. (2014), *Evenings, Nights and Weekends: Working Unsocial Hours and Penalty Rates*, Adelaide: Centre for Work and Life, University of South Australia.

Upward appraisal

Upward appraisal is a performance assessment conducted on by an employee on their supervisor or manager. The most positive element of the upward appraisal is its ability to instigate change, through providing feedback and perhaps a 'reality check' to management. Upward appraisals are often used to measure the effectiveness of management teams and to identify areas of improvement (Hall et al., 1996). Information from subordinates provide another useful dimension of information as subordinates are often in a prime position due to their frequent contact and interpersonal relations to evaluate supervisor performance and pinpoint problem areas.

Upward appraisals have been found to increase communication as it creates another avenue for which information can flow through the organization. Upward appraisals can also positively increase employee satisfaction as employees experience greater levels of involvement and empowerment if they are able to share their views and provide feedback upward in the organization. This signals to employees that the organization is paying attention to their needs and that it fosters and supports employee participation and voice. There are various arguments against upward appraisals, such as the fact that employees may not have the training and knowledge to accurately rate the performance of their supervisors. There may also be biases that may exist and this could negatively influence the integrity and validity of the appraisal process. Subordinates may inflate performance ratings for their own career development or fear being honest due to the risk of losing their job or other negative outcomes (Levy and Williams, 2004).

AMIE SOUTHCOMBE

See also:

Peer appraisal; Performance appraisal; 360-degree appraisal.

References and selected further readings

Antonioni, D. (1999), Predictors of upward appraisal ratings, *Journal of Managerial Issues*, **11**(1), pp. 26–36.

Bettenhausen, K.L. and D.B. Fedor (1997), Peer and upward appraisals: a comparison of their benefits and problems, *Group Organization Management*, **22**(2), pp. 236–263.

Hall, J.L., J.K. Leiaecker and C. DiMarco (1996), What we know about upward appraisals of management: facilitating the future use of UPAs, *Human Resource Development Quarterly*, **7**(3), pp. 209–226.

Levy, P.E. and J.R. Williams (2004), The social context of performance appraisal: a review and framework for the future, *Journal of Management*, **30**(6), pp. 881–905.

Mathews, B.P. and T. Redman (1997), The attitudes of service industry managers towards upward appraisal, *Career Development International*, **2**(1), pp. 46–53.

Upward problem-solving

Upward problem-solving is a form of direct employee voice that enables employees to identify work-related issues and concerns, and make suggestions to management that may in turn lead to organizational improvement. The focus on Japanese production methods including total quality management, quality circles and six sigma in the 1980s and 1990s, drove employer interest in the use of upward problem-solving (Ishikawa, 1985). Accordingly, employers saw value in enabling their employees to communicate upwards to management, as they were able to capture employees' ideas and suggestions to improve organizational performance.

Upward problem-solving differs to task-based participation in that these voice mechanisms operate independently of the work process. They can incorporate a range of voice mechanisms, designed to elicit employee knowledge and ideas, including off-line teams, quality circles, suggestion schemes, attitude surveys, problem-solving groups and two-way briefings (Marchington, 2007).

The extent to which the upward problem-solving mechanism genuinely allows an employee to participate and to have a say concerning work matters can be analysed based on a framework that measures the depth, level, scope and form of the scheme (Dundon and Wilkinson, 2009; Marchington and Wilkinson, 2005). A greater depth would enable employees to make suggestions on issues that would normally be made by management and that may otherwise have only been communicated downwards to employees. The level at which the upward problem-solving takes place may vary from employees contributing to their work group improvement through to issues that may be raised at the corporate level. The scope refers to the type of issues that employees can raise, such as minor canteen issues through to major problems such as plant relocation. The form that the upward problem-solving scheme takes could include posting ideas to an intranet, which may provide minimal employee influence, or through mechanisms such as a quality circle, which would provide greater employee autonomy and involvement in problem-solving and decision-making.

PAULA K. MOWBRAY

See also:

Attitude survey; Communication; Consultation; Employee involvement; Employee voice; Quality circles; Suggestion scheme.

References and selected further readings

Boxall, P. and K. Macky (2009), Research and theory on high performance work systems: progressing the high involvement stream, *Human Resource Management Journal*, **19**(1), pp. 3–23.

Dundon, T. and A. Wilkinson (2009), Employee participation, in T. Redman and A. Wilkinson (eds), *Contemporary Human Resource Management*, Harlow: Pearson.

Ishikawa, K. (1985), *What is Total Quality Control? The Japanese Way*, Englewood Cliffs, NJ: Prentice Hall.

Marchington, M. (2007), Employee voice systems, in P. Boxall, J. Purcell and P. Wright (eds), *The Oxford Handbook of Human Resource Management*, Oxford: Oxford University Press, pp. 231–250.

Marchington, M. and A. Wilkinson (2005), Direct participation, in S. Bach (ed.), *Personnel Management: A Comprehensive Guide to Theory and Practice*, 4th edn, Oxford: Blackwell.

Variable pay

'Variable pay' refers to those parts of the reward package that are not guaranteed to the employee but relate in some way to the achievement of productivity or performance improvements. Such payments would include bonuses, incentive schemes, 'payment by results' (PBR) and commission, but could also embrace other variable forms of pay such as profit-sharing, share ownership schemes, overtime and shift payments. These payments are often paid on top of basic pay, although in some cases workers may be paid entirely by their output or commission (although minimum wage entitlement must usually be met). Individual performance-related pay could be considered a form of variable pay but it is often in fact guaranteed in the sense that it is the form of progression through the salary band or scale and can be consolidated into base pay. In general, variable pay is not consolidated into base pay. While historically manual wage workers in manufacturing and construction received such payments in the form of output-based piecework or work-measured schemes, in recent times such variable pay systems have been increasingly applied to salaried workers. A major feature of the New Pay paradigm (see 'Reward management' in this volume) is the emphasis on a new relationship between fixed and variable remuneration, with increasing use of 'at risk' payments being advocated. Variable elements within the reward package can include individual, team and organization-wide rewards and a major area of growth in variable pay has been in the area of profit-sharing and share ownership schemes (Lowe et al., 2002).

A number of reasons have been identified why employers use variable or 'contingent' forms of remuneration. These include: to elicit greater work effort (input or output) from workers; to enhance employees' commitment; to attract higher quality workers; to retain workers when labour markets are tight; to introduce a greater element of equity into pay practices; or to act as a substitute for direct monitoring of worker performance by management (Pendleton et al., 2009). Research by IDS (2010) found that organizations adopted incentive or bonus schemes for the following reasons: to improve business performance; to focus employee efforts on key areas (e.g., health and safety, quality or customer care); to motivate staff; to assist recruitment and retention and to encourage specific behaviours in the workplace, such as teamwork. There is some confusion over the terms 'bonus' and 'incentive' and they are sometimes used interchangeably. Armstrong and Murlis (2007), however, argue that incentives are forward-looking and usually linked to measurable targets whereas bonuses are backward-looking and based on past performance.

There are five major dimensions to be considered in the design of variable pay elements:

1. What is being measured (inputs or outputs)?
2. What period of performance does the reward cover (short-term or long-term)?
3. Does the reward relate to the individual employee or to team or organization-wide success?
4. Is the performance measurement based on a single factor or multiple factors?
5. What form does the reward take (cash, shares or non-financial)?

GEOFF WHITE

See also:

Bonuses/incentives, Employee share ownership plans; Performance-related pay; Profit-sharing; Reward management; Team pay.

References and selected further reading

Armstrong, M. and H. Murlis (2007), *Reward Management: A Handbook of Remuneration Strategy and Practice*, 5th edn, London: Kogan Page.
Hyman, J. (2009), Financial participation schemes, in G. White and J. Druker (eds), *Reward Management: A Critical Text*, 2nd edn, London: Routledge.
IDS (2010), *Bonus Schemes*, IDS HR Study 911, London: Incomes Data Services.
Lowe, K.B., J. Milliman, H. DeCieri and P. Dowling (2002), International compensation practices: a ten-country comparative analysis, *Human Resource Management*, **41**(1), pp. 45–66.
Pendleton, A., K. Whitfield and A. Bryson (2009), The changing use of contingent pay at the modern British workplace, in W. Brown, A. Bryson, J. Forth and K. Whitfield (eds), *The Evolution of the Modern Workplace*, Cambridge: Cambridge University Press.
Shields, J. (2007), *Managing Employee Performance and Reward: Concepts, Practices, Strategies*, Cambridge: Cambridge University Press.

Varieties of capitalism

'Varieties of capitalism' (VoC) describes a theoretical approach to comparing market-based economic systems. It rejects the notion of a one-size-fits-all equilibrium model and recognizes diversity in the way that institutions operate in a capitalist economy. The term VoC was introduced by Hall and Soskice (2001) as a tool to distinguish the liberal market economies (LMEs) of English-speaking countries from the coordinated market economies (CMEs) of continental Europe. They are differentiated on the basis of institutional arrangements regarding: industrial relations, vocational training, corporate governance, inter-firm relations and employer–employee relations.

An LME such as the United Kingdom is characterized by a more deregulated, decentralized and adversarial employment relations landscape. Additionally, its employers place a greater emphasis on the acquisition of general and transferrable skills over industry-specific ones. Commercial operations and corporate governance in an LME are dominated by considerations regarding shareholder values. The interests of other stakeholders, therefore, play only an auxiliary role. Furthermore, relationships between firms in an industry tend to be competitive in nature. On the other hand, a CME such as Germany is characterized by a more regulated industrial relations landscape that fosters a cooperative approach to employee relations. Vocational training focuses on the acquisition of firm- and industry-specific skills. Stakeholder values, rather than those of shareholders alone, drive corporate governance and commercial operations. Relationships between firms in an industry tend to be collaborative in nature.

Much of the criticisms mounted at VoC revolve around its taxonomical approach (Peck and Theodore, 2007). Empirical findings (e.g., Schneider and Paunescu, 2012) support the view that the LME/CME dichotomy tends to oversimplify the subject matter and overlooks the tendency for institutions in an economy to change over time. There are calls for a more nuanced approach that acknowledges the applicability of the VoC framework in developed countries while recognizing diversity within each market cluster.

Commentators also criticize the Eurocentric nature of the VoC approach because the model does not adequately explain the operation of developing markets. Contributors to the VoC stream of literature are closing this gap, however, by expanding the framework to cover newly industrializing and developing markets (Schneider and Soskice, 2009; Witt and Redding, 2014).

KEVIN YOU

See also:

Coordinated market economy; Liberal market economy.

References and selected further readings

Hall, P.A. and D. Soskice (eds) (2001), *Varieties of Capitalism: The Institutional Foundations of Comparative Advantage*, Oxford: Oxford University Press.
Lane, C. and G.T. Wood (eds) (2012), *Capitalist Diversity and Diversity within Capitalism*, London: Routledge.
Peck, J. and N. Theodore (2007), Variegated capitalism, *Progress in Human Geography*, 31(6), pp. 731–772.
Schneider, M.R. and M. Paunescu (2012), Changing varieties of capitalism and revealed comparative advantages from 1990 to 2005: a test of the Hall and Soskice claims, *Socio-Economic Review*, 10(4), pp. 731–753.
Schneider, M.R. and D. Soskice (2009), Inequality in developed countries and Latin America: coordinated, liberal and hierarchical systems, *Economy and Society*, 38(1), pp. 17–52.
Witt, M.A. and G. Redding (eds) (2014), *The Oxford Handbook of Asian Business Systems*, Oxford: Oxford University Press.

Vocational education and training

Vocational education and training (VET) is generally regarded as a development activity that is aimed at preparing learners for employment or enhancing career prospects for those already employed. It is not about 'learning' per se but it is a focused activity of a practical nature designed for development and enhancement of skills leading toward practical or sometimes manual work in a specific trade or occupation. For example, within further education and some higher education institutions, vocational courses would be those classified as providing qualifications that would allow the successful student to enter or progress in a particular field. Bricklaying might be one example, social care another. At higher levels, VET examples might be surveying or social work. While VET has often been regarded as lower-level skill development, in its broader context it can be related to professional skills and technical (TVET) development and qualification at the postgraduate level. It is, however, generally perceived as different from academic learning and development and, while undeniably important, tends not to have the same cachet as more traditional forms of academic learning and development. VET has also been the focus of successive government initiatives seeking to reduce youth unemployment in particular.

VET is often delivered through further education, professional bodies and other educational and trade based providers such as City and Guilds. National Vocational Qualifications (NVQs) are also linked to VET and can be taken across a broad spectrum of occupations at a wide range of levels. The tradition and history of VET being linked with trades and apprenticeships, as well as the old technical schools, colleges and polytechnics, sees it being regarded as lower down on the spectrum of post-16 education. Nonetheless, it could be argued that training to be a medical doctor is in fact a form of VET.

ALISON SMITH

See also:

Training and development.

References and selected further readings

Anderson, D., M. Brown and P. Rushbrook (2004), *Vocational Education and Training*, Crows Nest: Allen & Unwin.

Edwards, R., S. Sieminski and D. Zeldin (eds) (2014), *Adult Learners, Education and Training*, London: Routledge.

Eichhorst, W., N. Rodriguez-Planas, R. Schmidle and K.F. Zimmerman (2015), A road map to vocational education and training in industrialized countries, *ILR Review*.

Hager, P. and T. Hyland (2003), Vocational education and training, in N. Blake, P. Smeyers, R. Smith and P. Standish (eds), *The Blackwell Guide to the Philosophy of Education*, Malden, MA: Blackwell Publishing, pp. 271–287.

Harris, R., M. Simons and K. Maher (2015), *New Directions in European Vocational Education and Training Policy and Practice: Lessons for Australia*, Adelaide: National Centre for Vocational Education Research Ltd.

Lucas, B., E. Spencer and G. Claxton (2012), *How to Teach Vocational Education: A Theory of Vocational Pedagogy*, London: City and Guilds.

Wages

Wages are a fixed regular payment earned for work or services, typically paid on a daily or weekly basis. The word is used so frequently that very few question its true meaning. It can have a broad or narrow meaning. At its widest it is a reward to the factor of production, labour, and includes any payment for work whether it is done for an employer or on a self-employed basis. When it is referring only to employees, it includes all forms of direct labour cost and is the cost of using labour as opposed to the cost of using capital or land.

As a price of labour, wages are said to be determined by the forces of demand and supply in the labour market, which in turn is affected by productivity levels and ability of the employers to substitute labour with other factors of production such as machinery. Since wage labour is the predominant form of work, the term 'wage' sometimes refers to all forms of employee compensation/remuneration.

So a wage is monetary compensation/remuneration paid by an employer to an employee in exchange for work done. Payment may be calculated as a fixed amount for each task completed (a task wage or piece rate), or at an hourly or daily rate, or based on an easily measured quantity of work done.

A fixed weekly or monthly wage is usually called a salary. Payment by wage contrasts with salaried work, in which the employer pays an arranged amount at steady intervals (such as a week or month) regardless of hours worked. Waged employees may also receive tips and employee benefits which are non-monetary forms of compensation. Wages may also refers to a single pay rate for each job or grade.

Wage is normally associated with manual work. Some argue that the difference between a wage and a salary is that wages tend to have less security of income and is often associated with incentive pay, overtime or shift pay on top of lower hourly rates.

You can also distinguish between a person's wage rate and their wages, which may be the amount they 'take home', but it could equally apply to a person's gross wage before social security and income tax deductions, etc.

MARK GILMAN

See also:
Payment system; Salary; Time-based pay.

References and selected further readings

Armstrong, M. (2012), *Armstrong's Handbook of Reward Management*, London: Kogan Page.
Gilman, M. (2013), Reward management, in T. Redman and A. Wilkinson (eds), *Contemporary Human Resource Management: Text and Cases*, New York: Pearson.
Perkins, S.J. and G. White (2008), *Employee Reward: Alternatives, Consequences and Contexts*, London: Chartered Institute of Personnel and Development.
White, G. and J. Drucker (2009), *Reward Management: A Critical Text*, London: Routledge.

Welfare

The Chartered Institute of Personnel and Development (CIPD, 2014) notes that welfare officers appeared around the end of the nineteenth century. Their original concern was for the protection of women and girls in industry, followed by a more general aim of 'industrial betterment'.

In prewar times, the idea of employee benefits began with some employers recognizing these as motivational factors in the recruitment, retention and wellbeing of their workforce. In the postwar era came the integration of general management with welfare at work, and so the concept of personnel management began. During the 1980s the term 'personnel management' began to be replaced by HRM, wherein manpower is seen as a business resource or an asset, albeit one that requires a range of human interventions at group and individual levels, such as training, motivation and welfare in order to function well.

In many organizations, welfare is now the shared responsibility of HR, occupational health and line management. Welfare in today's workplace tends to encompass the health and wellbeing of the workforce. The investment in employee welfare can effect positive employment relationships by engaging with employees to provide help and support at individual level. At an organizational level, positive outcomes are achieved through such initiatives as health and wellbeing-related policies, health promotion initiatives, rewards and benefits, etc. In its publication on health, work and wellbeing, Acas (2012) claims that healthy and motivated people will 'go the extra mile, give good customer service, take fewer sickies and provide commitment and creativity'.

Concern for the welfare of staff extends to employees and managers knowing how to help and where to seek advice. This will typically be to an HR and occupational health (OH) service when these are available. There are also government bodies available for employment advice. Policies play a major part in achieving fair and consistent best practice. Standard policies relating to employee welfare will cover: absence management, anti-bullying and discrimination, grievance and appeals, drugs and alcohol, etc.

Failure to invest in employee wellbeing and welfare can result in higher costs: for example, increased sickness absence, higher turnover, recruitment problems and low morale. Wellbeing initiatives focus on reducing absence and identifying causal factors. Research indicates that minor illness remains the most common cause of absence, followed by musculoskeletal injuries, back pain and stress.

Occupational health can play a major role in helping employees to take responsibility for their own wellbeing and advising employers on the health and welfare of staff. The confidential and impartial expertise of OH allows them to be a trusted and professional resource although ethical issues such as conflict of interest can be a concern.

JOAN LEWIS

See also:

Management style; Paternalism; Wellbeing.

References and selected further readings

Acas (2012), *Health, Work and Wellbeing*, www.acas.org.uk/media/pdf/3/t/Health-work-and-wellbeing-accessible-version.pdf.

CIPD (2014), *History of HR and the CIPD*, www.cipd.co.uk/hr-resources/factsheets/history-hr-cipd.aspx.

CIPD and Simply Health (2014), *Absence Management: Annual Survey Report 2014*, www.cipd.co.uk/research/absence-management-survey.aspx.

Griffiths, E. (2010), Managing for health, *Occupational Health*, **62**(5), pp. 14–15.

Russell, A. (1991), *The Growth of Occupational Welfare in Britain*, Aldershot: Avebury.
Tyson, S. (2006), *Essentials of Human Resource Management*, 5th edn, Oxford: Butterworth Heinemann.

Wellbeing

The term 'wellbeing' can be understood in many different ways. First, wellbeing can be measured in relation to life in general ('context-free' wellbeing) or in relation to a particular setting ('context-specific' wellbeing). In human resource management (HRM), attention has been directed mainly to work-related wellbeing, as HR interventions primarily target the workplace. Affective wellbeing at work can be defined as the overall quality of an individual's subjective experience and functioning at work (Warr, 1987). Grant et al. (2007) distinguish three dimensions of wellbeing in workers. The first type of wellbeing, happiness, refers to individual's subjective experiences at work. This type covers positive worker attitudes and psychological states (such as affective commitment, job satisfaction). Second, they distinguish a health-related type of wellbeing. This includes strain-related aspects of health, such as stress, burnout and exhaustion, and active health-related constructs such as work engagement. Third, relationship wellbeing focuses on interactions and the quality of relationships between employees, between employees and managers/the organization; for example, in terms of trust and cooperation. Employee wellbeing is an important end in itself. In addition, happiness, health and relationship wellbeing are positively associated with various forms of work behaviours (such as job performance, turnover and absenteeism). Hence, wellbeing has important individual and organizational consequences.

Starting in the late 1990s, greater attention has been paid to how HRM influences employee outcomes, including employee wellbeing. An important early contribution to this stream of literature 'building the worker into HRM' includes a paper by Guest (1999). In his 'worker's verdict' of HRM he found that the more HR practices employees experience, the higher their level of happiness and relationship wellbeing. However, both employees experiencing the fewest and the greatest number of HR practices reported a high degree of work pressure (which negatively impacts health-related wellbeing). The findings of this pioneering work indicate potential trade-offs between different wellbeing types: HR practices may benefit one type of wellbeing while harming another. The precise nature of the link between HRM and employee wellbeing is still under debate. Two main perspectives stand out in the literature. Central to the mainstream 'optimistic' perspective is the idea that HRM is beneficial for employees; the adoption of HR practices is expected to lead to higher levels of job discretion, more empowerment and a more supportive and rewarding work environment resulting in increased employee wellbeing. In contrast, the 'critical' perspective argues that while the adoption of HPWS leads to more discretion; it also leads to the intensification of work resulting in decreased employee wellbeing as employees are put under greater pressure at work. The results of the recent review by Van De Voorde et al. (2012) on the links between HRM, wellbeing and organizational performance support the idea of a positive relationship between HRM and happiness and relationship wellbeing. For health wellbeing, however, the majority of included studies demonstrated a negative effect of HRM, echoing the original work by Guest (1999).

Despite the growing evidence of a relationship between HRM and employee wellbeing, there is a general recognition in the literature that there remain two important theoretical issues that need to be addressed in order to gain a fuller understanding of this relationship. The first issue has to do with the processes and mechanisms that underpin the link between HRM and employee wellbeing. In particular, social exchange mechanisms and psychological empowerment are thought to act as mediators between HRM and happiness and relationship employee wellbeing (Jiang et al., 2013). According to social exchange theory, when employees perceive positive treatment and inducement via an investment in HRM, they will repay the organization by exerting positive feelings of wellbeing. Following empowerment theory, as HRM contributes to job control and discretion, feelings of empowerment and involvement will be enhanced, which in turn affect employee wellbeing positively. Regarding health-related wellbeing, a limited body of work investigated and confirmed the mediating role of increased workload in the HRM–employee health relationship. The second issue concerns the conditions under which HRM has an effect on employee wellbeing. Although workforce (such as employee age), organizational (such as leadership style), and institutional (such as trade union influence) factors are suggested to play a role in shaping the relationship between HRM and employee wellbeing in the literature, there has been very little research on these moderator effects to date. Recent work by Jensen and colleagues (2013) suggests that when employees have a sufficient amount of job control, the demands accompanying HRM translating into negative health effects are minimized.

In conclusion, employee wellbeing is a multidimensional construct, and the dimensions are differentially related to HRM. Our understanding of how HRM affects different aspects of employee wellbeing, and how these effects are influenced by boundary conditions is still limited.

KARINA VAN DE VOORDE AND MARC VAN VELDHOVEN

See also:

Burnout, Occupational health; Stress.

References and selected further readings

Grant, A.M., M.K. Christianson and R.H. Price (2007), Happiness, health, or relationships? Managerial practices and employee well-being tradeoffs, *Academy of Management Perspectives*, **21**(3), pp. 51–63.

Guest, D.E. (1999), Human resource management – the worker's verdict, *Human Resource Management Journal*, **9**(3), pp. 5–25.

Jensen, J.M., P.C. Patel and J.G. Messersmith (2013), High-performance work systems and job control: consequences for anxiety, role overload, and turnover intentions, *Journal of Management*, **39**(6), pp. 1699–1724.

Jiang, K., R. Takeuchi and D.P. Lepak (2013), Where do we go from here? New perspectives on the black boxes in strategic human resource management resource, *Journal of Management Studies*, **50**(8), pp. 1448–1480.

Van De Voorde, K., J. Paauwe and M. Van Veldhoven (2012), Employee well-being and the HRM–organisational performance relationship: a review of quantitative studies, *International Journal of Management Reviews*, **14**(4), pp. 391–407.

Warr, P.B. (ed.) (1987), *Work, Unemployment, and Mental Health*, Oxford: Clarendon Press.

Whistleblowing

Whistleblowers are organization members (including former members and job applicants) who disclose illegal, immoral or illegitimate practices (including omissions) under the control of their employers, to persons or organizations who may be able to effect action (Miceli and Near, 1984; Near and Miceli, 1985).

Whistleblowing is important because the social, financial and other costs of organizational wrongdoing are substantial (e.g., Katz et al., 2012), and insiders are often the first, best or only source of information that can lead to problem correction (e.g., Kaplan et al., 2010; Miceli et al., 2008). Interest in whistleblowing is growing, from a variety of disciplines (e.g., social sciences, management, law, ethics, accounting, etc.) and across many countries around the world (e.g., Brown et al., 2014).

Media reports on whistleblowing often speculate about why certain individuals come forward but others do not; for example, some suggest that there must be a 'whistleblowing personality' that leads some employees to risk retaliation to come forward. Some theories suggest that dispositions are important predictors of other workplace behaviours and may be related to whistleblowing. However, empirical research is not well-developed on the role of personality or disposition in whistleblowing; what currently exists generally suggests that situational factors are more important.

Organizations may ostensibly require employees to report perceived wrongdoing to parties in the organization, such as internal audit, or human resources professionals, in their job descriptions, ethical guidelines, etc. Important questions include: (a) In what ways does whistleblowing differ depending on the extent to which it is role-prescribed? (b) To what extent are prescriptions on paper supported by actual practice, for example, through responsiveness by the report recipient, or by the culture of the organization? (c) What variables predict whether managers in a particular organization are likely to retaliate against whistleblowers – characteristics of the manager, the organization, the whistleblower, or the wrongdoing itself?

A body of research investigating the predictors of whistleblowing and of retaliation has emerged over several decades. However, relatively little is known about the factors that cause whistleblowers to be effective in getting wrongdoing stopped.

Marcia P. Miceli and Janet P. Near

See also:

Conflict; Employee voice.

References and selected further readings

Brown, A.J. (ed.) (2008), *Whistleblowing in the Australian Public Sector: Enhancing the Theory and Practice of Internal Witness Management in Public Sector Organizations*, Canberra: ANU E-Press.

Brown, A.J., D. Lewis, R. Moberly and W. Vandekerckhove (eds) (2014), *International Handbook on Whistleblowing Research*, Cheltenham: Edward Elgar Publishing.

Ethics Resource Center (2012), *2011 National Business Ethics Survey: Workplace Ethics in Transition*, www.ethics.org.

Kaplan, S.E., K.R. Pope and J.A. Samuels (2010), The effect of social confrontation on individuals' intentions to internally report fraud, *Behavioral Research in Accounting*, 22, pp. 51–67.

Katz, M., H. LaVan and Y.P. Lopez (2012), Whistleblowing in organizations: Implications from litigation, *SAM Advanced Management Journal*, 77, pp. 4–17.

Miceli, M.P. and J.P. Near (1984), The relationships among beliefs, organizational position, and whistle-blowing status: a discriminant analysis, *Academy of Management Journal*, **27**, pp. 687–705.

Miceli, M.P., J.P. Near and T.M. Dworkin (2008), *Whistle-Blowing in Organizations*, New York: Routledge.

Miceli, M.P., J.P. Near, M.T. Rehg and J.R. Van Scotter (2012), Predicting employee reactions to perceived organizational wrongdoing: demoralization, justice, proactive personality, and whistle-blowing, *Human Relations*, **65**, pp. 923–954.

Near, J.P. and M.P. Miceli (1985), Organizational dissidence: the case of whistle-blowing, *Journal of Business Ethics*, **4**, pp. 1–16.

Near, J.P. and M.P. Miceli (2013), Whistleblowing, in R.W. Griffin (ed.), *Oxford Bibliographies Online Series: Management*, Oxford: Oxford University Press.

Work

Work can be defined as a purposeful human activity involving physical or mental exertion that is not undertaken solely for pleasure and that has economic or symbolic value. This includes paid employment and formal jobs, as well as unpaid forms of work such as household-based caring activities. What is valued as work in a specific time and place, however, is determined by complex factors including labour markets, legal regulations, managerial practices and cultural norms.

While the specific nature of work also varies across time and place, a deeper understanding of work is important for HRM because the diversity of meanings of work shape various HRM approaches. Work in a capitalist system is a commodity traded in labour markets, and some HRM strategies focus on buying labour as cheaply as possible. For some, work is a lousy activity tolerated to earn income, and this yields HRM approaches that emphasize economic incentives or penalties to motivate workers. High-engagement approaches to HRM, in contrast, try to make work a source of personal fulfilment and psychological rewards. HRM should also understand that work is embedded in complex social phenomena such that workers seek approval, status, sociability and power. Others argue that workers are human beings and are therefore entitled to rights and standards of dignity and self-determination irrespective of what the labour market or HRM might provide. This can lead to advocacy for protective labour legislation and trade unions.

The social context in which work occurs also generates social norms that define acceptable behaviors and work roles, and also create power relations that shape the allocation of resources and rewards. Feminist scholars and activists challenge traditional norms that reward paid employment and devalue reproductive work. Work that cares for others, it is then argued, should be recognized as 'real work' and therefore valued more fully. Karl Marx rejected capitalism because of the alienation that results from the commodification of work and because of the highly unequal nature of power relations between labour and capital.

Western meanings of work are typically individual-centric with an emphasis on a worker and their immediate family's needs for income, psychological fulfilment and caregiving. But work can also serve God, humanity or one's country, community or family in ways that go beyond serving the needs of an individual and his or her immediate family. HRM therefore has to consider the many different ways that employees think about what work means to them.

JOHN W. BUDD

See also:

Alienation; Employment relationship; Labour.

References and selected further readings

Applebaum, H. (1992), *The Concept of Work: Ancient, Medieval, and Modern*, Albany: State University of New York Press.
Budd, J.W. (2011), *The Thought of Work*, Ithaca, NY: Cornell University Press.
Korczynski, M., R. Hodson and P. Edwards (eds) (2006), *Social Theory at Work*, Oxford: Oxford University Press.
Michelson, G. and S. Ryan (2014), *Just Work: Narratives of Employment in the 21st Century*, Basingstoke: Palgrave Macmillan.
Spencer, D.A. (2009), *The Political Economy of Work*, London: Routledge.

Work–life balance

Work–life balance is concerned with the relationship between the work and non-work aspects of employees' lives. Over the past few decades, there has been a growing interest in what work–life balance means and how it can be achieved. Work–life balance has become a concern for employees, employers and policymakers. In most discussions of the subject, achieving a satisfactory work–life balance involves restricting work activity, in order to have more time for non-work activities. Generally speaking a good work–life balance is seen to be desirable, resulting in positive outcomes, such as job and life satisfaction, whereas a poor work–life balance is seen to be detrimental to wellbeing and to contribute to stress levels.

Scholarly interest in this field has tended to fall into three main categories. First, there is a body of research concerned with the outcomes associated with achieving (or otherwise) a satisfactory work–life balance. A good work–life balance has been found to be beneficial to wellbeing, both because there may be a buffering effect that protects the individual from negative experience in any one role and because it may reduce stress caused by tension between roles. Related to this, there has been considerable research examining the outcomes from employer policies, such as providing flexible work options, designed to help employees achieve a more satisfactory work–life balance. Second, there is research that has examined the relationship between the two domains of work and life and the extent to which conflict may arise and/or one domain may act as a source of enrichment to the other, where assets or resources are transferred between work and non-work roles. Third, there is research that explores how individuals manage the interface and the extent to which they 'integrate' and/or 'separate' the two (Ashforth et al., 2000).

Assisting employees to achieve a satisfactory work–life balance is advocated as good employment practice by bodies such as the European Union and there is also evidence to show that concern for work–life balance can assist in motivating, recruiting and retaining employees in competitive business environments. Research also shows that in order for these types of arrangements to be effective, it is important for employers to show respect for employees' other life commitments and to create an environment that is supportive of employees in this broader context.

While the notion of work–life balance may be easy to understand intuitively and most employees know whether or not they have it, defining work–life balance in the literature has not proved easy. There have been a number of controversies in this debate. First, the notion of balance has proved problematic. Some commentators have taken balance to mean equal distribution of time, energy and commitment between work and life. Greenhaus et al. (2003) use a definition where the individual is equally engaged in and satisfied by his or her work and non-work roles, whereas others have seen balance in a more subjective sense. Kirchmeyer (2000, p. 81) argues that it is where the individual 'achieves satisfying experiences in all life domains' and as a result needs to be able to commit resources, such as time, energy and commitment, across each domain. It has also been suggested that balance may be linked to the priority that an individual attributes to particular activities. As such the same allocation of resources – for example, of time and energy between work and non-work roles – might result in a satisfactory balance for one employee, but not for another. More recently, many studies have used the term integration rather than balance, to overcome the problems associated with the notion of balance.

Early concerns with work–life balance were mainly related to the challenges faced by parents, particularly mothers, balancing their work and caring commitments. This rather narrow conception of 'life' has been criticized by a number of scholars (see, e.g., Ozbilgin et al., 2011). It has been observed that the literature to date has paid little attention to other life activities including leisure, community involvement, participating in religious or volunteering activities or supporting extended families (Eby et al., 2005) and much of the research has been based on samples drawn from parents with dependent children (Casper et al., 2007). As such, there have been calls for future research to adopt a more holistic perspective that encompasses non-domestic activities and as a result includes all employees (Ozbilgin et al., 2011) reflecting the increasing diversity of the labour market.

CLARE KELLIHER

See also:

Family-friendly policies; Flexible working; Long hours culture.

References and selected further readings

Ashforth, B.E., G.E. Kreiner and M. Fugate (2000), All in a day's work: boundaries and micro role transitions, *Academy of Management Review*, **25**, pp. 472–491.
Casper, W.J., L.T. Eby, C. Bordeaux and A. Lockwood (2007), A review of methods in IO/OB work–family research, *Journal of Applied Psychology*, **92**, pp. 28–41.
Eby, L.T., W.J. Casper, A. Lockwood, C. Bordeaux and A. Brinley (2005), Work and family research in IO/OB: Content analysis and review of the literature (1989–2002), *Journal of Vocational Behavior*, **66**(1), pp. 124–197.
Greenhaus, J.H., K.M. Collins and J.D. Shaw (2003), The relationship between work–family balance and quality of life, *Journal of Vocational Behaviour*, **63**, pp. 510–531.
Kirchmeyer, C. (2000), Work–life initiatives: greed or benevolence regarding workers' time, in C.L. Cooper and D.M. Rousseau (eds), *Trends in Organisational Behaviour*, **7**, pp. 79–93.
Ozbilgin, M.F., T.A. Beauregard, A. Tali and M.P. Bell (2011), Work–life, diversity and intersectionality: a critical review and research agenda, *International Journal of Management Reviews*, **13**, pp. 177–198.

Work limitation

Work limitation is the practice of placing restrictions on the amount of effort expended in work and/or the time devoted to it. Some degree of work limitation is almost always present in the performance of work, whether it is freely undertaken or imposed. For almost all large tasks, to expend maximum effort from the start, without regard to the time available or the work necessary for completion, is to invite rapid exhaustion. An experienced person who is knowledgeable about the demands of a task will control the efforts they expend so as not to become so fatigued that they are unable to continue. Perhaps such a person might, like an athlete, periodically push the limits of their physical mental capability, but they will typically do so in such a way that the effort involved extends the limit of their ability to perform on future occasions. Baldamus (1963), for example, considers the balance operatives strike between the impairment of capability incurred by work and the inurement made possible by experience.

In history, leaving the design as well as the accomplishment of tasks to the person doing them has been a recurrent tendency. However, when this occurs, it is likely that the amounts of work accomplished are fixed by the capacity of the available technology and by custom and tradition concerning work performance. Almost certainly there will be little thought to maximizing output per unit of costs. By contrast with this, many if not most tasks that are undertaken for pay in the modern world, especially manual tasks and low-level service work, are designed by others and not the people doing these tasks. The early management consultants, such as such as Taylor, Gantt and the Gilbreths, thought that the traditional ways of defining work tasks were wasteful and allowed too much scope for work limitation, and so they took on the task of redesigning work in order to eliminate what they saw as waste and inefficiency. Taylor distinguished between what he called 'natural soldiering' (i.e., traditional work limitation) and 'systematic soldiering' (i.e., deliberate limitation in response to the new expectations and incentives imposed) (Taylor, 1947). Early management consultants attempted to define standard units of work and to design specific incentives to ensure high levels of effort in their completion. In so doing they changed the nature of modern work and the attitudes of people to it. For many commentators, especially sociologists of work, limitation is a part of resistance to managerial control regimes.

It is not an exaggeration to say that systematic and self-conscious work limitation was called into being by the modern practice work design. Furthermore, a struggle over various aspects of work accomplishment was initiated by the attempts to secure control of working effort. The control of work through incentives was often doubtful in effectiveness and where it was successful led to the growth of other areas in which they could be adjustment of the wage effort bargain, such as time indiscipline, destructiveness and fiddling (see Ackroyd and Thompson, 1999, pp. 90–98).

STEPHEN ACKROYD

See also:

Job design; Resistance; Work organization.

References and selected further readings

Ackroyd, S. and P. Thompson (1999), *Organisational Misbehaviour*, London: Sage.

Baldamus, W. (1963), *Efficiency and Effort*, London: Tavistock.
Taylor, F. (1947), *Scientific Management*, New York: Harper and Row.

Work organization

Work organization refers to the way in which individual tasks are combined into jobs within systems of production. That is, it is about the things that employees do in order to generate products or services and the ways in which these things fit together to make up their jobs. Work organization is a phenomenon that emerged with the birth of capitalist production and is central to management, because unless work is carried out effectively and efficiently and goods and services generated, organizations cannot function. In large part, scholars of work organization are concerned with how different approaches to organizing tasks into jobs have different impacts on employees and on organizational performance.

Since the early twentieth century, there have been two broad approaches to work organization. The first, which is associated with 'scientific management' or 'Taylorism' (Taylor, 1911) emphasizes a highly specialized and technical approach, in which individual workers perform jobs that involve repetition of the same simple task. Among the earliest and best-known discussions of work organization in the literature can be found in Adam Smith's *An Inquiry into the Nature and Causes of the Wealth of Nations* in 1776. Smith argued that the division of labour – the separation of work into specialist functions, with individual workers responsible for only one small part of production – led to efficiency gains and generated prosperity (Smith, 1993, pp. 11–25). In the early twentieth century, as factory production spread, organizations became larger and more complex and managers sought ways to increase productivity, work was increasingly organized around the principle of the division of labour.

The best-known and most influential thinker in this tradition was Frederick Winslow Taylor. Taylor's *The Principles of Scientific Management* (1911) promoted an approach to work organization characterized by individual workers undertaking narrow and specialized jobs, which were highly repetitive and involved little discretion. In Taylor's view, efficiency was promoted by a clear separation of conception – the role of managers – and execution – the role of employees. Managerial control of production was central to this approach, which was widely implemented during the twentieth century and was undoubtedly responsible for increased productivity and prosperity in the industrialized world. The benefits came with costs, however, in that jobs organized according to the principles of scientific management were boring, unfulfilling and alienating, and resulted in worker dissatisfaction, resistance and industrial unrest.

The second major approach to work organization emerged in part in response to the perceived negative outcomes of scientific management and is associated most closely with the 'human relations' school (see Mayo, 1919). Emerging in large part from the so-called Hawthorne Experiments (Roethlisberger and Dickson, 1939) the human relations approach to work organization, while motivated by a similar concern with productivity, emphasized the human aspects of organizational life. Approaches to work organization informed by human relations have emphasized the effectiveness of organizing work in ways that meet human needs. This has entailed the organization of work on a group rather than an individual basis. Further, this approach involves workers doing a range of tasks, moving between different jobs, and enjoying a degree of discretion to make decisions – more-or-less the antithesis of the Taylorist approach.

We can understand the history of work organization as largely reflecting a struggle between advocates of approaches informed by Taylorism on one hand and those influenced by the human relations approach on the other. Taylorism underpinned 'Fordist' mass production, which dominated manufacturing for much of the twentieth century (Legge, 2005, pp. 295–296). This approach to work organization can still be found in settings such as fast food and call centres and also underlies 'hard' HRM (Legge, 2005, p. 66). The human relations approach has underpinned 'soft' HRM, 'high-commitment management' and most recently 'high-performance work systems', all of which emphasize practices including team-based work, job rotation and employee 'empowerment' (Harley, 2011, p. 94). It would not be an exaggeration to say that most or all jobs in contemporary organizations reflect elements of one or both of the Taylorist and human relations approaches.

The key debates about work organization have reflected the struggle between these two schools of thought and have revolved around two questions. The first has concerned the extent to which different approaches to work organization contribute to organizational performance. There is a large and growing body of evidence that suggests that approaches informed by human relations are positively associated with a range of performance outcomes (Harley, 2011, p. 95). Nonetheless, it is also clear that Taylorist approaches deliver significant efficiency gains, particularly when applied to mass production, although it has inherent limits due to the aforementioned negative responses from workers (Ramsay et al., 2000). It appears clear that both approaches can deliver performance gains, although the extent of such gains may be contingent on the particular products or services being generated, and there would appear to be inherent limits to the potential of Taylorist approaches to delivering sustainable performance gains.

The second major debate has concerned the impact on employees of different approaches to work organization. It is widely acknowledged that Taylorist work organization has negative effects in terms of job satisfaction, commitment and stress. Advocates of humanistic approaches have argued that their approach overcomes these negative outcomes, while also generating superior performance, thereby solving an inherent problem with Taylorist approaches (Ramsay et al., 2000). Critical scholars have suggested that while humanistic approaches may increase employee satisfaction and commitment, at the same time they have the effect of increasing stress and burnout by shifting responsibility for decisions to workers and increasing work effort. Numerous studies have been conducted to assess the extent to which humanistic work organization is 'good' or 'bad' for employees, but the results have varied across different settings. A sensible conclusion would seem to be that the impact on employees varies depending on a range of factors in different settings and that it would be a mistake to assume uniform effects (Harley et al., 2010).

BILL HARLEY

See also:

Job design; Human relations movement; Scientific management.

References and selected further reading

Cordery, J. and S. Parker (2007), Work organisation, in P. Boxall, J. Purcell and P. Wright (eds), *The Oxford Handbook of Human Resource Management*, Oxford: Oxford University Press.

Harley, B. (2011), New work practices, participation and organisational performance: prospects for high performance work systems in Australia, in M. Baird, K. Hancock and J. Isaac (eds), *Work and Employment Relations: An Era of Change*, Sydney: Federation Press.

Harley, B., L. Sargent and B. Allen (2010), Employee responses to 'high performance work systems' practices: an empirical test of the 'disciplined worker thesis', *Work, Employment and Society*, **24**(4), pp. 740–760.

Legge, K. (2005), *Human Resource Management: Rhetorics and Realities*, London: Palgrave.

Mayo, E. (1919), *Democracy and Freedom: An Essay in Social Logic*, Melbourne: Macmillan.

Ramsay, H., D. Scholarios and B. Harley (2000), Employees and high performance work systems: testing inside the black box, *British Journal of Industrial Relations*, **38**(4), pp. 501–531.

Roethlisberger, F.J. and W.J. Dickson (1939), *Management and the Worker*, Cambridge MA: Harvard University Press.

Smith, A. (1993), *An Inquiry into the Nature and Causes of the Wealth of Nations*, Oxford: Oxford University Press.

Taylor, F.W. (1911), *The Principles of Scientific Management*, New York: Norton.

Thompson, P. and D. McHugh (2002), *Work Organisations: A Critical Introduction*, 3rd edn, London: Palgrave.

Workaholism

The term 'workaholism' was coined by the American minister and psychologist Wayne Oates in 1968 to refer to his own addiction to work. Workaholism is an individual difference characteristic referring to self-imposed demands, compulsive overworking, and an inability to regulate work habits (Robinson, 1997). Workaholics work beyond what is reasonably expected to meet organizational requirements. Their compulsive tendencies make workaholics devote more resources (e.g., time, effort, energy) to work, leaving them with fewer resources to devote to their family and private life. As a consequence, workaholics often neglect their life outside their job – their personal health, their family, and their community. Compulsive workers recognize that work is excessive but are unable to reduce or control it. They continue to work hard despite social or health problems, and they experience unpleasant withdrawal symptoms when away from work. Their motive to work excessively is not because they enjoy their work or their high achievement orientation, but because they are perfectionist and set overly stringent standards (Schaufeli et al., 2006).

There is accumulating evidence that workaholism is related to poorer psychological and physical wellbeing (Harpaz and Snir, 2015). Workaholics report relatively high levels of exhaustion, anxiety and depression, but also relatively low levels of work engagement and life satisfaction (Clark et al., forthcoming). Workaholics love to work, but the repetitive and addictive character of their behaviours seems to drain their psychological resources. Furthermore, because workaholics are willing to sacrifice personal relationships to derive satisfaction from work, it is not surprising that the spouses of workaholics report high levels of work–family conflict, low levels of social support and a low relationship quality (Bakker et al., 2009).

Despite their enormous investments in work, workaholics usually perform less well than non-workaholics. Working long hours diminishes both productivity and quality, because sleep-deprivation and fatigue make it hard to stay concentrated and increase the risk of mistakes. Moreover, workaholics are often self-centred and experience problems collaborating with colleagues, undermining team performance. There is still a debate in the literature regarding the most important causes of workaholism, and, consequently, the most important remedies. Whereas some scholars argue that workaholism is an individual difference variable that originates in employees, others have argued that the working environment is more important. Managers may create a culture that venerates overwork and stimulates excessive hard work. Working long days for a long period of time undermines opportunities for recovery and contributes to chronic exhaustion, the core symptom of job burnout.

ARNOLD B. BAKKER

See also:
Burnout; Employee engagement; Long hours culture; Stress.

References and selected further readings

Bakker, A.B., E. Demerouti and R. Burke (2009), Workaholism and relationship quality: a spillover-crossover perspective, *Journal of Occupational Health Psychology*, **14**, pp. 23–33.

Clark, M.A., J.S. Michel, L. Zhdanova, S.Y. Pui and B.B. Baltes (forthcoming), All work and no play: a meta-analytic examination of the correlates and outcomes of workaholism, *Journal of Management*.

Harpaz, I. and R. Snir (eds) (2015), *Heavy Work Investment: Its Nature, Sources, Outcomes and Future Directions*, New York: Routledge.

Robinson, B.E. (1997), Work addiction and the family: conceptual research considerations, *Early Child Development and Care*, **137**, pp. 77–92.

Schaufeli, W.B., T.W. Taris, and A.B. Bakker (2006), Dr Jeckyll or Mr Hyde: on the differences between work engagement and workaholism, in R.J. Burke (ed.), *Research Companion to Working Time and Work Addiction*, Cheltenham: Edward Elgar Publishing.

Worker

Section 230(3)(b) of the Employment Rights Act 1996 and section 296(1)(b) of the Trade Union and Labour Relations (Consolidation) Act 1992 both prescribe that an individual is a 'worker' if s/he has entered into or works under a contract, whether express or implied and (if it is express) whether oral or in writing, whereby the individual undertakes to do or perform personally any work or services for another party to the contract whose status is not by virtue of the contract that of a client or customer of any profession or business undertaking carried on by the individual. As such, in order to qualify as a 'worker', the individual must be engaged on the basis of a contract, involving the provision of personal services to the other party to the contract, and the latter must not be the individual's client or customer.

The significance of the statutory category of 'worker' lies in the fact that such an individual – while not qualifying as an 'employee' working for an employer on the basis of a contract of employment – is entitled to the benefit of some statutory employment rights, such as the right to be paid the national minimum wage under the National Minimum Wage Act 1998, and the right to holiday leave and pay under the Working Time Regulations 1998. This intermediate category lies somewhere between employment at one end of a spectrum and commercial self-employed independent contracting at the opposite end of that same spectrum. It was first introduced as a legal category by legislation in the mid-1980s and is intended to capture individuals who fail to make it to the 'finishing line' of employment status for one reason or another.

Much of the scholarship focusing on the 'worker' construct addresses whether it is a prerequisite that the individual is not performing services in the course of a business (Davidov, 2005; Brodie, 2005), and whether the individual ought to be subordinate to the will of the employing enterprise, in the sense that it is subject to the power of that enterprise to control how, where and when the work is done (Prassl, 2015).

DAVID CABRELLI

See also:

Employee; Self-employment; Temporary worker.

References and selected further readings

Brodie, D. (2005), Employees, workers and the self-employed, *Industrial Law Journal*, **34**(3), pp. 253–260.
Davidov, G. (2005), Who is a worker? *Industrial Law Journal*, **34**(1), pp. 57–71.
Prassl, J. (2015), Members, partners, employees, workers? Partnership law and employment status revised: *Clyde & Co. LLP v Bates van Winkelhof, Industrial Law Journal*, **43**(4), pp. 495–505.

Workforce intelligence planning

Workforce intelligence planning (WIP) has become an integral part of business planning in organizations. It is regarded as a core process of human resource management that ensures organizations having the right number of people at the right time, in the right place with the right skills, which are aligned with the organizational strategy (Baron et al., 2010; CIPD, 2012). The addition of behavioural considerations to the workforce plan, the creation of measures of effectiveness and, finally, the conversion of these into actions throughout the organization is known as workforce intelligence planning (WIP).

WIP is the essence of modern workforce planning shaped by the organization's business strategy. In terms of being able to forecast the number of people who will be in the workforce in future years, as well as understanding what skills the workforce should have. Traditionally, this process was known as manpower planning, then becoming known as human resource planning and forecasting (Turner, 2010).

The added value of the word 'intelligence' refers to the behavioural implications of organizational change. By combining quantitative analysis (headcount, labour turnover, etc.) of workforce planning (WP) together with management, staff behaviour and culture and change management implications, WIP provides a holistic view of the how an organization should craft its people strategy to deliver the organization's strategic objectives, of which there are several activities that might be included – for example, labour demand and supply forecasting, organization design, career planning and succession management, and skill needs and training requirements. Whichever HR activities are included, it's important to note that WP and WIP are dynamic HR tools and are integral to the organization's overall strategy of people management. These key activities also rely on analysing relevant internal data about workforce trends and relevant external data on such things as demographics and skills availability.

WP and WIP are important for the organization for three reasons. First, they are critical to the development of a competitive advantage and being agile in responding to the dynamic and fluid nature of the global economy. Second, WP and WIP require that HR professionals provide 'insight driven' HR in the development of the organization's strategy. Finally, the WP will ensure the reduction of 'business strategy execution risks associated with workforce capacity, capability, and flexibility' (Klosk, 2013).

JUDY SCULLY, MICHAEL GREGSON AND PAUL TURNER

See also:
Human resource planning.

References and selected further readings

Baron, A., R. Clarke, S. Pass and P. Turner (2010), *Workforce Planning: Right People, Right Time, Right Skills*, London: Chartered Institute of Personnel and Development.
CIPD (2012), *Workforce Planning Fact Sheet*, London: Chartered Institute of Personnel and Development.
Klosk, R. (2013), *Workforce Planning and Analytics Conference*, 5–7 February, Atlanta, GA: Human Capital Institute.
Nutt, C. (2010), Why workforce planning is a strategic imperative, in CIPD (ed.), *Reflections on Workforce Planning*, London: Chartered Institute of Personnel and Development.
Scully, J., P. Turner and M. Gregson (2014), Workforce intelligence planning, in J.R. Crawshaw, P. Budhwar and A. Davis (eds), *Human Resource Management: Strategic and International Perspectives*, London: Sage.
Turner, P. (2010), From manpower planning to capacity planning – why we need workforce planning, in CIPD (ed.), *Reflections on Workforce Planning*, London: Chartered Institute of Personnel and Development.

Working time

Working time, by definition, is fundamental to the notion of employment. The starting point for almost any job is that people agree to be available to work at certain times in return for 'compensation'. Working time thus comprises any periods spent in the service of an employer or, in the case of self-employment, dedicated to paid work. The European Union (EU) Working Time Directive (2003/88/EC) formally defines working time as 'any period during which the worker is working, at the employer's disposal and carrying out his activities or duties'. This is taken to include time spent on-call. Self-employment, which is growing as a result of subcontracting and precarious work, is usually excluded from the statutory regulation of working time.

The organization of working time is of central importance to employers and workers alike. It helps determine productivity and cost-efficiency and the ability to meet customer demands. The duration, distribution and intensity of working time also shape employees' experience of work and opportunities for family life, leisure and recreation. Working time is thus central to employee engagement, recruitment and retention.

Working time is also a significant health and safety matter, given the link to stress and fatigue. Certain patterns of working time, such as night work, are especially hazardous to health. Limiting working hours was a founding principle of trade unionism, and working time remains a key concern of collective bargaining. This includes rules around total basic weekly hours, paid leave, breaks, and overtime. The rise of trade unions helped ensure that the dramatic growth in productivity experienced in the nineteenth and twentieth centuries was realised in the form of a dramatic decline in overall hours spent at work (Arrowsmith, 2002).

State regulation also dates back to the nineteenth-century British Factory Acts. It is an important area of international law too. The very first Convention of the International Labour Organization, adopted in 1919, concerned working hours and rest breaks. The EU Working Time Directive provides for a maximum 48-hour working week, compulsory rest periods, limits to night work and at least four weeks' (pro rata) paid leave per year. Most developed countries have similar legal frameworks, except for the United States, which has some of the longest working hours in the world.

Patterns of working time vary by sector, occupation and gender. For example, firms in service sectors such as retail experience demand that is variable but largely predictable. This facilitates extensive part-time and temporary work to match daily, weekly and seasonal fluctuations as well as extended opening times. Organizational strategies include constructing jobs to meet the needs of those with childcare or educational commitments. Women are much more likely to work part-time, although most women are usually in full-time work. Female labour force participation expanded rapidly with the growth of the private and public service sectors, although this varies significantly between countries as a result of social mores and systems such as state childcare support.

Manufacturing firms usually have less predictable variation, which means greater reliance on overtime to adjust to fluctuations in demand. This applies especially in technical work, where there are skill barriers to occupational entry and a preference for full-time labour. Paid overtime is common for employees paid by the hour but less so for those in professional or 'white-collar' salaried jobs. Basic working hours may be less strictly monitored for these workers, leading to excessive working time. This is particularly the case for senior managers and professionals, but career pressures can also promote long hours further down the hierarchy, especially in a context of 'delayering' and job insecurity. This may be associated with the phenomenon of 'presenteeism', which refers to the physical-temporal demonstration of commitment.

Current developments in working time amount to a reversal of the secular trends of standardization and restriction that provided workers some protection from long and unpredictable hours. The fragmentation of working time reflects increased competition and deregulation, which is more permissive of the '24/7' economy. This has seen a growth of 'atypical' employment outside of the traditional 'nine to five' regimen, including shift work and shorter forms of part-time work culminating in 'zero-hours' contracts, in which no working time is actually guaranteed. The declining scope and weakening power of trade unions has led to even well-organized sectors facing more fragmented and vulnerable work. Employers have sought to raise the basic working week, as well as introduce more flexibility over scheduling through forms of 'annualization' in order to reduce overtime costs.

Another important driver of change is new technology. The microchip and digital revolutions enable remote working and wider use of flexitime and telecommuting schemes. This can promote better work–life balance for employees, but also risks a more or less informal extension of working time commitments through ever-present mobile communication. Countries such as Brazil, France and Germany have responded by introducing or proposing further regulations such as restricting the use of email at certain times.

Working time has long been neglected as an academic area of research but it is a fundamental strategy for organizations, both in terms of efficiency of work organization and furthering 'employee engagement' by meeting the needs and aspirations of staff.

According to the European Commission 'Flash Eurobarometer 398' survey, carried out in April 2014, one in five workers in the EU are dissatisfied with their working hours. Half of respondents not satisfied with their working hours (48 per cent) termed them 'excessive'. Other reasons cited were problems caused by shift work or irregular forms of working time, and inability to influence the work schedule (cited by 28 per cent of all respondents).

The control of working time is likely to be an increasingly contested area, if in less overt and collective terms as in the past. Competitive pressures have heightened employers' concerns with flexibility at the same time as workers seek more input and autonomy over their schedules to accommodate their lives outside of work. Employer strategies that neglect employee concerns are less likely to realise sustained competitive advantage.

JAMES ARROWSMITH

See also:
Annualized hours; Long hours culture; Overtime; Presenteeism; Shift work; Work–life balance.

References and selected further readings

Arrowsmith, J. (2002), The struggle over working time in nineteenth and twentieth century Britain, *Historical Studies in Industrial Relations*, **13**, pp. 83–117.
Arrowsmith, J. (2013), Working time in Europe, in J. Arrowsmith and V. Pulignano (eds), *The Transformation of Employment Relations in Europe*, New York and London: Routledge, pp. 111–132.

See Eurofound website (http://eurofound.europa.eu/) for a wide range of up-to-date and authoritative reports and articles on all aspects of working time in Europe.

Workplace democracy

Workplace democracy refers to the managerial delegation of decision-making power to an organization's employees. It is closely related to a wider set of terms, including, but not limited to: industrial democracy, worker participation, employee involvement, engagement and voice. The key distinguishing feature of workplace democracy within this wider nomenclature is that it emphasizes the politics of organizational decision-making. For this reason, the field of study has much in common with political science and political philosophy, but the unit of analysis is the organization, not the nation-state.

In theory, workplace democracy exists on a hypothetical continuum. On one end of the spectrum is the authoritarian organization where all managerial decisions are made by the chief executive officer. In such an organization, employees are simply expected to execute orders and follow directives. They have no 'say' over how to organize production. On the other end of the continuum is absolute worker control, where there is no distinction between managers and employees. In these types of organizations, the employees self-manage without any formal managerial structure. In practice, all organizations can be placed somewhere in between these two extremes, with some offering more and others less scope for employee participation in decision-making. The key political question centres around the ideal distribution of decision-making in organizations.

The study of workplace democracy is important because it is inextricably linked to wider debates surrounding firm performance and fairness at work. In respect to firm performance, it has been argued that delegating decision-making power to a company's employees can result in efficiency improvements because workers possess insight into some production problems that managers do not possess. Moreover, by giving employees a 'say' over strategic decision-making, they are likely to report higher satisfaction in their jobs and to be much more committed to the organization. In respect to fairness, it has been argued that employees have a human right to participate in decisions that affect them in the workplace. There are also fairness issues associated with managers giving some employees more 'say' than others. In short, workplace democracy has very real economic and moral implications.

ANDREW R. TIMMING

See also:

Employee involvement; Employee voice; Managerial control; Self-management.

References and selected further readings

Dundon, T., A. Wilkinson, M. Marchington and P. Ackers (2004), The meanings and purpose of employee voice, *International Journal of Human Resource Management*, **15**(6), pp.1149–1170.
Foley, J.R. and M. Polanyi (2006), Workplace democracy: why bother? *Economic and Industrial Democracy*, **27**(1), pp.173–191.
Timming, A.R. (2015), The 'reach' of employee participation in decision-making: exploring the Aristotelian roots of workplace democracy, *Human Resource Management Journal*, **25**(3), pp.382–396.
Webb, S and B.P. Webb (1897), *Industrial Democracy*, London: Longmans, Green and Co.
Wilkinson, A., J. Donaghey, T. Dundon and R.B. Freeman (eds) (2014), *Handbook of Research on Employee Voice*, Cheltenham: Edward Elgar.
Wilkinson, A., P.J. Gollan, M. Marchington and D. Lewin (2010), *The Oxford Handbook of Participation in Organizations*. Oxford: Oxford University Press.

Written warning

In Great Britain there is no legally binding disciplinary procedure that employers must follow (unless a contractual disciplinary procedure has been agreed). Nevertheless, where an employer ultimately decides to dismiss an employee who qualifies for the right not to be unfairly dismissed they should be aware that the reasonableness of their decision to dismiss will come under scrutiny (see 'Unfair dismissal' in this volume). Procedure is one of the factors to be weighed by an employment tribunal in deciding whether or not the decision to dismiss was reasonable. The Acas code of practice on disciplinary and grievance procedures (Acas, 2015) sets out good practice guidance to help employers, employees and their representatives to deal with disciplinary situations within the workplace. Although the code is not legally binding, it can be admitted as evidence in an employment tribunal and employment tribunals have the discretion to increase or decrease compensation awarded by up to 25 per cent where there has been an unreasonable failure to comply with the code (Trade Union and Labour Relations (Consolidation) Act 1992, section 207A).

Where a disciplinary issue arises, the Acas code suggests that employers take the following steps: establish the facts of the case, inform the employee of the problem, hold a meeting with the employee to discuss the problem, decide on appropriate action and provide an opportunity to appeal.

One form of action open to employers is a written warning. The Acas code notes that where misconduct is confirmed or where unsatisfactory performance is found, a written warning is usual. A final written warning would likely be given following a further act of misconduct, a failure to improve performance within a set period or where the employee's first act of misconduct was sufficiently serious to move directly to a final written warning (paragraphs 19–20). Guidance is given on the content of a first or final written warning. The code notes that a warning should set out the nature of the misconduct or poor performance and the change in behaviour or improvement in performance required along with information of the consequences of further misconduct, or failure to improve performance following a final warning. The guidance suggests that a written warning should also contain information about timescale; for example, the period of time within which the employee should change their behaviour or improve their performance and how long the warning will remain current.

Employers ought to be aware that workers have a statutory right to be accompanied to disciplinary and grievance hearings (Employment Relations Act 1999, section 10).

Liz Oliver

See also:

Disciplinary procedure; Discipline and grievance; Misconduct.

Reference list and selected further readings

Acas (2015), *Code of Practice 1: Disciplinary and Grievance Procedures*, London: Acas, www.acas.org.uk/dgcode.
Willey, B. (2012), *Employment Law in Context: An Introduction for HR Professionals*, 4th edn, Harlow: Pearson.

Wrongful dismissal

Wrongful dismissal is a common law concept. A wrongful dismissal occurs where a contract is terminated in a way that breaches the contract. A common example is where the contract contains a notice period but no notice is given. The remedy for wrongful dismissal is damages, a money payment to put the injured party in the position she or he would have been had the contract been properly performed; for example, the amount of pay that would have been received during the notice period. Wrongful dismissal is unlike unfair dismissal (see 'Unfair dismissal' in this volume) in that establishing a claim does not entail scrutiny of the reason for the dismissal or of the employer's decision to dismiss, the central question is simply whether the terms of the contract relating to termination have been breached.

Liz Oliver

See also:

Contract of employment; Dismissal; Unfair dismissal.

References and selected further readings

Emir, A. (2014), *Selwyn's Law of Employment*, 18th edn, Oxford: Oxford University Press.
Willey, B. (2012), *Employment Law in Context: An Introduction for HR Professionals*, 4th edn, Harlow: Pearson.

Young workers

Governments and international organizations tend to take 'young' as meaning those under 25 years old. 'Workers' is a more complex category, but is usually taken to mean people who are employed and self-employed. In some cases, it may or may not also include people who are in the armed services, people who are in training schemes that are provided by their employers, people who are unemployed but actively looking for work, and many other categories.

These definitional challenges have a particular impact on how we define 'young workers' because young people are much more likely than other groups to be in training (either paid by the state or by an employer), working as well as being students, or in unpaid work such as an internship and many other arrangements that are often not captured within official national statistics.

As a result, academics and policymakers often talk about young peoples' *transitions* into the labour market, recognising that transitions can be fragmented, can include periods of employment, unemployment, training and education, and may not always end in a young person finding a secure job. Increasing attention is being paid to evidence that in many industrialized countries, young people are finding it harder to find secure, full-time jobs in roles that pay enough to start an independent household.

Since the 2008 financial crisis, many industrialized countries have seen a jump in youth unemployment and downward trends in the quality of jobs available. Young workers are often hard hit in recessions because they have fewer skills than older workers, but the extended period of labour market challenges in a lot of EU countries has presented particular problems.

There is growing evidence that long periods of unemployment when someone is young have a negative or 'scarring' effect on many aspects of their later life. There is also some evidence that insecurity and experiences of poor quality work may also have problematic effects. Certainly a lack of job opportunities for young people in countries such as Spain and Greece has had considerable impact on peoples' lives, often meaning that they stay in the parental home longer, they delay starting their own family and they are dependent on the income of older family members.

Policy interventions tend to focus on ensuring that young people have 'employability skills' that show they are ready for work, but these are relatively ineffective if there are not enough jobs being created. One response can be to give incentives to employers to hire young workers, often by reducing the taxes they pay, or by subsidizing training; so-called 'active labour market policies'. These programmes are often expensive and have been cut back since 2008.

Most young workers do make successful transitions into work, but some do not and these people – often called NEETs or those 'not in employment, education or training' – are a growing concern to policymakers. And there is still significant debate about whether industrialized countries can create enough good quality jobs to sustain living standards in future.

MELANIE SIMMS

See also:
Employability; Skills; Training.

References and selected further readings

Bell, D. and D. Blanchflower (2011), Young people and the great recession, *Oxford Review of Economic Policy*, **27**(2), pp. 241–267.

Furlong, A. and F. Cartmel (2007), *Young People and Social Change: New Perspectives*, 2nd edn, Berkshire: Open University Press/McGraw Hill.

UKCES (2014), *Precarious Futures: Youth Employment in International Context*, London: United Kingdom Commission on Employment and Skills, www.gov.uk/government/publications/youth-employment-in-an-international-context.

Zero-hours contracts

Zero-hours contracts are working arrangements where a person is not contracted to work a set number of hours, and is only paid for the number of hours that they actually work. Casualized employment relationships with no guaranteed hours are not new. Indeed such arrangements are commonplace in some economies, such as the USA. It is their rising prevalence in the UK in recent years that has attracted particularly intense debate. There remain considerable gaps in knowledge about the true extent of zero-hours contracts, although more is known about the sectors where zero-hours contracts are concentrated, and the reasons why employers seek recourse to such arrangements. There is also a growing consensus about the relatively low quality of zero-hours contracts compared to other non-standard' and standard employment arrangements.

The hallmark features of zero-hours contracts are the limited mutuality of obligation and limited access to employment rights. While advocates of zero-hours contracts have argued that both the employer and the employee benefit from the limited mutuality of obligation under these arrangements, in reality, the social costs of employment are effectively transferred from employers onto workers, who tend to remain economically dependent upon a single employer (Brinkley, 2013). Availability and flexibility are key criteria used by employers to allocate hours to zero-hours contract workers on a daily or weekly basis (Bessa et al., 2013; Pennycook et al., 2013). 'Exclusivity clauses' in contracts have also been used to tie a zero-hours contract worker to a single employer, although legislation has been proposed to prohibit this practice. For employers, then, the use of zero-hours contracts offers an 'ultra-flexible' working arrangement. For workers, however, these contracts are largely highly precarious and of poor quality, with very little certainly over day-to-day working hours, limited employment security and relatively low levels of income (see Piper and Dar, 2015).

Estimates of the number of zero-hours contracts in the UK vary considerably, from 700,000 in the most recent Labour Force Survey (December 2014) to between 1.3 million and 2.7 million from a specially commissioned Office for National Statistics business survey (Piper and Dar, 2015). There are considerable overlaps in practice between zero-hours contracts and other contractual forms, such as agency working, and significant churn between zero-hours contract jobs, making precise figures hard to establish. It is clear, however, that in some sectors, such as health and social care, retail, hospitality and higher education, zero-hours contracts are commonplace. Indeed in some sectors, such as private sector domiciliary care, this form of contract has become the main form of employment arrangement (see Bessa et al, 2013).

IOULIA BESSA, CHRIS FORDE AND MARK STUART

See also:
Flexible working; Job security: Working time.

References and selected further readings

Bessa, I., C. Forde, S. Moore and M. Stuart (2013), *The National Minimum Wage, Earnings and Hours in the Domiciliary Care Sector*, Report for the Low Pay Commission, www.gov.uk/government/publications/national-minimum-wage-impact-on-the-domiciliary-care-sector.
Brinkley, I. (2013), *Flexibility or Insecurity? Exploring the Rise in Zero Hours Contracts*, London: The

Work Foundation, www.theworkfoundation.com/Reports/339/Flexibility-or-insecurity-Exploring-the-rise-in-zero-hours-contracts.

Pennycook, M., G. Cory and V. Alakeson (2013), *A Matter of Time: The Rise of Zero-Hours Contracts*, London: Resolution Foundation, www.resolutionfoundation.org/publications/matter-time-rise-zero-hours-contracts.

Piper, D. and A. Dar (2015), *Zero Hours Contracts: Standard Note*, Parliamentary Briefing 25 February, House of Commons Library, www.parliament.uk/briefing-papers/SN06553.pdf.

Index

Printed and bound by CPI Group (UK) Ltd, Croydon, CR0 4YY

13/02/2023

03191245-0001